Springer Proceedings in Business and Economics

More information about this series at http://www.springer.com/series/11960

Christopher F. Parmeter • Robin C. Sickles
Editors

Advances in Efficiency and Productivity Analysis

Springer

Editors
Christopher F. Parmeter
Miami Herbert Business School
University of Miami
Miami, FL, USA

Robin C. Sickles
Department of Economics
Rice University
Houston, TX, USA

ISSN 2198-7246 ISSN 2198-7254 (electronic)
Springer Proceedings in Business and Economics
ISBN 978-3-030-47105-7 ISBN 978-3-030-47106-4 (eBook)
https://doi.org/10.1007/978-3-030-47106-4

This Springer imprint is published by the registered company Springer Nature Switzerland AG
The registered company address is: Gewerbestrasse 11, 6330 Cham, Switzerland

Contents

Editors' Introduction

Christopher F. Parmeter and Robin C. Sickles

The papers in this collection, all works presented at the 2018 North American Productivity Workshop X hosted at the University of Miami, represent contributed, peer reviewed chapters across all areas of efficiency and productivity analysis. They offer new insights and perspectives into the modeling, identification, and estimation of productivity and its major components, efficiency and innovation. The collection is aptly titled *Advances in Efficiency and Productivity Analysis*. The contributions in this volume speak to firms or agencies that are privately or state-owned, capitalist or centrally planned economies, developed, developing or transitional countries–anywhere where the goal is to measure productivity and identify and explain possible inefficiencies and thus help a productive enterprise/entity improve and move to higher levels of efficiency and productivity and a more efficient utilization of valuable and costly resources. Productivity growth, as we know, is the main vehicle through which growth in living standards and welfare is achieved. Constraints on this growth, whether by ineffective or misguided regulatory oversight, maldistribution of productivity growth, failure to properly account for hidden costs and benefits of productive decisions and allocations, or market failures to accurately price current resources in light of how their depletion impacts future generations, all contribute to a diminution in productivity growth and thus in living standards. The papers in this volume provide new research findings on these issues.

We have grouped the 13 chapters into three main themes: measurement, econometrics, and applications. Each of these motifs are important to the field writ

C. F. Parmeter (✉)
Miami Herbert Business School, University of Miami, Miami, FL, USA
e-mail: cparmeter@bus.miami.edu

R. C. Sickles
Department of Economics, Rice University, Houston, TX, USA
e-mail: rsickles@rice.edu

C. F. Parmeter, R. C. Sickles (eds.), *Advances in Efficiency and Productivity Analysis*, Springer Proceedings in Business and Economics,
https://doi.org/10.1007/978-3-030-47106-4_1

large and the chapters within each make new contributions to the extant literature. The recent work of (Grifell-Tatjé et al. 2018; Sickles and Zelenyuk 2019) speaks to the steady popularity and importance of this area as well as to the speed at which contributions are arising. Collected works of this ilk are important to allow researchers to stay on the cutting edge and expand their knowledge. We are honored to have curated these chapters and indebted to the reviewers who graciously gave their time to provide feedback to improve the chapters and allowed us to put this book together.

1 Measurement

Before one can estimate and test and bring theory to the data, there is measurement. Just as good theory should provide a cogent explanation for some aspect of nature, good measurement details how best to think about the requirements for testing and assessing a theory, in our case productivity. The chapters in this collection on measurement all focus on different aspects of how best to measure productivity and to begin to think about what we can say about the productivity of some being (a firm, country, state, region, etc.)

Our first chapter on measurement is co-authored by Diewert and Fox and is entitled "The Difference Approach to Productivity Measurement and Exact Indicators." The authors point out that the number of productivity growth decompositions utilizing ratio forms is relatively large and they aim to reduce these to three analogous decompositions, based on a value added function for production, a cost constrained value added function, and a flexible functional form giving rise to an exact value added decomposition. The approaches range from one that is relatively transparent and easily implementable but restrictive to one that is more computationally challenging but has axiomatic advantages that are clearly spelled out in this well-written and accessible first chapter.

The second chapter on measurement by Triantis, "Efficiency Driven Socio-Technical System Design," takes a somewhat different approach to productivity measurement that is motivated more by industrial engineering than by neoclassical economic theory. An efficiency (productivity) measurement paradigm is recommended that is meant to evaluate the design of a system rather than rank different systems (aka firms), taking into consideration organizational design, enterprise systems engineering, and system complexity. This is referred to as a socio-technical system evaluation and contrasts with evaluations that rank different systems (firms, DMU's, etc.) based on prices and quantities of resources used and produced. Illustrations are provided. Stakeholder feedback and resource constraints are also factored into the socio-technical evaluation design.

Daraio's "A Framework for the Assessment and Consolidation of Productivity Stylized Facts," focuses on how researchers' perspectives and methods are framed by the traditions of their disciplines and the pedagogy therein, instead of by "scientific" approaches and experimentation that leave open methods of analysis and interpretation of results as an integral part of the measurement paradigm. She discusses how the research style adopted by productivity experts can be categorized in terms of mathematical theories of measurement, methods that rely on information theory, and model-based descriptions of a production system. As "stylized" heuristics often drive a researcher's predilection for adopting one approach versus another to measure productivity, a survey of such stylized heuristics and "facts" is an important read for any serious researcher in this field.

In Vrachioli and Stefanou contribution "Water's Contribution to Agricultural Productivity over Space," the authors look at both water and space when constructing measures of agricultural productivity. Noting that both an efficient and sustainable management of water resources is of pressing concern, they investigate how changes in farm-level productivity over space can reflect the economic performance of a public water infrastructure project. Their spatial optimal water allocation model provides users with the conditions needed to explain how water quantity and quality affect the economic performance of farmers. There model is important as the information it provides can be used by policymakers interested in maximizing the economic benefit of water allocation across farmers along an irrigation infrastructure project, where farmers make decisions on irrigation water use in sequence.

2 Econometrics

Outside of the theory of productivity and efficiency measurement is the means by which to estimate and conduct inference from data to assess the viability and reliability of theoretical predictions. The four chapters here speak to this theme. All four chapters touch on important, but different, aspects of modeling the production relationship and provide thorough reviews of the state of the art.

In Amsler and Schmidt's comprehensive chapter "A Survey of the Use of Copulas in Stochastic Frontier Models," the use of copulas in stochastic frontier models is detailed. The authors provide three different motivations for the use of copulas in the stochastic frontier literature, all of which are likely to arise in practical settings. Moreover, Amsler and Schmidt provide intuition and insight into several economic models that arise in the stochastic frontier literature that call for copulas with special characteristics. They provide rigorous details on copulas in general and how they can be deployed within the stochastic frontier setting. Another novel feature of the chapter is the discussion of how the practitioner goes about selecting the copula.

The second chapter in this section by Kumbhakar and Bernstein, "Does Xistence of Inefficiency Matter to a Neoclassical Xorcist? Some Econometric Issues in Panel Stochastic Frontier Models," the focus is on potential nonparametric identification and estimation when the practitioner has access to panel data. Specifically, they show that practitioners cannot simply ignore inefficiency when estimating the production function as this leads to severe inconsistency in the estimates of the technology parameters due to omitted variables which are determinants of inefficiency. Kumbhakar and Bernstein go on to provide practical solutions that researchers can rely on to both estimate the production frontier and recover the impact of various determinants of inefficiency in a panel data setting. Their work applies equally to those who may only be interested in the production function and those interested in both the production function and the impact of exogenous variables on inefficiency.

Papadopoulos provides the first comprehensive survey on the two-tier stochastic frontier model (2TSF) in "The two-tier stochastic frontier framework: measuring frontiers wherever they may exist." initially conceptualized by Polachek and Yoon (1987). This approach lied dormant for nearly two decades until it was revived by Kumbhakar and Parmeter (2009) and has since seen renewed interest in the field (both theoretically and empirically). Papadopoulos notes that at present the 2TSF inhabits only a small fraction of the field of efficiency analysis but that the frontier methodology extends far beyond the boundaries of cost and production. This work covers both the direct implementation of the 2TSF estimator as well as offering a variety of insights into when this methodology may be pertinent. The depth of the review should serve the profession well, both revealing the diversity of phenomena where the 2TSF can be deployed and promoting application of the 2TSF model by focusing on various implementation issues that are likely to arise for practitioners.

Kallio and Halme provide a new approach for estimating productivity/performance, focusing on the individual production possibility sets (PPS), in their chapter "Individual Efficient Frontiers in Performance Analysis." They model each production unit as somewhat unique in that each embodies outcomes from a set of different environmental factors and human resource constraints. Utilizing a partial equilibrium optimization framework they assume that each DMU is efficient relative to its PPS. They then derive a set of common prices that support the netputs across all DMUs, assuming that such prices are those most likely to occur when the DMU is optimizing its profits or returns. The framework is one in which the statistical data generating process is specified, although they do employ nonparametric methods to characterize their new performance measure. They compare their new methods with those from standard DEA and find strong rank correlations even though their approach does not rely on the radial distance metric that is DEA to measure performance.

Karagiannis, in "DEA models without inputs or outputs: A tour de force," discusses how pure input and/or output DEA models are suitable for applications other than those related to conventional production models and efficiency analysis. This significantly broadens the use of these models, opening other areas of science to their potential benefits to recover "boundaries." The focus of this chapter is the broad class of radial DEA models, either without inputs or outputs, or with fixed inputs or outputs. A detailed treatment of these DEA models with benefit-of-the-doubt (BoD) models is also provided. These comparisons are useful given the recent popularity of BoD models in constructing composite indices at various agencies, including the United Nations and the OECD.

3 Applications

Applications are the true mark of both good theory and good empirics. A well executed application can validate a theory, offer new avenues for improvement on an existing theory, pose questions that may lead to a new theory, or uncover areas where current theory is lacking. Without proper application, it is hard to quantify the impact that a theoretical curiosity has on the empirical literature at large.

Our first chapter in this group, "U.S. Banking in the Post-Crisis Era: New Results from New Methods," by Wilson examines the performance of US bank holding companies over the time frame bracketing the financial crisis. Given the well known importance of banks to the national and global economy, it seems reasonable to assess what happened to them throughout the global financial crises; this is exactly Wilson's focus. He provides estimates of technical, cost, and input allocative efficiency from 2006 to 2016. The results confirm to the implications from basic microeconomic theory of the firm. After the passage of the Dodd–Frank act, banks' costs were expected to increase due to substantial increases in regulatory oversight and burdensome reporting. These constraints on banking behavior effectively led to lower productivity and higher levels of inefficiency after the end of the global financial crisis. Thus, while there is need for regulatory oversight, it appears the effects of Dodd–Frank were to lead banks to take extreme measures to cut costs, which may have led to a delayed recovery of the national economy. Wilson's chapter is a paragon of theory and data coming together to confirm a widely believed story.

Next in this group is Bos and Zhang's contribution, titled "Room to Move: Why Some Industries Drive the Trade-Specialization Nexus and Others Do Not," where economic integration within the European Union (EU) is studied, with the aim to determine who drives the relationship between trade and specialization. Both Jones (2013) and Baqaee and Farhi (2019) have shown that large differences in growth outcomes (either at the sector, region, or country level) can be explained through resource misallocation. Bos and Zhang go a step further and document that subsequent resource reallocation can help explain industry growth, primarily through responses after trade barriers are reduced. They find that who drives the trade-specialization relationship are productive firms who benefit from the increase in trade-openness by appropriating resources from less productive firms. Bos and Zhang use latent class modeling approaches to determine those industries that require "room to move" so that increased trade-openness translates into increased specialization. Their application uses over 390,000 manufacturing firms spanning 18 industries in 14 EU countries. Bos and Zhang's application is an excellent example where estimates are consistent with the extant theoretical and empirical evidence in the international trade literature. Moreover, their findings have important policy recommendations: policies aimed at removing barriers are likely to enhance economic activity and the resulting gains in both technical efficiency and scale may represent an important source of economic growth in the EU.

Brinkerink, Chegut, and Letterie, in "Expansionary Investment Activities: Assessing Equipment and Buildings in Productivity," argue that buildings should be counted as a direct input factor to production (so-called investment spikes). They look at how investment in physical structures drives employment, production technology, and firm capacity in manufacturing industries in the Netherlands. They look at investment spikes in either equipment, buildings, or both. These spikes are important to account for when measuring productivity. Neglecting simultaneity of spikes in buildings and equipment inadequately represents the breadth of the extensive margin of productivity. Moreover, they document that firms which have investment spikes in both buildings and equipment experience higher ex post investment expansion in production and the number of workers relative to firms that experience a spike solely equipment or buildings.

Asmild, Kronborg, and Rønn-Nielsen's interesting application "Applying statistical methods to compare frontiers: Are organic dairy farms better than the conventional?" Utilizes permutation tests to provide inference on Malmquist index decompositions introduced by Färe et al. (1992) and more recently studied in terms of its asymptotic distribution by Kneip et al. (2018). Their study also examines statistical differences between organic and conventional dairy farms in Denmark. Bias correction procedures to address DEA finite sample biases in the estimation of the frontier technology are also pursued. Their applied analysis also has important implications for Danish competition policy in its agricultural sector and the authors stress the usefulness of their tests and inferences for informing public policy makers.

Our last chapter, "Nutrient Use and Precision Agriculture in Corn Production in the United States," by Mosheim and Schimmelpfennig tackles the role of precision agriculture in enhancing productivity in agriculture—this result has been shown for cost savings, profitability, and even farm resource stewardship, but has not been shown empirically for farm productivity. They use data on the corn sector in 2016 from the Agricultural Resource Management Survey, the largest farm production survey carried out by USDA in the USA. They employ a matching procedure where they match on observables to reduce the confoundedness of input choice with precision agriculture utilization.

References

Baqaee, D. R., & Farhi, E. (2019). Productivity and misallocation in general equilibrium. *The Quarterly Journal of Economics, 135*(1), 105–163.

Färe, R., Grosskopf, S., Lindgren, B., & Roos, P. (1992). Productivity changes in Swedish pharmacies 1980–1989: A non-parametric Malmquist approach. *Journal of Productivity Analysis, 3*(1), 85–101.

Grifell-Tatjé, E., Lovell, C. A. K., & Sickles, R. C. (2018). *The Oxford handbook of productivity analysis*. New York, NY: Oxford University Press.

Jones, C. I. (2013). Misallocation, economic growth, and input–output economics. In D. Acemoglu, M. Arellano, & E. Dekel (Eds.), *Advances in economics and econometrics: Tenth world congress* (vol. 2, pp. 419–456). Cambridge: Cambridge University Press.

Kneip, A., Simar, L., & Wilson, P. W. (2018). Inference in dynamic, nonparametric models of production: Central limit theorems for Malmquist indices. Discussion paper #2018/10. Institut de Statistique, Biostatistique et Sciences Actuarielles, Université Catholique de Louvain, Louvain-la-neuve, Belgium.

Kumbhakar, S. C., & Parmeter, C. F. (2009). The effects of match uncertainty and bargaining on labor market outcomes: Evidence from firm and worker specific estimates. *Journal of Productivity Analysis, 31*(1), 1–14.

Polachek, S. W., & Yoon, B. J. (1987). A two-tiered earnings frontier estimation of employer and employee information in the labor market. *The Review of Economics and Statistics, 69*(2), 296–302.

Sickles, R. C., & Zelenyuk, V. (2019). *Measurement of productivity and efficiency: Theory and practice*. Cambridge: Cambridge University Press.

The Difference Approach to Productivity Measurement and Exact Indicators

W. Erwin Diewert and Kevin J. Fox

Abstract There are many decompositions of productivity growth for a production unit that rely on the ratio approach to index number theory. In this paper, three analogous decompositions for productivity growth in a difference approach to index number theory are obtained. The first approach uses the production unit's value added function in order to obtain a suitable decomposition. It relies on various first order approximations to this function but in the end, the decomposition can be given an axiomatic interpretation. The second approach uses the cost constrained value added function and assumes that the reference technology for the production unit can be approximated by the free disposal conical hull of past observations of inputs used and outputs produced by the unit. The final approach uses a particular flexible functional form for the producer's value added function and provides an exact decomposition of normalized value added.

Keywords Productivity measurement · Index numbers · Indicator functions · The Bennet indicator · Flexible functional forms for value added functions · Technical and allocative efficiency · Nonparametric methods for production theory · Measures of technical progress

The authors thank Knox Lovell for helpful comments on this topic and related topics over the years. The first author gratefully acknowledges the financial support of the SSHRC of Canada, and both authors gratefully acknowledge the financial support of the Australian Research Council (DP150100830). This is an updated version of Discussion Paper 17-05, Vancouver School of Economics, University of British Columbia.

W. E. Diewert
School of Economics, University of British Columbia, Vancouver, BC, Canada
e-mail: erwin.diewert@ubc.ca

K. J. Fox (✉)
School of Economics, UNSW, Sydney, NSW, Australia
e-mail: K.Fox@unsw.edu.au

C. F. Parmeter, R. C. Sickles (eds.), *Advances in Efficiency and Productivity Analysis*, Springer Proceedings in Business and Economics,
https://doi.org/10.1007/978-3-030-47106-4_2

1 Introduction

Total factor productivity (TFP) growth is usually defined by economists as an output index divided by an input index. However, in the business and accounting literatures, there is more interest in measuring productivity growth in a difference framework.[1] Thus in the present paper, we will look at the value added produced by a production unit in two consecutive periods of time and we will attempt to find a decomposition of the value added difference into explanatory factors. One of these factors will be productivity growth measured in a difference framework.

As mentioned above, studying value added productivity growth in a difference framework is useful because this framework is consistent with business accounting practices which look at revenue, cost, and profit growth of a business enterprise in terms of differences rather than ratios. There is also a strong technical reason for taking a difference approach to productivity measurement as opposed to the usual ratio approach that was developed by Jorgenson and Griliches (1967, 1972), Caves et al. (1982), Diewert and Morrison (1986), Kohli (1990) and others: these approaches rely on some use of the translog functional form to describe technology and these approaches require *either* positivity of all outputs and inputs used by the production unit *or* at least positivity of all primary inputs used. This restriction is typically not problematic when dealing with sectoral or national data but when dealing with firm level data, the problem of new and disappearing outputs and inputs arises, leading to missing reservation prices and 0 outputs or inputs for the corresponding quantities. Thus the existing ratio type analysis for TFP growth cannot be applied. The difference approach developed in this paper can deal with this problem.

We will develop three separate approaches to the value added decomposition problem in difference format. The first approach will be explained in Sects. 2 and 3. This first approach relies on the assumption that observed production is always on the frontier of the production possibilities set and makes use of various first order approximations to the underlying value added functions. However, in the end, Approach 1 can be given an axiomatic interpretation which has some good properties. Section 4 notes a problem with the difference approach: nominal value added measured at two different points in time is measured in monetary units but the value of the monetary unit is not constant over time. Thus in Sect. 4, we suggest that all prices be deflated by a suitable general index of inflation.

Section 5 no longer assumes that producers are necessarily on the frontiers of their production possibility sets. The analysis here makes use of cost constrained value added functions and it also assumes that the producer's period t production possibilities set can be approximated by the free disposal conical hull of past observations on outputs produced and inputs used by the unit. Thus Approach 2 is a nonparametric one, as is Approach 1.

---

[1]See Grifell-Tatjé and Lovell (2015) for an extensive discussion of the difference approach to productivity measurement and its history.

Section 6 tries to develop a counterpart to the index number decompositions for value added growth that were obtained by Diewert and Morrison (1986) and Kohli (1990) that would be applicable in the difference approach to economic measurement (as opposed to the ratio approach that was used in these earlier studies). We succeed in providing a counterpart decomposition but in the end, it proves to be not very useful.

Section 7 concludes with some observations on the relative merits and demerits of the three approaches.

2 The First Order Approximation Approach

Let $y \equiv [y_1, \ldots, y_M]$ denote an M dimensional vector of net outputs (if $y_m > 0$, then net output m is an output, if $y_m < 0$, then net output m is an intermediate input) and let $x \equiv [x_1, \ldots, x_N] \geq 0_N$ denote a nonnegative N dimensional vector of primary inputs. We want to look at the productivity of a production unit that produces the M net outputs using the N primary inputs over periods $t = 0, 1, \ldots, T$. We assume that the period t production possibilities set is a set of feasible combinations of net outputs and primary inputs denoted by the set S^t. For each t, we assume a constant returns to scale production possibilities set so that S^t is a cone.[2] Suppose the producer faces the strictly positive vector of net output prices $p^t \equiv [p_1{}^t, \ldots, p_M{}^t] \gg 0_M$ in period t and has the nonnegative vector of primary inputs $x^t \equiv [x_1{}^t, \ldots, x_N{}^t]$ at its disposal. The maximum value added that the production unit can produce is $\Pi^t(p^t, x^t)$ defined as follows for $t = 0, 1, \ldots, T$:

$$\Pi^t\left(p^t, x^t\right) \equiv \max_y \left\{p^t \cdot y : \left(y, x^t\right) \in S^t\right\}, \tag{1}$$

where $\Pi^t(p, x)$ is the producer's *period t value added function*.[3] Let $w^t \equiv [w_1{}^t, \ldots, w_N{}^t] \gg 0_N$ be the period t vector of positive primary input prices. We assume that observed value added is equal to observed primary input cost in each period:[4]

[2]In addition to the cone property, we assume the weak regularity conditions P1–P7 on S^t that are listed in Diewert and Fox (2017, p. 277). Essentially, we assume that S^t is a nonempty closed cone which is subject to free disposal and $(0_M, 0_N) \in S^t$ for each t. It is not necessary to assume that S^t is a convex set. However, the assumption of constant returns to scale in production is restrictive (but necessary for our analysis).

[3]For the properties of value added functions, see McFadden (1966, 1978), Gorman (1968) and Diewert (1973). In this section, we will assume that first order partial derivatives of $\Pi^t(p, x)$ at $p = p^t$ and $x = x^t$ exist.

[4]In empirical applications, there are two main methods for ensuring that the value of outputs equals the value of inputs: (1) introduce a fixed factor that absorbs any pure profits or losses or (2) use a balancing rate of return in the user cost formula for durable inputs that will make the value of inputs equal to the value of outputs. For the early history of the first approach, see Grifell-Tatjé and Lovell (2015, p. 40) and for applications of the second approach, see Christensen and Jorgenson (1969) and Diewert and Fox (2016).

$$\Pi^t(p^t, x^t) \equiv p^t \cdot y^t = w^t \cdot x^t > 0;\ t = 0, 1, \ldots, T. \tag{2}$$

In this section, we also assume that $\Pi^t(p^t, x^t)$ is differentiable with respect to its components in each period so that we have (Hotelling 1932; Samuelson 1953):[5]

$$y^t = \nabla_p \Pi^t(p^t, x^t);\ t = 0, 1, \ldots, T;\ \text{(Hotellings (1932, p.594) Lemma)} \tag{3}$$

$$w^t = \nabla_x \Pi^t(p^t, x^t);\ t = 0, 1, \ldots, T;\ \text{(Samuelsons (1953, p.10) Lemma).} \tag{4}$$

We focus on the growth of value added going from period 0 to period 1. The growth analysis for other periods is entirely analogous. Assumptions (2) above plus simple algebra establishes the following *Laspeyres and Paasche type value added growth decompositions in ratio form*:

$$p^1 \cdot y^1 / p^0 \cdot y^0 = \left[\Pi^1(p^1, x^1)/\Pi^1(p^0, x^1)\right]\left[\Pi^1(p^0, x^1)/\Pi^0(p^0, x^1)\right] \left[\Pi^0(p^0, x^1)/\Pi^0(p^0, x^0)\right]; \tag{5}$$

$$p^1 \cdot y^1 / p^0 \cdot y^0 = \left[\Pi^0(p^1, x^0)/\Pi^0(p^0, x^0)\right]\left[\Pi^1(p^1, x^0)/\Pi^0(p^1, x^0)\right] \left[\Pi^1(p^1, x^1)/\Pi^1(p^1, x^0)\right]. \tag{6}$$

The terms $\Pi^t(p^1, x^t)/\Pi^t(p^0, x^t)$ for $t = 0, 1$ are *value added price indexes*, the terms $\Pi^1(p^0, x^1)/\Pi^0(p^0, x^1)$ and $\Pi^1(p^1, x^0)/\Pi^0(p^1, x^0)$ are *measures of technical progress* and the terms $\Pi^t(p^t, x^1)/\Pi^t(p^t, x^0)$ for $t = 0, 1$ are *input quantity indexes*. These ratio type decompositions have the following analogous *Laspeyres and Paasche type value added difference decompositions*:[6]

$$p^1 \cdot y^1 - p^0 \cdot y^0 = \left[\Pi^1(p^1, x^1) - \Pi^1(p^0, x^1)\right] + \left[\Pi^1(p^0, x^1) - \Pi^0(p^0, x^1)\right] + \left[\Pi^0(p^0, x^1) - \Pi^0(p^0, x^0)\right]; \tag{7}$$

[5]See also Diewert (1974, p. 140).

[6]Hicks (1941-42, pp. 127–134, 1945-46, pp. 72–73) was the first to see the analogy between index number theory and consumer surplus theory (a difference approach to welfare measurement) and he developed a first order Taylor series approximation method to obtain empirical counterparts to his theoretical difference measures of quantity and price change. Thus we are simply adapting his method to the producer context. See Diewert and Mizobuchi (2009, p. 367) for the early history of the contributions of Hicks to indicator theory in the consumer context.

$$p^1\cdot y^1 - p^0\cdot y^0 = \left[\Pi^0\left(p^1,x^0\right) - \Pi^0\left(p^0,x^0\right)\right] + \left[\Pi^1\left(p^1,x^0\right) - \Pi^0\left(p^1,x^0\right)\right] + \left[\Pi^1\left(p^1,x^1\right) - \Pi^1\left(p^1,x^0\right)\right]. \quad (8)$$

The terms $\Pi^t(p^1, x^t) - \Pi^t(p^0, x^t)$ are value added *indicators* of price change,[7] the terms $\Pi^1(p^0, x^1) - \Pi^0(p^0, x^1)$ and $\Pi^1(p^1, x^0) - \Pi^0(p^1, x^0)$ are measures of the absolute change in value added at constant net output prices and constant primary input quantities due to *technical progress* going from period 0 to 1 and the terms $\Pi^t(p^t, x^1) - \Pi^t(p^t, x^0)$ for $t = 0, 1$ are *indicators* of input growth at constant prices and constant technology in difference terms. Our problem is to obtain empirically observable estimates for the three sets of terms on the right-hand sides of (7) and (8).

We will use assumptions (2)–(4) in order to form first order Taylor series approximations to the various unobservable value added terms of the form $\Pi^r(p^s, x^t)$ for r, s, and t equal to 0 or 1. Thus we can derive the following first order approximations to the unobservable terms on the right-hand sides of the decompositions defined by (7) and (8):

$$\begin{aligned}\Pi^1\left(p^1,x^1\right) - \Pi^1\left(p^0,x^1\right) &\approx p^1\cdot y^1 - \left[\Pi^1\left(p^1,x^1\right) + \nabla_p\Pi^1\left(p^1,x^1\right)\cdot\left(p^0-p^1\right)\right] \\ &= p^1\cdot y^1 - \left[p^1\cdot y^1 + y^1\cdot\left(p^0-p^1\right)\right] \qquad \text{using (2) and (3)} \\ &= y^1\cdot\left(p^1-p^0\right).\end{aligned} \quad (9)$$

$$\begin{aligned}\Pi^1\left(p^0,x^1\right) - \Pi^0\left(p^0,x^1\right) &\approx \left[\Pi^1\left(p^1,x^1\right) + \nabla_p\Pi^1\left(p^1,x^1\right)\cdot\left(p^0-p^1\right)\right] \\ &\quad - \left[\Pi^0\left(p^0,x^0\right) + \nabla_x\Pi^0\left(p^0,x^0\right)\cdot\left(x^1-x^0\right)\right] \\ &= \left[p^1\cdot y^1 + y^1\cdot\left(p^0-p^1\right)\right] - \left[p^0\cdot y^0 + w^0\cdot\left(x^1-x^0\right)\right] \qquad \text{using (2)–(4)} \\ &= p^0\cdot y^1 - w^0\cdot x^1.\end{aligned} \quad (10)$$

[7]Diewert (1992, p. 556) introduced the term indicator to distinguish the difference concept from the usual ratio concept that is applied in index number theory. Diewert (2005, p. 317) also applied the indicator terminology in the context of measuring profit change over consecutive periods.

$$\begin{aligned}
&\Pi^0\left(p^0, x^1\right) - \Pi^0\left(p^0, x^0\right) \\
&\approx \left[\Pi^0\left(p^0, x^0\right) + \nabla_x \Pi^0\left(p^0, x^0\right) \cdot \left(x^1 - x^0\right)\right] - p^0 \cdot y^0 \quad \text{using (2)} \\
&= \left[p^0 \cdot y^0 + w^0 \cdot \left(x^1 - x^0\right)\right] - p^0 \cdot y^0 \qquad \text{using (4)} \\
&= w^0 \cdot \left(x^1 - x^0\right).
\end{aligned} \tag{11}$$

Substituting (9)–(11) into the decomposition (7) gives us the following approximate decomposition:[8]

$$\begin{aligned}
p^1 \cdot y^1 - p^0 \cdot y^0 \approx &\left[y^1 \cdot \left(p^1 - p^0\right)\right] + \left[p^0 \cdot y^1 - w^0 \cdot x^1\right] \\
&+ \left[w^0 \cdot \left(x^1 - x^0\right)\right] = p^1 \cdot y^1 - p^0 \cdot y^0.
\end{aligned} \tag{12}$$

Similar computations give us the following first order Taylor series approximations to the three terms on the right-hand side of decomposition (8):

$$\Pi^0\left(p^1, x^0\right) - \Pi^0\left(p^0, x^0\right) \approx y^0 \cdot \left(p^1 - p^0\right); \tag{13}$$

$$\Pi^1\left(p^1, x^0\right) - \Pi^0\left(p^1, x^0\right) \approx -\left[p^1 \cdot y^0 - w^1 \cdot x^0\right]; \tag{14}$$

$$\Pi^1\left(p^1, x^1\right) - \Pi^1\left(p^1, x^0\right) \approx w^1 \cdot \left(x^1 - x^0\right). \tag{15}$$

Substituting (13)–(15) into (8) gives us the following approximate decomposition:[9]

$$\begin{aligned}
p^1 \cdot y^1 - p^0 \cdot y^0 &\approx \left[y^0 \cdot \left(p^1 - p^0\right)\right] - \left[p^1 \cdot y^0 - w^1 \cdot x^0\right] + \left[w^1 \cdot \left(x^1 - x^0\right)\right] \\
&= p^1 \cdot y^1 - p^0 \cdot y^0.
\end{aligned} \tag{16}$$

Now take the arithmetic average of the two approximate decompositions (12) and (16) and we obtain the following Bennet (1920) type approximate decomposition:[10]

[8] We used $w^0 \cdot x^0 = p^0 \cdot y^0$ to derive the last equality in (12).

[9] We used $-p^0 \cdot y^0 = -w^0 \cdot x^0$ to derive the last equality in (16).

[10] This last equality follows by simply adding up the terms in the above expression.

$$\begin{aligned} p^1 \cdot y^1 - p^0 \cdot y^0 \approx & (1/2)\left(y^0 + y^1\right) \cdot \left(p^1 - p^0\right) \\ & + (1/2)\left[\left(p^0 \cdot y^1 - w^0 \cdot x^1\right) - \left(p^1 \cdot y^0 - w^1 \cdot x^0\right)\right] \\ & + (1/2)\left(w^0 + w^1\right) \cdot \left(x^1 - x^0\right) \\ = & p^1 \cdot y^1 - p^0 \cdot y^0. \end{aligned} \tag{17}$$

Define the *Bennet indicator of technical progress*, $B_\tau(p^0, p^1, w^0, w^1, y^0, y^1, x^0, x^1)$, as the middle term in the above decomposition:[11]

$$\begin{aligned} & B_\tau\left(p^0, p^1, w^0, w^1, y^0, y^1, x^0, x^1\right) \\ & \equiv (1/2)\left[\left(p^0 \cdot y^1 - w^0 \cdot x^1\right) - \left(p^1 \cdot y^0 - w^1 \cdot x^0\right)\right]. \end{aligned} \tag{18}$$

The last equality in (17) shows that the approximate decomposition (17) is in fact an exact one in the sense that the sum of the right-hand side terms equals the value added difference between the two periods. The first term on the right-hand side of (17), $(1/2)(y^0 + y^1)\cdot(p^1 - p^0)$, is the *Bennet indicator of value added price change*, the middle term, $(1/2)[(p^0\cdot y^1 - w^0\cdot x^1) - (p^1\cdot y^0 - w^1\cdot x^0)]$, is an *indicator of technical progress between periods 0 and 1*, and the last term, $(1/2)(w^0 + w^1)\cdot(x^1 - x^0)$, is the *Bennet indicator of input quantity change*. Note that the Bennet indicator of technical progress turns out to equal the arithmetic average of the hypothetical profit that the net output vector of period 1 would make if evaluated at the prices of period 0 and the negative of the hypothetical loss that the net output vector of period 0 would make if evaluated at the prices of period 1. This shows that there is a strong connection between measures of technical progress and of profitability.[12]

The classic *Bennet decomposition of value added change* into price change and quantity change components going from period 0 to 1 is the following one:

$$p^1 \cdot y^1 - p^0 \cdot y^0 = (1/2)\left(y^0 + y^1\right) \cdot \left(p^1 - p^0\right) + (1/2)\left(p^0 + p^1\right) \cdot \left(y^1 - y^0\right) \tag{19}$$

where the *Bennet indicator of value added quantity change* is defined as $(1/2)(p^0 + p^1)\cdot(y^1 - y^0)$. Substituting (19) into (17) and using definition (18) leads to the following two alternative expressions for the *Bennet indicator of technical progress*:

---

[11] Kurosawa (1975) recognized $p^0\cdot y^1 - w^0\cdot x^1$ as a measure of productivity growth (or technical progress); see also Grifell-Tatjé and Lovell (2015, pp. 177–185) for a discussion of this measure and related measures.

[12] See Grifell-Tatjé and Lovell (2015) for much more material on the relationships of profitability measures with measures of productivity growth.

$$\begin{aligned} &B_\tau\left(p^0, p^1, w^0, w^1, y^0, y^1, x^0, x^1\right) = (1/2)\left(p^0 + p^1\right)\cdot\left(y^1 - y^0\right) \\ &- (1/2)\left(w^0 + w^1\right)\cdot\left(x^1 - x^0\right) \\ &= (1/2)\left(p^0 + p^1\right)\cdot y^1 - (1/2)\left(w^0 + w^1\right)\cdot x^1 - \left[(1/2)\left(p^0 + p^1\right)\cdot y^0\right. \\ &\left. - (1/2)\left(w^0 + w^1\right)\cdot x^0\right] \end{aligned} \tag{20}$$

The first equality in (20) shows that the Bennet indicator of technical progress is also equal to the Bennet indicator of value added quantity change less the Bennet indicator of input quantity change. The second equality in (20) shows that the Bennet indicator of technical progress is equal to the hypothetical profitability of the overall period 1 net output vector, $[y^1, -x^1]$, evaluated at the average prices for period 0 and 1 net outputs, $(1/2)[p^0 + p^1, w^0 + w^1]$, less the hypothetical profitability of the overall period 0 net output vector, $[y^0, -x^0]$, evaluated at the same average prices for period 0 and 1 net outputs.

It is possible to obtain a fourth (dual) expression[13] for the Bennet indicator of technical progress. We know that value added change has the Bennet decomposition defined by (19) above and primary input cost change has the Bennet decomposition defined by (21) below:

$$w^1\cdot x^1 - w^0\cdot x^0 = (1/2)\left(w^0 + w^1\right)\cdot\left(x^1 - x^0\right) + (1/2)\left(x^0 + x^1\right)\cdot\left(w^1 - w^0\right). \tag{21}$$

Using (20), we have:

$$\begin{aligned} &B_\tau\left(p^0, p^1, w^0, w^1, y^0, y^1, x^0, x^1\right) \\ &= (1/2)\left(p^0 + p^1\right)\cdot\left(y^1 - y^0\right) - (1/2)\left(w^0 + w^1\right)\cdot\left(x^1 - x^0\right) \\ &= -\left[p^1\cdot y^1 - p^0\cdot y^0\right] + (1/2)\left(p^0 + p^1\right)\cdot\left(y^1 - y^0\right) + \left[w^1\cdot x^1 - w^0\cdot x^0\right] \\ &\quad - (1/2)\left(w^0 + w^1\right)\cdot\left(x^1 - x^0\right) \qquad \text{using (2) for } t = 0, 1 \\ &= -(1/2)\left(y^0 + y^1\right)\cdot\left(p^1 - p^0\right) \\ &\quad + (1/2)\left(x^0 + x^1\right)\cdot\left(w^1 - w^0\right) \qquad \text{using (19) and (21)} \\ &= -\Sigma_{m=1}{}^{M}(1/2)\left(y_m{}^1 + y_m{}^0\right)\left(p_m{}^1 - p_m{}^0\right) + \Sigma_{n=1}{}^{N}(1/2)\left(x_n{}^1\right. \\ &\quad \left. + x_n{}^0\right)\left(w_n{}^1 - w_n{}^0\right). \end{aligned} \tag{22}$$

Thus the empirical measure of technical progress $B_\tau(p^0, p^1, w^0, w^1, y^0, y^1, x^0, x^1)$ defined by (18) is also equal to the empirical Bennet measure of input price

[13]The dual approach to productivity measurement (in the ratio context) dates back to Siegel (1952, 1961, p. 27). See also Jorgenson and Griliches (1967, 1972) and Grifell-Tatjé and Lovell (2015, pp. 103–109) for more on the early history of this approach.

change $(1/2)(x^0 + x^1)\cdot(w^1 - w^0)$ less the Bennet measure of output price change, $(1/2)(y^0 + y^1)\cdot(p^1 - p^0)$.

The empirical decomposition of productivity growth defined by (22) is useful if one wishes to allocate aggregate productivity growth to purchasers of the production unit's outputs and to suppliers of primary inputs to the production unit. Thus the benefits of productivity growth flow through to (potentially) lower net output prices (this effect is captured by the terms—$\Sigma_{m=1}^{M}$ $(1/2)(y_m^{\ 1} + y_m^{\ 0})(p_m^{\ 1} - p_m^{\ 0})$ on the right-hand side of (22)) and to higher primary input prices (this effect is captured by the terms $\Sigma_{n=1}^{N}$ $(1/2)(x_n^{\ 1} + x_n^{\ 0})(w_n^{\ 1} - w_n^{\ 0})$ on the right-hand side of (22)).[14] Kendrick described in plain English the effects of productivity increases on factor incomes:

> Productivity gains provide the increments to real product out of which the real incomes of the factors are increased. If productivity advances, wage rates and capital return necessarily rise in relation to the general product price level, since this is the means whereby the fruits of productivity gains are distributed to workers and investors by the market mechanism. (John Kendrick 1961, p. 111).

Thus we have four alternative interpretations for the Bennet indicator of technical progress: the first one which flows from the original definition (18), two more interpretations which flow from the two equalities in (20), and the final dual interpretation defined by (22). All four interpretations are fairly simple and intuitively plausible.

3 Decomposing the Theoretical Indicators of Overall Output Price and Input Quantity Change into Individual Price and Quantity Indicators

Recall that the decomposition of value added growth defined by (7) had the overall output price change term $\Pi^1(p^1, x^1) - \Pi^1(p^0, x^1)$ on the right-hand side of the equation. It is useful to decompose this Paasche type *overall* measure of output price change into *separate* output price change contributions.[15] This task can be accomplished if we make use of the following decomposition of $\Pi^1(p^1, x^1) - \Pi^1(p^0, x^1)$:

[14]Grifell-Tatjé and Lovell (2015, pp. 36–41) devote many pages to alternative approaches to this distribution problem. They note the early contributions of Davis (1947) and Kendrick (1961) to this problem and their insights into many other aspects of productivity measurement. Grifell-Tatjé and Lovell do an excellent job on covering the history of productivity measurement and its connection with accounting theory. See also Lawrence et al. (2006) for a related exact index number application of this type of distributive analysis.

[15]As mentioned in the introduction, we are looking for a difference counterpart to the multiplicative decomposition of aggregate output price change into individual output price and input quantity change components that Diewert and Morrison (1986, pp. 666–667) and Kohli (1990) obtained in their traditional index number approach to the decomposition of value added growth.

$$\begin{aligned}\Pi^1\left(p^1,x^1\right)-\Pi^1\left(p^0,x^1\right)&=\Pi^1\left(p^1,x^1\right)-\Pi^1\left({p_1}^0,{p_2}^1,\ldots,{p_M}^1,x^1\right)\\&+\Pi^1\left({p_1}^0,{p_2}^1,\ldots,{p_M}^1,x^1\right)-\Pi^1\left({p_1}^0,{p_2}^0,{p_3}^1,\ldots,{p_M}^1,x^1\right)\\&+\Pi^1\left({p_1}^0,{p_2}^0,{p_3}^1,\ldots,{p_M}^1,x^1\right)-\Pi^1\left({p_1}^0,{p_2}^0,{p_3}^0,{p_4}^1,\ldots,{p_M}^1,x^1\right)\\&+\ldots\\&+\Pi^1\left({p_1}^0,\ldots,{p_{M-1}}^0,{p_M}^1,x^1\right)-\Pi^1\left(p^0,x^1\right).\end{aligned}\tag{23}$$

Thus the right-hand side of (23) consists of M differences in $\Pi^1(p, x^1)$ where each difference changes only one component of the p vector. We will approximate these terms by taking first order Taylor series approximations to the $\Pi^1(p, x^1)$ around the point $p = p^1$. Thus the first order approximation to $\Pi^1({p_1}^0, {p_2}^1, \ldots, {p_M}^1, x^1)$ is the following one:

$$\begin{aligned}\Pi^1\left({p_1}^0,{p_2}^1,\ldots,{p_M}^1,x^1\right)&\approx\Pi^1\left(p^1,x^1\right)+\left[\partial\Pi^1\left(p^1,x^1\right)/\partial p_1\right]\left[{p_1}^0-{p_1}^1\right]\\&=p^1\cdot y^1+{y_1}^1\left[{p_1}^0-{p_1}^1\right].\qquad\text{using (2) and (3)}\end{aligned}\tag{24}$$

Thus we have the following first order approximation to the first term on the right-hand side of (23):

$$\begin{aligned}&\Pi^1\left(p^1,x^1\right)-\Pi^1\left({p_1}^0,{p_2}^1,\ldots,{p_M}^1,x^1\right)\\&\quad\approx p^1\cdot y^1-\left\{p^1\cdot y^1+{y_1}^1\left[{p_1}^0-{p_1}^1\right]\right\}\qquad\text{using (2) and (24)}\\&\quad={y_1}^1\left[{p_1}^1-{p_1}^0\right].\end{aligned}\tag{25}$$

In a similar manner to the derivation of (24), we can derive the following first order approximation to $\Pi^1({p_1}^0, {p_2}^0, {p_3}^1, \ldots, {p_M}^1, x^1)$:

$$\begin{aligned}&\Pi^1\left({p_1}^0,{p_2}^0,{p_3}^1,\ldots,{p_M}^1,x^1\right)\approx\Pi^1\left(p^1,x^1\right)\\&+\left[\partial\Pi^1\left(p^1,x^1\right)/\partial p_1\right]\left[{p_1}^0-{p_1}^1\right]+\left[\partial\Pi^1\left(p^1,x^1\right)/\partial p_2\right]\left[{p_2}^0-{p_2}^1\right]\\&=p^1\cdot y^1+{y_1}^1\left[{p_1}^0-{p_1}^1\right]+{y_2}^1\left[{p_2}^0-{p_2}^1\right].\qquad\text{using (2) and (3)}\end{aligned}\tag{26}$$

Thus we have the following first order approximation to the second term on the right-hand side of (23):

$$\begin{aligned}&\Pi^1\left({p_1}^0,{p_2}^1,\ldots,{p_M}^1,x^1\right)-\Pi^1\left({p_1}^0,{p_2}^0,{p_3}^1,\ldots,{p_M}^1,x^1\right)\approx p^1\cdot y^1\\&+{y_1}^1\left[{p_1}^0-{p_1}^1\right]-\left\{p^1\cdot y^1+{y_1}^1\left[{p_1}^0-{p_1}^1\right]+{y_2}^1\left[{p_2}^0-{p_2}^1\right]\right\}\quad\text{using (24) and (26)}\\&={y_2}^1\left[{p_2}^1-{p_2}^0\right].\end{aligned}\tag{27}$$

In a similar fashion, it can be shown that the mth term on the right-hand side of (23) has the first order approximation ${y_m}^1[{p_m}^1 - {p_m}^0]$ for $m = 1, 2, \ldots, M$. The sum of these first order approximations is

$$\Sigma_{m=1}{}^{M} y_m{}^1 \left[p_m{}^1 - p_m{}^0\right] = y^1 \cdot \left(p^1 - p^0\right) \approx \Pi^1 \left(p^1, x^1\right) - \Pi^1 \left(p^0, x^1\right). \quad \text{using (9)} \tag{28}$$

Thus we have decomposed the Paasche type measure of aggregate price change, $\Pi^1(p^1, x^1) - \Pi^1(p^0, x^1)$, into the sum of the M individual price change measures on the right-hand side of (23) and the mth individual price change measure is approximately equal to $y_m{}^1[p_m{}^1 - p_m{}^0]$ for m = 1, 2, ..., M.

Recall that the decomposition of value added growth defined by (8) had the overall output price change term $\Pi^0(p^1, x^0) - \Pi^0(p^0, x^0)$ on the right-hand side of the equation. We want to decompose this Laspeyres type overall measure of price change into separate output price change contributions. We use the following decomposition:

$$\begin{aligned}\Pi^0 (p^1, x^0) - \Pi^0 (p^0, x^0) = {} & \Pi^0 (p^1, x^0) - \Pi^0 (p_1{}^0, p_2{}^1, \ldots, p_M{}^1, x^0) \\ & + \Pi^0 (p_1{}^0, p_2{}^1, \ldots, p_M{}^1, x^0) - \Pi^0 (p_1{}^0, p_2{}^0, p_3{}^1, \ldots, p_M{}^1, x^0) \\ & + \ldots \\ & + \Pi^0 (p_1{}^0, \ldots, p_{M-1}{}^0, p_M{}^1, x^0) - \Pi^0 (p^0, x^0).\end{aligned} \tag{29}$$

The right-hand side of (29) consists of M differences in $\Pi^0(p, x^0)$ where each difference changes only one component of the p vector. We will approximate these terms by taking first order Taylor series approximations to the $\Pi^0(p, x^0)$ around the point $p = p^0$. Thus the first order approximation to $\Pi^0(p_1{}^0, \ldots, p_{M-1}{}^0, p_M{}^1, x^0)$ is the following one:

$$\begin{aligned}& \Pi^0 \left(p_1{}^0, \ldots, p_{M-1}{}^0, p_M{}^1, x^0\right) \approx \Pi^0 \left(p^0, x^0\right) + \left[\partial \Pi^0 \left(p^0, x^0\right) / \partial p_M\right] \left[p_M{}^1 - p_M{}^0\right] \\ & = p^0 \cdot y^0 + y_M{}^0 \left[p_M{}^1 - p_M{}^0\right] \qquad \text{using (2) and (3)}\end{aligned} \tag{30}$$

Thus we have the following first order approximation to the last term on the right-hand side of (29):

$$\begin{aligned}& \Pi^0 (p_1{}^0, \ldots, p_{M-1}{}^0, p_M{}^1, x^0) \\ & - \Pi^0 (p^0, x^0) \approx p^0 \cdot y^0 + y_M{}^0 [p_M{}^1 - p_M{}^0] - p^0 \cdot y^0 \qquad \text{using (2) and (30)} \\ & = y_M{}^0 [p_M{}^1 - p_M{}^0].\end{aligned} \tag{31}$$

In a similar fashion, it can be shown that the mth term on the right-hand side of (29) has the first order approximation $y_m{}^0[p_m{}^1 - p_m{}^0]$ for m = 1,2, ..., M. The sum of these first order approximations is

$$\Sigma_{m=1}^{M} y_m^{0}\left[p_m^{1}-p_m^{0}\right]=y^0\cdot\left(p^1-p^0\right)\approx \Pi^0\left(p^1,x^0\right)-\Pi^0\left(p^0,x^0\right).\ \text{using (13)} \tag{32}$$

Thus we have decomposed the Laspeyres type measure of aggregate price change, $\Pi^0(p^1, x^0) - \Pi^0(p^0, x^0)$, into the sum of the M individual price change measures on the right-hand side of (29) and the mth individual price change measure is approximately equal to $y_m^0[p_m^1 - p_m^0]$ for $m = 1,2, \ldots, M$.

Recall that the overall Bennet indicator of value added price change was defined as $(1/2)(y^0+y^1)\cdot(p^1 - p^0)$ which is the arithmetic average of the Paasche and Laspeyres measures of price change, $\Sigma_{m=1}^{M} y_m^1[p_m^1 - p_m^0]$ and $\Sigma_{m=1}^{M} y_m^0[p_m^1 - p_m^0]$, respectively. Thus the mth term in the Bennet indicator of value added price change, $(1/2)y_m^1[p_m^1 - p_m^0] + (1/2)y_m^0[p_m^1 - p_m^0]$, can be interpreted as an approximation to the theoretical measure of change in the price of the mth output that is defined by the arithmetic average of the mth terms on the right-hand sides of (23) and (29).

The decomposition of value added growth defined by (7) had the overall input quantity change term $[\Pi^0(p^0, x^1) - \Pi^0(p^0, x^0)]$ on the right-hand side of the equation. We want to decompose this Laspeyres type overall measure of input quantity change into separate input quantity change contributions. We use the following decomposition:

$$\begin{aligned}\Pi^0\left(p^0,x^1\right)-\Pi^0\left(p^0,x^0\right)&=\Pi^0\left(p^0,x^1\right)-\Pi^0\left(p^0,x_1^0,x_2^1,\ldots,x_N^1\right)\\&+\Pi^0\left(p^0,x_1^0,x_2^1,\ldots,x_N^1\right)-\Pi^0\left(p^0,x_1^0,x_2^0,x_3^1,\ldots,x_N^1\right)\\&+\ldots\\&+\Pi^0\left(p^0,x_1^0,\ldots,x_{N-2}^0,x_{N-1}^1,x_N^1\right)-\Pi^0\left(p^0,x_1^0,\ldots,x_{N-1}^0,x_N^1\right)\\&+\Pi^0\left(p^0,x_1^0,\ldots,x_{N-1}^0,x_N^1\right)-\Pi^0\left(p^0,x^0\right)\end{aligned} \tag{33}$$

The right-hand side of (33) consists of N differences in $\Pi^0(p^0, x)$ where each difference changes only one component of the x vector. We will approximate these terms by taking first order Taylor series approximations to the $\Pi^0(p^0, x)$ around the point $x = x^0$. Thus the first order approximation to $\Pi^0(p^0, x_1^0, \ldots, x_{N-1}^0, x_N^1)$ is the following one:

$$\begin{aligned}&\Pi^0\left(p^0,x_1^0,\ldots,x_{N-1}^0,x_N^1\right)\approx \Pi^0\left(p^0,x^0\right)+\left[\partial \Pi^0\left(p^0,x^0\right)/\partial x_N\right]\left[x_N^1-x_N^0\right]\\&=p^0\cdot y^0+w_N^0\left[x_N^1-x_N^0\right].\qquad \text{using (2) and (4)}\end{aligned} \tag{34}$$

Thus we have the following first order approximation to the last term on the right-hand side of (33):

$$\begin{aligned}&\Pi^0\left(p^0, x_1{}^0, \ldots, x_{N-1}{}^0, x_N{}^1\right) - \Pi^0\left(p^0, x^0\right)\\ &\approx p^0 \cdot y^0 + w_N{}^0\left[x_N{}^1 - x_N{}^0\right] - p^0 \cdot y^0 \qquad \text{using (2) and (34)}\\ &= w_N{}^0\left[x_N{}^1 - x_N{}^0\right].\end{aligned} \tag{35}$$

In a similar fashion, it can be shown that the nth term on the right-hand side of (33) has the first order approximation $w_n{}^0[x_n{}^1 - x_n{}^0]$ for $n = 1, 2, \ldots, N$. The sum of these first order approximations is

$$\Sigma_{n=1}{}^N w_n{}^0\left[x_n{}^1 - x_n{}^0\right] = w^0 \cdot \left(x^1 - x^0\right) \approx \Pi^0\left(p^0, x^1\right) - \Pi^0\left(p^0, x^0\right). \quad \text{using (11)} \tag{36}$$

Thus we have decomposed the Laspeyres type measure of aggregate input quantity change, $\Pi^0(p^0, x^1) - \Pi^0(p^0, x^0)$, into the sum of the N individual input quantity change measures on the right-hand side of (33) and the nth individual quantity change measure is approximately equal to $w_n{}^0[x_n{}^1 - x_n{}^0]$ for $n = 1, 2, \ldots, N$.

The decomposition of value added growth defined by (8) had the overall input quantity change term $[\Pi^1(p^1, x^1) - \Pi^1(p^1, x^0)]$ on the right-hand side of the equation. We want to decompose this Paasche type overall measure of input quantity change into individual input quantity change contributions. We use the following decomposition:

$$\begin{aligned}\Pi^1\left(p^1, x^1\right) - \Pi^1\left(p^1, x^0\right) &= \Pi^1\left(p^1, x^1\right) - \Pi^1\left(p^1, x_1{}^0, x_2{}^1, \ldots, x_N{}^1\right)\\ &\quad + \Pi^1\left(p^1, x_1{}^0, x_2{}^1, \ldots, x_N{}^1\right) - \Pi^1\left(p^1, x_1{}^0, x_2{}^0, x_3{}^1, \ldots, x_N{}^1\right)\\ &\quad + \ldots\\ &\quad + \Pi^1\left(p^1, x_1{}^0, \ldots, x_{N-1}{}^0, x_N{}^1\right) - \Pi^1\left(p^1, x^0\right).\end{aligned} \tag{37}$$

The right-hand side of (37) consists of N differences in $\Pi^1(p^1, x)$ where each difference changes only one component of the x vector. As usual, we approximate these terms by taking first order Taylor series approximations to the $\Pi^1(p^1, x)$ around the point $x = x^1$. The observable first order approximation to the unobservable term $\Pi^1(p^1, x_1{}^0, x_2{}^1, \ldots, x_N{}^1)$ is the following one:

$$\begin{aligned}\Pi^1\left(p^1, x_1{}^0, x_2{}^1, \ldots, x_N{}^1\right) &\approx \Pi^1\left(p^1, x^1\right) + \left[\partial \Pi^1\left(p^1, x^1\right)/\partial x_1\right]\left[x_1{}^0 - x_1{}^1\right]\\ &= p^1 \cdot y^1 + w_1{}^1\left[x_1{}^0 - x_1{}^1\right]. \qquad \text{using (2) and (4)}\end{aligned} \tag{38}$$

Thus we have the following observable first order approximation to the unobservable first term on the right-hand side of (37):

$$\begin{aligned}\Pi^1(p^1, x^1) \; -\Pi^1(p^1, x_1{}^0, x_2{}^1, \ldots, x_N{}^1) &\approx p^1 \cdot y^1 \\ &- \{p^1 \cdot y^1 + w_1{}^1[x_1{}^0 - x_1{}^1]\} \qquad \text{using (2) and (38)} \qquad (39) \\ &= w_1{}^1[x_1{}^1 - x_1{}^0].\end{aligned}$$

In a similar fashion, it can be shown that the nth term on the right-hand side of (37) has the first order approximation $w_n{}^1[x_n{}^1 - x_n{}^0]$ for n = 1, 2, ..., N. The sum of these first order approximations is

$$\Sigma_{n=1}{}^N w_n{}^1[x_n{}^1 - x_n{}^0] = w^1 \cdot (x^1 - x^0) \approx \Pi^1(p^1, x^1) - \Pi^1(p^1, x^0). \quad \text{using (15)} \qquad (40)$$

We have decomposed the Paasche type measure of aggregate input quantity change, $\Pi^1(p^1, x^1)\Pi^1(p^1, x^0)$, into the sum of the N individual input quantity change measures defined on the right-hand side of (37) and the nth individual quantity change measure is approximately equal to $w_n{}^1[x_n{}^1 - x_n{}^0]$ for n = 1, 2, ..., N.

Recall that the overall Bennet indicator of input quantity change was defined as $(1/2)(w^0 + w^1) \cdot (x^1 - x^0)$ which is the arithmetic average of the Laspeyres and Paasche measures of input quantity change, $\Sigma_{n=1}{}^N w_n{}^0[x_n{}^1 - x_n{}^0]$ and $\Sigma_{n=1}{}^N w_n{}^1[x_n{}^1 - x_n{}^0]$, respectively. The nth term in the Bennet indicator of aggregate input quantity change, $(1/2)w_n{}^0[x_n{}^1 - x_n{}^0] + (1/2)w_n{}^1[x_n{}^1 - x_n{}^0]$, can be interpreted as an approximation to the theoretical measure of input n quantity change that is defined by the arithmetic average of the nth terms on the right-hand sides of (33) and (37).

4 The Problem of Adjusting the Measures for General Inflation

Today's dollar is, then, a totally different unit from the dollar of 1897. As the general price level fluctuates, the dollar is bound to become a unit of different magnitude. To mix these units is like mixing inches and centimeters or measuring a field with a rubber tape-line. Livingston Middleditch (1918, pp. 114–115).

Diewert (2005, p. 339) noted the above quotation by Middleditch in his discussion of the problem of adjusting for general inflation in making revenue, cost, and profit comparisons in difference form over two periods in time. Diewert noted that if there is a great change in the general purchasing power of money between the two periods being compared, then the Bennet indicators of quantity change may be "excessively" heavily weighted by the prices of the period with the highest general price level. His solution to this weighting problem was very simple: in each period, divide the period t nominal output and input prices, $p_m{}^t$ and $w_n{}^t$ by a suitable price index, say ρ^t. Thus define the period t *real output and input price vectors*, p^{t*} and w^{t*} as follows:

$$p^{t*} \equiv p^t/\rho^t;\ w^{t*} \equiv w^t/\rho^t;\ t = 0, 1, \ldots, T. \tag{41}$$

The period t value added function $\Pi^t(p, x)$ is linearly homogeneous in the components of p as are the derivatives $\partial\Pi^t(p, x)/\partial x_n$ for $n = 1, \ldots, T$. Using these homogeneity properties, we can establish the following counterparts to the Hotelling and Samuelson Lemma results (2) and (3):

$$\nabla_p \Pi^t\left(p^{t*}, x^t\right) \equiv \nabla_p \Pi^t\left(p^t/\rho^t, x^t\right) = \nabla_p \Pi^t\left(p^t, x^t\right) = y^t;\ t = 0, 1, \ldots, T; \tag{42}$$

$$\begin{aligned} \nabla_x \Pi^t\left(p^{t*}, x^t\right) &\equiv \nabla_x \Pi^t\left(p^t/\rho^t, x^t\right) = \left(1/\rho^t\right) \nabla_x \Pi^t\left(p^t, x^t\right) \\ &= \left(1/\rho^t\right) w^t = w^{t*};\ t = 0, 1, \ldots, T. \end{aligned} \tag{43}$$

Thus all of the nonparametric results established in Sects. 2 and 3 above go through unchanged if we replace p^t by p^{t*} and w^t by w^{t*}. The significance of this result is substantial: if we deflate nominal prices into real prices in each time period, it is almost certain that real price change from period to period will be less than the corresponding nominal price change. *Thus the first order approximations used in the previous sections will generally be subject to smaller errors and hence our decompositions using real prices are going to be more accurate.* This is particularly true if between period inflation is high. This is a powerful argument for using real prices.

There remains the problem of choosing the deflator, ρ^t. In order to determine an appropriate deflator, we need to ask what is the purpose of the analysis or what is the application of the theory? In most applications, the task at hand is the measurement of the productivity growth of the production unit under consideration. If the production unit is a firm, investors will be interested in revenues and costs deflated by a suitable consumer price index. Factors of production will be interested in the growth of their real compensation; i.e., how many bundles of consumption can their present period compensation purchase relative to the previous period. Again, deflation by a consumer price index seems appropriate. Some policy makers may argue for a broader deflator such as a deflator for domestic output or absorption.

In summary, the choice of the deflator will depend on the purpose of the exercise but in most cases, deflation by a consumer price index (or a consumption deflator) will probably be appropriate.[16] However, the accounting profession has resisted moving to this type of accounting, even when general inflation was high so we do not expect that productivity decompositions that use the difference approach adjusted for general inflation will become a routine part of the quarterly and

[16]This type of accounting for general price level changes was first suggested by Middleditch (1918) and by Sweeny (1927, 1931). Sweeny called his method "stabilized accounting" as opposed to the usual historical cost accounting.

annual reports of corporations.[17] But governments and business economists are interested in productivity decompositions and so in the future, we think it is likely that decompositions similar to the ones we propose in this paper will be made, particularly for firm level data where the problems associated with the treatment of new and disappearing products emerge.

The analysis presented up to this point suffers from (at least) two problems:

- We have assumed constant returns to scale and
- We have assumed (competitive) profit maximizing behavior and hence there is no possibility of technical inefficiency.

In the following section, we develop an alternative methodology that allows for the possibility of technical inefficiency.[18]

5 The Difference Approach to Productivity Measurement Using the Nonparametric Cost Constrained Value Added Function

The approach used in this section can be explained in a few sentences. Diewert and Fox (2018) worked out an approach to the measurement of productivity in a constant returns to scale context that was based on traditional multiplicative index number theory.[19] The theoretical indexes used in that paper could be calculated using the concept of a cost constrained value added function that made use of a particular nonparametric approximation to the true technology of a production unit. The nonparametric approximation to the true technology is the set of all

[17]In the 1970s and 1980s when inflation was high in most OECD countries, there was some interest by academic accountants in moving away from historical cost accounting and towards what was called "current value accounting"; see Baxter (1975), Whittington (1980), and Zeff (1982). However, the issues associated with adjusting for price level changes between accounting periods are complex: there was controversy between those who advocated specific price level changes (for the treatment of durable asset price changes) and those who advocated general price level changes of the type considered by Sweeney. As a result, historical cost accounting was not overturned and as inflation died down in OECD countries, the issues associated with adjusting for general inflation were forgotten. We believe that these issues will become important again in the future as more and more microeconomic data on the inputs used and outputs produced by production units become available. For the record, we agree with the approach taken by the accountant Sterling (1975, p. 51): "It follows that the appropriate procedure is to (1) adjust the present statement to current values and (2) adjust the previous statement by a price index. It is important to recognize that *both* adjustments are necessary and that neither is a substitute for the other. Confusion on this point is widespread."

[18]We are not able to relax the assumption of constant returns to scale because the nonparametric cost constrained value added function that we use in our analysis in the following section is not always well defined unless we assume constant returns to scale in production.

[19]This paper drew heavily on the earlier papers by Balk (2003) and Diewert (2014).

nonnegative linear combinations of past production vectors. This section simply reworks their multiplicative index number decompositions into difference form. The details follow.

Define the production unit's *period t cost constrained value added function*, $R^t(p, w, x)$ as follows:[20]

$$R^t(p, w, x) \equiv \max_{y,z} \{p \cdot y : (y, z) \in S^t; w \cdot z \leq w \cdot x\}. \tag{44}$$

If (y^*, z^*) solves the constrained maximization problem defined by (44), then the value added $p \cdot y$ of the production unit is maximized subject to the constraints that (y, z) is a feasible production vector and primary input expenditure $w \cdot z$ is equal to or less than "observed" primary input expenditure $w \cdot x$. Thus if the sector faces the prices $p^t \gg 0_M$ and $w^t \gg 0_N$ during period t and (y^t, x^t) is the sector's observed production vector, then production will be *value added efficient* if the observed value added, $p^t \cdot y^t$, is equal to the optimal value added, $R^t(p^t, w^t, x^t)$. However, production may not be efficient and so the following inequality will hold:

$$p^t \cdot y^t \leq R^t(p^t, w^t, x^t); t = 0, 1, \ldots, T. \tag{45}$$

Adapting the ratio definition of Balk (1998, p. 143) to the difference context, we define the *value added* or *net revenue efficiency* of the production unit during period t, e^t, as follows:

$$e^t \equiv p^t \cdot y^t - R^t(p^t, w^t, x^t) \leq 0; t = 0, 1, \ldots, T \tag{46}$$

where the inequality in (46) follows from (45). Thus if $e^t = 0$, then production is allocatively efficient in period t and if $e^t < 0$, then production during period t is allocatively inefficient. Note that the above definition of value added efficiency is a net revenue difference counterpart to Farrell's (1957, p. 255) cost based measure of *overall efficiency* in the DEA context, which combined his measures of technical and (cost) allocative efficiency. DEA or *Data Envelopment Analysis* is the term used by Charnes and Cooper (1985) and their co-workers to denote an area of analysis which

---

[20]The cost constrained value added function is analogous to Diewert's (1983, p. 1086) *balance of trade restricted value added function* and Diewert and Morrison's (1986, p. 669) *domestic sales function*. However, the basic idea can be traced back to Shephard's (1974) *maximal return function*, Fisher and Shell's (1998, p. 48) *cost restricted sales function*, and Balk's (2003, p. 34) *indirect revenue function*. See also Färe et al. (1992, p. 286) and Färe and Primont (1994, p. 203) on Shephard's formulation. Shephard, Fisher and Shell, and Balk defined their functions as $IR^t(p, w, c) \equiv \max_{y,z} \{p \cdot y: w \cdot z \leq c; (y, z) \in S^t\}$ where $c > 0$ is a scalar cost constraint. It can be seen that our cost constrained value added function replaces c in the above definition by $w \cdot x$, a difference which will be important in forming our input indexes and hence our value added decompositions. Another difference is that our y vector is a net output vector; i.e., some components of y can be negative. Excluding Diewert and Morrison (1986) and Diewert (1983), the other authors required that y be nonnegative. This makes a difference to our analysis. Also, our regularity conditions are weaker than the ones that are usually used.

is called the nonparametric approach to production theory or the measurement of the efficiency of production by economists.[21]

We assume that the production unit's period t production possibilities set S^t is the conical free disposal hull of the period t actual production vector and past production vectors that are in our sample of time series observations for the unit.[22] Using this assumption about S^t, for strictly positive price vectors p and w and nonnegative input quantity vector x, we define the *period t cost constrained value added function* $R^t(p, w, x)$ for the production unit as follows:

$$\begin{aligned} R^t(p, w, x) &\equiv \max_{y,z}\left\{p\cdot y : w\cdot z \le w\cdot x; (y, z) \in S^t\right\} \\ &\ge \max_\lambda \{p\cdot \lambda y^s : w\cdot \lambda x^s \le w\cdot x; \lambda \ge 0\} \quad \text{since } (\lambda y^s, \lambda x^s) \in S^t \text{ for all } \lambda \ge 0 \\ &= \max_\lambda \{\lambda p\cdot y^s : \lambda w\cdot x^s \le w\cdot x; \lambda \ge 0\} \\ &= (w\cdot x/w\cdot x^s)\, p\cdot y^s. \end{aligned} \tag{47}$$

The inequality in (47) will hold for all s = 1, 2, ..., t. Thus we have

$$R^t(p, w, x) \ge \max_s \left\{p\cdot y^s\, w\cdot x/w\cdot x^s : s = 1, 2, \ldots, t\right\}. \tag{48}$$

The rays $(\lambda y^s, \lambda x^s) \in S^t$ for $\lambda \ge 0$ generate the efficient points in the set S^t so the strict inequality in (42) cannot hold and so we have

$$\begin{aligned} R^t(p, w, x) &\equiv \max_{y,z}\left\{p\cdot y : w\cdot z \le w\cdot x; (y, z) \in S^t\right\} \\ &= \max_s \{p\cdot y^s w\cdot x/w\cdot x^s : s = 1, 2, \ldots, t\} \\ &= w\cdot x \max_s \{p\cdot y^s/w\cdot x^s : s = 1, 2, \ldots, t\} \\ &= \max_{\lambda_1,\ldots,\lambda_t} p\cdot \left(\Sigma_{s=1}{}^t y^s\lambda_s\right); w\cdot \left(\Sigma_{s=1}{}^t x^s\lambda_s\right) \\ &\le w\cdot x; \lambda_1 \ge 0, \ldots, \lambda_t \ge 0\Big\} \end{aligned} \tag{49}$$

where the last line in (49) follows from the fact that the solution to the linear programming problem is an extreme point and thus its solution is equal to the second line in (49). Thus all three equalities in (49) can serve to define $R^t(p, w, x)$. We assume that all inner products of the form $p\cdot y^s$ and $w\cdot x^s$ are positive and

[21] The early contributors to this literature were Farrell (1957), Afriat (1972), Hanoch and Rothschild (1972), Färe and Lovell (1978), Diewert and Parkan (1983), Varian (1984), and Färe et al. (1985).

[22] Diewert (1980, p. 264) suggested that the convex, conical, free disposal hull of past and current production vectors be used as an approximation to the period t technology set S^t when measuring TFP growth. Tulkens (1993, pp. 201–206) and Diewert and Fox (2014, 2017) dropped the convexity and constant returns to scale assumptions and used free disposal hulls of past and current production vectors to represent the period t technology sets. In this paper, we also drop the convexity assumption but maintain the free disposal and constant returns to scale assumptions. We also follow Diewert and Parkan (1983, pp. 153–157), Balk (2003, p. 37), and Diewert and Mendoza (2007) in introducing price data into the computations.

this assumption rules out the possibility of a $\lambda_s = 0$ solution to the third line in (49). The last expression in (49) can be used to show that when we assume constant returns to scale for our nonparametric representation for S^t, the resulting $R^t(p, w, x)$ is linear and nondecreasing in x, is convex and linearly homogeneous in p, and is homogeneous of degree 0 in w. The bottom line is that the third equality in (49) can be used to evaluate the function $R^t(p, w, x)$ as p, w, and x take on the observable values in the definitions which follow.

Our task in this section is to decompose the growth in observed nominal value added over the two periods, $p^t \cdot y^t - p^{t-1} \cdot y^{t-1}$, into explanatory growth factors.

One of the explanatory factors will be the *growth in the value added efficiency* of the sector or production unit. Above, we defined the period t value added efficiency as $e^t \equiv p^t \cdot y^t - R^t(p^t, w^t, x^t)$. Define the corresponding period $t - 1$ efficiency as $e^{t-1} \equiv p^{t-1} \cdot y^{t-1} - R^{t-1}(p^{t-1}, w^{t-1}, x^{t-1})$. Given the above definitions of value added efficiency in periods t−1 and t, we can define an index of the *change in value added efficiency* ε^t for the sector over the two periods as follows:

$$\varepsilon^t \equiv e^t - e^{t-1} = p^t \cdot y^t - p^{t-1} \cdot y^{t-1} - \left[R^t\left(p^t, w^t, x^t\right) - R^{t-1}\left(p^{t-1}, w^{t-1}, x^{t-1}\right)\right]; \quad t=1, 2, \ldots, T. \tag{50}$$

The above equations can be rewritten as follows:

$$p^t \cdot y^t - p^{t-1} \cdot y^{t-1} = \varepsilon^t + R^t\left(p^t, w^t, x^t\right) - R^{t-1}\left(p^{t-1}, w^{t-1}, x^{t-1}\right); \; t=1, 2, \ldots, T. \tag{51}$$

Notice that the cost constrained value added function for the production unit in period t, $R^t(p, w, x)$, depends on four sets of variables:

- The time period t and this index t serves to indicate that the period t technology set S^t is used to define the period t value added function;
- The vector of net output prices p that the production unit faces;
- The vector of primary input prices w that the production unit faces, and
- The vector of primary inputs x which is available for use by the production unit during period t.

At this point, we will follow the methodology that is used in the economic approach to index number theory that originated with Konüs (1939) and Allen (1949) and we will use the value added function to define various *families of indexes* that vary only *one* of the four sets of variables, t, p, w, and x, between the two periods under consideration and hold constant the other sets of variables.

Our first family of factors that explain sectoral value added growth is a family of *net output price indicators*, $\alpha(p^{t-1}, p^t, w, x, t)$:

$$\alpha\left(p^{t-1}, p^t, w, x, s\right) \equiv R^s\left(p^t, w, x\right) - R^s\left(p^{t-1}, w, x\right). \tag{52}$$

Following the example of Konüs (1939) in his analysis of the true cost of living index, it is natural to single out two special cases of the family of net output price indicators defined by (52): one choice where we use the period t − 1 technology and set the reference input prices and quantities equal to the period t − 1 input prices and quantities w^{t-1} and x^{t-1} (which gives rise to a *Laspeyres type net output price indicator*) and another choice where we use the period t technology and set the reference input prices and quantities equal to the period t prices and quantities w^t and x^t (which gives rise to a *Paasche type net output price indicator*). We define these special cases $\alpha_L{}^t$ and $\alpha_P{}^t$ for t = 1, …, T as follows:

$$\alpha_L{}^t \equiv \alpha\left(p^{t-1}, p^t, w^{t-1}, x^{t-1}, t-1\right) \equiv R^{t-1}\left(p^t, w^{t-1}, x^{t-1}\right) - R^{t-1}\left(p^{t-1}, w^{t-1}, x^{t-1}\right); \quad (53)$$

$$\alpha_P{}^t \equiv \alpha\left(p^{t-1}, p^t, w^t, x^t, t\right) \equiv R^t\left(p^t, w^t, x^t\right) - R^t\left(p^{t-1}, w^t, x^t\right). \quad (54)$$

Our second family of factors that explain value added growth is a family of *input quantity indicators*, $\beta(x^{t-1}, x^t, p, w, s)$:

$$\beta\left(x^{t-1}, x^t, p, w, s\right) \equiv R^s\left(p, w, x^t\right) - R^s\left(p, w, x^{t-1}\right) \quad (55)$$

It is natural to single out two special cases of the family of input quantity indexes defined by (55): one choice where we use the period t − 1 technology, input prices and output prices as the reference p, w, and s which gives rise to the *Laspeyres input quantity indicator* $\beta_L{}^t$ and another choice where we set the reference p, w equal to p^t and w^t and set s equal to t which gives rise to the *Paasche input quantity indicator* $\beta_P{}^t$. Thus define these special cases $\beta_L{}^t$ and $\beta_P{}^t$ for t = 1, …, T as follows:

$$\beta_L{}^t \equiv R^{t-1}\left(p^{t-1}, w^{t-1}, x^t\right) - R^{t-1}\left(p^{t-1}, w^{t-1}, x^{t-1}\right); \quad (56)$$

$$\beta_P{}^t \equiv R^t\left(p^t, w^t, x^t\right) - R^t\left(p^t, w^t, x^{t-1}\right). \quad (57)$$

Our next family of indexes will measure the effects on cost constrained value added of a change in input prices going from period t − 1 to t. We consider a family of measures of the relative change in cost constrained value added of the form $R^s(p, w^t, x) - R^s(p, w^{t-1}, x)$. Since $R^s(p, w, x)$ is homogeneous of degree 0 in the components of w, it can be seen that we cannot interpret $R^s(p, w^t, x)/R^s(p, w^{t-1}, x)$ as an input price index and hence $R^s(p, w^t, x) - R^s(p, w^{t-1}, x)$ cannot be interpreted as an input price indicator. It is best to interpret $R^s(p, w^t, x) - R^s(p, w^{t-1}, x)$ as measuring the effects on cost constrained value added of a change in the relative proportions of inputs and outputs used in production or in the *mix* of inputs and outputs used in production that is induced by a change in relative input prices when there is more than one primary input. Thus define the family of *input mix indicators* $\gamma(w^{t-1}, w^t, p, x, s)$ as follows:[23]

$$\gamma\left(w^{t-1}, w^t, p, x, s\right) \equiv R^s\left(p, w^t, x\right) - R^s\left(p, w^{t-1}, x\right). \tag{58}$$

We will consider two special cases of the above family of input mix indicators, neither of which is a "pure" Laspeyres or Paasche type indicator:

$$\begin{aligned}\gamma_{LP}{}^t \equiv \gamma\left(w^{t-1}, w^t, p^{t-1}, x^t, t\right) &\equiv R^t\left(p^{t-1}, w^t, x^t\right) \\ &-R^t\left(p^{t-1}, w^{t-1}, x^t\right); t = 1, \ldots, T;\end{aligned} \tag{59}$$

$$\gamma_{PL}{}^t \equiv \gamma\left(w^{t-1}, w^t, p^t, x^{t-1}, t-1\right) \equiv R^{t-1}\left(p^t, w^t, x^{t-1}\right) - R^{t-1}\left(p^t, w^{t-1}, x^{t-1}\right); \quad t=1, \ldots, T. \tag{60}$$

The reason for these rather odd looking choices for reference vectors will become apparent below because they lead to exact decompositions of the difference in observed value added between two successive periods.

Finally, we use the cost constrained value added function in order to define a family of *technical progress indicators* going from period $t-1$ to t, $\tau(t, p, w, x)$, for reference vectors of output and input prices, p and w, and a reference vector of input quantities x as follows:[24]

$$\tau\left(t, p, w, x\right) \equiv R^t\left(p, w, x\right) - R^{t-1}\left(p, w, x\right). \tag{61}$$

If there is positive technical progress going from period $t-1$ to t, then $R^t(t, p, w, x)$ will generally be greater than $R^{t-1}(p, w, x)$ and hence $\tau(t, p, w, x)$ will be greater

[23]It would be more accurate to say that $\gamma(w^{t-1}, w^t, p, x, s)$ represents the hypothetical change in cost constrained value added for the period s reference technology due to the effects of a change in the input price vector from w^{t-1} to w^t when facing the reference net output prices p and the reference vector of inputs x. Thus we shorten this description to say that γ is an "input mix indicator." If there is only one primary input, then since $R^s(p, w, x)$ is homogeneous of degree 0 in w, $R^s(p, w, x)$ does not vary as the scalar w varies and hence $\gamma(w^{t-1}, w^t, p, x, s) \equiv 0$; i.e., if there is only one primary input, then the input mix index is identically equal to 0. For alternative mix definitions in the index number context, see Balk (2001) and Diewert (2014, p. 62).

[24]The counterpart to this family of technical progress indicators was defined in the index number context by Diewert and Morrison (1986, p. 662) using the value added function $\Pi^t(p, x)$. A special case of this ratio family was defined earlier by Diewert (1983, p. 1063). Balk (1998, p. 99) also used this definition and Balk (1998, p. 58), following the example of Salter (1960), also used the joint cost function to define a similar family of technical progress indexes.

than zero. If S^{t-1} is a subset of S^t (so that technologies are not forgotten), then $\tau(t, p, w, x) \geq 0$.

Again, we will consider two special cases of the above family of technical progress indexes, a "mixed" Laspeyres case and a "mixed" Paasche case. The Laspeyres Paasche case $\tau_{LP}{}^t$ will use the period t − 1 reference output and input price vectors p^{t-1} and w^{t-1} and the period t input vector x^t as the reference input vector while the Paasche Laspeyres case $\tau_{PL}{}^t$ will use the period t reference output and input price vectors p^t and w^t and use the period t − 1 input vector x^{t-1} as the reference input vector:

$$\tau_{LP}{}^t \equiv \tau\left(t, p^{t-1}, w^{t-1}, x^t\right) \equiv R^t\left(p^{t-1}, w^{t-1}, x^t\right) - R^{t-1}\left(p^{t-1}, w^{t-1}, x^t\right). \tag{62}$$

$$\tau_{PL}{}^t \equiv \tau\left(t, p^t, w^t, x^{t-1}\right) \equiv R^t\left(p^t, w^t, x^{t-1}\right) - R^{t-1}\left(p^t, w^t, x^{t-1}\right). \tag{63}$$

We are now in a position to decompose the growth in nominal value added for the production unit going from period t − 1 to t as the sum of five explanatory indicators of change:

- The change in cost constrained value added efficiency over the two periods; i.e., $\varepsilon^t \equiv e^t - e^{t-1}$ defined by (50) above;
- Changes in net output prices; i.e., an indicator of the form $\alpha(p^{t-1}, p^t, w, x, s)$ defined above by (52);
- Changes in input quantities; i.e., an indicator of the form $\beta(x^{t-1}, x^t, p, w, s)$ defined by (55);
- Changes in input prices; i.e., an input mix indicator of the form $\gamma(w^{t-1}, w^t, p, x, s)$ defined by (58), and
- Changes due to technical progress; i.e., an indicator of the form $\tau(t, p, w, x)$ defined by (61).

Straightforward algebra using the above definitions shows that we have the following exact decompositions of the observed value added difference going from period t − 1 to t into explanatory indicators of the above type for $t = 1, \ldots, T$:[25]

$$p^t \cdot y^t - p^{t-1} \cdot y^{t-1} = \varepsilon^t + \alpha_P{}^t + \beta_L{}^t + \gamma_{LP}{}^t + \tau_{LP}{}^t; \tag{64}$$

$$p^t \cdot y^t - p^{t-1} \cdot y^{t-1} = \varepsilon^t + \alpha_L{}^t + \beta_P{}^t + \gamma_{PL}{}^t + \tau_{PL}{}^t. \tag{65}$$

Define the period t arithmetic averages of the above α, β, γ, and τ indicators as follows for $t = 1, \ldots, T$:

[25]These decompositions are the difference analogues to the ratio decompositions obtained by Diewert and Fox (2018).

$$\alpha^t \equiv (1/2)\left(\alpha_L{}^t + \alpha_P{}^t\right); \beta^t \equiv (1/2)\left(\beta_L{}^t + \beta_P{}^t\right); \gamma^t \equiv (1/2)\left(\gamma_{LP}{}^t + \gamma_{PL}{}^t\right);$$
$$\tau^t \equiv (1/2)\left(\tau_{LP}{}^t + \tau_{PL}{}^t\right). \quad (66)$$

Each of the exact decompositions defined by (64) and (65) gives a somewhat different picture of the growth process. If we take the arithmetic average of these decompositions, we will obtain a decomposition that will give the same results whether we measure time going forward or backwards. Hence our preferred growth decomposition is the following one which averages the two decompositions:

$$p^t \cdot y^t - p^{t-1} \cdot y^{t-1} = \varepsilon^t + \alpha^t + \beta^t + \gamma^t + \tau^t; t = 1, \ldots, T. \quad (67)$$

Following Jorgenson and Griliches (1967), a total factor productivity (TFP) growth index can be defined as an output quantity index divided by an input quantity index.[26] Translating this concept into the difference context, we define a TFP indicator as an output quantity indicator less an input quantity indicator. An implicit output quantity indicator is value added growth less an output price indicator. Thus we define our *TFP indicator for period t* as follows:[27]

$$\begin{aligned} TFP^t &\equiv p^t \cdot y^t - p^{t-1} \cdot y^{t-1} - \alpha^t - \beta^t; t = 1, \ldots, T \\ &= \varepsilon^t + \gamma^t + \tau^t. \qquad \text{using (67)} \end{aligned} \quad (68)$$

Thus the indicator of period t Ttotal factor productivity growth, TFP^t, is equal to the sum of period t value added efficiency change ε^t, the period t input mix indicator γ^t (which typically will be close to 0)[28] and the period t indicator of technical progress τ^t. All of the terms in (68) can be measured under our assumptions on the technology sets S^t. The advantage of the decomposition of TFP growth defined by (68) compared to the decomposition (20) that was defined in Sect. 2 above is that the technical change indicator τ^t that appears in (68) is always nonnegative whereas the Bennet indicator of technical progress $B_\tau(p^0, p^1, w^0, w^1, y^0, y^1, x^0, x^1)$ defined by (20) will usually become negative when there is a severe recession. Using the decomposition defined by (68) will avoid this problem: when there is a recession, the efficiency indicator ε^t will typically become negative, indicating that the production unit is no longer on its production frontier. Put another way, the approach outlined in Sect. 2 assumes that the observed output and input vectors for period t, y^t and

[26]This definition of TFP growth can be traced back to Copeland (1937, p. 31) and Siegel (1952, 1961); see Grifell-Tatjé and Lovell (2015, p. 69) for additional references to the early literature on definitions of TFP growth.

[27]The difference decomposition defined by (68) is the difference counterpart to the ratio type decomposition that was obtained by Diewert and Fox (2018).

[28]In the empirical estimates made by Diewert and Fox (2018), the mix index counterpart to our present indicator γ^t was always close to 1, implying that its difference counterpart will be close to 0.

x^t, are always on the frontier of the period t production possibilities set S^t. This assumption is not plausible during recessions because firms cannot instantaneously dispose of their fixed inputs (land and structures) and they often employ more labor input than is efficient because it is not costless to fire and then rehire workers when the recession ends.

It is possible to decompose the overall output price indicator defined by the difference $R^s(p^t, w, x) - R^s(p^{t-1}, w, x)$ into a sum of M commodity specific price indicators if we use the same type of decomposition of $\Pi^0(p^1,x^0) - \Pi^0(p^0,x^0)$ into individual price change components that was defined by (29) in Sect. 3. Similarly, it is possible to decompose the overall input quantity indicator defined by the difference $R^s(p, w, x^t) - R^s(p, w, x^{t-1})$ into a sum of N commodity specific quantity indicators if we use the same type of decomposition of $\Pi^0(p^0,x^1) - \Pi^0(p^0,x^0)$ into individual quantity change components that was defined by (33) in Sect. 3.

Finally, our discussion at the end of Sect. 4 on the usefulness of replacing the nominal price vectors, p^t and w^t, by their deflated counterparts, $p^t/\rho^t \equiv p^{t*}$ and $w^t/\rho^t \equiv w^{t*}$, is still relevant in the present context (where ρ^t is a suitable period t deflator). Using the approach outlined in this section, we no longer have to worry about the accuracy of first order approximations since under our assumptions, we can compute all manner of hypothetical net revenues using the formula for $R^s(p, w, x)$ defined by the third equation in (49). However, the Middleditch quotation is still relevant; it does not make sense to compare nominal amounts of money across time periods when there is general inflation. Thus we recommend that the deflated prices, p^{t*} and w^{t*}, be used in place of the nominal prices, p^t and w^t, in the above definitions and decompositions in order to obtain more meaningful difference type comparisons.

In the following section, we outline our final approach to decomposing value added change into explanatory components.[29]

6 An Exact Indicator Approach to the Decomposition of Value Added Change

Suppose the period t value added function has the following *normalized quadratic* functional form:[30]

$$\begin{aligned}\Pi^t(p, x) \equiv{}& (1/2)\, p^T A p\ (\alpha\cdot p)^{-1}(\beta\cdot x) + (1/2)\, x^T B x\ (\alpha\cdot p)(\beta\cdot x)^{-1} + p^T C x \\ &+ (a\cdot p)(\beta\cdot x)\, t + (\alpha\cdot p)(b\cdot x)\, t\end{aligned} \tag{69}$$

[29]Balk et al. (2004) also used related techniques in an attempt to obtain an exact economic decomposition of a cost difference into Bennet type explanatory factors.

[30]See Diewert and Wales (1987, 1992) for applications of the normalized quadratic functional form to production theory.

where A is an M by M symmetric positive semidefinite matrix of parameters, B is a symmetric N by N matrix of parameters where B has one positive eigenvalue and $N - 1$ nonpositive eigenvalues, C is an M by N matrix of parameters, a and $\alpha > 0_M$ are M dimensional vectors of parameters and b and $\beta > 0_N$ are N dimensional vectors of parameters. It can be shown that the Π defined by (69) is a flexible functional form (in the class of functional forms that are dual to technology sets that are subject to constant returns to scale) for a twice continuously differentiable value added function for any predetermined α and β vectors. Moreover, this functional form allows for commodity specific biased technical charge (the a and b parameter vectors accomplish this). We note that $\Pi^t(\lambda p, x) = \lambda\Pi^t(p, x)$ and $\Pi^t(p, \lambda x) = \lambda\Pi^t(p, x)$ for all scalars $\lambda > 0$; i.e., $\Pi^t(p, x)$ is linearly homogeneous in the components of p and x separately.

The term $(\alpha \cdot p)$ can be regarded as a fixed basket price index and the term $(\beta \cdot x)$ can be regarded as a linear input quantity index. We use these indexes to form the *normalized price and quantity vectors*, ρ and χ:[31]

$$\rho^t \equiv p^t/\alpha \cdot p^t;\ \chi^t \equiv x^t/\beta \cdot x^t;\ t = 0, 1. \tag{70}$$

Using the linear homogeneity properties of $\Pi^t(p^t, x^t)$ and definitions (70), it can be seen that $\Pi^t(\rho^t, \chi^t)$ is equal to the following expression:

$$\Pi^t\left(\rho^t, \chi^t\right) = (1/2)\ \rho^t \cdot A\rho^t + (1/2)\ \chi^t \cdot B\chi^t + \rho^t \cdot C\chi^t + \ \left(a \cdot \rho^t\right) t + \left(b \cdot \chi^t\right) t;\ t = 0, 1. \tag{71}$$

It can be seen that $\Pi(\rho, \chi^t, t)$ is a quadratic function in ρ, χ, and t. Thus we have the following identities:[32]

$$\begin{aligned}&\left[\Pi^0\left(\rho^1, \chi^0\right) - \Pi^0\left(\rho^0, \chi^0\right)\right] + \left[\Pi^1\left(\rho^1, \chi^1\right) - \Pi^1\left(\rho^0, \chi^1\right)\right]\\ &\quad = \left[\nabla_\rho \Pi^0\left(\rho^0, \chi^0\right) + \nabla_\rho \Pi^1\left(\rho^1, \chi^1\right)\right] \cdot \left[\rho^1 - \rho^0\right];\end{aligned} \tag{72}$$

$$\begin{aligned}&\left[\Pi^0\left(\rho^0, \chi^1\right) - \Pi^0\left(\rho^0, \chi^0\right)\right] + \left[\Pi^1\left(\rho^1, \chi^1\right) - \Pi^1\left(\rho^1, \chi^0\right)\right]\\ &\quad = \left[\nabla_\chi \Pi^0\left(\rho^0, \chi^0\right) + \nabla_\chi \Pi^1\left(\rho^1, \chi^1\right)\right] \cdot \left[\chi^1 - \chi^0\right]\end{aligned} \tag{73}$$

We can evaluate the derivatives in (72) and (73) using observed data plus a knowledge of the parameter vectors α and β. Using Hotelling's Lemma, we have

$$y^t = \nabla_\rho \Pi^t\left(p^t, x^t\right);\ t = 0, 1. \tag{74}$$

[31]The new definition for ρ^t is different from the previous definition for ρ^t.

[32]This identity is a generalization of Diewert's (1976, p. 118) *quadratic identity*. A logarithmic version of the above identity corresponds to the *translog identity* which was established in the Appendix to Caves et al. (1982, pp. 1412–1413).

Using Samuelson's Lemma, we have

$$w^t = \nabla_x \Pi^t(p^t, x^t)\,;\, t = 0, 1. \tag{75}$$

Using (74) and (75), definitions (70), and the homogeneity properties of Π, we can establish the following results:

$$\nabla_\rho \Pi^t(\rho^t, \chi^t) = \nabla_p \Pi^t(p^t, x^t/\beta\cdot x^t) = (\beta\cdot x^t)^{-1}\nabla_p \Pi^t(p^t, x^t) = y^t/\beta\cdot x^t;\, t = 0, 1; \tag{76}$$

$$\nabla_\chi \Pi^t(\rho^t, \chi^t) = \nabla_x \Pi^t(p^t/\alpha\cdot p^t, x^t) = (\alpha\cdot p^t)^{-1}\nabla_x \Pi^t(p^t, x^t) = w^t/\alpha\cdot p^t;\, t = 0, 1. \tag{77}$$

(76) and (77) and the homogeneity properties of $\Pi^t(p, x)$ also imply the following relations:

$$\begin{aligned}\Pi^t(\rho^t, \chi^t) &= p^t\cdot y^t/(\alpha\cdot p^t\beta\cdot x^t) = \rho^t\cdot y^t/\beta\cdot x^t = w^t\cdot x^t/(\alpha\cdot p^t\beta\cdot x^t)\\ &= w^t\cdot \chi^t/\alpha\cdot p^t;\, t = 0, 1.\end{aligned} \tag{78}$$

It is convenient to define the inflation adjusted input prices for period t, w^{t*}, as the unadjusted prices w^t divided by the exogenous price index for period t, $\alpha\cdot p^t$.[33] It is also convenient to define the normalized net output quantity vector for period t, y^{t*}, as the unadjusted net output vector y^t divided by the exogenous input index, $\beta\cdot x^t$. Thus we have

$$w^{t*} \equiv w^t/\alpha\cdot p^t;\; y^{t*} \equiv y^t/\beta\cdot x^t;\, t = 0, 1. \tag{79}$$

Using definitions (79), Eqs. (76)–(78) simplify to the following equations:

$$\nabla_\rho \Pi^t(\rho^t, \chi^t) = y^{t*};\, t = 0, 1; \tag{80}$$

$$\nabla_\chi \Pi^t(\rho^t, \chi^t) = w^{t*};\, t = 0, 1; \tag{81}$$

$$\Pi^t(\rho^t, \chi^t) = \rho^t\cdot y^{t*} = w^{t*}\cdot \chi^t;\, t = 0, 1. \tag{82}$$

We will call $\rho^t\cdot y^{t*} = w^{t*}\cdot \chi^t$ the *period t normalized value added* for the production unit. It is equal to unnormalized period t value added, $p^t\cdot y^t = w^t\cdot x^t$, divided by $\alpha\cdot p^t\beta\cdot x^t$.

[33] This definition for w^{t*} is also different from the definition used in the previous section.

Substituting (76) and (77) into (72) and (73) and using (79)–(82) leads to the following identities for the *Bennet indicators of normalized output price change and normalized input quantity change*:

$$\begin{aligned}
&(1/2)\left[\Pi^0(\rho^1,\chi^0)-\Pi^0\left(\rho^0,\chi^0\right)\right]+(1/2)\left[\Pi^1(\rho^1,\chi^1)-\Pi^1\left(\rho^0,\chi^1\right)\right]\\
&=(1/2)\left[(y^0/\beta\cdot x^0)+(y^1/\beta\cdot x^1)\right]\cdot\left[(p^1/\alpha\cdot p^1)-(p^0/\alpha\cdot p^0)\right]\\
&=(1/2)\left[y^{0*}+y^{1*}\right]\cdot\left[\rho^1-\rho^0\right]\\
&\equiv B_\rho\left(\rho^0,\rho^1,y^{0*},y^{1*}\right);
\end{aligned} \tag{83}$$

$$\begin{aligned}
&(1/2)\left[\Pi^0(\rho^0,\chi^1)-\Pi^0(\rho^0,\chi^0)\right]+(1/2)\left[\Pi^1(\rho^1,\chi^1)-\Pi^1(\rho^1,\chi^0)\right]\\
&=(1/2)\left[(w^0/\alpha\cdot p^0)+(w^1/\alpha\cdot p^1)\right]\cdot\left[(x^1/\beta\cdot x^1)-(x^0/\beta\cdot x^0)\right]\\
&=(1/2)\left[w^{0*}+w^{1*}\right]\cdot\left[\chi^1-\chi^0\right]\\
&\equiv B_\chi\left(\chi^0,\chi^1,w^{0*},w^{1*}\right).
\end{aligned} \tag{84}$$

Recall the identities that were defined by Eqs. (7) and (8). Similar decompositions can be applied to the normalized value added difference, $\Pi^1(\rho^1,\chi^1)-\Pi^0(\rho^0,\chi^0)$. Taking the arithmetic average of these two decompositions leads to the following decomposition:

$$\begin{aligned}
\Pi^1(\rho^1,\chi^1)-\Pi^0(\rho^0,\chi^0)&=(1/2)\left[\Pi^1(\rho^1,\chi^1)-\Pi^1\left(\rho^0,\chi^1\right)\right]\\
&+(1/2)\left[\Pi^0(\rho^1,\chi^0)-\Pi^0\left(\rho^0,\chi^0\right)\right]\\
&+(1/2)\left[\Pi^1(\rho^0,\chi^1)-\Pi^0\left(\rho^0,\chi^1\right)\right]+(1/2)\left[\Pi^1(\rho^1,\chi^0)-\Pi^0\left(\rho^1,\chi^0\right)\right]\\
&+(1/2)\left[\Pi^0(\rho^0,\chi^1)-\Pi^0\left(\rho^0,\chi^0\right)\right]+(1/2)\left[\Pi^1(\rho^1,\chi^1)-\Pi^1\left(\rho^1,\chi^0\right)\right]\\
&=(1/2)\left[y^{0*}+y^{1*}\right]\cdot\left[\rho^1-\rho^0\right]+(1/2)\left[\Pi^1(\rho^0,\chi^1)-\Pi^0\left(\rho^0,\chi^1\right)\right]\\
&+(1/2)\left[\Pi^1(\rho^1,\chi^0)-\Pi^0\left(\rho^1,\chi^0\right)\right]\\
&+(1/2)\left[w^{0*}+w^{1*}\right]\cdot\left[\chi^1-\chi^0\right] \quad \text{using (83) and (84)}\\
&=\rho^1\cdot y^{1*}-w^{0*}\cdot\chi^0
\end{aligned} \tag{85}$$

where the last equality follows using (82). The middle term in the above decomposition is a theoretical measure of technical progress going from period 0 to 1. We can use the last equation in (85) to obtain an empirical expression for this theoretical measure, the *normalized Bennet indicator of technical progress*, $B_\tau(\rho^0,\rho^1,w^{0*},w^{1*},y^{0*},y^{1*},\chi^0,\chi^1)$:

$$
\begin{aligned}
&(1/2)\left[\Pi^1\left(\rho^0,\chi^1\right)-\Pi^0\left(\rho^0,\chi^1\right)\right]+(1/2)\left[\Pi^1\left(\rho^1,\chi^0\right)-\Pi^0\left(\rho^1,\chi^0\right)\right]\\
&=\rho^1\cdot y^{1*}-w^{0*}\cdot\chi^0-(1/2)\left[y^{0*}+y^{1*}\right]\cdot\left[\rho^1-\rho^0\right]-(1/2)\left[w^{0*}+w^{1*}\right]\cdot\left[\chi^1-\chi^0\right]\\
&=(1/2)\left[\rho^0\cdot y^{1*}-w^{0*}\cdot\chi^1\right]-(1/2)\left[\rho^1\cdot y^{0*}-w^{1*}\cdot\chi^0\right]\\
&\equiv B_\tau\left(\rho^0,\rho^1,w^{0*},w^{1*},y^{0*},y^{1*},\chi^0,\chi^1\right).
\end{aligned}
\tag{86}
$$

Note that definition (86) is analogous to definition (18). Substituting (86) into (85) and making use of definitions (83) and (84) leads to the following *Bennet type exact decomposition of normalized value added growth* into explanatory components going from period 0 to 1 under our functional form assumptions:

$$
\begin{aligned}
\Pi^1\left(\rho^1,\chi^1\right)-\Pi^0\left(\rho^0,\chi^0\right)&=B_\rho\left(\rho^0,\rho^1,y^{0*},y^{1*}\right)\\
+\ B_\chi\left(\chi^0,\chi^1,w^{0*},w^{1*}\right)&+B_\tau\left(\rho^0,\rho^1,w^{0*},w^{1*},y^{0*},y^{1*},\chi^0,\chi^1\right).
\end{aligned}
\tag{87}
$$

The above exact decomposition of the difference in normalized value added is a difference counterpart to the exact ratio decomposition of nominal value added that was obtained by Diewert and Morrison (1986) and Kohli (1990) where the translog value added function was the underlying functional form for the nominal value added function. However, the decomposition (87) is not as useful as these earlier decompositions for two reasons:

- It is somewhat complicated to go from (87) back to the nominal value added difference; i.e., we want a nice decomposition of $\Pi^1(p^1,x^1) - \Pi^0(p^0,x^0)$ whereas we have a nice decomposition of $\Pi^1(\rho^1,\chi^1) - \Pi^0(\rho^0,\chi^0)$;
- More fundamentally, the decomposition will depend on the analyst's choice of the α and β vectors and there is no clear rational for any particular specific choice.[34]

7 Conclusion

We have outlined three different approaches to the problem of decomposing the difference in a value added aggregate into explanatory components that are also differences. The third approach outlined in the previous section does not seem promising from an empirical point of view since different choices of the reference vectors α and β can lead to very different decompositions.

[34]This is the same problem that makes applications of directional distance function productivity studies problematic; there is no clear rational for any particular choice of the chosen direction and results are very much dependent on this choice.

The first approach leads to very simple intuitively plausible decompositions but it has the disadvantage of being an approximate approach. It also assumes technical efficiency which is problematic when recessions occur. However, it is possible to reinterpret the first approach as an axiomatic approach where we choose the Bennet indicators of price and quantity change as being "best" from the viewpoint of the test approach.[35] The resulting productivity index combines the effects of technical progress and improvements in technical and allocative efficiency. Thus from the viewpoint of the test approach to indicators, one might view Approach 1 as "best."

The second approach seems "best" from the viewpoint of the economic approach to indicators. The drawback to the approach is that it is somewhat computationally intensive. It is also the case that our assumption that the actual period t production possibilities set can be well approximated by the free disposal conical hull of past observations may not be an accurate assumption. However, we like the fact that the approach is able to separate out the effects of technical progress and inefficiency, at least to some extent.

Finally, we recommend that Approaches 1 and 2 be implemented using prices that are deflated by a consumer price index or some other exogenous deflator that is suitable for the purpose at hand. This is particularly important for Approach 1 because the accuracy of the first order approximations used in this approach will be greatly improved by the removal of general inflation from the nominal prices.

References

Afriat, S. N. (1972). Efficiency estimation of production function. *International Economic Review, 13*, 568–598.

Allen, R. D. G. (1949). The economic theory of index numbers. *Economica, 16*, 197–203.

Balk, B. M. (1998). *Industrial price, quantity and productivity indices*. Boston: Kluwer Academic Publishers.

Balk, B. M. (2001). Scale efficiency and productivity change. *Journal of Productivity Analysis, 15*, 159–183.

Balk, B. M. (2003). The residual: On monitoring and benchmarking firms, industries and economies with respect to productivity. *Journal of Productivity Analysis, 20*, 5–47.

Balk, B. M., Färe, R., & Grosskopf, S. (2004). The theory of economic price and quantity indicators. *Economic Theory, 23*(1), 149–164.

Baxter, W. T. (1975). *Accounting values and inflation*. London: McGraw-Hill.

Bennet, T. L. (1920). The theory of measurement of changes in cost of living. *Journal of the Royal Statistical Society, 83*, 455–462.

Caves, D. W., Christensen, L. R., & Diewert, W. E. (1982). The economic theory of index numbers and the measurement of input, output and productivity. *Econometrica, 50*, 1393–1414.

Charnes, A., & Cooper, W. W. (1985). Preface to topics in data envelopment analysis. *Annals of Operations Research, 2*, 59–94.

[35] See Diewert (2005) who developed a test approach for indicators and found that the Bennet indicators seemed "best" from the viewpoint of the test approach to indicators just as the Fisher index seems "best" from the viewpoint of the usual index number test approach.

Christensen, L. R., & Jorgenson, D. W. (1969). The measurement of U.S. real capital input, 1929-1967. *Review of Income and Wealth, 15*, 293–320.

Copeland, M. (1937). Concepts of national income. In *Studies in income and wealth, volume 1* (pp. 3–63). Chicago: National Bureau of Economic Research, University of Chicago Press.

Davis, H. S. (1947). *The industrial study of economic progress*. Philadelphia: University of Pennsylvania Press.

Diewert, W. E. (1973). Functional forms for profit and transformation functions. *Journal of Economic Theory, 6*, 284–316.

Diewert, W. E. (1974). Applications of duality theory. In M. D. Intriligator & D. A. Kendrick (Eds.), *Frontiers of quantitative economics, volume 2* (pp. 106–171). Amsterdam: North-Holland.

Diewert, W. E. (1976). Exact and superlative index numbers. *Journal of Econometrics, 4*, 114–145.

Diewert, W. E. (1980). Capital and the theory of productivity measurement. *American Economic Review, 70*, 260–267.

Diewert, W. E. (1983). The theory of the output price index and the measurement of real output change. In W. E. Diewert & C. Montmarquette (Eds.), *Price level measurement* (pp. 1049–1113). Ottawa: Statistics Canada.

Diewert, W. E. (1992). Exact and superlative welfare change indicators. *Economic Inquiry, 30*, 565–582.

Diewert, W. E. (2005). Index number theory using differences rather than ratios. *American Journal of Economics and Sociology, 64*(1), 311–360.

Diewert, W. E. (2014). Decompositions of profitability change using cost functions. *Journal of Econometrics, 183*, 58–66.

Diewert, W. E., & Fox, K. J. (2016). Alternative user costs, rates of return and TFP growth rates for the US nonfinancial corporate and noncorporate business sectors: 1960-2014, Discussion Paper 16-03, Vancouver School of Economics, The University of British Columbia, Vancouver, Canada.

Diewert, W. E., & Fox, K. J. (2014). Reference technology sets, free disposal hulls and productivity decompositions. *Economics Letters, 122*, 238–242.

Diewert, W. E., & Fox, K. J. (2017). Decomposing productivity indexes into explanatory factors. *European Journal of Operational Research, 256*, 275–291.

Diewert, W. E., & Fox, K. J. (2018). Decomposing value added growth into explanatory factors. In E. Grifell-Tatjé, C. A. K. Lovell, & R. Sickles (Eds.), *The Oxford handbook of productivity analysis* (pp. 625–662). New York: Oxford University Press.

Diewert, W. E., & Mendoza, N. F. (2007). The Le Chatelier principle in data envelopment analysis. In R. Färe, S. Grosskopf, & D. Primont (Eds.), *Aggregation, efficiency, and measurement* (pp. 63–82). New York: Springer.

Diewert, W. E., & Mizobuchi, H. (2009). "Exact and superlative Price and quantity indicators", *Macroeconomic Dynamics* 13. *Supplement, 2*, 335–380.

Diewert, W. E., & Morrison, C. J. (1986). Adjusting output and productivity indexes for changes in the terms of trade. *The Economic Journal, 96*, 659–679.

Diewert, W. E., & Parkan, C. (1983). Linear programming tests of regularity conditions for production functions. In W. Eichhorn, R. Henn, K. Neumann, & R. W. Shephard (Eds.), *Quantitative studies on production and prices* (pp. 131–158). Vienna: Physica Verlag.

Diewert, W. E., & Wales, T. J. (1987). Flexible functional forms and global curvature conditions. *Econometrica, 55*, 43–68.

Diewert, W. E., & Wales, T. J. (1992). Quadratic spline models for producer's supply and demand functions. *International Economic Review, 33*, 705–722.

Färe, R., Grosskopf, S., & Lovell, C. A. K. (1985). *The measurement of efficiency of production*. Boston: Kluwer-Nijhoff.

Färe, R., Grosskopf, S., & Lovell, C. A. K. (1992). Indirect productivity measurement. *Journal of Productivity Analysis, 2*, 283–298.

Färe, R., & Lovell, C. A. K. (1978). Measuring the technical efficiency of production. *Journal of Economic Theory, 19*, 150–162.

Färe, R., & Primont, D. (1994). The unification of Ronald W. Shephard's duality theory. *Journal of Economics, 60*, 199–207.

Farrell, M. J. (1957). The measurement of production efficiency. *Journal of the Royal Statistical Society, Series A, 120*, 253–278.

Fisher, F. M., & Shell, K. (1998). *Economic analysis of production price indexes*. New York: Cambridge University Press.

Gorman, W. M. (1968). Measuring the quantities of fixed factors. In J. N. Wolfe (Ed.), *Value, capital and growth: Papers in Honour of Sir John Hicks* (pp. 141–172). Chicago: Aldine.

Grifell-Tatjé, E., & Lovell, C. A. K. (2015). *Productivity accounting: The economics of business performance*. New York: Cambridge University Press.

Hanoch, G., & Rothschild, M. (1972). Testing the assumptions of production theory: A nonparametric approach. *Journal of Political Economy, 80*, 256–275.

Hicks, J. R. (1941-42). Consumers' surplus and index numbers. *The Review of Economic Studies 9*, 126–137.

Hicks, J. R. (1945-46). The generalized theory of consumers' surplus. *The Review of Economic Studies 13*, 68–74.

Hotelling, H. (1932). Edgeworth's taxation paradox and the nature of demand and supply functions. *Journal of Political Economy, 40*, 577–616.

Jorgenson, D. W., & Griliches, Z. (1967). The explanation of productivity change. *Review of Economic Studies, 34*, 249–283.

Jorgenson, D. W., & Griliches, Z. (1972). Issues of growth accounting: A reply to Edward F. Denison. *Survey of Current Business, 55*(5, part II), 65–94.

Kendrick, J. W. (1961). *Productivity trends in the United States*. Princeton: Princeton University Press.

Kohli, U. (1990). Growth accounting in the open economy: Parametric and nonparametric estimates. *Journal of Economic and Social Measurement, 16*, 125–136.

Konüs, A. A. (1939). The problem of the true index of the cost of living. *Econometrica, 7*, 10–29.

Kurosawa, K. (1975). An aggregate index for the analysis of productivity and profitability. *Omega, 3*(2), 157–168.

Lawrence, D., Diewert, W. E., & Fox, K. J. (2006). The contributions of productivity, price changes and firm size to profitability. *Journal of Productivity Analysis, 26*, 1–13.

McFadden, D. (1966). *Cost, revenue and profit functions: A cursory review* (IBER Working Paper No. 86). University of California, Berkeley.

McFadden, D. (1978). Cost, revenue and profit functions. In M. Fuss & D. McFadden (Eds.), *Production economics: A dual approach, volume 1* (pp. 3–109). Amsterdam: North-Holland.

Middleditch, L. (1918). Should accounts reflect the changing value of the dollar? *Journal of Accountancy, 25*, 114–120.

Salter, W. E. G. (1960). *Productivity and technical change*. Cambridge: Cambridge University Press.

Samuelson, P. A. (1953). Prices of factors and goods in general equilibrium. *Review of Economic Studies, 21*, 1–20.

Shephard, R. W. (1974). *Indirect production functions*. Meisenheim Am Glan: Verlag Anton Hain.

Siegel, I. H. (1952). *Concepts and measurement of production and productivity*. Washington, DC: Bureau of Labor Statistics.

Siegel, I. H. (1961). On the design of consistent output and input indexes for productivity measurement. In The Conference on Research in Income and Wealth (Ed.), *Output, input and productivity measurement* (pp. 23–46). Princeton, NJ: Princeton University Press.

Sterling, R. R. (1975). Relevant financial reporting in an age of price changes. *Journal of Accountancy, 139*(February), 42–51.

Sweeney, H. W. (1927). Effects of inflation on German accounting. *Journal of Accountancy, 43*, 180–191.

Sweeney, H. W. (1931). Stabilized depreciation. *The Accounting Review, 6*, 165–178.

Tulkens, H. (1993). On FDH efficiency analysis: Some methodological issues and application to retail banking, courts, and urban transit. *Journal of Productivity Analysis, 4*, 183–210.

Varian, H. R. (1984). The nonparametric approach to production analysis. *Econometrica, 52*, 579–597.

Whittington, G. (1980). Pioneers of income measurement and price-level accounting: A review article. *Accounting and Business Research, 10*(38), 232–240.

Zeff, S. A. (1982). Truth in accounting: The ordeal of Kenneth MacNeal. *The Accounting Review, 57*, 528–553.

Efficiency Driven Socio-Technical System Design

Konstantinos Triantis

Abstract In this paper we advocate that the efficiency measurement paradigm could transition from an evaluation-to-rank towards an evaluation-to-design paradigm. We suggest that this transition can inform the design of socio-technical systems. In order to achieve this type of design would require the consideration of issues associated with organizational design, enterprise systems engineering along with system complexity. We recommend that the required research be conducted within inter- or trans-disciplinary context with all of their benefits and challenges to achieve high quality application results. We describe five illustrations conducted over the years at Virginia Tech's System Performance Laboratory. We present these illustrations by describing the societal or socio-technical system needs that drove the research, the research constraints and considerations, the stakeholders affected by the research, the approach or approaches used, the feedback to theory and open modeling issues, and a description of societal and socio-technical system impacts. We describe the potential of a complex adaptive systems approach as an enabler of socio-technical system design and conclude with a series of open-ended questions and issues.

Keywords Efficiency driven design · Socio-technical systems · Complexity · Trans-disciplinary application research

1 Introduction and Context

What makes the efficiency measurement paradigm a compelling precursor for the design of future socio-technical systems? The quest to answer this question drives the content of this document. In many instances, researchers, analysts, and decision-makers use efficiency measurement as a mechanism to define and evaluate

K. Triantis (✉)
Grado Department of Industrial and Systems Engineering, Virginia Tech, Blacksburg, VA, USA
e-mail: triantis@vt.edu

C. F. Parmeter, R. C. Sickles (eds.), *Advances in Efficiency and Productivity Analysis*, Springer Proceedings in Business and Economics,
https://doi.org/10.1007/978-3-030-47106-4_3

appropriate interventions (e.g., organizational policies that drive enterprise and sector environmental sustainability). In most cases, they use ex-post data for their analyses and then given their analytical results, define the suggested interventions. We take an alternative approach by considering efficiency measurement as a design requirement even before the socio-technical system is built and operated. Nevertheless, our focus is on socio-technical systems given that we are simultaneously considering their technologies along with their behavioral counter-parts.

The thinking that led to this document has been influenced over the years by many divergent disciplines and individuals in these disciplines as part of ongoing research at Virginia Tech's System Performance Laboratory (SPL). What we offer in this paper is a set of illustrations (Sect. 3) where efficiency measurement was used to varying degrees to evaluate and design socio-technical systems. Each illustration has a unique story behind it. What we have tried to describe as part of each individual story is the societal or socio-technical system need that drove the research, the research constraints and considerations, the stakeholders affected by the research, the approach or approaches used, how each research project benefited from the other research projects (synergies, learning, and project management), the feedback to theory and open modeling issues, and a description of societal and socio-technical system impacts. Two of the stories (Sects. 3.4 and 3.5) are currently ongoing and final conclusions have not been reached. The references cited at the end of this paper provide the technical details associated with each illustration. We will not replicate the technical details in this paper. Our intent is to provide an overview of each story and to suggest future research opportunities and challenges.

1.1 Systems and System Design

But before we begin, it is important to discuss a number of issues that are pertinent to our discussion. Our perspective and assumption is that the efficiency measurement paradigm can inform future socio-technical system designs. This means that we assume an ex-ante point of view. "By 'system' we mean a group of interrelated, interacting, or interdependent constituents forming a complex whole" (Webster 1998) to achieve some defined objective. An example objective could be efficiency maximization. But as seen in the illustrations discussed in Sect. 3, is that efficiency achievement is one of many objectives that are relevant and important for the design of socio-technical systems. We advocate that the approach or approaches provided by our research illustrations that focus on efficiency measurement can be used to measure the achievement of other objectives. As suggested by the American Red Cross research (Sect. 3.1) the concurrent achievement of financial performance, efficiency, quality, and effectiveness was necessary and desirable for this socio-technical system.

By "design" we mean the implementation of classical systems engineering and organizational theory principles to derive alternative socio-technical system configurations. We assume that we either use a requirements-based or value-based approach for this design. With the requirements-based approach we consider all the characteristics and their interactions that we wish our socio-technical system to possess. We then proceed with the usual systems engineering life-cycle that includes conceptual, preliminary, and detailed design, production/construction, utilization/support, phase out, and disposal. While with the value-based approach (Deshmukh and Collopy 2010), we substitute the allocated requirements with an objective function over the same set of attributes.

As part of the overall system design, one needs to consider the relationship between the efficiency performance objectives of individual DMUs that constitute a system to the efficiency performance objective of the overall system. It is not obvious that for a system where each individual DMU maximizes its efficiency, it will achieve the same efficiency performance outcome as an overall system, when the efficiency performance of its individual DMUs are not considered. For example, from the research projects discussed in Sect. 3, one would need to investigate the performance (efficiency, financial, quality, and outcome) objectives of chapters versus the same performance objectives of the overall American Red Cross organization (Sect. 3.1), the relationship between performance (safety, financial, efficiency) objectives of households versus the same performance objectives of the community (Sect. 3.4), and the performance (workload, financial, safety) objectives of individual controller workstations versus the same performance objectives of the traffic control centers (Sect. 3.5). The examples of the interdependencies of objectives are part of the operational realities of most socio-technical systems (Sect. 1.2). This issue among others motivated our thinking to pursue research where coordination (of objectives among other issues) among DMUs exhibits the features of connectivity, feedback, and adaptation as part of a complex adaptive systems representation (Sect. 4). Nevertheless, the relationship of overall system efficiency goals to the efficiency goals of the DMUs that constitute the system remains an open theoretical and empirical issue.

1.2 Socio-Technical Systems and Complexity

We consider a *socio-technical system* as one that consists of one or more social networks and one or more physical networks that interact with each other (Van Dam 2009). One could consider them as different networks where one follows social laws (e.g., behavioral response theory in disaster management (Sect. 3.4)) and the other follows the physical laws (e.g., traffic flow theory (Sect. 3.2); asphalt deterioration theory (Sect. 3.3)) (Van Dam 2009). In a socio-technical system both types of laws influence the system such as in disaster planning (Sect. 3.4) (Kroes et al. 2006; Van Dam 2009).

Additionally, socio-technical system design provides the opportunity to challenge the limits of economic production theory. In other words to what extent does the axiomatic economic production theory framework hold in different socio-technical contexts? The answer to this question gives us an opportunity to modify or expand the axiomatic framework of production theory (Vaneman and Triantis 2003). Additionally, we need to consider and integrate other disciplinary theoretical frameworks that describe processes and systems being designed. Within a trans-disciplinary context (Sect. 1.3), we could relax assumptions and explore alternative theoretical abstractions and elaborations of the various socio-technical design configurations.

Typically, these socio-technical systems are described as complex. We first refer to Simon (1962, p. 468) "Roughly, by a *complex system* I mean one made up of a large number of parts that interact in a non-simple way. In such systems, the whole is more than the sum of the parts, not in an ultimate, metaphysical sense, but in the important pragmatic sense that, given the properties of the parts and the laws of their interaction, it is not a trivial matter to infer the properties of the whole. In the face of complexity, an in-principle reductionist may be at the same time a pragmatic holist."

Some key takeaways from this definition are as follows. First, the relationship between the whole and its parts. Finding and describing this relationship is not a trivial matter especially when we abstract and elaborate on the socio-technical system design. Second is the description of the interactions/interdependencies of the socio-technical system components. Understanding, describing, and predicting the behaviors associated with the interactions/interdependencies is ongoing research that affects, for example, the understanding of system resilience in terms of extreme events (Sect. 3.4; Mili et al. 2018), the sustainability and resilience of coastal communities, the assessment of "smart" technologies and their unintended consequences, among other research topics that are driven by basic societal needs. Third, researchers are being challenged to come up with approaches that offer unique yet simpler representations that can be described in terms of other more basic phenomena (Holland 1999). An example where we describe the dynamics of production systems that learn from one another to achieve an efficiency objective uses a biological metaphor of "flocking" (Dougherty et al. 2017; see Sect. 4).

The attempted interaction between complexity theory and economic production theory is driven in part by the characteristics of complex systems. Two such important characteristics include the following. First, the non-linear dynamic behavior associated with production and service systems. This characteristic inspired our complex adaptive system approach (CAS) where we model the movement of the (agent) decision-making units in the production possibility space as they approach the frontier (Sect. 4). Second is the possibility that the production or service system has more than one equilibrium point (Vaneman and Triantis 2007). This is not frequently addressed. We typically assume that the production or service system is in equilibrium and as such is a singular one.

1.3 *Trans-disciplinary, Multi-disciplinary, and Inter-disciplinary Research*

Given the nature of the socio-technical systems that we have researched (Sect. 3), we have reached out to other disciplines in engineering (e.g., transportation engineering) but also to other domains in the social and behavioral sciences (e.g., disaster management). Over the years, we have shifted from multi-disciplinary to inter-disciplinary approaches and currently aspiring to conduct research in a trans-disciplinary fashion. A few definitions are in order.

In multi-disciplinary research, each discipline and the researchers associated with the discipline, maintains its assumptions, methodologies, and understanding without important changes. Researchers understand that the relationships between disciplines are cumulative but not interactive. On the other hand, in inter-disciplinary research we assume the interdependence of the disciplines, suggesting that they are interactive. This leads to changes in disciplinary understanding. In this context, researchers integrate disciplines, where each discipline's assumptions and methodologies are interdependent on the other disciplines. Additionally, researchers *interactively* fuse practices in an interactive way so that researchers change the disciplines during the integrative research process.[1]

Finally, "transdisciplinary research is, essentially, team science. In a transdisciplinary research endeavor, scientists contribute their unique expertise but work entirely outside their own discipline. They strive to understand the complexities of the whole project, rather than one part of it. Transdisciplinary research allows investigators to transcend their own disciplines to inform one another's work, capture complexity, and create new intellectual spaces." (Washington University School of Medicine in Saint Louis Transdisciplinary Research on Energetics and Cancer Center n.d.).

One of the difficult issues is how to conduct inter- or trans-disciplinary research effectively. This is not a trivial matter. It requires considerable work to reach a consensus for different and often times conflicting perspectives, to define holistic, rigorous, and systematic approaches, and to revise mental models and deal with domain-related biases to reach an overall consensus. Our contention is that we need additional applications to explore the limits of economic production theory as we build bridges to other disciplines. We face at least two difficulties or limitations. First, to find socio-technical systems that will allow access to information, data, and decision-makers. Second to establish validation mechanisms to reinforce the connection between theory and practice.

The focus of our illustrations has been to interact with other disciplines in a multi- or inter-disciplinary fashion. The disciplines that we have interacted with in addition to economic production theory are the following: service science (Sect. 3.1), transportation science and engineering (Sects. 3.2 and 3.4), asset management (Sect.

[1]Other general, good reference Haythornthwaite et al. (2006).

3.3), disaster management (Sect. 3.4), decision theory (Sect. 3.5), human factors engineering (Sect. 3.5), systems engineering and systems science (all illustrations and Sect. 2), and complexity science (Sect. 4).

1.4 Application Research and Application Issues

All of the illustrations described in this paper (Sect. 3) were motivated by societal/socio-technical system needs. Readers may view the illustrations as application studies. Therefore, we ask the fundamental question as to what constitutes "good" application research. There are a number of criteria that we ascribe to "good" application research. We highlight the ones that our illustrations have attempted to adhere to.

These include: (a) *the uniqueness of the application domain*: A number if not all of our research studies have addressed unique application domains. For example, we highlight the downtown space reservation system (Sect. 3.2) as a system that was not built at the time we conducted our research yet it addressed a significant societal issue, that of traffic congestion; (b) *the innovation and thoroughness associated with the methods and models used*: A number of studies have relied on the combination of efficiency analysis with other methods from other disciplines. Examples include the integration with system dynamics modeling (Sect. 3.3), survey research (Sects. 3.1, 3.4, and 3.5), transportation simulation modeling (Sects. 3.2 and 3.4), transportation demand modeling (Sect. 3.4), multivariate statistical modeling (Sect. 3.5), human factors simulation studies (Sect. 3.5), and asphalt deterioration modeling (Sect. 3.3); (c) *the uniqueness, completeness, and precision of the data used*: The data used for all studies are unique and are a combination of data existing in databases and newly collected data. We have relied on data that were shared with us by enterprises (American Red Cross (Sect. 3.1); INFRABEL (Sect. 3.5)), newly collected survey data (Sects. 3.1 and 3.4), agency data (Sects. 3.3 (Virginia Department of Transportation) and 3.4 (Virginia transportation agency in Hampton Roads)), and simulation data (Sects. 3.2 and 3.4); (d) *the validation and replication of the results obtained*: face validation has been the approach used for four of the studies where we have consulted with engineers at INFRABEL (Sect. 3.5), transportation engineers at the Virginia Department of Transportation (Sect. 3.3), policy decision-makers at the American Red Cross both at the chapter and headquarter levels (Sect. 3.1), and households and transportation agency personnel through focus groups (Sect. 3.4). We have used analytical methods such as sensitivity analysis to evaluate the sensitivity of the results that we have obtained (Sect. 3.3); (e) *the contribution to theory*: In terms of service science, we focused on establishing the determinants of efficient and effective social service provision (Sect. 3.1). We are in the process of gaining insights as to the possible admissible tradeoffs among workload, safety, and economic performance when establishing a safety "envelope" (Rasmussen 1997) (Sect. 3.5). Additionally, we are assessing the determinants of effective evacuation strategies for disaster management's protective action theory (Sect. 3.4); (f) *unique and relevant policy insights*: We have investigated resource allocation (Sect. 3.1), travel demand management (Sect. 3.2), maintenance, evacuation (Sect. 3.4), and safety (Sect. 3.5) policies or interventions as part of our research; (g) and *relevance to the literature and useful societal impacts*: Some enterprises have acted on the proposed policies such as the American Red Cross (Sect. 3.1) and INFRABEL (Sect. 3.5) with discernable gains.

In each illustration we faced unique and substantive application issues and research challenges. (a) We always need to ask what constitutes the production possibility set and do the production axioms hold. The answer to this question is never inherently obvious; (b) we struggled and continue to struggle with the definition of what constitutes a reasonable unit of analysis. For example, in our evacuation planning research (Sect. 3.4), we oscillate between considering individual households versus the community as an aggregate construct; (c) the specification of the input, output, and contextual (e.g., environmental) representations/variables over the life-cycle of the socio-technical system is never obvious especially when considering the provision of services (e.g., social services (Sect. 3.1) or transportation services (Sects. 3.2, 3.4, and 3.5)); (d) in socio-technical systems we need to connect the underlying technologies, the behavioral considerations, the transformation process (es) with the defined variables; (e) additionally, the measurement of behavioral variables pose their own unique challenge. Typically, information systems are not designed to facilitate operational performance analyses. This leads to difficulties in gathering and using data to evaluate alternative socio-technical system design configurations; (f) in almost all of the illustrations presented in this paper, the linkage to decision-making is ambiguous and requires a separate yet rigorous assessment and modeling. This is something that we are undertaking with our study of traffic control centers (Sect. 3.5); (g) finally, we need to keep the mapping between the modeling world and the "real world" at the forefront of our thinking since this is not inherently obvious.

The conceptual mapping between the production axioms to the system dynamic behaviors (Vaneman and Triantis 2003) and the production axioms to the characteristics of complex adaptive systems (Dougherty et al. 2017) is part of the foundational work needed for the effective application of the efficiency measurement paradigm to the design of socio-technical systems using alternative techniques (system dynamics (Sect. 3.3) and agent-based modeling (Sect. 4), respectively) to the traditional efficiency measurement techniques.

Furthermore, as part of the research process, it was important for each of the examples described in Sect. 3 to question the relevance of the production axioms. This was done in part through observation and through careful analysis of the production/service data. Even though there were no apparent departures from the axioms per se in each of the examples, there were issues that pertained to the acceptance and use of specific modeling assumptions. For example, in the traffic control center work (Sect. 3.5) the analysis of the data suggests non-linear relationships among the key variables that we use for workload modeling. This also holds true for the implementation of the agent-based modeling of Sect. 4.

Therefore, the foundational assumptions of linearity, convexity, independence of DMUs among other assumptions require careful consideration for the underlying production processes of the socio-technical systems. This is where we can introduce alternative modeling frameworks (for example, machine learning techniques for the evaluation of the workload performance of traffic control centers (Sect. 3.5)) that can complement the traditional efficiency measurement analysis approaches. In addition, it is important to conduct a rigorous verification and validation analysis (as systems engineers typically do) that can serve as a point of reference when questioning the appropriateness of the production axioms along with other hypotheses/assumptions for specific socio-technical systems. Nevertheless, the formalization of rigorous verification and validation analysis techniques remains an open-ended research endeavor in this research domain. In the end, our objective is to generate relevant and useful results.

2 Efficiency Measurement and Socio-Technical System Design[2]

Socio-technical system design decisions include among other items allocating scarce resources and coordinating actions toward the achievement of common goals taking into account technological, organizational, and behavioral realities. In this document, we suggest that the efficiency performance measurement paradigm can be used to inform socio-technical system design. As suggested by Herrera-Restrepo and Triantis (2018), efficiency performance measurement has been primarily used to *describe* how well a system has performed, i.e., focusing on an ex-post assessment. However, investigating on "what could happen" when making operational changes, i.e., an ex-ante evaluation, has received less attention. To address this gap Herrera-Restrepo and Triantis (2018) synthesized literature findings pertaining to socio-technical system design from the organizational design, enterprise systems engineering, and efficiency performance measurement literatures. This synthesis allowed them to identify the integrative role that the efficiency performance measurement paradigm plays when informing socio-technical system transformation/change decisions. In other words, the focus is on how the efficiency performance measurement paradigm can ascertain how well a socio-technical system could perform if certain design decisions are made up-front.

The synthesis from the organizational design, enterprise design, and performance measurement literatures resulted in conclusions that our illustrations in part show. There are five steps that a number of studies follow where efficiency performance measurement plays an integrative role between organizational design and enterprise systems engineering for socio-technical design. These include: the identification and analysis of needs for design; the identification and analysis of

[2]The discussion of this section has been modified from Herrera-Restrepo and Triantis (2018).

socio-technical system components; the identification and analysis of interactions among components; modeling and evaluation of socio-technical system performance; and informing of the socio-technical system design. The literature shows that performance measurement objectives and drivers in efficiency performance measurement can be framed into performance measurement objectives and drivers for both organizational design and enterprise systems engineering. For example, the illustration of Sect. 3.4 (Herrera-Restrepo et al. 2016) provides a theoretical conceptualization of an evacuation management socio-technical system through the prism of a dynamic network DEA approach (Tone and Tsutsui 2014). The representation includes many stakeholder perspectives, systems, processes, and their inter-relationships. Additionally, the study links the measurement approach results to choices among evacuation management strategies.

Nevertheless, we need to consider and address a number of challenges to move the efficiency performance measurement paradigm from an evaluation-to-rank towards an evaluation-to-design approach (Herrera-Restrepo and Triantis 2018). We begin with the modeling assumptions and decisions we make. For modelers, it is important to think about socio-technical systems as open systems given that they are subject to always changing contextual/environmental conditions. This suggests that socio-technical systems cannot be holistically engineered for predictability. However, we can use analytical and simulation approaches to capture important key relationships among performance drivers to explore the future uncertainty associated with design decisions. As stated earlier, we need to ensure that modeling assumptions and decisions are logical and can be mapped into the real world. In conjunction with the modeling assumptions and decisions we make, we deal with the challenge of how we treat data. This is extremely important given that data in most cases come from different sources (e.g., surveys, simulations, databases, etc.) and need to be fused. Finally, we need to consider the level of aggregation at which the analyses will be conducted and how we will deal with influential or unusual observations (Seaver and Triantis 1992).

3 Efficiency Driven Socio-Technical System Design: Five Illustrations

We provide five illustrations of socio-technical system designs researched over the years at Virginia Tech's System Performance Laboratory (SPL). We do not focus on the technical details since these are provided by the references at the end of the document. Our intention is to be concise and to give five different stories supporting the overall theme of this document, i.e., that the efficiency performance measurement paradigm can be used to inform socio-technical system design.

3.1 Social Service Provision: The American Red Cross (Medina-Borja et al. 2007; Medina-Borja and Triantis 2011; ARC Grant)

3.1.1 Societal/Socio-Technical System Need

In the early to mid-nineties the United Way as a major funder of the American Red Cross (ARC) requested that the ARC demonstrate the outcomes achieved by the provision of its major social services. In addition with this initiative, the ARC, which is one of the largest social service organizations in the USA, was faced with the challenge to develop and implement an integrated performance measurement system. What was meant by integration was the consideration of the following requirements. First was the alignment of multiple performance dimensions, i.e., financial performance, capacity building, efficiency, service quality, and outcome achievement. Second was the use of the performance measurement system by the field chapters and headquarters. Third was the consideration of data from diverse sources (databases, customer satisfaction, and outcome surveys).

3.1.2 Research Constraints/Considerations

A key consideration was the measurement system needed to be designed and implemented to measure and evaluate performance metrics for a network of over 1000 field units (chapters) nationwide. We needed to consider that not all units (chapters) have the same operating environments and to account for these differences. Therefore, this was the first time we practically faced the issue of how we could meaningfully evaluate efficiency performance given the heterogeneity of operating environments. We also needed to measure the desired outcomes of programs and services (program effectiveness) because of the social nonprofit nature of the organization and because of the requirement defined by the United Way. The management at the ARC wished to have a basis for comparisons and benchmarking among its chapters considering the multiple dimensions of performance. This would allow for analytically grounded resource allocation decisions. Management both at headquarters and at the chapters wished for us to provide easy to understand and valid performance improvement recommendations. This was the first time we were confronted with the issue of validating our analytical results from a very practical point of view given that decision-makers at the ARC would implement some of our recommendations. Finally, the ARC did not wish to invest many resources in collecting new data. This was a concern especially for the chapters since most of them had very limited labor resources and did not wish to undertake an additional administrative burden.

3.1.3 Stakeholders

There were four major stakeholders. The first was the United Way, which provided the impetus for the ARC to embark on this initiative. The second was ARC headquarters, which over the years had initiated multiple yet unsuccessful efforts to measure outcomes and the design and implementation of an integrated performance measurement system. The third were the ARC chapters who would use the information generated by the performance measurement system to manage their operations and to learn best practices from other chapters. Last but not least were the recipients of ARC services. While they were always appreciative of ARC's efforts and services they frequently were interested in providing input for improvement.

3.1.4 Approach

The first major task was to capture the achievement of outcomes and service quality for each chapter. This required a number of subtasks. First, we designed and provided a framework for the measurement of outcome objectives and outcomes. Second, we held four workshops one for each major ARC line of service where participants from the field and headquarter representatives participated. The objective of each workshop was to obtain preliminary definitions of the outcome objectives and outcomes for each line of service. Third, we designed outcome measurement and customer satisfaction survey instruments for each line of service. We then formulated a four-stage nested DEA model to measure the performance of chapters where the actual occurrences (values) of the output variables of each stage were considered as inputs in the successive linked stage. Each DEA formulation was a non-radial output-maximization DEA model that assumed variable returns to scale. Central to each DEA formulation was the need to account for the influence of socio-economic factors (environment) in both, the selection of peers and target calculations.

3.1.5 Synergies and Learning from Other Projects

This was one of the first research projects in the area of socio-technical system design. It drew from multiple and concurrent research initiatives. Initial research on the application of efficiency measurement paradigm to manufacturing firms (Triantis 1984, 1987, 1990) focused on conceptual, data, and managerial issues. As part of this experience and dealing with real ("messy") manufacturing data led to the research on influential observations and their relationship with efficiency measures (Seaver and Triantis 1989, 1992). These application and data issues helped inform our approach taken with the American Red Cross (ARC). The research was driven by the needs of the ARC and consequently ensured effective project management and the delivery of project outputs in a timely fashion.

3.1.6 Feedback to Theory/Open Modeling Issues

As noted earlier, a modeling challenge that we faced was how to deal with the environmental heterogeneity of each chapter. While we implemented the Banker and Morey (1986) approach, we understood that this remained an open modeling issue. Another challenge that we did not handle systematically or rigorously was the integration of survey data in DEA. This remains an open issue that we are investigating as part of the evacuation planning research (Sect. 3.4). We also stumbled from a practical point of view, on the issue of validation. Our approach was to use face validation since we had access to decision-makers both at the chapter as well as at the headquarter levels. Finally, it became apparent that there is a need for a theoretical framework that incorporates the determinants of effective and efficient social service provision. This would directly contribute to the discipline of service science.

3.1.7 Societal/Socio-Technical System Impact

Our approach was used by chapters to address the United Way requirements. Additionally, our results were used by the ARC strategy department to make important decisions with respect to chapter mergers, closings, and organization-wide allocation of resources.

3.2 *Traffic Congestion: The Downtown Space Reservation System (Zhao et al. 2010a, b, 2011; NSF Grant # 0527252)*

3.2.1 Societal/Socio-Technical System Need

Traffic congestion is an ongoing societal issue that continues to require significant policy interventions. On the demand side, researchers have investigated travel demand mitigation strategies (e.g., congestion pricing) that induce travelers to use existing road networks in alternative ways. One such policy is the downtown space reservation system (DSRS) where travelers who want to drive to an urban downtown area have to reserve their time slots in advance before embarking on their trips. The transportation agency who operates the DSRS allocates time slots to travelers based on the availability of the road network capacity. Only the travelers who get permission from the transportation agency can drive in the downtown area during the requested time period. This idea builds on the literature of revenue management and is analogous to the way travelers make reservations on various modes of transportation (airplane, train, etc.). At the time that the research was conducted, a DSRS did not exist.

3.2.2 Research Constraints/Considerations

Since the system was not yet built and operated, ex-post data were not available. Our efficiency measurement approach assumed an ex-ante (design) point of view as described in this document. We relied on transportation simulation data to populate the production possibility space for our efficiency measurement formulations. The most difficult issues were in relation to the definition of the unit of analysis as well as the definition of the input/output/outcome variables. We ended by comparing 28 different simulated DSRS transportation scenarios as the unit of analyses. We assumed that the users of the system were relatively homogenous and could aggregate their physical realities.

3.2.3 Stakeholders

The two main stakeholder groups that we considered were the transportation agency who would design, build, and manage the DSRS and the users who participated in this strategy. Thus, it became extremely important to take into account both points of view in our modeling formulations and the assessment of our results.

3.2.4 Approach

We considered four modeling approaches. We handled these in a sequential fashion so there was no need to integrate them concurrently. We relied on data exchanges among modeling approaches as needed. The first modeling approach was the formulation and solution of an offline optimization module. We solved this optimization module based on historical travel demand information. We considered two objectives as part of the objective function. First, the total number of travelers that the transportation system handles during a certain time period and second the revenue obtained from the downtown space reservation system. We wished to maximize both objectives with an understanding that there were tradeoffs between the two objectives that we needed to consider.

The second modeling approach was the formulation of an online decision-making module based on neural networks that considered the stochastic variations in travel demand. We assumed hundreds of historical demand scenarios, and we obtained optimal solutions for each scenario. From the learning process, the system was able to recognize a situation characterized by the number of reservations that already have been made for each vehicle class during each time period and the corresponding revenue generated from the reservations. When a new request was provided, the neural network could rely on this historical information to provide a real-time decision.

Third, a microscopic traffic simulation approach executed in VISSIM was used to evaluate the DSRS. This traffic simulation approach relied on the physics of traffic flow at a microscopic level. The simulation was conducted for a revised road network representing downtown Boise, Idaho. We conducted a number of simulations to test various scenarios. For example, the transportation network performance with and without the DSRS and the DSRS versus First Come First Serve (FCFS) principle. We also evaluated specific DSRS parameters using the simulations, such as the relative importance of traveler throughput versus revenue generation.

The fourth modeling approach was the efficiency performance assessment. We modeled and implemented a network DEA approach. We considered three perspectives. Namely, the agency's/provider's perspective to evaluate operational issues and the provision of services. The travelers'/users' perspective to assess the quality of service (e.g., mobility issues) by considering the consumption technology. The community's perspective where we considered the DSRS social welfare impact (e.g., sustainability and environmental considerations).

The variability associated with the various scenarios was a function of total demand, the assigned weights to traveler throughput and revenue in the objective function of the optimization model, and the inherent stochastic behavior of the traffic assignments and traffic flow. The data from the simulation model were complemented with revenue data from the original optimization model of the DSRS. Travel time, vehicle miles, average speed, fuel costs, emissions, and personal miles (calculated from total vehicle miles and average occupancy) were obtained from the micro-simulation. We obtained revenue data from the DSRS optimization.

3.2.5 Synergies and Learning from Other Projects

The ARC project (Sect. 3.1) highlighted the idea of considering multiple performance dimensions (efficiency, financial, quality, and outcome). In the case of this research project, the relationship between efficiency and the level of transportation service (effectiveness) became important. However, not only did we consider multiple dimensions, but also multiple perspectives, which in this research project translated into the transportation agency and user (traveler) perspectives. The ARC project also highlighted the importance of looking at the overall system in addition to the individual DMUs (chapters). However, in the context of this research project, what constituted a DMU for the overall transportation system became a conceptual and modeling challenge. What we ended up defining as a DMU was an instantiation of a micro traffic simulation of a downtown transportation network. An additional challenge became the definition of meaningful improvement strategies for a system not built or operated yet. Consequently, using the simulation of an engineered system not yet built or operated to generate operational data became an intriguing concept that we continue to pursue as part of our research efforts in the System Performance Lab. Project management was driven as part of the NSF annual report delivery process.

3.2.6 Feedback to Theory/Open Modeling Issues

The formulated network DEA structure implied the performance behavior that we were able to observe as part of our analysis. What remained an open research question was what would happen if the performance network structure was altered? Would the efficiency performance results change in a meaningful way? Additionally, node dominance varied based on the computational approach (radial versus slacks based) approach. This result could be explained computationally but not from a policy point of view. This limited the confidence in the recommended interventions or improvements.

3.2.7 Societal/Socio-Technical System Impact

The validation of the approach could not be carried out at the time of the research, given that the system had not been built and operated. Prototyping would help determine the operational and economic feasibility of the system. Nevertheless, absent any real data we could not predict if traffic congestion would be mitigated.

3.3 *Asset Management: Highway Maintenance (Fallah-Fini et al. 2010, 2012, 2014, 2017; NSF Grant # 0726789)*

3.3.1 Societal/Socio-Technical System Need

One of the key societal challenges remains the deterioration of US road infrastructure. Due to major budgetary restrictions and the significant growth in traffic demand, there is an emerging need to improve the performance of highway maintenance practices. At the time when we undertook this research, the underlying premise was that privatizing portions of road maintenance operations by state Departments of Transportation (DOTs) under performance-based contracts would result in improved performance. Performance-based contracts had been one of the innovative initiatives in response to better highway maintenance practices. Successful implementation of new maintenance policies required state DOTs to measure the performance of performance-based contracts (public-private partnerships) versus traditional contracting approaches.

3.3.2 Research Constraints/Considerations

We relied on the data that the engineers at the Virginia Department of Transportation (VDOT) provided for us. The data collection was laborious and limited the number of DMUs that we could have for our analytical approaches. There were issues and difficulties associated with the definition of the unit of analysis, which in our case were highway segments, as well as the definition of the input/output variables. We started with a total of 25 variables but because of the curse of dimensionality, we restricted the number of input and output variables to three. Nevertheless in the end, we provided an adequate representation of the transformation process. The physical process that we needed to understand and incorporate in our modeling was asphalt deterioration and renewal. Thus, we consulted with civil and material engineers who shared with us the requisite empirical relationships of the process. The other challenge that we faced was that of environmental heterogeneity, i.e., climate considerations that were pervasive for the different geographically diverse counties of the Commonwealth of Virginia. Last but not least was the consideration of the dynamics of the physical process. We built off the Dynamic Productive Efficiency Model (Vaneman and Triantis 2007) and consulted with the non-parametric approaches in the literature (Fallah-Fini et al. 2014).

3.3.3 Stakeholders

The Virginia Department of Transportation (VDOT) was the main beneficiary of our research. This research provided a modeling approach that could be used by agencies that are confronted with the following issues: (1) agencies that want to use their existing databases; (2) agencies that have databases that provide a considerable amount of data and information but do not isolate all critical data and information that decision-makers need to focus on, and (3) decision-makers that need to identify the boundary of best practice performance. The other key stakeholder groups are the highway maintenance contractors and the highway drivers.

3.3.4 Approach

As was the case in the previous illustration, we again used a mixed methods approach in this research. We started out with a physics based micro system dynamics simulation approach (Fallah-Fini et al. 2010) where we represent the "development over time" of the road condition. As an outcome of the modeling approach we find the optimal highway maintenance budget allocation given a set of environmental and operational conditions. We then used a non-parametric meta-frontier framework that was adjusted by the two-stage bootstrapping approach (Fallah-Fini et al. 2012). The original non-parametric efficiency scores were obtained using only controllable inputs/outputs. On the input side we considered maintenance expenditures, while on the output side we considered the change in the condition of road sections that have been maintained and the area of road sections that have been maintained. We used the meta-frontier framework in order to group the DMUs based on their contract type and then applied the two-stage bootstrapping technique to the DMUs in each group to estimate the non-parametric efficiency scores with respect to group frontiers and to find the relation between efficiency scores and uncontrollable factors. We corrected for the bias of the estimated efficiency scores and constructed their confidence intervals. We then applied the two-stage bootstrapping technique to DMUs in the pooled data set to estimate the Meta Technology Ratio to evaluate how performance contracting group performed with respect to the traditional contracting group.

3.3.5 Synergies and Learning from Other Projects

We continued to build on the previous two projects and more specifically, on the ideas of multiple dimensions (efficiency and level of service (effectiveness)), multiple perspectives (transportation agency, drivers) and disaggregated processes (DMUs) as part of the overall system (in this case the road maintenance system) efficiency evaluation. What constituted a challenge again in this research project was the appropriate consideration of a DMU, which was finally defined as a highway segment. In this project, we built off and expanded on research associated with dynamic efficiency (Vaneman and Triantis 2007). What became apparent from the research was the need to explicitly consider the physics associated with road maintenance as part of the research design (Fallah-Fini et al. 2010). Furthermore, we faced curse of dimensionality issues since we had a limited data set that was obtained from the Virginia Department of Transportation (VDOT). The other issue that was highlighted (as was the case with the ARC project (Sect. 3.1)) is the necessity to consider environmental/contextual conditions (in this case climate conditions of the highway network). Project management was driven as part of the NSF annual report delivery process and the promised feedback to VDOT.

3.3.6 Feedback to Theory/Open Modeling Issues

Our findings indicated that the optimum maintenance policy suggested preventive maintenance to be preferred over corrective maintenance. The overlap in the priority of preventive and corrective maintenance operations increased as the total maintenance budget decreased. Also, there is a need to share the budget between preventive maintenance and corrective maintenance. Additionally, road authorities that have used traditional contracting can be as efficient as road authorities that have used performance-based contracting. Minimum/maximum temperatures and snowfall stood out as significant factors explaining the differences among efficiency scores of road authorities that are using the same type of contract. Nevertheless, the research suggests that there is a need to further elaborate on the concept of dynamic efficiency beyond what the literature offers to date. We were very effective in using complementary modeling approaches (system dynamics modeling, bootstrapping, non-parametric efficiency analysis). However, for real socio-technical systems (as was the case in our first illustration) the data collection, cleaning, and use were extremely time consuming and expensive to maintain. Given the limited number of DMUs associated with the analysis, the curse of dimensionality required fundamental adjustments to the specifications of our models.

3.3.7 Societal/Socio-Technical System Impact

The research results were validated by VDOT maintenance engineers. Yet there was reluctance to use the research recommendations. Nevertheless, we could potentially provide benefits to the society at large by defining and suggesting strategies that have immediate and long-term impacts on the ways a critical civil infrastructure is maintained.

3.4 Disaster Management: Evacuation Planning (Herrera-Restrepo et al. 2016; NSF Grant # 1536808 (Ongoing))

3.4.1 Societal/Socio-Technical System Need

The frequency and intensity of extreme events (e.g., hurricanes) are growing. Public agencies are tasked to accomplish more with less. However, there is a limited consensus as to what determines a successful evacuation among different stakeholder groups. Our research addresses the following questions. What constitutes a good evacuation? Does this concept change during the evacuation and how? Who determines what a good evacuation means? Given this context, our research focuses on the assessment of transportation evacuation strategies and more specifically ramp closures and contraflow lanes with crossovers. To address our questions, we are engaged in an inter-disciplinary research project. We engage economic production theory (efficiency measurement), sociology (disaster management), and transportation engineering (transportation management). We focus our research on two perspectives, i.e., that of transportation engineers (agency focus) and that of social scientists (household focus). Neither of these perspectives have fully and systematically addressed evacuation performance either individually or together. Identifying and understanding the links between the two perspectives and how they contribute to the understanding of what constitutes a good evacuation is our research motivation.

Our research is an attempt not only to represent stakeholder perspectives in an integrated fashion, but to explore the interdependencies of the physical infrastructures and social systems in the context of evacuation planning. Our premise is that these interdependencies affect performance substantially. The transportation engineers (agency focus) typically view evacuation as an optimization problem that addresses a specific traffic problem. They adhere to a problem-solving approach driven by time-based and aggregate household measures. On the other hand, the social scientists (household focus) view evacuation as a social and cognitive phenomenon and they attempt to understand how individuals and households are affected by a host of very specific variables or factors. They use theories to derive and test falsifiable hypotheses. Our contribution is to address evacuation as a multi-perspective, multi-system, and multi-process concept.

3.4.2 Research Constraints/Considerations

We consider the transportation engineering (transportation management), disaster management (protective behavioral response), and economic production theory (efficiency measurement) domains. In this context, we integrate behavioral considerations, transportation engineering along with data envelopment analysis (DEA) representations. In order to populate our models (transportation demand, transportation simulation, and DEA modeling) we fuse data from different sources (focus groups; surveys; optimization demand modeling; mesoscopic traffic simulations). The conceptual linkages among the various models remain an open research challenge. Finally, providing an appropriate survey design to accommodate the data requirements for our normative models has not yet been resolved.

3.4.3 Stakeholders

There are two primary stakeholder groups. First are the transportation (Virginia Department of Transportation (VDOT) and the Florida Department of Transportation (FDOT)) and the emergency management agencies. Second are the households and their communities. The first community that we collected data from is the Hampton Roads area in Virginia and the second community that we are collecting data from are households from Florida where we will capture information on the hurricane IRMA experience.

3.4.4 Approach

In our preliminary research (Herrera-Restrepo et al. 2016), we proposed a theoretical representation of a slacks-based dynamic network DEA approach for measuring evacuation performance when we consider a ramp closure evacuation traffic management strategy to deal with a hypothetical no-notice threat (e.g., chemical spill) triggering an evacuation in Blacksburg, VA. A no-notice threat is an extreme event of unexpected occurrence. The evacuation due to this type of threat typically occurs after the event has taken place. This research combined the dynamic network DEA approach with traffic engineering and socio-behavioral theory of protective action. Our approach allowed for the discovery of efficiency interdependencies among perspectives (agency and household), which in turn provided useful information and insights for the future design of holistic evacuation traffic management strategies. We continue to build on this preliminary research by focusing on the fundamental phenomena of evacuation and reconsidering how good or bad outcomes of that phenomena are evaluated and measured. At this junction, it is not clear how our evolving efficiency modeling conceptualizations will materialize given some of the open modeling issues.

3.4.5 Synergies and Learning from Other Projects

We continue to build from the previous projects and more specifically, on the ideas of multiple dimensions (efficiency, safety, and level of service (effectiveness)), multiple perspectives (transportation agency, household) and disaggregated processes (DMUs) as part of the overall system (in this case the hurricane evacuation system) efficiency evaluation. What we continue to struggle with are the appropriate definitions of a DMU, where we have considered households, the community and instances of the transportation simulation as DMUs (a similar concept that was introduced in the downtown space reservation project (Sect. 3.2)). The choice of a DMU definition depends on the research questions we wish to address. We face curse of dimensionality issues since our data set is limited by the number of times that we can execute the transportation simulation (each DMU requires 3 days of computational time). The other issue that is highlighted that is quite different than the previous projects is the conceptual/modeling/data integration across different research domains (disaster management, transportation engineering, and economic production theory). Project management has been driven as part of the NSF annual report delivery process.

3.4.6 Feedback to Theory/Open Modeling Issues

There are a number of open questions that remain as we are working on this research. How should we incorporate data collected from surveys into our DEA analysis? How do we formulate meaningful hypotheses and what is the resulting theory? Is the dynamic network DEA approach the most appropriate framework to capture the interactions and the resulting complexity between stakeholder perspectives and their dynamics? What is the appropriate unit of analysis (e.g., manifestation of the strategy? household? community?)? Finally, what are the key considerations that define homogeneity of the households and at an aggregate level of the communities that we use for our analysis? How do we consider dynamic behaviors and stochastic representations consistently across our modeling approaches?

3.4.7 Societal/Socio-Technical System Impact

Our suggestion to represent an evacuation as a network composed of perspectives by considering systems, and systems containing processes (linked through efficiency measures) is the point of departure for disaster management, transportation engineering and efficiency measurement literatures on evacuation planning. Given that the research information/data of this research is based on agency and household responses and transportation occurrences calibrated in realistic scenarios (e.g., hurricane IRMA) suggests that approach and research results targets could be adapted by both agencies, households, and communities.

3.5 Supervision of Autonomous Systems: Railway Traffic Control Centers (Topcu et al. 2019) (Ongoing)

3.5.1 Societal/Socio-Technical System Need

The design and operation of critical infrastructure systems face competing performance pressures of efficiency and safety, along with uncontrollable environmental phenomena and societal demands. In order to design and operate these complex socio-technical systems, we need to effectively model the inter-relationships derived from these considerations. This is a very difficult complex modeling problem that exceeds the reach of any single research domain. Thus, in our research, we consider the domains of decision theory, human factors engineering, infrastructure systems, and economic production theory. For various modes of transportation safe and efficient control room operation is paramount. For these control room operations, various infrastructure providers are continuously introducing new technologies, procedures, and processes. The impact of these technologies on the quality of the decisions made, the quality of controller work life, the safety associated with the controller room operations, and the economic efficiency of the control room operations is not well understood. Additionally, there is a growing need to balance efficient staff alignment with safe operations.

3.5.2 Research Constraints/Considerations

This is our first attempt to conduct trans-disciplinary research in the sense that we contribute by our own unique expertise but we also work entirely outside of our own disciplines. We need to concurrently consider human factors engineering to explore issues related to distributed situational awareness and mental workload as controllers experience these in the control centers, decision theory to investigate the stated and revealed preferences of controllers and management, and economic production theory to explore real-time production control. Each one of us will try to understand the complexity associated with the whole traffic control center socio-technical system and we transcend our own disciplines to inform and alter one another's work. One of the challenges that we face from the beginning is that we need to create a decision-support system for management in part because of the requirements of one of our key collaborators (INFRABEL). As is the case with the evacuation planning research (Sect. 3.4), it is not entirely clear how we will fuse production data, survey data, on-site interviews and data from simulator studies.

3.5.3 Stakeholders

Two US universities along with a group of key industry collaborators is undertaking this research. All of our research collaborators (INFRABEL, ProRail, Network

Rail, TU Delft, German Aerospace Agency, and the European Union agency for railways) will provide input to research tasks and the validation and verification of our research. INFRABEL as our main collaborator will manage large-scale and comprehensive socio-technical database and provide real-life and simulator environments. TU Delft will be the liaison with the Next Generation Infrastructure program, which is a joint initiative of the Dutch National Science Foundation and the Next Generation Infrastructures foundation (a not-for-profit legal entity). Other important stakeholder groups include other infrastructure providers and the users of the infrastructure systems (e.g., passenger trains, airplanes, etc.).

3.5.4 Approach

We use a combination of normative and inductive approaches (as is the case with the evacuation planning research (Sect. 3.4)). For the two important macro-ergonomic factors of situational awareness (SA) and mental workload (MWL), our work will utilize the theoretical construct of distributed situational awareness to develop a systems-model of SA for control rooms. In decision theory we study the interaction of decisions at multiple levels (individuals interacting with autonomous systems, teams, and overall control rooms). We are reconsidering for the first time, the notion of a "frontier" from economic production theory as a "boundary" by integrating workload, safety, and economic perspectives in support of achieving a "safety envelope" (Rasmussen 1997).

3.5.5 Synergies and Learning from Other Projects

We continue to build from all previous projects and more specifically, on the ideas of multiple dimensions (safety, workload, economic efficiency), multiple perspectives (controllers, traffic control centers, and riders) and disaggregated processes (DMUs) as part of the overall system (in this case the traffic control center) efficiency evaluation. We use different definitions of a DMU (workstation and traffic control centers). The operational data set we are using is rich so there is no curse of dimensionality issue. The other issue that is highlighted as was the case with the ARC (Sect. 3.1) and the highway maintenance (Sect. 3.3) projects is the necessity to consider contextual factors (in this case transportation network conditions (e.g., network complexity)). The other issue that is highlighted as is in the evacuation performance project (Sect. 3.4) is the conceptual/modeling/data integration across different domains (human factors, decision theory, and economic production theory). Project management is driven by reporting back to our key collaborator INFRABEL (Belgian railways) who also provides the rich data set.

3.5.6 Feedback to Theory/Open Modeling Issues

We are investigating the limits of economic production theory by addressing issues of real-time production control as this control is informed by the preferences (stated or revealed) of the decision-makers (controllers and management), is constrained by physiological and cognitive limitations (situational awareness and mental workload), and is limited and influenced by new technologies. At this junction, it is not clear to what extent the production axioms assumed by economic production theory will hold. Additionally, in the spirit of going from an ex-post to ex-ante (design) perspective as we suggested throughout this paper, we will need to reconsider some of the dynamic approaches in the non-parametric efficiency literature (Fallah-Fini et al. 2014). Within this context, we need to augment the integration of efficiency analysis with dynamic modeling (Vaneman and Triantis 2007) and invest further in our exploratory research where we consider the marriage of complex adaptive systems as a mechanism to address efficiency goals (Sect. 4). These approaches could potentially shift our exploration of the causes of efficiency under-performance from a meta-analysis perspective (e.g., finding best practices from our peers) to a more predictive point of view. In other words, anticipating and predicting the influence of potential factors on the performance of infrastructure systems.

3.5.7 Societal/Socio-Technical System Impact

This research is aligned with the investigation of the human-technology frontier. As an outcome of the research, we could investigate the effect of various interventions (e.g., merging of traffic control centers) on the overall infrastructure system performance. This research provides an application platform (Sect. 1.4) anchored in the real world to study how the impact of individual and group decision making in a safety critical environment affects socio-technical system performance.

4 Complex Adaptive Systems and Efficiency Measurement[3]

A key assumption of efficiency analysis is the independence of the decision-making units (DMUs). In other words, DMUs typically do not interact or learn from one another at least when the initial analysis is performed. The learning takes place as a meta-analytic activity when best practices are identified from the identified peers. One possible mechanism to address the interactions and learning among decision-making units as part of the initial analysis is to follow an alternative approach. We bridge the complex adaptive systems (CAS) paradigm (Holland 1999) with

[3]This section is adapted from Dougherty et al. (2017) and Herrera-Restrepo and Triantis (2019).

economic production theory (Dougherty et al. 2017; Herrera-Restrepo and Triantis 2019).

Within this framework we assume that the decision-making units (agent DMUs) are individual autonomous, goal seeking decision-makers within a larger complex socio-technical system. The autonomous DMUs interact with one another and with their environment. We build from Holland (1999) and propose an agent-based simulation modeling approach labeled as the Complex Adaptive Performance Efficiency Model (CAPEM) (Dougherty et al. 2017). This simulation environment is used as a mechanism to conduct exploratory research to investigate the notion of productive efficiency "emergence" when complex socio-technical systems interact with one another and with their environments.

We consider the collection of agent DMUs representing a CAS. The agent DMUs use "flocking" (Reynolds 1987) as their decision-making paradigm. We assume that for these agent DMUs, flocking on an individual level takes into account the autonomy of an agent DMU but at a collective level captures aggregate interactions and interdependencies. Flocking explicitly represents agent DMUs own goal seeking behaviors (e.g., risk avoidance, continuous improvement among others) where each agent DMU uses identical rules (e.g., alignment with others who share the same goals, cohering with others who exhibit successful and effective behaviors, and independence in decision-making).

The CAPEM simulation framework allows us to study managerial policies and their effect on socio-technical system efficiency performance. These socio-technical systems operate on their own or could also be part of a group of interacting systems that we could represent as a network. For socio-technical systems that operate under a similar or a complementary mission and under the same or different ownership, the coordination of decisions and actions is vital. We consider that this coordination exhibits the features of connectivity, feedback, and adaptation, which are also characteristic of complex adaptive systems (CAS).

We can represent socio-technical system networks as CAS and then study managerial policies that affect the coordination among the socio-technical systems and its subsequent effect on technical efficiency. This effect takes place both at the individual and at the aggregate network levels. We assume that flocking can be used as a proxy for managerial policies. Up until recently, we have conducted simulation experiments using a socio-technical network of deregulated power plants. In more recent research, we are investigating a network of regulated banks. Our experimental results demonstrate when and how managerial policies augment the coordination among network members and allow for the exploration of the inter-relationships and interactions that exist between individual decisions and collective interdependencies. The inter-relationships among the deregulated power plants result in an emergent goal seeking aggregate network behavior with respect to achieving technical efficiency.

5 Conclusions and Future Directions

The research that we summarized in this paper represents evolving thinking as to how to meaningfully integrate the efficiency measurement paradigm as a vital consideration in socio-technical system design. In order to go down this path, we need to take into account a number of issues.

First that this research requires an inter- or trans-disciplinary approach. Integrating multiple domains along with the consideration of translation relevance makes the feedback from theory to implementation and then back to theory a challenge. This last statement implies that there is some degree of consensus among disciplines as to what constitutes theory, good research, theoretical, translational, and application research. This is rarely the case but offers an opportunity to challenge our collective mental models.

Second, by their very nature, socio-technical systems are complex. The interactions between the technologies and human behaviors in these systems are rarely understood. This offers an opportunity for many future research investigations where hypotheses can be tested and evaluated.

Third, the collection, cleaning, understanding, and use of the data are paramount. One may suggest that the evolving field of machine learning can assist to clarify and challenge some of the basic premises/axioms of our disciplines. Additionally, within the context of complex adaptive systems as described in the previous section, machine learning may provide the means to understand the meaning of productive efficiency "emergence" when complex socio-technical systems interact with one another and with their environments.

Fourth, in all illustrations of Sect. 3, we identified the impact or the potential impact of the research for the socio-technical systems and/or society. This is not to imply that meaningful research cannot be conducted without an "eye" for its impact. Our bias is that in all illustrations, the research problem originated with societal and/or socio-technical system needs and resulted in recommendations for improved system performance. This provided the context for our research and for the approaches that we undertook where the mapping between the "virtual" and "real" worlds was paramount.

There are many research problems for which our framework could be of use. We will refer only to the following three. (a) The modeling and understanding of the resilience of interdependent critical infrastructure systems as a reaction to extreme events is ongoing (Mili et al. 2018). This is not surprising given the growing frequency and intensity of extreme climate events; (b) the interactions of infrastructure, human and natural systems in coastal areas and the prediction of their future behaviors in light of a series of mitigating strategies to extreme events and disasters is of great societal concern; (c) the modeling and prediction of the performance of research enterprises is an important issue for universities, government agencies, and learning communities. The intense competition for research funding is the main motivator for the understanding and modeling of this issue.

Acknowledgements None of the research described in this paper would have been achieved without the significant contributions of former students, current students, and colleagues that are co-authors in the references cited at the end of this document. Additionally, I would like to acknowledge the funding support of the American Red Cross and the National Science Foundation (grants # 0527252, # 0726789, # 1536808).

References

Banker, R. D., & Morey, R. C. (1986). Efficiency analysis for exogenously fixed inputs and outputs. *Operations Research, 34*(4), 513–521.

Deshmukh, A., & Collopy, P. (2010). Fundamental research into the design of large-scale complex systems. In *13th AIAA/ISSMO Multidisciplinary Analysis Optimization Conference*. Texas: Fort Worth.

Dougherty, F., Ambler, N., & Triantis, K. (2017). A complex adaptive systems approach for productive efficiency analysis: Building blocks and associative inferences. *Annals of Operations Research, 250*(1), 45–63. https://doi.org/10.1007/s10479-016-2134-3.

Fallah-Fini, S., O'Donell, C., & Triantis, K. (2017). Comparing firm performance using transitive productivity index numbers in a meta-frontier framework. *Journal of Productivity Analysis, 47*(2), 117–128. (supported by NSF grant # 0726789).

Fallah-Fini, S., Rahmandad, H., Triantis, K., & de la Garza, J. (2010). Optimizing highway maintenance policies and practices: Operational and dynamic considerations. *System Dynamics Review, 26*(3), 216–238. https://doi.org/10.1002/sdr.449. (supported by NSF grant # 0726789).

Fallah-Fini, S., Triantis, K., de la Garza, J., & Seaver, B. (2012). Measuring the efficiency of highway maintenance contracting strategies: A bootstrapped non-parametric meta-frontier approach. *European Journal of Operational Research, 219*(1), 134–145. https://doi.org/10.1016/j.ejor.2011.12.009. (supported by NSF grant # 0726789).

Fallah-Fini, S., Triantis, K., & Johnson, A. (2014). Efficiency performance: State-of-the-art. *Journal of Productivity Analysis, 41*(1), 51–67. (supported by NSF grant # 0726789).

Haythornthwaite, C., Lunsford, K. J., Bowker, G. C., & Bruce, B. C. (2006). Challenges for research and practice in distributed, interdisciplinary collaboration. In H. Christine (Ed.), *New infrastructures for knowledge production: Understanding E-science* (pp. 143–166). Hershey: IGI Global. https://doi.org/10.4018/978-1-59140-717-1.

Herrera-Restrepo, O., & Triantis, K. (2018). Efficiency-driven enterprise design: A synthesis of studies. *IEEE Transactions on Engineering Management, 65*(3), 363–378.

Herrera-Restrepo, O., & Triantis, K. (2019). Enterprise design through complex adaptive systems and efficiency measurement. *European Journal of Operational Research, 278*(2), 481–497. https://doi.org/10.1016/j.ejor.2018.12.002.

Herrera-Restrepo, O., Triantis, K., Trainor, J., Murray-Tuite, P., & Edara, P. (2016). A multi-perspective dynamic network performance measurement of an evacuation: A dynamic network-DEA approach. *Omega, 60*, 54–59. https://doi.org/10.1016/j.omega.2015.04.019.

Holland, J. H. (1999). *Emergence: From chaos to order*. Oxford: Oxford University Press.

Kroes, P., Franssen, M., van de Poel, I., & Ottens, M. (2006). Treating socio-technical systems as engineering systems: Some conceptual problems. *Systems Research and Behavioral Science, 23*(6), 803–814.

Medina-Borja, A., & Triantis, K. (2011). Modeling social services performance: A four-stage DEA approach to evaluate fundraising efficiency, capacity building, service quality, and effectiveness in the nonprofit sector. *Annals of Operations Research, 221*(1), 285–307. https://doi.org/10.1007/s10479-011-0917-0. (supported in part by a grant by the American Red Cross).

Medina-Borja, A. M., Pasupathy, K. S., & Triantis, K. (2007). Large-scale data envelopment analysis (DEA) implementation: A strategic performance management approach. *Journal of the*

Operational Research Society, 58, 1084–1098. (Goodeve Award, Operational Research Society, UK) (supported in part by a grant by the American Red Cross).

Mili, L., Triantis, K., & Greer, A. (2018). Integrating community resilience in power system planning. In V. Badescu, C. Lazaroiu, & L. Barelli (Eds.), *Advanced power engineering*. New York: CRC Press, Taylor & Francis.

Rasmussen, J. (1997). Risk management in a dynamic society: A modelling problem. *Safety Science, 27*(2), 183–213.

Reynolds, C. W. (1987). Flocks, herds, and schools: A distributed behavioral model. *ACM SIGGRAPH Computer Graphics, 21*(4), 25–34.

Seaver, B., & Triantis, K. (1989). The implications of using messy data to estimate production frontier based technical efficiency measures. *Journal of Business and Economic Statistics, 7*(1), 51–59.

Seaver, B., & Triantis, K. (1992). A fuzzy clustering approach used in evaluating technical efficiency measures in manufacturing. *Journal of Productivity Analysis, 3*, 337–363.

Simon, H. (1962). The architecture of complexity. *Proceedings of the American Philosophical Society, 106*(6), 467–482.

Tone, K., & Tsutsui, M. (2014). Dynamic DEA with network structure: A slacks-based measure approach. *Omega, 42*(1), 124–131.

Topcu, T. G., Triantis, K., & Roets, B. (2019). Estimation of the workload boundary in socio-technical infrastructure management systems: The case of Belgian railroads. *European Journal of Operational Research, 278*(1), 314–329. https://doi.org/10.1016/j.ejor.2019.04.009.

Triantis, K. (1984). *Measurement of efficiency of production: The case of pulp and linerboard manufacturing*. Ph.D. Dissertation, Columbia University, Department of Industrial Engineering and Operations Research.

Triantis, K. (1987). Total and partial productivity measurement at the plant level: Empirical evidence for linerboard manufacturing. In D. Sumanth (Ed.), *Productivity management frontiers - I* (pp. 113–123). Amsterdam: Elsevier Science Publishers.

Triantis, K. (1990). An assessment of technical efficiency measures for manufacturing plants. In J. A. Edosomwan (Ed.), *People and product management in manufacturing* (Advances in industrial engineering, no. 9) (pp. 149–166). Amsterdam: Elsevier Science Publishers.

Van Dam, K. (2009). *Capturing socio-technical systems with agent based systems* (Ph.D. thesis, TU Delft).

Vaneman, W., & Triantis, K. (2003). The dynamic production axioms and system dynamics behaviors: The foundation for future integration. *Journal of Productivity Analysis, 19*(1), 93–113.

Vaneman, W., & Triantis, K. (2007). Evaluating the productive efficiency of dynamical systems. *IEEE Transactions on Engineering Management, 54*(3), 600–612.

Washington University School of Medicine in Saint Louis Transdisciplinary Research on Energetics and Cancer Center. (n.d.). *Trans-disciplinary, multi-disciplinary, and inter-disciplinary research: What is the difference*? Retrieved from https://obesity-cancer.wustl.edu/about/what-is-transdisciplinary-research/

Webster. (1998). *Webster's II new riverside desk dictionary*. Boston: Houghton Mifflin, ISBN 0395483689.

Zhao, Y., Triantis, K., & Edara, P. (2010b). Evaluation of travel demand strategies: A microscopic traffic simulation approach. *Transportation, 37*(3), 549–571. https://doi.org/10.1007/s11116-010-9258-0. (supported by NSF grant # 0527252).

Zhao, Y., Triantis, K., Murray-Tuite, P., & Edara, P. (2011). Performance measurement of a transportation network with a downtown space reservation system: A network-DEA approach. *Transportation Research: Part E, 47*(6), 1140–1159. https://doi.org/10.1016/j.tre.2011.02.088. (supported by NSF grant # 0527252).

Zhao, Y., Triantis, K., Teodorović, D., & Edara, P. (2010a). A travel demand management strategy: The downtown space reservation system. *European Journal of Operational Research, 205*(3), 584–594. https://doi.org/10.1016/j.ejor.2010.01.026. (supported by NSF grant # 0527252).

A Framework for the Assessment and Consolidation of Productivity Stylized Facts

Cinzia Daraio

Abstract This chapter tackles the little-treated subject of how productivity and efficiency stylized facts are measured and consolidated. We show that measurement requires the formulation of a model starting from a general framework. We propose a doubly conditional performance evaluation model for the measurement of productivity stylized facts and an econometric approach for consolidating stylized facts. The proposed framework can complement recent methodological works guiding the users to describe and choose the most appropriate method for their context of analysis. Our performance measurement framework may act as a leading thread for bringing together different strands of literature that are outlined in the concluding section.

Keywords Performance · Productivity · Nonparametric · Efficiency · Heterogeneity · Innovation

1 Introduction

> Knowing how to bake a cake is knowing how to execute the sequence of operations that are specified…in a cake recipe. […] But the recipe is not fully revealed by the list of ingredients.
>
> An even more serious limitation of the list of ingredients approach …[appears] when we are asking not about the ability to execute a given recipe but about the ability to create the recipe"… Winter (2006, pp. 131–133)

C. Daraio (✉)
Department of Computer, Control and Management Engineering A. Ruberti (DIAG), Sapienza University of Rome, Rome, Italy
e-mail: cinzia.daraio@uniroma1.it

C. F. Parmeter, R. C. Sickles (eds.), *Advances in Efficiency and Productivity Analysis*, Springer Proceedings in Business and Economics,
https://doi.org/10.1007/978-3-030-47106-4_4

1.1 Stylized Facts and Productivity/Efficiency Stylized Facts

Stylized facts (Kaldor 1963; Lawson 1989; Boland 1994) are observations that have been made in so many contexts that they are widely understood to be empirical truths, to which theories must fit. In social sciences, especially economics, a *stylized fact* is a simplified presentation of an empirical finding. While results in statistics can only be shown to be highly probable, in a stylized fact, they are presented as true. A stylized fact is often a broad generalization, which although essentially true may have inaccuracies in the detail.

In literature, especially growth and financial economics, there are several articles that survey stylized facts. Very little attention is devoted instead on how these facts are observed, measured, and consolidated.

Stylized facts on productivity and efficiency differentials (*productivity* or *efficiency stylized facts*) are central to economic theory. What is usually done by economists is to start the investigation by setting a set of stylized facts and then propose a theoretical model able to reproduce them. After that, the theoretical model is used to explain the functioning mechanisms and to make prediction (in the best cases and when it is not too complicate).

Stylized facts are measured on an attempt to measure reality. Measurement can be defined in different ways. One commonly agreed definition of measurement among philosophers is as "an activity that involves interaction with a concrete system with the aim of representing aspects of that system in abstract term" (Tal 2015). In our case, concrete implies real, and hence, measurement of stylized facts involves the *representation* of ideal systems. Complementary aspects of measurement and modern philosophical discussions about the nature of measurement and the conditions that make measurement possible and reliable are surveyed in Tal (2015). Of interest to our analysis are mathematical theories of measurement, information theoretic and model-based accounts, and epistemology of measurement (which includes standardization, theory-ladenness of measurement, accuracy, and precision). Quantification or measurement is then a critical issue as we will see in the following of this chapter (Sect. 2). An underpinning question to applied economic modeling concerns the *method* or *approach* used by applied economists to gauge productivity/efficiency differentials,[1] that is to measure these stylized facts, based on observation (data) coming from the real world. Problems related to productivity

[1]For productivity of a unit we mean the the ratio of its output to its input. This ratio is easy to compute if the unit uses a single input to produce a single output. Otherwise, for multiple outputs—multiple inputs cases, the inputs and outputs have to be aggregated so that productivity remains the ratio of two scalars. We can distinguish between a partial productivity, when it concerns a sole production factor, and a total factor (or global) productivity, when referred to all factors. Similar, but not equal, is the concept of efficiency, although, in the literature many authors consider the terms productivity and efficiency as synonyms. Following Daraio and Simar (2007, p. 14), we define efficiency of a unit as the distance between its output/input ratio, and the output/input value that defines the best practice frontier, or the most efficient frontier. Efficiency and productivity, anyway, are two cooperating concepts. The measures of efficiency are more accurate than those of

and production efficiency[2] are at the core of the interest of economic analysis since the time of Adam Smith's study on the *Wealth of Nations*, if not even before.

Usually, researchers make surveys of existing studies, taking into account the results of previous analyses without considering the methods used and the implicit assumptions that were made. Moreover, quality, availability, and data problems are often underestimated and only skimmed in empirical works. Griliches (1994) calls "data woes" the problems of empirical data and his analysis is still valid today.[3] Data constraints are really fundamental for empirical evidence on productivity differentials and have been analyzed in various contexts (e.g. Bartelsman and Beaulieu 2007). Bartelsman et al. (2005) investigate comparability problems of microdata.

Another fundamental question, for theoretical development in economics, is related to *how* these stylized facts are consolidated. This is connected to the methodology of economics and the role of theory to interpret and explain the real world, that is at the core of different investigations including, without claiming of completeness: (1) *philosophy of science*, (2) works asking for more empirical-based evidence in economics (e.g. Anand 2003; Dosi 2004, Fagiolo et al. 2006), (3) *economic methodology* and *econometric approaches* (e.g., Hendry 1980, 2001; Pagan 1987; Hendry and Mizon 2000; Hoover and Perez 1999; Spanos 1999, 2000; Hoover 2005; Doornik and Hendry 2015), (4) *management approaches* (Davis et al. 2007) as summarized by Maanen et al. (2007) that survey how theory and method have been treated in management studies and suggest that respecting both

productivity in the sense that they involve a comparison with the most efficient frontier, and for that they can complete those of productivity, based on the ratio of outputs on inputs.

[2]In this chapter we consider production activity as a broad activity involving not only the realization of material goods but also intangibles and services.

[3]Griliches (1994, p. 14) states: *Why are the data not better? [...] at least three observations come to mind: (1) The measurement problems are really hard. (2) Economists have little clout in Washington, especially as far as data-collection activities are concerned. Moreover, the governmental agencies in these areas are balkanized and underfunded. (3) We ourselves do not put enough emphasis on the value of data and data collection in our training of graduate students and in the reward structure of our profession. It is the preparation skill of the econometric chef that catches the professional eye, not the quality of the raw materials in the meal, or the effort that went into procuring them (Griliches 1986). In many cases the desired data are unavailable because their measurement is really difficult. After decades of discussion we are not even close to a professional agreement on how to define and measure the output of banking, insurance, or the stock market (see Griliches 1994). Similar difficulties arise in conceptualizing the output of health services, lawyers, and other consultants, or the capital stock of R&D. While the tasks are difficult, progress has been made on such topics. The work of Jorgenson and Fraumeni (1992) on the measurement of educational output is an example both of what can be done and of the difficulties that still remain. But it is not reasonable for us to expect the government to produce statistics in areas where the concepts are mushy and where there is little professional agreement on what is to be measured and how. Much more could be done, however, in an exploratory and research mode. Unfortunately, the various statistical agencies have been both starved for funds and badly led, with the existing bureaucratic structure downplaying the research components of their enterprise when not being outright hostile to them, research being cut first when a budget crunch happens (Triplett 1991).*"

the primacy of theory and the primacy of evidence is not an easy task but a necessary balancing practice that characterizes high-quality research.

1.2 Productivity and Efficiency Measurement

Theoretical mainstream production analysis has always focused on production activity as an optimization process. Conventional microeconomic theory assumes that producers optimize by not wasting resources in a systematic way: producers operate on the boundary of their production possibility sets (see, e.g., Varian 1992). However, numerous and various empirical evidences show that not all producers optimize in all circumstances. Hence, it is important to analyze the degree to which producers fail to optimize and the extent of departures from technical and economic efficiency.

Available empirical evidence shows wide and persistent "asymmetries" in efficiency among firms within the same industry (e.g. Cimoli and Dosi 1996). Mainstream empirical production has concentrated its analysis on central tendency, or "average" or "most likely" relationship constructed by intersecting data with a function rather than surrounding data with a frontier. Available evidence (Bartelsman and Doms 2000; Bartelsman et al. 2004, 2005) seems not coherent with some of the most entrenched economic assumptions,[4] such as the aggregate production function based on the notion of *representative agent*, and the transient nature of asymmetries in production efficiency. These evidences may give impetus to the competing evolutionary theory of production and technical change (Winter 2017). On the other hand, evolutionary theory suffers from some limitations that are at the core of recent developments.

The approach of production frontiers (e.g. Färe et al. 1994) is an effort to empirically define an envelopment of production data. This approach combines the construction of production frontiers with the measurement and interpretation of efficiency relative to the constructed frontiers. Best practices (captured by the frontier approach) may be better than average practices (measured in a regression-based framework) in the sense that best practices exploit available substitution possibilities or scale opportunities that average practices do not. Griliches and Mairesse (1983) observed that "the simple *production function* model, even when augmented by additional variables and further nonlinear terms, is at best just an approximation to a much more complex and changing reality at the firm, product,

[4]The stylized facts surveyed by Bartelsman and Doms (2000), for instance, point up largely that "*productivity levels are quite dispersed, that productivity differences between plants may be very persistent, that entry and exit of plants with different productivity levels is an important source of productivity growth, and that plants long-run employment changes and productivity changes are not correlated. The existence of productivity heterogeneity, even among producers of comparable products with comparable equipment, has forced analysts to rethink and reassess some old truths that find no support in the microdata. For instance, these results begin to cast doubt on the appropriateness of an aggregate production function that is based on a representative firm.*"

and factory floor level." The approach of *production frontiers*, instead, is based on the envelopment of production data. From the empirical point of view, a frontier approach allows for estimating the "efficient" production frontier and for measuring and interpreting the *relative* efficiency of each individual unit with respect to this estimated frontier, instead of relying on standard or *typical* (representative) behavior.

As we will see in Sect. 2, the measurement of productivity/efficiency is a complex task that is included in the broader activity of the management of the performance. There are many techniques for the estimation of the efficiency/productivity differentials and many software that implement these techniques (see Daraio et al. 2019 for a survey of existing software options). Surveys and presentation of the existing methods can be found in Parmeter and Kumbhakar (2014), Simar and Wilson (2013, 2015), and Sickles and Zelenyuk (2019). We may classify efficient frontier models according to the three *criteria* listed in Table 1.

In *Parametric* models, the attainable set is defined trough a *production frontier function* which is a known mathematical function depending on some unknown parameters, where generally the output is univariate. The main advantages of this approach are the economic interpretation of parameters and the statistical properties of estimators; the main drawbacks are the choice of the function for the frontier and the handling of multiple inputs, multiple outputs cases. *Nonparametric* models do not assume any particular functional form for the frontier. The main strengths of this approach are the robustness to model choice and the easy handling of multiple inputs, multiple outputs case. The main limitations of nonparametric models are the estimation of unknown functional and the so-called *curse* of dimensionality,[5] typical of nonparametric methods. *Deterministic Models* assume that all observations belong to the production set with probability one. The main weakness of this approach is the influence of "super-efficient" outliers. *Stochastic Models* instead allow for noise in the data, i.e. some observations might lie outside the production set. The main problem of this approach is the identification of noise from inefficiency. In *Cross-sectional* models the data sample is composed

Table 1 A taxonomy of efficient frontier models

Criterium	Model type
Functional form specification of the frontier	Parametric
	Nonparametric
	Semi-parametric
Presence of noise	Deterministic
	Stochastic
	Robust
Type of data	Cross-section
	Panel data

[5]The "course of dimensionality," shared by many nonparametric methods means that to avoid large variances and wide confidence interval estimates a large quantity of data is needed.

by observations on a given number of units, while *Panel Data* models include observations on a given number of units that are available over a number of periods of time. Panel data allow the measurement of *productivity change* as well as the estimation of technical progress or regress.

The limitations of the parametric approach are mainly related to the additional assumptions on the functional specification of the frontier and the functional specification of the inefficiency term. These assumptions/specifications may strongly affect the efficiency estimates. The preference of the nonparametric approach over the parametric approach is due to the small amount of assumptions required and mainly to the fact that we do not have to specify the functional form of the relation inputs-outputs and we do not need to specify a distributional form for the inefficiency term. Nonetheless, traditional nonparametric estimators based on envelopment techniques (i.e., Data Envelopment (DEA)/Free Disposal Hull (FDH) types) were for a long time limited by several drawbacks: deterministic (meaning that all deviations from the efficient frontier are considered as inefficiency, and no noise is allowed) and non-statistical nature; influence of outliers and extreme values; lack of parameters for the economic interpretation; unsatisfactory techniques for the introduction of environmental or external variables in the measurement of the efficiency. See, e.g., Daraio and Simar (2007) that provide an overview of some advances to overcome the limits of nonparametric frontier models. Stock (2010) identifies one of the causes of the development of nonparametric models in the *dissatisfaction* towards traditional parametric models.

Figure 1 shows a schematic evolution of the methods of frontier estimation. At the beginning, the parametric approach was mainly developed and adopted by economists, while the nonparametric approach was developed and used in

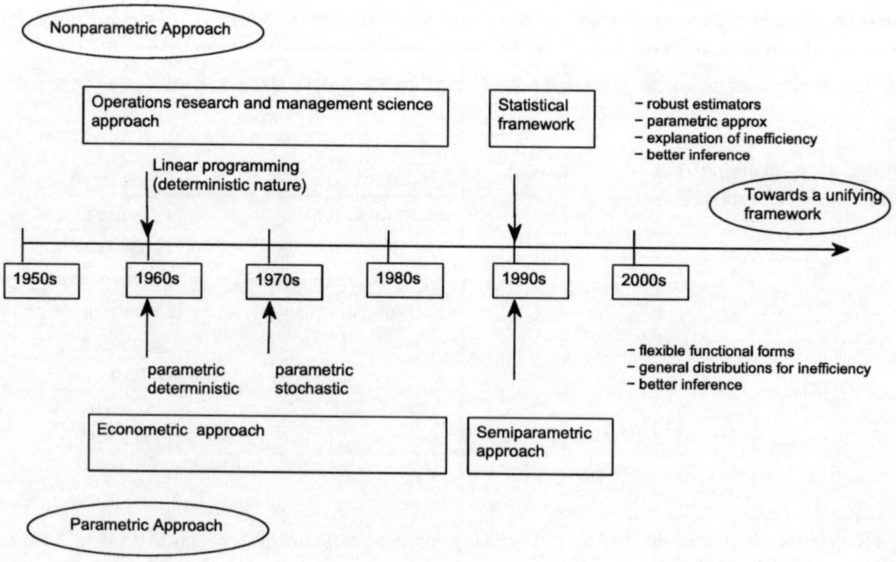

Fig. 1 Convergence of methods for frontier estimation

the operational research literature. Later, different semi-parametric approaches were introduced, with the aim of providing more flexible functional forms, more general distributions for inefficiency and better inference. Parmeter and Zelenyuk (2019) survey recent methodological advances that try to combine the virtues of nonparametric approaches with those of parametric ones, confirming our view, illustrated in Fig. 1, that shows a trend towards a unifying approach in which parametric and nonparametric approaches tend to converge overcoming their own specific limitations. Parmeter and Zelenyuk (2019) discuss the operationalization of the new methods introduced in the literature based on local likelihood estimation and other semi-parametric approaches and their implementation and admit that these new approaches are not yet used in the empirical literature. One reason for this may be the neglected importance of the need to specify a framework for the assessment of productivity and the consequent missing description of the production process that is a current practice in empirical works.

Choosing a model for the assessment of productivity and efficiency means to specify the main features of a data generating process (DGP) that can be used to carry out the estimation of the inefficiency differentials. Table 2 summarizes the main options that are available and that should be carefully described and discussed in the specific application context. Moving from the North-West towards the South-East part of Table 2 implies an increasing difficulty in running inference as the problems of estimation become more complex. Obviously, if the representation of the production process is not discussed and described, it is difficult to choose a model for the assessment of productivity that identifies a reasonable DGP appropriate for the empirical context.

Table 2 Specifying a data generating process: the options available

	Parametric	Semi-parametric	Nonparametric
Deterministic	Analytical models for frontier	Some parametric specifications	No specific model for frontier
	And for distance from it	No noise allowed	No noise allowed
	(No noise allowed)		
Robust	Analytical models for frontier	Some parametric specifications	No specific model for frontier
	Some deviations	Some deviations	Some deviations
	(Outliers) allowed	(Outliers) allowed	(Outliers) allowed
Stochastic	Analytical models for frontier	Some parametric specifications	No specific model for frontier
	Including noise	Including noise	Some structure on noise for identification

1.3 *Main Aim and Organization of the Paper*

The main objective of this paper is to propose a framework for the development of models of performance that permits the correct description of the hypotheses and correct specification of the DGP to make an appropriate measurement of productivity/efficiency stylized facts. This work can complement recent methodological works surveyed, e.g., in Simar and Wilson (2015), Parmeter and Zelenyuk (2019), and Sickles and Zelenyuk (2019), guiding the users to describe and choose the most appropriate method for the analysis taking into account all the other relevant dimensions and conditions.

In the next section, we analyze in details the need to specify a framework for developing performance measurement models and discuss the implementation problem. Section 3 proposes a doubly conditional performance measurement model. The following section deals with the important role played by the representation of the production process. After that, Sect. 5 introduces recent advances in modeling coming from computer science at the intersection with statistics and behavioral economics.

Section 6 proposes a general econometric methodology for deriving economic regularities and let empirical evidence contribute to the advancements of economic theory. Section 7 shows that our approach to measuring and consolidating performance can be a valuable tool for bringing together different strands of literature.

2 The Need for a Framework to Assess Productivity

The evaluation of productivity and efficiency is a complex task for many reasons, as we have seen in the previous section. The evaluation of productivity falls within the field of performance measurement and management. *Performance* may be defined as "an organization's ability to achieve its goals and objectives measurably, reliably, and sustainably through intentional actions" (Hunter and Nielsen 2013, p. 10). Performance management includes several constitutive elements, such as performance leadership, operational leaders, operational managers, management structure, accountability systems, performance budgeting, information and knowledge production, measuring and monitoring systems (for more information, see, e.g., Hunter and Nielsen 2013). Figure 2 illustrates the main elements involved in performance evaluation starting with the evaluative purposes that are formulated within a policy-making process, or by the governance of institutions, or may arise from research questions. Performance evaluation includes also development of models and methodological choices.

Generally, the main purposes of productivity and efficiency analyses are the comparative evaluation of the performance of production units, the investigation on the explicative factors, a benchmarking of the units analyzed, the contribution to relevant economic issues, with rigorous empirically based evidence. There are

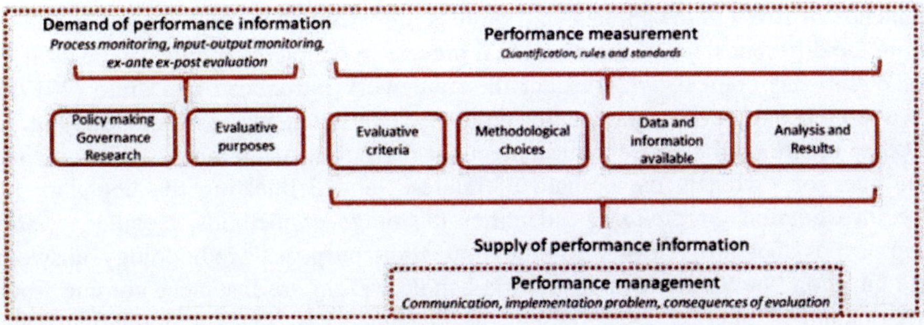

Fig. 2 An outline of the performance evaluation setup. This is composed by three blocks. Performance measurement is in the middle between demand and supply of performance information

several possible reasons for *comparative efficiency (productivity) analysis* in a wide range of empirical applications (see Daraio et al. 2020, for a survey of existing surveys).

Figure 2 shows how the process of providing information related to performance, included in the broader performance management, is connected to performance measurement. The latter represents the focus of our discussion. To perform a measurement of the performance appropriate to the evaluative purposes, we support the need to have a reference *framework*. A framework is necessary to develop models of performance that are as close as possible to the reality being assessed. Identifying a model and describing its constitutive elements and basic hypotheses (DGP) are necessary for being able to check the robustness of the model and its coherence with its purposes. In the next section, we describe the importance of the issue of designing *relevant and appropriate models* to assess productivity and efficiency which are at the core of the stylized facts.

2.1 *Developing Models*

A *model* is an abstract representation of an object or real phenomenon. A model is built on the reality, from some point of view, and has some aims. The representation of reality is achieved through the *analogy* established between aspects of reality and aspects of the model. We can state that a model is a tool for understanding reality (Gibbard and Varian 1978). *Econometric* models are quantitative models of economic variables. These are models in which the analogy with the real world takes place through the quantification of objects, facts, and phenomena and the identification of the relationships existing between the previously identified objects, and the reality that is the object of the model (see also Sugden 2000; Viskovatoff 2003). The practical use of a model depends on the different *roles* that the model can have including interpretation, forecasting, and/or intervention (here the famous sentence of Box (1976) applies: "all models are wrong, but some are useful") and from the different *steps* of the decisional process in which the model can be used.

Within this context, we consider the framework introduced in Daraio (2017a) as a reference to develop models for productivity/efficiency assessment. See Fig. 3. *Theory* identifies the conceptual content (background) of the analysis, answering the question "what is the domain of interest" and delineating the boundary of the investigation. *Methodology* identifies the range of methods, techniques, and approaches that are relevant for the evaluation purpose. Methodology answers the question "how" the investigation is handled. *Data* are instances coming from the domain of interest and represent the raw materials (or basic ingredients) on which the empirical evidence is built. Data are a relevant dimension which has a problematic definition. This is because the definition of data depends on their use and not on the inherent characteristics of the data (Borgman 2015, p. 74).

The *development of a model* requires the understanding of the theoretical background of the problem (or analyzed reality). From a methodological point of view, developing a model is connected to the identification of the subject (*what to assess*) of the analysis and of the means (*how to assess*) or methods of the analysis. The *subject of the analysis* may be: (1) the *output* or the result of a transformation process which uses inputs to produce products or services, (2) *partial or total factor productivity* or/ *efficiency* (productivity with respect to a reference), (3) *effectiveness* which considers inputs, outputs and account for the aims of the activity, and (4) *impact* including contributions outside the production activity, to the general economy or society. The *means* of the assessment may be quantitative,

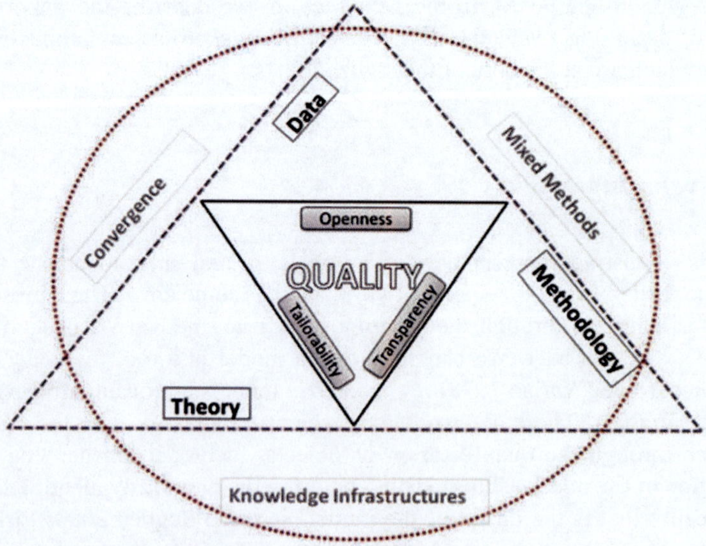

Fig. 3 A three-dimensional framework for the development of models for productivity/efficiency assessment. Adapted from Daraio (2017a)

qualitative, or mixed approaches. Finally, it is important to assess the availability, the usability of data, together with their interoperability and the level of objectiveness of the considered information (independence from the unit of analysis or *unit free property* of data in Daraio 2017a).

As observed in Daraio (2017a), each quantitative evaluation is based on a model that can be implicitly or explicitly defined and discussed. If the model underlying the assessment is not described, this does not allow clarifying and accounting for the underlying theoretical choices, methodological assumptions, and data limits, in an explicit way. As a consequence, when the model related to the quantitative assessment is not explicitly described, it is not possible to check its robustness.

Developing models is important for (1) learning about the explicit consequences of assumptions, test the assumptions, highlight relevant relations; and for (2) improving, to better operate, document/verify the assumptions, decompose analysis and synthesis, systematize the problem and the evaluation/choice done, explicit the dependence of the choice to the scenario. There are however several *pitfalls* and difficulties in modeling that should be taken into account, namely: (1) the possibility that the targets are not quantifiable, (2) the complexity, uncertainty, and changeability of the environment in which the controlled system works, (3) the limits in the decision context, (4) the intrinsic complexity of calculation.

We support that the ability to develop (and afterwards understand and use effectively) models for the assessment of productivity/efficiency is linked and depends, among other factors, on the degree or depth of the conceptualization and formalization, in an unambiguous way, of the underlying idea of *quality*. Quality is the overarching concept of this framework. It is intended as "fitness for purpose" and is also an attribute of the different dimensions of the framework. The framework includes also three implementation factors, namely *Tailorability* (the adaptability to the features of the problem at hand), *Transparency* (that relates to the description of the choices made and underlying hypothesis masked in the proposed/selected theory/methodology/data combination), and *Openness* (accessibility to the main elements of the modeling). Factors supporting model development (the so-called *enabling conditions*) include: mixed methods, convergence, and knowledge infrastructure. According to Daraio (2017a), *Mixed Methods* refer to the intelligent combination of qualitative and quantitative approaches, *Convergence* is the evolution of the *transdisciplinary* approach, which allows for overcoming the traditional paradigms, increasing the dimensional space of thinking, and *Knowledge infrastructures* refer to networks of people that interacts with artifacts, tools, and data infrastructures. As we will see in the following, these attributes are included in the broader implementation problem.

2.2 The Implementation Problem

Once we have introduced a framework for the development of productivity assessment models, we have to deal with the implementation problem, already mentioned in Fig. 2, in which it is part of the performance management activities. The *problem of implementation* refers to the application of methods developed as *basic research* for assessing the productivity/efficiency in a concrete organization and/or context.

Figure 4 outlines the generalized implementation problem proposed in Daraio (2017b).[6] Panel A of Fig. 4, on the top-left side, shows three systems, which constitute the context of the intervention. According to Mingers (2006) the three systems are the agents undertaking the intervention (*intervention*), the real-world situation of concern (*problem content*), and the available theories and methodologies (*intellectual resources*). The right and bottom part of Panel A of Fig. 4 illustrates the approach of the Level of Abstraction (LoA, Floridi 2008). According to this approach, reality can be viewed from different perspectives or levels and the identification relation between two observables is always contextual. The context is a function of the level of abstraction chosen for the required analysis. This contextualization permits the configuration of a model specifying its ontological commitment. The LoA (the Ontological committing step) generates the model (the ontological committed outcome) which is used to identify the properties that are attributed to the application context. Panel B of Fig. 4 adds to the previous figure the *translations* that are related to the configurations and reconfigurations of mediations originated by the movements of the instantiation and abstraction which transform the actors involved in the process (Latour 2005).

From this illustration it clearly appears the complexity of the model development phase and the difficulties that may arise in each step of the implementation. Difficulties may arise in setting the correct LoA that is connected with the ontological commitment of the modeling phase, in identifying the properties of the model that can be attributed to the context of intervention and in the movements (or translations) of the abstraction and instantiation from the global to the local context of intervention.

3 A Doubly Conditional Performance Model

For the assessment of productivity and efficiency stylized facts we propose the *doubly conditional* performance evaluation model introduced by Daraio (2017b) and illustrated in Fig. 5. This performance model is called *doubly conditional* because the evaluation is conditioned two times: on the available information and on the information that are not available. The model distinguishes two kinds of conditioning: (1) Internal conditioning or *normalization*; (2) External conditioning or *contextualization*. Internal conditioning factors are the items reported in the bottom of Fig. 5 (actors, processes, and results). Normalization means to compare

[6]It is called generalized problem because it considers (1) the interaction of method development with its useful application; (2) the implementation which changes the unit of assessment and includes (3) knowledge and technological innovation (see Daraio 2017b).

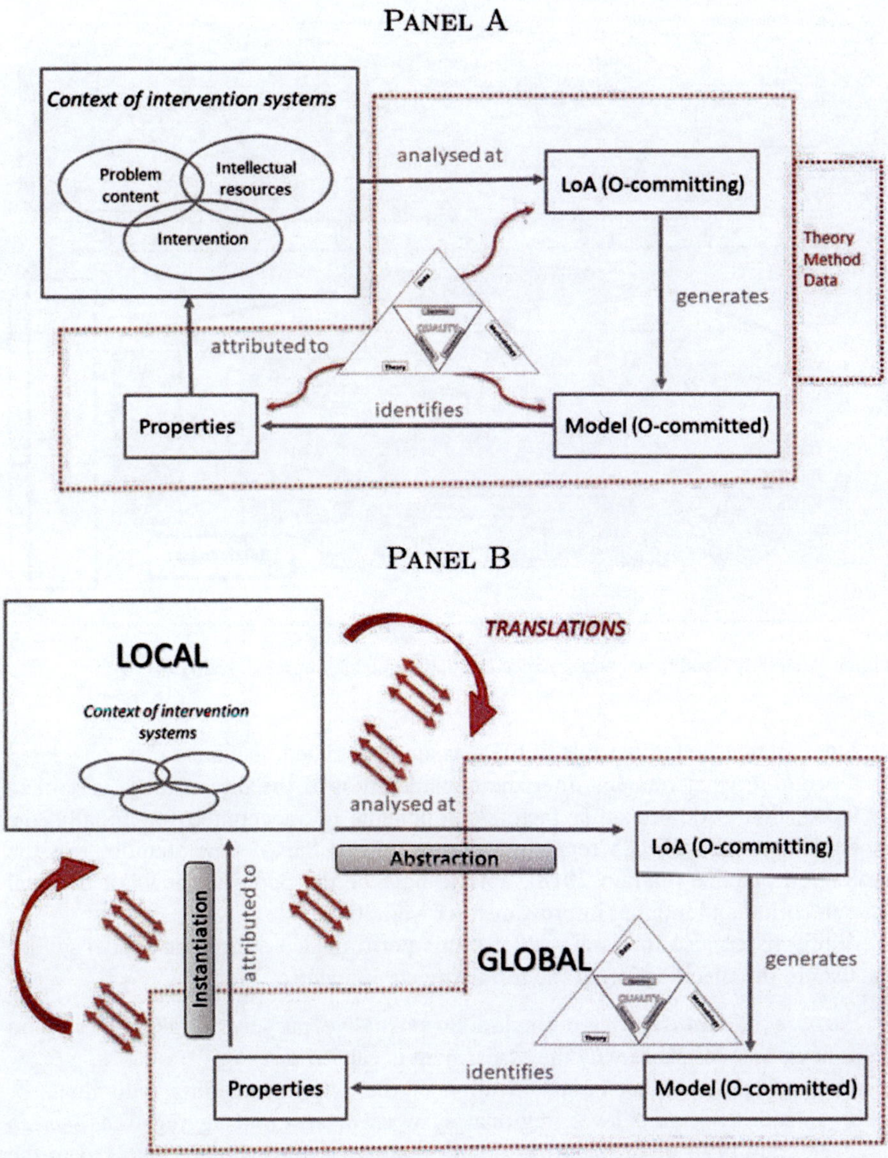

Fig. 4 An illustration of the generalized implementation problem. Source: Daraio (2017b)

comparable entities, setting appropriate reference sets. External conditioning factors are the items reported in the top of Fig. 5. Contextualization corresponds to accounting for heterogeneity factors. This model allows us to identify the components of the analysis (in terms of theory-method-data characterization) that are excluded (i.e., what remains outside) from the specific context of the evaluation. The model

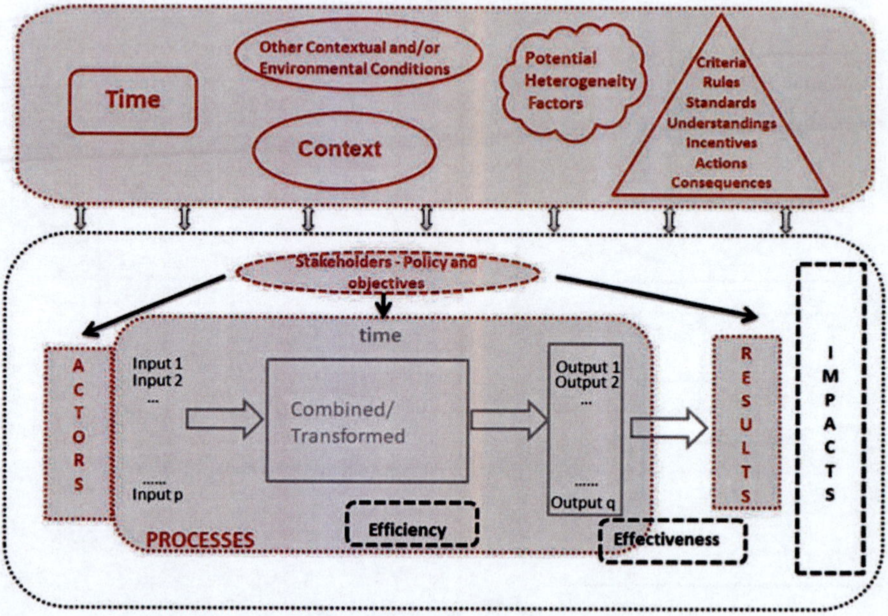

Fig. 5 A Doubly Conditional performance evaluation model. Source: Daraio (2017b)

provides an interpretative value of the measure calculated, that has to be considered as a *residual*, what remains after the consideration of the dimensions (variables) included, that is due to other factors/components not accounted for. Finally, the model illustrated in Fig. 5 represents a step toward the "democratization" of the evaluation practice (Daraio 2018), able to balance the opposite views of external accountability and internal improvement (Ewell 2009).

As discussed also in Daraio (2019), this performance evaluation model guides the user to the specification of the following components:

- *Purpose of the assessment* (including evaluative purposes, stakeholders, and policy), that describes why the assessment is carried out;
- *Level of analysis*, that is specification of the actors (including individuals or organizations—*micro* level, regional systems or sectorial aggregations—*meso* level, country or other macro aggregate—*macro* level) who are involved in the assessment;
- *Object of the evaluation* (including outputs, efficiency, results, effectiveness, and impact) that identifies what is assessed;
- *Means of the evaluation* (including (1) qualitative, (2) quantitative, and (3) mixed methods and data) that specifies how the assessment is carried out;
- *Internal conditional factors* (including actors, processes, and results) considering how, when, and where the assessment is done;

- *External conditional factors* (including time, context, other contextual factors, potential heterogeneity, criteria, rules, standards, understandings, incentives, actions, and consequences) considering how, when, and where the assessment is done.

At this point, a question arises: What is the relationship between the framework illustrated in Fig. 3 and the performance evaluation model shown in Fig. 5? The link between these two is given by the *representation* of the production process that is illustrated in the next section.

4 The Representation of the Production Process

Productivity seems a simple concept although its *operationalization* and application are difficult including some critical issues, such as the definition of the *production process* that is the set of knowledge about production. We need to specify a model of the production process, select a representation of the production process, and have to measure the inputs, outputs, and other factors.

A production process may be represented in different ways, including the neoclassical production function (defined as the maximum value of output associated to a given value of input), according to the accounting view in monetary values, according to an engineering production function approach (Chenery 1949, based on production functions rewritten in terms of cost per unit of engineering variables), through a frontier approach (in particular the nonparametric frontier approach that does not rely on the specification of a functional form for the frontier) which departs from the mainstream economics based on production function specification, and finally, based on the flows and funds model of Georgescu Roegen (1971).

Georgescu Roegen (1971) describes at length his ideas about the economic process as a process dominated by a qualitative change (transformation) making a close connection between the entropy law and the economic process. Georgescu Roegen (1971) makes a distinction between *arithmomorphic* characteristics (of mathematical models) typical of *mechanistic-deductive* knowledge and *dialectical* characteristics of *dialectic-evolutionary* knowledge. He strongly criticizes the neoclassical production function approach, with its arithmomorphic characteristics, because it is not able to account for *time* and the *boundary* of the production process. In fact, in order to perform an analytical study, the process shall be separated from its environment by identifying a boundary. Only analyzing the elements crossing the boundary permits to understand what is happening in the process. The elements crossing the boundary can be either inputs or outputs and may be characterized in two types: *stock* (all material inputs or outputs that physically takes part of the transformation due to the process; they can be stored and are measured in terms of *flow*, i.e. volume of material per unit of time) and *services* (these are used, not consumed by the process; they cannot be stored and are supplied by *fund* of services; they are measured as size of the used fund of service times the used period of time).

This representation of the production process suggests the following elements *to improve productivity*: (1) organizational changes, to improve the activities on the line; (2) increase of the time in which the funds are used; (3) faster execution of the operations on the flows; (4) changes on the relations of inputs and outputs.

Georgescu Roegen (1971) proposes a more general production function in which time is integrated and this lead to a production function that is not anymore a single point function but is a functional, defined in a given interval of time and determined by the nature of the process. Fioretti (2007) shows that this model of production, which accounts for organizational aspects of the production, has some connections with recent neural network developments. Morroni (1992, 2006, 2014) highlights the organizational aspects of the production process present in the Georgescu-Roegen's (1971) funds and flows model and their interactions at different levels of analysis. The different productivity network models introduced in the data envelopment analysis literature (see Kao 2017 for an encyclopedic overview) are an implementation of the funds and flows model. Daraio et al. (2017) and Daraio (2019) propose a new more general framework for modeling the production process which is based on Georgescu-Roegen's (1971) model of production, includes nonparametric productivity networks, combines information theoretic approaches to econometrics, machine learning, and statistical inference from the physics of complex systems.

The approach that we consider suitable to analytically represent the production process for measuring the stylized productivity/efficiency facts is the one described by Georgescu Roegen (1971). This is the most general approach, currently available, to analytically represent a production process. This approach, moreover, is closely connected to our framework (Fig. 3): it links the enabling conditions of our framework illustrated in Fig. 3 with the doubly conditional performance measurement model of Fig. 5. Georgescu Roegen (1971) in fact criticizes the merely quantitative (arithmomorphic or mathematical) models, favoring a qualitative-quantitative approach (mixed methods); proposes to overcome the disciplinary limits ranging from philosophy to physics and supports the combination of multiple monoprospective visions (convergence); highlights the importance of the human factor and the need for a conceptual dialectical reasoning (knowledge infrastructure), finally discusses the important role of *quality* that represents the overarching concept of our framework (see Fig. 3).

5 Behavioral Economics and Behavioral Model Building

The role of human behavior in the development of models for the measurement of performance is important and has been illustrated in Sect. 2 discussing the implementation problem. This connects our discussion with behavioral economics, that is according to Thaler (2016, p. 1577) the "mixture of psychology and economics." Tversky and Kahneman (1974) introduce three heuristics that are employed in taking decisions under uncertainty, usually neglected in mainstream economic models, namely (1) *representativeness*, related to the use of categories to evaluate the probability that a given event belongs to a given class or a given process; (2) *availability of instances or scenarios*, related to the evaluation the frequency of a given class or the likelihood of a particular progress; and (3) *adjustment from an anchor*, related to numerical prediction, when a pertinent value is available. These heuristics that are generally effective lead to regular and expected biases. The study of heuristics in decision making introduced by Tversky and Kahneman (1974) extended Simon's research on human bounded rationality in problem solving (see, e.g., Simon 1969, 1982, 2000) which lead to the *satisficing* situation where people seek solutions or accept choices or judgments that are "good enough" for their purposes, instead of maximizing behavior. The discussion on heuristics in human decision making and of their inherent biases is extended in Kahneman (2011) that describes two different ways of thinking, a "fast system," characterized by fast, automatic, frequent, emotional, stereotypic, subconscious, and a "slow system," characterized by slow, effortful, infrequent, logical, calculating, conscious. On the base of heuristics, Kahneman (2011) asserts that the fast system involves the association of new information with existing patterns instead of building new patterns for each new event.

These recent developments in behavioral economics decision making may be further explored in combination with recently developed statistical and machine learning approaches (see, e.g., Mezard and Montanari 2009; Barber 2012). Machine learning techniques, lying at the intersection of computer science and statistics, are at the core of artificial intelligence and data science, and are showing increasing potentialities (Jordan and Mitchell 2015). Thaler (2016) considers behavioral economics as an empirical and evidence based discipline able to exploit the most sophisticated statistical techniques having access to increasingly large and rich datasets.

In the previous sections we illustrated the importance of describing a model of the production process to have an appropriate measurement of productivity stylized facts. We have seen (see Sect. 2) how complex is the implementation of a model and the importance of considering the information that are available in the model together with the information that could be relevant but are not available for the analysis (see Sect. 3). The proposed doubly conditional model shows how each model is conditioned by the information contained in the variables used by the model, but also by the relevant information not considered in the model. The framework described in the previous sections is therefore necessary to formulate a model to be used to quantify the stylized facts of productivity.

Model identification requires specifying the relationships that exist among the variables. An important role in this context is represented by causal relationships. Structural causal model is nicely discussed in Pearl (2000), which provides a mathematical foundation for the analysis of causes and counterfactuals, including and unifying other approaches to causation (for a review see Pearl 2010). In concluding the survey on recent advances in causal analysis, Pearl (2010) states that "*Causal inference requires two additional ingredients: a science-friendly language for articulating causal knowledge, and a mathematical machinery for processing that knowledge, combining it with data and drawing new causal conclusions about a phenomenon. This paper [...] shows how statistical methods can be supplemented with the needed ingredients. The theory invokes nonparametric structural equations models as a formal and meaningful language for defining causal quantities, formulating causal assumptions, testing identifiability, and explicating many concepts used in causal discourse. These include: randomization, intervention, direct and indirect effects, confounding, counterfactuals, and attribution. The algebraic component of the structural language coincides with the potential-outcome framework, and its graphical component embraces Wright's method of path diagrams. When unified and synthesized, the two components offer statistical investigators a powerful and comprehensive methodology for empirical research.*"

The identification and estimation of causal relationships, based on clearly defined assumptions in a behavioral (structural) model, is a relevant part of the modelling exercise. Identifying restrictions that are not testable but are necessary to allow for the interpretation of coefficients in a production function or frontier, or for the role of unobserved heterogeneity as fixed or random is an important investigation to carry out in the selection of the method of analysis to apply for the measurement of the productivity stylized fact.

Geffner (2018) shows that in artificial intelligence there is a need to combine model-free learners and model-based solvers to have intelligent systems that are robust and general. Model-free learners are based on black-boxes that do not have the flexibility, transparency, and generality of their model-based counterparts. Model-based approaches require the specification of models. These two models are connected to the two systems of human mind developed in Kahneman (2011), a "fast" system and a "slow" system. The next section proposes a methodology to consolidate productivity stylized facts which combines "General to Specific" with "Specific to General" approaches in econometrics.

6 The Accumulation of Productivity Stylized Facts

In order to carry out an empirical study we need to follow a methodological framework. As pointed out by Hendry (2001, p. 7), "there can be little dispute that econometric methodology lacks a consensus." The traditional econometric methodology illustrated in the top panel of Fig. 6 has been the reference methodology for a large number of econometric applications, starting from the consumer-income relations modeling and going to other applied economics exercises.

Meanwhile, several factors of changes have emerged. According to Lütkepohl (2001), some of these are the advances in computer technology, the data availability, some new developments in statistical theory (e.g. bootstrap), some new ideas in economic theory, the dissatisfaction with unexplained phenomena or poorly modeled data characteristics, some problems in the economic conditions. These forces have played and are going to play a central role in the development of the econometric methodology. They contribute to amplify the gap existing between econometric theory and applied economics. On the origin of this increasing gap, Heckman

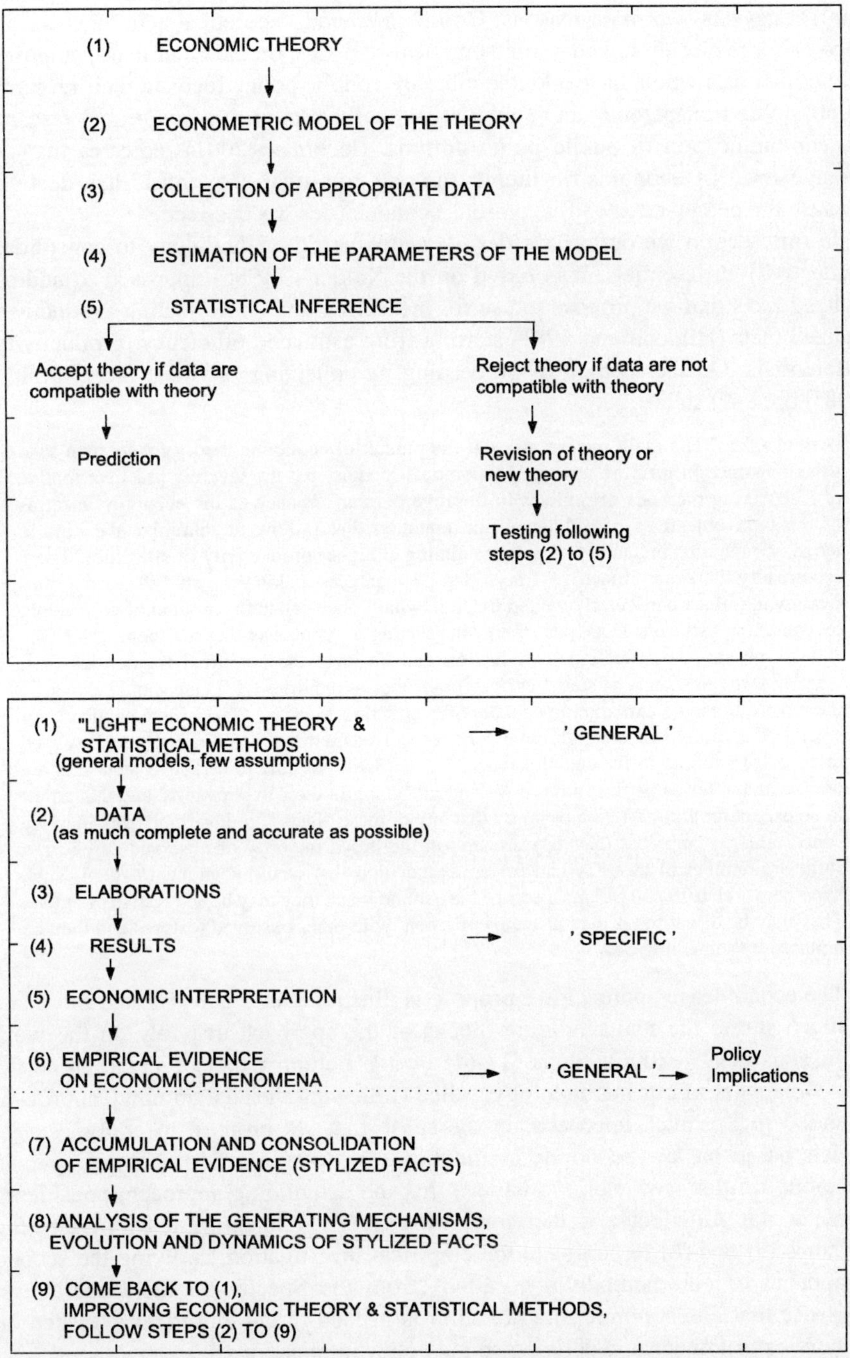

Fig. 6 Evolution of the Econometric methodology: from a traditional perspective (e.g. Gujarati 1978) toward a more flexible "general to specific"–"specific to general" approach

(2001) suggests two main reasons. On the one hand, theoretical econometrics has become more closely linked to mathematical statistics; on the other hand, empirical economists as a whole have adopted more of a public policy focus in their research, emphasizing transparency and simplicity as hallmarks of good empirical research for communication in public policy forums. Heckman (2001) indicates that the average level of econometric literacy among empirical economists has declined because the perceived need for rigorous econometrics has declined.

In this section we describe a *flexible* econometric methodology to consolidate productivity differentials. It is based on the Kaldor's (1985) approach to address stylized facts that we propose to use for measuring and consolidating productivity stylized facts (Hildenbrand 1981) starting from estimated efficiency (productivity) differentials. On the method of proceeding by collecting "stylized facts," Kaldor (1985, pp. 8–9) states:

> [Arthur Okun] His main motive was not the pursuit of economic theory for its own sake - the construction of more advanced theoretical models- but the severely practical motive of discovering methods or policies to improve the performance of the economy in terms of the twin objectives of efficiency and equality, that is how to minimize the cost in terms of economic inequality of policies aiming at higher productivity or efficiency. There are broadly the same objectives I myself [...] regard as making the study of economics worthwhile. But I particularly valued in Okun what I once called the method of proceeding by collecting "stylized facts" and then constructing a hypothesis that fits them. [...] One should subordinate deduction to induction and discover the empirical regularities first, whether through a study of statistics or through special inquiries [...] One should also seek the most reasonable explanation capable of accounting for these "facts," independently of whether they fit into the general framework of received theory or not. I called them "stylized facts" [...] because in the social sciences [...] it is impossible to establish facts that are precise and at the same time suggestive and intriguing in their implications, and that admit to no exception. [...] We do not imply that any of these "facts" are invariably true in every conceivable instance but that they are true in the broad majority of observed cases- in a sufficient number of cases to call for an explanation that would account for them. Such hypotheses relate to particular aspects of the economy and they may be suggestive of others. They may be discarded if they prove inconsistent with other observed features and then be replaced by something else.

The econometric approach we propose is illustrated in Fig. 6. The bottom panel of Fig. 6 shows the main building blocks of the approach that rely on the work of Juselius (1999, 2006). Steps (1)–(4) on the bottom panel of Fig. 6 show the first component of our methodology, called (following the "datamining" approach) "General to Specific" approach, in the sense that we propose to apply *general* models based on few economic assumptions on data, in order to obtain *specific* economic results. However, we believe that the datamining approach, considered alone, is not sufficient and therefore, we suggest to integrate it by performing the steps (5) and (6) to complete the empirical investigation, applying the second component of our methodology, called "from the Specific to the General," in the sense that an economic interpretation is needed to get empirical evidence on economic phenomena and deriving sound policy implications.[7]

---

[7] At this purpose, we report the conclusions of Heckman (2001, p. 5): *If the limits of mathematical statistics as a guide to empirical analysis and interpretation of economic data are appreciated and*

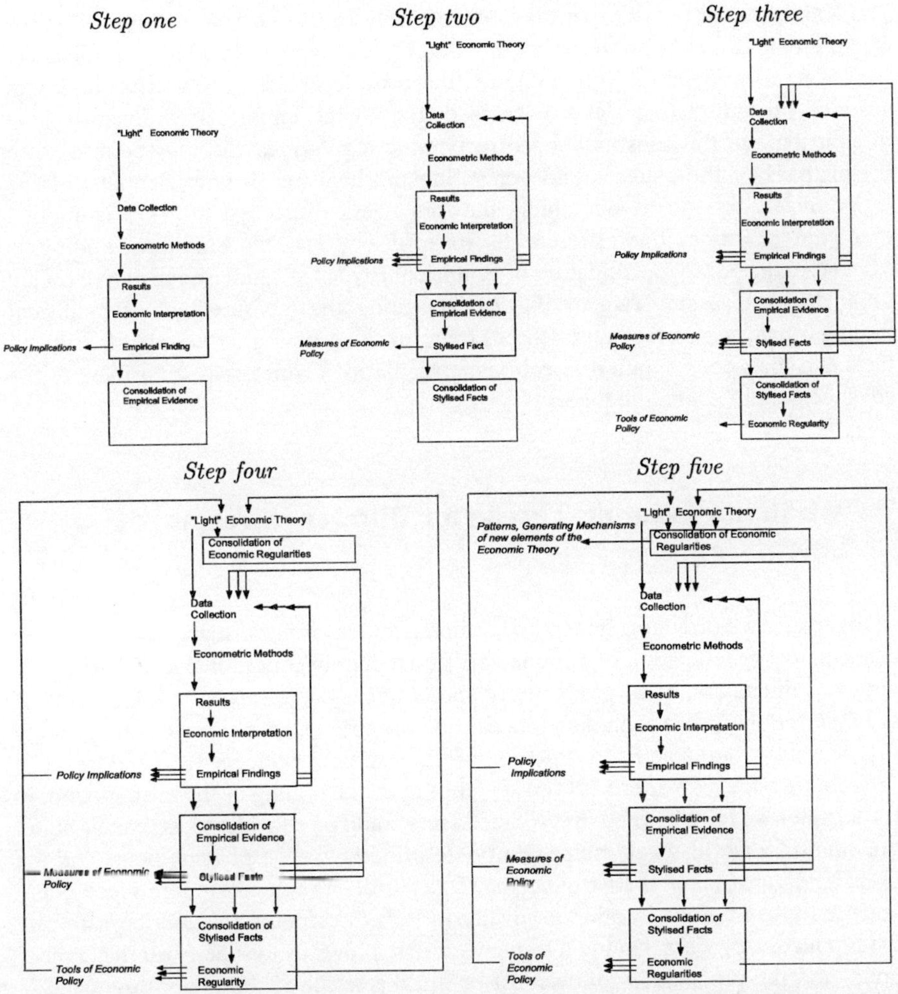

Fig. 7 Illustration of a flexible econometric methodology to consolidate productivity stylized facts

This methodology offers a way for consolidating empirical evidence and analyzing its generating mechanisms, patterns, and dynamics.[8]

In the following Fig. 7 we illustrate how productivity/efficiency differentials (measured by an efficient frontier model, see Tables 1 and 2) may be consolidated

---

economics is more closely integrated into the development of and justification for estimators, then the gap between econometric theory and applied work will diminish and econometrics will reassert itself as an important part of the corpus of economics.

[8]In the end, *econometrics is useful only if it helps economists conduct and interpret empirical research on economic data. Empirical research is intrinsically an inductive activity, building up generalizations from data, and using data to test competing models, to evaluate policies and to forecast the effects of new policies or modifications of existing policies (Heckman 2001, p. 3).*

in a Kaldor's (1985) approach: the stylized facts come out from the consolidation of the empirical findings and economic regularities are generated by consolidating the observed stylized facts. In so doing, there are feedbacks mechanisms and with a *spiral* procedure (see the five steps in Fig. 7) the empirical evidence is able to contribute to the consolidation of economic regularities and may contribute to the analysis of the patterns and generating mechanisms of new elements of the economic theory. At the beginning, the framework illustrated in Fig. 3 is applied to obtain empirical finding (see step one of Fig. 7). This empirical finding is stocked in the box "Consolidation of Empirical Evidence" and used to derive policy implications (see step two of Fig. 7). Repeating the measurement of empirical findings many times (see steps three, four, and five of Fig. 7) we obtain stylized facts and their consolidation in economic regularities which may contribute to the advancement of economic theory.

7 A Unifying Leading-Thread for Different Streams of Literature

In this paper we provide a general operationalization of performance measurement based on the specification of a framework and a doubly conditional model to assess and consolidate empirical productivity and efficiency. We detail the importance of the description of the production process and propose an econometric methodology for the accumulation and consolidation of the empirical evidence (stylized facts).

Coming back to Winter's (2006) sentence at the beginning of the introduction, in this chapter we have learned that stylized facts could be considered as recipes about the empirical world. Each recipe can be described by a list of ingredients and the preparation method. To better understand the recipe, its content, to reproduce it and potentially to improve it, adding novelty in it, it is essential to describe carefully the production process, having a framework that allows us to specify all the choices done, and the procedures followed to obtain the result of the recipe (the cake in Winter's 2006 words).

The proposed framework may act as a leading-thread for different streams of literature in economics, management, and political science which may all take advantage from our general operationalization of performance measurement.

Section 5 introduced behavioral economics and its connection to the development of models for performance evaluation. Tomer (2007) identifies and compares different strands of behavioral economics against mainstream economic theory, including Simon (1969, 1982) bounded rationality and satisficing objective; psychological economics (Kahneman 2011; Nelson and Winter 1982) evolutionary theory, as well as Leibenstein (1966) X-efficiency theory looking at understanding why less than optimal internal efficiency is the usual state of affairs in firms. While Simon and psychological economics were described in Sect. 5, in the following we describe the other streams of behavioral economics that can be unified by our framework and introduce other strands of literature that may be included as well, which are resource-based view of the firm, complementarity theory, variety of governance, and design of evaluation and control systems.

7.1 Evolutionary Theory of the Firm

The notion of technological paradigm (Dosi 1982, 1988) has been introduced in literature to develop an "alternative" theoretical framework with respect to the conventional (neoclassical) production theory, largely criticized on the ground of its strong assumptions (maximizing behavior, functional specification of the relation inputs-outputs, representative agent, and so on). It is based on a view of technology grounded on the following three fundamental ideas. First, it suggests that any satisfactory description of what technology is and how it changes must also embody the representation of the specific forms of knowledge on which a particular activity is based and cannot be reduced to a set of well-defined blueprints. It primarily concerns problem-solving activities involving—to varying degrees—also tacit forms of knowledge embodied in individuals and organizational procedures. Second, paradigms entail specific heuristic and visions on "how to do things" and how to improve them, often shared by the community of practitioners in each particular activity. Third, paradigms often also define basic templates of artifacts and systems, which over time are progressively modified and improved. As highlighted in Nelson and Winter (1982, 2002) technical change and market structure must be understood as mutually interactive, with each affecting the other. In the evolutionary theory, technical change and production activities play a central role in explaining economic change. Evolutionary thinking sees questions of production as tightly and reciprocally connected with questions of coordination, organization, and incentives. Also production activity is embedded in a variety of processes of knowledge creation. The knowledge invoked in productive performances resides for the most part in individual skills. Skills are formed in individuals, and routines in organizations, largely through "learning by doing." These concepts are related to the evolutionary theory of the firm that characterizes the firm for the "specificity" of the competencies of problem solving that organizations incorporate (Metcalfe 2018). This theory considers the firm as a behavioral organization characterized by specific competencies incorporated in its *operational routines*, which evolve over time, partly for their internal learning and partly in answer to environmental changing (Dosi and Malerba 1996). The increasing of *structural diversity* in the firms and the simultaneously reduction of the efficacy of the formal ways of coordination and controls can explain the great emphasis given by the firms to the informal means of control (Chandler, Hagström and Sölvell 1999). The firm is then considered as a depository of knowledge, for a great extent incorporated in its operational routines, which evolves over time influenced by its behavioral and strategic "meta-rules." Competencies of the firm, its ability of learning and problem solving, the rules of the internal organization are then considered as "specific" of the firm. They are mainly tacit and not formalized, very often difficult to copy or transfer. It is this "competence specificity" on the base of the corporate and national system diversity (Coriat and Dosi 2000).

Nevertheless, evolutionary theory suffers from some limitations. First, there is not a fully developed formal theory based on assumptions of bounded rationality and learning applied to production. This makes extremely difficult to introduce notions of efficiency in production (Winter 2005). Second, the theory captures the notion of realized production at the level of individual firms, conditional on idiosyncratic knowledge, but fails to identify a frontier of potential production, based on the pool of productive knowledge available at the industry level. Some recent attempts (e.g., Dosi and Grazzi 2006) discuss technologies as problem-solving procedures and as input-output relations but do not provide any rigorous and coherent approach (alternative to the standard regression-based production function approach) which can be used for consolidating empirical evidence on productivity differentials. Our framework may be useful to provide such approach.

7.2 X-Inefficiency and Resource-Based View of the Firm

X-(in)efficiency theory of the firm is developed by Leibenstein (1966), Leibenstein (1979) tries to capture the performance of the management at a micro-micro level of analysis, trying to explore and characterize individual productivity differentials.[9]

A related stream of literature is the resource-based view (RBV) of the firm (Barney 1991; Barney and Arikan 2001; Rumelt 1987; Dierickx and Cool 1989; Peteraf 1993) which is based on the existence of sustained differences in firms' resources and capabilities. In this field, researchers have proposed definitions of resources and capabilities and the conditions under which they contribute to competitive advantage. For instance, Makadok (2001) defines "resources" as observable assets that can be individually valued and traded; "capabilities" as organizationally embedded; Hoopes et al. (2003) suggest that scale advantages are

[9]It is interesting to recall here Griliches (1994) about Leibenstein's X-inefficiency and the lack of quantitative operationalization:

> Our theories tend to assume that we are, indeed, at the frontier and that we can only either move along it or try to shift it, the latter being a difficult and chancy business. In fact we may be far from our existing "frontiers." Harvey Leibenstein's (1966) ideas about X-efficiency, or more correctly X-inefficiency, did not get much of a sympathetic ear from us. They were inconsistent with notions of equilibrium, the absence of unexploited profit opportunities, and the possibilities for economic arbitrage. But real economic growth is the consequence of both the appearance of such disequilibria and the devising of ways of closing them. How quickly they are eliminated depends on the strength of incentive systems within enterprises, and on their organizational quality. In spite of the large growth in the literature on organizations, we have not yet developed useful ways of quantifying their strengths and weaknesses (Griliches 1994, pp. 15–16). See also Griliches (2003).

neither resources nor capabilities, but fall in a separate category of "cost drivers." Even so, the RBV has lacked the clarity required for empirical specification, it has proved difficult to operationalize. Empirical work, such as Lieberman and Dhawan (2005), has been largely ad hoc, lacking common approaches to modeling, measures, and testing (Barney and Mackey 2005). A subsequent contribution by Leibenstein and Maital (1992) suggests the data envelopment analysis (DEA) approach to empirically estimate X-(in)efficiency differentials and hence links this literature to the quantitative framework proposed in this chapter that may be well suited for the operationalization of the performance measurement.

7.3 *Economic Theory, Complementarity, and Innovation in Production*

Complementarity is an economic property opposite to substitutability and is a classic topic in the theory of production. Factors of production (e.g., capital, labor) are said to be complementary when they are jointly necessary for production. Milgrom and Roberts (1990, 1995) have introduced a more sophisticated notion, suggesting that firms may increase their production more than proportionally if they achieve complementarity between sub-systems of the organization. Generally speaking, complementarity involves the interactions among changes in different variables in affecting performance. Two choice variables are complements when doing (more of) one of them increases the returns to doing (more of) the other. In more mathematical language, the incremental or marginal return to one choice variable increases in the level of any complementary choice variable (Roberts 2007, p. 34).

The conventional theory of the firm based on microeconomics offers a very poor representation of complementarities. Marginal rates of substitution between inputs, on the one hand, and economies of scope in multi-product firms, on the other hand, are the only analytical tools available to explore complementary relations. The only analytical treatment of complementarity in the mainstream theory of the firm was proposed by Milgrom and Roberts (1990, 1995). More recently, the mathematical theory of supermodularity has been employed to model complementary relations also in a non-mainstream framework (e.g. Buenstorf 2005); however, this theory is far from being full developed. Lindbeck and Snower (2003) showed that factor complementarities together with transaction costs can determine the boundary of the firm. Even if it is a nice attempt to integrate recent theories of the firm that emphasize communication and coordination costs, principal-agent problems, and so on, in the paper there is not an operationalization of this idea for empirical work.

An attempt to recognize a central role of production activities inside the theory of the firm can be found in Morroni (2006). The flows and funds model of Georgescu-Roegen is a representation of the production process that takes into account the actual characteristics of production elements and processes such as indivisibility, complementarity, tacitness, and heterogeneity productive knowledge. In most literature, capabilities, transactions, and scale-scope are considered rival explanations of firm competitiveness and organizational boundaries. Morroni (2006) shows that these three aspects are not rivals, but they interplay in explaining the boundaries and the competitiveness of the firm. Under radical uncertainty, complementarity between inputs, indivisibility of inputs, and setup processes, the weight and the interplay of these three aspects are significant; firm competitiveness is linked to its ability of coordinating the development of capabilities, the arrangement of transactions, and the design of the scale of production.

Morroni (2014) shows that there are three levels of analysis. The analysis of inputs-outputs (first level) is encompassed in the analysis that is carried out by the flow funds model that includes the organizational aspects of production and the time dimension. This second level of analysis, the representation of the production process with the flow funds model is then encompassed in the third level of analysis that consider the theory of the firm and the production of new knowledge in which processes (represented with the flow fund model) take place in historical time with productive knowledge that is tacit, local, non-tradable, and heterogeneous across firms. The implication for the theory of the firm is that innovative activity creates: (1) tacit and heterogeneous knowledge; (2) unexpected outcomes (radical uncertainty); (3) new processes that are characterized by indivisible and complementary funds. The framework described in this paper encompasses the general representation of the production process (see Sect. 4) required by Morroni (2014).

7.4 Comparative Institutional Analysis

The framework proposed in this chapter is particularly suited for comparative institutional analysis. There has been an attempt to integrate the literature on institutions, firm strategy, and technological innovation (see e.g. Nelson 1994, 1995; Mowery and Nelson 1999; Tushman and Murmann 1998). This effort has developed descriptive studies of how institutions, firm capabilities, and technologies co-evolve so that particular societies and firms at specific moments in time excel in particular kinds of innovations.

Even though there are innumerable discussions on institutional change, the ability to measure the rate of institutional change is very limited. As pointed out by Hollingsworth (2000), one of the reasons for this shortcoming is that the social sciences are deficient in a theory of institutions, and there is a need to define the parameters of institutional analysis. Therefore, Hollingsworth (2000) proposes a map, with multiple levels at which institutional analysis occurs, see Table 3. Theoretically, each of these areas on the map is interrelated with each other level.

Table 3 Components of institutional analysis (Source: Hollingsworth 2000, p. 601)

1	Institutions	Norms, rules, conventions, habits and values
2	Institutional arrangements	Markets, states, corporate hierarchies, networks, associations, communities
3	Institutional sectors	Financial system, system of education, business system, system of research
4	Organizations	
5	Outputs and performance	Statutes; administrative decisions, the nature, quantity and the quality of industrial products, sectoral and societal performance

Note The five components in this table are arranged in descending order of permanence and stability. That is, norms, conventions, etc. are more enduring and persistent than each of the other components of institutional analysis. Each component is interrelated with every other component, and changes in one are highly likely to have some effect in bringing about change in each of the other components. For references on each component see Hollingsworth (2000, p. 601)

7.5 *Design of Evaluation and Control Systems*

As we have seen in Sect. 2", the assessment of productivity and efficiency is a component of a broader process of performance assessment and management. Within this process, the design of evaluation and control mechanisms is crucial. Ouchi (1979) frames the problem of evaluation and control of organizations proposing three mechanisms through which organizations obtain cooperations among a collection of individuals that have only partially congruent objectives: (1) *markets* that deal with the control problem through their ability to precisely measure and reward individual contributions; (2) *bureaucracies* (Weber 1947, 2009) that rely instead upon a mixture of closed evaluation with a socialized acceptance of common objectives; and (3) *clans* that rely upon a relatively complete socialization process which effectively eliminates goal incongruence between individuals (suited for loosely coupled systems, see Weick 1976).

Ouchi (1979) states that the essential element which underlies any bureaucratic or market form of control is the assumption that it is feasible to measure the performance (output or behavior) with reasonable precision. He identifies two conditions determining the measurement of behavior and of output: (1) the ability to measure outputs and (2) knowledge of the transformation process. Under conditions of ambiguity, loose coupling (Weick 1976) and uncertainty, measurement with reliability and precision is not possible. In this case, the clan form of control which operates by stressing values and objectives as much as behavior is preferable.

7.6 Varieties of Governance

In the previous section, we introduced the classification of evaluation, coordinating and control systems in *market* (based on worth), *hierarchy* (evenness) and *network* or *clan* (appropriateness). This was developed in Ouchi's (1979) and is at the base of the recent theories of governance. Governance is necessary for analyzing the complexity of contemporary policy-making that is the way in which a society and its political processes are organized and steered. Governance is included in the performance evaluation setup illustrated in Fig. 2. Recent trends include fragmentation of the policy-making process (new stakeholders, NGOs, public opinion, and general public), new governance arrangements, as responses to changes in state-societal arrangements (characterized by policentrism, flexibility, co-operation, deliberation, non-coerciveness). New actors enter in the policy arena, new policy instruments are added: contracts, partnership, recommendations, participation, benchmarking, learning. New policy tools emerge from these recent trends and should start to be addressed by various other policy instruments, including financial incentives, periodic evaluation, and request for transparent processes.

Governance is a heuristic tool with which to describe some of the complexity of political processes. There is a variety of governance characterized by *dynamics*, *ability of government to change strategy* (actions and interactions) and *capacity* that is its effectiveness in achieving their objectives. A mode of governance is an equilibrium of these three components at a moment (Capano et al. 2015). Empirical oriented focus, policy mixes/instruments, connected to the performance. Governance arrangements are usually composed by a prevailing coordinating principle (hierarchy) accompanied by other principles (market and network). Real governance arrangements consist of complex policy mixes, that is a blend of different coordinating principles and their respective policy instruments (Capano et al. 2012). The increasing role of *market* principles of coordination is an effect of the financial crisis and the new public management policy instruments. Public administration, more accountable and responsible, is needed to legitimize their decisions outside the normal route of democratic parliamentary procedures. The knowledge governance approach (Foss 2007) emerges to study how governance mechanisms influence knowledge processes.

Governance is a *problem solving* activity in a *dynamic* context accounting for *strategy* and *capacity* (Capano et al. 2015). The connection of governance to performance measurement is an important issue, still rarely explored (Peters et al. 2018). The comprehensive approach we propose in this chapter may be a useful reference for the operationalization of the performance measurement within the varieties of governance.

Acknowledgments The financial support of the Italian Ministry of Education and Research (through the PRIN Project N. 2015RJARX7) and of Sapienza University of Rome (through the Sapienza Awards no. PH11715C8239C105) is gratefully acknowledged. This chapter is the methodological base of the plenary presentation on "New Perspectives on Estimation and Inference about Research Productivity" done by the author at the X NAPW 2018 Conference, June 12–15

2018, at Miami Herbert Business School. The chapter draws upon an introductory chapter of the author's Ph.D. thesis (Daraio 2003). Previous versions have been presented at the Sixth European Meeting on Applied Evolutionary Economics, DIME Special Session on "Production, Product Design and Organization", May 21–23, 2009, Jena, AiIG 2009 Conference, October 2009 Udine, 26th EURO INFORMS Workshop, Rome, 2 July 2013, and during seminars at the University of Bologna (Department of Management), University of Bari (Department of Economics), Max Planck Institute of Economics (Jena), Politecnico di Milano (DIG, Department of Management Engineering), University of Bergamo (Department of Management Engineering), university of Pisa and Lund university. It relies on some recent works of Daraio (2017a,b, 2018, 2019). This chapter is dedicated to Claudio Leporelli.

References

Anand P. (2003). Does economic theory need more evidence? A balancing of arguments. *Journal of Economic Methodology, 10*(4), 441–463.

Barber, D. (2012). *Bayesian reasoning and machine learning*. Cambridge: Cambridge University Press.

Barney, J. (1991). Firm resources and sustained competitive advantage. *Journal of Management, 17*(1), 99–120.

Barney, J. B., & Arikan, A. M. (2001). The resource-based view: Origins and implications. In *Handbook of strategic management* (pp. 124–188).

Barney, J. B., & Mackey, T. B. (2005). Testing resource-based theory. In *Research methodology in strategy and management* (pp. 1–13). Bingley: Emerald Group Publishing.

Bartelsman, E. J., & Beaulieu, J. J. (2007). A consistent accounting of US productivity growth. In *Hard-to-measure goods and services: Essays in Honor of Zvi Griliches* (pp. 449–482). Chicago, IL: University of Chicago Press.

Bartelsman E., Haltiwanger J., & Scarpetta S. (2005). *Measuring and analyzing cross-country differences in firm dynamics*. Paper prepared for NBER Conference on Research in Income and Wealth Producer Dynamics: New Evidence from Micro Data, April 8 and 9, 2005.

Bartelsman, E., & Doms, M. (2000). Understanding productivity: Lessons from longitudinal data. *Journal of Economic Literature, 38*, 569–594.

Bartelsman, E., Haltiwanger, J., Scarpetta, S. (2004). *Microeconomic evidence of creative destruction in industrial and developing countries*. Discussion Paper 2004-114/3, Tinbergen Institute, Amsterdam.

Bartelsman, E., Scarpetta, S., & Schivardi, F. (2005). Comparative analysis of firm demographics and survival: Evidence from micro-level sources in OECD countries. *Industrial and Corporate Change, 14*, 365–391.

Boland, L. A. (1994). Stylized facts. In *The new Palgrave a dictionary of economics* (pp. 535–536). New York, NY: Palgrave Publishers.

Borgman, C. L. (2015). *Big data, little data, no data: Scholarship in the networked world.* Cambridge, MA: MIT Press.

Box, G. E. (1976). Science and statistics. *Journal of the American Statistical Association, 71*(356), 791–799.

Buenstorf, G. (2005). Sequential production, modularity and technological change. *Structural Change and Economic Dynamics, 16*(2), 221–241.

Capano, G., Howlett, M., & Ramesh, M. (Eds.). (2015). *Varieties of governance*. Hampshire: Palgrave Macmillan.

Capano, G., Rayner, J., & Zito, A. R. (2012). Governance from the bottom up: Complexity and divergence in comparative perspective. *Public Administration, 90*(1), 56–73.

Chandler, A. D., Hagström, P., & Sölvell, Ö. (Eds.). (1999). *The dynamic firm: The role of technology, strategy, organization and regions*. Oxford: Oxford University Press.

Chenery, H. B. (1949). Engineering production functions. *The Quarterly Journal of Economics, 63*(4), 507–531.
Cimoli, M., Dosi, G. (1996). Technological paradigms, patterns of learning and development: An introductory roadmap. In Dopfer, K.(Ed.), *The global dimension of economic evolution. Knowledge variety and diffusion in economic growth and development* (pp. 63–88).
Coriat, B., & Dosi, G. (2000). *The Institutional Embeddedness of Economic Change. An Appraisal of the 'Evolutionary' and 'Regulationist' Research Programmes* (pp. 347–376). Cheltenham: Edward Elgar Publishing.
Daraio C. (2003). *Comparative efficiency and productivity analysis based on nonparametric and robust nonparametric methods. Methodology and Applications*. Ph.D. Dissertation, Sant'Anna School of Advanced Studies, Pisa.
Daraio C. (2017a). A framework for the assessment of research and its impacts. *Journal of Data and Information Science, 2*(4), 7–42.
Daraio C. (2017b). Assessing research and its impacts: The generalized implementation problem and a doubly-conditional performance evaluation model. In *Proceedings of the 16th International Conference on Scientometrics and Informetrics, ISSI 2017* (pp. 1546–1557).
Daraio C. (2018). The democratization of evaluation and altmetrics, Technical Report DIAG, 01/2018.
Daraio, C., et al. (2017). Inference for nonparametric productivity networks: A pseudo-likelihood approach. In *Proceedings of the 10th International Conference of the ERCIM WG on Computational and Methodological Statistics (CMStatistics 2017)*.
Daraio C. (2019). Econometric approaches to the measurement of research productivity. In W. Glänzel, H. F. Moed, H. Schmoch, & M. Thelwall (Eds.), *Springer handbook of science and technology indicators* (pp. 633–666).
Daraio, C., Kerstens, K., Nepomuceno, T., & Sickles, R. C. (2020). Empirical surveys of Frontier applications: A meta-review. *International Transactions in Operational Research*. https://doi.org/10.1111/itor.12649
Daraio, C., Kerstens, K., Nepomuceno, T., & Sickles, R. C. (2019). Productivity and efficiency analysis software: An exploratory bibliographical survey of the options. *Journal of Economic Surveys, 33*(1), 85–100.
Daraio, C., & Simar, L. (2007). *Advanced robust and nonparametric methods in efficiency analysis. Methodology and applications*. New York, NY: Springer.
Davis, J. P., Eisenhardt, K. M., & Bingham C. B. (2007). Developing theory through simulation methods *Academy of Management Review, 32*(2), 480–499.
Dierickx, I., & Cool, K. (1989). Asset stock accumulation and sustainability of competitive advantage. *Management Science, 35*(12), 1504–1511.
Doornik, J. A., Hendry, D. F. (2015). Statistical model selection with Big Data. *Cogent Economics & Finance, 3*(1), 1045216.
Dosi, G. (1982). Technological paradigms and technological trajectories: A suggested interpretation of the determinants and directions of technical change. *Research Policy, 11*(3), 147–162.
Dosi, G. (1988). Sources, procedures, and microeconomic effects of innovation. *Journal of Economic Literature, 26*(3), 1120–1171.
Dosi, G. (2004). A very reasonable objective still beyond our reach: Economics as an empirically disciplined social science. In *Models of a man: Essays in memory of Herbert A. Simon* (pp. 211–226).
Dosi, G., & Grazzi, M. (2006). Technologies as problem-solving procedures and technologies as input-output relations: Some perspectives on the theory of production. *Industrial and Corporate Change, 15*(1), 173–202.
Dosi, G., & Malerba, F. (1996). Organizational learning and institutional embeddedness. In *Organization and strategy in the evolution of the enterprise* (pp. 1–24). London: Palgrave Macmillan.
Ewell, P. (2009). *Assessment, accountability and improvement: Revisiting the tension*. National Institute for Learning Outcomes Assessment. http://www.learningoutcomesassessment.org/. Retrieved September 28, 2016.

Fagiolo, G., Moneta, A., & Windrum, P. (2006). Confronting agent-based models with data: Methodological issues and open problems. In *Advances in Artificial Economics* (pp. 255–267). Berlin: Springer.

Färe, R., Grosskopf, S., & Lovell, C.A.K. (1994). *Production Frontiers*. Cambridge: Cambridge University Press.

Fioretti, G. (2007). The production function. *Physica A: Statistical Mechanics and its Applications, 374*(2), 707–714.

Floridi, L. (2008). The method of levels of abstraction. *Minds and Machines, 18*(3), 303–329.

Foss, N. J. (2007). The emerging knowledge governance approach: Challenges and characteristics. *Organization, 14*(1), 29–52.

Geffner, H. (2018). Model-free, model-based, and general intelligence. arXiv:1806.02308.

Georgescu-Roegen, N. (1971), *Entropy law and the economic process*. Cambridge, MA: Harvard University Press.

Gibbard, A., & Varian, H. (1978). Economic models. *Journal of Philosophy, 75*, 664–677.

Griliches Z. (1994). Productivity, R&D, and the data constraint. *American Economic Review, 84*(1), 1–23.

Griliches Z. (2003). Zvi Griliches contributions to economic measurement. In CRIW Conference in Memory of Zvi Griliches, Bethesda, Maryland.

Griliches, Z., & Mairesse, J. (1983). Comparing productivity growth: An exploration of French and US industrial and firm data. *European Economic Review, 21*(1–2), 89–119.

Griliches, Z. (1986). Economic data issues. *Handbook of econometrics, 3*, 1465–1514.

Gujarati, D. N. (1978). *Basic econometrics*. New York, NY: McGraw-Hill.

Heckman, J. J. (2001). Econometrics and empirical economics. *Journal of Econometrics, 100*(1), 3–5.

Hendry, D. F. (1980). Econometrics-alchemy or science? *Economica, 47*(188), 387–406.

Hendry, D. F. (2001). Achievements and challenges in econometric methodology. *Journal of Econometrics, 100*(1), 7–10.

Hendry, D., & Mizon, G. (2000). Reformulation empirical macroeconomic modelling. *Oxford Review of Economic Policy, 16*(4), 138–159.

Hildenbrand, W. (1981). Short-run production functions based on microdata. *Econometrica, 49*, 1095–1125.

Hollingsworth, J. R. (2000). Doing institutional analysis: Implications for the study of innovations. *Review of International Political Economy, 7*(4), 595–644.

Hoopes, D. G., Madsen, T. L., & Walker, G. (2003). Why is there a resource-based view? Toward a theory of competitive heterogeneity. *Strategic Management Journal, 24*, 889–902.

Hoover K. D. (2005). The methodology of econometrics. In *Handbook of econometrics* (Vol. 1). Theoretical econometrics. London: Palgrave.

Hoover, K. D., & Perez, S. J. (1999). Data mining reconsidered: Encompassing and the general-to-specific approach to specification search. *The Econometrics Journal, 2*(2), 167–191.

Hunter, D. E., & Nielsen, S. B. (2013). Performance management and evaluation: Exploring complementarities. *New Directions for Evaluation, 2013*(137), 7–17.

Jordan, M. I., & Mitchell, T. M. (2015). Machine learning: Trends, perspectives, and prospects. *Science, 349*(6245), 255–260.

Jorgenson, D. W., & Fraumeni, B. M. (1992). The output of the education sector. In Output measurement in the service sectors (pp. 303–341). University of Chicago Press.

Juselius, K. (1999). Models and relations in economics and econometrics. *Journal of Economic Methodology, 6*(2), 259–290.

Juselius, K. (2006). *The cointegrated VAR model: Methodology and applications*. Oxford: Oxford University Press.

Kaldor, N. (1963). Capital accumulation and economic growth. In F. Lutz (Ed.), *The theory of capital* (pp. 177–222). London: Macmillan.

Kaldor, N. (1985). *Economics without equilibrium* (pp. 8–9). Armonk, NY: M. E. Sharpe.

Kahneman, D. (2011). *Thinking, fast and slow.* New York, NY: Farrar, Straus and Giroux.

Kao, C. (2017). *Network data envelopment analysis; Foundations and extensions*. Berlin: Springer.

Latour, B. (2005). *Reassembling the social: An introduction to actor-network-theory*. Oxford: Oxford University Press.

Lawson, T. (1989). Abstraction, tendencies and stylised facts: A realist approach to economic analysis. *Cambridge Journal of Economics, 13*(1), 59–78.

Leibenstein, H. (1966). Allocative efficiency vs. X-efficiency. *American Economic Review, 56*, 392–415.

Leibenstein, H. (1979). A branch of economics is missing: Micro-micro theory. *Journal of Economic Literature, 17*(2), 477–502.

Leibenstein, H., & Maital, S. (1992). Empirical estimation and partitioning of X-inefficiency: A data-envelopment approach. *The American Economic Review, 82*(2), 428–433.

Lieberman, M. B., & Dhawan, R. (2005). Assessing the resource base of Japanese and US auto producers: A stochastic frontier production function approach. *Management Science, 51*(7), 1060–1075.

Lindbeck, A., & Snower, D. J. (2003). The firm as a pool of factor complementarities. IUI, The Research Institute of Industrial Economics (No. 598). Working Paper.

Lütkepohl, H. (2001). Comment on essays on current state and future challenges of econometrics. *Journal of Econometrics, 100*(1), 81–82.

Maanen, J. V., Sorensen J. B., & Mitchell T. R. (2007). The interplay between theory and method, introduction to special topic forum. *Academy of Management Review, 32*(4), 1145–1154.

Makadok, R. (2001). Toward a synthesis of the resource-based and dynamic-capability views of rent creation. *Strategic Management Journal, 22*, 387–401.

Metcalfe, S. (Ed.). (2018). *Evolutionary theories of economic and technological change: Present status and future prospects* (Vol. 44). Abingdon: Routledge.

Mezard, M., & Montanari, A. (2009). *Information, physics, and computation*. Oxford: Oxford University Press.

Milgrom, P., & Roberts, J. (1990). The economics and modern manufacturing: Technology strategy, and organization. *American Economic Review, 80*, 511–528.

Milgrom, P., & Roberts, J. (1995). Complementarity and fit: Strategy, structure and organizational change in manufacturing. *Journal of Accounting and Economics, 19*, 178–208.

Mingers, J. (2006). *Realising systems thinking: Knowledge and action in management science*. Berlin: Springer.

Morroni, M. (1992). *Production process and technical change*. Cambridge: Cambridge University Press, repr. 2009.

Morroni, M. (2006). *Knowledge, scale and transactions in the theory of the firm*. Cambridge: Cambridge University Press, repr. 2009.

Morroni, M. (2014). Production of commodities by means of processes. The flow-fund model, input-output relations and the cognitive aspects of production. *Structural Change and Economic Dynamics, 29*, 5–18.

Mowery, D. C., & Nelson, R. R. (Eds.). (1999). *Sources of industrial leadership: Studies of seven industries*. Cambridge: Cambridge University Press.

Nelson, R. R. (1994). The co-evolution of technology, industrial structure, and supporting institutions. *Industrial and Corporate Change, 3*(1), 47–63.

Nelson, R. R. (1995). Recent evolutionary theorizing about economic change. *Journal of Economic Literature, 33*(1), 48–90

Nelson, R. R., & Winter, S. G. (1982). *An evolutionary theory of economic change*. Cambridge, MA: Harvard University Press.

Nelson, R. R., & Winter, S. G. (2002). Evolutionary theorizing in economics. *Journal of Economic Perspectives, 16*(2), 23–46.

Ouchi, W. G. (1979). A conceptual framework for the design of organizational control mechanisms. *Management Science, 25*(9), 833–848.

Pagan, A. (1987). Three econometric methodologies: A critical appraisal 1. *Journal of Economic Surveys, 1*(1–2), 3–23.

Parmeter, C. F., & Kumbhakar, S. C. (2014). Efficiency analysis: A primer on recent advances. *Foundations and Trends in Econometrics, 7*(3–4), 191–385.

Parmeter, C. F., & Zelenyuk, V. (2019). Combining the virtues of stochastic Frontier and data envelopment analysis. *Operations Research, 67*(6), 1503–1782.
Pearl, J. (2010). An introduction to causal inference. *The international journal of biostatistics, 6*(2), 51.
Pearl, J. (2000). *Causality: Models, reasoning and inference*. Cambridge, MA: MIT Press.
Peteraf, M. A. (1993). The cornerstones of competitive advantage: A resource-based view. *Strategic Management Journal, 14*(3), 179–191.
Peters, B. G., Capano, G., Howlett, M., Mukherjee, I., Chou, M. H., & Ravinet, P. (2018). Designing for policy effectiveness: Defining and understanding a concept. In *Elements in Public Policy*. Cambridge: Cambridge University Press
Roberts, J. (2007). *The modern firm: Organizational design for performance and growth*. Oxford: Oxford University Press.
Rumelt, R. P. (1987). Theory, strategy, and entrepreneurship. *The Competitive Challenge, 137*, 158.
Sickles, R. C., & Zelenyuk, V. (2019). *Measurement of productivity and efficiency: Theory and practice*. Cambridge: Cambridge University Press.
Simar, L., & Wilson, P. W. (2013). Estimation and inference in nonparametric frontier models: Recent developments and perspectives. *Foundations and Trends in Econometrics, 5*(3-4), 183–337.
Simar, L., & Wilson, P. W. (2015). Statistical approaches for non-parametric Frontier models: A guided tour. *International Statistical Review, 83*(1), 77–110.
Simon, H. A. (1969). *The sciences of the artificial*. Cambridge, MA: MIT Press.
Simon, H. A. (1982). *Models of bounded rationality: Empirically grounded economic reason* (Vol. 3). Cambridge, MA: MIT Press.
Simon, H. A. (2000). Bounded rationality in social science: Today and tomorrow. *Mind & Society, 1*(1), 25–39.
Spanos, A. (1999). *Probability theory and statistical inference: Econometric modeling with observational data*. Cambridge: Cambridge University Press.
Spanos, A. (2000). Revisiting data mining: 'Hunting' with or without a license. *Journal of Economic Methodology, 7*(2), 231–264.
Stock, J. H. (2010). The other transformation in econometric practice: Robust tools for inference. *The Journal of Economic Perspectives, 24*(2), 83–94.
Sugden, R. (2000), Credible worlds: The status of theoretical models in economics. *Journal of Economic Methodology, 7*(1), 1–31.
Tal, E. (2015). Measurement in science. In *Stanford encyclopedia of philosophy*.
Thaler, R. H. (2016). Behavioral economics: Past, present, and future. *American Economic Review, 106*(7), 1577–1600.
Tomer, J. F. (2007). What is behavioral economics? *The Journal of Socio-Economics, 36*(3), 463–479.
Triplett, J. E. (1991). Measuring the output of banks: what do banks do?. In Western Economic Association meetings in Seattle, Washington, June (Vol. 29).
Tushman, M. L., & Murmann, J. P. (1998). Dominant designs, technology cycles, and organization outcomes. In *Academy of Management Proceedings* (Vol. 1998, No. 1, pp. A1–A33). Briarcliff Manor, NY: Academy of Management.
Tversky, A., & Kahneman, D. (1974). Judgment under uncertainty: Heuristics and biases. *Science (New York, NY), 185*(4157), 1124–1131.
Varian, H. R. (1992). *Microeconomic analysis*. Norton
Viskovatoff A. (2003). Rationalism and mainstream economics. *Journal of Economic Methodology, 10*(3), 397–415.
Weber, M. (1947). *The theory of economic and social organization*. Trans. AM Henderson and Talcott Parsons. New York, NY: Oxford University Press.
Weber, M. (2009). *The theory of social and economic organization*. New York, NY: Simon and Schuster.
Weick, K. E. (1976). Educational organizations as loosely coupled systems. *Administrative Science Quarterly, 21*(1) (Mar., 1976), 1–19.

Winter, S. G. (2005), Toward an evolutionary theory of production. In Dopfer (Ed.), *The evolutionary foundations of economics* (pp. 223–254).

Winter, S. G. (2006). Toward a neo-Schumpeterian theory of the firm. *Industrial and Corporate Change, 15*(1), 125–141.

Winter, S. G. (2017). Pursuing the evolutionary agenda in economics and management research. *Cambridge Journal of Economics, 41*(3), 721–747.

Water's Contribution to Agricultural Productivity over Space

Maria Vrachioli and Spiro E. Stefanou

Abstract After recent projections for food and agricultural production for the next three decades, water is at the centre of the discussion. Given the increase in population growth, food demand will increase and the agricultural sector will likely have to expand the use of irrigation water to meet this rising demand. However, water scarcity leads to significant water management issues in the agricultural sector. With agriculture playing an important role in the water crisis as it is by far the largest user of water, the emphasis is finding ways to allocate this scarce resource more efficiently and to produce increasing quantities of food with decreasing quantities of water. The improved effectiveness of water conveyance, the efficiency in its use, and the associated impact on non-water input and output choices have the potential to impact the economic well-being of the farming community and promote the sustainability of agricultural production. The objective of this paper is to contribute toward productivity-enhancing policies by estimating the magnitude of gains from the more effective use of water in agriculture. The effectiveness of these policies depends on the proper measurement of water's contribution to agricultural efficiency and productivity. This paper develops a measure of water's contribution to total factor productivity (TFP) change that accounts for spatial water quantity and quality adjustments. This spatial model is a first attempt to estimate the contribution of water use to agricultural productivity and to capture differences in farm-level productivity due to head versus tail disparities in water allocation and water quality. Water policy strategies should aim toward internalizing the spatial externalities and encouraging productivity-enhancing techniques allowing the farmers to produce more output with the same or even less water and to improve the quality of water

M. Vrachioli (✉)
Production and Resource Economics, Technical University of Munich, Munich, Germany
e-mail: maria.vrachioli@tum.de

S. E. Stefanou
Food and Resource Economics Department, University of Florida, Gainesville, FL, USA

Business Economics Group, Wageningen University, Wageningen, Netherlands

C. F. Parmeter, R. C. Sickles (eds.), *Advances in Efficiency and Productivity Analysis*, Springer Proceedings in Business and Economics,
https://doi.org/10.1007/978-3-030-47106-4_5

used in the agricultural sector by deploying sustainable management practice and promoting community engagement.

Keywords Agricultural water use · Total factor productivity · Spatial optimization · Quantity and quality of agricultural water

1 Introduction to the Theoretical Framework

Sustainable and efficient water management constitutes one of the greatest twenty-first century challenges that the world faces to ensure prosperity for all, address poverty, and build resilient communities. With the world population projected to reach 8.6 billion by 2030 (United Nations 2017), the demand for fresh water is expected to increase exponentially. At the same time, the supply of water is becoming less predictable due to climate change, and competition among different users is rising. Energy and sanitization needs in expanding cities and rising food demand in the agricultural sector will exacerbate global water stress, which can hinder economic growth and shared prosperity.

Water touches practically every aspect of development, but puts particular pressure on agriculture. Population growth, in combination with increasing incomes, is leading to an increasing food demand with a higher nutritional quality that has driven the agricultural sector to expand the use of water for irrigation, bringing the water crisis to the center of the global debate (United Nations 2015). Water shortages and fresh water competition from other sectors are two serious risks for the sustainable development of agriculture. Thus, the next years are crucial for the immediate implementation of policy scenarios that can establish not only food and nutrition security but also promote water security and conserve water resources.

The current direction of projects related to sustainable agricultural water management practices suggests that shifting to more productive, water-saving technologies is the cornerstone to achieving effective use of agricultural water (IFPRI 2017; World Bank 2017; United Nations 2015; FAO 2012). The improved effectiveness of water conveyance, the efficiency in its use, and the associated impact on non-water input and output choices have the potential to impact the economic well-being of the farming community and promote the sustainability of agricultural production.

At a global level, 70–90% of fresh water withdrawals are used for agricultural irrigation (Molden and Oweis 2007). In addition, irrigated land accounts for 20% of the total cultivated land and for 40% of the total agricultural production (Rosegrant et al. 2009). Thus, even small improvements in water productivity can have a significant effect on the local and global water supply. In 2000, the UN Secretary General in his Report to the Millennium Conference mentioned "*We need a Blue Revolution in agriculture that focuses on increasing productivity per unit of water—more crop per drop*" (Kofie A. Annan 2000). Also, FAO (2012) considers "*an increase in agricultural water productivity as the single most important avenue for managing water demand in agriculture.*"

This paper uses a spatial model to examine water's contribution to agricultural productivity by assuming that water follows a gravity system where individual farms draw this resource along a path (i.e. irrigation canal) extending from the water source and ending at the last farm. The quantity of water in the canal decreases with distance from the water source, with farmers at the tail end of the canal facing potential water scarcity. Farmers near the water source are said to consume a disproportionate share of irrigation water, while tail farmers are left with limited and unreliable residual supplies (Wade 1982). Except for the water scarcity, farmers at the tail end can face potential water quality degradation (Sigman 2002).

The model used in this paper follows the approach proposed by Chakravorty and Roumasset (1991) and Chakravorty et al. (1995) augmented with irrigation return flows as modelled by Huffaker and Whittlesey (2000). Based on Isard and Liossatos (1979) and Knapp and Schwabe (2008), we address the spatial water allocation model and we derive the rules for the economic optimization of water supplied to the farmers at various distances from the water source. We next use the solutions of the spatial optimal water allocation model to decompose total factor productivity change over space at the farm level, and analyse water's contribution and its shadow value impact on agricultural productivity while we are accounting for spatial water quantity and quality adjustments.

In the literature, the majority of the studies that use a spatial model of a water project focus mainly on the efficient allocation of water (or allocative inefficiencies) among farmers along an irrigation shared canal based on different investment scenarios in on-farm irrigation efficiency as a mechanism to control water use in agriculture. Our model differs from past spatial models of water conveyance along a unidirectional irrigation canal with a fixed supply of water resources by examining how agricultural water productivity changes over space including irrigation return flows. In this paper, we investigate how changes in farm-level productivity over space can reflect the economic performance of a water public infrastructure project. The spatial optimal water allocation model provides us with the conditions needed to explain how water quantity, water quality, and shadow value of water affect the economic performance of the farmers (measured by productivity), while we are moving away from the water source. This information can be used by policymakers or social planners who are interested in maximizing the economic benefit of water allocation across farmers along an irrigation infrastructure project, where farmers make decisions on irrigation water use in sequence. This policy intervention can be achieved, for example, by adjusting the water quantity received by the farmer at each location and by charging farmers water permit prices according to the spatial shadow values of water, when a water market exists. These shadow values of water can also be adjusted to capture changes in the quality of water over space.

Agricultural water productivity ("*crop per drop*") is a partial measure of economic performance that focuses on a single input, water, and it is defined as the ratio of total output produced to the water used. However, when the partial factor productivity is estimated for variable inputs like water, misleading and biased performance indicators may be produced. For example, a gain in agricultural water productivity can come at the expense of agricultural labour productivity. In Fig. 1,

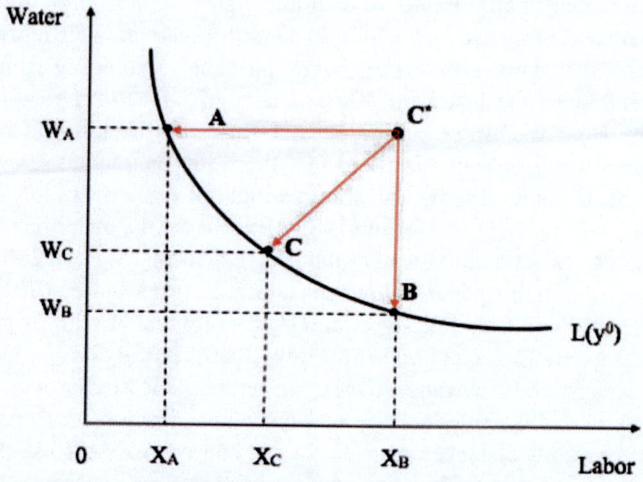

Fig. 1 Agricultural water and labour productivity

moving from point A to point B decreases the amount of water used, which increases the agricultural water productivity, but this also leads to a decrease in the partial measure of agricultural labour productivity. To overcome the issue of biased estimators, total factor productivity (TFP) measures that account for all the inputs should be considered. This paper contributes to the existing literature of total factor productivity assessment in the agricultural sector by isolating and studying the effect of water use. While most of the studies attribute TFP growth to land productivity, there is little or no evidence on how water affects agricultural productivity despite its importance in the agricultural production process.

The remainder of this paper is organized as follows. The second Section presents the optimization framework of the spatial model, and the derivation and decomposition of agricultural productivity change over space into various components, emphasizing on the contribution of water. We next solve the optimal water allocation model by accounting for water quality changes over space, and then decompose the quality adjusted productivity index. The fourth Section provides some concluding remarks, policy recommendations, and suggestions for further research.

2 Model Specification

2.1 Spatial Optimization Problem

Following Chakravorty et al. (1995), we consider a single cropping season model of a water distribution system conveying water from a source (e.g. a dam or an aquifer) into an irrigation canal.[1] Farms are located on either side of this canal and draw water from it for agricultural purposes. Also, farmers are assumed to be identical in all aspects except for their distance from the head of the canal and that no investment is made from the water distributor for improving the canal quality (e.g. earthen canal). Departing from Chakravorty et al. (1995) and using Huffaker and Whittlesey (2000), we assume that there is a portion (β) of the delivered water that has not been consumed by the crops on the farm and re-enters the irrigation system. If $\beta = 1$, all the unconsumed water is available as irrigation return flow; while when $\beta = 0$, all the water that has not been used by the crops cannot be reused and it is lost in the system. However, these are two extreme cases and in reality β takes values between 0 and 1, where part of the unconsumed water returns to the system and can be reused, while the other part cannot be retrieved and it is lost.

With $w(r)$ being the quantity of water delivered to a farm at location r and $\Omega(r)$ being the volume of instream flow at the same location, then the relationship between instream flow and diverted water in a two-farm case framework (farms A and B, with farm A located upstream) is given by

$$\Omega_B\ (r) = \Omega_A\ (r) - w_A(r) + \beta w_A(r) \tag{1}$$

Changes in water diversion (w) upstream can lead to changes in the reliability of water supplies downstream. The presence of return flows in Eq. (1) highlights the linkage between upstream and downstream water use capturing potential water quantity and quality externalities along an irrigation canal. These spatial trade-off externalities can likely affect other water users further downstream at the end of the irrigation canal, including other water utilities or environmental uses.

All farms produce the same output (y) using two inputs, the quantity of water delivered to the farm (w) and an aggregate index of all the other inputs used by the farmer in the production process (x). Let p denote the output price of the crop, z the aggregate input price, and τ the price of water. Let r represent the distance of each farm from the source, with $r = 0$ denoting the first farm. There is no loss of water from the source to the first farm of the system, and r increases while we are moving away from the source. The variable r can take values from the interval $[0, R]$, where R denotes the fixed length of the system. Also, the amount of water available at the source, $\Omega(0)$, is exogenously determined and is equal to w_0. The production function, $f(x, w, \Omega, r)$, has the usual properties that apply to stage II of the neoclassical production function:

$$f(x, w, \Omega, r) > 0\ ;\ \ f'\ (x, w, \Omega, r) > 0\ ;\ \ f''\ (x, w, \Omega, r) < 0 \tag{2}$$

[1]To assess agricultural water productivity change over space, we assume that water resource availability follows a unidirectional flow with an exogenously determined and fixed initial supply, and the source of water is external to the spatial model framework.

where $f(x, w, \Omega, r)$ is a twice continuous differentiable, strictly increasing and concave function in inputs and represents the maximum amount of output than can be produced using aggregate input, x, and water, w, given the distance from the water source, r. Also, the production function will be strictly increasing in the instream flow, Ω.

The spatially optimal maximization problem of an irrigation water shared infrastructure represents the value generating from the irrigation canal by aggregating the individual maximum profits of farmers, considering the impact that distance has on the availability of water along the canal, and is given by

$$\max_{(x,w)} \pi = \int_0^R [pf(x(r), w(r), \Omega(r), r) - zx(r) - \tau w(r)]\,\mathrm{d}r \tag{3}$$

$$s.t.\ \dot{\Omega}(r) = -w(r) + \beta w(r) \tag{4}$$

$$\Omega(0) = w_0 \tag{5}$$

$$x(r), w(r) \geq 0 \tag{6}$$

where $\dot{\Omega}$ is the spatial rate of change of instream flow at point r.

The objective of the above maximization problem (Eqs. (3)–(6)) is to define the amount of delivered water, $w(r)$, and the level of input use, $x(r)$, to maximize farmers' profits, π, along an irrigation canal in a single cropping period, subject to the equation of motion (Eq. (4)). The profit function, $\pi(p, z, \tau, \Omega, r)$, is non-decreasing in output prices, p, and non-increasing in aggregate input price, z, and the price of water, τ. It is also convex in p, z, τ (Chambers 1988). Based on the equation of motion, the instream flow adjusts to each location r according to the volume of water diverted to the farm, $w(r)$, and the portion of unconsumed water that re-enters the system as irrigation return flow, $\beta w(r)$. Finally, we assume that the canal inflow at $r = 0$ is fixed at an exogenously determined level w_0 (Eq. (5)). For the profit maximization problem, the first order conditions are given as follows:

$$pf_x - z = 0 \tag{7}$$

$$pf_w - \tau - (1 - \beta)\pi_\Omega = 0 \tag{8}$$

The marginal value product of input use is equal to the input price (Eq. (7)), while Eq. (8) shows that the marginal value product of water use is equal to the water price plus the shadow value of instream flow (π_Ω) weighted by the term $(1-\beta)$ accounting for the extent to which unconsumed water at the farm level re-enters the system as irrigation return flow. In the case that the system is characterized by irrigation return flows ($\beta = 1$), the marginal value product of water use will be equally to the externally determined price of water, τ (Eq. (9)). On the other hand, with no irrigation return flows ($\beta = 0$), the marginal value product of water use will be equal to the externally determined water price, τ, plus the internally defined water price, which is the shadow value of instream flow, π_Ω (Eq. (10)). From Eqs. (9) and (10), we can conclude that the marginal value product of water use in the absence of irrigation return flows will be associated with a higher marginal cost of water use.

$$pf_w = \tau \qquad , \text{if} \beta = 1 \tag{9}$$

$$pf_w = \tau + \pi_\Omega \text{ , if} \beta = 0 \tag{10}$$

An approach to spatial optimization problem is the Bellman's dynamic programming equation (Kamien and Schwartz 1991). With sufficient differentiability, the dynamic programming approach presented by Kamien and Schwartz (1991) can be applied to a spatial framework and used to develop the necessary conditions of optimal control. For the case of spatial adjustment:

$$0 = \max_{x,w}(pf(x, w, \Omega, r) - zx - \tau w - \pi_\Omega w + \beta \pi_\Omega w + \pi_r) \tag{11}$$

where the optimal choices are expressed as $x^* = x(p, z, \tau, \Omega, r)$ and $w^* = w(p, z, \tau, \Omega, r)$. The optimized programming equation is given by

$$0 = (pf(x^*, w^*, \Omega, r) - zx^* - \tau w^* - \pi_\Omega w^* + \beta \pi_\Omega w^* + \pi_r) \tag{12}$$

where $\pi_\Omega = \pi_\Omega(p, z, \tau, \Omega, r)$ and $\pi_r = \pi_r(p, z, \tau, \Omega, r)$. While π_Ω captures changes in profit given a change in instream flow level (Ω); π_r captures changes in farmer's profit given a change in location (r).

From Eq. (12) and the optimal solutions for x, w, π_Ω, π_r, we will obtain the fundamental partial differential equation of the value function $\pi(p, z, \tau, \Omega, r)$:

$$\begin{aligned} 0 = {} & pf(x(p, z, \tau, \Omega, r), w(p, z, \tau, \Omega, r), \Omega, r) - zx(p, z, \tau, \Omega, r) - \tau w(p, z, \tau, \Omega, r) \\ & - \pi_\Omega\ (p, z, \tau, \Omega, r) w(p, z, \tau, \Omega, r) + \beta\ \pi_\Omega(p, z, \tau, \Omega, r) w(p, z, \tau, \Omega, r) \\ & + \pi_r\ (p, z, \tau, \Omega, r) \end{aligned} \tag{13}$$

Differentiating the optimized partial differential Eq. (13) at the optimal point with respect to aggregate input price (z) yields

$$\begin{aligned} 0 = {} & pf_x \frac{\partial x^*}{\partial z} + pf_w \frac{\partial w^*}{\partial z} - x^* - z \frac{\partial x^*}{\partial z} - \tau \frac{\partial w^*}{\partial z} - \pi_\Omega \frac{\partial w^*}{\partial z} + \beta \pi_\Omega \frac{\partial w^*}{\partial z} - \pi_{\Omega z} w^* \\ & + \beta \pi_{\Omega z} w^* + \pi_{rz} \end{aligned} \tag{14}$$

Using Eqs. (14), (7), and (8), the optimal level of aggregate input use, x, can be expressed as follows:

$$x^* = -\pi_{\Omega z} w^* + \beta \pi_{\Omega z} w^* + \pi_{rz} \tag{15}$$

Differentiating the optimized partial differential Eq. (13) at the optimal point with respect to water price (τ) gives

$$0 = pf_x \frac{\partial x^*}{\partial \tau} + pf_w \frac{\partial w^*}{\partial \tau} - w^* - z\frac{\partial x^*}{\partial \tau} - \tau\frac{\partial w^*}{\partial \tau} - \pi_\Omega \frac{\partial w^*}{\partial \tau} + \beta\pi_\Omega \frac{\partial w^*}{\partial \tau} - \pi_{\Omega\tau} w^*$$
$$+ \beta\pi_{\Omega\tau} w^* + \pi_{r\tau} \quad (16)$$

From Eqs. (16), (7), and (8), the optimal level of water diverted to the farm is given by

$$w^* = -\pi_{\Omega\tau} w^* + \beta\pi_{\Omega\tau} w^* + \pi_{r\tau} \quad (17)$$

Rearranging Eq. (17) and substituting to Eq. (15), we have the following optimal solutions for x and w:

$$x^* = x(p, z, \tau, \Omega, r) = \frac{(\beta - 1)\pi_{\Omega z}}{1 + (1 - \beta)\pi_{\Omega\tau}} \pi_{r\tau} + \pi_{rz} \quad (18)$$

$$w^* = w(p, z, \tau, \Omega, r) = \frac{1}{1 + (1 - \beta)\pi_{\Omega\tau}} \pi_{r\tau} \quad (19)$$

These optimal solutions, (x^*, w^*), exploit the derivative property of the value function akin to a Hotelling's lemma in the presence of change over space. Epstein (1981) presents the duality properties for an optimization problem similar to this type presented in Eqs. (3)–(6), along with candidate functional forms amenable to econometric estimation.

Finally, differentiating the optimized partial differential Eq. (13) at the optimal point with respect to the instream flow (Ω) leads to:

$$0 = pf_x \frac{\partial x^*}{\partial \Omega} + pf_w \frac{\partial w^*}{\partial \Omega} + pf_\Omega - z\frac{\partial x^*}{\partial \Omega} - \tau\frac{\partial w^*}{\partial \Omega} - \pi_\Omega \frac{\partial w^*}{\partial \Omega} + \beta\pi_\Omega \frac{\partial w^*}{\partial \Omega} - \pi_{\Omega\Omega} w^*$$
$$+ \beta\pi_{\Omega\Omega} w^* + \pi_{r\Omega} \quad (20)$$

Applying the first order conditions Eqs. (7) and (8) in Eq. (20) lead to

$$pf_\Omega = -[(1 - \beta)w^* \pi_{\Omega\Omega} + \pi_{r\Omega}] \quad (21)$$

and using Eq. (4)

$$pf_\Omega = -\left(\pi_{\Omega\Omega} \frac{d\Omega}{dr} + \pi_{r\Omega}\right) \quad (22)$$

To facilitate interpretation of Eq. (22), we can differentiate the shadow value of water, π_Ω, with respect to the change over space, r, to yield:

$$\frac{d\pi_\Omega}{dr} = \pi_{\Omega\Omega} \frac{d\Omega}{dr} + \pi_{\Omega r} \quad (23)$$

Using Eq. (23), this leads to Eq. (22) being expressed as

$$pf_{\Omega} = -\frac{d\pi_{\Omega}}{dr} \tag{24}$$

which implies that the marginal value product of an additional unit of water at the source equals the change in the shadow value of water available at the source over space along the irrigation canal. As we are moving away from the source, the water available to the farmers for irrigation purposes decreases and fewer farmers are able to access it and gain value from it. Despite there is change in the shadow value of instream flow while we are moving along the canal, this change is getting smaller and smaller as we are getting away from the source.

2.2 *Contribution of Agricultural Water to Total Factor Productivity*

The measure of the partial agricultural water productivity is defined as output per unit of water used (y_i/w_i), where $i = 1, 2, \ldots, N$. In Fig. 2, consider a starting point A (w_A, y_A) that corresponds to a hypothetical farm. We can define two different possible scenarios that lead to an increase in the agricultural productivity. Under the first scenario, the farmer is moving from point A(w_A, y_A) to point B(w_A, y_B), which

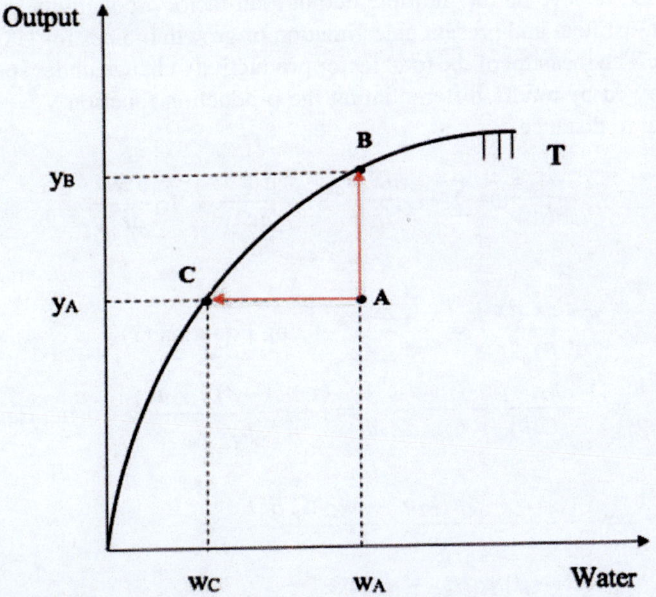

Fig. 2 Agricultural water productivity

in economic terms means higher output production with the same amount of water. In this case, agricultural water productivity is defined as y_B/w_A, with $y_B > y_A$. Then, based on the second scenario, the farmer instead of producing in point A, she is now producing in point C(w_C, y_A), which implies same output production with less amount of water and now agricultural water productivity is defined as y_A/w_C, with $w_A > w_C$. Consequently, an improvement in agricultural water productivity can be occurred either by increasing output holding water usage constant, or by decreasing water usage while the output level remains the same.

Total factor productivity change over space, $T\hat{F}P$, is the change in outputs explained by the change in water use over space ($T\hat{F}P_w$), or by the change in both aggregate input index and water use over space ($T\hat{F}P$). Under the framework of spatial adjustment, the formulas of total factor agricultural productivity change over space with an emphasis in water use and with respect to all the inputs are given by Eqs. (25) and (26), respectively:

$$T\hat{F}P_w = \frac{dy}{dr}\frac{1}{y} - \frac{dw}{dr}\frac{1}{w} \tag{25}$$

$$T\hat{F}P = \frac{dy}{dr}\frac{1}{y} - \left(\sum \frac{dx}{dr}\frac{1}{x} + \frac{dw}{dr}\frac{1}{w}\right) \tag{26}$$

where $y = f(x, w, \Omega, r)$ represents the production technology, which is the same for all the farms along the irrigation canal.

Solow (1957), Jorgenson and Griliches (1967) and Christensen and Jorgenson (1970) pioneered efforts in multiple factor definitions of productivity. Luh and Stefanou (1991) develop the multiple output total factor productivity growth under dynamic adjustment and present an estimation of growth indices for US production agriculture. The measure of the total factor productivity change under spatial adjustment is derived by totally differentiating the production function $y = f(x, w, \Omega)$ with respect to distance, r:

$$\frac{dy}{dr}\frac{1}{y} = \sum f_x \frac{dx}{dr}\frac{1}{y} + f_w \frac{dw}{dr}\frac{1}{y} + f_\Omega \frac{d\Omega}{dr}\frac{1}{y} \tag{27}$$

where

$$\sum f_x \frac{dx}{dr}\frac{1}{y} = \sum \frac{zx}{py}\frac{dx}{dr}\frac{1}{x} = \sum \frac{zx}{py}\hat{x}, \quad \text{using Equation (7)} \tag{28}$$

$$f_w \frac{dw}{dr}\frac{1}{y} = \frac{(\tau + \pi_\Omega - \beta\pi_\Omega)w}{py}\frac{dw}{dr}\frac{1}{w} = \frac{(\tau + (1-\beta)\pi_\Omega)w}{py}\hat{w}, \quad \text{using Equation (8)} \tag{29}$$

$$\begin{aligned} f_\Omega \frac{d\Omega}{dr}\frac{1}{y} &= \frac{(\pi_{\Omega\Omega}w - \beta\pi_{\Omega\Omega}w - \pi_{r\Omega})\Omega}{py}\frac{d\Omega}{dr}\frac{1}{\Omega} \\ &= \frac{((1-\beta)\pi_{\Omega\Omega}w - \pi_{r\Omega})\Omega}{py}\hat{\Omega}, \quad \text{using Equation (21)} \end{aligned} \tag{30}$$

where ˆ indicates the proportional rate of change over space.

From Eqs. (25) and (28) to (30), the total factor productivity change over space with an emphasis in water use, $T\hat{F}P_w$, can be decomposed as

$$T\hat{F}P_w = \sum \frac{zx}{py}\hat{x} + \frac{(\tau + \pi_\Omega - \beta)w}{py}\hat{w} + \frac{((1-\beta)\pi_{\Omega\Omega}w - \pi_{r\Omega})\Omega}{py}\hat{\Omega} - \hat{w} \tag{31}$$

$$T\hat{F}P_w = \sum \frac{zx}{py}\hat{x} + \frac{\tau w}{py}\hat{w} + \frac{\pi_\Omega(1-\beta)w}{py}\hat{w} + \frac{\pi_\Omega(w(1-\beta) - \dot{\Omega})}{py}\hat{\pi_\Omega} - \hat{w} \tag{32}$$

Defining total factor productivity spatial change as the difference between output change and input change over space (aggregate input use, $\hat{x}$, and water use, $\hat{w}$), we obtain from Eqs. (26) and (28)–(30):

$$T\hat{F}P = \sum \frac{zx}{py}\hat{x} + \frac{(\tau + \pi_\Omega - \beta\pi_\Omega)w}{py}\hat{w} + \frac{((1-\beta)\pi_{\Omega\Omega}w - \pi_{r\Omega})\Omega}{py}\hat{\Omega} - \hat{x} - \hat{w} \tag{33}$$

$$T\hat{F}P = \left(\sum \frac{zx}{py} - 1\right)\hat{x} + \left(\frac{\tau w}{py} - 1\right)\hat{w} + \frac{\pi_\Omega(1-\beta)w}{py}\hat{w} + \frac{\pi_\Omega(w(1-\beta) - \dot{\Omega})}{py}\hat{\pi_\Omega} \tag{34}$$

$$T\hat{F}P = \left(\frac{1}{\epsilon_c} - 1\right)\hat{F} + \frac{\pi_\Omega(1-\beta)w}{py}\hat{w} + \frac{\pi_\Omega(w(1-\beta) - \dot{\Omega})}{py}\hat{\pi_\Omega} \tag{35}$$

where $\hat{F}$ is the change in all the inputs used in the production process and is defined as the summation of input change, $\hat{x}$, and water change, $\hat{w}$, along the irrigation canal; and ϵ_c is the scale elasticity and is defined as the ratio of average cost (AC) to marginal cost (MC). When the scale elasticity is equal to one, the production technology is characterized by constant returns to scale and there is no scale effect. In the case that scale elasticity is greater than 1 (less than 1), the farm operates under increasing (decreasing) returns to scale.

Table 1 presents the interpretation of all the components of $T\hat{F}P_w$ and $T\hat{F}P$. The additional total factor productivity components that are associated with the change of water use along the irrigation canal, comparing to the traditional total factor productivity, are: (1) the change in the water use with internal values, $\frac{\pi_\Omega(1-\beta)w}{py}\hat{w}$, and (2) the change in the shadow value of water, $\frac{\pi_\Omega(w(1-\beta)-\dot{\Omega})}{py}\hat{\pi_\Omega}$. Both of these components are also weighted by the extent to which unconsumed water returns to the system and can be used by other farmers downstream, β.

The components of total factor productivity in Eqs. (32) and (35) can be estimated either computationally or involving restrictive production function specification for a closed form solution. For the latter case, farm-level data on the full range of farm inputs, including water conveyed, and output choices are needed in a spatial framework in which the exact position of each farm along the irrigation canal

Table 1 Definition of the components of spatial total factor productivity decomposition

Expression	Description	
$\sum \frac{zx}{py}\hat{x}$	Change in **variable input use**	The change in the use of variable inputs along the canal, excluding water
$\frac{\tau w}{py}\hat{w}$	Change in **water use** with *external values*	The change in water use along the canal using externally determined prices for water (τ)
$\frac{\pi_\Omega(1-\beta)w}{py}\hat{w}$	Change in **water use** with *internal values*	The change in water use along the canal using internally determined prices for water (π_Ω)
$\frac{\pi_\Omega(w(1-\beta)-\dot{\Omega})}{py}\hat{\pi}_\Omega$	Change in **shadow value of water**	The change in shadow value of water from moving along the canal
$\left(\frac{1}{\epsilon_c}-1\right)\hat{F}$	**Total input scale effect**	The scale effect captured by changes in the use of inputs, including water, along the canal
Quality adjustment		
$\frac{\tilde{\pi}_\Omega(1-\beta(q_w w-q))w}{py}\hat{w}$	Change in **water use** with *internal values*	The change in water use along the canal using internally determined prices for water (π_Ω)
	- QUALITY ADJUSTED -	
$\frac{\tilde{\pi}_\Omega(w(1-\beta q)-\dot{\Omega})}{py}\hat{\tilde{\pi}}_\Omega$	Change in **shadow value of water**	The change in shadow value of water from moving along the canal
	- QUALITY ADJUSTED -	
$\frac{\beta w\tilde{\pi}_\Omega q}{py}\hat{q}$	Change in **water quality**	The change in quality of water from moving along the canal

is reported. However, the availability of data for modelling purposes at different spatial scales can be an issue.

3 Accounting for Water Quality Adjustments over Space

Apart from capturing the quantity aspect of water, the proposed model can also be extended by considering debates about agricultural water quality, as the head versus tail conflict not only affects the quantity of water but also its quality. The reusable property of water can suffer from externalities related to salinity from irrigation and nitrate pollution from the use of fertilizers. Deterioration in the agricultural water quality can lead to decreasing water productivity, as upstream water use can have spillover effects on downstream farmers. The proposed spatial framework can incorporate water quality adjustments in the agricultural water productivity measurement and enable policy makers to examine the effect of advancing agricultural water management on both water quantity and quality.

Disputes over water quality along a canal have recently been the source of international or intra-national conflicts over water rights. The increasing use of chemicals and the intensification of agriculture due to higher food demand can result in water quality issues. For studying the spatial patterns of pollution along a canal, we can model the behaviour of the farmer who wants to optimally increase her profits, but she does not take into consideration the external effects on downstream farmers. As a result, upstream water use can have spillover effects on downstream farmers (Sigman 2002). Despite the fact that the farmers can face the same technology and output prices along a canal, due to externalities, the allocation of clean water among them is not efficient and market failure can arise.

The water quality dimension enters the spatial optimization model described above by using a water quality indicator, q, that can vary over space and is a function of the amount of water diverted, w, and the volume of water in the canal, Ω (Kanazawa 1991). While on the one hand, upstream water diversions can affect the quality of water in the canal due to the amounts of dissolved solids that are discharged back into the canal, on the other hand, reducing volume of instream flow downstream can also be associated with diminishing surface water quality. In particular, water quality spatially diminishes with increases in upstream water diversions ($q_w < 0$) and with decreases in the volume of instream flow in the canal ($q_\Omega > 0$).

To model the water quality impact on TFP change over space, it will be assumed that the quality of water in the canal is directly associated with the quantity of the return flow, $\beta w(r)$. This implies that the equation of motion of the spatial optimization model will be given by

$$\dot{\Omega}(r) = -w(r) + q(w, \Omega)\beta w(r) \tag{36}$$

In this case, the new spatial optimization problem, where $\widetilde{\pi}(p, z, t, \Omega, r, g(.))$ reflects the water quality adjusted profit, is given by

$$\max_{(x,w)} \widetilde{\pi} = \int_0^R [pf(x(r), w(r), \Omega(r), r) - zx(r) - \tau w(r)]\,\mathrm{d}r \tag{37}$$

$$s.t.\;\; \dot{\Omega}(r) = -w(r) + q(w, \Omega)\beta w(r) \tag{38}$$

$$\Omega(0) = w_0 \tag{39}$$

$$x(r), w(r) \geq 0 \tag{40}$$

The first order condition with respect to the aggregate input use, x, remains the same like in Eq. (9), while the one with respect to the water use, w, changes to the following expression:

$$pf_w - \tau - (1 - q\beta - q_w \beta w)\widetilde{\pi}_\Omega = 0 \tag{41}$$

The quality adjusted marginal value product of water use is equal to the water price plus the shadow value of instream flow adjusted for changes in water quality over space. This quality adjustment is captured by the term $(1 - q\beta - q_w\beta w)$ showing that water quality changes over space due to the quality of the irrigation return flow. The optimal solutions for the aggregate input use, x, and for the water diverted to the farm, w, can be expressed as follows:

$$x^* = -\widetilde{\pi}_{\Omega z} w^* + q\beta\widetilde{\pi}_{\Omega z} w^* + \widetilde{\pi}_{rz} \tag{42}$$

$$w^* = -\widetilde{\pi}_{\Omega \tau} w^* + q\beta\widetilde{\pi}_{\Omega \tau} w^* + \widetilde{\pi}_{r\tau} \tag{43}$$

Rearranging Eq. (43) and substituting to Eq. (42), we have the following optimal solutions for x and w that account for both water quantity and quality spatial adjustments:

$$x^* = x(p, z, \tau, \Omega, r) = \frac{(q\beta - 1)\widetilde{\pi}_{\Omega z}}{1 + (1 - q\beta)\widetilde{\pi}_{\Omega \tau}}\widetilde{\pi}_{r\tau} + \widetilde{\pi}_{rz} \tag{44}$$

$$w^* = w(p, z, \tau, \Omega, r) = \frac{1}{1 + (1 - q\beta)\widetilde{\pi}_{\Omega \tau}}\widetilde{\pi}_{r\tau} \tag{45}$$

In addition, Eq. (46) shows that the quality adjusted marginal value product of an additional unit of water at the source equals the change in the shadow value of water available at the source plus a quality adjusted shadow value of water associated with the change in the quality of water given a change in the volume of instream flow (Eq. (46)).

$$pf_\Omega = -\left(\frac{d\widetilde{\pi}_\Omega}{dr} + q_\Omega \beta w^* \widetilde{\pi}_\Omega\right) \tag{46}$$

Then, the total factor productivity change over space with an emphasis in water use with water quality adjustments will be decomposed as follows:

$$T\hat{F}P_w^q = \sum \frac{zx}{py}\hat{x} + \frac{\tau w}{py}\hat{w} + \frac{\widetilde{\pi}_\Omega(1 - \beta(q_w w - q))w}{py}\hat{w} + \frac{\widetilde{\pi}_\Omega(w(1 - \beta q) - \dot{\Omega})}{py}\hat{\widetilde{\pi}}_\Omega - \frac{\beta w \widetilde{\pi}_\Omega q}{py}\hat{q} - \hat{w} \tag{47}$$

The water quality adjusted total factor productivity spatial change, accounting for both aggregate input and water change, can be given by the following expression:

$$T\hat{F}P^q = \left(\frac{1}{\epsilon_c} - 1\right)\hat{F} + \frac{\widetilde{\pi}_\Omega(1 - \beta(q_w w - q))w}{py}\hat{w} + \frac{\widetilde{\pi}_\Omega(w(1 - \beta q) - \dot{\Omega})}{py}\hat{\widetilde{\pi}}_\Omega - \frac{\beta w \widetilde{\pi}_\Omega q}{py}\hat{q} \tag{48}$$

The lower part of Table 1 presents the three components of the quality adjusted TFP and their interpretation. In the case that the water quality dimension is not ignored, the change in the water use with internal values ($\frac{\tilde{\pi}_{\Omega}(1-\beta(q_w w-q))w}{py}\hat{w}$) and the change in the shadow value of water ($\frac{\tilde{\pi}_{\Omega}(w(1-\beta q)-\dot{\Omega})}{py}\hat{\tilde{\pi}}_{\Omega}$) are weighted by the water quality indicator, q. Further exploring the water quality adjusted TFP change over space, there is an extra component that captures the direct impact of changing water quality over space ($\frac{\beta w\tilde{\pi}_{\Omega}q}{py}\hat{q}$). This component indicates that agricultural productivity can be negatively affected by changes in the quality of water while we are moving away from the water source, and the magnitude of this effect is related to the quality of the return flows and the shadow value of water.

4 Discussion and Further Remarks

4.1 Irrigation Efficiency, Technical Efficiency, and Water Productivity

In the context of sustainable agriculture and water resources, many empirical studies have focused on measuring agricultural water efficiency and productivity that are essential aspects of sustainable agricultural production. However, among these studies there is no consensus on the definitions and estimation procedures of these performance indicators in agriculture (Giordano et al. 2017). This heterogeneity stems from the complex nature of water and its numerous users (farmers, municipal water utilities, industries, and recreational users) in different geographical scales. For this reason, the absence of common measures of agricultural water efficiency and productivity has led to different results. Based on Van Halsema and Vincent (2012), the content and the purpose of each study are the main drivers of which measure is used.

While irrigation efficiency can provide useful information regarding the performance of the irrigation system, its economic rationale is suspect. In the engineering field, irrigation efficiency is defined as the ratio of the water diverted from a specific source to the water received at the farm level and contributed to output growth. In this case, irrigation efficiency is measured in physical units of water without accounting for output value, allocation of inputs, or even environmental externalities. However, when crop production or farm profitability is the items of interest, economic efficiency is the concept to be used to enable the measurement and interpretation of the economic implications of an irrigation system.

Economic efficiency can be defined as the maximum attainable output that can be produced (technical efficiency) and the optimal allocation of inputs (allocative efficiency) when the farmer exploits the full potential of the available production technology. Input-specific efficiency can be a special case of the input-oriented measure of efficiency with the only difference that we are interested in a single input, i.e. irrigation water (Lansink et al. 2002; Kapelko et al. 2015). While input-specific efficiency measures can be a useful tool for policy makers, their use in the efficiency literature is limited. Water-specific efficiency in the agricultural economics literature has mainly be limited to the context of technical efficiency measures examining the impact of different irrigation systems on technical efficiency levels (Bravo-Ureta 2014).

In addition, productivity also plays an important role in the economic literature and is defined as the ratio of output(s) to inputs(s) and serves as measure of how well economic units can transform inputs into output(s). Agricultural water productivity ("*crop per drop*") is a partial productivity measure of economic performance that focuses on a single input, water, and is affected by the farmers' managerial abilities among other factors. However, the criticism is whether it can serve as a useful agricultural performance measure. Partial factor productivity can produce unbiased performance measures when it accounts for quasi-fixed input changes. However, when the partial factor productivity is estimated for variable inputs, like water, misleading and biased performance indicators may be produced. To address the problem of biased estimators, total factor productivity measures that account by definition for all input adjustments need to be considered.

Regardless of which measure the analyst selects, irrigation efficiency, (input-specific) technical efficiency, and agricultural (total factor or partial) productivity are three different measures assessing performance. While most of the research has been focused on measuring the impact of spatial allocation of water on irrigation or technical efficiency, this paper applies the spatial optimization framework with return flows to assess the impact of water allocation along a canal to agricultural total factor productivity. We highlight the role of water in the measurement of agricultural productivity by decomposing the productivity measurement into components associated with changes in shadow value of water, and water quantity and quality over space. We are able to identify costs associated with both water quantity and water quality changes due to upstream–downstream externalities through the change in the shadow values of water along the canal.

4.2 Future Outlook

Although the study in this paper is static, the dynamic nature of water highlights that water lost in seepage often ends up as groundwater recharge and is available for pumping. In this case, the proposed model can be extended to include not only the use of surface irrigation water from the canal but also groundwater from the aquifer with the irrigation technology at each location being determined as a function of the irrigation return flow (Umetsu and Chakravorty 1998; Chakravorty and Umetsu 2003). According to Chakravorty and Umetsu (2003), the optimal water allocation suggests specialization: upstream farmers tend to use surface water for irrigation while downstream farmers pump from the aquifer as very often they do not have access to secure supplies of canal water. In reality, farmers usually drew on a mix of surface water and groundwater irrigation with the portion of surface water relative to groundwater decreasing along the irrigation canal. Irrigation return flows can have a significant economic value (Griffin and Hsu 1993) and including them in the spatial modelling framework can affect the level of productivity at the farm level, and alter the spatial distribution of water and its shadow value across space. Also, high water table elevation and transfer of water between locations can affect the decision of farmers to pump groundwater from the aquifer as the pumping costs can vary with location and the stock of groundwater.[2]

Studying the allocation of water over space and time in the same framework will allow future work where the agricultural land allocation/conversion effect due to changes in water access can be modelled.[3] This land reallocation effect due to water availability can be included as a state variable in the proposed optimization model and then the land/farm size effect can be incorporated in the total factor productivity decomposition. While this can be a very interesting extension of the current paper with important policy implications as most of the total factor productivity growth in the agricultural sector comes from land productivity, it comes with some limitations that need to be addressed. First, the reality of land transfers/allocations in the agricultural sector is not frequent. And if these land size changes occur under variable returns to scale, this can adversely affect the economic performance of the farmers. In addition, land reallocations can be difficult due to spatial constraints and land market imperfections that can lead to land transfer/allocation inertia.

Some of the simplifying assumptions of the model in this paper could be relaxed in future work with the spatial model of water use to accommodate multiple-input and multiple-output production technologies. In addition, the spatial model proposed in this paper can be extended by considering the possibility of changing the production technology over space. Due to the head versus tail water disparities, farmers can decide to use another production technology as the distance from the water source is changing. For example, within the conjunctive surface water and groundwater regime, farmers may choose to use a different production technology (i.e. invest in groundwater pumping equipment) to assure water supplies.

Finally, scaling-up the spatial change of total factor productivity in unidirectional framework could be of great importance for policy analysis; however, there may be many obstacles in this attempt. While this paper is purely characterized by a micro-level, project-specific framework, it can be scaled-up to a watershed level. However, assessing the impact of agricultural water quantity and quality to productivity change over space at the country level can suffer from modelling and data limitations. Regarding the modelling aspects, the assumption of a unidirectional flow with exogenously determined initial water supply needs to be relaxed in future work. In this way, we can expand the optimization modelling framework in a

[2]The use of both surface and ground water in the same spatial optimization framework needs to be augmented by the inherent quality differences between these two different water sources.

[3]We thank two anonymous referees for raising the issue of agricultural land change due to water availability. This suggestion can make the current proposed modelling framework more intricate and open the door for future extensions.

more aggregated level (i.e. country) when multiple sources of water with different geographical and political boundaries are shaping the supply of water. In addition, while water plays an important role in the agricultural production and the impact of water stress due to climatic variability on agricultural productivity has been extensively highlighted in the last decade. However, information on water quantity and quality is not included in the productivity accounts of the countries. When this information will be available in more aggregated levels, this will allow us to scale-up the framework and analysis presented in this paper.

5 Conclusion

Current discussions on agricultural water management issues, due to irrigation water scarcity, have resulted in many policy recommendations aiming to enhance effective water use in agriculture. The magnitude of gains from the more effective use of agricultural water imply that water policy can aim toward efficiency- and productivity-enhancing techniques that can lead to better use of scarce water resources and sustainability of the ecosystems. However, the effectiveness of these policies depends on the proper measurement of water's contribution to agricultural productivity. Given the intensity of water used in agriculture, even small improvements in agricultural productivity associated with irrigation water use can have a significant impact on local and global water resources. The water savings can be used to improve water allocation on a local level, and farms that utilize the same water source can have access to reliable water allocations regardless of being placed close to or far away from the water source.

This paper presents a unique framework for measuring the contribution of water to total factor productivity in the agricultural sector. The analysis is carried out within a spatial framework, which enables the measurement of productivity along an irrigation canal accounting for both quantity and quality aspects of water. Improving water's contribution to productivity under the water scarcity constraint must address the issue that not all individuals or regions experience the water shortages when taking a global perspective. Those at the head of the water source have access to abundant clean water relative to the other downstream users, and thus have no incentive to limit their consumption, or alter their current practices to the detriment of producers downstream. A spatial model generating measures of water's contribution to productivity along a canal by determining optimal water allocation can accommodate this externality.

The proposed spatial model in this paper captures the differences in productivity in the agricultural sector due to head versus tails discrepancies in water allocation, while at the same time it accounts for irrigation return flows and their impact on water quality. The results of the spatial optimization model suggest that in the absence of irrigation return flows the farmer faces a higher marginal cost of irrigation water use. In addition, the spatially adjusted total factor productivity index provides insight on how a change in location can affect the shadow value of water and the water use based on this value, when both elements are weighted by the level of irrigation return flows. More specifically, the quantity of water decreases and the shadow value of water increases at a decreasing rate as we are moving away from the source. The shadow value of water within the proposed framework captures the extra cost that the farmer needs to absorb due to the change in the quantity of water while we are moving along the canal.

With water quality deterioration being another major concern related to the management of water resources in agriculture, the proposed spatial model is enhanced on accounting for changes in the quality of water over space. The water quantity and quality adjusted TFP decomposition reveals the impact of diminishing water quality over space in agricultural productivity given a change both in the quantity of water diverted in each location, and consequently the quantity of return flows, and in the volume of instream flow while the distance from the water source is increasing. It has been found that agricultural productivity is negatively affected by changes in the quality of water while we are moving along the canal with the magnitude of this effect related to the shadow value of water and the extent of return flows. The quality adjusted shadow value of water captures the effect of water quality externalities on farmer's economic performance due to the spatial water trade-off.

Water policy strategies should aim toward internalizing the spatial externalities and encouraging productivity-enhancing techniques allowing the farmers to produce more output with the same or even less water and to improve the quality of water used in the agricultural sector by deploying sustainable management practice and promoting community engagement. Policy makers can improve water use efficiency and productivity, spatial water allocation and management through different mechanisms. Attention should be paid on aligning the water management strategies of producers with the overall goal of socially efficient water use (Wichelns 2003). This can be achieved through economic instruments (Huffaker and Whittlesey 2003; Tiwari and Dinar 2000) such as water pricing (Dinar and Subramanian 1997) or subsidies for improved irrigation technologies that can enhance the spatial allocation of water resources and the choice of technologies upstream that ensure not only adequate quantity of water for downstream farmers but also diminishing return flows and run-off that can directly affect the quality of water downstream. In addition, regulatory approaches related to the management of water rights (Meinzen-Dick and Bakker 2001) and permits on performance-based norms and standards can encourage farmers to achieve higher water productivity levels that can offset the cost of the water rights and permits.

References

Annan, K., & United Nations. Department of Public Information. & United Nations. Secretary-General. (2000). *We the peoples: The role of the United Nations in the 21st century*. New York: United Nations Dept. of Public Information.

Bravo-Ureta, B. E. (2014). Stochastic frontiers, productivity effects and development projects. *Economics and Business Letters, 3*, 51–58.

Chakravorty, U., & Roumasset, J. (1991). Efficient spatial allocation of irrigation water. *American Journal of Agricultural Economics, 73*, 165–173.

Chakravorty, U., & Umetsu, C. (2003). Basinwide water management: A spatial model. *Journal of Environmental Economics and Management, 45*, 1–23.

Chakravorty, U., Hochman, E., & Zilberman, D. (1995). A spatial model of optimal water conveyance. *Journal of Environmental Economics and Management, 29*, 25–41.

Chambers, R. G. (1988). *Applied production analysis: A dual approach*. Cambridge: Cambridge University Press.

Christensen, L. R., & Jorgenson, D. W. (1970). The measurement of U.S. Real capital input, 1929-1967. *Review of Income and Wealth, 15*, 293–320.

Dinar, A., & Subramanian, A. (1997). Water pricing experiences: An international perspective. In *World Bank Technical Paper* (pp. 1–178).

Epstein, L. G. (1981). Duality theory and functional forms for dynamic factor demands. *The Review of Economic Studies, 48*(1), 81–95.

FAO (2012). *Coping with water scarcity: An action framework for agriculture and food security*. FAO Water Reports.

Giordano, M., Turral, H., Scheierling, S. M., Tréguer, D. O., & McCornick, P. G. (2017). *Beyond more crop per drop: Evolving thinking on agricultural water productivity*. Technical report, IWMI Research Report 169.

Griffin, R., & Hsu, S.-H. (1993). The potential for water market-efficiency when instream flows have value. *American Journal of Agricultural Economics, 75*, 292–303.

Huffaker, R., & Whittlesey, N. (2000). The allocative efficiency and conservation potential of water laws encouraging investments in on-farm irrigation technology. *Agricultural Economics, 24*, 47–60.

Huffaker, R., & Whittlesey, N. (2003). A theoretical analysis of economic incentive policies encouraging agricultural water conservation. *Water Resources Development, 19*, 37–53.

IFPRI (2017). *Global Food policy report 2017*. Washington: IFPRI.

Isard, W., & Liossatos, P. (1979). *Spatial dynamics and optimal space-time development*. New York: North-Holland.

Jorgenson, D. W., & Griliches, Z. (1967). The explanation of change productivity. *The Review of Economic Studies, 34*, 249–283.

Kamien, M., & Schwartz, N. (1991). *Dynamic optimization: The calculus of variations and optimal control in economics and management* (2nd ed.). Amsterdam: Elsevier.

Kanazawa, M. (1991). Water quality and the economic efficiency of appropriative water rights. In A. Dinar, & D. Zilberman (Eds), *The economics and management of water and drainage in agriculture*. Boston: Kluwer Academic Publishers, chap. 41.

Kapelko, M., Horta, I. M., Camanho, A. S., & Lansink, A. O. (2015). Measurement of input-specific productivity growth with an application to the construction industry in Spain and Portugal. *International Journal of Production Economics, 166*, 64–71.

Knapp, K. C., & Schwabe, K. a. (2008). Spatial dynamics of water and nitrogen management in irrigated agriculture. *American Journal of Agricultural Economics, 90*, 524–539.

Lansink, A. O., Pietola, K., & Backman, S. (2002). Efficiency and productivity of conventional and organic farms in Finland 1994-1997. *European Review of Agricultural Economics, 29*, 51–65.

Luh, Y.-h., & Stefanou, S. E. (1991). Productivity growth in U.S. agriculture under dynamic adjustment. *American Journal of Agricultural Economics, 73*, 1116–1125.

Meinzen-Dick, R., & Bakker, M. (2001). Water rights and multiple water uses: Framework and application to Kirindi Oya irrigation system Sri Lanka. *Irrigation and Drainage Systems, 15*, 129–148.

Molden, D., & Oweis, T. Y. (2007). Pathways for increasing agricultural water productivity. In *Water for food, water for life: A comprehensive assessment of water management in agriculture* (pp. 278–310).

Rosegrant, M. W., Ringler, C., & Zhu, T. (2009). Water for agriculture: Maintaining food security under growing scarcity. *Annual Review of Environment and Resources, 34*, 205–222.

Sigman, H. (2002). International Spillovers and water quality in rivers: Do countries free ride? *American Economic Review, 92*, 1152–1159.

Solow, R. M. (1957). Technical change and the Aggregate production function. *Review of Economic Studies, 39*, 312–320.

Tiwari, D., & Dinar, A. (2000). Role and use of economic incentives in irrigated agriculture. *World Bank Research Paper*.

Umetsu, C., & Chakravorty, U. (1998). Water conveyance, return flows and technology choice. *Agricultural Economics, 19*, 181–191.

United Nations (2015). *The United Nations world water development report 2015: Water for a sustainable world*. New York: United Nations.

United Nations (2017). *World population prospects: The 2017 revision*. New York: United Nations.

Van Halsema, G. E., & Vincent, L. (2012). Efficiency and productivity terms for water management: A matter of contextual relativism versus general absolutism. *Agricultural Water Management, 108*, 9–15.

Wade, R. (1982). The system of administrative and political corruption: Canal irrigation in South India. *Journal of Development Studies, 18*, 287–328.

Wichelns, D. (2003). Enhancing water policy discussions by including analysis of non-water inputs and farm-level constraints. *Agricultural Water Management, 62*, 93–103.

World Bank (2017). *Beyond scarcity: Water security in the Middle East and North Africa*. Washington DC: World Bank.

A Survey of the Use of Copulas in Stochastic Frontier Models

Christine Amsler and Peter Schmidt

1 Introduction

Copulas are used to create joint distributions with specified marginal distributions. The copula models the dependence between the corresponding marginal random variables. In the normal case, the multivariate normal distribution is a natural choice of joint distribution with normal marginals and its covariance matrix parameterizes the dependence between the individual marginal normals. But how would we specify a joint distribution for a normal and a half-normal, where these two random variables are allowed to be dependent? We can do this using copulas.

We will distinguish three different motivations for the use of copulas in the stochastic frontier literature. (1) Allowing statistical noise and inefficiency to be dependent (correlated) in an otherwise standard stochastic frontier model (SFM). (2) Allowing dependence between different composed errors and/or other types of errors; for example, with panel data, or across different equations in a multi-equation model. (3) Allowing non-standard types of dependence between the errors in a multi-equation system. We will discuss papers that fit into each of these categories.

Although this is a survey, we will try to make it more than a list of papers. We will discuss some important issues that arise as a consequence of different modeling strategies and which have not previously been systematically addressed.

The plan of the paper is as follows: Section 2 gives a few basic results about copulas. Section 3 discusses dependence between noise and inefficiency in an otherwise standard SFM. Section 4 covers panel data and errors in different equations in a multi-equation system. Section 5 discusses non-standard types of

C. Amsler · P. Schmidt (✉)
Michigan State University, East Lansing, MI, USA
e-mail: schmidtp@msu.edu

C. F. Parmeter, R. C. Sickles (eds.), *Advances in Efficiency and Productivity Analysis*, Springer Proceedings in Business and Economics,
https://doi.org/10.1007/978-3-030-47106-4_6

dependence. Section 6 discusses the problem of choosing a copula. Finally, Section 7 gives some concluding remarks.

2 Copula Basics

We begin with two basic facts. (1) If Z has cdf F, then $W \equiv F(Z)$ is uniform on [0,1]. (2) If W is uniform on [0,1] and F is a cdf, then $Z \equiv F^{-1}(W)$ has cdf F.

Definition A copula is a multivariate distribution whose marginal distributions are uniform.

The copula, therefore, is the distribution of the cdf values (W, above) of a set of random variables.

We will use the following standard notation. The copula cdf is $C(w_1, \ldots, w_n)$ and the copula density is $c(w_1, \ldots, w_n)$, where n is the number of random variables linked by the copula.

Here are some examples (all for $n = 2$).

Independence: $c(w_1, w_2) = 1$

Farlie–Gumbel–Morgenstern (FGM):

$$c\,(w_1, w_2) = 1 + \theta\,(1 - 2w_1)\,(1 - 2w_2)$$

Normal:

$$c\,(w_1, w_2) = \left(1 - \rho^2\right)^{-\frac{1}{2}} \exp\left[-\frac{1}{2}\left(1 - \rho^2\right)^{-1} \left(\rho^2 w_1^2 + \rho^2 w_2^2 - 2\rho w_1 w_2\right)\right]$$

These are prominent examples, but there are many, many more copulas. For one (long) list of copulas, see Nadarajah et al. (2017).

The basis for most uses of copulas is the following important result. We state it somewhat informally. For a more technically detailed statement, see, for example, Nelson (2006, p. 18).

Sklar's Theorem

Suppose that $Z_1, \ldots, Z_n$ have marginal cdfs $F_1(z_1), \ldots F_n(z_n)$; marginal densities $f_1(z_1), \ldots f_n(z_n)$; joint cdf $H(z_1, \ldots, z_n)$; and joint density $h(z_1, \ldots, z_n)$. Then

$$h\,(z_1, \ldots, z_n) = \prod\nolimits_{j=1}^{n} f_j\,(z_j) \cdot c\,(w_1, \ldots, w_n)\,, \tag{1}$$

where $w_j = F_j(z_j), j = 1, \ldots, n$.

We note that we have $h\,(z_1, \ldots, z_n) = \prod_{j=1}^{n} f_j\,(z_j)$ if $Z_1, \ldots, Z_n$ are mutually independent. If they are not mutually independent, the extra term $c(w_1, \ldots, w_n)$ in (1) quantifies their dependence.

This theorem has two parts: First, if we specify a joint distribution h for continuous random variables $Z_1, \ldots, Z_n$, the marginal distributions and the copula are uniquely defined. The uniqueness of the copula depends on these being continuous random variables. Second, and for our purposes more importantly, if we specify the marginal distributions and a copula, then h as defined above is a joint distribution, and it has the correct marginals and it implies the correct copula. So, to construct a joint distribution with specified marginal distributions, we just need to choose a copula.

The first use of copulas in econometrics appears to be Lee (1983). He has a selectivity model with non-normal errors that he wants to be correlated. So, in generic terms, he wants random variables U_1 and U_2 to have cdfs F_1 and F_2. To do this he assumes the representation

$$U_1 = F_1^{-1}\left(\Phi\left(V_1\right)\right), U_2 = F_2^{-1}\left(\Phi\left(V_2\right)\right), \tag{2}$$

where (V_1, V_2) has a standard bivariate normal distribution (means equal to 0, variances equal to 1, correlation ρ) and where Φ is the standard univariate normal cdf. Lee was not aware of copulas, and he (correctly) reinvented the normal copula.

3 Allowing Dependence Between Noise and Inefficiency

The first use of copulas in the stochastic frontier literature appears to be Smith (2008). He considers a SFM with composed error $\varepsilon = v - u$, where v is noise and $u \geq 0$ is inefficiency. (For notational simplicity we suppress the observational subscript "i.") He does not want to assume that v and u are independent, so he uses a copula to model their dependence.

The most standard case in the SF literature is that v is normal and u is half-normal, in which case it is well known that if v and u are independent, ε has a skew-normal distribution. If v and u are dependent, the distribution of ε is generally intractable. However, in the case that v is logistic and u is exponential and the FGM copula is assumed, Smith derives closed-form expressions for the density of ε and for the usual predictor of u, $\hat{u} = E\left(u|\varepsilon\right)$. He also considers the normal/half-normal model with three different copulas where these closed-form expressions are analytically intractable.

If the density of ε is analytically intractable, it can be calculated by numerical integration, or by simulation, leading to a simulated likelihood function. The marginal distributions for v and u and the assumed copula yield a joint density $h(v, u)$. Then the joint density of ε and u is

$h(\varepsilon + u, u)$ and the marginal density of ε is

$$f_\varepsilon\left(\varepsilon\right) = \int_0^\infty h\left(\varepsilon + u, u\right) du.$$

This can be calculated by numerical quadrature, which is what Smith does. Alternatively,

$$f_{\varepsilon}(\varepsilon) = \int_0^{\infty} \frac{h(\varepsilon + u, u)}{f_u(u)} \cdot f_u(u)du = E_u \frac{h(\varepsilon + u, u)}{f_u(u)}, \tag{3}$$

where "E_u" means the expectation over the distribution of u. This corresponds to Eq. (3.6) of Smith. We can calculate (estimate) this density as the average of $\frac{h(\varepsilon+u,u)}{f_u(u)}$ over a large number of draws from the distribution of u. This is a slight generalization of the method of simulated likelihood in the case of independence of v and u, for which a standard reference is Greene (2003).

This can be simplified (or at least rewritten) by noting that $h(v, u) = f_v(v) \cdot f_u(u) \cdot c(F_v(v), F_u(u))$ and therefore

$$f_{\varepsilon}(\varepsilon) = \int_0^{\infty} c\left(F_v(\varepsilon + u), F_u(u)\right) \cdot f_v(\varepsilon + u) \cdot f_u(u)du \tag{4}$$

$$= E_u \left[c\left(F_v(\varepsilon + u), F_u(u)\right) \cdot f_v(\varepsilon + u)\right].$$

This may or may not be easier to simulate than the expression in (3).

We note that the simulation based on (3) does not require that $f_u(u)$ be the correct marginal density of u. That is, for an arbitrary density $p(u)$, we can write

$$f_{\varepsilon}(\varepsilon) = \int_0^{\infty} \frac{h(\varepsilon + u, u)}{p(u)} \cdot p(u)du = E_{p(u)} \frac{h(\varepsilon + u, u)}{p(u)}, \tag{5}$$

where the notation $E_{p(u)}$ indicates the expectation over the distribution $p(u)$. This is called *importance sampling*. It could be useful in cases in which it is difficult to sample from the true density $f_u(u)$, or we do not know how to do so, but there is a similar density $p(u)$ from which it is easy to sample. Similarity of $p(u)$ and $f_u(u)$ is important so that the ratio $\frac{h(\varepsilon+u,u)}{p(u)}$ is not close to 0 or infinity.

For the calculation of $\hat{u} = E(u|\varepsilon)$, similar considerations apply. The joint density of ε and u is $h(\varepsilon + u, u)$, as above. The density of u conditional on ε is $h(\varepsilon + u, u)/f_{\varepsilon}(\varepsilon)$ and

$$E(u|\varepsilon) = \int_0^{\infty} u \frac{h(\varepsilon + u, u)}{f_{\varepsilon}(\varepsilon)} du = \frac{1}{f_{\varepsilon}(\varepsilon)} \int_0^{\infty} uh(\varepsilon + u, u)\, du.$$

This corresponds to Eq. (3.7) of Smith. It can be calculated numerically, or by simulation. To calculate it by simulation, note

$$E(u|\varepsilon) = \frac{1}{f_{\varepsilon}(\varepsilon)} \int_0^{\infty} u \frac{h(\varepsilon + u, u)}{f_u(u)} f_u(u)du = \frac{1}{f_{\varepsilon}(\varepsilon)} E_u\, u \frac{h(\varepsilon + u, u)}{f_u(u)} \tag{6}$$

As in the calculation of the density of ε, we can calculate the last term by averaging over a large number of draws from the distribution of u. However, this requires two separate simulations: one to obtain the density of ε and a second one to obtain the last term in the equation above.

An alternative is to estimate $E(u|\,\varepsilon)$ nonparametrically. If we can make draws from the joint distribution of (v, u), then we can construct draws from the joint distribution of (ε, u), just by calculating $\varepsilon = v - u$. From a sample of such draws, we can estimate $E(u|\,\varepsilon)$ using nonparametric methods such as kernels or nearest neighbors. This procedure is used (in a different context) by Amsler et al. (2014).

Quite a few other papers use copulas to allow for dependence between v and u. A few of these papers choose the marginal distributions and copula in such a way that analytical expressions can be found for the density of ε and/or the value of $E(u|\,\varepsilon)$. For example, Gomez-Deniz and Perez-Rodriguez (2015) consider the normal/half-normal model with a Sarmanov copula, which allows closed-form expressions. Gomez-Deniz and Perez-Rodriguez (2017) also consider the normal/exponential model in which a different Sarmanov copula allows analytical expressions. Similarly, Bonanno et al. (2017) assume that noise is Type 1 logistic, inefficiency is exponential, and the copula is the FGM copula, which also allows closed-form expressions. Their motivation is to allow the possibility of either positive or negative skew for ε.

Other examples include El Mehdi and Hafner (2014), who suggest inference via bootstrapping; Kinaci et al. (2016), Najjari et al. (2016), Pipitpojanakarn et al. (2016), who consider a stochastic frontier quantile model; and Tibprasorn et al. (2017).

4 Allowing Dependence Between Different Composed Errors or Composed Errors and Other Errors

4.1 *Panel Data*

Suppose that we have panel data consisting of T observations on each cross-sectional unit. So (again suppressing the cross-sectional subscript) we have ε but now $\varepsilon = (\varepsilon_1, \ldots, \varepsilon_T)'$, and similarly for v and u. Suppose that the ε_t $(t = 1, \ldots, T)$ are identically distributed as skew-normal, the standard composed error distribution. So we are assuming that v_t and u_t are independent. The only issue is correlation of v or u over different values of t.

An important point is that we can ignore this correlation. The quasi-MLE based on the likelihood that (incorrectly) assumes independence over t is consistent. The conventional standard errors would be incorrect, but they can be corrected using the familiar HAC standard errors. Also the usual Jondow et al. (1982) form of $\hat{u}_t = E\,(u_t|\varepsilon_t)$ applies.

So why use a copula? There are two possible reasons: First, by accounting for the autocorrelation, we can have a more efficient estimation. Second, and more importantly, in some models we can have a better prediction of the u_t.

Amsler et al. (2014) discuss both of these points. They consider two models: In Model 1, they assume a copula for the joint distribution of ε. In Model 2, the v_t are i.i.d. (over t) and they assume a copula for the joint distribution of u.

Model 1 was previously considered by Shi and Zhang (2011). The advantage of Model 1 is that it is straightforward. A closed-form expression exists for the joint distribution of ε and therefore for the likelihood. This yields more efficient estimates than the quasi-MLE that assumes independence. The disadvantage is that we still must use the Jondow et al. (1982) expression for $\hat{u}_t = E(u_t|\varepsilon_t)$. The values of the other ε_s $(s \neq t)$ are not informative because the model does not specify whether the correlation over t is due to v or u.

The disadvantage of Model 2 is that it is numerically complicated. Amsler et al. (2014) suggest estimation by simulated MLE, assuming that the copula is one that we can draw from. In their case it was the multivariate normal copula which is easy to draw from. In other cases they suggest importance sampling. But in any case this is harder than Model 1 where there is a closed-form expression for the likelihood. The advantage of Model 2 is that it leads to improved predictions of u. Specifically, now we have $\tilde{u}_t = E(u_t|\varepsilon_1, \ldots, \varepsilon_T)$ which is better (more explained variation and less unexplained variation) than $\hat{u}_t = E(u_t|\varepsilon_t)$. The calculation (estimation) of $\tilde{u}_t$ is based on kernels or nearest neighbors and is more complicated than before because we now have a conditioning set of T dimensions.

More complicated models are possible. Das (2015) has a model where v_t and u_t are correlated; the v_t are not autocorrelated; and the u_t are autocorrelated but u_t and u_s are correlated only for $|t - s| \leq 1$.

Even less restrictive models could be formulated, but there are unexplored issues of identification and possible numerical difficulties. At the extreme, if we do not put any restrictions on the covariance structure of v and u, we have ½$T(T + 1)$ distinct covariances for each, for a total of $T(T + 1)$ covariances to identify. We "observe" ε and can estimate its ½$T(T + 1)$ distinct covariances. Clearly without some sort of restrictions we cannot identify this unrestricted model. (And this count does not take into account any additional parameters that may arise if v and u are correlated.)

4.2 *Correlation of Errors Across Equations*

Next we will discuss multi-equation models in which some or all of the errors are non-normal and we do not want to assume independence across equations. These models are similar to the panel data models just discussed, in that the quasi-likelihood maximum likelihood estimator based on the false assumption of independence is still consistent.

An early paper with this kind of model is Genius et al. (2012). They have a set of stochastic frontier models for input demands. Each equation (input) has a composed error and a copula is used to allow dependence across equations. A somewhat similar paper is Lai and Huang (2013), in which each firm has J divisions. They assume a stochastic frontier model for each division and the normal copula is used to model correlation across divisions. Carta and Steel (2012) have a multiple output production function where there is an equation with a composed error for each output. Only the one-sided component is correlated across equations, so this is similar to Model 2 of Amsler et al. (2014). They use a Bayesian treatment of the model and it is not entirely clear (at least to us) how this correlation affects the posterior distributions of the inefficiencies. Repkine (2014) has a metafrontier model in which the inefficiency of a firm relative to its group frontier and the metafrontier distance (inefficiency of the group frontier relative to the metafrontier), both of which are non-negative, are correlated using a copula. Amsler et al. (2016, 2017) consider endogeneity in stochastic frontier models, so they have a production frontier with a composed error and reduced-form equations for the endogenous explanatory variables, with normal errors. Huang et al. (2018b) have two equations, one for cost efficiency and one for market power, each of which has a composed error, and the two composed errors are linked using the normal copula.

There is a long list of other papers that have multiple equations with various kinds of errors, some or all of which are composed errors, where a copula is used to model correlation across the errors. Examples include Tran and Tsionas (2015), Huang et al. (2017a, b, 2018a), and Sriboonchitta et al. (2017).

5 Copulas Designed to Handle Specific Non-Standard Types of Dependence

There may be special aspects of dependence that call for specific types of copulas. As a prominent example, in the copula literature there is a feature of the copula called "tail dependence." Lower tail dependence is defined as

$$\lambda_L = \lim_{s \to 0} P\left[Z_2 \leq F_2^{-1}(s) | Z_1 \leq F_1^{-1}(s)\right] \tag{7}$$

(Nelson 2006, p. 214). It is a measure of how likely it is that an event in the extreme left tail of Z_1 occurs along with an event in the extreme left tail of Z_2. That is, it is a measure of how likely it is that a very low probability Z_1 event occurs in conjunction with a very low probability Z_2 event. The Gaussian (normal) copula has tail dependence equal to 0, whereas some other copulas, notably the Clayton copula, allow for positive tail dependence. This distinction came to the fore in the 2008 financial crisis. Starting with Li (2000), the Gaussian copula was used to model the probability of simultaneous defaults on mortgages and therefore to construct and price mortgage-based derivatives. However, because it has no tail dependence, the Gaussian copula is thought to have understated the probability of a large number of simultaneous defaults and thus to have led to the collapse of mortgage-based derivatives. This is perhaps the only time that the concept of a copula has made it into the popular press. See, e.g., Jones (2009), "The Formula that Felled Wall Street." Subsequent work has used copulas with positive tail dependence, such as the Clayton copula, to better allow for the prospect of many simultaneous mortgage defaults.

The last paragraph has nothing to do with stochastic frontier models, other than to argue that one should ask whether the dependence implied by standard copulas is appropriate for an intended application. One case in which it is arguably not appropriate is the estimation of a system consisting of a cost function (or production function) plus a set of first-order conditions (e.g., for cost minimization). This issue is sometimes referred to as the "Greene Problem." Christensen and Greene (1976) estimate a system with a translog cost function and equations for the optimal shares. The errors in these equations are correlated in the usual way. The "Greene problem" is that this is not reasonable. Incorrect shares (too big or too small) raise costs. The error in the cost function should be correlated with the absolute value of the share equation errors. A normal copula or other standard copulas cannot accomplish this.

An early paper that deals with this problem is Schmidt and Lovell (1980). They have a stochastic frontier production function model

$$y_i = \alpha + x_i'\beta + v_i - u_i = \alpha + x_i'\beta + \varepsilon_i, i = 1, \ldots, N \tag{8}$$

with y and x in logs, where $\varepsilon_i = v_i - u_i$, and equations for the optimal input ratios

$$x_{i1} - x_{ij} = B_{ij} + \omega_{ij}, j = 2, \ldots, K, \tag{9}$$

where K is the number of inputs and $B_{ij} = p_{ij} - p_{i1} + \ln(\beta_1) - \ln(\beta_j)$. They want technical inefficiency and allocative inefficiency to be dependent. But they want u_i to be correlated with $|\omega_{ij}|$, not with ω_{ij}.

Dropping the subscript i for simplicity, Schmidt and Lovell assume that $u = |u^*|$, where $\begin{bmatrix} u^* \\ \omega \end{bmatrix} \sim N(0, \Sigma)$ and where $\Sigma = \begin{bmatrix} \sigma_u^2 & \Sigma_{\omega u}' \\ \Sigma_{\omega u} & \Sigma_{\omega\omega} \end{bmatrix}$. Then u is half-normal and ω is multivariate normal; u and ω are uncorrelated, and the correlation between u and $|\omega_j|$ is

$$(2/\pi)\left[\sqrt{1 - \rho_j^2} + \rho_j \arcsin(\rho_j) - 1\right] \geq 0,$$

where ρ_j is the correlation between u^* and ω_j.

The connection of this to copulas is that clearly there must be a copula implicit in this construction. Amsler et al. (2018) show that this copula is the mixture (with weights equal to ½) of the Gaussian copula with variance matrix Σ and the Gaussian copula with variance matrix $\Sigma^* = \begin{bmatrix} \sigma_u^2 & -\Sigma_{\omega u}' \\ -\Sigma_{\omega u} & \Sigma_{\omega\omega} \end{bmatrix}$. This is a copula that could be used in other settings, as long as one wants a random variable to be uncorrelated with another random variable, but correlated with its absolute value.

Of course, there must be other copulas with the same property. For now, consider the case of two inputs so that ω is a scalar. In generic notation, we have a copula density $c(w_1, w_2)$, where w_1 and w_2 are scalars. The relevant random variables are u and scalar ω; then the copula arguments are $w_1 = F_u(u)$ and $w_2 = F_\omega(\omega)$. For any two random variables, Spearman's rho is the correlation between the copula arguments. We are interested in copulas such that Spearman's rho equals 0, that is, $w_1 = F_u(u)$ and $w_2 = F_\omega(\omega)$ are uncorrelated. (The covariance between the original random variables u and ω depends on the marginal distributions F_u and F_ω). However, we want copulas such that Spearman's rho equals 0, but $\mathrm{cov}(w_1, |w_2 - ½|) \neq 0$. For the case that ω has a symmetric distribution around 0, $w_2 = ½$ corresponds to $\omega = 0$, which explains our interest in $|w_2 - ½|$.

Amsler et al. (2018) define a family of copulas with this property, as follows.

Definition An APS-2 copula is a copula of the form $c(w_1, w_2) = 1 + \theta(1 - 2w_1)\left(1 - k_q^{-1} q(w_2)\right)$, where $q(s)$ is integrable on [0,1]; $q(s)$ is symmetric around $s = ½$, that is, $q(s) = q(1 - s)$; $q(s)$ is monotonically decreasing on [0, ½] and therefore monotonically increasing on [½, 1]; and $k_q = \int_0^1 q(s)ds$.

Two specific members of this family are as follows.

APS-2-A $c(w_1, w_2) = 1 + \theta(1 - 2w_1)[1 - 12(w_2 - ½)^2]$, $|\theta| \leq ½$

APS-2-B $c(w_1, w_2) = 1 + \theta(1 - 2w_1)(1 - 4|w_2 - ½|)$, $|\theta| \leq 1$.

They establish a number of results for this family of copula, including the following. (The numbering of these results follows the numbering in Amsler et al. (2018).)

Result 1. For any APS-2 copula, $\mathrm{cov}(w_1, w_2) = 0$.

Result 4. (i) The APS-2-A copula is a copula for $|\theta| \leq ½$.

(ii) $\mathrm{cov}\left[w_1, \left(w_2 - \frac{1}{2}\right)^2\right] = \frac{1}{90}\theta$.(iii) $\mathrm{var}\left[\left(w_2 - \frac{1}{2}\right)^2\right] = \frac{1}{180}$.

(iv) $\mathrm{corr}[w_1, (w_2 - ½)^2] = \frac{2}{\sqrt{15}}\theta \cong 0.516\,\theta$.

Result 5. (i) The APS-2-B copula is a copula for $|\theta| \leq 1$.

(ii) $\mathrm{cov}\left[w_1, |w_2 - \frac{1}{2}|\right] = \frac{1}{72}\theta$.(iii) $\mathrm{var}\left(|w_2 - \frac{1}{2}|\right) = \frac{1}{48}$.

(iv) $\mathrm{corr}[w_1, |w_2 - ½|] = \frac{1}{3}\theta$.

They also consider the three-dimensional case. This corresponds to three inputs, so two equations for the optimal input ratios, as in Schmidt and Lovell. They propose the following:

APS-3-A $c^*(w_1, w_2, w_3) = 1 + (c_{12} - 1) + (c_{13} - 1) + (c_{23} - 1)$, where

$c_{12}(w_1, w_2) = 1 + \theta_{12}(1 - 2w_1)\left[1 - 12\left(w_2 - \frac{1}{2}\right)^2\right]$

$c_{13}(w_1, w_3) = 1 + \theta_{13}(1 - 2w_1)\left[1 - 12\left(w_3 - \frac{1}{2}\right)^2\right]$

$c_{23}(w_2, w_3) =$ bivariate normal copula

APS-3-B $c^*(w_1, w_2, w_3) = 1 + (c_{12} - 1) + (c_{13} - 1) + (c_{23} - 1)$, where

$c_{12}(w_1, w_2) = 1 + \theta_{12}(1 - 2w_1)\left(1 - 4\left|w_2 - \frac{1}{2}\right|\right)$

$c_{13}(w_1, w_3) = 1 + \theta_{13}(1 - 2w_1)\left(1 - 4\left|w_3 - \frac{1}{2}\right|\right)$

$c_{23}(w_2, w_3) =$ bivariate normal copula.
See Amsler et al. (2018) for more details.

6 Choosing the Copula

There are many different copulas and it is not altogether clear how one should be chosen. Often they appear to be chosen on the basis of algebraic tractability or computational simplicity. At a more statistical level, we can consider two alternatives: (1) Use an explicit model-choice procedure, such as the Akaike Information Criterion (AIC) or the Bayes Information Criterion (BIC) to choose one copula from a set of possible copulas. (2) Pick a copula (or a small number of possible copulas) and then apply a goodness-of-fit test to see if it is rejected by the data.

6.1 Information Criteria

The use of information criteria for copula choice was apparently first suggested by Joe (1997, Sect. 10.3). A few stochastic frontiers papers have used AIC to pick a copula. For example, Smith (2008) used AIC to choose among the AMH, Frank, Plackett, and independence copulas. Das (2015) used AIC to choose between the FGM and normal copulas. Sriboonchitta, Liu, Wiboonpongas, and Denoeux (Sriboonchitta et al. 2017) used AIC to choose a copula from a large set of different copulas (Gaussian, Frank, Clayton, Gumbel, Joe, rotated Clayton, rotated Gumbel, and rotated Joe).

The value of AIC is $2k - 2 \ln \hat{L}$, where k is the number of parameters in the model and $\hat{L}$ is the maximized value of the likelihood. We pick the model with the smallest value of AIC. If we are comparing models with the same marginal distributions, then if the various copulas have the same number of parameters, comparing the AIC values is the same as comparing the likelihood values. BIC could also be used. The value of BIC is $(\ln N)\, k - 2 \ln \hat{L}$, where k and $\hat{L}$ are as above and N is the sample size (not to be confused with n, the number of variables being linked). So, again, if we are comparing models with the same marginal distributions, and if the various copulas have the same number of parameters, a comparison of the BIC values will be the same as a comparison of the AIC values or the likelihood values.

In the previous paragraph, the likelihood values come from the estimation of the model based on the joint distribution of the random variables. That is, we estimate the models for the marginal distributions along with the copula. An appealing alternative is to estimate the distributions of the marginal variables nonparametrically, so as to choose the copula without requiring correct specification of the marginal distributions. Suppose that the variables we are linking with the copula are $Z_1, \cdots, Z_n$, and the copula density is defined as $c(F_1(z_1), \cdots, F_n(z_n))$, as in Eq. (1) above. Then for each observation we replace each cdf value $F_j(z_j)$ with $\hat{F}_j\left(z_j\right)$, the value of the empirical cdf at z_j for that observation. This amounts to reducing the data to ranks. The ranked empirical cdf values are actually taken to be $\frac{1}{N+1}, \frac{2}{N+1}, \cdots, \frac{N}{N+1}$, where N is the sample size; these equal the $\hat{F}_j\left(z_j\right)$ scaled by $\frac{N}{N+1}$, so as to avoid values of 0 or 1. A likelihood constructed from $c\left(\hat{F}_1\left(z_1\right), \cdots, \hat{F}_n\left(z_n\right)\right)$ is called the pseudo-likelihood (e.g., Gronneberg and Hjort 2014) and the AIC criterion can be calculated from the pseudo-likelihood. However, Gronneberg and Hjort point out that the standard formula for AIC no longer applies. The effects of using the empirical (estimated) cdf need to be taken into account, and they propose a Copula Information Criterion (CIC) and a Cross-Validation Information Criterion (xv-CIC) which do so. These criteria were evaluated in simulations by Jordanger and Tjostheim (2014). So far as we know these new methods have not been applied in the stochastic frontiers setting.

6.2 Goodness-of-Fit Tests

There is surprisingly little discussion of goodness-of-fit testing in stochastic frontier models. The only systematic treatment that we are aware of is Wang et al. (2011). There do not appear to be any applications of goodness-of-fit tests for the copula in a stochastic frontier model.

However, there is a relevant statistical literature on goodness-of-fit tests for copulas. This includes good surveys by Berg (2009) and Genest et al. (2009) and more recent papers by Genest et al. (2013) and Huang and Prokhorov (2014). Similar considerations to those of the previous subsection apply when we consider goodness-of-fit (GOF) testing. If we specify the marginal distributions and the copula, then we have specified the joint distribution for the data and we have a standard GOF problem. However, we may want to test the adequacy of the copula independently of the correctness of the marginal distributions. To do so we once again consider the ranks $\hat{F}_j\left(z_j\right)$ which will be the basis of the test. The term "blanket test" is used to describe a test that does not require the specification of the marginal distributions, is applicable to any copula family, and does not require the choice of tuning parameters like kernels or bandwidths. Genest, Rémillard, and Beaudoin discuss and compare five different blanket tests. See also Genest, Huang, and Dufour. A problem with these tests is that they have non-standard asymptotic distributions and bootstrap methods are required to achieve correct size. Huang and Prokhorov suggest a test based on the information matrix equality, similarly to the famous test of White (1982) but using the pseudo-likelihood. This is a blanket test that is notable because it has a standard chi-squared asymptotic distribution under the null, so there is no need for bootstrapping.

7 Concluding Remarks

We have tried to provide a reasonably comprehensive survey of previous uses of copulas in stochastic frontier models. We have also tried to explain some issues in the use of copulas, notably whether the copula should be applied to the technical inefficiency term u or the composed error $\varepsilon = v - u$. This distinction leads to computational issues, such as the need for simulated maximum likelihood and importance sampling.

We have also discussed the sense in which the economic models that arise in the stochastic frontier literature call for copulas with special characteristics. For normal random variables, the multivariate normal distribution is a natural choice to model their dependence. The multivariate normal distribution has normal marginals and the Gaussian (normal) copula. We could have normal marginals and a different copula, but the multivariate normal distribution is natural because of the multivariate central limit theorem. For non-normal marginals, the Gaussian copula is still popular, because it is simple and because it has a non-controversial definition in the case of more than two dimensions. But it is not so natural as in the case of normal marginals, and in some cases (like the Greene problem) it does not seem appropriate. So there is scope for the invention of new copulas as well as new uses of existing copulas.

References

Amsler, C., Prokhorov, A., & Schmidt, P. (2014). Using copulas to model time dependence in stochastic frontier models. *Econometric Reviews, 33*, 497–522.

Amsler, C., Prokhorov, A., & Schmidt, P. (2016). Endogeneity in stochastic frontier models. *Journal of Econometrics, 190*, 280–288.

Amsler, C., Prokhorov, A., & Schmidt, P. (2017). Endogenous environmental variables in stochastic frontier models. *Journal of Econometrics, 199*, 131–140.

Amsler, C., Prokhorov, A., & Schmidt, P. (2018). *A new copula, with application to estimation of a production frontier system*. University of Sydney Business School, Discipline of Business Analytics.

Berg, D. (2009). Copula goodness-of-fit testing: An overview and power comparison. *The European Journal of Finance, 15*, 675–701.

Bonanno, G., De Giovanni, D., & Domma, F. (2017). The 'wrong skewness' problem: A re-specification of stochastic frontiers. *Journal of Productivity Analysis, 47*, 49–64.

Carta, A., & Steel, M. F. J. (2012). Modelling multi-output stochastic frontiers using copulas. *Computational Statistics and Data Analysis, 56*, 3757–3773.

Christensen, L., & Greene, W. H. (1976). Economies of scale in U.S. electric power generation. *Journal of Political Economy, 84*, 655–676.

Das, A. (2015). Copula-based stochastic frontier model with autocorrelated inefficiency. *Central European Journal of Economic Modelling and Econometrics, 7*, 111–126.

El Mehdi, R., & Hafner, C. M. (2014). Inference in stochastic frontier analysis with dependent error terms. *Mathematics and Computers in Simulation, 102*, 104–116.

Genest, C., Huang, W., & Dufour, J.-M. (2013). A regularized goodness-of-fit test for copulas. *Journal de la Société Française de Statistique, 154*, 64–77.

Genest, C., Rémillard, B., & Beaudoin, D. (2009). Goodness-of-fit tests for copulas: A review and a power study. *Insurance: Mathematics and Economics, 44*, 199–213.

Genius, M., Stefanou, S., & Tzouvelekas, V. (2012). Measuring productivity growth under factor non-substitution: An application to US steam-electric power generation utilities. *European Journal of Operational Research, 220*, 844–852.

Gomez-Deniz, E., & Perez-Rodriguez, J. V. (2017). Maximum likelihood estimation of stochastic frontier models with dependent errors. unpublished manuscript.

Gomez-Deniz, E., & Perez-Rodriquez, J. V. (2015). Closed-form solution for a bivariate distribution in stochastic frontier models with dependent errors. *Journal of Productivity Analysis, 43*, 215–223.

Greene, W. H. (2003). Simulated likelihood estimation of the normal-gamma stochastic frontier function. *Journal of Productivity Analysis, 19*, 179–190.

Gronneberg, S., & Hjort, N. L. (2014). The copula information criterion. *Scandinavian Journal of Statistics, 41*, 436–459.

Huang, T.-H., Chen, K.-C., & Lin, C.-I. (2018a). An extension from network DEA to copula-based network SFA: Evidence from the U.S. commercial banks in 2009. *The Quarterly Review of Economics and Finance, 67*, 51–62.

Huang, T.-H., Chiang, D.-L., & Chao, S.-W. (2017a). A new approach to jointly estimating the Lerner index and cost efficiency for multi-output banks under a stochastic meta-frontier framework. *The Quarterly Review of Economics and Finance, 65*, 212–226.

Huang, T.-H., Lin, C.-I., & Chen, K.-C. (2017b). Evaluating efficiencies of Chinese commercial banks in the context of stochastic multistage technologies. *Pacific-Basin Finance Journal, 41*, 93–110.

Huang, T.-H., Liu, N.-H., & Kumbhakar, S. C. (2018b). Joint estimation of the Lerner index and cost efficiency using copula methods. *Empirical Economics, 54*, 799–822.

Huang, W., & Prokhorov, A. (2014). A goodness-of-fit test for copulas. *Econometric Reviews, 33*, 751–771.

Joe, H. (1997). *Multivariate models and dependence concepts*. Boca Raton, FL: Chapman and Hall/CRC.

Jondow, J., Lovell, C. A. K., Materov, I. S., & Schmidt, P. (1982). On the estimation of technical inefficiency in the stochastic frontier production function model. *Journal of Econometrics, 19*, 233–238.

Jones, S. (2009, April 24). The formula that felled Wall Street. *Financial Times*.

Jordanger, L. A., & Tjostheim, D. (2014). Model selection of copulas: AIC versus a cross-validation copula information criterion. *Statistics and Probability Letters, 92*, 249–255.

Kinaci, H., Najjari, V., & Alp, I. (2016). Using data envelopment analysis and stochastic frontier analysis methods to evaluate efficiency of hydroelectricity centers. *Gazi University Journal of Science, 29*, 167–176.

Lai, H.-P., & Huang, C. J. (2013). Maximum likelihood estimation of seemingly unrelated stochastic frontier regressions. *Journal of Productivity Analysis, 40*, 1–14.

Lee, L.-F. (1983). Generalized econometric models with selectivity. *Econometrica, 51*, 507–512.

Li, D. X. (2000). On default correlation: A copula function approach. *Journal of Fixed Income, 9*, 43–54.

Nadarajah, S., Afuecheta, E., & Chan, S. (2017). A compendium of copulas. *Statistica, 77*, 279–329.

Najjari, V., Bal, H., Ozturk, F., & Alp, I. (2016). Stochastic frontier models by copulas and an application. *U.P.B. Scientific Bulletin, 78*, 31–41.

Nelson, R. B. (2006). *An introduction to copulas*. London: Springer.

Pipitpojanakarn, V., Maneejuk, P., Yamaka, W., & Sriboonchitta, S. (2016). Analysis of agricultural production in Asia and measurement of technical efficiency using copula-based stochastic frontier quantile model. In H. Inuiguichi, L. Le, & Denoeux (Eds.), *Integrated uncertainty in knowledge modelling and decision making, Lecture Notes in Computer Science* (Vol. 9978, pp. 701–714). Berlin: Springer.

Repkine, A. (2014). A copula-based approach to the simultaneous estimation of group and meta-frontiers by constrained maximum likelihood. *Australian Journal of Agricultural and Resource Economics, 58*, 90–110.

Schmidt, P., & Lovell, C. A. K. (1980). Estimating stochastic production and cost frontiers when technical and allocative inefficiency are correlated. *Journal of Econometrics, 13*, 83–100.

Shi, P., & Zhang, W. (2011). A copula regression model for estimating firm efficiency in the insurance industry. *Journal of Applied Statistics, 38*, 2271–2287.

Smith, M. D. (2008). Stochastic frontier models with dependent error components. *Econometrics Journal, 11*, 172–192.

Sriboonchitta, S., Liu, J., Wiboonpongse, A., & Denoeux, T. (2017). A double-copula stochastic frontier model with dependent error components and correction for sample selection. *International Journal of Approximate Reasoning, 80*, 174–184.

Tibprasorn, P., Autchariyapanitkul, K., & Sriboonchitta, S. (2017). Stochastic frontier model in financial econometrics: A copula-based approach. In Kreinovich, Sriboonchitta, & Huynh (Eds.), *Robustness in Econometrics* (Vol. 692, pp. 575–586). Cham: Springer.

Tran, K. C., & Tsionas, E. G. (2015). Endogeneity in stochastic frontier models: Copula approach without external instruments. *Economics Letters, 133*, 85–88.

Wang, W. S., Amsler, C., & Schmidt, P. (2011). Goodness of fit tests in stochastic frontier models. *Journal of Productivity Analysis, 35*, 95–118.

White, H. (1982). Maximum likelihood estimation of misspecified models. *Econometrica, 50*, 1–26.

Does Xistence of Inefficiency Matter to a Neoclassical Xorcist? Some Econometric Issues in Panel Stochastic Frontier Models

Subal C. Kumbhakar and David H. Bernstein

Abstract Does the presence of inefficiency affect estimation of the production function? This paper shows that one cannot ignore inefficiency in estimating the production function simply because standard neoclassical production theory does not recognize its existence. Exclusion of inefficiency can cause inconsistency in the estimates of the technology parameters due to omitted variables which are determinants of inefficiency. We show how one can avoid this inconsistency in estimating the production technology irrespective of whether one is interested in estimating inefficiency or not. Our proposed estimation methods use two state-of-the-art stochastic frontier (SF) panel models. Since distributional assumptions are often a bone of contention even among the followers of the SF approach, we focus on estimation methods that do not rely on distributional assumptions for the inefficiency and noise components.

Keywords Panel data · Random effects · Fixed effects · Semiparametric · Nonparametric · Omitted variables

Presented at the North American Productivity Workshop X held at the University of Miami, Coral Gables, Florida, June 12–15, 2018. The authors are grateful for the comments and suggestions by the participants. We also thank Chris Parmeter and an anonymous referee for valuable feedback which has greatly improved the paper. Any errors that remain are ours alone.

S. C. Kumbhakar (✉)
Department of Economics, State University of New York at Binghamton, Binghamton, NY, USA

University of Stavanger, Business School, Stavanger, Norway
e-mail: kkar@binghamton.edu

D. H. Bernstein
Department of Economics, University of Miami, Coral Gables, FL, USA
e-mail: dbernstein@bus.miami.edu

C. F. Parmeter, R. C. Sickles (eds.), *Advances in Efficiency and Productivity Analysis*, Springer Proceedings in Business and Economics,
https://doi.org/10.1007/978-3-030-47106-4_7

1 Introduction

To dogmatic neoclassical economists who believe in perfectly competitive markets, inefficiency is "non-existent." This is especially true in the long-run. That is, an inefficient firm cannot survive in the long-run in a competitive market. Thus, one often justifies the presence of inefficiency in regulated markets when the rules of competitive markets do not apply. In the 1970s, Leibenstein (1973) had testy exchanges with Stigler (1976) on the "xistence" of inefficiency. Stigler was a strong believer in neoclassical production theory with full efficiency. To him, inefficiency, if any, is nothing but representation of unmeasured/unobserved inputs.

The term "inefficiency" may be unfortunate, although its theoretical underpinning does not go against neoclassical production theory. In fact the textbook definition of a production function is the upper bound (maximum of output) for a given vector of inputs. We define this upper bound as the production "frontier." Thus, the neoclassical theory acknowledges the possibility that some producers may not be able to operate at the production frontier, given their input usage. The production technology is often defined in terms of a production set for a given input vector. This definition allows existence of technical inefficiency—failure to attain the production frontier (given the inputs), although there is no universally accepted theory to justify why a producer is unable to attain the production frontier.

Thus, modeling inefficiency does not go against the neoclassical theory—in fact it complements the neoclassical production theory. If all the producers operate on the production frontier, one gets back to the neoclassical production theory of full efficiency. *This is a testable hypothesis in econometrics.* That is, inclusion of inefficiency if firms are fully efficient can easily be tested, and if the test shows no inefficiency, the standard neoclassical theory holds. So the empirical question is whether ignoring inefficiency creates any econometric problems in estimating the production frontier consistently. In particular, one may not be interested in estimating inefficiency per se but everyone is interested in estimating the technology consistently. So the issue is whether consistency is affected by the omission of inefficiency in the econometric model. That is, whether there is omitted variable bias arising from ignoring inefficiency from the estimating equation.

To address this issue we consider two widely used state-of-the-art panel data stochastic frontier (SF) models. In doing this we want to accomplish two goals. First, to obtain consistent estimates of the technology parameters in the presence of inefficiency that is explained by exogenous (environmental) factors, although one may not be interested in estimating inefficiency. Second, to produce estimates of inefficiency and the marginal effects of the determinants of inefficiency after estimating the technology. In addressing these issues we do not make any distributional assumptions on the noise and inefficiency components. To estimate inefficiency, we consider a two-step procedure. The first step is focused on estimating only the technology, although in doing so one may need to include inefficiency in the estimating equation. The second-step is for estimating inefficiency and might not be of interest to those (e.g., ardent followers of Stigler) who are not into inefficiency alone.

The rest of the paper proceeds as follows. Section 2 specifies the panel SF models and derives the estimating equations to show whether exclusion of inefficiency creates inconsistency problems. Estimation issues are discussed in Sect. 3. Section 4 presents Monte Carlo simulations. Section 5 concludes the paper.

2 Model Specification

We consider two state-of-the-art and widely used panel SF models to illustrate the main points of the paper. The first model separates transient inefficiency from the firm effects. The second model does the same but adds an extra inefficiency component, viz. persistent inefficiency. We treat firm effects as either fixed or random.[1] In the fixed effects setting, we allow for possible correlation between the firm effects and the inputs. Following the SF literature, the noise and transient inefficiency components are assumed to be uncorrelated with the inputs in all the models we consider, although this assumption can be relaxed (Lai and Kumbhakar 2019).

2.1 *The Model with Firm Effects and iid Transient Inefficiency*

2.1.1 Random Firm Effects

First, we consider the case where firm effects are random and specify the production function as

$$y_{it} = \beta_0 + x_{it}'\beta + b_i + v_{it} - u_{it}, i = 1, \cdots, n; t = 1, \cdots, T \tag{2.1}$$

where y_{it} is log output for firm i at time t, x_{it} is a vector of inputs for firm i at time t (which include inputs in logarithm if the production function is Cobb–Douglas, and log inputs, their squares and cross-product terms for a translog production function), v_{it} is the noise term that is iid over i and t with zero mean and constant variance, b_i are firm effects, and $u_{it} \geq 0$ are transient inefficiency. Initially, we assume the transient inefficiency u_{it} to be iid over i and t. Since u_{it} are iid and non-negative, we assume that $E(u_{it}|x_{it}) = \mu_u > 0$ where μ_u is a constant.

Rewrite (2.1) as

$$y_{it} = (\beta_0 - \mu_u) + x_{it}'\beta + b_i + [v_{it} - \{u_{it} - \mu_u\}] \equiv \beta_0^* + x_{it}'\beta + b_i + \epsilon_{it} \tag{2.2}$$

[1] In practice, a simple Hausman test may not suffice, see, for example, (Guggenberger 2010; Amini et al. 2012).

where the error term ϵ_{it} has zero mean by construction. The model in (2.2) fits into a standard random effects (RE) panel data model, which can be estimated to produce consistent estimator of β. Thus proponents of Stigler can rightfully argue that there is no penalty in the econometric estimation of (2.2) ignoring inefficiency. In fact one will use Eq. (2.2) to estimate the parameters even if there is no inefficiency. Thus the presence of inefficiency does not change the estimating equation, except for the intercept.

2.1.2 Fixed Firm Effects

We now consider the case where the firm effects b_i are correlated with x_{it}. Although (2.2) fits into a random effects (RE) panel model, the use of GLS will give inconsistent parameter estimates because of the correlation between b_i and x_{it}. One can avoid this inconsistency problem by considering either a first difference (FD) or within transformation. The FD transformation to (2.1) gives

$$\Delta y_{it} = \Delta x_{it}'\beta + \Delta v_{it} - \Delta u_{it} \equiv \Delta x_{it}'\beta + \Delta\epsilon_{it} \tag{2.3}$$

Note that $\Delta\epsilon_{it}$ has zero mean and is uncorrelated with x_{it} under the standard assumptions. Thus one can use OLS to (2.3) to get consistent estimates of the technology parameters β. And there is no penalty in the econometric estimation of (2.3), which would be the estimating equation without inefficiency. In other words, ignoring the presence of inefficiency, if any, does not cost consistency of the parameter estimates.

2.2 *The Model with Determinants of Inefficiency and Firm Effects*

Here we consider the same two specifications discussed earlier but allow transient inefficiency to be non-iid. That is, we assume that there are exogenous variables that can explain inefficiency.

2.2.1 Random Firm Effects

The model is the same as (2.1)

$$y_{it} = \beta_0 + x_{it}'\beta + v_{it} + b_i - u_{it}, \tag{2.4}$$

but we allow the transient inefficiency u_{it} to depend on z_{it} so that $E(u_{it}|x_{it}, z_{it}) = h(z_{it}) \geq 0$ (Parmeter et al. 2017). If we rewrite (2.4) as

$$y_{it} = \beta_0 - h(z_{it}) + x_{it}'\beta + b_i + [v_{it} - \{u_{it} - h(z_{it})\}] \equiv [\beta_0 - h(z_{it})] + x_{it}'\beta + b_i + \xi_{it}, \quad (2.5)$$

so that $\xi_{it} = [v_{it} - \{u_{it} - h(z_{it})\}]$ is a zero mean random variable, (2.5) cannot be treated as a standard RE model as in (2.2) because of the presence of $h(z_{it})$ in (2.5) which cannot be subsumed by the intercept. Thus use of the RE model cannot give a consistent estimate of β unless the x and z variables are uncorrelated. And the standard RE model will suffer from omitted variable bias if inefficiency is ignored. In other words, even if one is not interested in estimating inefficiency per se, its presence cannot be ignored from the econometric model if the objective is to estimate β consistently. To put it differently, the presence of inefficiency matters in estimating the technology parameters whether one is interested in estimating it or not.

2.2.2 Fixed Firm Effects

As before we assume firm effects b_i to have zero mean, but are correlated with x_{it}. To purge this correlation we take a FD of the model in (2.4) which gives

$$\Delta y_{it} = \Delta x_{it}'\beta + \Delta v_{it} - \Delta u_{it} \equiv \Delta x_{it}'\beta - [h(z_{it}) - h(z_{it-1})] + \{\Delta v_{it} - [\Delta u_{it} - E(\Delta u_{it-1})]\} \quad (2.6)$$

Note that the error term $\{\Delta v_{it} - [\Delta u_{it} - E(\Delta u_{it-1})]\}$ has a zero mean by construction and is uncorrelated with Δx_{it}. However, one cannot use OLS to estimate (2.6) because of the presence of the unknown function $[h(z_{it}) - h(z_{it-1})]$. Note that without inefficiency the nonparametric function $[h(z_{it}) - h(z_{it-1})]$ will be absent from (2.6) and one could use OLS to estimate it. Thus, the estimating equation with and without inefficiency will be different and using OLS ignoring inefficiency (meaning excluding the nonparametric function $[h(z_{it}) - h(z_{it-1})]$) will lead to biased and inconsistent estimates of β. That is to say, inefficiency matters in getting consistent estimates of β whether one is interested in estimating it or not.

2.3 *The Model with iid Persistent and Transient Inefficiency and Firm Effects*

Now we consider the second model that generalizes the previous model by allowing an extra component of inefficiency which is time invariant (labeled as persistent technical inefficiency in Colombi et al. (2014), Kumbhakar et al. (2014), and Tsionas and Kumbhakar (2014); Filippini and Greene 2016). Although this model is proposed with random firm effects, we discuss both fixed and random firm effects.

2.3.1 Random Firm Effects

The new model is

$$y_{it} = \beta_0 + x_{it}'\beta + b_i - \eta_i + v_{it} - u_{it}, \tag{2.7}$$

where $\eta_i \geq 0$ is persistent inefficiency. All other variables are the same as before. If both the inefficiency components are iid with constant means, i.e., $E(u_{it}|x_{it}) = \mu_u$ and $E(\eta_i) = \mu_\eta$, then we can rewrite (2.7) as

$$y_{it} = \beta_0^* + x_{it}'\beta + b_i + \epsilon_{it}, \tag{2.8}$$

where $\beta_0^* = [\beta_0 - \mu_u - \mu_\eta]$ and $\epsilon_{it} = [v_{it} - (u_{it} - \mu_u) - (\eta_i - \mu_\eta)]$. Thus, ignoring both persistent and transient inefficiency will not affect consistency of the β parameters when (2.1) is estimated (instead of (2.8)) using a RE approach, provided that η_i are uncorrelated with x_{it}. That is, there is no econometric problem in estimating the technology parameters (viz. β) consistently using the RE approach when inefficiencies are excluded from the estimating equation in (2.8). This is good news for the proponents of Stigler because there is no penalty (econometrically speaking) in ignoring both components of inefficiency.

2.3.2 Fixed Firm Effects

If the firm effects b_i in (2.7) are correlated with x_{it}, the use of the GLS procedure to (2.8) will give inconsistent parameter estimates because of the correlation between b_i and x_{it}. As before one can avoid this inconsistency problem by considering the FD transformed model in (2.3) or in (2.8) and apply OLS to it to get consistent estimates of the technology parameters β. Again nothing is lost econometrically (so far as consistent estimation of β is concerned) if one ignores both persistent and transient inefficiency and estimates the FD transformed model. This is because both persistent inefficiency and firm effects are eliminated by the FD transformation.

2.4 The Model with Determinants of Persistent and Transient Inefficiency and Firm Effects

2.4.1 Random Firm Effects

We now extend the model in the preceding subsection by allowing exogenous determinants of persistent inefficiency η_i and transient inefficiency u_{it} (Badunenko and Kumbhakar 2017; Lai and Kumbhakar 2019). We do this by assuming $E(\eta_i) = g(w_i) \geq 0$ and $E(u_{it}|x_{it}, z_{it}) = h(z_{it}) \geq 0$ and rewrite the model in (2.7) as

$$y_{it} = \beta_0 - g(w_i) - h(z_{it}) + x'_{it}\beta + b_i + \tilde{\epsilon}_{it}, \tag{2.9}$$

where $\tilde{\epsilon}_{it} = [v_{it} - (\eta_i - g(w_i)) - (u_{it} - h(z_{it}))]$. It is clear that (2.9) is not a standard RE panel model and estimating it ignoring $g(w_i)$ and $h(z_{it})$ will lead to inconsistency in the estimates of the technology parameters so long as z and x are correlated. There is an endogeneity issue if persistent inefficiency (which is included in the error term) is correlated with x_{it}. Thus, as before one cannot exclude inefficiency from the estimating equation in (2.9) even if the objective is to estimate only the technology parameters. That is, a neoclassical economist cannot remove the inefficiency effects from the estimating equation, and therefore their exclusion from (2.9) will lead to inconsistency in the estimate of β parameters.

2.4.2 Fixed Firm Effects

Here the model is the same as in (2.9) above except that b_i are correlated with x_{it}. To purge this correlation we consider the FD transformation which gives

$$\Delta y_{it} = \Delta x'_{it}\beta - [h(z_{it}) - h(z_{it-1})] + \{\Delta v_{it} - [\Delta u_{it} - E(\Delta u_{it-1})]\}, \tag{2.10}$$

which is identical to the model without persistent inefficiency. This is because the persistent inefficiency (no matter whether it is iid or its mean is a function of time-constant variables, w_i) is eliminated upon the FD transformation. Even after the FD transformation one cannot ignore inefficiency because of the presence of the $-[h(z_{it}) - h(z_{it-1})]$ term in (2.10).

The model with determinants of inefficiency is more realistic because it allows both components of inefficiency to be systematically related to exogenous variables. It can explain why some firms are more or less efficient than others, and more importantly how inefficiency can be altered by changing the use of the z and w variables. For example, $\frac{\partial h(z_{it})}{\partial z_{kit}} = \frac{\partial E(u_{it})}{\partial z_{kit}}, k = 1, \cdots, K$ shows whether the kth z variable is transient efficiency enhancing or not. Similar arguments can be made about the w variables affecting persistent inefficiency. Again this might not be important to the followers of Stigler who are not interested in estimating inefficiency components and their marginal effects, but their presence cannot be ignored from the estimating Eq. (2.5) or (2.10) without affecting consistency of the β parameters.

We now summarize the main issues in terms of the two state-of-the-art SF panel models. (1) When there are factors that determine inefficiency, the technology parameters cannot be consistently estimated by ignoring/excluding inefficiency from the econometric model (estimating equation). (2) One needs to model inefficiency and it has to be included in the estimating equation in order to estimate the technology parameters consistently.

3 Estimation

In this section we consider estimation of the models discussed in the preceding section. We consider procedures to get consistent estimates of the technology parameters irrespective of whether one wants to estimate inefficiency or not. Since ignoring the presence of iid inefficiency does not matter in estimating the technology parameters, we only consider the cases where there are exogenous determinants of inefficiency.

3.1 *Models with Determinants of Inefficiency and Firm Effects*

3.1.1 Fixed Firm Effects

The estimating equation for this model specified in (2.4) is

$$y_{it} = \beta_0 - h(z_{it}) + x_{it}'\beta + b_i + [v_{it} - \{u_{it} - h(z_{it})\}], \tag{3.1}$$

where $E(u_{it}|x_{it}, z_{it}) \equiv h(z_{it}) \geq 0$ is fully nonparametric. We assume that x and z variables are separated and do not assume any functional form for the $h(z_{it})$ function.[2]

Take expectation of (2.4) conditional on z_{it}, i.e.,

$$E(y_{it}|z_{it}) = \beta_0 + E(x_{it}'|z_{it})\beta + b_i - E(u_{it}|z_{it}) = \beta_0 + E(x_{it}'|z_{it})\beta + b_i - h(z_{it}) \tag{3.2}$$

assuming that $E(v_{it}|z_{it}) = 0$. Subtracting (3.2) from (2.4) gives

$$\tilde{y}_{it} = \tilde{x}_{it}'\beta + [v_{it} - \{u_{it} - h(z_{it})\}] \equiv \tilde{x}_{it}'\beta + \xi_{it}, \tag{3.3}$$

where $\tilde{y}_{it} = y_{it} - E(y_{it}|z_{it})$ and the same for each $\tilde{x}_{it}$. By construction $E(\xi_{it}) = 0$ and therefore the model in (3.3) can be estimated using OLS. That is, OLS applied to (3.3) will give consistent estimates of the technology parameters. Note that the "tilde" transformation requires computation of conditional expectation of the y and x variables using nonparametric methods. Thus if someone is interested in only estimating the technology parameters, the story ends with the use of OLS on (3.3). This is step 1.

There are alternative estimation methods if one prefers estimating the technology parameters and inefficiency jointly. For this we consider (2.5) and write it as

$$y_{it} = \mu_i - h(z_{it}) + x_{it}'\beta + \xi_{it}, \tag{3.4}$$

[2] See Parmeter et al. (2017) for details on the estimation of this model.

where $\mu_i = \beta_0 + b_i$. In the panel data literature this model is considered both in Baltagi and Li (2002) and in Su and Ullah (2007). Following the procedure in Su and Ullah, one can get a consistent estimate of the β parameters and the $h(z_{it})$ function. To the neoclassical economists, estimation of the $h(z_{it})$ function is not of interest but its presence cannot be ignored. Since the estimate of $h(z_{it})$ comes as a by-product and we are treating $h(z_{it})$ as an estimator of inefficiency (barring the intercept which is not identified), we can estimate inefficiency from $\hat{u}_{it} = \max_i \{h(z_{it})\} - h(z_{it})$ for each t. That is, inefficiency is relative to the best firm in the sample for each year and we do this to ensure that estimated inefficiency is non-negative. Another advantage of estimating $h(z_{it})$ and the partial derivatives of it is that the derivatives are marginal effects of the z variables on inefficiency which are of interest to policy makers and practitioners.

If one prefers to estimate β in complete isolation (not in the presence of inefficiency), then the "tilde" transformation à la (Robinson 1988) in (3.3) might be preferred. Since the "tilde" transformation gives consistent estimates of β, estimation ends here for those who are interested in the estimation of the technology parameter. However, for those who also want to estimate inefficiency there is one additional step. For this we define the residuals (plugging in the estimated value of β) in (3.1),

$$r_{it} = y_{it} - x_{it}'\beta = \mu_i - h(z_{it}) + \xi_{it}. \tag{3.5}$$

This is a nonparametric FE model, estimation of which is considered by Henderson et al. (2008) and by Parmeter and Racine (2018) in the panel data literature. Thus we can obtain estimates of $h(z_{it})$ and its derivatives with respect to each z from (3.5). These derivatives are the marginal effect of each z on the mean inefficiency, and are robust to distributional assumptions. If the interest is to get relative inefficiency, then we can estimate them, as before, from $\hat{u}_{it} = \max_i \{h(z_{it})\} - h(z_{it})$ for each t.

3.1.2 Random Firm Effects

If firm effects b_i are correlated with x_{it}, then "tilde" transformation à la (Robinson 1988) still works to estimate the β parameters consistently. That is, one can use the model in (3.4) to estimate the technology parameters irrespective of whether firm effects are fixed or random. Thus step 1 is identical to the case discussed above.

Step 2: To estimate u_{it}, we need to change the equation in (3.5) and rewrite is as

$$r_{it} = y_{it} - x_{it}'\beta = [\beta_0 - h(z_{it})] + [\xi_{it} + bi] \equiv h^*(z_{it}) + \xi_{it}^*, \tag{3.6}$$

where the random firm effects term is added to the error term, and β_0 is added to the nonparametric function $h(z_{it})$ since it cannot be separated from the intercept term in $h(z_{it})$. To define r_{it} we plug in the estimated value of β. The above model can be estimated nonparametrically (see Li and Racine 2006) but it only gives estimates of relative inefficiency as before. However, in both cases one can compute the marginal effects of the z_{it} variables on inefficiency from the derivatives of $h(z_{it})$.

3.2 Models with Determinants of Persistent and Transient Inefficiency and Firm Effects

3.2.1 Fixed Firm Effects

When there are determinants of both persistent and transient inefficiency, and b_i are correlated with x_{it}, a two-step procedure can be utilized as follows.

Step 1: Following Sect. 2.4 we write the estimating equation as

$$y_{it} = \mu_i^* - h(z_{it}) + x_{it}'\beta + \epsilon_{it}, \tag{3.7}$$

where $\mu_i^* = [\beta_0 - g(w_i) + b_i]$ and $\epsilon_{it} = [v_{it} - (\eta_i - g(w_i)) - (u_{it} - h(z_{it})]$. Note that (3.7) is similar to (3.4), except for the definition of μ_i^* and the error term ϵ_{it}. Thus we can estimate (3.7) using the "tilde" transformation à la (Robinson 1988) to get consistent estimates of β. Since η_i is part of the error term, we need to make an additional assumption that it is uncorrelated with x_{it}.

Step 2: To estimate $h(z_{it})$ we consider the nonparametric FE model $r_{it} = y_{it} - x_{it}'\beta = \mu_i^* - h(z_{it}) + \epsilon_{it}$, after plugging in the estimated value of β. This can be estimated, for example, using the approach in Parmeter and Racine (2018). From the estimator of $h(z_{it})$ one can estimate marginal effect of z_k on inefficiency from $\frac{\partial h(z_{it})}{\partial z_{kit}} = \frac{\partial E(u_{it})}{\partial z_{kit}}$. Relative inefficiency can be obtained from $\hat{u}_{it} = \max_i \{h(z_{it})\} - h(z_{it})$ for each t. This part is similar to the model without persistent inefficiency.

The steps above do not give an estimate of persistent inefficiency. In fact, there is a problem in estimating persistent inefficiency η_i from $r_{it} + h(z_{it}) = \beta_0 + b_i - g(w_i) + [v_{it} - (\eta_i - g(w_i)) - (u_{it} - h(z_{it}))]$. If b_i are fixed parameters, one cannot separate (identify) b_i from η_i, since there is no cross-sectional variations left in $[v_{it} - (\eta_i - g(w_i)) - (u_{it} - h(z_{it}))]$ after the fixed effects $\mu_i^* = [\beta_0 - g(w_i) + b_i]$ are removed. Thus, although the presence of fixed b_i together with random η_i do not create any problem in estimating β and $h(z_{it})$ in the steps above, the model cannot separate (identify) η_i when b_i are fixed parameters irrespective of whether the mean of η_i is a constant or a function of some w_i variables.

3.2.2 Random Firm Effects

Given the identification problem, it is necessary to assume b_i to be random (although it can be correlated with x_{it}), if one is interested in estimating η_i. Since the "tilde" transformation removes both η_i and b_i, estimation of β in step 1 and estimation $h(z_{it})$ in step 2 remain unchanged.

Step 3: To estimate persistent inefficiency η_i from $g(w_i)$,we plug in the estimates of β and $h(z_{it})$ to get

$$\tilde{r}_{it} = y_{it} - x_{it}'\beta + h(z_{it}) = [\beta_0 - g(w_i)] + [\xi_{it} + bi - (\eta_i - g(w_i))] \equiv g^*(w_i) + \tilde{\xi}_{it}. \tag{3.8}$$

Since $g^*(w_i)$ varies cross-sectionally we can consider the following nonparametric regression to estimate $g^*(w_i)$.

$$\tilde{r}_{i.} = g^*(w_i) + \tilde{\xi}_{i.}, \tag{3.9}$$

where $\tilde{r}_{i.} = \sum_t \tilde{r}_{it}/T$ and $\tilde{\xi}_{i.} = \sum_t \tilde{\xi}_{it}/T$.
Note that β_0 cannot be separated from the nonparametric functions $g^*(w_i)$ and it is not possible to estimate persistent inefficiency absolutely. However, one can estimate marginal effects of the w_i from the estimates of $g^*(w_i)$.

4 Monte Carlo Simulations

The Monte Carlo design herein follows Badunenko and Kumbhakar (2016) for the sample sizes $n \in \{50, 100, 500\}$, time periods $t \in \{3, 6, 10\}$, and replications $R = 1000$. These results indicate that the structural parameters of a Cobb–Douglas production function will be poorly estimated under particular settings discussed in the previous sections, but perform relatively well in the null situation where the z_{it} are absent from the underlying data generating process (DGP).

4.1 *Specific Equation*

A two input production DGP with constant returns to scale is selected:

$$y_{it} = \beta_0 + \beta_1 x_{1,it} + \beta_2 x_{2,it} + b_i - 1_\eta \eta_i + v_{it} - h(z_{it})u_i^*, \tag{4.1}$$

where $X_{1,it} \sim \mathcal{U}[3, 10]$, $X_{2,it} \sim \mathcal{U}[1, 50]$, $x_{k,it} = \log(X_{k,it})$ for $k \in \{1, 2\}$, $b_i \sim \mathcal{N}(0, 0.08)$, 1_η is a zero-one indicator variable, $\beta_0 = 0.5$, $\beta_1 = 0.6$, and $\beta_2 = 0.4$. The covariates and individual effects, b_i, are fixed across all replications, whereas all other shocks change for each replication based on the seed selected. Thus, $v_{it} \sim \mathcal{N}(0, 0.08)$, $\eta_i \sim \mathcal{N}^+(0, \sigma_\eta)$, $u_i^* \sim \mathcal{N}^+(\mu, \sigma_{u^*})$ and several different assumptions are made on z_{it}:

$$\text{DGP}_0 := z_{it} \sim \mathcal{N}^+(0, 0.4) \text{ and } h(z)u^* = u, \text{ where } u_{it} \sim \mathcal{N}^+(0, 0.4) \text{ and } z \perp u;$$
$$\text{DGP}_1 := z_{it} \sim \mathcal{N}^+(0, 1) \text{ where } h(z) = e^z, \text{ and } \mu = 0;$$
$$\text{DGP}_2 := z_{it} \sim \mathcal{U}[2, 7] \text{ where } h(z) = |\sin(z)|, \text{ and } \mu = 0;$$
$$\text{DGP}_3 := z_{it} \sim \mathcal{U}[2, 5] \text{ where } h(z) = 0.2e^{0.5z}, \text{ and } \mu = 0.5.$$

Two regions for the signal to noise ratio are selected. In the first case, $\sigma_{u^*} = \sigma_\eta = 0.1$, so the signal to noise ratios are close to unity. In the second case, $\sigma_{u^*} = \sigma_\eta = 0.4$, (i.e., $\sigma_u >> \sigma_v$ and $\sigma_\eta >> \sigma_b$) to see how well the model performs when the signal to noise ratios are far from unity. DGP_0 describes the null situation where the model follows a classic stochastic frontier panel model, so that the z_{it} is uninformative about the underlying process. DGP_1 is an ordinary exponential model. DGP_2 is selected given the popularity of estimating the sin function in nonparametric settings. DGP_3 modifies the functional form of DGP_1 slightly. Lastly, the model in Eq. (4.1) is considered under both a RE framework and a FE framework along the lines of Chen et al. (2014), so that, in the FE setting:

$$x_{k,it}^{fe} = \tau b_i + \sqrt{(1 - \tau^2)} x_{k_it}, \text{ where } \tau = 0.5, \text{ for } k \in \{1, 2\},$$

while this is not the case in the RE setting. Simulation results with $\tau = 0.1$ indicate that the lower degree of correlation tends to favor conventional methods (as in Tables 2, 3, and 4). The level of MSE (as in Tables 7, 8, and 9) is also consistently lower for the "tilde" method when $\tau = 0.1$.[3] While it is also possible to introduce other forms of dependence among the covariates and transient effects, this is not necessary to illustrate the magnitude of estimation issues induced by nonlinearities in u_{it}.

4.2 Estimation and Results

This Monte Carlo experiment examines the extent to which a neoclassical economist might err in ignoring possible nonlinearities in the functional form of the z_{it}. Thus, two different possible neoclassical economists are considered. Namely, the pure xorcist ("P" before either FE or RE in Tables 1, 2, 3, and 4) estimates the model in Eq. (4.1) by standard panel methods, completely ignoring z_{it}, and the linear xorcist ("L" in Tables 1, 2, 3, and 4) estimates this model including z_{it} as a covariate. More explicitly, the estimating equations assumed by the xorcists are the following:

$$\text{pure}: y_{it} = \beta_0 + \beta_1 x_{1,it} + \beta_2 x_{2,it} + b_i + v_{it};$$
$$\text{linear}: y_{it} = \beta_0 + \beta_1 x_{1,it} + \beta_2 x_{2,it} + \beta_3 z_{it} + b_i + v_{it},$$

[3]These results are available upon request.

Table 1 DGP_0: Ratio of MSE of standard panel models to MSE of model with nonparametric 'tilde' transformation multiplied by 100 across various sample sizes

		$\sigma_{u^*} = \sigma_\eta = 0.1$								$\sigma_{u^*} = \sigma_\eta = 0.4$							
		PRE		PFE		LRE		LFE		PRE		PFE		LRE		LFE	
n	t	β_1	β_2	β_1	β_2	β_1	β_2	β_1	β_2	β_1	β_2	β_1	β_2	β_1	β_2	β_1	β_2
$1_\eta = 1$																	
50	3	76	74	83	75	77	74	84	76	93	90	95	93	94	92	96	95
100		84	68	90	81	84	68	90	81	97	89	98	93	96	90	98	94
500		94	86	96	93	94	86	96	94	100	97	100	99	100	97	100	98
50	6	81	73	85	78	81	73	85	78	97	91	98	93	96	92	98	94
100		92	83	96	87	92	84	96	87	97	96	97	97	97	97	97	97
500		99	97	98	95	99	97	98	95	100	99	99	99	100	99	99	99
50	10	88	79	90	85	89	79	90	85	97	96	98	97	98	97	98	97
100		94	86	96	89	94	86	97	89	99	94	99	95	99	95	99	95
500		95	95	97	97	95	95	97	97	100	99	100	99	100	99	100	99
$1_\eta = 0$																	
50	3	79	76	82	76	80	77	83	77	94	91	97	94	95	92	98	96
100		86	71	90	81	86	71	90	81	98	88	99	94	98	88	99	95
500		94	85	96	93	94	85	96	93	100	96	101	98	100	96	101	98
50	6	82	73	86	80	82	73	86	80	96	90	98	93	96	91	98	94
100		91	80	95	85	91	80	95	85	96	93	98	96	97	94	98	96
500		98	96	99	97	98	97	99	97	100	99	99	99	100	99	99	99
50	10	89	77	90	84	90	77	90	84	99	96	99	96	100	97	99	97
100		94	85	95	88	94	86	95	88	98	95	99	96	99	96	99	96
500		95	95	97	96	95	95	97	96	100	99	100	100	100	99	100	99

Numbers greater than 100 indicate greater performance of nonparametric 'tilde' transformation

for both the FE and RE settings. The pure and linear settings are compared to an econometrician who estimates the model with the same standard methods, for both FE and RE in the second stage, but by first performing the nonparametric "tilde" transformation on all covariates and on the dependent variable with the z_{it}. All bandwidths for the nonparametric regressions are selected using least-squares cross-validation. Furthermore, the local-linear regression has a Gaussian kernel.[4] Then, the squared error for all 1000 replications of the estimates for β_1 and β_2 is computed, and the average of the squared errors is compared as a ratio multiplied by 100. When this ratio is greater than 100, this means that the "tilde" method outperforms the pure xorcist or linear xorcist.

Prior to illustrating the strength of the "tilde" transformation method, it is important to understand how this method performs in the null setting. The null

[4]Regressions are run in R using the np package (Hayfield and Racine 2008).

Table 2 DGP_1: Ratio of MSE of standard panel models to MSE of model with nonparametric 'tilde' transformation multiplied by 100 across various sample sizes

		$\sigma_{u^*} = \sigma_\eta = 0.1$								$\sigma_{u^*} = \sigma_\eta = 0.4$							
		PRE		PFE		LRE		LFE		PRE		PFE		LRE		LFE	
n	t	β_1	β_2	β_1	β_2	β_1	β_2	β_1	β_2	β_1	β_2	β_1	β_2	β_1	β_2	β_1	β_2
$1_\eta = 1$																	
50	3	242	203	289	227	125	117	142	123	382	326	445	372	184	171	198	182
100		223	200	255	265	140	119	153	147	333	348	360	407	197	193	206	213
500		261	220	285	238	150	139	155	146	314	296	346	301	171	174	177	170
50	6	271	230	283	249	153	122	163	130	383	353	394	373	204	173	212	180
100		275	220	271	245	146	137	144	152	364	329	352	339	176	194	171	200
500		284	256	292	264	164	137	165	139	340	321	347	330	185	159	185	160
50	10	252	243	257	259	142	128	144	136	338	388	337	382	176	186	175	182
100		247	229	261	251	148	125	154	138	333	332	340	334	186	170	186	173
500		255	255	259	256	137	146	139	146	304	316	309	319	152	166	154	166
$1_\eta = 0$																	
50	3	242	206	291	232	126	119	142	126	386	331	447	380	188	174	199	185
100		225	207	252	259	142	122	151	144	336	351	366	414	201	194	210	217
500		260	215	286	237	150	135	155	145	314	294	348	301	171	171	178	170
50	6	274	240	291	253	155	126	167	132	380	356	394	375	202	173	212	181
100		275	215	271	238	146	134	144	147	363	327	350	337	176	192	170	199
500		284	253	293	263	164	135	166	138	340	321	345	330	185	158	184	160
50	10	248	238	259	256	140	126	145	134	334	380	336	394	175	183	174	188
100		245	235	261	248	147	129	154	137	335	330	340	332	187	169	187	172
500		257	252	261	259	138	144	140	148	303	317	308	318	152	165	154	166

Numbers greater than 100 indicate greater performance of nonparametric 'tilde' transformation

setting following DGP_0 exactly nests Eq. (2.7) for both the FE and RE assumptions. Thus, Table 1 shows that in the worst case scenario when $\sigma_{u^*} = \sigma_\eta = 0.4$, for $n = 100$ and $T = 3$, the "tilde" method would be nearly 12% worse at estimating β_2 relative to the pure xorcist who correctly, in this case, estimates the model, while β_1 is only 3% off in terms of mean squared error (MSE). When $\sigma_{u^*} = \sigma_\eta = 0.1$ this method becomes less accurate, given the difficulty of separating signal from noise. For moderate sample sizes, the "tilde" method becomes more accurate, eventually reaching parity both when $\sigma_{u^*} = \sigma_\eta = 0.1$ and when $\sigma_{u^*} = \sigma_\eta = 0.4$.

For DGP_1 in Table 2, when $n = 50$, $T = 3$, $\sigma_{u^*} = \sigma_\eta = 0.4$ and $1_\eta = 1$, the MSE ratio is 171 for β_2 under the linear xorcist for the RE setting. This means that the linear xorcist estimates β_2 with 71% higher MSE than the econometrician who first performs the nonparametric "tilde" transformation. The dramatic increase in MSE for the RE setting can be entirely attributed to the nonlinear nature of the conditional mean of u_{it}. When the RE assumption is relaxed, some deviance stems from the particular relationship between b_i and the covariates. The linear xorcist in

Table 3 DGP$_2$: Ratio of MSE of standard panel models to MSE of model with nonparametric 'tilde' transformation multiplied by 100 across various sample sizes

		$\sigma_{u^*} = \sigma_\eta = 0.1$								$\sigma_{u^*} = \sigma_\eta = 0.4$							
		PRE		PFE		LRE		LFE		PRE		PFE		LRE		LFE	
n	t	β_1	β_2	β_1	β_2	β_1	β_2	β_1	β_2	β_1	β_2	β_1	β_2	β_1	β_2	β_1	β_2
$1_\eta = 1$																	
50	3	63	61	77	70	64	62	78	72	103	94	112	92	103	96	111	94
100		82	59	87	69	82	60	87	70	124	89	129	95	124	90	131	96
500		101	91	103	96	102	90	104	96	162	137	169	150	160	136	167	149
50	6	71	56	80	64	72	56	81	64	117	84	128	98	118	84	129	98
100		81	70	89	81	81	70	89	81	121	100	130	112	120	99	129	111
500		105	98	106	97	105	98	105	97	163	137	167	142	161	137	166	142
50	10	95	87	96	89	95	87	96	88	130	98	137	106	129	97	137	105
100		93	81	98	86	93	81	98	86	149	120	155	132	147	119	154	131
500		101	97	103	99	101	97	103	99	169	159	173	163	169	158	172	162
$1_\eta = 0$																	
50	3	59	58	77	71	60	59	78	72	87	88	113	102	86	89	112	105
100		78	57	88	70	78	58	89	71	123	88	138	108	124	88	140	108
500		102	88	104	98	102	87	105	98	157	124	170	149	155	123	168	148
50	6	74	60	84	67	74	60	84	67	117	76	132	92	118	76	133	92
100		82	69	89	78	82	69	89	78	126	94	136	106	125	94	136	106
500		105	99	106	98	105	99	106	99	167	139	170	144	165	139	168	144
50	10	97	88	96	89	97	87	97	89	143	108	146	117	143	108	146	117
100		93	81	98	86	92	81	98	85	141	113	157	128	140	112	155	126
500		100	96	103	98	100	96	103	98	168	155	174	162	168	154	173	161

Numbers greater than 100 indicate greater performance of nonparametric 'tilde' transformation

Table 2 performs dramatically better than the pure xorcist owing to the fact that a first order approximation is better than nothing in this setting.

For DGP$_2$ in Table 3, it is interesting to note that unlike in Table 2, the linear xorcist performs almost identically to the pure xorcist, owing to the fact that a sin function is selected. Therefore, DGP$_2$ elucidates the fact that merely including the inefficiency term as a covariate may have little impact on correctly estimating the technology parameters. Further, though DGP$_1$ approximations for linear and pure estimates improve as the sample grows, DGP$_2$ estimates become worse. This demonstrates the fact that in many settings, the standard methods are not consistent.

For DGP$_2$ and DGP$_3$, Tables 3 and 4 demonstrate that for small sample sizes, neither method may be totally reliable, indicating the presence of a finite sample bias. Nonetheless, comparing outcomes as the sample size increases, it is apparent that the "tilde" method vastly outperforms the null setting described in DGP$_0$, in almost all of the settings considered.

In summary, this section covers four different DGPs, across a range of sample sizes. These four DGPs demonstrate the importance of applying advanced SFA tools. In the null situation where z_{it} is completely uninformative about the underly-

Table 4 DGP3: Ratio of MSE of standard panel models to MSE of model with nonparametric 'tilde' transformation multiplied by 100 across various sample sizes

n		$\sigma_{u^*} = \sigma_\eta = 0.1$								$\sigma_{u^*} = \sigma_\eta = 0.4$							
		PRE		PFE		LRE		LFE		PRE		PFE		LRE		LFE	
n	t	β_1	β_2	β_1	β_2	β_1	β_2	β_1	β_2	β_1	β_2	β_1	β_2	β_1	β_2	β_1	β_2
$1_\eta = 1$																	
50	3	514	525	651	655	92	86	101	88	229	248	247	275	90	87	92	91
100		579	513	731	671	97	84	103	92	271	267	288	284	96	94	98	96
500		661	621	799	793	119	116	124	122	282	260	295	280	106	105	107	106
50	6	585	476	657	611	97	75	104	91	271	262	282	275	99	92	101	95
100		672	750	761	812	108	99	113	104	299	317	309	320	102	99	103	100
500		801	750	837	818	132	125	131	127	282	306	285	313	110	107	110	107
50	10	773	646	796	701	112	98	114	104	298	243	304	252	97	87	99	91
100		773	711	820	782	121	108	123	114	309	293	315	302	105	101	105	103
500		784	748	824	781	121	113	124	114	296	287	299	288	107	102	108	102
$1_\eta = 0$																	
50	3	502	501	635	665	91	82	98	89	233	252	255	283	93	89	95	93
100		583	511	736	695	97	84	104	95	272	259	288	287	96	93	98	97
500		655	613	801	787	119	115	124	121	279	257	297	279	107	105	107	106
50	6	590	471	664	576	97	75	105	86	271	261	283	278	99	91	102	96
100		655	736	766	818	107	97	114	105	299	316	309	317	103	98	103	99
500		800	749	839	819	132	126	131	128	282	304	286	313	111	107	111	107
50	10	776	640	789	688	112	97	113	102	311	251	314	262	101	91	102	94
100		759	707	820	777	119	108	123	113	307	290	314	297	104	99	105	101
500		776	743	818	782	122	112	124	114	295	285	300	287	107	101	108	101

Numbers greater than 100 indicate greater performance of nonparametric 'tilde' transformation

ing process, very little is lost for sufficiently large sample sizes. Alternatively, when z_{it} does impact the underlying process, much can be gained from SFA methods, and recognizing the presence of inefficiency.

4.3 *State-of-the-art Methods*

Whereas Sect. 4.2 establishes superior performance of the "tilde" method to conventional methods in instances of inefficiency, and for large enough sample sizes, Sect. 4.3 focuses on the state-of-the-art. After estimation of the Cobb–Douglas parameters, one can take the resulting residuals and estimate Eq. (3.6) from Sect. 3.1, with the same nonparametric methods as in Sect. 4.2, in order to approximate the shape of $h(z)$. For simulations in Tables 5 and 6, the intercept is excluded and only the RE setting is considered. Nonetheless, the level of MSE and ρ varies from DGP to DGP.

Table 5 DGP$_1$–DGP$_3$: MSE and correlation (ρ) of $h(z)$ to $\hat{h}(z)$ across various sample sizes as well as adjusted R^2 from first stage, RE. ($\sigma_{u^*} = \sigma_\eta = 0.4$)

		DGP$_1$			DGP$_2$			DGP$_3$		
n	T	$\bar{R}^2$	ρ	MSE	$\bar{R}^2$	ρ	MSE	$\bar{R}^2$	ρ	MSE
$1_\eta = 1$										
50	3	0.33	0.93	5.99	0.85	0.76	0.08	0.69	0.97	0.17
100	3	0.28	0.94	5.97	0.86	0.88	0.07	0.68	0.98	0.15
500	3	0.26	0.96	5.65	0.89	0.97	0.05	0.72	1.00	0.13
50	6	0.33	0.94	5.86	0.88	0.88	0.07	0.73	0.98	0.15
100	6	0.33	0.95	5.71	0.91	0.93	0.06	0.76	0.99	0.13
500	6	0.29	0.97	5.60	0.91	0.98	0.05	0.76	1.00	0.13
50	10	0.35	0.95	5.74	0.91	0.92	0.06	0.78	0.99	0.14
100	10	0.32	0.96	5.69	0.91	0.95	0.05	0.76	0.99	0.13
500	10	0.28	0.98	5.58	0.92	0.99	0.05	0.77	1.00	0.13
$1_\eta = 0$										
50	3	0.34	0.93	7.10	0.86	0.90	0.25	0.70	0.97	0.45
100	3	0.29	0.94	7.08	0.87	0.94	0.23	0.69	0.98	0.42
500	3	0.27	0.96	6.74	0.90	0.98	0.20	0.72	1.00	0.39
50	6	0.33	0.94	6.96	0.89	0.94	0.23	0.73	0.98	0.42
100	6	0.33	0.95	6.81	0.91	0.97	0.21	0.77	0.99	0.39
500	6	0.29	0.97	6.69	0.91	0.99	0.20	0.76	1.00	0.39
50	10	0.35	0.95	6.82	0.91	0.96	0.21	0.78	0.99	0.41
100	10	0.32	0.96	6.78	0.91	0.98	0.20	0.76	0.99	0.39
500	10	0.28	0.98	6.68	0.92	0.99	0.20	0.77	1.00	0.40

Table 6 DGP$_1$–DGP$_3$: MSE and correlation (ρ) of $h(z)$ to $\hat{h}(z)$ across various sample sizes as well as adjusted R^2 from first stage, RE. ($\sigma_{u^*} = \sigma_\eta = 0.1$)

		DGP$_1$			DGP$_2$			DGP$_3$		
n	T	$\bar{R}^2$	ρ	MSE	$\bar{R}^2$	ρ	MSE	$\bar{R}^2$	ρ	MSE
$1_\eta = 1$										
50	3	0.82	0.93	11.88	0.93	0.45	0.31	0.90	0.99	0.40
100		0.80	0.93	11.92	0.93	0.66	0.29	0.90	1.00	0.39
500		0.81	0.96	11.81	0.94	0.92	0.28	0.92	1.00	0.38
50	6	0.83	0.94	11.90	0.94	0.69	0.30	0.92	1.00	0.39
100		0.84	0.95	11.78	0.95	0.83	0.28	0.93	1.00	0.37
500		0.83	0.97	11.79	0.95	0.95	0.28	0.93	1.00	0.38
50	10	0.85	0.95	11.82	0.95	0.80	0.28	0.94	1.00	0.38
100		0.84	0.95	11.78	0.95	0.89	0.27	0.93	1.00	0.37
500		0.82	0.97	11.81	0.95	0.97	0.28	0.93	1.00	0.38
$1_\eta = 0$										
50	3	0.82	0.92	12.28	0.93	0.48	0.39	0.90	0.99	0.50
100		0.80	0.93	12.33	0.93	0.72	0.37	0.90	1.00	0.48
500		0.81	0.96	12.22	0.94	0.93	0.36	0.92	1.00	0.47
50	6	0.83	0.94	12.30	0.94	0.75	0.38	0.92	1.00	0.49
100		0.84	0.95	12.18	0.95	0.86	0.36	0.93	1.00	0.47
500		0.83	0.97	12.19	0.95	0.96	0.35	0.93	1.00	0.47
50	10	0.85	0.95	12.21	0.95	0.84	0.35	0.94	1.00	0.47
100		0.84	0.95	12.18	0.95	0.91	0.35	0.93	1.00	0.46
500		0.83	0.97	12.21	0.95	0.97	0.36	0.93	1.00	0.47

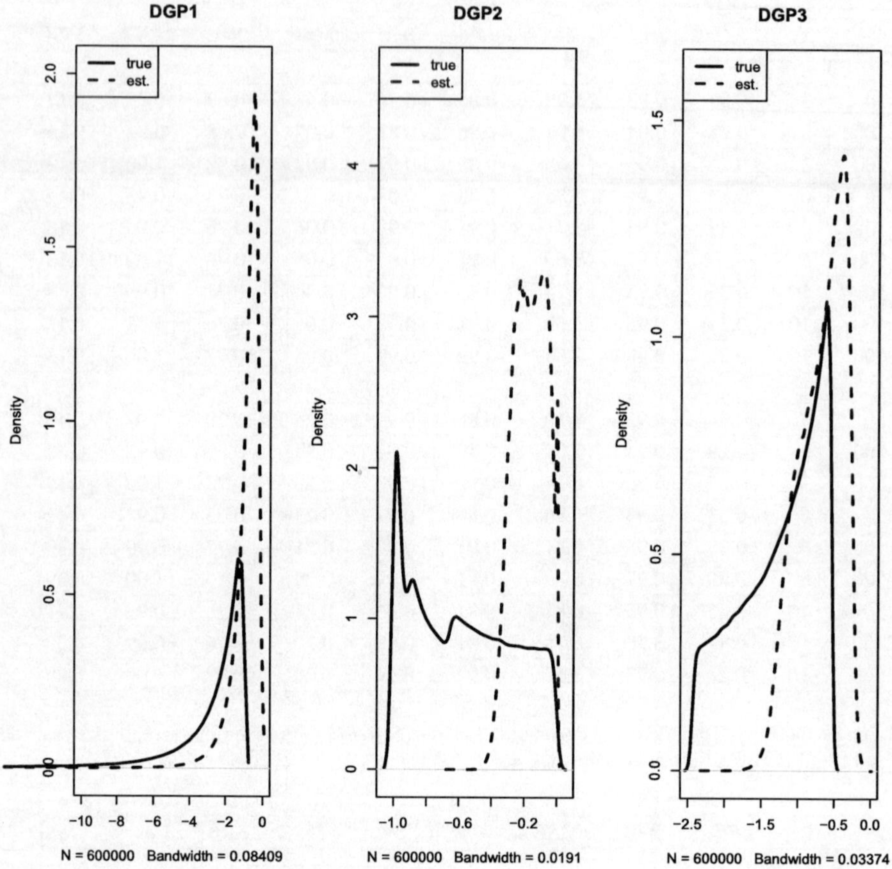

Fig. 1 Density plots of $h(z)$ and $\hat{h}(z)$ for DGP$_1$–DGP$_3$, for $T = 6$, $n = 100$, $\sigma_{u^*} = \sigma_\eta = 0.4$

Tables 5 and 6 give the MSE and correlation (ρ) between the true value of $h(z)$ and the estimated values for DGP$_1$-DGP$_3$. Additionally, the adjusted R-squared ($\bar{R}^2$) from the first stage is given. For each DGP, it can be seen that both correlation and MSE are roughly converging with the sample size. When $1_\eta = 1$, $h(z)$ is estimated up to a constant. Equation (3.6) would not work to estimate $h(z)$ when $1_\eta = 1$ if η_i contained nonlinearities such as u_{it}, and results from Sect. 3.2 would be necessary. However, as $\eta_i \sim \mathcal{N}^+(0, 0.4)$ across all simulations, this is not a concern.

Figures 1 and 2 illustrate how the average density (using all 1000 replications: i.e., $6 \times 10 \times 1000 = 600{,}000$ data points) of estimated values of $\hat{h}(z)$ deviates from

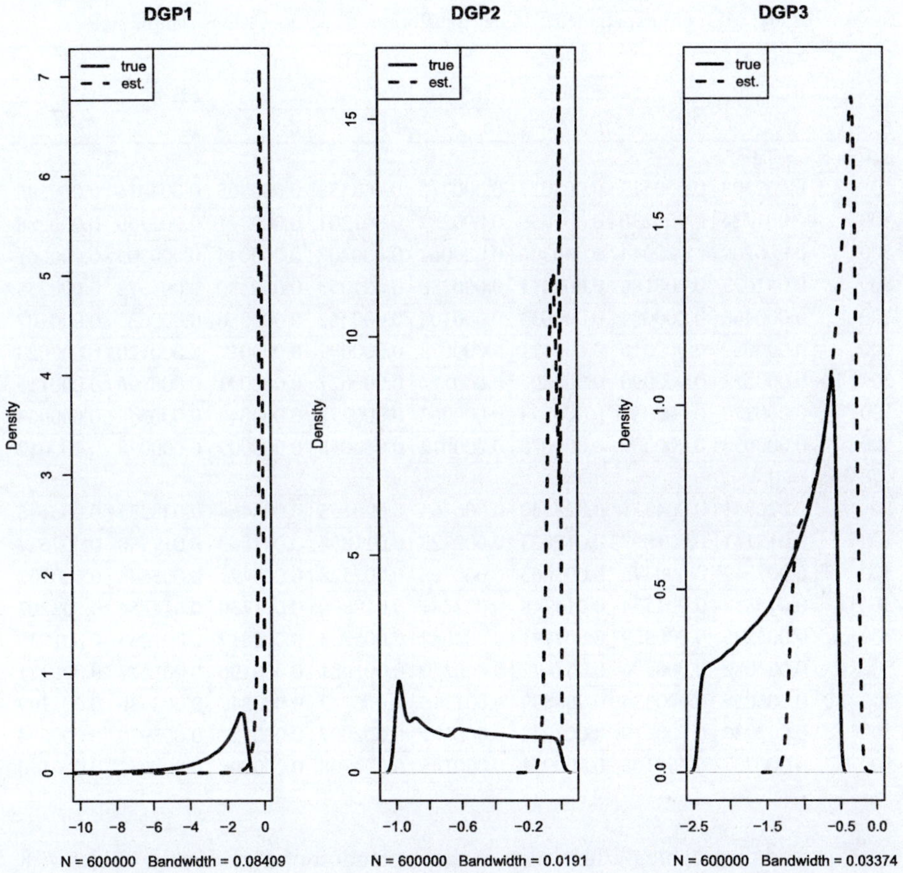

Fig. 2 Density plots of $h(z)$ and $\hat{h}(z)$ for DGP$_1$–DGP$_3$, for $T = 6$, $n = 100$, $\sigma_{u^*} = \sigma_\eta = 0.1$

the true density $h(z)$ for DGP$_1$–DGP$_3$, $T = 6$, $n = 100$, and assuming RE with $1_\eta = 0$. These figures also demonstrate that being in a large signal to noise setting is crucial in obtaining a small MSE, despite the strong performance of correlation. Tables 7, 8, and 9 demonstrate the rate of convergence of DGP$_1$–DGP$_3$, respectively. It can be seen that the functional form as well as degree of noise impacts the level of MSE, but that both β_1 and β_2 are clearly converging for each DGP, regardless of the signal to noise ratio.

In summary, this section covers the three non-null DGPs, across a range of sample sizes. Tables 5 and 6 illustrate that the level of MSE decreases across all simulations as the sample size increases, and the correlation also increases. Figures 1

Table 7 DGP$_1$: MSE of nonparametric 'tilde' transformation across various sample sizes

		$1_\eta = 1$				$1_\eta = 0$			
		RE		FE		RE		FE	
n	t	β_1	β_2	β_1	β_2	β_1	β_2	β_1	β_2
$\sigma_{u^*} = \sigma_\eta = 0.1$									
50	3	0.002393	0.000513	0.003027	0.000713	0.002358	0.000505	0.003014	0.000696
100		0.001224	0.000230	0.001736	0.000282	0.001201	0.000221	0.001759	0.000288
500		0.000209	0.000044	0.000304	0.000061	0.000207	0.000044	0.000303	0.000061
50	6	0.001073	0.000186	0.001411	0.000238	0.001053	0.000180	0.001373	0.000235
100		0.000466	0.000084	0.000634	0.000104	0.000462	0.000086	0.000633	0.000107
500		0.000089	0.000016	0.000121	0.000023	0.000089	0.000017	0.000120	0.000023
50	10	0.000617	0.000090	0.000802	0.000114	0.000627	0.000091	0.000796	0.000115
100		0.000270	0.000051	0.000348	0.000062	0.000272	0.000049	0.000348	0.000063
500		0.000058	0.000009	0.000078	0.000012	0.000058	0.000009	0.000078	0.000012
$\sigma_{u^*} = \sigma_\eta = 0.4$									
50	3	0.020741	0.004521	0.028450	0.006264	0.020165	0.004464	0.028335	0.006146
100		0.012141	0.001897	0.017823	0.002723	0.011854	0.001863	0.017548	0.002677
500		0.002542	0.000475	0.003663	0.000703	0.002528	0.000471	0.003644	0.000702
50	6	0.010837	0.001734	0.014748	0.002281	0.010860	0.001730	0.014754	0.002267
100		0.005275	0.000809	0.007191	0.001082	0.005233	0.000817	0.007233	0.001085
500		0.001082	0.000196	0.001472	0.000270	0.001081	0.000196	0.001477	0.000271
50	10	0.006654	0.000834	0.008899	0.001146	0.006727	0.000848	0.008936	0.001109
100		0.002930	0.000519	0.003922	0.000691	0.002907	0.000521	0.003920	0.000694
500		0.000707	0.000108	0.000951	0.000145	0.000708	0.000108	0.000953	0.000146

and 2 provide a graphical illustration of the estimation of $h(z)$. Lastly, Tables 7, 8, and 9 in Sect. 4.3 can also be viewed as the denominators of Tables 2, 3, and 4 in Sect. 4.2, so one can get an idea of the degree of accuracy these methods have intrinsically.

5 Conclusion

This paper showed that one cannot ignore inefficiency in estimating the production function just because the standard neoclassical production theory does not recognize its existence, especially when inefficiency can be explained by some exogenous variables. We showed that exclusion of inefficiency causes inconsistency in the estimate

Table 8 DGP$_2$: MSE of nonparametric 'tilde' transformation across various sample sizes

		$1_\eta = 1$				$1_\eta = 0$			
		RE		FE		RE		FE	
n	t	β_1	β_2	β_1	β_2	β_1	β_2	β_1	β_2
$\sigma_{u^*} = \sigma_\eta = 0.1$									
50	3	0.000967	0.000201	0.001066	0.000252	0.001079	0.000202	0.001062	0.000250
100		0.000373	0.000084	0.000529	0.000099	0.000361	0.000084	0.000519	0.000098
500		0.000057	0.000012	0.000085	0.000016	0.000054	0.000012	0.000084	0.000016
50	6	0.000441	0.000074	0.000515	0.000089	0.000436	0.000070	0.000493	0.000084
100		0.000158	0.000026	0.000196	0.000031	0.000153	0.000026	0.000195	0.000032
500		0.000025	0.000004	0.000034	0.000006	0.000025	0.000004	0.000034	0.000006
50	10	0.000170	0.000024	0.000224	0.000032	0.000166	0.000024	0.000224	0.000032
100		0.000076	0.000014	0.000097	0.000018	0.000075	0.000014	0.000098	0.000018
500		0.000014	0.000002	0.000019	0.000003	0.000015	0.000002	0.000019	0.000003
$\sigma_{u^*} = \sigma_\eta = 0.4$									
50	3	0.001722	0.000407	0.002208	0.000578	0.002017	0.000403	0.002196	0.000519
100		0.000828	0.000165	0.001083	0.000210	0.000735	0.000161	0.001013	0.000185
500		0.000114	0.000024	0.000152	0.000030	0.000108	0.000024	0.000152	0.000031
50	6	0.000730	0.000143	0.000890	0.000165	0.000735	0.000158	0.000861	0.000175
100		0.000316	0.000054	0.000395	0.000065	0.000301	0.000056	0.000377	0.000068
500		0.000048	0.000008	0.000063	0.000011	0.000047	0.000008	0.000062	0.000011
50	10	0.000374	0.000065	0.000472	0.000080	0.000334	0.000058	0.000442	0.000073
100		0.000139	0.000029	0.000178	0.000036	0.000144	0.000031	0.000176	0.000037
500		0.000025	0.000005	0.000033	0.000006	0.000025	0.000005	0.000033	0.000006

of the technology (parameters) due to omitted variables which are determinants of inefficiency. Finally, using two widely used state-of-the-art stochastic frontier panel models, we showed how one can avoid this inconsistency irrespective of whether one is interested in estimating inefficiency or not. Monte Carlo simulations help to elucidate these findings and shed some light on how to estimate the components of transient inefficiency. Unlike the existing stochastic frontier models, our proposed estimation methods do not use distributional assumptions on firm effects, noise and inefficiency components.

Table 9 DGP_3: MSE of nonparametric 'tilde' transformation across various sample sizes

		$1_\eta = 1$				$1_\eta = 0$			
		RE		FE		RE		FE	
n	t	β_1	β_2	β_1	β_2	β_1	β_2	β_1	β_2
$\sigma_{u^*} = \sigma_\eta = 0.1$									
50	3	0.001181	0.000226	0.001412	0.000306	0.001200	0.000232	0.001447	0.000301
100		0.000519	0.000100	0.000712	0.000131	0.000509	0.000098	0.000707	0.000126
500		0.000085	0.000016	0.000115	0.000022	0.000084	0.000016	0.000115	0.000022
50	6	0.000520	0.000097	0.000653	0.000107	0.000516	0.000097	0.000646	0.000114
100		0.000211	0.000029	0.000271	0.000037	0.000213	0.000030	0.000269	0.000037
500		0.000034	0.000006	0.000045	0.000008	0.000033	0.000006	0.000045	0.000008
50	10	0.000234	0.000035	0.000303	0.000044	0.000233	0.000035	0.000306	0.000045
100		0.000097	0.000018	0.000130	0.000023	0.000098	0.000018	0.000130	0.000023
500		0.000020	0.000003	0.000027	0.000005	0.000020	0.000003	0.000027	0.000005
$\sigma_{u^*} = \sigma_\eta = 0.4$									
50	3	0.004404	0.000873	0.005791	0.001119	0.004285	0.000848	0.005615	0.001089
100		0.002084	0.000351	0.002857	0.000473	0.002064	0.000352	0.002852	0.000469
500		0.000374	0.000068	0.000503	0.000093	0.000368	0.000068	0.000500	0.000093
50	6	0.001781	0.000284	0.002348	0.000363	0.001777	0.000284	0.002339	0.000360
100		0.000816	0.000105	0.001081	0.000139	0.000805	0.000106	0.001082	0.000140
500		0.000152	0.000025	0.000204	0.000034	0.000151	0.000025	0.000203	0.000034
50	10	0.000943	0.000147	0.001227	0.000190	0.000905	0.000142	0.001186	0.000183
100		0.000389	0.000071	0.000519	0.000093	0.000389	0.000072	0.000521	0.000094
500		0.000085	0.000014	0.000113	0.000019	0.000085	0.000014	0.000112	0.000019

References

Amini, S., Delgado, M. S., Henderson, D. J., & Parmeter, C. F. (2012). Fixed vs Random: The Hausman test four decades later. *Essays in Honor of Jerry Hausman, 29*, 479–513.

Badunenko, O., & Kumbhakar, S.C. (2016). When, where and how to estimate persistent and transient efficiency in stochastic frontier panel data models. *European Journal of Operational Research, 255*, 272–287.

Badunenko, O., & Kumbhakar, S.C. (2017). Economies of scale, technical change and persistent and time-varying cost efficiency in Indian banking: Do ownership, regulation and heterogeneity matter? *European Journal of Operational Research, 260*(2), 789–803. https://doi.org/10.1016/j.ejor.2017.01.025.

Baltagi, B.H., & Li, D. (2002). Series estimation of partially linear panel data models with fixed effects. *Annals of Economics and Finance, 3*, 103–116.

Chen, Y., Schmidt, P., & Wang, H., (2014). Consistent estimation of the fixed effects stochastic frontier model. *Journal of Econometrics, 181*, 65–76.

Colombi, R., Kumbhakar, S.C., Martini, G., & Vittadini, G. (2014). Closed-skew normality in stochastic frontiers with individual Effects and Long/Short-run Efficiency. *Journal of Productivity Analysis, 42*, 123–136.

Filippini, M., & Greene, W.H. (2016). Persistent and transient productive inefficiency: A maximum simulated likelihood approach. *Journal of Productivity Analysis, 45*, 187–196.

Guggenberger, P. (2010). The impact of a Hausman pretest on the size of a hypothesis test: The panel data case. *Journal of Econometrics, 156*, 337–343.

Hayfield, T., & Racine, J. S. (2008). Nonparametric econometrics: The NP package. *Journal of Statistical Software, 27*(5), 1–32.

Henderson, D. J, Carroll, R. J., & Li, Q. (2008). Nonparametric estimation and testing of fixed effects panel data models. *Journal of Econometrics, 144*, 257–275.

Kumbhakar, S. C., Lien, G., & Hardaker, J. B. (2014). Technical efficiency in competing panel data models: A study of Norwegian Grain Farming. *Journal of Productivity Analysis, 41*, 321–337.

Lai, H., & Kumbhakar, S. C. (2019). Technical and allocative efficiency in a panel stochastic production frontier system model. *European Journal of Operational Research, 278*(1), 255–265. https://doi.org/10.1016/j.ejor.2019.04.001.

Leibenstein, H. (1973). Competition and X-Efficiency: Reply. *Journal of Political Economy, 81*, 765–77.

Li, Q., & Racine, J. S. (2006). *Nonparametric econometrics theory and practice*. Princeton, NJ: Princeton University Press.

Parmeter, C. F., & Racine, J. (2018). Nonparametric estimation and inference for panel data models. In *McMaster University - Department of Economics Working Paper* (2018–02).

Parmeter, C. F., Wang, H., & Kumbhakar, S. C. (2017). Nonparametric estimation of the determinants of inefficiency. *Journal of Productivity Analysis, 47*, 205–221.

Robinson, P. M. (1988). Root-N-Consistent semiparametric regression. *Econometrica, 56*, 931–954.

Stigler, G. J. (1976). The Xistence of X-Efficiency. *American Economic Review, 66*, 213–216.

Su, L., & Ullah, A. (2007). More efficient estimation of nonparametric panel data models with random effects. *Economics Letters, 96*, 375–380.

Tsionas, E. G., & Kumbhakar, S. C. (2014). Firm heterogeneity, persistent and transient technical inefficiency: A generalized true random effects model. *Journal of Applied Econometrics, 29*, 110–132.

The Two-Tier Stochastic Frontier Framework (2TSF): Measuring Frontiers Wherever They May Exist

Alecos Papadopoulos

1 Introduction

Stochastic frontier analysis (SFA) focuses mostly on measuring and analyzing matters of efficiency in production and in cost decisions, based on the conceptual and modeling device of a *frontier*, a boundary beyond which a firm can find itself only by chance, literally. But the existence of frontiers in human activity is a consequence of physical and of *economic* scarcity: the fact that resources are always less than what we would desire to have available in order to fulfill whatever needs and wants we are able to imagine (or cannot ignore no matter how hard we try). Scarcity creates restrictions, constraints, bounds, boundaries... frontiers. Therefore "frontier modeling" is not constrained to be a specialized tool for efficiency and productivity analysis but can be used as a general methodological approach to formulate and then study economic phenomena (and not only).

The two-tier stochastic frontier model (2TSF henceforth) occupies a rather small place in the SFA field. But it shows in a tangible way how the concept of efficiency goes beyond direct matters of production and cost, and more generally, it is the clearest and most colorful example of how frontier modeling can be applied to very diverse situations, economic and non-economic alike. For this reason we will often call it the 2TSF *framework*. It has been proposed in the literature 30 years

This review paper draws material from my PhD thesis Papadopoulos (2018), where one can find all necessary tools to implement in empirical studies the various models that are presented here summarily for matters of space.

A. Papadopoulos (✉)
Athens University of Economics and Business, Athens, Greece
e-mail: papadopalex@aueb.gr

C. F. Parmeter, R. C. Sickles (eds.), *Advances in Efficiency and Productivity Analysis*, Springer Proceedings in Business and Economics,
https://doi.org/10.1007/978-3-030-47106-4_8

ago, lying rather dormant for its first two decades of existence. But in the last ten years researchers have started to realize its flexibility and potential and many applications and theoretical extensions have been published, while this newfound interest appears to be accelerating. Still, a review of the 2TSF framework has yet to be written, and this is the purpose of the present work: to provide an overview of the empirical applications, the theoretical foundations, and the technical tools that currently constitute the 2TSF framework.

The generating mechanism of our object of study can be very simple: suppose that we have an outcome/dependent variable y for which we postulate that it is a function $f(\cdot)$ of a vector of explanatory variables/regressors $\mathbf{x}$ on which we have data. The dependent variable is further affected by a stochastic noise/disturbance/shock/error denoted v. Suppose now that we know (or that we can adequately argue) that apart from $\mathbf{x}$ and v, there exist two forces that affect y each in the opposite direction, but for which we possess no data. Denote the positive influence w and the negative influence u. Since we have no data on them, it is natural to treat them both as one-sided (positive) latent random variables attaching a negative sign to the one representing the negative influence. Then the expression for the dependent variable becomes

$$y = f(\mathbf{x}) + \varepsilon, \quad \varepsilon = v + w - u.$$

Single-tier SF models in their various incarnations use either u or w. By using both, the 2TSF framework transforms the representation of the frontier: in a single-tier model $f(\mathbf{x})$ is the deterministic frontier, and $f(\mathbf{x}) + v$ is its stochastic counterpart, while w or u (which one is present) measure the distance from it. In the 2TSF context there are *two inherently stochastic* frontiers and w or u *take part in determining the one while measuring the distance from the other:* $f(\mathbf{x}) + v + w$ represents the stochastic upper frontier (or the frontier of the "seller" in an economic exchange) while u represents the distance from it. At the same time, $f(\mathbf{x}) + v - u$ represents the stochastic lower frontier (or the frontier of the buyer), and here it is w that measures the distance from the latter.

This is the 2TSF model, characterized by its three-component composite error term, its two-sided frontier concept, and its applicability to a large number of circumstances. And indeed researchers have used it to model all sort of situations, as the literature review in Sect. 2 makes evident. Section 3 analyzes specific structural foundations that have been proposed in order to rationalize the 2TSF model more concretely, while Sect. 4 presents the technical tools available for its implementation in empirical studies. A final section discusses some novel applications of the 2TSF approach, as well as suggesting how the many new methods that have been developed rather recently in its context can be used to revisit familiar domains with new eyes and knives.

2 Roads Taken: Applications of the 2TSF Framework

2.1 Labor Market

The 2TSF model was introduced by Polachek and Yoon (1987) with a focus on the labor market. The authors pointed to the fact that even in relatively homogeneous competitive labor markets we observe wage variation and not a single equilibrium wage as standard theory would predict. Based on search theory premises, they attributed this phenomenon to the (optimal) existence of incomplete information: employees searching for work do not know of all the opportunities and work offers (because it would be costly to obtain such information). On the other hand, employers do not know all workers that search for work, and what they would be willing to supply at any given wage. And because incomplete information is heterogeneous and varies from employer to employer and from employee to employee, we also observe wage dispersion.

In order to estimate both effects, the authors extended previous work by Hofler and Polachek (1982) where a single-tier SF model with a negative one-sided term was used to estimate the effects of "employee ignorance" only, to which they added an additional one-sided unobservable term representing now the "employer ignorance" and having a positive effect on the realized wage, arriving at a composite error term of the form $\varepsilon = v + w - u$. The systematic part of the regression equation represented the wage under full information but taking into account individual heterogeneity and variation around the observable characteristics of the "average" firm-worker pair. And thus, the 2TSF model was born, technically as a combination of a "production" and a "cost" frontier in the same equation.

The authors assumed that the two one-sided error terms each followed an Exponential distribution, derived the density of the three-component error term (the third one being the random disturbance, assumed to follow a zero-mean Normal distribution), and applied maximum likelihood estimation. They also stratified their sample and calculated measures of employee and employer ignorance for various subsamples partitioned according to characteristics like gender, race, education, and tenure. In all cases, the realized wage was on average below the full-information estimated level.

The stratification exercise in the foundational 2TSF paper accounted up to a degree for the existence of heterogeneity that was used to rationalize the observed wage dispersion. 2TSF models that directly allowed for heterogeneity at the observation level came later. Groot and Oosterbeek (1994) extended the model in order to explain information effects through individual attributes, by assuming that the moments of each one-sided disturbance is a linear function of the regressors and/or other variables.[1] Since the assumed distributions have a single parameter, this

[1]From a technical point of view one can object to the linear formulation used by the authors, since these parameters should be constrained to be positive, as noted in Parmeter (2018). Specifying an exponential function instead solves this issue.

setup not only allowed for individual heterogeneity regarding the mean value, but also accommodated conditional heteroskedasticity. Using data from the Netherlands the authors found that average realized wages were *above* the full-information wage.

Polachek and Yoon (1996) extended their original model to accommodate earnings-related panel data in order to disentangle *unobserved* individual heterogeneity from the informational imperfections. They found that the panel-data approach improved the quality of the results, and that the significance of incomplete information, although it was reduced, persisted.

Polachek (2017) digs more deeply into the relation between unobservable individual heterogeneity and incomplete information by combining the 2TSF model with research from Polachek et al. (2013, 2015) that exploited the fact that, as the years pass, long-enough time-series data on *individuals* have become available, allowing the authors to estimate five key individual parameters for a specific sample of persons. Three of these parameters measure two types of ability, another quantifies skill depreciation, and the last one constitutes the respondent's time discount rate. Polachek (2017) estimates then a 2TSF model for the same individuals, while using these five parameters to stratify the data and obtain how incomplete information may change in each subgroup.

Kumbhakar and Parmeter (2009) proposed a different reason why variations around the full-information wage exist: they pointed out that the value of an employer–employee match is uncertain and remains so, and it is this uncertainty that creates the necessary space for *bargaining* to take place. And in a bargaining situation over some price, each side tries to pull the outcome in opposing directions: a framework suitable for the 2TSF approach. Their model estimates the expected value of the match (the observable systematic component of the regression equation), and, through the two one-sided error components, the monetary value of the gap claimed by the two negotiating parties (depending on their relative bargaining power). Regarding quantitative findings, they obtained that the bargaining power of buyers (employers) was relatively higher than that of sellers (employees), leading the realized wage to be on average below the expected value of the match.

Blanco (2017) focused on the market for job placement services. He found that employees that used these services are not more informed about wage offers than employees that did not use them, while firms that employed individuals through job placement agencies are more informed about reservation wages relative to firms that did not use such services. Combined, these results tell us that job placement services tend to benefit more the employer side.

Das and Polachek (2017a, b) developed a new panel-data 2TSF model in order to estimate *gross* flows in and out of the labor market, employment and unemployment ("Joiners and Leavers"), flows that are more important (compared to net ones) in order to understand the actual dynamics of this market. The model embeds heterogeneity directly into the composite error term of the 2TSF specification.

Other studies of the labor market and the wage equation using the basic or heteroskedastic 2TSF framework are Sharif and Dar (2007), Murphy and Strobl (2008), and Dar (2014).

2.2 Health Services Market

The 2TSF model has also seen applications in the health services market, where informational asymmetries and inefficiencies are believed to abound, favoring the supply side of the market. Gaynor and Polachek (1994) applied it to the physician services' market in the USA arguing that the observed wide variations in physician fees went beyond differences in quality-of-service, and part of them were to be explained by the incomplete and asymmetric information of the market participants. Their findings aligned with conventional wisdom, estimating that the monetary effects of the incomplete patient information were approximately 50 percent greater than those of the incomplete physician information. The paper also contained a new structural 2TSF framework that we will present in the next section.

In a purely empirical paper Chawla (2002) used the original 2TSF model on health services data from Egypt, and also found that doctors were extracting a larger surplus in their transactions with the patients.

Tomini et al. (2012) estimated the effects of incomplete information on the informal ("under-the-table") payments made to physicians, using a sample from Albania. They found that prices were *below* full-information levels, meaning that patients were better informed than doctors in these transactions, and this has intuition: in the absence of a public market and price system, buyers–patients tend to exchange more information regarding informal costs, while on the other hand sellers–doctors possess less information for the same reasons, and also tend to avoid exchanging information because informal revenues are considered unethical and usually are illegal. The fundamental asymmetry here is the fact that patients are not saddled with the moral burden of participating in an illegal/unethical transaction, because they are the ones in need. Nevertheless, the inherent asymmetry in the *bargaining* power that favors the physicians should still be present, implying that the informational advantage of the patients is strong enough to more than offset it.

2.3 A Lot of Other Markets (And Not Only Markets)

Kumbhakar and Parmeter (2010) developed a 2TSF hedonic price framework for the house-selling market, and applied it to the US data. As Pope (2008) observes, it is reasonable to expect incomplete and asymmetric information in the housing market, since sellers have lower search costs and are more informed than buyers by virtue of knowing the property beforehand and/or actually living in the area.

Rajapaksa (2015) applied their model to the housing market in Brisbane, Australia and found that the incomplete information of the buyer was higher than that of the seller's, leading to a price above the full-information level, in accordance with the argument in Pope (2008). But in the empirical study in the Kumbhakar and Parmeter paper, the selling price was found to be somewhat *below* the full-information one, showing that buyers are in a better position than sellers (in both the standard model as well as in its heteroskedastic variant).

We can rationalize this result by observing that sometimes houses are sold under financial distress for the sellers, creating an unfavorable *bargaining* situation for their side that may mitigate and even reverse their informational advantage. We encountered an analogous situation just previously in the health services market, where information and bargaining effects may "compete" with each other in the *same* side of the transaction. This creates an interesting identification and measurement challenge for which we will have more to say later on.

The 2TSF Nash bargaining framework mentioned previously has seen many applications to other markets and situations. Kinukawa and Motohashi (2010, 2016) applied the model to the biotechnology market and the trading of biotechnologies/knowledge assets through company alliances/collaborations that are very common in this market. They too found that buyers had greater bargaining power than sellers.

Wang (2016a) applied it to the field of bilateral aid to developing countries. The related literature has identified different setups in which aid takes place. One of them is the "aid-for-policy" framework, where aid is conditioned on the recipient countries implementing specific policies, either because the donors are self-interested and they require something in return, or because they are altruistic but have specific opinions as to what policies would benefit the population of the recipient country. Here the donors are the "buyers," "buying" the aid-recipients' government command over local resources and the authority to implement policies. The author found that donor countries enjoyed more bargaining power in surplus division than recipients. This conclusion was reinforced by the empirical study in Wang (2016b) related to the US economic aid for the period 1976–2011.

Zhang et al. (2017) applied the bargaining model to the tourism industry in relation to tourist shopping. They found that tourists (buyers) extract a *higher* surplus compared to the sellers, which perhaps runs against widely held expectations that picture tourists as temporary customers, outside their comfort zone and their supporting social networks, and so in a "weaker" position than sellers and ripe for exploitation. But on a second thought the results have intuition. Doing business with tourists is a high-volume short-length activity and so sellers are pressed to complete a high volume of transactions in a short period of time. This weakens *their* position in a bargaining situation, since they will bear the hidden cost of losing business if each individual negotiation is protracted. On the other hand tourists come in the negotiation with a bias that sellers will try to "rip them off" and so we may expect that they will put up a tough negotiating stance from the beginning.

Ferona and Tsionas (2012) examined auctions in order to assess the extent of *systematic* underbidding and overbidding behavior. Using data from timber auctions, they found that overbidding behavior dominated. In a tasty paper, Fried and Tauer (2019) applied the model to study over-pricing and under-pricing in the wine market of US Rieslings in the period 2000–2016. Their empirical finding of average over-pricing was not so tasty.

These applications already exemplify the wide reach of the 2TSF framework, outside the traditional topics of research in SFA. But there is more.

Researchers in China have taken a strong interest in the model, and although at times their approach is lacking as regards the conceptual and/or formal justification of its use, their work certainly exemplifies the ability of the model to analyze very diverse situations:[2] Lian and Chung (2008), Yu and Liang (2012), Zhang and Zheng (2012), Li et al. (2014), and Wen et al. (2016) used it to investigate the effects of financing constraints and agency costs on investment behavior and also on dividend policies, of listed Chinese firms. Lv (2013) investigated volume and efficiency in R&D investment of Chinese listed companies, pitting agency conflicts against incentive compatibility through a 2TSF model. The effects were reported as large but diminishing through time. Wei (2015) studied the opposing forces of financial constraints and government subsidies on R&D investment. Lin et al. (2017) synthesized these topics by examining the effects of financing constraints and agency costs on R&D investment specifically. Liu (2017) examined the internal struggles in corporations that may lead to over-investment, while Xie and Li (2018) applied the model in order to measure investment efficiency and test whether equity-incentives to management had an effect on the former.

Zheng and Zhang (2012a), Huang (2013), and Liu and Liu (2014) used the model to separate the "premium" effect from the "under-pricing" effect in Initial Public Offerings (IPOs) of Chinese firms. All three studies found that the under-pricing effect dominated in the samples examined. Huang et al. (2017) went one step deeper and decomposed the under-pricing effect into a discount effect from the primary market and a premium effect from the secondary market. Zheng and Zhang (2012b) examined extreme IPO returns. Tao et al. (2014) examined the allocation of bargaining power between listed companies and banks in the credit market (and found that banks had the upper hand). Du and Wei (2014) used the model to measure the efficiency of urban industrial emissions. Zhang and Sun (2015) investigated the exchange rate of China's currency RBM using the 2TSF model, and found evidence that, if anything, the intervention of the Chinese government in the exchange market tends to *overvalue* the currency, contrary to the predominant belief. Xu et al. (2016) identified a dual effect of government intervention on the real-estate market in China, one tending to increase prices and one tending to decrease them, and used the 2TSF model to quantify them. Yan and Qi (2017) used the 2TSF model to study the effects of asymmetric information and bargaining power in the fruit export market in China. Lyu et al. (2018) visited the labor market and examined the compensation of CEOs in Chinese firms using the 2TSF Nash bargaining model.

And then, we have the truly exotic applications.

Groot and van den Brink (2007) used the 2TSF framework to measure the effects of "optimism" and "pessimism" in self-reported quality of life. Compared to the estimated "realistic" (mean) values of life satisfaction, they found that "optimistic"

[2] We were not able to obtain full English copies for some of the papers from China referenced here, so for them we rely on the available abstracts.

people are *too* optimistic, while "pessimistic" people tend in comparison to be below of, but much closer to, the realistic value of life satisfaction. Other findings of their study were that men are relatively more optimistic and less pessimistic than women. Also, that cardiovascular disease makes people both less optimistic and less pessimistic, i.e. it dampens the intensity of these psychological tendencies, which is a reasonable result considering that people with such health issues are advised and usually do try to avoid strong emotional states.

Poggi (2010) went back to the labor market, but this time in order to measure "perceived job satisfaction" and how it is affected by downward and upward biases created by peoples' aspirations. She found that perceived job satisfaction languished on average a good 13% below its realistic level, a result that is consistent with the findings of the previous study: optimism (high aspirations) leads to disappointment and downward bias in evaluating the actual situation.

2.4 The DEA Connection

We close this section with the sister field of Data Envelopment Analysis (DEA), where there also exist papers similar in spirit to the 2TSF framework that model various situations as "double price frontiers."[3] Lins et al. (2005) introduced the "Double Perspective" DEA model (DP-DEA), in order to study the housing market in Brazil but also to provide a real-estate value assessment tool. The authors essentially created an equivalent of the core of an Edgeworth's exchange box by taking an input-oriented DEA model, transposing it and super-imposing it on an output-oriented DEA model. Hadley and Ruggiero (2006) applied the same approach to study the arbitraged salary negotiations in the market for Major League Baseball players in the USA. Mouchart and Vandresse (2007, 2010) studied the freight market in Belgium, modeling the contract space of the related negotiations as a "maximum willingness to pay/minimum willingness to sell" double frontier, an approach that is conceptually analogous to that of Gaynor and Polachek (1994). Mouchart and Vandresse estimated their model by an extension of the standard DEA approach using "bidirectional" free disposability, and it is interesting that the estimated densities (p. 1301, Fig. 3 in the 2007 paper) of what in their model corresponds to the positive and negative one-sided error components in the 2TSF approach, roughly indicate an Exponential-like distribution for both.

Lakhdar et al. (2013) studied the illicit drug trade. They abandon the convexity assumption of DEA and formulate a double-frontier model using a free disposal hull (FDH) model. They explicitly invoke incomplete information as the force that drives price up or down from a perfect-information equilibrium. Wolff (2016) also adopts an FDH approach to study "bargaining power" in on-line diamond markets. The author first runs a standard hedonic price regression in order to select

[3] I would like to thank professor Kristiaan Kerstens for bringing this literature to my attention.

the most important features that influence the buying-selling decision, which are subsequently used in his main model. This is similar in spirit to the 2TSF "scaling property" approach proposed by Parmeter (2018) that we will present in a while, where covariates are used as "determinants of inefficiency."

Finally Shabanpur et al. (2017) apply a multistage Goal Programming-DEA model to estimate a double frontier, this time around the *same* "decision making unit" (this is structurally analogous to the situations examined by Groot and van den Brink 2007 and Poggi 2010). Their case study concerns estimating the "sustainability" of a sample of suppliers, creating in the process upper and lower boundaries for (in)efficiency using data on "inputs" like price, environmental and work-safety indices, and on "outputs" like quality of products, financial stability, and efficiency in energy consumption.

It is natural to envision a comparative study of these methods together with the 2TSF approach, in the sense of applying all of them on the same data set(s) and explore and understand the differences in the obtained results (or marvel at their similarity). This would best be a collaborative effort.

3 Structural Foundations

3.1 *The "Incomplete Information" Framework of Polachek and Yoon (1987)*

In the first paper to introduce the 2TSF model, Polachek and Yoon (1987) had the insight that incomplete information on the one side of the market essentially affects the effective presence of the *other* side in the market: if employers do not know all labor supplied at a given wage, then the effective labor supplied by workers is only what the employers know. And if workers do not know all the labor demanded at a given price, the effective labor demanded is what the workers know. In short: "If the other side does not know that I exist, I don't." This turns the complete-information supply and demand schedules into *frontiers* with the distance from the frontier determined by the degree of incomplete information of the other side. The effective demand and supply functions were stochastically modeled as

$$L^D = f\left(\mathbf{x}^D, \omega\right) - e^D,\ \partial f/\partial\omega < 0, L^S = g\left(\mathbf{x}^S, \omega\right) - e^S,\ \partial g/\partial\omega > 0$$

where ω equals wage; e^D is a non-negative random variable, reflecting the part of labor demanded not seen by workers due to their incomplete information; the vector $\mathbf{x}^D$ lists the determinants of $f(\mathbf{x}^D, \omega)$ other than ω. Similarly for the supply curve, the actual quantity supplied L^S is below the maximum labor quantity $g(\mathbf{x}^S, \omega)$ which will be supplied at any wage level. The term e^S is a non-negative random variable to reflect the amount of labor supplied not seen by employers due to their incomplete information. Defining the non-stochastic portion of excess labor demand

$$h(\mathbf{x}, \omega) \equiv f\left(\mathbf{x}^D, \omega\right) - g\left(\mathbf{x}^S, \omega\right), \; \mathbf{x} = \left(\mathbf{x}^D, \mathbf{x}^S\right),$$

imposing the market-clearing condition $L^D = L^S$, and manipulating the relation lead to a wage determination equation where the error term has the composite 2TSF structure,

$$\omega_i \;=\; \omega_{FI} \;+\; (\mathbf{x}_i - E(\mathbf{x}_i))'\boldsymbol{\beta} \;+\; v_i \;+ w_i - u_i, \tag{1}$$

$$w = \left|\frac{\partial h(\mathbf{x}_{FI}, \omega_{FI})}{\partial \omega}\right|^{-1} \cdot e^S, \quad u = \left|\frac{\partial h(\mathbf{x}_{FI}, \omega_{FI})}{\partial \omega}\right|^{-1} \cdot e^D,$$

and where ω_{FI} is the full-information wage (for the average worker in the average firm). It can be consistently estimated as the constant term of the regression (with centered regressors and uncentered dependent variable), as long as we apply maximum likelihood estimation and estimate directly the parameters of the distribution of the composite error term. Equilibrium in such a market can intuitively be drawn in a diagram (Fig. 1).

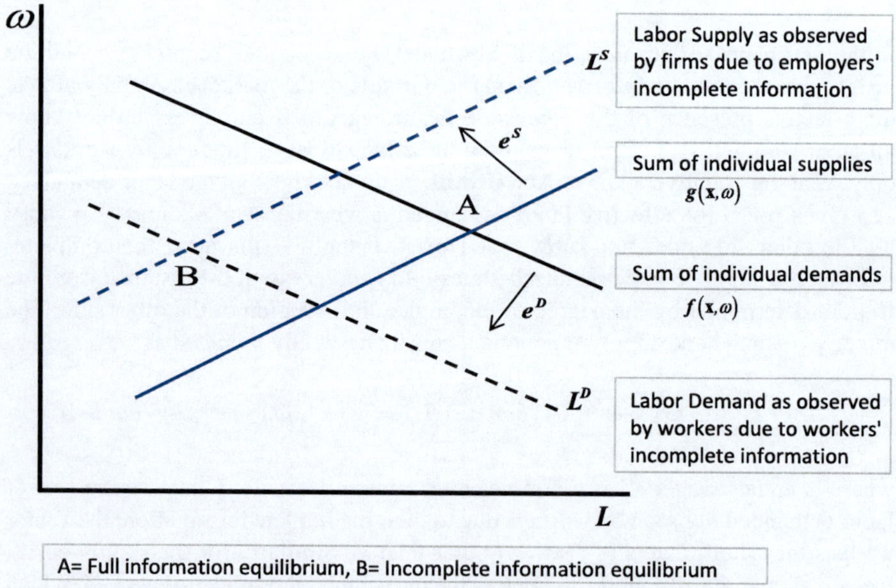

Fig. 1 Incomplete information at market level as failure to know the whole market

From the diagram it is clear that the unambiguous effect of incomplete information is to depress the equilibrium employment level. The effect on the equilibrium wage is ambiguous: it may be higher, lower, or equal to the full-information wage.

The incomplete information interpretation has received empirical validation in Polachek and Robst (1998). The authors used independent direct measures of workers' "knowledge of the world of work" obtained from the National Longitudinal Survey of Young Men (NLSYM) in the USA. They compared frontier estimates of incomplete information to these direct measures of workers' knowledge and verified that stochastic frontier analysis provides a reasonable measure of a worker's incomplete information.

3.2 *The "Reservation Price" Framework of Gaynor and Polachek (1994)*

This was the first paper to apply the 2TSF model to the health services market. The authors started their build-up toward the 2TSF reduced form by assuming structural regression equations for the reservation prices of both buyer (patient) and seller (physician). Namely, here the model starts at the individual level, imagining a bilateral transaction between buyer and seller. The equations take the usual linear form (subscript "b" for the buyer and "s" for the supplier),

$$P_b = \mathbf{x}_b'\beta_b + v_b, \quad P_s = \mathbf{x}_s'\beta_s + v_s. \tag{2}$$

The vector $\mathbf{x}_b$ contains the factors that affect the maximum fee the patient will be willing to pay (such as the extent of insurance coverage, the patient's education and income, the severity of the patient's illness, and the frequency with which the physician's services are needed), and v_b is a random disturbance. Analogously for the physician, the vector $\mathbf{x}_s$ contains regressors such as input prices, technology, age of equipment, and factors affecting efficiency, that determine the minimum fee a physician is willing to accept. The authors then define "gains" for the buyer and the seller, as the distance between reservation prices and actual price P. Each gain is a consequence of the incomplete information of the other side of the transaction. These gains are defined for the buyer and seller, respectively, as

$$U \equiv P_b - P \geq 0, \quad W \equiv P - P_s \geq 0. \tag{3}$$

Combining with the expressions for the reservation prices we get

$$P = \mathbf{x}_b'\beta_b + v_b - U, \quad P = \mathbf{x}_s'\beta_s + v_s + W. \tag{4}$$

Summing up and dividing by 2 we obtain

$$P = \mathbf{x}'\beta + v + w - u, \tag{5}$$

$$\mathbf{x}' = \left(\mathbf{x}_s', \mathbf{x}_b'\right), \ \beta = \frac{1}{2}\left(\beta_s{}', \beta_b{}'\right)', v = \frac{1}{2}\left(v_s + v_b\right), \ \ w = W/2, \ \ u = U/2.$$

Equation (5) has the structure of a 2TSF reduced-form equation. It is important to point out that the definitions for W and U are *ex post representations*, and not ex ante structural relations. If they were the latter, they would render Eq. (5) an identity let alone inducing all sorts of statistical dependencies that would threaten the reliability of the estimation results. In other words, W and U are only *measured ex post* as indicated by the right-hand sides of the equations in (3), they are not *caused* by these expressions, but rather, they arise due to the incomplete information of the participants in the transaction.

This is a foundation for the 2TSF model that can be used for any market/transaction where we can argue for the existence of reservation prices on both sides of the market (and have some covariates to express them). In applying this framework, we should not forget the factor 1/2 when we quantitatively assess the effects of incomplete information on price, since in expected-value terms we have $\hat{E}(W) = 2\hat{E}(w)$, $\hat{E}(U) = 2\hat{E}(u)$, and it is $\hat{E}(w)$, $\hat{E}(u)$ that we will obtain from the estimation procedure, while it is $E(W)$, $E(U)$ that we are interested in.

3.3 The "Hedonic Price" Framework of Kumbhakar and Parmeter (2010)

In this paper the authors applied the 2TSF model in the house-selling market, in a hedonic analysis framework. Superficially, their approach may appear similar with the one in Gaynor and Polachek (1994) analyzed just above, but it is not, quite the contrary, and it leads to different quantitative consequences.

The authors define the gains to the buyer and the seller due to the incomplete information of the other in the same way as in Gaynor and Polachek (1994), but they do *not* construct structural equations for the reservation prices of buyers ("willingness to pay") and sellers ("willingness to accept").

When they impose the necessary condition that price received must equal price paid, they essentially *add* the loss to the seller to, and *subtract* the loss to the buyer from, the transaction price, thus creating a "full-information" price expression. In the notation of the previous part we have

$$P_{FI} = P + u - w, \quad u = U, \ w = W. \tag{6}$$

They then point out that in a hedonic analysis approach we have the hedonic function decomposition of *full-information* price (not actual price) $P_{FI} = h(\mathbf{z}) + v$, where $\mathbf{z}$ is a vector of characteristics of the house on sale, $h(\cdot)$ is the hedonic function, and v is a random disturbance. Equating the two and rearranging we get

$$P = h(\mathbf{z}) + v + w - u, \quad u = U, \; w = W, \tag{7}$$

which is a 2TSF reduced-form equation.

The evident difference from the "reservation price" framework of Gaynor and Polachek (1994) analyzed previously is that here the one-sided error terms in the 2TSF model *equal* the gains of the parties due to incomplete information of the other, while previously each was only *half* of them (compare Eq. (7) with Eq. (5)). This is certainly crucial when using the model to obtain quantitative results. So it is important to understand clearly why do these frameworks differ, and so when it is appropriate to use the one or the other.

The fundamental difference is that Kumbhakar and Parmeter (2010) obtain two equations for the *full-information* price, something that allows them to eliminate it and obtain a single expression for the *transaction* price. Gaynor and Polachek (1994) do *not* assume the existence of an "independent" expression for the "full-information" price (physician's fee) as Kumbhakar and Parmeter do (the hedonic equation). But they do assume the existence of structural equations for the *reservation* prices (while Kumbhakar and Parmeter do not). Consequently, what Gaynor and Polachek obtain is two expressions for the *transaction* price (Eq. 4) and they have to add them and divide by 2 to arrive at a single expression that can be implemented econometrically.

Both frameworks are valid. As for which one to use, it will depend on the data available and the model developed in each case.

3.4 The Nash Bargaining 2TSF Framework

In Kumbhakar and Parmeter (2009), the authors made the first attempt to build a 2TSF model for a bilateral wage bargaining situation. They assumed realistically that since the productivity/output of the worker lies in the future, it is uncertain. To analyze this they adjusted the benchmark deterministic search and match labor market model of Pissarides (2000, chap. 1) that uses reservation prices to form the negotiation space and a Nash bargaining solution concept, substituting expected output for its deterministic counterpart. But as we show in Papadopoulos (2018, chap. 2), the end result was really a single-tier SF model, despite its 2TSF appearance. Specifically, the fundamental issue is that in order to obtain the 2TSF structure, the authors had to assume that the maximum wage that the firm is willing to pay is *equal or greater* than the expected output of the worker (as expected by the firm). But this means that the firm is a priori prepared to incur a loss by hiring the worker, which cannot be an accurate description for the bulk of the situations encountered in the real world.[4] Once we acknowledge this and postulate that the maximum wage the firm is willing to pay is equal to the expected output of the worker, the model collapses to a single-tier SF one.

But a bargaining situation is without any doubt a natural place for the 2TSF approach to emerge, so we tried again. First, we used the fact that as bargaining unfolds in cases where we ultimately reach an agreement, the initial reservation prices become non-binding and irrelevant for the outcome since the two parties are moving closer and so bargain in the interior of the feasible space defined by these initial prices. This led us to formulate the equilibrium situation as depending on the *targets* that each party formulates as regards the desired outcome. Denoting ω_e^T the target of the employee and ω_f^T the target of the firm, the Nash bargaining solution can now be expressed as

$$\omega^* = \eta\omega_e^T + (1-\eta)\,\omega_f^T,$$

where ω^* is the observed equilibrium wage, and η the relative bargaining power of the employee. Next, we acknowledge the existence of heterogeneous information in the two bargaining parties, as well as a non-empty common information set, $I_f \neq I_e$, $I_f \cap I_e \neq \varnothing$. This permits us to define the *symmetric-information expected value of the match, $E(p|I_f \cap I_e)$*, which may change somehow during the bargaining process as more information is exchanged. So the *equilibrium* common-information expected value is

$$\mu(\mathbf{x}) = E\left(p\,|I_f \cap I_e\right) + v.$$

This cannot be the conditional expectation of any of the parties, since it does not use the full information of either, but it is reasonable to model their targets as pivoting off from this common base. For the sellers, the target tends to be always higher than $\mu(\mathbf{x})$, either for strategic reasons or because of a "own-evaluation premium" that arises from the private information they have on themselves or on what they sell,

$$\omega_e^T \equiv \mu_p(\mathbf{x}) + g = E\left(p\,|I_f \cap I_e\right) + v + g,\ g \geq 0.$$

For the buyers, their target will always be below $\mu(\mathbf{x})$, either again due to strategic bargaining considerations, or due to a "prudential discount" ("it is never as good as it looks"),

$$\omega_f^T \equiv \mu_p(\mathbf{x}) - d = E\left(p\,|I_f \cap I_e\right) + v - d,\ d \geq 0.$$

[4]One may think of cases where the firm will incur a tangible loss (like a contract penalty) if it does not fill a position. In such a case, it could hire the worker at a loss, as long as the latter loss is smaller than the former. But these are rather exceptional cases.

Inserting this into the targets-based Nash bargaining solution we obtain

$$\omega^* = E\left(p \left| I_f \cap I_e\right.\right) + v + \eta g - (1-\eta)\, d. \tag{8}$$

$E(p|I_f \cap I_e)$ is the systematic part of the regression, and $v + \eta g - (1-\eta)d$ is a proper 2TSF composite error term. The relative bargaining power of the employees η is not a constant but a random variable, since we expect that in principle it will vary in each separate bilateral bargaining that takes place. The same holds for the variables g and d.

The products $\eta_i g_i$ and $(1-\eta_i)d_i$ achieve separate representation (if not identification) of the *information* effect (g_i and d_i) from the *bargaining power* effect (η_i and $1-\eta_i$), providing the theoretical base of the earlier discussion related to empirical results from the health services and housing markets.

We make a note that informational aspects here are used in a totally different way than in the original 2TSF paper of Polachek and Yoon (1987). As we have analyzed earlier, there the focus was on incomplete information of each party, and how this affected the other party. Here, the focus is on *private* information and how it affects the behavior of its owner.

We stress that the model is not just a re-writing of an earnings relation *a la* Mincer. In an empirical application, one should use here a data set that includes variables reflecting characteristics of both bargaining parties (namely, a matched employer–employee data set), in order to represent and estimate properly the common-information expected value $E(p|I_f \cap I_e)$. The good news is that since the systematic part represents the common information, it should be adequately represented by covariates that are generally available in accessible data bases.

On the other hand, characterizing the properties of η_i separately from the own-evaluation premium g_i and the prudential discount d_i appears infeasible without additional information/restrictions on the model. In Sect. 4.2.3 we discuss a possible way forward on this issue.

The above targets-based 2TSF Nash bargaining framework is generally applicable, beyond the labor market, and it validates ex post the various 2TSF empirical applications in other bargaining situations that were mentioned earlier. The model is fully developed and presented in Papadopoulos (2020c).

4 Tools of the Trade

4.1 Distributional Specifications

4.1.1 The Exponential 2TSF Specification

2TSF models come equipped with distributional assumptions on the composite error term. All applied studies up to now have used the Exponential 2TSF specification, where the assumptions on the composite error term $\varepsilon = v + w - u$ are

$$v \sim \mathrm{N}\left(0, \sigma_v^2\right), w \sim \mathrm{Exp}\left(\sigma_w\right), \quad u \sim \mathrm{Exp}\left(\sigma_u\right),$$

where σ_w, σ_u are scale parameters of Exponential distributions. The three components are assumed to be jointly independent. The density of the composite error term, as obtained in Kumbhakar and Parmeter (2009), is

$$f_\varepsilon(\varepsilon) = \frac{\exp\{a_1\}\Phi(b_1) + \exp\{a_2\}\Phi(b_2)}{\sigma_w + \sigma_u}, \tag{9}$$

where $\Phi(\cdot)$ is the standard normal distribution function and where

$$a_1 = \frac{\sigma_v^2}{2\sigma_u^2} + \frac{\varepsilon}{\sigma_u}, \quad b_1 = -\left(\frac{\varepsilon}{\sigma_v} + \frac{\sigma_v}{\sigma_u}\right), \quad a_2 = \frac{\sigma_v^2}{2\sigma_w^2} - \frac{\varepsilon}{\sigma_w}, \quad b_2 = \frac{\varepsilon}{\sigma_v} - \frac{\sigma_v}{\sigma_w}. \tag{10}$$

As with the single-tier SF models, of importance are also individual measures (i.e., at the observation level), usually in the form of conditional expected values. Kumbhakar and Parmeter (2009) provide these expressions[5] that are based on the approach of Jondrow et al. (1982), sometimes called the JLMS measures. Some additional results and formulas related to the 2TSF Exponential specification can be found in Papadopoulos (2018).

An issue specific to the 2TSF models, and related to the JLMS measures arises when we regress the dependent variable in logarithmic form. Then the ultimate individual measures will be based on the exponentiated variables, e^w, e^{-u}. Naturally we would like to consider their net effect. But $E(e^w e^{-u}|\varepsilon) \neq E(e^w|\varepsilon) \cdot E(e^{-u}|\varepsilon)$ because, even though we assume that w and u are independent, they stop being independent when conditioned on ε, something that have escaped notice in the literature. To obtain $E(e^w e^{-u}|\varepsilon)$ directly, we need first to derive the distribution of the variable $z = w - u$. For w and u Exponential, their difference is an asymmetric Laplace distribution, except if w, u have the same parameter.

4.1.2 The Half-Normal 2TSF Specification

Papadopoulos (2015a) presented an alternative distributional specification for the 2TSF composite error term, where the one-sided error terms are assumed to follow each a Half-Normal distribution instead of the Exponential one. Here the distributional assumptions for $\varepsilon = v + w - u$ are

[5] And, as luck would have it, it contains typographical errors in two formulas in the main text (Eqs. 11 and 12). The corresponding formulas in their Appendix (Eqs. A.10 and A.13) are the correct ones and should be used instead.

$$v \sim \mathrm{N}\left(0, \sigma_v^2\right), w \sim \mathrm{HN}\left(\sigma_w\right), \quad u \sim \mathrm{HN}\left(\sigma_u\right),$$

where σ_w, σ_u are the standard deviations of the symmetric zero-mean Normals of which the two Half-Normals are their absolute values. Joint independence is again assumed. The density of the composite error term is

$$f_\varepsilon\left(\varepsilon_i\right) = \frac{2}{s}\phi\left(\varepsilon_i/s\right)\left[G_1\left(\varepsilon_i; 0, \omega_1, -\lambda_1\right) \;-\; G_2\left(\varepsilon_i; 0, \omega_2, \lambda_2\right)\right], \tag{11}$$

with

$$\theta_1 \equiv \frac{\sigma_w}{\sigma_v}, \; \theta_2 \equiv \frac{\sigma_u}{\sigma_v}, s \equiv \sqrt{\sigma_v^2 + \sigma_w^2 + \sigma_u^2} \;=\; \sigma_v\sqrt{1+\theta_1^2+\theta_2^2},$$

and

$$\omega_1 \equiv \frac{s\sqrt{1+\theta_2^2}}{\theta_1}, \; \omega_2 \equiv \frac{s\sqrt{1+\theta_1^2}}{\theta_2}, \lambda_1 \equiv \frac{\theta_2}{\theta_1}\sqrt{1+\theta_1^2+\theta_2^2}, \; \lambda_2 \equiv \frac{\theta_1}{\theta_2}\sqrt{1+\theta_1^2+\theta_2^2}$$

and where $\phi(\cdot)$ is the standard Normal density while $G(z; \mathit{location}, \mathit{scale}, \mathit{skew})$ is the distribution function of a univariate Skew Normal random variable. An alternative way to express this distribution function is in terms of the correlated bivariate standard normal integral Φ_2,

$$G\left(\varepsilon_i; \xi, \omega, \lambda\right) \;=\; 2\Phi_2\left(\frac{\varepsilon_i - \xi}{\omega}, 0; \rho = \frac{-\lambda}{\sqrt{1+\lambda^2}}\right). \tag{12}$$

In our case, $\xi = 0$. This is convenient for empirical implementation, since $\Phi_2(\cdot)$ is widely available in software packages as a special function. Using this we can re-write the density of the composite error as

$$f_\varepsilon\left(\varepsilon_i\right) = \frac{4}{s}\phi\left(\varepsilon_i/s\right)\left[\Phi_2\left(\frac{\varepsilon_i}{\omega_1}, 0; \rho = \frac{\lambda_1}{\sqrt{1+\lambda_1^2}}\right) - \Phi_2\left(\frac{\varepsilon_i}{\omega_2}, 0; \rho = \frac{-\lambda_2}{\sqrt{1+\lambda_2^2}}\right)\right]. \tag{13}$$

The paper also includes formulas for the JLMS observation-specific measures, either for a specification in levels or for the semi-log and log-log regression specifications that are commonly found in the literature. The density of the difference $z = w - u$ has been derived in Papadopoulos (2015b).

4.1.3 The Truncated Normal 2TSF Specification

As a by-product of a panel-data 2TSF model, Wang (2017) presented the 2TSF Truncated Normal specification for cross-sectional data, where the one-sided terms follow the Truncated Normal distribution (rather than the Exponential or the Half-normal). Unfortunately, the provided expression for the density of the composite error term was wrong. The assumptions here for $\varepsilon = v + w - u$ are

$$v \sim \mathrm{N}\left(0, \sigma_v^2\right), w \sim \mathrm{TN}_{\geq 0}\left(\mu_w, \sigma_w\right), \quad u \sim \mathrm{TN}_{\geq 0}\left(\mu_u, \sigma_u\right),$$

where $\mathrm{TN}_{\geq 0}(\mu, \sigma)$ stands for a Normal distribution truncated from below at zero with non-zero location parameter. Then, using the same notations and shorthands that we used for the Half-Normal 2TSF specification, the correct density of the composite error term is

$$\begin{aligned} f_\varepsilon(\varepsilon) =& \frac{\left[\Phi\left(\mu_w/\sigma_w\right)\Phi\left(\mu_u/\sigma_u\right)\right]^{-1}}{s}\phi\left(\frac{\varepsilon_i - (\mu_w - \mu_u)}{s}\right) \\ & \times \left\{\Phi_2\left[\frac{1}{\omega_1}\left(\varepsilon + \frac{(\sigma_v^2 + \sigma_u^2)}{\sigma_w^2}\mu_w + \mu_u\right), \lambda_0; \rho = \frac{\lambda_1}{\sqrt{1+\lambda_1^2}}\right]\right. \\ & \left. -\Phi_2\left[\frac{1}{\omega_2}\left(\varepsilon - \mu_w - \frac{\sigma_v^2 + \sigma_w^2}{\sigma_u^2}\mu_u\right), \lambda_0; \rho = \frac{-\lambda_2}{\sqrt{1+\lambda_2^2}}\right]\right\}, \end{aligned} \tag{14}$$

$$\lambda_0 = \frac{(\sigma_u/\sigma_w)\,\mu_w + (\sigma_w/\sigma_u)\,\mu_u}{s_0}, \quad s_0 \equiv \sqrt{\sigma_w^2 + \sigma_u^2}.$$

If $\mu_w = \mu_u = 0$ the density collapses to the density of the 2TSF Half-Normal specification, as should be expected.

4.1.4 The Semi-Gamma 2TSF Specification

An early criticism by Stevenson (1980) was that by using the Exponential or the Half-normal distribution in SF models we impose the assumption that the most likely values for these components are near zero, something not necessarily true or justifiable in all cases. Responding to this criticism, Papadopoulos (2018) presented two new specifications that relax this constraint.

The first one is the semi-Gamma specification that comes in two variants.

One variant is the Gamma-Exponential 2TSF specification where we have for $\varepsilon = v + w - u$,

$$v \sim \mathrm{N}\left(0, \sigma_v^2\right), w \sim \text{Gamma}\left(k_w, \theta_w\right), \quad u \sim \text{Exp}\left(\sigma_u\right).$$

For the Gamma distribution we adopt the shape-scale parametrization. Here the positive one-sided component is allowed to have its mode away from zero. The density of the composite error term is

$$f_\varepsilon(\varepsilon) = \frac{\sigma_u^{k_w-1}}{(\sigma_u+\theta_w)^{k_w}} \left[\exp\left\{\frac{\varepsilon}{\sigma_u} + \frac{\sigma_v^2}{2\sigma_u^2}\right\} - \int_0^\infty \exp\{z/\sigma_u\} \frac{1}{\sigma_v}\phi\left(\frac{\varepsilon - z}{\sigma_v}\right) F_G(z; k_w, \delta)\, dz \right]. \tag{15}$$

where $F_G(z; k_w, \delta)$ is the Gamma distribution function with shape parameter k and scale parameter$\delta \equiv \sigma_u\theta_w/(\sigma_u+\theta_w)$. The density does not have a closed form and so the model requires other estimation methods than standard maximum likelihood.[6] Individual measures are also of non-closed form, and can be computed by Gauss–Laguerre or Newton–Cotes quadrature.

The second variant of the semi-Gamma specification is the Exponential-Gamma,where

$$v \sim \mathrm{N}\left(0, \sigma_v^2\right), w \sim \text{Exp}\left(\sigma_w\right), \quad u \sim \text{Gamma}\left(k_u, \theta_u\right).$$

The density of the composite error term is

$$f_\varepsilon(\varepsilon) = \frac{\sigma_w^{k_u-1}}{(\sigma_w+\theta_u)^{k_u}} \left[\exp\left\{-\frac{\varepsilon}{\sigma_w} + \frac{\sigma_v^2}{2\sigma_w^2}\right\} - \int_0^\infty \exp\{z/\sigma_w\} \frac{1}{\sigma_v}\phi\left(\frac{\varepsilon + z}{\sigma_v}\right) F_G(z; k_u, \delta)\, dz \right]. \tag{16}$$

with $\delta \equiv \sigma_w\theta_u/(\sigma_w+\theta_u)$, and the same comments apply.

The semi-Gamma specification is the only one where the one-sided components follow different distributions (although of the same family). Evidently, such cross-breeding can be extended and applied to the other specifications as well, at least to those that assume independence between the two terms.

---

[6]Using the Fast Fourier Transform, Tsionas (2012) estimated a model where both one-sided errors were initially specified as following the Gamma distribution. For the sample he used, he found that the negative component was actually an Exponential random variable, thus ending up with the Gamma-Exponential specification.

4.1.5 The Generalized Exponential 2TSF Specification

The semi-Gamma specification allows only one of the non-negative error components to have its mode away from zero. Moreover, Ritter and Simar (1997) have shown that the Gamma distribution may be a risky choice, because its shape parameter (the one that structurally provides its shape flexibility) is weakly identifiable, even for large samples. To allow for both error components to possess the non-zero mode property, we have also developed the Generalized Exponential 2TSF specification. The marginal density, say for w is

$$f_w(w) = \frac{2}{\theta_w} \exp\{-w/\theta_w\} (1 - \exp\{-w/\theta_w\}), \quad \theta_w > 0, \; w \geq 0, \tag{17}$$

and analogously for u. It can be seen as a special case of the three-parameter "Generalized Exponential" distribution of Gupta and Kundu (1999) and we will write w~GE$(2, \theta_w, 0)$. But there is a price to pay: The strictly positive mode is an inherent property and it does not nest the Exponential case (so in a sense "Generalized Exponential" is an inaccurate name). This is a specification that has to be supported by economic and behavioral arguments—and once it does, this statistical inflexibility does not loom large over the model.

We see that the GE density equals $2f_E(x)F_E(x)$, where $f_E(x)$is the density and $F_E(x)$ is the distribution function of an Exponential random variable. But then $2f_E(x)F_E(x)$ is the density of the maximum of two i.i.d Exponentials. This carries over to the case of a logarithmic specification, where we are ultimately interested in $\exp\{w\}$, $\exp\{u\}$ and the measures derived from them. These measures each follow the distribution of the maximum of two i.i.d. random variables. So if we mentally picture two possible outcomes for each variable, the model will give us the stronger of the two. We can say then that the 2TSF Generalized Exponential specification pictures the real world as operating at maximum intensity, something not incompatible with fundamental ideas in economic theory.

For $\varepsilon = v + w - u$ with $v \sim \mathrm{N}\left(0, \sigma_v^2\right), \; w \sim \mathrm{GE}\left(2, \theta_w, 0\right), \; u \sim \mathrm{GE}\left(2, \theta_u, 0\right)$, jointly independent, we have the density function

$$\begin{aligned} f_\varepsilon(\varepsilon) = \frac{2}{\theta_w+\theta_u} \Bigg[& \frac{2\theta_u \exp\{a_u\}\Phi(b_u)}{\theta_w+2\theta_u} - \frac{\theta_u \exp\{2a_u+(\sigma_v/\theta_u)^2\}\Phi(b_u-\sigma_v/\theta_u)}{2\theta_w+\theta_u} \\ & + \frac{2\theta_w \exp\{a_w\}\Phi(b_w)}{2\theta_w+\theta_u} - \frac{\theta_w \exp\{2a_w+(\sigma_v/\theta_w)^2\}\Phi(b_w-\sigma_v/\theta_w)}{\theta_w+2\theta_u} \Bigg] \end{aligned} \tag{18}$$

with

$$a_u = \frac{\varepsilon}{\theta_u} + \frac{\sigma_v^2}{2\theta_u^2}, \quad b_u = -\left(\frac{\varepsilon}{\sigma_v} + \frac{\sigma_v}{\theta_u}\right), \quad a_w = \frac{\sigma_v^2}{2\theta_w^2} - \frac{\varepsilon}{\theta_w}, \quad b_w = \frac{\varepsilon}{\sigma_v} - \frac{\sigma_v}{\theta_w}.$$

This specification was developed in order to focus on the modes of the distributions, and so it seemed appropriate to do the same as regards measures at the observation level. We derived the conditional densities for $w|\varepsilon$, $u|\varepsilon$, as well as for $\exp\{\pm w\}|\varepsilon$, $\exp\{-u\}|\varepsilon$. Then, computing the conditional mode for each $\hat{\varepsilon}_i$ is done by iterative non-linear maximization. This specification is presented in detail, also for single-tier SF models, in Papadopoulos (2020a).

4.1.6 Dependence Between the One-Sided Error Components: The 2TSF Correlated Exponential Specification

In many cases, maintaining the assumption that the three error components are jointly independent is indefensible. For example, in the 2TSF Nash bargaining framework, the two one-sided components are functions of the relative bargaining power of the employee η which is not a constant but a random variable, and dependence is inescapable. To cover these situations, we developed the 2TSF Correlated Exponential specification, where the two one-sided components are assumed to follow jointly the bivariate Exponential extension of Freund (1961). We maintain the assumption that $v \sim \mathrm{N}\left(0, \sigma_v^2\right)$, while the joint density of w and u is

$$f_{wu}(w,u) = \begin{cases} ab' \exp\left\{-b'u - \left(a+b-b'\right)w\right\} & 0 < w < u \\ a'b \exp\left\{-a'w - \left(a+b-a'\right)u\right\} & 0 < u < w \end{cases} \qquad a, a', b, b' > 0$$

The Pearson's correlation coefficient range allowed by this bivariate distribution is $(-1/3, 1)$ which is respectable, taking into account that we are talking about the correlation of two non-negative random variables (that cannot reach -1). Setting $m \equiv a/(a+b)$, the density of the composite error term $\varepsilon = v + w - u$ is

$$f_\varepsilon(\varepsilon) = \sqrt{2\pi}\varphi\left(\varepsilon/\sigma_v\right)$$
$$\left[mb' \exp\left\{\frac{1}{2}\omega_2^2\right\} \Phi\left(-\omega_2\right) + (1-m)\,a' \exp\left\{\frac{1}{2}\omega_3^2\right\} \Phi\left(\omega_3\right)\right]$$

$$\omega_2 \equiv \frac{\varepsilon}{\sigma_v} + b'\sigma_v, \quad \omega_3 \equiv \frac{\varepsilon}{\sigma_v} - a'\sigma_v.$$

Note that in the regression context with the composite error term, (a, b) are not separately identifiable, only $m \equiv a/(a+b)$ is. Introducing intra-dependence weakens the role of skewness of the residuals as an indication of the relative strengths of the one-sided components: we can show that for certain combinations of parameter values, we may have $E(w-u) > 0$ together with negative third cumulant $\kappa_3(\varepsilon) < 0$ and vice versa. This result is analogous with what Smith (2008) found for single-tier SF specifications under dependence.

Papadopoulos (2018, chap. 4.1) completes the specification with individual JLMS measures, the distribution of $z = w - u$, as well as a formal statistical test for the postulated dependence.[7]

4.2 *Estimation Methods*

4.2.1 Maximum Likelihood

Maximum likelihood is the dominant method of estimation for 2TSF models. Compared to single-tier SF models, the 2TSF framework provides an additional flexibility regarding the composite error term from a technical point of view: in $\varepsilon = v + w - u$, the v term is no longer needed to ensure that the regularity conditions of ML estimation are satisfied (as is the case for single-tier SF models). Of course, the presence of this term is justified also by real-world considerations: random shocks do happen. Still, if in the process of an empirical study we obtain a nearly zero-variance for v, implying that its effect compared to w and u is negligible, we can safely discard it and re-estimate. In fact if we do not do this, our ML estimator will be non-standard (although now with known properties), since we have the true value of one of the parameters on the boundary of its parameter space, and a singular Hessian matrix. Discarding the v term will restore the standard properties of the MLE, while the regularity conditions will be respected too. This is another reason why having available the distribution of $z = w - u$ is useful—we may need to use it in the core estimation step of a study, and not just for calculating individual measures.

The maximum likelihood framework is also the one that can be used in order to account for regressor endogeneity using Copulas rather than instrumental variables. In Papadopoulos (2019) we expand on the work of Tran and Tsionas (2015) and detail the application of the Gaussian Copula for this purpose.

Previously, we have also presented densities for the composite error term that are not in closed form and cannot be estimated by the usual ML estimator. A solution here is to use simulated maximum likelihood. The first application in a 2TSF context appears to be Murphy and Strobl (2008). The authors used for their main work the 2TSF Exponential specification, but they reported a specification test where they estimated by simulated maximum likelihood a full Gamma specification for the model (i.e., where both one-sided error components are assumed to follow Gamma distributions, that nests the Exponential). Blanco (2017) adjusted the 2TSF model to take into account sample-selection bias, and extended and applied the simulated maximum likelihood methodology that Greene (2010) has developed for the single-tier SF framework. Another approach is to use the Fast Fourier Transform algorithm

[7] For additional 2TSF specifications with intra-error dependence, see Papadopoulos, Parmeter and Kumbhakar (2020).

as proposed in Tsionas (2012). Scaling back on technical sophistication, we have also developed a Corrected OLS/Method-of-Moments estimator, which we present next.

4.2.2 Corrected OLS/Method of Moments.

It is a known result that the residuals from OLS estimation of a single-tier or two-tier SF model converge in probability to the true *centered* composite error term, $\hat{\varepsilon}_{OLS} \xrightarrow{p} \varepsilon - E(\varepsilon)$. Therefore the residual moments are consistent estimators of the central error moments. But the central error moments are functions of the unknown parameters of the composite error distribution. This allows us to construct an estimator that is based on the method of moments: in the first stage we estimate the model with OLS, obtaining consistent estimates for the regressor coefficients, an estimate for the constant term that is biased because it includes also the estimated mean of the error term, and a series of residuals. In the second step, we formulate a method-of-moments estimator, using the error moment equations and the OLS residual series to obtain consistent estimates for these unknown error distribution parameters. With these we can obtain a consistent estimate for the mean of the error term. In the third step, we use this to correct the OLS estimate of the constant term, and subsequently to correct also the OLS residual series. Then we can also proceed with calculating the various individual measures using the corrected OLS residuals.

Various studies have developed method-of-moments estimators for single-tier SF models, starting with Olson et al. (1980), and continuing with Greene (1990), Kopp and Mullahy (1990), Coelli (1995) and Chen and Wang (2004). The 2TSF composite error term has at least three unknown parameters in its distribution and in the semi-Gamma specification, it has four. The first-order moment equation cannot be used since the sum and mean of the OLS residuals will be by construction zero. So in order to estimate four unknown parameters, we need to use the moment equations for the second, third, fourth, and fifth central moment. For small and medium sized samples, the downward bias of central sample moments of higher order is well known, and it gets worse as the order of the moment increases. When we deal with regression residuals the downward bias increases also with the number of regressors. Fisher's (1930) unbiased estimators for the central error moments and the cumulants, the latter going by the name "*k*-statistics," do not account for the bias in our case, since they assume that we have data from the true distribution. To offset the bias, we derived unbiased estimators for the central error moments, $\hat{\mu}_j(\varepsilon)$ and also for their cumulants $\hat{\kappa}_j(\varepsilon)$, up to and including the fifth order.

We called the unbiased cumulant estimators the "kapa-statistics" and it is those that we used to formulate our COLS/MM estimator, rather than the central moments (they are the same though for the second and third order). Erickson et al. (2014) provide Monte Carlo evidence that cumulant estimators perform better than moment estimators when used in a regression estimation.

The COLS/MM estimator can be implemented with any specification that satisfies the following for $\varepsilon = v + w - u$: v has zero mean, is symmetric around zero and so it has all odd moments equal to zero, w and u have non-zero mean and non-zero third, fourth, and fifth central moments, the three random variables are jointly independent, and the unknown parameters are no more than four.

In practice, this can be implemented as an exactly identified GMM estimator. Starting values can be provided by numerically solving the system of cumulant equations. This will essentially give us almost exactly the final estimates, but the application of the GMM routine is required in order to obtain standard errors for the estimates. The use of the unbiased kapa-statistics makes the application of the Analogy Principle exact in finite samples also, while the COLS/MM estimator is consistent and asymptotically Normal.

4.2.3 Non-linear Least Squares

In a purely methodological paper, Parmeter (2018) exploits the "scaling property" that characterizes all single-parameter distributions (and not only), in order to make feasible a non-linear least squares (NLS) estimator, thus doing away with the distributional assumptions that are needed for maximum likelihood and can cause misspecification. The approach has similarities with the heteroskedastic extension of the 2TSF model discussed earlier, since it can be implemented only if we have available covariates to use as determinants of the one-sided error components. But here, the functional specification is non-linear, and it guarantees identification even if it so happens that the two one-sided unobservables are symmetric. Contrast this with the work of Harding et al. (2003). They essentially apply the 2TSF philosophy in order to measure bargaining power in a hedonic framework for existing homes. But they model the bargaining power of buyers and sellers as linear functions of observable individual characteristics, and so for identification they need these characteristics to take different values for the two sides of the transaction.

Another important property of the NLS approach is that it allows automatically for the existence of dependence between the error terms and between them and the regressors, since in essence, *the one-sided error terms become composite regressors themselves*, leaving only the random symmetric disturbance as unobservable: the regression equation here looks like

$$y = \mathbf{x}'\beta + \exp\left\{\mathbf{z}_w'\delta_w\right\} - \exp\left\{\mathbf{z}_u'\delta_u\right\} + v,$$

$$E\left(w \,|\mathbf{x}, \mathbf{z}_w, \mathbf{z}_u\right) = \exp\left\{\mathbf{z}_w'\delta_w\right\}, \quad E\left(u \,|\mathbf{x}, \mathbf{z}_w, \mathbf{z}_u\right) = \exp\left\{\mathbf{z}_u'\delta_u\right\}.$$

Now, consider again the Nash bargaining regression Eq (8): for estimation purposes, we make the mappings $\eta_i g_i \equiv w_i, \quad (1 - \eta_i)d_i \equiv u_i$, namely we map products of random variables to a single random variable. The relative bargaining power variable η_i ranges in $(0, 1)$ while the variables g_i, d_i that represent private information effects are non-negative. It could reasonably be argued that the distribution of their product will not be adequately approximated by any one of the familiar non-negative distributions (and using non-standard distributions would most likely make the composite density intractable). So applying the distribution-free NLS estimator appears even more justified in this case.

Moreover, if we have *distinct* covariates to use as explanatory variables for the bargaining power and the information effects, we can obtain separate estimations on how each factor affects the conditional mean of the product variables.

For example, "length of unemployment spell" or "number of dependents in the household" would probably affect negatively the bargaining power of a prospective employee, while the self-evaluation premium will tend to co-vary positively with "length of experience" since the longer the experience the more information about professional achievements stays out of a resumé (even though previous job positions may all be listed).

For the side of the employer, strong product demand may negatively affect its bargaining position (due to prospective loss of profits if vacancies persist), while a high employee turn-over rate would tend to strengthen the prudential discount.

4.3 Panel Data

The Exponential 2TSF specification has initially been extended for panel data in Polachek and Yoon (1996). The authors applied a fixed-effects model and a two-step estimation procedure. Das and Polachek (2017a, b) introduced heterogeneity in the following way: although they assume that the one-sided error components each follow an Exponential distribution as in the benchmark model, one of them is no longer identically distributed because it contains a group-specific heterogeneity parameter (so it remains an Exponential distribution but with changing parameter). This leads to a different likelihood function and a different estimation algorithm than the usual one.

Wang (2017) extends the four-component single-tier SF panel-data model of Kumbhakar et al. (2014), and formulates an all-encompassing six-component 2TSF model for panel data: it includes an individual heterogeneity component, the random disturbance, and two one-sided effects where each is decomposed into a time-varying and a time-invariant part. We have the specification

$$\begin{aligned} y_{it} &= \alpha_0 + \mathbf{x}_{it}'\beta + (\theta_i + v_{it}) + \ (\gamma_i + w_{it}) - (\eta_i + u_{it})\,, \\ i &= 1, \ldots, N,\ t = 1, \ldots, T. \end{aligned} \tag{19}$$

The terms v_{it}, w_{it}, u_{it} are now the time-varying components of their cross-sectional selves, while θ_i, γ_i, η_i are the time-invariant parts (with θ_i being the "individual heterogeneity" parameter). All are treated as random variables. We assume that $E(\theta_i) = E(v_{it}) = 0$ and Normally distributed. Let a tilde above a variable denote that the variable is centered on its mean, $\tilde{x} = x - E(x)$. Estimation can proceed in two stages as in Kumbhakar et al. (2014). In the first stage, we define

$$\alpha_0^* \equiv \alpha_0 + E(\gamma_i) - E(\eta_i) + E(w_{it}) - E(u_{it}),$$
$$\alpha_i \equiv \theta_i + \tilde{\gamma}_i - \tilde{\eta}_i, \quad \varepsilon_{it} \equiv v_{it} + \tilde{w}_{it} - \tilde{u}_{it}.$$

Then the main equation can be written

$$y_{it} = \alpha_0^* + \mathbf{x}'_{it}\beta + \alpha_i + \varepsilon_{it}, \quad i = 1, \ldots, N, \; t = 1, \ldots, T.$$

This is a standard random-effects panel-data model, and can be estimated as usual, which, among other estimates, it will provide an estimated set of values $\{\hat{\alpha}_i\}$ over cross-sections and an estimated panel $\{\hat{\varepsilon}_{it}\}$.

In the second stage, we perform two separate maximum likelihood estimations. For the time-invariant components, we have (subject to estimation error),

$$\hat{\alpha}_i + E(\gamma_i) - E(\eta_i) = \theta_i + \gamma_i - \eta_i \equiv \psi_i.$$

The right-hand side is a 2TSF composite error term, and we have by now alternative distributional specifications to choose from. Selecting one of them gives us the density of the left-hand side,

$$f_\psi(\psi_i) = f_\psi\left(\hat{\alpha}_i + E(\gamma_i) - E(\eta_i)\right).$$

Here the $\{\hat{\alpha}_i\}$ estimates are treated as the sample (no regression relation is involved), while $E(\gamma_i)$, $E(\eta_i)$ are simple or composite functions of the unknown parameters already present in f_ψ. The sum of $\ln f_\psi(\psi_i)$'s forms the log-likelihood. We apply the same method for the time-varying components since

$$\hat{\varepsilon}_{it} + E(w_{it}) - E(u_{it}) \equiv v_{it} + w_{it} - u_{it}.$$

The panel aspect of $\{\hat{\varepsilon}_{it}\}$ is not taken into account and the data are pooled to function as the sample based on which we can estimate the parameters of the 2TSF density.

In principle, the 2TSF distributional specifications may differ in the two legs of the second stage. This may have a behavioral justification. For example, the researcher may have reasons to believe that the time-invariant components have their mode away from zero and/or are correlated, while the time-varying components have zero modes and are independent (or vice versa, depending on the real-world situation).

This estimation method ignores the estimation error of the first stage, but also the fact that the series used in the second stage, being estimated series, no longer form an independent sample (although the elements of the series are identically distributed). Still, under consistency, this dependence vanishes asymptotically.

5 Moving Forward

After a 20-year period of rather sparse application, the 2TSF approach has started to increasingly attract the attention of researchers. The present review hopes to reinforce this trend by accomplishing two things: first, reveal the diversity of the real-world phenomena that can be fruitfully formulated as 2TSF situations, and promote in this way the application of the model to these areas, but also others as yet uncovered. Indicatively, our own research has led us to apply the model in the most traditional single-tier SF situation, the production function, where we use it in order to capture the effects on output of the ever-intriguing management factor (Papadopoulos 2020b). This allows us to offer a simple and intuitive explanation of the "wrong skewness" issue that appears often in production data samples. As another example of an application that expands the horizon of frontier analysis beyond matters of efficiency, one can identify two main opposing forces in the pricing decisions of a firm: brand loyalty and the fear of competition, both as assessed by the firm. These may make observed prices deviate from their hedonic level that is based on the "objective" characteristics of a product. A 2TSF model would be immediately applicable here, revealing important aspects of the "mind of the firm" that are never available as data. Yet one more unexpected area where the model has been applied is Huang et al. (2018), which combine the 2TSF approach with a business cycle model with autocorrelation, opening at once two new territories to the 2TSF treatment: serial correlation, and macroeconomics.

The second thing that we hope we have accomplished here, and perhaps even more important, is to clearly signal that the 2TSF framework is no longer a poor relative as regards the tools available to dissect and interpret the data. While virtually all empirical studies up to now have been conducted on cross-sectional data using standard maximum likelihood and the Exponential specification, the 2TSF framework nowadays includes many more weapons in its arsenal to accommodate data sets that are richer and statistical structures that are more demanding, as well as to offer more concrete interpretations.

It appears worthwhile to revisit the birthplace of the 2TSF model, the labor market, in order to re-examine the determination of the wage using the robust bilateral Nash bargaining framework as the interpretation tool, a matched employer–employee data set, and the Correlated Exponential specification to account for statistical dependence between the one-sided error components.

If data on determinants of the one-sided term are available, the use of Parmeter's (2018) non-linear least squares estimator guards against regressor endogeneity with respect to these terms, frees us from the need of possibly unrealistic distributional assumptions, and may also allow us to separate and identify separately the informational effects from the bargaining power effects, as has been discussed in the relevant section. This applies not just to the labor market and wage determination, but to any situation where bilateral bargaining takes place and both bargaining power and private information affect the outcome.

Markets with complex goods like houses and information technology products are expected to be characterized by incomplete and asymmetric information, and most likely non-zero, especially from the side of the buyers. To do justice to such an unbalanced structure requires one of the one-sided distributions to have its mode away from zero, like the Gamma-Exponential variant of the semi-Gamma specification that moreover can be estimated relatively effortlessly with the method-of-moments/COLS estimator and the kapa-statistics.

Analogous thoughts apply to the markets for health services. Their perennial status as a sensitive sociopolitical issue makes the insightful analysis of the data in order to inform the public dialogue even more crucial than what scientific principles would alone dictate. Using the Generalized Exponential specification with its many individual measures of informational inefficiencies (expected values, modes, and medians) would provide a rich characterization of this group of idiosyncratic markets.

All the above can immediately translate to a panel-data environment using the approach described earlier that allows for flexible modeling and estimation. Panel-data samples enhance our ability to separate concurrent latent forces and this is the ever-present challenge that the 2TSF framework faces: the accurate separation, identification, and measurement of what is actually at work behind the data.

References

Blanco, G. (2017). Who benefits from job placement services? A two-sided analysis. *Journal of Productivity Analysis, 47*(1), 33–47.

Chawla, M. (2002). Estimating the extent of patient ignorance of the health care market. In S. Devarajan & F. Halsey Rogers (Eds.), *World Bank economists' forum* (Vol. 2, pp. 3–24). Washington, DC: World Bank.

Chen, Y. Y., & Wang, H. J. (2004). A method of moments estimator for a stochastic frontier model with errors in variables. *Economics Letters, 85*(2), 221–228.

Coelli, T. (1995). Estimators and hypothesis tests for a stochastic frontier function: A Monte Carlo analysis. *Journal of Productivity Analysis, 6*(3), 247–268.

Dar, A. (2014). The impact of imperfect information on the wages of native-born and immigrant workers: Evidence from the 2006 Canadian census. *Proceedings of 2nd Economics & Finance Conference*, Vienna, 215–232. International Institute of Social and Economic Sciences.

Das, T., & Polachek, S. W. (2017a). *Estimating labor force joiners and leavers using a heterogeneity augmented two-tier stochastic frontier* (IZA Discussion Paper #10534).

Das, T., & Polachek, S. W. (2017b). Estimating labor force joiners and leavers using a heterogeneity augmented two-tier stochastic frontier. *Journal of Econometrics, 199*(2), 93–232.

Du, Z., & Wei, P. (2014). Agglomeration economy, external governance and the efficiency of urban industrial emissions. *Urban Problems, 2014*, 10.

Erickson, T., Jiang, C. H., & Whited, T. M. (2014). Minimum distance estimation of the errors-in-variables model using linear cumulant equations. *Journal of Econometrics, 183*(2), 211–221.

Ferona, A., & Tsionas, E. G. (2012). Measurement of excess bidding in auctions. *Economics Letters, 116*(3), 377–380.

Fisher, R. A. (1930). Moments and product moments of sampling distributions. *Proceedings of the London Mathematical Society, 2*(1), 199–238.

Freund, J. E. (1961). A bivariate extension of the exponential distribution. *Journal of the American Statistical Association, 56*(296), 971–977.
Fried, H., & Tauer, L. (2019). Efficient wine pricing using stochastic frontier models. *Journal of Wine Economics, 14*(2), 164–181. https://doi.org/10.1017/jwe.2019.16.
Gaynor, M., & Polachek, S. W. (1994). Measuring information in the market: An application to physician services. *Southern Economic Journal, 60*(4), 815–831.
Greene, W. (2010). A stochastic frontier model with correction for sample selection. *Journal of Productivity Analysis, 34*(1), 15–24.
Greene, W. H. (1990). A gamma-distributed stochastic frontier model. *Journal of Econometrics, 46*(1-2), 141–163.
Groot, W., & Oosterbeek, H. (1994). Stochastic reservation and offer wages. *Labour Economics, 1*(3), 383–390.
Groot, W., & van den Brink, H. M. (2007). Optimism, pessimism and the compensating income variation of cardiovascular disease: A two-tiered quality of life stochastic frontier model. *Social Science & Medicine, 65*(7), 1479–1489.
Gupta, R. D., & Kundu, D. (1999). Theory & methods: Generalized exponential distributions. *Australian & New Zealand Journal of Statistics, 41*(2), 173–188.
Hadley, L., & Ruggiero, J. (2006). Final-offer arbitration in major league baseball: A nonparametric analysis. *Annals of Operations Research, 145*(1), 201–209.
Harding, J. P., Rosenthal, S. S., & Sirmans, C. F. (2003). Estimating bargaining power in the market for existing homes. *Review of Economics and Statistics, 85*(1), 178–188.
Hofler, R., & Polachek, S. W. (1982). Ignorance in the labor market: A new approach for measuring information content. *Proceedings of the American Statistical Association*, 422–425.
Huang, S., Jia, J., & Wang, W. (2017). Research of IPO underpricing decomposition based on two-tiered stochastic frontier model: Evidence from Chinese growth enterprises market. *CMS, 25*(2), 21–29.
Huang, Y., Luo, S., & Wang, H. (2018). Asymmetric business cycles and economic uncertainties: An application of two-tier stochastic frontier model. In *Paper presented at the Asia Pacific productivity conference 2018*. Seoul National: University.
Huang, Z. (2013). The study of IPO pricing efficiency in Chinese GEM market: An empirical measure based on two-tier stochastic frontier model. *Journal of Guangdong University of Finance and Economics, 2*. http://en.cnki.com.cn/Article_en/CJFDTOTAL-SONG201302006.htm.
Jondrow, J., Knox Lovell, C. A., Materov, I. S., & Schmidt, P. (1982). On the estimation of technical inefficiency in the stochastic frontier production function model. *Journal of Econometrics, 19*(2), 233–238.
Kinukawa, S., & Motohashi, K. (2010). *Bargaining in technology markets: An empirical study of biotechnology alliances* (RIETI Discussion Paper Series 10-E-200).
Kinukawa, S., & Motohashi, K. (2016). What determines the outcome of licensing deals in market for technology? Empirical analysis of sellers and buyers in biotechnology alliances. *International Journal of Technology Management, 70*(4), 257–280.
Kopp, R. J., & Mullahy, J. (1990). Moment-based estimation and testing of stochastic frontier models. *Journal of Econometrics, 46*(1-2), 165–183.
Kumbhakar, S. C., Lien, G., & Hardaker, J. B. (2014). Technical efficiency in competing panel data models: A study of Norwegian grain farming. *Journal of Productivity Analysis, 41*(2), 321–337.
Kumbhakar, S. C., & Parmeter, C. F. (2009). The effects of match uncertainty and bargaining on labor market outcomes: Evidence from firm and worker specific estimates. *Journal of Productivity Analysis, 31*(1), 1–14.
Kumbhakar, S. C., & Parmeter, C. F. (2010). Estimation of hedonic price functions with incomplete information. *Empirical Economics, 39*(1), 1–25.
Lakhdar, B., Leleu, C. H., Vaillant, N. G., & Wolff, F. C. (2013). Efficiency of purchasing and selling agents in markets with quality uncertainty: The case of illicit drug transactions. *European Journal of Operational Research, 226*(3), 646–657.

Li, C., Wang, Y., & Zheng, Z. (2014). The path analysis of the dual principal-agent problem affects the over-investment of listed companies: Based on the two-tier heterogeneity stochastic frontier model. *CMS, 22*(11), 131–139. https://doi.org/10.16381/j.cnki.issn1003-207x.2014.11.014.

Lian, Y. & Chung, C-F. (2008). Are Chinese Listed Firms Over-Investing?. Available at https://doi.org/10.2139/ssrn.1296462.

Lin, Z. J., Liu, S., & Sun, F. (2017). The impact of financing constraints and agency costs on corporate R&D investment: Evidence from China. *International Review of Finance, 17*(1), 3–42.

Lins, M. P. E., de Lyra Novaes, L. F., & Legey, L. F. L. (2005). Real estate appraisal: A double perspective data envelopment analysis approach. *Annals of Operations Research, 138*(1), 79–96.

Liu, H. (2017). Dynamic identification and early-warning of inefficient investment carried out by listed companies based on the stochastic and PVAR model. *Boletín Técnico, 55*(8), 708–717.

Liu, X., & Liu, F. (2014). IPO pricing efficiency measurement on listed SMEs in China: Under the condition of asymmetric information. *Review of Investment studies, 6*, 1. http://en.cnki.com.cn/Article_en/CJFDTotal-TZYJ201406010.htm.

Lv, X. (2013). Agency conflicts, incentive compatibility and technology innovation of Chinese listed companies: Empirical analysis based on two-tier stochastic frontier model. *Modern Finance and Economics–Journal of Tianjin University of Finance and Economics*, 11. http://en.cnki.com.cn/Article_en/CJFDTOTAL-XCXB201311012.htm.

Lyu, X., Decker, C., & Ni, J. (2018). Compensation negotiation and corporate governance: The evidence from China. *Journal of Chinese Economic and Business Studies, 12*(2), 193–213. https://doi.org/10.1080/14765284.2018.1445081.

Mouchart, M., & Vandresse, M. (2007). Bargaining powers and market segmentation in freight transport. *Journal of Applied Econometrics, 22*(7), 1295–1313.

Mouchart, M., & Vandresse, M. (2010). A double-frontier approach for measuring market imperfection. *Annals of Operations Research, 173*(1), 137–144.

Murphy, A., & Strobl, E. (2008). Employer and employee ignorance in developing countries: The case of Trinidad and Tobago. *Review of Development Economics, 12*(2), 339–353.

Olson, J. A., Schmidt, P., & Waldman, D. M. (1980). A Monte Carlo study of estimators of stochastic frontier production functions. *Journal of Econometrics, 13*(1), 67–82.

Papadopoulos, A. (2015a). The half-normal specification for the two-tier stochastic frontier model. *Journal of Productivity Analysis, 43*(2), 225–230.

Papadopoulos, A. (2015b). *The double half-normal distribution and its extensions*. Research Report. Athens University of Economics and Business.

Papadopoulos, A. (2018). *The two-tier stochastic frontier framework: Theory and applications, models and tools*. PhD Thesis. Athens University of Economics and Business. http://www.pyxida.aueb.gr/getfile.php?object_id=iid:6525&ds_id=PDF1

Papadopoulos, A. (2019). Accounting for endogeneity in regression models using Copulas: A step-by-step guide for empirical studies. Submitted manuscript under review.

Papadopoulos, A (2020a). Stochastic frontier models using the generalized exponential distribution. Submitted manuscript under review.

Papadopoulos, A. (2020b). Measuring the effect of management on production: A two-tier stochastic frontier approach.. Submitted manuscript under review.

Papadopoulos, A. (2020c). Matched employer-employee data sets in action: A Nash bargaining model for wage determination under productivity uncertainty and information asymmetry. Submitted manuscript under review.

Papadopoulos, A., Parmeter, C., and Kumbhakar, S. (2020). Modeling dependence in two-tier stochastic frontier models. Submitted manuscript under review.

Parmeter, C. F. (2018). Estimation of the two-tiered stochastic frontier model with the scaling property. *Journal of Productivity Analysis, 49*(1), 37–47.

Pissarides, C. A. (2000). *Equilibrium unemployment theory* (2nd ed.). Cambridge, MA: MIT.

Poggi, A. (2010). Job satisfaction, working conditions and aspirations. *Journal of Economic Psychology, 31*(6), 936–949.

Polachek, S., Das, T., & Thamma-Apiroam, R. (2013). *Heterogeneity in the production of human capital* (IZA Discussion Paper #7335).

Polachek, S., Das, T., & Thamma-Apiroam, R. (2015). Micro- and macroeconomics implications of heterogeneity in the production of human capital. *Journal of Political Economy, 128*(6), 1410–1455.

Polachek, S. W. (2017). Heterogeneity in the labor market: Ability and information acquisition. *Eastern Economic Journal, 43*(3), 377–390.

Polachek, S. W., & Robst, J. (1998). Employee labor market information: Comparing direct world of work measures of workers' knowledge to stochastic frontier estimates. *Labour Economics, 5*, 231–242.

Polachek, S. W., & Yoon, B. J. (1987). A two-tiered earnings frontier estimation of employer and employee information in the labor market. *The Review of Economics and Statistics, 69*(2), 296–302.

Polachek, S. W., & Yoon, B. J. (1996). Panel estimates of a two-tiered earnings frontier. *Journal of Applied Econometrics, 11*(2), 169–178.

Pope, J. C. (2008). Do seller disclosures affect property values?: Buyer information and the hedonic model. *Land Economics, 84*(4), 551–572.

Rajapaksa, D. P. (2015). *Floods and property values: A hedonic property and efficiency analysis*. Doctoral dissertation. Queensland University of Technology.

Ritter, C., & Simar, L. (1997). Pitfalls of normal-gamma stochastic frontier models. *Journal of Productivity Analysis, 8*(2), 167–182.

Shabanpour, H., Yousefi, S., & Saen, R. F. (2017). Future planning for benchmarking and ranking sustainable suppliers using goal programming and robust double frontiers DEA. *Transportation Research, 50D*, 129–143.

Sharif, N. R., & Dar, A. A. (2007). An empirical investigation of the impact of imperfect information on wages in Canada. *Review of Applied Economics, 3*(1-2), 137–155.

Smith, M. D. (2008). Stochastic frontier models with dependent error components. *The Econometrics Journal, 11*(1), 172–192.

Stevenson, R. E. (1980). Likelihood functions for generalized stochastic frontier estimation. *Journal of Econometrics, 13*, 57–66.

Tao, J., Xin, B., & Lian, Y. (2014). Measurement of listed company's bargaining power in the credit market: Based on two-tier stochastic model. *Review of Investment Studies, 4*, 1. http://en.cnki.com.cn/Article_en/CJFDTOTAL-TZYJ201408006.htm.

Tomini, S., Groot, W., & Pavlova, M. (2012). Paying informally in the Albanian health care sector: A two-tiered stochastic frontier model. *The European Journal of Health Economics, 13*, 777–788.

Tran, K. C., & Tsionas, E. G. (2015). Endogeneity in stochastic frontier models: Copula approach without external instruments. *Economics Letters, 133*, 85–88.

Tsionas, E. G. (2012). Maximum likelihood estimation of stochastic frontier models by the Fourier transform. *Journal of Econometrics, 170*, 234–248.

Wang, P. Y. (2017). *A six component panel stochastic model*. Master Thesis. National Taiwan University.

Wang, Y. (2016a). Bargaining matters: An analysis of bilateral aid to developing countries. *Journal of International Relations and Development, 21*, 1–21. https://doi.org/10.1057/jird.2016.8.

Wang, Y. (2016b). The effect of bargaining on US economic aid. *International Interactions, 42*(3), 479–502.

Wei, Z. (2015). Financial constraint, government R&D subsidies and corporate R&D investment: An empirical study of China's strategic emerging industries. *Contemporary Finance & Economics*, 11, 86–97.

Wen, H. X., Liu, X. J., Wang, H., & Caputo, Y. (2016). The influence of financial constraint and agency cost on investment inefficiency of gem listed firms–based on two-tier stochastic frontier model. *Journal of Mechanical Engineering Research and Developments, 39*(2), 584–592. https://doi.org/10.7508/jmerd.2016.02.038.

Wolff, F. C. (2016). Bargaining powers of buyers and sellers on the online diamond market: A double perspective non-parametric analysis. *Annals of Operations Research, 244*(2), 697–718.

Xie, C., & Li, L. (2018). The empirical test on investment efficiency and influence of equity incentive in supply-side structural reform: Based on the two-tier stochastic frontier approach. *Applied Stochastic Models in Business and Industry, 34*, 5. https://doi.org/10.1002/asmb.2304.

Xu, H., Wang, H., Zhou, C., & Geng, Z. (2016). Dual attributes of government intervention and China's real estate prices—Is Chinese government a promoter of the real estate prices? *Accounting and Finance Research, 5*(3), 29–36.

Yan, X., & Qi, C. (2017). Asymmetric information, bargaining power and the formation of Chinese export fruit price: based on the two-tier stochastic frontier model. *Statistics Forum, 32*, 46–54.

Yu, L., & Liang, T. (2012). *The performance of dividend policy–Based on financing constraints and agency cost trade-off.* In Proceedings of 2012 international conference on information management, innovation management and industrial engineering (ICIII), pp. 455–459.

Zhang, H., Zhang, J., Yang, Y., & Zhou, Q. (2017). Bargaining power in tourist shopping. *Journal of Travel Research, 57*(7), 947–961. https://doi.org/10.1177/0047287517724917.

Zhang, X., & Sun, G. (2015). Dual characteristics of exchange rate and the dispute on RMB between China and the US—Is China a currency manipulator? *Finance & Trade Economics, 8*, 1.

Zhang, Z., & Zheng, Z. (2012). The Influence of financial constraint and agency cost on investment inefficiency of listed firms: An empirical measurement based on two-tier stochastic frontier model. *Journal of Industrial Engineering and Engineering Management, 2*, 119–126.

Zheng, Z., & Zhang, Z. (2012a). IPO bookbuilding and issue: Underpricing effect or overpricing effect? An empirical measure based on two-tier stochastic frontier model. *Systems Engineering, 3*. http://en.cnki.com.cn/Article_en/CJFDTOTAL-GCXT201203004.htm.

Zheng, Z., & Zhang, Z. (2012b). Cause decomposition and re-examination of Chinese extreme IPO returns—Evidence from Chinese hybrid verification-bookbuilding method offerings. *Journal of Shanxi Finance and Economics University, 4*, 37–47.

Individual Efficient Frontiers in Performance Analysis

Markku Kallio and Merja Halme

Abstract We propose a new approach for performance comparisons with a goal similar to the DEA or efficiency analysis based on stochastic frontiers. Our approach accounts for varying environmental factors and human resources among the units under consideration by assuming individual production possibility sets (PPS). In a partial equilibrium framework we assume that the observed netputs represent an equilibrium. Thus, each DMU is efficient with respect to its individual PPS. The netputs and estimated prices common for all units reveal characteristics of the individual PPSs and assess the units' relative performance. To obtain such prices from scarce data we assume that the observed netput vectors represent a random sample of netput vectors. We use prices which render the realizations of individual profits or returns of the DMUs most likely. We compare the DEA based efficiency rankings with our performance rankings. Strong rank correlation is observed between the two. The discriminatory power of our ranking is superior to conventional DEA methods.

Keywords Performance analysis · Partial equilibrium · Production analysis · Evolutionary computation

Electronic Supplementary Material The online version of this chapter (https://doi.org/10.1007/978-3-030-47106-4_9) contains supplementary material, which is available to authorized users.

M. Kallio · M. Halme (✉)
Department of Information and Service Management, Aalto University School of Business, Espoo, Finland
e-mail: markku.kallio@aalto.fi; merja.halme@aalto.fi

C. F. Parmeter, R. C. Sickles (eds.), *Advances in Efficiency and Productivity Analysis*, Springer Proceedings in Business and Economics,
https://doi.org/10.1007/978-3-030-47106-4_9

1 Introduction

Financial accounting figures, such as profit, return on assets, etc., remain widely used and easily understandable performance measures of firms, for instance, in annual and quarterly reports. They are commonly used for performance comparisons of individual firms as well. On the other hand, since the introduction of DEA by Charnes et al. (1978), we have witnessed the success of efficiency analysis both in academic and in field studies. DEA provides a simple framework to compare the efficiency of units with multiple inputs and outputs. Commonly, a production possibility set (PPS) is defined by feasible combinations of input and output vectors, and using some distance function, the efficiency score of a DMU is based on how far its netput vector is from the efficient frontier of the PPS. A number of articles involve a stochastic production frontier which may be parametric or non-parametric; see e.g., Kumbhakar and Lovell (2000), and Kumbhakar et al. (2015).

The approach we put forward does not fall in the domain of DEA or stochastic frontier approaches but it has common goals with them: to produce for units under consideration scores ranking their performance. It includes two important advantages that are not present in the simple original DEA models: first, our approach takes care of different environments and human resources of the units and, second, has superior discriminatory power. Additional elements have been suggested for taking care of the varying environments and lack of discriminations in DEA models.

When productivity analysis is carried out the assumption of units functioning in similar environments is rarely close to the true situation. In the DEA several additions have been suggested (e.g. Ruggiero 1998; Fried et al. 2002; Banker and Natarajan 2008) as a remedy, while our approach deals with different environments assuming individual production possibility sets (PPS). The discriminatory power of DEA related to the scores of the units can been increased by the inclusion of preference information (weight restrictions or benchmarks, see Pedjara-Chaparro et al. 1997; Halme et al. 1999), or by e.g. second stage DEA (e.g. Ramalho et al. 2010). Our approach considers value (profit) or return efficiency (for corresponding DEA formulations see Halme et al. 1999; Kuosmanen et al. 2010, Eskelinen et al. 2014) instead of dealing with technical efficiency. The approach uses the same prices for all units.

One major factor that apparently increases the variety of the units is the quality of the management. Personnel economics research provides strong evidence that a firm's productivity and its production possibility set (PPS) can be strongly influenced by human resources, such as management skills; for an extensive survey, see Bloom and Van Reenen (2011). Furthermore, there are other DMU-specific environmental factors, such as those determined by location. A single PPS may not be entirely feasible for any DMU. Motivated by the above, we assume an individual (possibly unobservable) PPS^j for each DMU^j, $j = 1, \ldots, n$, and propose an approach where performance scores are not based on some common efficient frontier. To avoid confusion, our methodology is introduced as *performance analysis (PA)* to distinguish it from frontier based *efficiency analysis (EA)*.

In a partial equilibrium framework, given prices of inputs and outputs, we assume that each DMU^j chooses the best feasible netput vector; i.e., given the resources and environment of DMU^j, the management and employers do the best within their skills. Noting that each PPS^j is assumed to account for human resource capabilities and other differing factors of the environment for each DMU^j, we assume that the observed choices of the DMUs are equilibrium netput vectors. To obtain estimates for equilibrium prices from the scarce data of netput vectors, we assume that the observed netput vectors represent a random sample of netput vectors.

We use profit or return as a performance measure, which depends on the prices of inputs and outputs. From an admissible set we look for a price vector which renders the realizations of individual performance measures of the DMUs most likely. Such prices are used as estimates for equilibrium prices. Optimality conditions together with such prices and the netput vectors yield an estimated PPS for each DMU^j individually. The generally non-convex likelihood maximization problem for price estimates is solved using an evolutionary algorithm of Deb et al. (2002).

In our performance measurement—unlike typically in DEA approaches—the prices used for evaluation of the DMUs are common for each unit. Profit or return is used as a performance measure. The fact that market conditions are present today everywhere, also in public organizations, supports the one-price-for-all choice as an approximation of real world.

Our approach suffers neither from the lack of discriminatory power often encountered by DEA applications nor from the problems related to economies of scale (DEA can use some tests for diagnosing the returns to scale assumption such as suggested by Kneip et al. 2016). For instance, in the field study discussed in this article, 28–32% of the $DMUs$ are found efficient by DEA.

Since both the frontier based methods and our approach provide a basis of ranking for the DMUs, we compare the rankings of a field study whose results qualitatively represent well numerous other cases we have considered. Despite the differences our test results of the two approaches show a strong correlation of rankings; however, a stronger discriminatory power is achieved by PA.

The rest of the article proceeds as follows. In Sect. 2 we introduce performance analysis (PA). Section 3 reviews traditional efficiency analysis (EA) methods to be used for comparison with PA in Sect. 4. Section 5 concludes. Supplementary material is in the Appendix: an evolutionary optimization procedure for price estimation is presented in Appendix A illustrative simulated examples of PA are in Appendix B; data and results of a field study are shown in the Appendix C.

2 Performance Analysis

We begin by introducing the economic basis of PA in Sect. 2.1. The principle of estimating the price vector is introduced in Sect. 2.2. Thereafter we define PA scores in Sect. 2.3, propose density estimates of profit and return in Sect. 2.4, and discuss computational considerations in Sect. 2.5.

2.1 Economic Foundation

Consider firms or other decision-making units DMU^j for $j = 1, 2, \ldots, n$. Because of differing availability of resources (including human resources) and environmental considerations, we assume a specific production possibility set PPS^j for each DMU^j. In a partial equilibrium framework, consider profit maximizing producers DMU^j, $j = 1, \ldots, n$. For each DMU^j, there are m inputs and k outputs. Let $\xi^j \leq 0$ denote the input vector and $\eta^j \geq 0$ the output vector of DMU^j. For all j, let $g^j(\xi^j, \eta^j)$ be a multi-input multi-output transformation function of DMU^j such that PPS^j is defined by $g^j(\xi^j, \eta^j) \leq 0$. Transformation function $g^j(\xi^j, \eta^j)$ may represent, for instance, CET-GD technology (e.g., Kumbhakar et al. 2015). Let $p(\eta)$ be an integrable price function (inverse demand function) facing aggregate output supply $\eta = \sum_j \eta^j$ and let $c(\xi)$ be an integrable marginal cost function (supply function) facing aggregate input demand $\xi = \sum_j \xi^j$.

Assuming price taking behavior[1] for each DMU^j, consider a competitive equilibrium. For each DMU^j, the *observed inputs* $\xi^j = -x^j \in R^m_+$ and *outputs* $\eta^j = y^j \in R^k_+$ represent equilibrium choices lying on the efficient frontier of PPS^j. For a non-negative input vector $x \in R^m_+$ and a non-negative output vector $y \in R^k_+$, the netput vector z is defined by

$$z^t = (-x^t, y^t), \tag{1}$$

where superscript t refers to a transpose. For all j, z^j is the observed equilibrium netput vector of DMU^j with input vector x^j and output vector y^j.

Given an equilibrium price vector μ^*_x for inputs and μ^*_y for outputs with $\mu^* = (\mu^*_x, \mu^*_y)$, the performance of DMU^k in terms of profit or return may appear superior to DMU^j because of the differences in PPS^k and PPS^j. Using optimality conditions of each DMU^j, we note that price estimates for μ^* together with inputs x^j and outputs y^j imply the individual transformation functions—provided that the number of parameters of each transformation function is not excessive—and thereby the production possibility sets PPS^j are revealed. For numerical examples, see Appendix B.

2.2 Estimating Prices

The price function for outputs, the cost function for inputs, and transformation functions for the DMUs are not known; in addition to observed inputs and outputs, we may only have partial price information which imposes some conditions for

[1]If prices of some products or services are not observable in the market, we interpret the prices resulting from rational expectations equilibrium.

price relationships and possibly takes into account some price observations, for instance. Therefore, to estimate the prices we assume that observed netput vectors z^j represent a random sample from netput vector $\tilde{z}$ with a multivariate pdf $\Phi(z)$. While an efficient production frontier characterizes each PPS^j, we need not assume a bounded support for $\tilde{z}$.

Let row vector $\mu = (\mu_x, \mu_y) \in R^{m+k}$ denote the vector of prices with input prices $\mu_x \in R^m$ and output prices $\mu_y \in R^k$. The prices are expressed in monetary units per unit of product. Partial price information is given by the *admissible set of prices* P. We require $\mu \geq \epsilon$, for some $\epsilon \geq 0$. Prices are restricted by other means as well. For scaling the prices, we may fix the value of some cost and/or revenue component. Some prices may be fixed or restricted to some interval and price ratios may be bounded. We may also employ subjective judgment. For instance, if z^j is seen superior to z^k in terms of profit in a pair-wise comparison among two netput vectors, we may include such judgmental information in the analysis. In this case we require $\mu(z^j - z^k) \geq 0$. We assume that the set of admissible prices P is a non-empty compact and convex set defined by linear equations and linear inequalities.

We now turn to an estimate $\hat{\mu}$ of μ^* to be used in PA. For netput vector $z^t = (-x^t, y^t)$ with $x \geq 0$ and $y \geq 0$, given a price vector $\mu = (\mu_x, \mu_y) \in P$ we determine a performance measure $\kappa = \kappa(\mu, z)$. Subsequently κ stands for profit $\pi = r - c$ or return $\rho = r/c$ with revenue $r = \mu_y y$ and cost $c = \mu_x x$. Given pdf $\Phi(z)$, price vector μ, and the definition of κ, a pdf $\psi(\kappa; \mu)$ of κ is implied for each μ. Of course, $\psi(\kappa; \mu)$ may not have an analytical expression even if $\Phi(z)$ has one. An estimate of $\psi(\kappa; \mu)$ is denoted by $\hat{\psi}(\kappa; \mu)$ and it will be discussed in Sect. 2.4. Prices are parameters of such a pdf and we look for prices which make the individual performance figures of the DMUs most likely. For DMU^j, the performance measure $\kappa_j = \kappa_j(\mu, z^j)$ depends on prices $\mu \in P$ whose values we determine by log-likelihood maximization:

$$\max_{\mu \in P} \sum_{j=1}^{n} \log \hat{\psi}(\kappa_j(\mu, z^j); \mu). \tag{2}$$

An optimal price vector in (2) is denoted by $\hat{\mu}$ and it is used to evaluate the return and value performance scores defined in Sect. 2.3.

2.3 Return and Value Performance Scores

Given an estimate $\hat{\mu}$ of the equilibrium price vector and the netput vector z^j we can evaluate return and profit. Thereby we may state alternative scores for return and value performance.

For *return performance analysis (RPA)*, return ρ plays the role of performance measure κ. Given estimate $\hat{\mu}$ for the equilibrium price vector with components $\hat{\mu}_x$ for inputs and $\hat{\mu}_y$ for outputs, the random return is $\tilde{\rho} = \hat{\mu}_y \tilde{y} / \hat{\mu}_x \tilde{x}$ and we calculate the return $\hat{\rho}_j$ of each DMU^j. Then the *return performance* (RP) score of DMU^j is the probability of $\tilde{\rho} \leq \hat{\rho}_j$. A score 0.68 of DMU^j means that 68% of the realizations of $\tilde{z}$ are inferior or as good as DMU^j or that DMU^j is ranked among top 32%; see Fig. 1.

For *value performance analysis (VPA)* measure κ is profit π. Given price vector estimate $\hat{\mu}$, we obtain the random profit $\tilde{\pi} = \hat{\mu}\tilde{z}$ and we calculate profit $\hat{\pi}_j$ of each DMU^j. Then the *value performance* (VP) score of DMU^j is the probability of $\tilde{\pi} \leq \hat{\pi}_j$.

2.4 Density Estimates of Profit and Return

Consider three cases for the distribution of netput vector $\tilde{z}$: Case 1, $\tilde{z}$ is multivariate normal; Case 2, no distributional assumption is made; Case 3, a parametric family of multivariate distributions is adopted. Case 1 in Sect. 2.4.1 applies to VPA but not for RPA. In Sect. 2.4.2 of Case 2, a kernel density estimate is employed for pdf $\hat{\psi}(\kappa; \mu)$ of the performance measure κ. In Sect. 2.4.3 of Case 3, parameters of pdf $\Phi(z)$ are estimated first to obtain $\hat{\Phi}(z)$ and $\hat{\psi}(\kappa; \mu)$ is derived thereafter. At the first reading, one may proceed directly to Sect. 2.5.

2.4.1 Multivariate Normal Distribution of Netput Vectors

In this section we assume $\tilde{z}$ has a multivariate normal pdf $\Phi(z)$.[2] Maximum likelihood estimates $\bar{z}$ and V for the expected value and the covariance matrix of $\tilde{z}$ are

$$\bar{z} = \frac{1}{n}\sum_j z^j$$

$$V = \frac{1}{n}\sum_j (z^j - \bar{z})(z^j - \bar{z})^t.$$

Hence pdf $\hat{\Phi}(z)$, the estimate of Φ, is the pdf $N(\bar{z}, V)$, and given a price vector $\mu \in P$, the random profit $\pi = \mu\tilde{z}$ has the pdf $N(\bar{\pi}, \sigma^2)$, where $\bar{\pi} = \mu\bar{z}$ and $\sigma^2 = \mu V \mu^t$. Therefore, in case of VPA, $\hat{\psi}(\pi; \mu)$ has a normal distribution. For each DMU^j, price vector $\mu \in P$ and netput vector z^j yield profit $\pi_j = \mu z^j$. Thus the log-likelihood function in (2) for profits π_j (omitting constant terms) is $-(n/2)\log(\sigma^2)$. Hence, the estimate for price vector μ is obtained by minimizing the variance σ^2; i.e. our problem is to find price vector μ to

$$\min_{\mu \in P} \mu V \mu^t. \tag{3}$$

[2] In this case we expect that the likelihood for $x \ngeq 0$ and $y \ngeq 0$ is small.

Given optimal price vector $\hat{\mu}$ in (3), we obtain the normal pdf for the random profit $\tilde{\pi} = \hat{\mu}z$, whose expected value is $\hat{\mu}\bar{z}$ and variance is the optimal objective function value in (3).

2.4.2 Kernel Density Estimate of $\psi(\kappa; \mu)$

Kernel density estimate with Gaussian kernel and bandwidth δ is a standard approach which may be adopted for estimating univariate distribution ψ; see e.g., Rosenblatt (1956) and Silverman (1998). Given price vector μ and netput vectors z^j, with $\kappa_j = \kappa(\mu, z^j)$ we define

$$\hat{\psi}(\kappa; \mu) = \frac{1}{n} \sum_{j=1}^{n} \frac{1}{\sqrt{2\pi}\delta} \exp[-\frac{(\kappa - \kappa_j)^2}{2\delta^2}]. \tag{4}$$

We employ the following result in Silverman (1998): if the pdf to be estimated is normal with variance σ^2, then an approximate optimal bandwidth δ minimizing the mean integrated square error is

$$\delta = \sigma(4/3n)^{1/5}. \tag{5}$$

Figure 1 shows the kernel density estimate $\hat{\psi}(\rho; \hat{\mu})$ with bandwidth $\delta = 0.088$ in the grocery stores case study of Sect. 4.

We use (5) where σ^2 is replaced with the variance $\hat{\sigma}^2$ of the sample $\{\kappa_j\}$. Since $\hat{\sigma}$ depends on prices, we need to search for a suitable bandwidth δ to satisfy (5) with sample variance associated with the estimate $\hat{\mu}$ of equilibrium prices. In the case studies in Sect. 4 such values of δ range from 0.063 to 0.158.

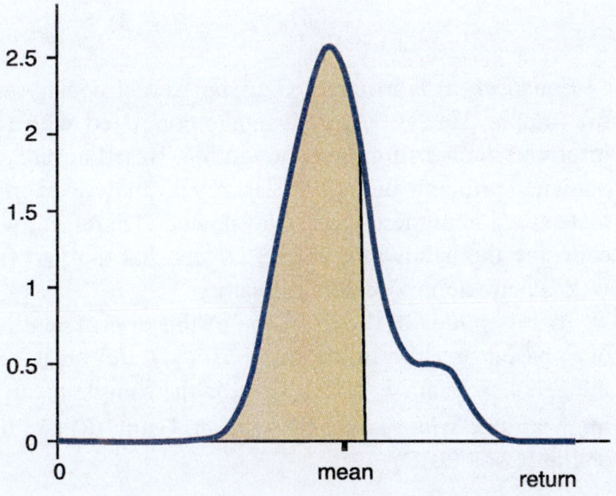

Fig. 1 Kernel density estimate of probability density function $\hat{\psi}(\rho; \hat{\mu})$ of return for RPA in the grocery stores case study of Sect. 4. The shaded area is the return performance (RP) score 0.68 of the DMU ranking eighth among the 25 DMUs

2.4.3 Parametric Distribution of Netput Vectors

Next, consider a family of multivariate pdfs for $\Phi(z)$ with some set of parameters (a multivariate log-normal distribution, for example). The observations z^j, $j = 1, \ldots, n$, are used for parameter estimation and $\hat{\Phi}(z)$ denotes the estimated pdf of $\tilde{z}$. Given pdf $\hat{\Phi}(z)$, price vector μ and the definition of κ, let $\phi(\kappa; \mu)$ denote the associated pdf of the measure κ given price vector μ.

Typically an analytical expression for $\phi(\kappa; \mu)$ is not available, wherefore we employ an approximation $\hat{\psi}$ of ϕ. To derive $\hat{\psi}$, consider a family of normal pdfs $f(\kappa; \kappa', \delta^2)$ of κ with expected values κ' and variance δ^2. In this family, let $\phi(\kappa'; \mu)$ be the pdf of expected values κ'. Then expected pdf at κ is

$$E(\kappa, \delta) \equiv E[f(\kappa; \kappa', \delta^2)] = \int_{\kappa'} f(\kappa; \kappa', \delta^2)\phi(\kappa'; \mu)d\kappa'. \tag{6}$$

As δ approaches zero, $f(\kappa; \kappa', \delta^2)$ approaches the Dirac delta function, and therefore

$$\lim_{\delta \to 0} E(\kappa, \delta) = \phi(\kappa; \mu). \tag{7}$$

We approximate the integral in (6) by a sample average. Using a random sample $\{z^s\}$ of S independent draws from $\hat{\Phi}(z)$, define $\kappa_s = \kappa(\mu, z^s)$. Then $\{\kappa_s\}$ is a random sample of S draws from $\phi(\kappa; \mu)$ and the sample average pdf is

$$\hat{\psi}(\kappa; \mu) = \frac{1}{S}\sum_s f(\kappa; \kappa_s, \delta^2) = \frac{1}{S}\sum_s \frac{1}{\sqrt{2\pi}\delta}\exp[-\frac{(\kappa - \kappa_s)^2}{2\delta^2}]. \tag{8}$$

By (6)–(8), for large S and small $\delta > 0$ we have

$$\hat{\psi}(\kappa; \mu) \approx E(\kappa, \delta) \approx \phi(\kappa; \mu). \tag{9}$$

Equation (8) is in fact a Gaussian kernel density estimate of $\phi(\kappa; \mu)$ based on the sample. However, an advantage compared with (4) is that we now are better informed in choosing the bandwidth δ. Based on pdf $\hat{\Phi}(z)$, the true pdf $\phi(\kappa; \mu)$ is known in principle but not necessarily its analytic expression. However, sample estimates for its moments can be evaluated. Therefore, we employ approximation (8) choosing the bandwidth in such a way that the first few moments of $\phi(\kappa; \mu)$ and $\hat{\psi}(\kappa; \mu)$ are approximately the same.

To get an idea of the precision of this approximation, we compare the moments of κ based on the sample from $\phi(\kappa; \mu)$ and on the approximation $\hat{\psi}(\kappa; \mu)$. For integers $l > 0$, $\hat{m}_l = (1/S)\sum_s \kappa_s^l$ is the sample mean of κ^l and m_l denotes the lth moment of κ with respect to $\hat{\psi}(\kappa; \mu)$. Using (8) and the moments of $N(\kappa_s, \delta^2)$ we obtain (Cook 2012)

$$m_l = \frac{1}{S}\sum_s \sum_{i=0}^{[l/2]} \binom{l}{2i} (2i-1)!!\,\delta^{2i}\,\kappa_s^{(l-2i)} = \sum_{i=0}^{[l/2]} \binom{l}{2i} (2i-1)!!\,\delta^{2i}\,\hat{m}_{(l-2i)}$$
$$= \hat{m}_l + O(\delta^2), \tag{10}$$

where $[\cdot]$ denotes rounding down and $(\cdot)!!$ denotes double factorial.[3] The residual term $O(\delta^2)$ is of the order of δ^2. For example, $m_1 = \hat{m}_1$, $m_2 = \hat{m}_2 + \delta^2$, $m_3 = \hat{m}_3 + 3\hat{m}_1\delta^2$ $m_4 = \hat{m}_4 + 6\hat{m}_2\delta^2 + 3\delta^4$, etc. For large S, the sample means $\hat{m}_l$ approach the respective moments based on $\phi(\kappa; \mu)$, and for small δ, the moments m_l are close to respective moments $\hat{m}_l$. Silverman's rule (5) here matches the moments unsatisfactory.

Note that for the first moments, $m_1 = \hat{m}_1$. Let $\hat{\sigma}^2 = \hat{m}_2 - \hat{m}_1^2$ denote the sample variance of κ and $\sigma^2 = m_2 - m_1^2$ the variance based on $\hat{\psi}(\kappa; \mu)$. Their relative difference is $\delta^2/\hat{\sigma}^2$. For computations in Sect. 4, we use sample size $S = 1000$ and $1/2\delta^2 = 10^5$. For these choices the relative difference $\delta^2/\hat{\sigma}^2$ of the variances is less than 0.03% in all cases considered. Furthermore, in Sect. 2.4.1

A test of approximation (8) is as follows. In the multivariate normal case for VPA an approximation is not needed but can be used; an optimal price estimate is obtained from (3), while near optimal prices are obtained using the sample approximation (8) in (2). With sample size $S = 1000$ and $1/2\delta^2 = 10^5$ we solve (2) in two cases of Sect. 4 where the distribution of netput vectors most closely resembles a multivariate normal distribution. These cases refer to bank branches and grocery stores. Based on the results we rank the DMUs according to VP scores. Then the ranking is done based on the scores obtained from the "exact" problem (3). The Spearman rank correlation (of approximate vs. "exact") is 1.00 both for bank branches and grocery stores.

2.5 *Price Computations*

Finally, we discuss computations for obtaining a price vector estimate $\hat{\mu}$ from the likelihood problem (2). In the special and simple case of VPA assuming the netput vector $\tilde{z}$ is multivariate normal an optimal solution for (2) is obtained solving the convex problem (3). For other cases we use evolutionary optimization. Using approximation (8) for pdf $\hat{\psi}$ in (2) the objective function may become highly nonlinear with plenty of local optima; for an illustration of RPA, see Fig. 2 (right) concerning the grocery stores case in Sect. 4. Instead, using the kernel density estimate (4) the objective can be relatively smooth; see Fig. 2 (left). In both cases we end up with a non-convex problem. For global optimization we employ an implementation of the evolutionary optimization procedure PCX-$G3$ (see Deb et al. 2002). The algorithmic steps are presented in Appendix A including some

[3]For integer $k \geq 1$, $k!!$ is the product of positive integers up to k with the same parity as k, and $0!!=(-1)!!=1$.

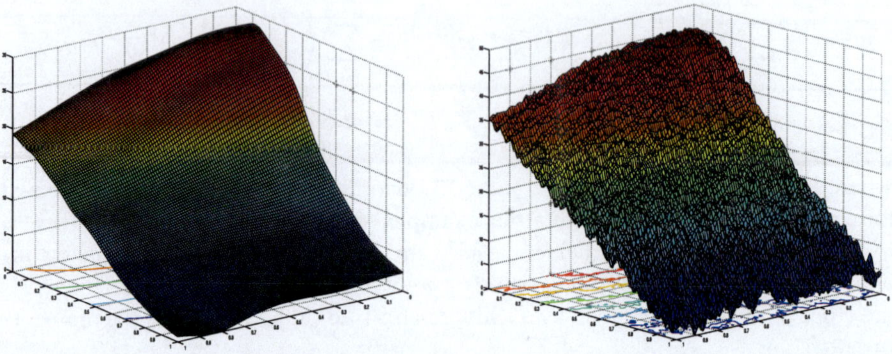

Fig. 2 Log-likelihood functions for RPA in the grocery stores case study with two inputs, two outputs, and price constraints $\mu_1 + \mu_2 = 1$ and $\mu_3 + \mu_4 = 1$. On the left, kernel density estimate (4) with bandwidth $\delta = 0.088$. On the right, multivariate log-normal distribution for netput vectors is employed and approximation (8) with sample size $S = 1000$ and $1/2\delta^2 = 10^5$. Both figures show the log-likelihood in (2) as a function of price vector μ. The horizontal coordinates refer to μ_2 (increasing to the left) and μ_4, both ranging from 0 to 1. Optimal price vector on the left is $\hat{\mu} = (0.914, 0.086, 0.892, 0.108)$ and on the right $\hat{\mu} = (0.912, 0.088, 0.921, 0.079)$

sensitivity analysis for the control parameters of evolutionary optimization. For computations we use $AMPL$ (Fourer et al. 2003) and $MINOS$ (Murtagh and Saunders 1978).

3 Conventional DEA Based Methods

We now review two DEA based approaches for EA, *value (or profit) efficiency analysis* (VEA) based on profit (see e.g., Nerlove 1965, Chambers et al. 1998 and Halme et al. 1999) and *return efficiency analysis* (REA) based on return (see e.g., CCR by Charnes et al. 1978 and BCC by Banker et al. 1984). The rankings based on these methods are used for comparisons with VPA and RPA in Sect. 4 using five real cases of efficiency analysis.

We adopt the presentation of VEA and REA from Kallio and Kallio (2002). We begin by introducing the set of feasible netput vectors (PPS). We judge DMU^r in terms of its netput vector z^r with respect to a production possibility set T of feasible netput vectors z and (as in Sect. 2.2) a set P of admissible price vectors μ. For each DMU^j, we assume that $z^j \in T$.

Consider feasible netput vectors, which are linear combinations of the netput vectors z^j; i.e., for a set $\Lambda \subset R^n$ of weight vectors $\lambda = (\lambda_j)$, we define

$$T = \{z \mid z = \sum_j \lambda_j z^j,\ \lambda \in \Lambda\}. \tag{11}$$

Choices of Λ result in alternative sets T of which one is adopted for efficiency evaluation. In our comparisons of Sect. 4 we use two alternatives. Under a constant returns to scale (CRS) hypothesis,

$$\Lambda = \{\lambda \in R^n |\ \lambda \geq 0\}, \tag{12}$$

and under a variable returns to scale (VRS) hypothesis,

$$\Lambda = \{\lambda \in R^n |\ \sum_j \lambda_j = 1,\ \lambda \geq 0\}. \tag{13}$$

In value efficiency analysis (VEA) the *difference measure of efficiency* of DMU^r is the difference of the best profit achievable by netput vectors in T and the profit of DMU^r and the prices are chosen from the admissible set P to minimize the difference. To test for profit efficiency of DMU^r we solve the problem of finding admissible prices $\mu \in P$ and a scalar θ to

$$\min_{\theta,\mu}\{\theta - \mu z^r \mid \mu \in P \text{ and } \mu z \leq \theta \text{ for all } z \in T\}. \tag{14}$$

At an optimal solution of (14), θ is the maximum profit over T and $\theta - \mu z^r \geq 0$ because $z^r \in T$. If $\theta - \mu z^r = 0$, then z^r maximizes μz over T and DMU^r is profit efficient. The optimal objective function value $\theta - \mu z^r$ in (14) is the difference measure of profit efficiency.

In return efficiency analysis REA, the *ratio measure of return efficiency* of DMU^r is the return (productivity) relative to the best return taking into account all netput vectors in T, and the prices are chosen from the admissible set P to maximize return ratio for DMU^r. To test for return efficiency of netput vector z^r of DMU^r, we solve the problem of finding admissible prices $\mu = (\mu_x, \mu_y) \in P$ and a scalar θ, recalling decomposition of netput vector z in (1), to

$$\max_{\theta,\mu_x,\mu_y} \{\frac{\mu_y y^r}{\mu_x x^r}\frac{1}{\theta} \mid \mu \in P \text{ and } \frac{\mu_y y}{\mu_x x} \leq \theta \text{ for all } z \in T\}. \tag{15}$$

At the optimal solution of (15), θ is the maximum return over T and the optimal objective function value in (15) is the ratio measure of return efficiency. This measure is at most one because $z^r \in T$, and it is equal to one if z^r maximizes the return over T in which case DMU^r is return efficient. As usual, LP is applied to solve (14) and (15).

4 Comparison of PA and EA Methods

For comparisons of VEA and REA with VPA and RPA, we used five published field studies concerning (i) bank branches (Eskelinen et al. 2014), (ii) parishes (Halme and Korhonen 2015), (iii) dental care units (Halme and Korhonen 2000), (iv) grocery stores (Korhonen et al. 2002), and (v) power plants (Kuosmanen 2012). Here we only discuss case (i) in some detail; results from the other four cases were very similar.

The bank branch study by Eskelinen et al. (2014) concerns sales performance of branches in the Helsinki OP Bank. The analysis covers the years 2007–2010 in the 25 branches operating in the Helsinki metropolitan area. The bank considers financing and investment services as outputs in the model. The output quantities by bank branch are shown in the Appendix C where both output figures are in average number of aggregated transactions per annum. There are five inputs: total work time in five categories of the sales force. The input figures in average full-time years per annum for each branch are shown as well. For VEA and REA, a constant returns to scale (CRS) hypothesis is adopted for the set T of feasible netput vectors. Hence, T is defined by (11) and (12).

For PA we consider both a multivariate log-normal distribution $\tilde{z}$ and a kernel density estimate for the performance measure (return or profit). We use a set of admissible prices with a lower limit 10^{-6} for all prices and we scale the input prices such that the average cost $\mu_x \bar{x} = 1$, where $\bar{x}$ is the average of input vectors x^j in the sample. Additionally for REA and RPA, we require that the revenue $\mu_y \bar{y} \geq 1$, where $\bar{y}$ is the average of output vectors y^j.[4]

For the bank branch case the Appendix C shows PA and EA based efficiency scores as well as ranking of DMUs based on different methods. Figure 3 (top) shows the comparisons of conventional REA efficiency (horizontal axis in each diagram) vs. return performance of RPA (vertical axis). Figure 3 (bottom) displays a similar comparison of VEA and VPA. In each case, results based on both density estimates (log-Normal/kernel) are depicted.[5] In these figures, one can see the correlation between the pairs of scores. The corresponding Spearman rank correlation ranges from 0.80 to 0.91. The number of efficient DMUs is 9 for both VEA and REA. The ranking based on PA is nearly independent of the distributional assumption of $\tilde{z}$.

[4]For VEA this additional requirement under CRS leads to infeasibility.

[5]Note that in Fig. 3 the REA and RPA scores are positively correlated whereas in Fig. 3 the VEA and VPA scores have negative correlation because high VEA score means poor performance.

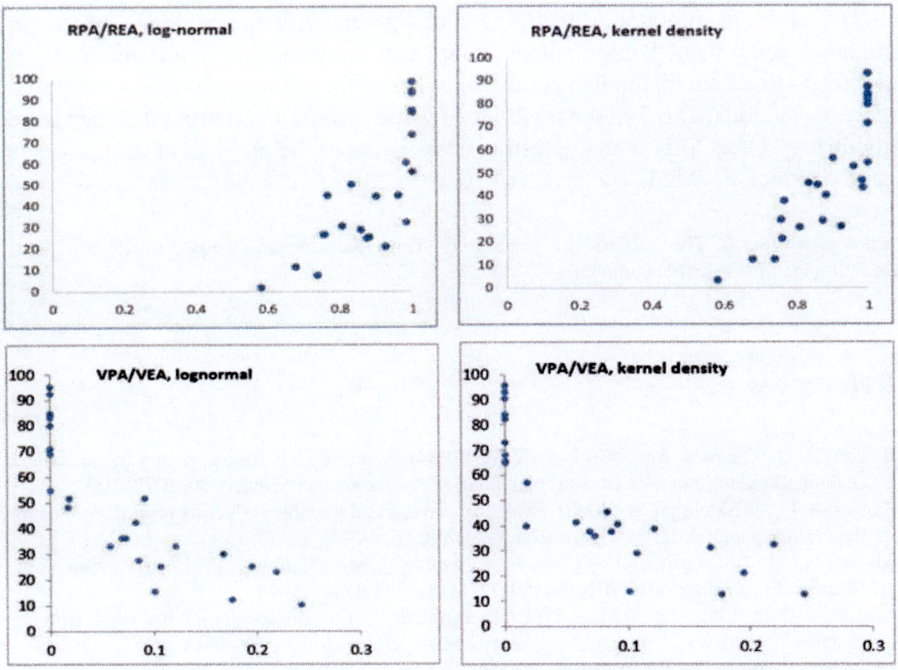

Fig. 3 The bank branches case with 25 units. Top: Correlation diagrams of REA scores (horizontal axis in each diagram) and return performance (vertical axis) of RPA. REA employs the ratio measure of return efficiency. Bottom: Correlation diagrams of VEA scores (horizontal axis in each diagram) and value performance (vertical axis) of VPA. VEA shows the difference measure of profit efficiency

5 Conclusions

We propose a novel approach to measure value (profit) and return performance of decision-making units. The method does not rely on distances from an efficient frontier. Therefore, for the sake of clarity, we discuss performance analysis (PA) instead of frontier based efficiency analysis. Contrary to the assumption made by DEA the units considered typically function in various environments which is why we assume the production possibility sets are individual for each unit. We adopt a partial equilibrium perspective wherefore the observed netput vector of each unit is assumed to be on the efficient frontier of the individual production possibility set. Common prices are calculated for all the units and they represent estimates for equilibrium prices. Our single-price requirement is justified, for instance, by the market forces confronting all kinds of organizations today. Price restrictions can be employed to account for partial price information. The discriminatory power is superior to DEA based methods.

The rankings produced by PA are compared with the rankings based on efficiency analysis of DEA methods. In spite of the significantly different starting points, it turned out that in five published case studies our ranking results compared with conventional DEA based methods of value (profit) and return efficiency were highly correlated. This is an interesting observation as the problem of zero prices is quite common in DEA.

Acknowledgments The authors are grateful to Timo Kuosmanen, Knox Lovell, and Antti Saastamoinen for valuable comments.

References

Banker, R. D., Charnes, A., & Cooper, W. W. (1984). Some models for estimating technical and scale inefficiencies in data envelopment analysis. *Management Science, 30*, 1078–1092.

Banker, R. D., & Natarajan, R. (2008). Evaluating contextual variables affecting productivity using data envelopment analysis. *Operations Research, 56*, 48–58.

Bloom, N., & Van Reenen, J. (2011). *Handbook of labor economics* (Vol. 4b). Amsterdam: Elsevier. https://doi.org/10.1016/S0169-7218(11)02417-8

Chambers, R. G., Chung, Y., & Färe, R. (1998). Profit, directional distance functions, and Nerlovian efficiency. *Journal of Optimization Theory and Applications, 98*, 351–364.

Charnes, A., Cooper, W. W., & Rhodes, E. (1978). Measuring efficiency of decision making units. *European Journal of Operational Research, 2*(6), 429–444.

Cook, J. (2012). *General formula for normal moments*. http://www.johndcook.com/blog/2012/11/06/general-formula-for-normal-moments/

Deb, K., Anand, A., & Joshi, D. (2002). A computationally efficient evolutionary algorithm for real-parameter optimization. *Journal of Evolutionary Computation, 10*(4), 371–395.

Eskelinen, J., Halme, M., & Kallio, M. (2014). Bank branch sales evaluation using extended value efficiency analysis. *European Journal of Operational Research, 232*, 654–663.

Fourer, R., Gay, D., & Kernighan, B.W. (2003). *AMPL, a modeling language for mathematical programming* (2nd ed.). Pacific Grove: Brooks/Cole Thomson Learning.

Fried, H. O., Lovell, C. A. K., Schmidt, S. S., & Yaisawarng, S. (2002). Accounting for environmental effects and statistical noise in data envelopment analysis. *Journal of Productivity Analysis, 17*, 157–174.

Halme, M., Joro, T., Korhonen, P., Salo, S., & Wallenius, J. (1999). A value efficiency approach to incorporating preference information in data envelopment analysis. *Management Science, 45*(1), 103–115.

Halme, M., & Korhonen, P. (2000). Restricting weights in value efficiency analysis. *European Journal of Operational Research, 126*, 175–188.

Halme, M., & Korhonen, P. (2015). Using value efficiency analysis to benchmark non-homogeneous units. *International Journal of Information Technology & Decision Making, 14*, 727–745. https://doi.org/10.1142/S0219622014500916

Kallio, A. M. I., & Kallio, M. J. (2002). Nonparametric models for evaluating economic efficiency and imperfect competition. *Journal of Productivity Analysis, 18*, 171–189.

Kneip, A., Simar, L., & Wilson, P. W. (2016). Testing hypotheses in nonparametric models of production. *Journal of Business & Economic Statistics, 34*(3), 435–456.

Korhonen, P., Soismaa, M., & Siljamäki, A. (2002). On the use of value efficiency analysis and some further developments. *Journal of Productivity Analysis, 17*, 49–65.

Kumbhakar, S. C., & Lovell, C. A. K. (2000). *Stochastic frontier analysis*. Cambridge: Cambridge University Press.

Kumbhakar, S. C., Wang, H.-J., & Horncastle, A. (2015). *A practitioner's guide to stochastic frontier analysis using stata*. Cambridge: Cambridge University Press.

Kuosmanen, T. (2012). Stochastic semi-nonparametric frontier estimation of electricity distribution networks: Application of the StoNED method in the Finnish regulatory model. *Energy Economics, 34*(6), 2189–2199.

Kuosmanen, T., Kortelainen, M., Sipiläinen, T., & Cherchye, L. (2010). Firm and industry level profit efficiency analysis using absolute and uniform shadow prices. *European Journal of Operational Research, 202*, 584–594.

Murtagh, B., & Saunders, M. (1978). Large-scale linearly constrained optimization. *Mathematical Programming, 14*, 41–72.

Nerlove, K. (1965). *Estimation and identification of Cobb-Douglas production functions*. Chicago: Rand Mcnally.

Pedjara-Chaparro, F., Salinas-Jimenez, J., & Smith, P. (1997). On the role of weight restrictions in data envelopment analysis. *European Journal of Operational Research, 8*, 215–230.

Ramalho, E. A., Ramalho, J. J. S., & Henriques, P. D. (2010). Fractional regression models for second stage DEA efficiency analyses. *Journal of Productivity Analysis, 34*, 239–255.

Rosenblatt, M. (1956). Remarks on some nonparametric estimates of a density function. *The Annals of Mathematical Statistics, 27*(3), 832–837.

Ruggiero, J. (1998). Non-discretionary inputs in data envelopment analysis. *European Journal of Operational Research, 111*(3), 461–469.

Silverman, B. W. (1998). *Density estimation for statistics and data analysis*. Boca Raton: Chapman & Hall.

DEA Models Without Inputs or Outputs: A Tour de Force

Giannis Karagiannis

Abstract In this paper we review DEA models without outputs or inputs and models with a single constant input or output and we explore their properties and relations. Then we summarize their potential usefulness in several applications, including (a) multiple criteria decision-making (MCDM) such as supplier selection and ABC inventory classification, (b) construction of composite indicators (environmental, sustainability, subjective well being, etc.), (c) ratio analysis, and (d) spatial efficiency. We further consider the cases of optimistic versus pessimistic composite indicators and of intra- and inter-group composite indicators. We also explore the usefulness of these models in other topics of performance evaluation such as cross efficiency, efficiency based on common weights, and productivity analysis. Lastly, we consider their aggregation across DMUs rules.

Keywords Data envelopment analysis · Radial models without inputs or outputs · Radial models with single constant input or output

1 Introduction

Besides its main use as a tool for estimating efficiency, Data Envelopment Analysis (DEA), in contrast to its econometric rival (i.e., stochastic production frontier), has been used in a number of other applications. These include (1) multi-criteria decision-making (MCDM) problems, such as inventory classification (Ramanathan 2006a; Ng 2007) and vendor/supplier selection (Weber and Desai 1996; Seydel 2006; Ng 2008), (2) derivation of local and global priority weights in the Analytic Hierarchy Process (AHP) (Ramanathan 2006b; Wang and Chin 2009), (3) determination of design requirements' relative importance in quality function deployment (referred to as house of quality) (Ramanathan and Yunfeng 2009), (4) derivation of

G. Karagiannis (✉)
Department of Economics, University of Macedonia, Thessaloniki, Greece
e-mail: karagian@uom.edu.gr

C. F. Parmeter, R. C. Sickles (eds.), *Advances in Efficiency and Productivity Analysis*, Springer Proceedings in Business and Economics,
https://doi.org/10.1007/978-3-030-47106-4_10

weights for Grey Relational Analysis (GRA) (Huang et al. 2015), (5) assessment of quality perception (i.e., SERVQUAL and SERVPREF) (Lee and Kim 2014; Charles and Kumar 2014), (6) construction of composite indicators (Cherchye et al. 2007a; OECD 2008) and quantity/quality indices (Sahoo and Acharya 2010; O'Donnell and Nguyen 2013; Whittaker et al. 2015; Molinos-Senante et al. 2017), (7) location choice and spatial efficiency (Thompson et al. 1986; Desai and Storbeck 1990; Adolphson et al. 1991), (8) analysis of preference voting for election and product or project ranking (Cook and Kress 1990; Green et al. 1996; Hashimoto 1997), (9) ratio analysis when the underlying data do not allow splitting ratio variables into numerators (outputs) and denominators (inputs) (i.e., DEA-R) (Despic et al. 2007; Wei et al. 2011), (10) game theory (e.g., Banker 1980; Lins et al. 2003; Nakabayashi and Tone 2006; Xu et al. 2013), (11) extended (multiple attribute) utility theory (Yang et al. 2014), (12) price and attributes efficiency (Kamakura et al. 1988; Doyle and Green 1991; Fernandez-Castro and Smith 2000), and (13) portfolio evaluation (Morey and Morey 1999; Murthi et al. 1997).

Interestingly, in all but the last two of the aforementioned applications, pure input or output DEA models or their equivalent single constant input or output models have been used. These two special cases of DEA models contain either only input or output variables or restrict the value of inputs or outputs to be constant (i.e., invariant) across decision-making units (DMUs) (see Lovell and Pastor 1999; Caporaletti et al. 1999; Liu et al. 2011).[1] The underlying logic and intuition of these models is related to assessment without inputs or assuming that all DMUs use the same amount of input(s) or, on the other hand, performance evaluation without outputs or assuming that all DMUs produce the same quantity of output(s). They are thus compatible with Koopman's idea of a helmsman who has at his/her disposal a unitary quantity of an aggregate input (output) and attempts to steer (squeeze) all outputs (inputs) toward their maximum (minimum) levels. Consequently, the pure input or output DEA models are suitable for applications other than those related to conventional production models and efficiency analysis. Such applications include the following: *first*, estimating effectiveness (i.e., ability to state and achieve goals) rather than efficiency (i.e., benefits realized versus resources used), where goals are determined by observed behavior (i.e., best practice) and our objective is to evaluate the extent to which they are achieved (Prieto and Zofio 2001). *Second*, evaluating the performance of DMUs in relation to targets set by stakeholders or experts, where the outputs are the percentage of target coverage (Lovell and Pastor 1997). *Third*, accessing performance by means of ratios, as in some business and management studies, where it is difficult (if not impossible) to reformulate the data into original input and output variables and apply conventional DEA (Yang et al. 2014). *Fourth*, determining the ideal or most preferred alternative in MCDM problems where we

[1]The value of inputs or outputs is set usually to one but this is not necessary, it has only to be the same for all DMUs.

do not need to consider input (sometimes output) variables (Yang et al. 2014).[2] *Fifth*, aggregating indicators, indices, or votes by means of an additive linear share-weighting scheme, where the weights are determined endogenously and are not *a priori* equal.

The increasing popularity in recent years of the DEA models considered here is related to the construction of composite indicators as one of their variants, namely the Benefit-of-the-Doubt (BoD) model—an input-oriented DEA model with a single constant input, has been included in OECD (2008) manual as one of four statistical models recommended for constructing composite indicators. The BoD model has been used in a large number of applications, including (but not limiting to) the Human Development Index (e.g., Despotis 2005), the OECD Better Life Index (Mizobuchi 2014), the Quality of Life Indicator (e.g., Morais and Camanho 2011), several life satisfaction indices (see e.g. Guardiola and Picazo-Tadeo (2014), the Internal Market Index (e.g., Cherchye et al. 2007b), the Competitiveness Index (e.g., Bowen and Moesen 2011), the Digital Access Indicator (e.g., Gaaloul and Khalfallah 2014), the Technology Achievement Index (e.g., Cherchye et al. 2008), Students' Evaluation of Teaching indicators (e.g., de Witte and Rogge 2011), educational quality indicators (Murias et al. 2008), the Health System Performance Index (e.g., Lauer et al. 2004), and the Environmental Performance Index (e.g., Zanella et al. 2013).

The aim of this paper is to provide a critical survey of radial DEA models without inputs and outputs or their equivalent single constant input or output models. In that respect, we provide a feat of their strength in terms of their relations with other DEA models and the great number of different applications that may be used. We review the existing literature to provide the main features of these models and discuss some recent extensions. Even though there are some work on non-radial DEA models without inputs and outputs, the main body of existing work is on radial models. We focus on the theoretical aspects of these models and we present a selection of the most interesting applications to illustrate their relevance and usefulness in empirical analysis.

In the next section, we present the main models, we explore the relations among them, and we highlight some of their most interesting applications. In the third section, we examine their relation with other DEA and linear programming models while in the fourth section we consider several extensions. Aggregation (across DMUs) issues are discussed in the fifth section and results related to productivity analysis are presented in the sixth section. Concluding remarks follow in the last section.

[2]In MCDM analysis, alternatives can be seen as DMUs and attributes or criteria for evaluating the alternatives as inputs or outputs, with the former corresponding to the less-is-better type criteria and the latter to the more-is-better type criteria.

2 Models Presentation and Uses

The various DEA models without inputs or outputs and with single constant input or output are presented, respectively, in the upper and the lower panel of Table 1.[3] They are distinguished by orientation, i.e., input- versus output-oriented, and by the type of returns to scale, i.e., constant-returns-to-scale (CRS) versus variable-returns-to-scale (VRS). Since it makes no sense to have an input-oriented model without inputs and an output-oriented model without outputs, and given that a CRS input-oriented (output-oriented) model without outputs (inputs) rates all DMUs as infinitely inefficient, as Lovell and Pastor (1999) shown (see their proposition 1), we are left with only two usable pure input or output DEA models, namely the VRS output-oriented model without inputs, which in its multiplier and envelopment form is given as:

Table 1 DEA models without input and outputs and with single constant input or output

	Input-oriented		Output-oriented	
	CRS	VRS	CRS	VRS
No inputs			Infinitely inefficient	×
No outputs	Infinitely inefficient	◎		
Single constant input	×	All efficient	×	×
Single constant output	◎	◎	◎	All efficient

[3]As Lovell and Pastor (1999, p. 51) claimed, "considering a single constant input (output) is equivalent to considering multiple constant inputs (outputs)."

$$
\begin{array}{llll}
\min\limits_{u_j^k, v_0^k} - v_0^k & & \max\limits_{\lambda_j^k, \theta^k} \theta^k & \\
st \quad \sum_{j=1}^{J} u_j^k y_j^k = 1 & & st \quad \sum_{h=1}^{K} \lambda_h^k y_j^h \geq \theta^k y_j^k & j = 1, \ldots, J \\
-\sum_{j=1}^{J} u_j^k y_j^h - v_0^k \geq 0 & h = 1, \ldots, K & \sum_{h=1}^{K} \lambda_h^k = 1 & \\
u_j^k \geq 0 & j = 1, \ldots, J & \lambda_h^k \geq 0 & h = 1, \ldots, K \\
v_0^k \; free \; in \text{ sign} & & &
\end{array}
\qquad (1)
$$

and the VRS input-oriented DEA model without outputs, which is its multiplier and envelopment form is given as:

$$
\begin{array}{llll}
\max\limits_{v_i^k, u_0^k} - u_0^k & & \min\limits_{\lambda_j^k, \phi^k} \phi^k & \\
st \quad \sum_{i=1}^{I} v_i^k x_i^k = 1 & & st \quad \sum_{h=1}^{K} \mu_h^k x_i^h \leq \phi^k x_i^k & i = 1, \ldots, I \\
\sum_{i=1}^{I} v_i^k x_i^h + u_0^k \geq 0 & h = 1, \ldots, K & \sum_{h=1}^{K} \mu_h^k = 1 & \\
v_i^k \geq 0 & i = 1, \ldots, I & \mu_h^k \geq 0 & h = 1, \ldots, K \\
u_0^k \; free \; in \text{ sign} & & &
\end{array}
\qquad (2)
$$

where y and x refer to output and input quantities, u and v to output and input multipliers, v_0 and u_0 to parameters related to returns to scale, θ and ϕ to input- and output-oriented technical efficiency scores, λ and μ to intensity variables, $j = 1, \ldots, J$ is used to index outputs, $i = 1, \ldots, I$ to index inputs and $h = 1, \ldots, k, \ldots, K$ to index DMUs.

The VRS output-oriented DEA model without inputs in (1) was firstly used by Lovell and Pastor (1997) for target setting while the VRS input-oriented DEA model without outputs in (2) was firstly employed by Adolphson et al. (1991) for location choice.

In contrast, there are more modeling options in the class of models with a single constant input or output. Notice however that, as Gomes et al. (2012) shown, a VRS input-oriented model with a single constant input rates all DMUs as fully efficient and thus it is not really useful for performance evaluation.[4] One can easily verify

[4]It is only the slacks that render a DMU inefficient in this case as in regard to ordinal factors DEA model.

that a similar result holds for the corresponding output-oriented model: that is, a VRS output-oriented model with a single constant output rates all DMUs as fully efficient.

Considering first the models with a single constant input, we have the CRS output-oriented model, which in its multiplier and envelopment form is given as:

$$
\begin{array}{llll}
\min\limits_{u_j^k, v^k} v^k & & \max\limits_{\lambda_j^k, \theta^k} \theta^k & \\
st \ \sum\limits_{j=1}^{J} u_j^k y_j^k = 1 & & st \ \sum\limits_{h=1}^{K} \lambda_h^k y_j^h \geq \theta^k y_j^k & j = 1, \ldots, J \\
v^k - \sum\limits_{j=1}^{J} u_j^k y_j^h \geq 0 & h = 1, \ldots, K & \sum\limits_{h=1}^{K} \lambda_h^k = 1 & \\
u_j^k \geq 0 & j = 1, \ldots, J & \lambda_h^k \geq 0 & h = 1, \ldots, K \\
v^k \geq 0 & & &
\end{array}
\tag{3}
$$

and the corresponding VRS model given as:

$$
\begin{array}{llll}
\min\limits_{u_j^k, v^k, v_0^k} \ v^k - v_0^k & & \max\limits_{\lambda_j^k, \theta^k} \theta^k & \\
st \ \sum\limits_{j=1}^{J} u_j^k y_j^k = 1 & & st \ \sum\limits_{h=1}^{K} \lambda_h^k y_j^h \geq \theta^k y_j^k & j = 1, \ldots, J \\
v^k - \sum\limits_{j=1}^{J} u_j^k y_j^h - v_0^k \geq 0 & h = 1, \ldots, K & \sum\limits_{h=1}^{K} \lambda_h^k \leq 1 & \\
u_j^k \geq 0 & j = 1, \ldots, J & \sum\limits_{h=1}^{K} \lambda_h^k = 1 & \\
v^k \geq 0 & & \lambda_h^k \geq 0 & h = 1, \ldots, K \\
v_0^k \ \textit{free in} \ \text{sign} & & &
\end{array}
\tag{4}
$$

According to Lovell and Pastor (1999, proposition 2) and Caporaletti et al. (1999, Appendix A), the CRS output-oriented model with a single constant input in (3) is equivalent to the VRS output-oriented model with a single constant input in (4). To verify this notice *first* that the presence of the convexity constraint, i.e., $\sum_{h=1}^{K} \lambda_h^k = 1$, in (4) renders the constraint associated with the single constant input, i.e., $\sum_{h=1}^{K} \lambda_h^k \leq 1$, redundant (Ferrier and Trivitt 2013) and *second*, that the input constraint in (3) must be binding and thus should be replaced by an equality, i.e., $\sum_{h=1}^{K} \lambda_h^k = 1$ (Liu et al. 2011). For the multiplier form, v^k in (3) should be equal to $v^k - v_0^k$ in (4) for all k.

The CRS output-oriented DEA model with a single constant input in (3) was firstly used by Mahlberg and Obersteiner (2001) for constructing composite indicators (the HDI in particular) while the VRS output DEA model with a single constant input in (4) was firstly employed by Fernandez-Castro and Smith (1994) to analyze financial ratios. Later, the CRS output-oriented DEA model with a single constant input in (3) was used by Xu et al. (2013) to analyze min-max strategy games, where the evaluated DMU freely selects weights to maximize its output score and the evaluator select among competitive DMUS to increase the relative loss function in order to force the evaluated DMU to change its output weights.[5]

On the other hand, the CRS input-oriented model with a single constant input is given as:

$$
\begin{array}{llll}
\max\limits_{u_j^k, v^k} \sum\limits_{j=1}^{J} u_j^k y_j^k & & \min\limits_{\mu_j^k, \phi^k} \phi^k & \\
st \;\; v^k = 1 & & st \;\; \sum\limits_{h=1}^{K} \mu_h^k y_j^h \geq \phi^k y_j^k & j = 1, \ldots, J \\
v^k - \sum\limits_{j=1}^{J} u_j^k y_j^h \geq 0 & h = 1, \ldots, K & \sum\limits_{h=1}^{K} \mu_h^k \leq \phi^k & \\
u_j^k \geq 0 & j = 1, \ldots, J & \mu_h^k \geq 0 & h = 1, \ldots, K \\
v^k \geq 0 & & &
\end{array}
\tag{5}
$$

in its multiplier and envelopment form, respectively. This model was firstly used by Greenberg and Nunamaker (1987) to aggregate ratio indicators and since then, it has been used in several other applications including (1) modeling of preference voting for election (Cook and Kress 1990; Hashimoto 1997) or product/project ranking (Doyle et al. 1995), (2) construction of composite indicators, where it is known as the Benefit-of-the-Doubt (BoD) model (Cherchye et al. 2007a), (3) effectiveness evaluation (Prieto and Zofio 2001), e.g. research and teaching activities of faculty members (de Witte and Rogge 2010, 2011; Kao et al. 2012; Karagiannis and Paschalidou 2017), libraries (Kao and Lin 2004), and sports (Cooper et al. 2009; Ruiz et al., 2013), (4) MCDM applications, such as inventory classification (Ramanathan 2006a) and supplier selection (Seydel 2006), (5) construction of output quantity indices (O'Donnell and Nguyen 2013) and monetary aggregation (Sahoo and Acharya 2010), (6) construction of quality indices (Molinos-Senante et al. 2017), (7) assessment of quality perception (i.e., SERVQUAL and SERVPREF)

[5]In their set-up, there are two players in the game: one player is the DMU under evaluation who attempts to max (min) its gain (loss) and the other player is a central evaluator who wants to min (max) its loss (gains). On the other hand, there are two strategy spaces in the game: one is related to the weights in the multiplier form of the DEA model and the other to the index h, which selects a competitive DMU.

(Lee and Kim 2014; Charles and Kumar 2014), (8) in AHP analysis (Ramanathan 2006b; Wang and Chin 2009), (9) in GRA (Huang et al. 2015), and (10) estimating overall efficiency for grouping on levels (Cook et al. 1998).

Regarding next the models with a single constant output, we have the CRS input-oriented model, which in its multiplier and envelopment form is given as:

$$\begin{array}{llll}
\max\limits_{v_i^k, u_0^k} u^k & & \min\limits_{\lambda_j^k, \phi^k} \phi^k & \\
st \ \sum\limits_{i=1}^{I} v_i^k x_i^k = 1 & & st \ \sum\limits_{h=1}^{K} \mu_h^k x_i^h \leq \phi^k x_i^k & i = 1, \ldots, I \\
\sum\limits_{i=1}^{I} v_i^k x_i^h - u^k \geq 0 & h = 1, \ldots, K & \sum\limits_{h=1}^{K} \mu_h^k \geq 1 & \\
v_i^k \geq 0 & i = 1, \ldots, I & \mu_h^k \geq 0 & h = 1, \ldots, K \\
u^k \geq 0 & & &
\end{array} \tag{6}$$

and the corresponding VRS model is:

$$\begin{array}{llll}
\max\limits_{v_i^k, u^k, u_0^k} u^k - u_0^k & & \min\limits_{\mu_j^k, \phi^k} \phi^k & \\
st \ \sum\limits_{i=1}^{I} v_i^k x_i^k = 1 & & st \ \sum\limits_{h=1}^{K} \mu_h^k x_i^h \leq \phi^k x_i^k & i = 1, \ldots, I \\
\sum\limits_{i=1}^{I} v_i^k x_i^h - u^k + u_0^k \geq 0 & h = 1, \ldots, K & \sum\limits_{h=1}^{K} \mu_h^k \geq 1 & \\
v_i^k \geq 0 & i = 1, \ldots, I & \sum\limits_{h=1}^{K} \mu_h^k = 1 & \\
u^k \geq 0 & & \mu_h^k \geq 0 & h = 1, \ldots, K \\
u_0^k \ \mathit{free\ in} \ \text{sign} & & &
\end{array} \tag{7}$$

According to Lovell and Pastor (1999, proposition 2), which is based on a reasoning similar to the one used for (3) and (4), one can verify that the CRS input-oriented DEA model with a single constant output in (6) is equivalent to the VRS input-oriented DEA model with a single constant output in (7).

The CRS input-oriented DEA model with a single constant output in (6) was firstly used by Thompson et al. (1986) for comparative site evaluation (i.e., location choice) and the VRS input-oriented DEA model with a single constant output in (7) was employed by Desai and Storbeck (1990) for the same purpose. Later, the CRS input-oriented DEA model with a single constant output in (6) was used by Xu et al. (2013) to analyze max-min strategy games, where the evaluated DMU selects the worst practice DMU and the evaluator would choose the best weights.

On the other hand, the CRS output-oriented model with a single constant output is given as:

$$
\begin{array}{llll}
\min\limits_{v_i^k, u^k} \sum\limits_{i=1}^{I} v_i^k x_i^k & & \max\limits_{\lambda_j^k, \theta^k} \theta^k & \\
st\ u^k = 1 & & st\ \sum\limits_{h=1}^{K} \lambda_h^k \geq \theta^k & \\
\sum\limits_{i=1}^{I} v_i^k x_i^h - u^k \geq 0 & h = 1, \ldots, K & \sum\limits_{h=1}^{K} \lambda_h^k x_i^h \geq x_i^k & i = 1, \ldots, I \\
v_i^k \geq 0 & i = 1, \ldots, I & \lambda_h^k \geq 0 & h = 1, \ldots, K \\
u^k \geq 0 & & &
\end{array}
\tag{8}
$$

in its multiplier and envelopment form, respectively. This model was firstly used by Doyle et al. (1995) in a multiple attributes problem (see also Caporaletti et al. 1999) and then by Weber and Desai (1996) for supplier selection and Takamura and Tone (2003) for cite selection. It is known as the inverted BoD model and it has been used in conjunction with the BoD model to compare composite indicators based on the most and least favorable weights; see for example Zhou and Fan (2007) for multi-criteria ABC inventory classification and Zhou et al. (2007) for constructing composite indicators. It was also employed for constructing input quantity and quality indices; see respectively O'Donnell and Nguyen (2013) and Whittaker et al. (2015).

Interestingly, models in the upper and the lower panel of Fig. 1 are related to each other: as Lovell and Pastor (1999) have shown (see their proposition 3), a VRS input-oriented (output-oriented) model with a single constant output (input) is equivalent to a VRS input oriented (output-oriented) model without output (inputs). This establishes the equivalence between (1) and (4) and between (2) and (7). Given in addition the equivalence between (3) and (4) and between (6) and (7), due to Lovell and Pastor (1999) proposition 2, one can verify the equivalence between (1) and (3) and between (2) and (6); this is corollary 3.1 in Lovell and Pastor (1999). On the other hand, due to CRS, one can verify that (3) and (5) as well as (6) and (8) are reciprocal to each other (Caporaletti et al. 1999; Yang et al. 2014, theorem 1).

Thus, we end up with two quadrat equivalencies: *first*, the VRS input-oriented model without outputs in (1), the VRS input-oriented model with a single constant output in (7), the CRS input-oriented model with a single constant output in (6), and the inverse of the CRS output-oriented model with a single constant output in (8) are all equivalent to each other (this equivalence is depicted by the yellow line in Fig. 1).[6] *Second*, the VRS output-oriented model without inputs in (2), the VRS output-

[6]Interestingly, the three models that have been used for site evaluation, namely the VRS input-oriented model without outputs in (1) used by Adolphson et al. (1991), the VRS input-oriented model with a single constant output in (7) used by Desai and Storbeck (1990), the CRS input-

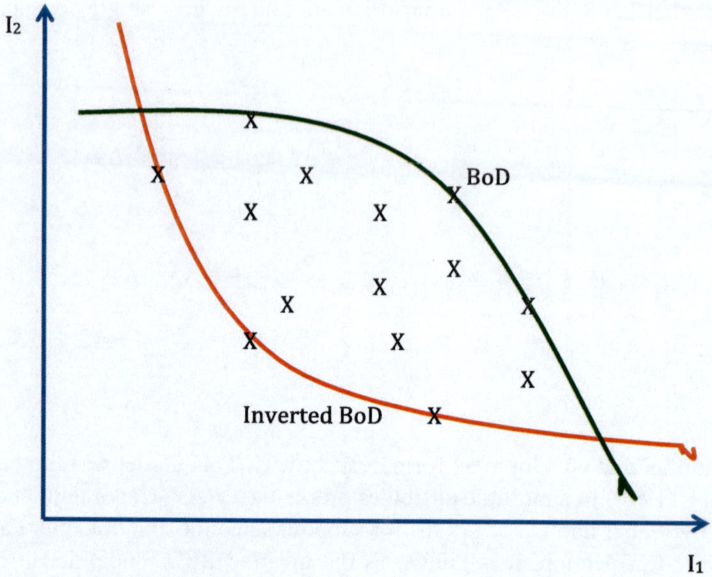

Fig. 1 The BoD and the inverted BoD models

oriented model with a single constant input in (4), the CRS output-oriented model with a single constant input in (3), and the inverse of the CRS input-oriented model with a single constant input in (5) are all equivalent to each other (this equivalence is depicted by the red line in Fig. 1). Thus, we actually have only two models in the class of the pure and single constant input or output DEA models.

From now on, these two models will generically be referred to as the BoD and the inverted BoD model, respectively. Their multiplier and envelopment forms in (5) and (8) may be rewritten after few manipulations as:

$$\begin{aligned} &\max_{u_j^k} \sum_{j=1}^{J} u_j^k y_j^k && \min_{\mu_j^k} \sum_{h=1}^{K} \mu_h^k \\ &st \quad \sum_{j=1}^{J} u_j^k y_j^h \le 1 \quad h = 1, \ldots, K && st \quad \sum_{h=1}^{K} \mu_h^k y_j^h \ge \phi^k y_j^k \quad j = 1, \ldots, J \\ &u_j^k \ge 0 \qquad j = 1, \ldots, J && \mu_h^k \ge 0 \qquad h = 1, \ldots, K \end{aligned} \tag{9}$$

and

oriented model with a single constant output in (6) used Thompson et al. (1986), and the CRS output-oriented model with a single constant output in (8) used by Takamura and Tone (2003) are equivalent to each other and result in the same assessment results.

$$\begin{array}{llll} \min\limits_{v_i^k} \sum\limits_{i=1}^{I} v_i^k x_i^k & & \max\limits_{\lambda_j^k} \sum\limits_{h=1}^{K} \lambda_h^k & \\ st \ \sum\limits_{i=1}^{I} v_i^k x_i^h \geq 1 & h = 1, \ldots, K & st \ \sum\limits_{h=1}^{K} \lambda_h^k x_i^h \geq x_i^k & i = 1, \ldots, I \\ v_i^k \geq 0 & i = 1, \ldots, I & \lambda_h^k \geq 0 & h = 1, \ldots, K \end{array} \tag{10}$$

By disregarding inputs and outputs in (9) and (10) and instead considering both of them as indicators, attributes, or criteria, we can see from their multiplier formulation that the BoD and the inverted BoD models provide, respectively, an optimistic and a pessimistic perspective of performance evaluation. This is also reflected in their two-dimensional graphical representation in Fig. 1, where the values of indicators, attributes, or criteria (*I*) are measured in the two axes. From there we can see that the BoD model may be viewed as an upper envelop of data points (it is presented here as a CRS output-oriented model with indicators as outputs and a unitary input) while the inverted BoD model as lower envelop (it is represented here as a CRS input-oriented model with indicators as inputs and a unitary output).[7] Moreover, in Table 2 we summarize all possible up-to-now uses of these two models.

Table 2 Applications of the BoD and the inverted BoD models

BoD model	Inverted BoD model
1. Composite indicators	1. Composite indicators
2. Inventory classification	2. Inventory classification
3. Supplier selection	3. Supplier selection
4. Min-max strategy games	4. Min-max strategy games
5. Output indices	5. Input indices
6. Quality indices	6. Quality indices
7. Long-run output-oriented CU	7. Long-run input-oriented CU
8. Quality perception	8. Spatial efficiency
9. Aggregating preference voting	
10. Ratio analysis—DEA-R	
11. Target setting	
12. Effectiveness	
13. AHP analysis	
14. GRA	
15. Multiple attribute utility theory	
16. Group efficiency	

[7]See van Puyenbroeck (2018) for a discussion on the output orientation of the BoD model.

3 Relations with Other Models

In this section we consider the relation of the DEA models without inputs or outputs with other DEA formulations and linear programming models. *First*, consider what we referred to as the normalized BoD model. This model can be obtained from the multiplier form of (9) by assuming that either all indicators are measured in a common scale or they are normalized to range between zero and one and in addition, we require output multipliers to sum up to one. Then, the second constraint in the multiplier form of (9) becomes redundant and we get the following model:

$$\begin{aligned} &\max_{u_j^k} \sum_{j=1}^{J} u_j^k I_j^k \\ &st \sum_{j=1}^{J} u_j^k = 1 \\ &u_j^k \geq 0 \qquad \forall j = 1, \ldots, J \end{aligned} \tag{11}$$

which was firstly used by Melyn and Moesen (1991) and later by Kao and Hung (2003).[8] Even though (9) and (11) have the same objective function they differ in terms of the model's constraints. In (11) there is only one (equality) constraint, besides the non-negativity constraints on the weights, while the number of inequality constraints in the multiplier form of (9) is equal to the number of DMUs. Besides these differences, Kao et al. (2008) have shown that they result in the same value of the objective function, i.e., in the same estimated value of the composite indicator so long as the weights in (9) sum up to one, which holds by default in (11). In addition, Karagiannis and Paschalidou (2017) have noticed that, once we estimate the weights in (9) we can use them to obtain the weights in (11) but the opposite is not possible. This asymmetry is due to the type and the number of constraints in (11).

Nakabayashi and Tone (2006) considered a special case of (11) where in addition, $\sum_{j=1}^{J} I_j^k = 1$. On the other hand, Ng (2007, 2008) considered a variant of (11) with the following descending order weighting scheme, $u_1^k > u_2^k > u_3^k \ldots$, and Hadi-Vencheh (2010) a distance-based version of it.

On the other hand, the normalized inverted BoD model, which is related to (10) above, is given as:

[8] Melyn and Moesen (1991) were the first to use the name BoD model but they did so for (11) not for (9), as it is common now days.

$$
\begin{aligned}
&\min_{v_i^k} \sum_{i=1}^{I} v_i^k I_i^k \\
&st \sum_{i=1}^{I} v_i^k = 1 \\
&v_i^k \geq 0 \qquad \forall i = 1, \ldots, I
\end{aligned}
\tag{12}
$$

and was firstly used by Nakabayashi et al. (2009).

Second, the BoD (inverted BoD) model is equivalent to the input-oriented (output-oriented) DEA-R model (Mozaffari et al. 2014).

Third, following Färe and Karagiannis (2014), the diet problem (the first linear programming problem—see Stigler (1945) for its formulation) and the BoD model are linear programming duals. That is, the primal (dual) formulation of the diet problem is equivalent to the dual (primal) formulation of the BoD model so long as food prices are set equal to one.[9] In addition, the diet problem and the inverted BoD are linear programming equivalent so long as the nutritional requirements are set equal to one. That is, the primal (dual) formulation of the diet problem is equivalent to the primal (dual) formulation of the inverted BoD model so long as the nutritional requirements are set equal to one.

Fourth, according to Yang et al. (2014), the linear form of the multi-attribute utility model with variable weights (see Keeney and Raiffa 1976) coincides with the BoD model.

Fifth, the long-run plant capacity utilization (CU) measures, introduced by Cesaroni et al. (2019), are identical to models of a VRS technology without inputs or outputs. In particular, the long-run output-oriented CU measure is obtained by estimating the BoD model while the long-run input-oriented CU measure by estimating the inverted BoD model.

4 Some Extensions

In this section we summarize the results of some extensions of the models presented in the second section. These extensions concern:

4.1 Weak Disposability and Non-isotonic Indicators

In nonparametric production models, weak disposability of outputs may be modeled by means of either a uniform or a multiple abatement factor specification; see e.g.

[9]For the BoD and the inverted BoD models, the primal formulation corresponds to the multiplier form and the dual to the envelopment form.

Färe and Grosskopf (2003) and Kuosmanen (2005). Kuosmanen and Podinovski (2009) have shown that in the case of a single constant input (or equivalently if all DMUs use the same input quantity) the abatement factors in the multiple abatement factor specification of production technology collapse to a single one as it is the case in the uniform abatement factor specification.

In the case of composite indicators, bad outputs correspond to indicators that are not isotonic and increasing values are considered as unfortunate events. There are two modeling strategies for treating non-isotonic indicators: *first*, the directional BoD model (Fusco 2015; Vidoli et al. 2015; Zanella et al. 2015a, 2015b; Charles et al. 2016) treats non-isotonic indicators as undesirable outputs by means of weak disposability. Implicit in this modeling choice is the assumption of null-jointness, namely that desirable outputs cannot be produced without the production of undesirable outputs, which is a rather reasonable assumption for conventional production processes but less justifiable in the context of the BoD model.

Alternatively, Färe et al. (2019) suggest treating non-isotonic indicators as reverse rather than undesirable outputs. The main difference is that reverse outputs might not be accompanied by desirable outputs. That is, the presence of forward indicators does not imply nor it is implied by the presence of reverse indicators. The proposed BoD model is the single-constant-input version of Lewis and Sexton (2004) CRS input-oriented DEA model with forward inputs and forward and reverse outputs. The multiplier and the envelopment form of the BoD model with forward and reverse indicators are given as:

$$\begin{aligned}
&\max_{u_j} \sum_{j=1}^{m} u_j y_{k'j} - \sum_{j=m+1}^{J} u_j y_{k'j} \min_{\lambda_k} \sum_{h=1}^{K} \lambda_h^k \\
&st \sum_{j=1}^{m} u_j y_{k'j} - \sum_{j=m+1}^{J} u_j y_{k'j} \leq 1^k \quad h = 1, \ldots, K \\
&st \sum_{h=1}^{K} \lambda_h^k y_{kj} \geq y_{k'j} \quad j = 1, \ldots, m \\
&u_j \geq 0 \qquad j = 1, \ldots, J \quad \sum_{h=1}^{K} \lambda_h^k y_{kj} \leq y_{k'j} \qquad j = m+1, \ldots, J \\
&\lambda_h^k \geq 0 \qquad h = 1, \ldots, K
\end{aligned} \tag{13}$$

where $y_{k'j}$ refers to forward indicators and $y_{k'j}$'s to reverse indicators.

4.2 Intra- and Inter-Group BoD Models

The primary models presented in the second section assume implicitly a common set of environmental or contextual conditions for all DMUs. These factors are related to the conditions surrounding the performance of the evaluated DMUs.

Assessing performance across different environments requires splitting the sample of DMUs into separate groups and then analyzing performance differences within and between groups. Intra-group composite indicators are estimated using the conventional BoD model in (9) by restricting the reference set into DMUs that belong to a particular group.

Inspired from the notion of programmatic efficiency (see Charnes et al. 1981), Karagiannis and Karagiannis (2018) have proposed two alternative approaches for estimating inter-group composite indicators. The first approach proceeds in three steps: *first*, estimate the intra-group composite indicators separately for each group; *second*, adjust the "unitary input" to eliminate any intra-group inefficiency, which means replacing I^j with I^j_m / I^k_m in the conventional BoD; *third*, estimate the following form of the conventional BoD model (the multiplier and the envelopment form of which is given in (14) below) for the pooled data (including all groups) to obtain the values of the inter-group composite indicators:

$$
\begin{array}{llll}
\max\limits_{s_i^k} \sum\limits_{i=1}^{N} s_i^k I_i^k & & \min\limits_{\lambda_j^k} \sum\limits_{h=1}^{K} \lambda_h^k \left({}^g I_m^j / {}^g I_m^k \right) & \\
st \ \sum\limits_{i=1}^{N} s_i^k I_i^h \leq \left(\dfrac{{}^g I_m^h}{{}^g I_m^k} \right) & h = 1, \ldots, K & st \ \sum\limits_{h=1}^{K} \lambda_h^k I_i^j \geq I_i^k & i = 1, \ldots, N \\
 & g = 1, \ldots, G & & \\
s_i^k \geq 0 & i = 1, \ldots, N & \lambda_h^k \geq 0 & h = 1, \ldots, K
\end{array}
\tag{14}
$$

The second approach also proceeds in three steps: *first*, estimate the intra-group composite indicators separately for each group; *second*, estimate the conventional BoD model for the pooled data (including all DMUs); and *third*, calculate the inter-group composite indicator by the ratio of the latter to the former.

One can easily verify that the two approaches result in the same inter-group composite indicators. However, the second is easier to implement, but it provides no insights about the identification of peers and/or the estimated component weights because the values of the inter-group composite indicator are calculated residually instead of being estimated as in the first alternative (Karagiannis and Karagiannis 2018). In addition, the second approach does not provide any insights for the aggregation of inter-group composite indicators, in which we will turn after the next sub-section.

4.3 Average Cross Efficiency in the BoD Model

Another interesting implication of the BoD model is in terms of the average cross efficiency. Cross efficiency is a peer-appraisal performance measure that is obtained by using the optimal weights of all DMUs to evaluate the performance of a particular DMU. Then average cross efficiency (ACE) results by computing the simple average of these cross efficiency scores (Doyle and Green 1994). The ACE in the BoD model is computed based on a common set of weights given by the simple arithmetic average of the weights obtained from the self-appraisal version of the model as in (9) (Karagiannis and Paleologou 2014; Rogge 2018). These common weights allow for complete ranking and comparison of all (efficient and inefficient) DMUs and they can be applied to calculate performance indices for DMUs not in the sample.

5 Aggregation Across DMUs

In several empirical applications we are interesting on the performance of the group that the evaluated units belong to instead of the units themselves. To proceed in this direction one needs a theoretically consistent way to aggregate across all or some of the DMUs. By theoretically consistent way we mean that the resulting aggregate composite indicator will have exactly the same intuitive interpretation as the individual ones. This necessitates the development of an aggregation scheme that is compatible with the BoD and the inverted models and which involves the choice of aggregation weights as well as the type of average to be used.

According to Färe and Karagiannis (2017, 2020) denominator rule, consistency in aggregation of ratio-type performance measures, including efficiency indices, is ensured so long as the weights are defined in terms of the denominator variable of the relevant index. This, which constitutes the practical counterpart of Koopmans theorem (Koopmans 1957) in aggregating ratio-type performance indices, refers to arithmetic aggregation. For harmonic aggregation one should use the numerator rule and define the aggregation weights in term of the numerator variable of the relevant index.

Following the denominator rule, Karagiannis (2017) has shown that the arithmetic average is the theoretically consistent aggregation rule for the BoD model and thus, for the input-oriented DEA model with a single constant input. Then, the aggregate composite indicator equals the simple (un-weighted) arithmetic average of the estimated individual DMU's composite indicators. As an input-oriented model, the aggregation weights for the BoD model should be defined by means of the input variables and in particular, by means of actual input values, which is the variable in the denominator of the corresponding efficiency score. However, in the case of the BoD model there is only one input that is equal to one across all DMUs. This implies that the aggregation weights equal to one over the number of the evaluated DMUs, which in turn implies that the aggregate composite indicator is equal to the arithmetic average of DMU's composite indicators. This holds without requiring the relative weights of each indicator to be the same across DMUs, as Morais and Camanho (2011) have claimed. On the other hand, considering the BoD as an output-oriented model, Rogge (2018) argued that the aggregation weights are equal to the arithmetic mean of the share of every DMU in each indicator. The relation (if any) between these two results needs further investigation.

6 Productivity Analysis

The use of radial DEA models without inputs or outputs can be taken one step further by considering their potential use in inter-temporal performance evaluation by means of productivity indices. Using an output-oriented model with a single constant input, Karagiannis and Lovell (2016) have shown that in this case (a) the Malmquist and Hicks–Moorsteen productivity indices coincide, (b) they are multiplicatively complete, and (c) the choice of orientation for the measurement of productivity change does not matter.[10] In addition, there is a unique decomposition of the sources of productivity change containing three independent components, i.e., technical efficiency change, neutral technical change, and output-biased technical change. Lastly, the aggregate output-oriented Malmquist productivity index is given by the geometric average between any two periods of the simple (un-weighted) arithmetic average of the individual contemporaneous and mixed period distance functions. A similar analysis can be conducted in the case of an input-oriented model with a single constant output.

7 Concluding Remarks

The aim of this paper is to provide a critical review of the radial DEA models without input or outputs as well as their equivalent single constant input or output models and to summarize the fields that they have been applied so far. This literature review is by no means complete, as we have only focused on radial models. There are in the literature several papers dealing with non-radial as the additive model without inputs (Cai and Wu 2001; Liu et al. 2011), the output-oriented slack based model without outputs (Sahoo and Acharya 2010; Liu et al. 2011), and the Russell measure (Liu et al. 2011; Yang et al. 2014). On the other hand, we have implicitly assumed convexity, which is not necessary in this kind of models: see for example, the works of Athanassopoulos and Storbeck (1995), Bardhan et al. (1996) and Garcia-Romero et al. (2016), which used a free disposal hull model. The former has used an input-oriented model without outputs to estimate spatial efficiency and the other two an output-oriented model without inputs and with a single constant input, respectively. In addition, Xu et al. (2013) have used a free disposal hull model without inputs or outputs to analyze max-min strategy games. Finally, we did not also consider models with weight restrictions (see e.g. Cook and Kress 1990; Cherchye et al. 2007a) and several variants of the BoD model that result in common weights such as the one based on the goal programming approach

[10]This simply means that the aforementioned result also holds for an input-oriented model with a single constant input, i.e., the BoD model.

(Despotis 2005; Bernini et al. 2013; Sayed et al. 2018) and the one based on the meta-goal programming approach (Sayed et al. 2015). All these are left for future work.

Acknowledgment An earlier version of this paper was presented in the 15th International Conference on Data Envelopment Analysis hold at Prague, July 9-11, 2017. I would like to thank session participants for a constructive and stimulating discussion and an anonymous referee for helpful comments and suggestions.

References

Adolphson, D. L., Cornia, G. C., & Walters, L. C. (1991). A unified framework for classifying DEA models. In *Operational research '90* (pp. 647–657). New York: Pergamon Press.

Athanassopoulos, A. D., & Storbeck, J. E. (1995). Non-parametric models for spatial efficiency. *Journal of Productivity Analysis, 6*, 225–245.

Banker, R. D. (1980). A game theoretic approach to measuring efficiency. *European Journal of Operational Research, 5*, 262–268.

Bardhan, I., Bowlin, W. F., Cooper, W. W., & Sueyoshi, T. (1996). Models and measures of efficiency dominance in DEA: Part II: free disposal hull and Russell measure approaches. *Journal of the Operational Research Society of Japan, 39*, 333–344.

Bernini, C., Guizzardi, A., & Angelini, G. (2013). DEA-like model and common weights approach for the construction of a subjective community well-being indicator. *Social Indicators Research, 114*, 405–424.

Bowen, H. P., & Moesen, W. (2011). Composite competitiveness indicators with endogenous versus predetermined weights: An application to the world economic forum's global competiveness index. *Competitiveness Review: An International Business Journal, 21*, 129–151.

Cai, Y., & Wu, W. (2001). Synthetic financial evaluation by a method combining DEA with AHP. *International Transactions in Operational Research, 8*, 603–609.

Caporaletti, L. E., Dula, J. H., & Womer, N. K. (1999). Performance evaluation based on multiple attributes with nonparametric frontiers. *Omega, 27*, 637–645.

Cesaroni, G., Kerstens, K., & van de Woestyne, I. (2019). Short- and long-run plant capacity notions: definitions and comparison. *European Journal of Operational Research, 275*, 387–397.

Charles, V., & Kumar, M. (2014). Satisficing data envelopment analysis: an application to SERVQUAL efficiency. *Measurement, 51*, 71–80.

Charles, V., Fare, R., & Grosskpf, S. (2016). A translation invariant pure DEA model. *European journal of Operational Research, 249*, 390–392.

Charnes, A., Cooper, W. W., & Rhodes, E. (1981). Evaluating program and managerial efficiency: an application of data envelopment analysis to program follow through. *Management Science, 27*, 668–697.

Cherchye, L., Lovell, C. A. K., Moesen, W., & van Puyenbroeck, T. (2007). One market, one number? A composite indicator assessment of EU internal market dynamics. *European Economic Review, 51*, 749–779.

Cherchye, L., Moesen, W., Rogge, N., & van Puyenbroeck, T. (2007a). An introduction to "benefit of the doubt" composite indicators. *Social Indicators Research, 82*, 111–145.

Cherchye, L., Lovell, C. A. K., Moesen, W., & van Puyenbroeck, T. (2007b). One market, one number? A composite indicator assessment of EU internal market dynamics. *European Economic Review, 51*, 749–779.

Cherchye, L., Moesen, W., Rogge, N., van Puyenbroeck, T., Saisana, M., Saltelli, A., Liska, R., & Tarantola, S. (2008). Creating composite indicators with DEA and robustness analysis: the case of the technology achievement index. *Journal of Operational Research Society, 59*, 239–253.

Cook, W. D., & Kress, M. (1990). A data envelopment model for aggregating preference rankings. *Management Science, 36*, 1302–1310.

Cook, W. D., Chai, D., Doyle, J. R., & Green, R. H. (1998). Hierarchies and groups in DEA. *Journal of Productivity Analysis, 10*, 177–198.

Cooper, W. W., Ruiz, J. L., & Sirvent, I. (2009). Selecting non-zero weights to evaluate effectiveness of basketball players with DEA. *European Journal of Operational Research, 195*, 563–574.

de Witte, K., & Rogge, N. (2010). To publish or not to publish: on the aggregation and drivers of research performance. *Scientometrics, 85*, 657–680.

de Witte, K., & Rogge, N. (2011). Accounting for exogenous influences in performance evaluations of teachers. *Economics of Education Review, 30*, 641–653.

Desai, A., & Storbeck, J. E. (1990). A data envelopment analysis for spatial efficiency. *Computers, Environment and Urban Systems, 14*, 145–156.

Despic, O., Despic, M., & Paradi, J. C. (2007). DEA-R: ratio-based comparative efficiency model, its mathematical relation to DEA and its use in applications. *Journal of Productivity Analysis, 28*, 33–44.

Despotis, D. K. (2005). A reassessment of the human development index via data envelopment analysis. *Journal of Operational Research Society, 56*, 969–980.

Doyle, J. R., & Green, R. H. (1991). Comparing products using data envelopment analysis. *Omega, 19*, 631–638.

Doyle, J. R., & Green, R. H. (1994). Efficiency and cross efficiency in DEA: derivation, meanings and uses. *Journal of Operational Research Society, 45*, 567–578.

Doyle, J. R., Green, R. H., & Cook, W. D. (1995). Upper and lower bound evaluation for multiattribute objects: Comparison models using linear programming. *Organizational Behavior and Human Decision Processes, 64*, 261–273.

Färe, R., & Grosskopf, S. (2003). Nonparametric productivity analysis with undesirable outputs: comment. *American Journal of Agricultural Economics, 85*, 1070–1074.

Fernandez-Castro, A.S. and P.C. Smith. Towards a general non-parametric model of corporate performance, *Omega*, 1994, 22, 237-49.

Fernandez-Castro, A. S., & Smith, P. C. (2000). Lancaster's characteristics approach revisited: product selection using non-parametric methods. *Managerial and Decision Economics, 23*, 83–91.

Ferrier, G. D., & Trivitt, J. S. (2013). Incorporating quality in the measurement of hospital efficiency: a double DEA approach. *Journal of Productivity Analysis, 40*, 337–355.

Fusco, E. (2015). Enhancing Non-compensatory composite indicators: a directional proposal. *European Journal of Operational Research, 242*, 620–630.

Färe, R., & Karagiannis, G. (2014). Benefit-of-the-doubt aggregation and the diet problem. *Omega, 47*, 33–35.

Färe, R., & Karagiannis, G. (2017). The denominator rule for share-weighting aggregation. *European Journal of Operational Research, 260*, 1175–1180.

Färe, R., & Karagiannis, G. (2020). The denominator rule and a theorem by Janos Aczel. *European Journal of Operational Research, 282*, 398–400.

Färe, R., Karagiannis, G., Hassanasab, M., & Margaritis, D. (2019). A benefit-of-the-doubt model with reverse indicators. *European Journal of Operational Research, 278*, 394–400.

Gaaloul, H., & Khalfallah, S. (2014). Application of the "Benefit-of-the-Doubt" approach for the construction of a digital access indicator: a revaluation of the "Digital Access Index". *Social Indicators Research, 118*, 45–56.

Garcia-Romero, A., Santin, D., & Sicilla, G. (2016). Another brick in the wall: a new ranking of academic journal in economics using FDH. *Scientometrics, 107*, 91–101.

Gomes, E. G., de Abreu, U. G. P., de Mello, J. C. C. B. S., de Carvalho, T. B., & de Zen, S. (2012). Unitary input DEA model to identify beef cattle production systems typologies. *Pesquisa Operacional, 32*, 389–406.

Green, R. H., Doyle, J. R., & Cook, W. D. (1996). Preference voting and project ranking using DEA and cross evaluation. *European Journal of Operational Research, 90*, 461–472.

Greenberg, R., & Nunamaker, T. (1987). A Generalized multiple criteria model for control and evaluation of nonprofit organizations. *Financial Accountability and Management, 3*, 331–342.

Guardiola, J., & Picazo-Tadeo, A. (2014). Building weighted-domain composite indices of life satisfaction with data envelopment analysis. *Social Indicators Research, 117*, 257–274.

Hadi-Vencheh, A. (2010). An improvement to the multiple criteria ABC inventory classification. *European Journal of Operational Research, 201*, 962–965.

Hashimoto, A. (1997). A ranked voting system using a DEA/AR exclusion model: a note. *European Journal of Operational Research, 97*, 600–604.

Huang, C., Dai, C., & Guo, M. (2015). A hybrid approach using two-level DEA for financial failure prediction and integrated SE-DEA and GCA for indicators selection. *Applied Mathematics and Computation, 251*, 431–441.

Kamakura, W. A., Ratchford, B. T., & Agrawal, J. (1988). Measuring market efficiency and welfare loss. *Journal of Consumer Research, 15*, 289–302.

Kao, C., & Hung, H. T. (2003). Ranking university libraries with a posteriori weights. *Libri, 53*, 282–289.

Kao, C., & Lin, Y. C. (2004). Evaluation of the university libraries in Taiwan: total measure versus ratio measure. *Journal of Operational Research Society, 55*, 1256–1265.

Kao, C., Wu, W. Y., Hsieh, W. J., Wang, T. Y., Lin, C., & Chen, L. H. (2008). Measuring the national competitiveness of Southeast Asian countries. *European Journal of Operational Research, 187*, 613–628.

Kao, C., Liu, S. T., & Pao, H. L. (2012). Assessing improvement in management research in Taiwan. *Scientometrics, 92*, 75–87.

Karagiannis, G. (2017). On aggregate composite indicators. *Journal of Operational Research Society, 68*, 741–746.

Karagiannis, R., & Karagiannis, G. (2018). Intra- and inter-group composite indicators using the BoD model. *Socio-economic Planning Sciences, 61*, 44–51.

Karagiannis, G., & Lovell, C. A. K. (2016). Productivity measurement in radial DEA models with a single constant input. *European Journal of Operational Research, 251*, 323–328.

Karagiannis, G., & Paleologou, S. M. (2014). Towards a composite public sector performance indicator. In: Paper presented in the 2014 Asia Pacific productivity conference, Brisbane, July 2-4, 2014.

Karagiannis, G., & Paschalidou, G. (2017). Assessing research effectiveness: A comparison of alternative nonparametric models. *Journal of the Operational Research Society, 68*, 456–468.

Keeney, R. L., & Raiffa, H. (1976). *Decisions with multiple objectives*. New York: Wiley.

Koopmans, T. C. (1957). *Three essays on the state of economic science*. New York: McGraw-Hill.

Kuosmanen, T. (2005). Weak disposability in nonparametric production analysis with undesirable outputs. *American Journal of Agricultural Economics, 87*, 1077–1082.

Kuosmanen, T., & Podinovski, V. (2009). Weak disposability in nonparametric production analysis: Reply to Färe and Grosskopf. *American Journal of Agricultural Economics, 91*, 539–545.

Lauer, J. A., Lovell, C. A. K., Murray, C. J. L., & Evans, D. B. (2004). World health system performance revisited: the impact of varying the relative importance of health system goals. *BMC Health Services Research*.

Lewis, H. F., & Sexton, T. R. (2004). Data envelopment Analysis with reverse inputs and outputs. *Journal of Productivity Analysis, 21*, 113–132.

Lee, H., & Kim, C. (2014). Benchmarking of service quality with data envelopment analysis. *Expert Systems with Applications, 41*, 3761–3768.

Lins, M. P. E., Gomes, E. G., Soares de Mello, J. C. C. B., & de Mello, A. J. R. S. (2003). Olympic ranking based on a zero sum gains DEA model. *European Journal of Operational Research, 148*, 312–322.

Liu, W. B., Zhang, D. Q., Meng, W., Li, X. X., & Xu, F. (2011). A study of DEA models without explicit inputs. *Omega, 39*, 472–480.

Lovell, C. A. K., & Pastor, J. T. (1997). Target setting: an application to a bank branch network. *European Journal of Operational Research, 98*, 290–299.

Lovell, C. A. K., & Pastor, J. T. (1999). Radial DEA models without inputs or without outputs. *European Journal of Operational Research, 118*, 46–51.
Mahlberg, B., & Obersteiner, M. (2001). Re-measuring the HDI by data envelopment analysis. In: IIASA interim report IR-01-069, Luxemburg.
Melyn, W., & Moesen, W. (1991). *Towards a synthetic indicator for macroeconomic performance: unequal weighting when limited information is available, Public Economics Research Paper Nr 17*. Katholieke Universiteit Leuven.
Mizobuchi, H. (2014). Measuring world better life frontier: a composite indicator for OECD better life index. *Social Indicators Research, 118*, 987–1007.
Molinos-Senante, M., Gomez, T., Caballero, R., & Sala-Garrido, R. (2017). Assessing the quality of service to consumers provided by water utilities: a synthetic index approach. *Ecological Indicators, 78*, 214–220.
Morais, P., & Camanho, A. S. (2011). Evaluation of performance of European cities with the aim to promote quality of life improvements. *Omega, 39*, 398–409.
Morey, M. R., & Morey, R. C. (1999). Mutual fund performance appraisals: A multi-horizon perspective with endogenous benchmarking. *Omega, 27*, 241–258.
Mozaffari, M. R., Gerami, J., & Jablonsky, J. (2014). Relationship between DEA models without explicit inputs and DEA-R models. *Central European Journal of Operational Research, 22*, 1–12.
Murias, P., de Miguel, J. C., & Rodriguez, D. (2008). A composite indicator for university quality assessment: the case of Spanish higher education system. *Social Indicators Research, 89*, 129–146.
Murthi, B. P. S., Choi, Y. K., & Desai, P. (1997). Efficiency of mutual funds and portfolio performance measurement: a non-parametric approach. *European Journal of Operational Research, 98*, 408–418.
Nakabayashi, K., & Tone, K. (2006). Egoist's dilemma: a DEA game. *Omega, 34*, 135–148.
Nakabayashi, K., Sahoo, B. K., & Tone, K. (2009). Fair allocation based on two criteria: A DEA game view of "add them up and divide by two". *Journal of the Operational Research Society of Japan, 52*, 131–146.
Ng, W. L. (2007). A simple classifier for multiple criteria ABC analysis. *European Journal of Operational Research, 177*, 344–353.
Ng, W. L. (2008). An efficient and simple model for multiple criteria supplier selection problem. *European Journal of Operational Research, 186*, 1059–1067.
O'Donnell, C. J., & Nguyen, K. (2013). An econometric approach to estimating support prices and measures of productivity change in public hospitals. *Journal of Productivity Analysis, 40*, 323–335.
OECD. (2008). *Handbook on constructing composite indicators: Methodology and user guide*. Paris.
Prieto, A. M., & Zofio, J. L. (2001). Evaluating effectiveness in public provision of infrastructure and equipment: The case of Spanish municipalities. *Journal of Productivity Analysis, 15*, 41–58.
Ramanathan, R. (2006a). ABC inventory classification with multiple-criteria using weighted linear optimization. *Computers and Operations Research, 33*, 695–700.
Ramanathan, R. (2006b). Data envelopment analysis for weight derivation and aggregation in the analytical hierarchy process. *Computers and Operations Research, 33*, 1289–1307.
Ramanathan, R., & Yunfeng, J. (2009). Incorporating cost and environmental factors in quality function deployment using data envelopment analysis. *Omega, 37*, 711–723.
Rogge, N. (2018). On aggregating benefit of the doubt composite indicators. *European Journal of Operational Research, 264*, 364–369.
Ruiz, J. L., Pastor, D., & Pastor, J. T. (2013). Assessing professional tennis players using data envelopment analysis (DEA). *Journal of Sports Economics, 14*, 276–302.
Sahoo, B. K., & Acharya, D. (2010). An alternative approach to monetary aggregation in DEA. *European Journal of Operational Research, 204*, 672–682.

Sayed, H., Hamed, R., Abdelhamid, A. H., & Hosny, S. H. (2015). Using meta-goal programming for a new Human Development Indicator with distinguishable country ranks. *Social Indicators Research, 123*, 1–27.

Sayed, H., Hamed, R., Hosny, S. H., & Abdelhamid, A. H. (2018). Avoiding ranking contradictions in human development index using goal programming. *Social Indicators Research, 138*, 405–442.

Seydel, J. (2006). Data envelopment analysis for decision support. *Industrial Management and Data Systems, 106*, 81–95.

Stigler, G. J. (1945). The cost of subsistence. *Journal of Farm Economics, 27*, 303–314.

Takamura, Y., & Tone, K. (2003). A comparative site evaluation study for relocating Japanese government agencies out of Tokyo. *Socio-economic Planning Sciences, 37*, 85–102.

Thompson, R. G., Singleton, F. D., Jr., Thrall, R. M., & Smith, B. A. (1986). Comparative site evaluation for locating a high-energy physics lab in Texas. *Interfaces, 16*, 35–49.

van Puyenbroeck, T. (2018). On the output orientation of the benefit-of-the-doubt model. *Social Indicators Research, 139*, 415–431.

Vidoli, F., Fusco, E., & Mazziota, C. (2015). Non-compensability in composite indicators: a robust directional frontier model. *Social Indicators Research, 122*, 635–652.

Wang, Y. M., & Chin, K. S. (2009). A new data envelopment analysis method for priority determination and group decision making in the analytic hierarchy process. *European Journal of Operational Research, 195*, 239–250.

Weber, C. A., & Desai, A. (1996). Determination of paths to vendor market efficiency using parallel coordinates representation: A negotiation tool for buyers. *European Journal of Operational Research, 90*, 142–155.

Wei, C. K., Chen, L. C., Li, R. K., & Tsai, C. H. (2011). A study of developing an input-oriented ratio-based comparative efficiency model. *Experts Systems with Applications, 38*, 2473–2477.

Whittaker, G., Barnhart, B., Färe, R., & Grosskopf, S. (2015). Application of index number theory to the construction of a water quality index: Aggregated nutrient loadings related to the areal extent of hypoxia in the northern Gulf of Mexico. *Ecological Indicators, 49*, 162–168.

Xu, F., Zhang, D., Yang, G., & Liu, W. (2013). Game perspectives of DEA models and their duals. *Journal of Applied Mathematics*.

Yang, G., Shen, W., Zhang, D., & Liu, W. (2014). Extended utility and DEA models without explicit input. *Journal of Operational Research Society, 65*, 1212–1220.

Zanella, A., Camanho, A. S., & Dias, T. G. (2013). Benchmarking countries' environmental performance. *Journal of Operational Research Society, 64*, 426–438.

Zanella, A., Camanho, A. S., & Dias, T. G. (2015a). Undesirable outputs and weighting schemes in composite indicators based on data envelopment analysis. *European Journal of Operational Research, 245*, 517–530.

Zanella, A., Camanho, A. S., & Dias, T. G. (2015b). The assessment of cities' livability integrating human wellbeing and environmental impact. *Annals of Operation Research, 226*, 695–726.

Zhou, P., & Fan, L. (2007). A note on multi-criteria ABC inventory classification using weighted linear optimization. *European Journal of Operational Research, 182*, 1488–1491.

Zhou, P., Ang, B. W., & Poh, K. L. (2007). A mathematical programming approach to constructing composite indicators. *Ecological Economics*, 291–297.

U.S. Banking in the Post-Crisis Era: New Results from New Methods

Paul W. Wilson

Abstract This paper examines the performance of U.S. bank holding companies before, during, and after the 2007–2012 financial crisis. Fully nonparametric methods are used to estimate technical, cost, and input allocative efficiencies. Recently developed statistical results are used to test for changes in efficiencies as well as productivity over time, and to test for changes in technology over time. I find evidence of non-convexity of banks' production set is found. In addition, the data reveal that mean technical efficiency declined during the financial crisis, but recovered in the years after, ending higher in 2016 than in 2006, while both cost and input allocative efficiencies declined from 2006 to 2016. Statistical tests indicate that technology shifted downward throughout the period 2006–2016.

1 Introduction

The financial crisis of 2007–2012 began ostensibly, in the USA, with problems in housing mortgage markets.[1] On 27 February 2007, The Federal Home Loan Mortgage Corporation announced that it would no longer buy the most risky

[1]Gorton (2018) refers to the financial crisis of 2007–2008, while Bolt et al. (2012) and others refer to the crisis of 2008. The National Bureau of Economic Research lists the corresponding peak-to-trough business cycle contraction as fourth-quarter 2007 through second-quarter 2009. Many of the effects of the recent financial crisis lasted beyond 2009.

P. W. Wilson (✉)
Department of Economics and School of Computing, Division of Computer Science, Clemson University, Clemson, SC, USA
e-mail: pww@clemson.edu

C. F. Parmeter, R. C. Sickles (eds.), *Advances in Efficiency and Productivity Analysis*, Springer Proceedings in Business and Economics,
https://doi.org/10.1007/978-3-030-47106-4_11

sub-prime mortgages and mortgage-related securities. Just over a month later, on 2 April 2007, New Century Financial Corporation, a leading player in the sub-prime mortgage market, filed for chapter "U.S. Banking in the Post-Crisis Era: New Results from New Methods" bankruptcy protection. On 7 June 2007 Bear Stearns suspended redemptions from its High-Grade Structured Credit Strategies Enhanced Leverage Fund; later, on 31 July, the company liquidated two hedge funds that invested in various types of mortgage-backed securities. Countrywide Financial Corporation warned of "difficult conditions" in Securities and Exchange Commission Filing on 24 July. Problems accelerated in the second half of 2007 and during 2008, with Lehman Brothers Holdings Inc. filing for chapter "U.S. Banking in the Post-Crisis Era: New Results from New Methods" bankruptcy protection on 15 September 2008.

As with other financial crises, the crisis that began in 2007 started with a credit boom likely related to a glut of global savings as described by Bernanke (2005). Gorton et al. (2012) note that the rise of the shadow banking system had by 2007 significantly and permanently changed the U.S. financial system. Bernanke (2013) defines shadow banking as comprising "a diverse set of institutions and markets that, collectively, carry out traditional banking functions—but do so outside, or in ways only loosely linked to, the traditional system of regulated depository institutions. Examples of important components of the shadow banking system include securitization vehicles, asset-backed commercial paper conduits, money market funds, markets for repurchase (repo) agreements, investment banks, and mortgage companies." Yet as of 2007, there were almost no data available to measure or monitor activities within the shadow banking system.

Hördahl and King (2008) note that repo markets doubled in size between 2002 and year-end 2007, amounting to roughly \$10 trillion in each of the U.S. and Euro repo markets, and another \$1 trillion in the U.K. repo market by the end of 2007. A repo involves the sale of a security with an agreement to repurchase the same security at a specified price at the end of the contract. Repo markets are an important source of secured financing for both banks and non-bank financial institutions (including those in the shadow banking system), as well as a key tool for the implementation of monetary policy. Despite the presence of collateral, repo markets are sensitive to financial turmoil.

Gorton (2018, Section 4) describes how the financial crisis began in 2007 with runs on asset-backed commercial paper, repo, and money market mutual funds. In the first two markets, short-term debt holders became concerned that privately produced asset- and mortgage-backed securities rated AAA or Aaa were not as safe as their ratings implied. Consequently, starting in mid-2007, repo transactions became increasingly limited to short-term maturities involving only the highest-quality securities, making lesser-quality securities increasingly illiquid. Financing in unsecured markets became more expensive or unavailable, forcing financial institutions needing funds to bid more aggressively in repo markets or to turn to foreign exchange swaps and cross-currency swaps as noted by Baba et al. (2008). At the same time, repo investors withdrew cash from the repo market, further reducing the quantity of financing available. The simultaneous flight to and hoarding of U.S. Treasury securities by investors created a scarcity of top-quality collateral, causing repo rates (i.e., the difference between sale and buy-back prices) for U.S. Treasuries to fall to levels close to zero. Hördahl and King (2008) note that the U.S. repo market suffered significantly more disruption than either the Euro or the U.K. markets. The repo market in mid-2007 was in turmoil and was the seed of the financial crisis, but this was noticed by few who were not trading in the repo market.[2]

The period 2007–2012 and beyond was very disruptive to the banking industry. The period is remarkable for its historically low interest rates, large numbers of bank failures, forced mergers, and eventually an increase in regulatory burden with enactment of the Dodd-Frank Wall Street Reform and Consumer Protection Act in 2010 (otherwise known as the "Dodd-Frank Act"). Although banks eventually became awash in cash, with large excess reserves, the demand for loans fell, thereby impacting opportunities for banks to earn revenue.[3]

Banks are an important component of nations' economies. The business of banking involves transforming short-term debt into longer-term loans. Banks facilitate "cash smoothing" between depositors and borrowers, thereby contributing to economic growth. Bankers make profits (when they can) by managing risk and the spread between interest rates on deposits and loans. As Diamond and Rajan (2001) observe, banks perform valuable functions on both sides of their balance sheets. They make loans to illiquid borrowers, enhancing the flow of credit in the economy, and they provide liquidity on demand to depositors. Although both of these actions are important, it makes banks inherently risky and potentially unstable. Banks may have different *business plans*, and may change their business plans over time. Given the importance of banks in the economy, it is reasonable to ask what happened to the U.S. banking industry following 2006, the last year before the financial crisis.

This paper provides evidence on the performance of large U.S. banks just before, during, and after the 2007–2012 financial crisis. The approach is fully nonparametric, and exploits new theoretical results that have been recently developed. Estimates

[2]See Hördahl and King (2008), Bernanke (2018) and Gorton (2018) for additional discussion. See also the comprehensive timeline of the financial crisis provided by the Federal Reserve Bank of St. Louis at https://www.stlouisfed.org/financial-crisis/full-timeline.

[3]Total loans and leases, net of unearned income for U.S. commercial banks reached a peak of 6.807 trillion dollars in 2008Q3, fell to 6.415 trillion dollars by 2009Q4, and did not reach the level of 2008Q3 until 2012Q4. All real estate loans reached a peak of 3.835 trillion in July 2009, fell to 3.491 trillion in September 2011, and did not reach the July 2009 level until November 2015. Commercial real estate loans reached a peak of 1.730 trillion in December 2008, fell to 1.419 trillion in January 2012, and did not reach the level of December 2008 again until September 2015. The levels of loans outstanding reflect in large part past loan-making activity; i.e., there is a good deal of inertia reflected in the values given here. The decline in values of loans originating during the financial crisis is likely far larger than the levels of loans outstanding, but is harder to measure.

of technical, cost, and input allocative efficiency at 2-year intervals from 2006 to 2016 are examined in a statistical paradigm permitting inference and hypothesis testing. As such, this paper both (1) contributes to the banking literature by shedding light on the reaction of large U.S. banks to the recent financial crisis and (2) provides an illustration of state-of-the art nonparametric, statistical methods for performance benchmarking.

The primary regulatory response to the financial crisis that began near the end of 2007 was enactment of the Dodd-Frank Act. The Dodd-Frank Act contains 845 pages, 16 titles, and 225 new rules to be implemented by 11 government agencies; see U.S. Congress (2010) for details. The Dodd-Frank Act is the largest, most far-reaching financial regulation passed by the U.S. Congress since the Banking Act of 1933. Among other things, the Dodd-Frank Act addresses systemic risk by imposing (1) capital requirements that are supposed to increase during times of financial stress and (2) restrictions on certain asset holdings (e.g., using the Volcker rule outlined in Section 619 of the Act). However, as discussed by Acharya and Richardson (2012), capital regulation may be ineffective due to financial activities involving regulatory capital arbitrage and carry trades.[4] To protect against systemic risk in the financial sector, regulators must require banks to hold sufficient capital to cover large losses that may occur with only small probability and when aggregate risk in the financial system is present. This implies banks must hold excess capital more or less continuously, even during (most) times when the probability of failure is small or even zero (see Kashyap et al. 2008 for discussion).[5] Consequently, subsequent to passage of the Dodd-Frank Act, one might expect banks' costs to increase due to the increased regulatory and reporting burdens imposed by the Act.[6] In addition, one might expect a downward shift in banks' production frontier, i.e., a contraction of their production possibilities set due to the requirements for increased capitalization of banks, as well as perhaps decreased productivity. These effects and others are investigated below.

The paper proceeds as follows. A statistical model, essential for statistical inference, is presented in the next section. Estimators of technical, cost, and input allocative efficiency and their properties are discussed in Sect. 3. In addition, various

[4]Carry trades are those trades with an initial return or "carry," but with large tail risks involving losses in the future which have low probability but which are perhaps catastrophically large.

[5]An unintended consequence of burdensome capital requirements may be to induce movement of financial intermediation out of regulated entities into weakly or unregulated entities. This in large part gave rise to shadow banking that existed by 2007.

[6]Patel (2014) reports that JP Morgan Chase & Co.'s chief executive officer, Jamie Dimon, stated in mid-2014 that JP Morgan would hire 13,000 new staff in compliance, audit, and other areas by year-end, increasing the bank's risk control staff by 30%. The number of audit staff at Bank of America Corp. roughly doubled from mid-2011 to mid-2014. Between the end of 2011 and mid-2014, Citigroup Inc. increased its staff working on regulatory and compliance issues by 33% for a total of about 30,000 employees, representing 12.3% of Citi's 244,000 total employees at the end of second-quarter 2014. Patel (2014) observes that these increases represent "the new normal for banks as they grapple with a host of new regulations and capital requirements in the wake of the financial crisis, according to analysts."

statistical results needed for testing hypotheses about model features are also discussed in Sect. 3. The data used for estimation and inference are discussed in Sect. 4, and empirical results are presented in Sect. 5. Summary and conclusions are given in Sect. 6.

2 The Statistical Model

To establish notation, let $X \in \mathbb{R}_+^p$ and $Y \in \mathbb{R}_+^q$ denote (random) vectors of input and output quantities, respectively. Let $W \in \mathbb{R}_{++}^p$ denote random vectors of input prices. Similarly, let $x \in \mathbb{R}_+^p$, $y \in \mathbb{R}_+^q$ and $w \in \mathbb{R}_{++}^p$ denote fixed, nonstochastic vectors of input and output quantities and input prices. The production set

$$\Psi := \{(x, y) \mid x \text{ can produce } y\} \tag{2.1}$$

gives the set of feasible combinations of inputs and outputs. Several assumptions on Ψ are common in the literature. The assumptions of Shephard (1970) and Färe (1988) are typical in microeconomic theory of the firm and are used here.

Assumption 21 *Ψ is closed.*

Assumption 22 $(x, y) \notin \Psi$ *if* $x = 0,\ y \geq 0,\ \ y \neq 0$*; i.e., all production requires use of some inputs.*

Assumption 23 *Both inputs and outputs are strongly disposable, i.e.,* $\forall\,(x, y) \in \Psi$*, (i)* $\widetilde{x} \geq x \Rightarrow (\widetilde{x}, y) \in \Psi$ *and (ii)* $\widetilde{y} \leq y \Rightarrow (x, \widetilde{y}) \in \Psi$.

Here and throughout, inequalities involving vectors are defined on an element-by-element basis, as is standard. Assumption 21 ensures that the *efficient frontier* (or *technology*) Ψ^∂

$$\Psi^\partial := \left\{(x, y) \mid (x, y) \in \Psi,\ (\gamma^{-1}x, \gamma y) \notin \Psi \text{ for any } \alpha \in (1, \infty)\right\} \tag{2.2}$$

is the set of extreme points of Ψ and is contained in Ψ. Assumption 22 means that production of any output quantities greater than 0 requires use of some inputs so that there can be no free lunches. Assumption 23 imposes weak monotonicity on the frontier.

The Farrell (1957) input efficiency measure

$$\theta(x, y \mid \Psi) := \inf\{\theta \mid (\theta x, y) \in \Psi\} \tag{2.3}$$

gives the amount by which input levels can feasibly be scaled downward, proportionately by the same factor, without reducing output levels. The Farrell (1957) output efficiency measure gives the feasible, proportionate expansion of output quantities and is defined by

$$\lambda(x, y \mid \Psi) := \sup\{\lambda \mid (x, \lambda y) \in \Psi\}. \tag{2.4}$$

Both (2.3) and (2.4) provide *radial* measures of efficiency since all input or output quantities are scaled by the same factor θ or λ, holding output or input quantities fixed (respectively). Clearly, $\lambda(x, y \mid \Psi) \geq 1$ and $\theta(x, y \mid \Psi) \leq 1$ for all $(x, y) \in \Psi$.

Alternatively, Färe et al. (1985) provide a hyperbolic, graph measure of efficiency defined by

$$\gamma(x, y \mid \Psi) := \inf\left\{\gamma > 0 \mid (\gamma x, \gamma^{-1} y) \in \Psi\right\}. \tag{2.5}$$

By construction, $\gamma(x, y \mid \Psi) \leq 1$ for $(x, y) \in \Psi$. Just as the measures $\theta(x, y \mid \Psi)$ and $\lambda(x, y \mid \Psi)$ provide measures of the *technical efficiency* of a firm operating at a point $(x, y) \in \Psi$, so does $\gamma(x, y \mid \Psi)$, but along the hyperbolic path from (x, y) to the frontier of Ψ. The measure $\gamma(x, y \mid \Psi)$ gives the amount by which input levels can be feasibly, proportionately scaled downward while simultaneously scaling output levels upward by the same proportion.

Given a vector $w \in \mathbb{R}^p_+$ of input prices, the minimum cost of producing a specific vector y_0 of output quantities from a given vector x_0 of input quantities is

$$\mathcal{C}_{\min}(x_0, y_0 \mid \Psi, w) = \min_x\{w'x \mid (x, y_0) \in \Psi,\ x \in \mathbb{R}^p_+,\ w \in \mathbb{R}^p_{++}\}. \tag{2.6}$$

Cost efficiency (sometimes called input overall efficiency) for the firm operating at $(x_0, y_0) \in \Psi$ and facing input prices w is then defined by

$$C(x_0, y_0 \mid \Psi, w) := \frac{\mathcal{C}_{\min}(x_0, y_0 \mid \Psi, w)}{w'x_0} = \frac{w'x_*}{w'x_0} \tag{2.7}$$

where x_* is the argmin of the expression on the right-hand side (RHS) of (2.6). The cost efficiency measure in (2.7) gives the fraction by which cost of producing output quantities y_0 could be reduced when facing input prices w; achieving this reduction might require altering the mix of inputs used to produce y_0.

Simar and Wilson (2020) define the set

$$\Psi_w := h_w(\Psi) = \{(c, y) \mid (c, y) = h_w(x, y)\ \forall\ (x, y) \in \Psi\} \tag{2.8}$$

where $h_w : \mathbb{R}^{p+q}_+ \mapsto \mathbb{R}^{1+q}_+$ is the affine function such that $h_w(x, y) = A_w \left[x'\ y'\right]'$ where

$$A_w = \begin{bmatrix} w' & 0'_q \\ 0'_{p\times q} & I_q \end{bmatrix}, \tag{2.9}$$

0_q is a $(q \times 1)$ vector of zeros, $0_{p\times q}$ is a $(p \times q)$ matrix of zeros, and I_q is a $(q \times q)$ identity matrix. Due to the properties of affine functions (e.g., see Boyd and Vandenberghe 2004, pp. 36–38), it is clear that since h_w is affine, Ψ_w is convex if and only if Ψ is convex. The set $\Psi_w \subset \mathbb{R}_+^{q+1}$ gives the set of feasible pairs of cost and output quantities. Simar and Wilson (2020, Lemma 3.2) prove that for $(x, y) \in \Psi$ and $c = w'x$,

$$\mathcal{C}(x, y \mid \Psi, w) = \theta(c, y \mid \Psi_w). \tag{2.10}$$

Then the input allocative efficiency defined by Färe et al. (1985) can be written as

$$\begin{aligned} \mathcal{A}_x(x_0, y_0 \mid \Psi, w) :=& \frac{\mathcal{C}(x, y \mid \Psi, w)}{\theta(x_0, y_0 \mid \Psi)} \\ =& \frac{\theta(c, y \mid \Psi_w)}{\theta(x_0, y_0 \mid \Psi)}. \end{aligned} \tag{2.11}$$

Input allocative efficiency measures the amount of cost inefficiency that would remain if any technical inefficiency was eliminated by proportionately reducing input quantities by the factor $\theta(x_0, y_0 \mid \Psi)$.

All of the quantities and model features defined so far are unobservable, and therefore must be estimated. The sets Ψ and Ψ_w can be estimated using the free-disposal hull (FDH) estimator introduced by Deprins et al. (1984) or either the variable returns to scale (VRS) or constant returns to scale (CRS) versions of the data envelopment analysis (DEA) estimator proposed by Farrell (1957). But, inference is needed in order to know what might be learned from data, and inference requires a well-defined statistical model. The assumptions that follow are similar to Assumptions 3.1–3.4 of Kneip et al. (2015) and complete the statistical model. The first two assumptions that follow are needed for both FDH and VRS estimators.

Assumption 24 *(i) The random variables (X, Y) possess a joint density f with support $\mathcal{D} \subset \Psi$ and (ii) f is continuously differentiable on $\mathcal{D}$.*

Assumption 25 *(i) $\mathcal{D}^* := \{\theta(x, y \mid \Psi)x,\ y) \mid (x, y) \in \mathcal{D}\} = \{(x,\ \lambda(x, y \mid \Psi)y) \mid (x, y) \in \mathcal{D}\} = \big\{(\gamma(x, y \mid \Psi)x,\ \gamma(x, y \mid \Psi)^{-1}y) \mid (x, y) \in \mathcal{D}\big\} \subset \mathcal{D}$; (ii) $\mathcal{D}^*$ is compact; and (iii) $f(\theta(x, y \mid \Psi)x, y) > 0$ for all $(x, y) \in \mathcal{D}$.*

The next two assumptions are needed when VRS estimators are used. Assumption 26 imposes some smoothness on the frontier. Kneip et al. (2008) required only two-times differentiability to establish the existence of a limiting distribution for VRS estimators, by the stronger assumption that follows is needed to establish results on moments of the VRS estimators.

Assumption 26 *$\theta(x, y \mid \Psi)$, $\lambda(x, y \mid \Psi)$ and $\gamma(x, y \mid \Psi)$ are three times continuously differentiable on $\mathcal{D}$.*

Recalling that the strong (i.e., free) disposability assumed in Assumption 23 implies that the frontier is weakly monotone, the next assumption strengthens this by requiring the frontier to be strictly monotone with no constant segments. This is also needed to establish properties of moments of the VRS estimators.

Assumption 27 *$\mathcal{D}$ is* almost strictly convex*; i.e., for any* $(x, y), (\tilde{x}, \tilde{y}) \in \mathcal{D}$ *with* $(\frac{x}{\|x\|}, y) \neq (\frac{\tilde{x}}{\|\tilde{x}\|}, \tilde{y})$*, the set* $\{(x^*, y^*) \mid (x^*, y^*) = (x, y) + \alpha((\tilde{x}, \tilde{y}) - (x, y))$ *for some* $0 < \alpha < 1\}$ *is a subset of the* interior *of* $\mathcal{D}$.

Alternatively, when FDH estimators are used, Assumptions 26 and 27 can be replaced by the following assumption.

Assumption 28 *(i)* $\theta(x, y \mid \Psi)$, $\lambda(x, y \mid \Psi)$ *and* $\gamma(x, y \mid \Psi)$ *are twice continuously differentiable on* $\mathcal{D}$ *and (ii) all the first-order partial derivatives of* $\theta(x, y \mid \Psi)$, $\lambda(x, y \mid \Psi)$ *and* $\gamma(x, y \mid \Psi)$ *with respect to x and y are nonzero at any point* $(x, y) \in \mathcal{D}$.

Assumption 28 strengthens the assumption of strong disposability in 23 by requiring that the frontier is strictly monotone and does not possess constant segments (which would be the case, for example, if outputs are discrete as opposed to continuous, as in the case of ships produced by shipyards). Finally, part (i) of Assumption 28 is weaker than Assumption 26; here the frontier is required to be smooth, but not as smooth as required by Assumption 26.[7] Assumptions 21–25 and 28 comprise a statistical model appropriate for use of FDH estimators of technical efficiency, while Assumptions 21–27 comprise a statistical model appropriate for use of VRS estimators of technical efficiency.[8]

Regardless of whether VRS or FDH estimators are used, and additional assumption regarding input prices is needed. The assumption here is similar to Assumption 2.9 of Simar and Wilson (2020).

Assumption 29 *(i) The random variable* (W) *has probability density* f_W *with compact support* $\mathcal{D}_W \subset \mathbb{R}^p_{++}$ *and (ii) The random variables* (X, Y, W) *are defined on an appropriate probability space such that the joint density* $f_{X,Y,W}(x, y, w)$ *exists and is well-defined with support* $\mathcal{D} \times \mathcal{D}_W$.

Assumption 29 ensures that all prices are strictly positive and have finite upper bounds. In some situations firms may face the same prices. In such cases f_W is degenerate with mass at a single point.

3 Estimation and Inference

Let $\mathcal{S}_{XYW,n} = \{(X_i, Y_i, W_i)\}_{i=1}^n$ be a random sample drawn from the density $f_{X,Y,W}$ introduced in Assumption 29, and let $\mathcal{S}_n = \{(X_i, Y_i)\}_{i=1}^n$ be the corresponding set of input-output pairs. Given a random sample $\mathcal{S}_n = \{(X_i, Y_i)\}$,

---

[7] Assumption 28 is slightly stronger, but much simpler than assumptions AII–AIII in Park et al. (2000).

[8] Additional assumptions are needed for CRS efficiency estimators. See Kneip et al. (2015) for additional discussion.

the production set Ψ can by estimated by the free-disposal hull of the sample observations in $\mathcal{S}_n$,

$$\widehat{\Psi}_{\mathrm{FDH}},n := \bigcup_{(X_i,Y_i)\in\mathcal{S}_n} \left\{(x,y) \in \mathbb{R}_+^{p+q} \mid x \geq X_i,\ y \leq Y_i\right\}, \tag{3.1}$$

proposed by Deprins et al. (1984). Alternatively, Ψ can be estimated by the convex hull of $\widehat{\Psi}_{\mathrm{FDH}}$ of the free-disposal hull of the sample observations in $\mathcal{S}_n$, i.e., by

$$\widehat{\Psi}_{\mathrm{VRS},n} := \left\{(x,y) \in \mathbb{R}^{p+q} \mid y \leq \boldsymbol{Y}\boldsymbol{\omega},\ x \geq \boldsymbol{X}\boldsymbol{\omega},\ \boldsymbol{i}_n'\boldsymbol{\omega} = 1,\ \boldsymbol{\omega} \in \mathbb{R}_+^n\right\}, \tag{3.2}$$

where $\boldsymbol{X} = \left(X_1,\ \ldots,\ X_n\right)$ and $\boldsymbol{Y} = \left(Y_1,\ \ldots,\ Y_n\right)$ are $(p \times n)$ and $(q \times n)$ matrices of input and output vectors, respectively; $\boldsymbol{i}_n$ is an $(n \times 1)$ vector of ones, and $\boldsymbol{\omega}$ is a $(n \times 1)$ vector of weights. The estimator $\widehat{\Psi}_{\mathrm{VRS}}$ imposes convexity, but allows for VRS. This is the VRS, DEA estimator of Ψ proposed by Farrell (1957) and popularized by Banker et al. (1984). The CRS, DEA estimator $\widehat{\Psi}_{\mathrm{CRS},n}$ of Ψ is obtained by dropping the constraint $\boldsymbol{i}_n'\boldsymbol{\omega} = 1$ in (3.2). FDH, VRS, or CRS estimators of $\theta(x, y \mid \Psi)$, $\lambda(x, y \mid \Psi)$ and $\gamma(x, y \mid \Psi)$ defined in Sect. 2 are obtained by substituting $\widehat{\Psi}_{\mathrm{FDH},n}$, $\widehat{\Psi}_{\mathrm{VRS},n}$, or $\widehat{\Psi}_{\mathrm{CRS},n}$ for Ψ in (2.3)–(2.5) (respectively). In the case of VRS estimators, this results in

$$\widehat{\theta}_{\mathrm{VRS}}(x, y \mid \mathcal{S}_n) = \min_{\theta,\boldsymbol{\omega}} \left\{\theta \mid y \leq \boldsymbol{Y}\boldsymbol{\omega},\ \theta x \geq \boldsymbol{X}\boldsymbol{\omega},\ \boldsymbol{i}_n'\boldsymbol{\omega} = 1,\ \boldsymbol{\omega} \in \mathbb{R}_+^n\right\}, \tag{3.3}$$

$$\widehat{\lambda}_{\mathrm{VRS}}(x, y \mid \mathcal{S}_n) = \max_{\lambda,\boldsymbol{\omega}} \left\{\lambda \mid \lambda y \leq \boldsymbol{Y}\boldsymbol{\omega},\ x \geq \boldsymbol{X}\boldsymbol{\omega},\ \boldsymbol{i}_n'\boldsymbol{\omega} = 1,\ \boldsymbol{\omega} \in \mathbb{R}_+^n\right\} \tag{3.4}$$

and

$$\widehat{\gamma}_{\mathrm{VRS}}(x, y \mid \mathcal{S}_n) = \min_{\gamma,\boldsymbol{\omega}} \left\{\gamma \mid \gamma^{-1} y \leq \boldsymbol{Y}\boldsymbol{\omega},\ \gamma x \geq \boldsymbol{X}\boldsymbol{\omega},\ \boldsymbol{i}_n'\boldsymbol{\omega} = 1,\ \boldsymbol{\omega} \in \mathbb{R}_+^n\right\}. \tag{3.5}$$

The corresponding CRS estimators $\widehat{\theta}_{CRS}(x, y \mid \mathcal{S}_n)$, $\widehat{\lambda}_{CRS}(x, y \mid \mathcal{S}_n)$ and $\widehat{\gamma}_{CRS}(x, y \mid \mathcal{S}_n)$ are obtained by dropping the constraint $\boldsymbol{i}_n'\boldsymbol{\omega}$ in (3.3)–(3.5). The estimators in (3.3)–(3.4) can be computed using linear programming methods, but the hyperbolic estimator in (3.5) is a non-linear program. Nonetheless, estimates can be computed easily using the numerical algorithm developed by Wilson (2011).

Substituting $\widehat{\Psi}_{\mathrm{FDH}}$ into (2.3)–(2.5) (respectively) leads to integer programming problems, but the estimators can be computed using simple numerical methods. In particular, let $D_{x,y}$ denote the set indices of points in $\mathcal{S}_n$ dominating (x, y), i.e., $D_{x,y} = \{i \mid (X_i, Y_i) \in \mathcal{S}_n,\ X_i \leq x,\ Y_i \geq y\}$. Then

$$\widehat{\theta}_{\mathrm{FDH}}(x, y \mid \mathcal{S}_n) = \min_{i \in D_{x,y}} \max_{j=1,\ldots,p} \left(\frac{X_i^j}{x^j}\right), \tag{3.6}$$

where for a vector a, a^j denotes its j-th component. The output-oriented estimator can be computed by solving

$$\lambda_{\text{FDH}}(\boldsymbol{x}, \boldsymbol{y} \mid \mathcal{S}_n) = \max_{i \in D(\boldsymbol{x},\boldsymbol{y})} \min_{j=1,\ldots,q} \left(\frac{\boldsymbol{Y}_i^j}{\boldsymbol{y}^j} \right), \tag{3.7}$$

and Wilson (2011) shows that the hyperbolic estimator can be computed by solving

$$\widehat{\gamma}_{\text{FDH}}(\boldsymbol{x}, \boldsymbol{y} \mid \mathcal{S}_n) = \min_{i=1,\ldots,n} \left(\max_{\substack{j=1,\ldots,p \\ k=1,\ldots,q}} \left(\frac{\boldsymbol{x}_i^j}{\boldsymbol{x}^j}, \frac{\boldsymbol{y}^k}{\boldsymbol{y}_i^k} \right) \right). \tag{3.8}$$

The statistical properties of these efficiency estimators are well-developed. Kneip et al. (1998) derive the rate of convergence of the input-oriented VRS estimator, while Kneip et al. (2008) derive its limiting distribution. Park et al. (2010) derive the rate of convergence of the input-oriented CRS estimator and establish its limiting distribution. Park et al. (2000) and Daouia et al. (2017) derive both the rate of convergence and limiting distribution of the input-oriented FDH estimator. These results extend trivially to the output orientation after straightforward (but perhaps tedious) changes in notation. Wheelock and Wilson (2008) extend these results to the hyperbolic FDH estimator, and Wilson (2011) extends the results to the hyperbolic DEA estimator.

Kneip et al. (2015) derive moment properties of both the input-oriented FDH, VRS and CRS estimators and establish central limit theorem (CLT) results for mean input-oriented efficiency after showing that the usual CLT results (e.g., the Lindeberg-Feller CLT) do not hold unless $(p + q) < 3$ in the DEA case, or unless $p + q < 2$ in the FDH case.[9] Kneip et al. (2015) use these CLT results to establish asymptotically normal test statistics for testing differences in mean efficiency across two groups, convexity versus non-convexity of Ψ, and CRS versus VRS. All of these results extend trivially (but again, tediously) to the output-oriented FDH, VRS, and CRS estimators. Kneip et al. (2020) extend these results to the hyperbolic VRS and CRS estimators. Moment results for the hyperbolic FDH estimator are provided by the following result.

Theorem 31 *Under Assumptions 21–25 and 28, there exists a constant* $0 < \mathfrak{C} < \infty$ *such that for all* $i, j \in \{1, \ldots, n\}$, $i \neq j$,

$$E\left(\widehat{\gamma}_{FDH}(X_i, Y_i \mid \mathcal{S}_n) - \gamma(X_i, Y_i)\right) = \mathfrak{C}n^{-\frac{1}{p+q}} + O\left(n^{-\frac{2}{p+q}}(\log n)^{\frac{p+q+2}{p+q}}\right), \tag{3.9}$$

[9]In other words, standard CLT results hold in the FDH case if and only if $p = 1$ and output is fixed and constant, or $q = 1$ and input is fixed and constant.

$$VAR\left(\widehat{\gamma}_{FDH}(X_i, Y_i \mid \mathcal{S}_n) - \gamma(X_i, Y_i)\right) = O\left(n^{-\frac{2}{p+q}} (\log n)^{\frac{2}{p+q}}\right), \tag{3.10}$$

and

$$\left|COV\left(\widehat{\gamma}_{FDH}(X_i, Y_i \mid \mathcal{S}_n) - \gamma(X_i, Y_i), \widehat{\gamma}_{FDH}(X_j, Y_j \mid \mathcal{S}_n) - \gamma(X_j, Y_j)\right)\right|$$
$$= O\left(n^{-\frac{p+q+1}{p+q}} (\log n)^{\frac{p+q+1}{p+q}}\right) = o\left(n^{-1}\right). \tag{3.11}$$

The value of the constant $\mathfrak{C}$ depends on f and on the structure of the set $\mathcal{D} \subset \Psi$.

Proof Define the mapping $\phi\colon \mathbb{R}_{+}^{(p+q)} \mapsto \mathbb{R}_{+}^{(p+q)}$ such that $(x, y) \mapsto (x, y^{-1})$ where y^{-1} is the vector whose elements are the inverses of the corresponding elements of y. Denote $z = \phi(x, y)$. and note that ϕ is a continuous, one-to-one transformation. Hence $(x, y) = \phi^{-1}(z)$.

Clearly,

$$\widehat{\gamma}_{\text{FDH}}(x, y) = \min_{i=1, \ldots, n} \left(\max_{j=1, \ldots, (p+q)} \left(\frac{z_i^j}{z^j} \right) \right). \tag{3.12}$$

This is identical in form to the input-oriented estimator in (3.3) in (x, y)-space with $(p + q)$ input dimensions and no output dimensions. Obviously, it makes no difference whether the hyperbolic FDH estimator is computed in (x, y)-space or in z-space. In either case, the resulting estimate is the same due to the fact that the transformation ϕ preserves the ordering of the observations in $\mathcal{S}_n$ in each of the $(p + q)$ dimensions, and the estimator is computed in terms of distance to the free-disposal hull of the sample observations in either case. Consequently, the results hold using the arguments in the proof of Kneip et al. (2015, Theorem 3.3). ■

Theorem 31 and the argument in the proof showing that the hyperbolic FDH estimator can be viewed as an input-oriented FDH estimator in a transformed space make clear that the CLT results of Kneip et al. (2015) as well as the results from Kneip et al. (2016) on tests of differences in means, returns to scale, and convexity of Ψ carry over to the hyperbolic FDH estimator.

To summarize, in all cases, the FDH, VRS, and CRS estimators are consistent, converge at rate n^{κ} (where $\kappa = 1/(p+q)$ for the FDH estimators, $\kappa = 2/(p+q+1)$ for the VRS estimators and $\kappa = 2/(p + q)$ for the CRS estimators) and possess non-degenerate limiting distributions under the appropriate set of assumptions. In addition, the bias of each of the three estimators is of order $O\left(n^{-\kappa}\right)$. Bootstrap methods proposed by Kneip et al. (2008, 2011) and Simar and Wilson (2011a) provide consistent inference about $\theta(x, y \mid \Psi)$, $\lambda(x, y \mid \Psi)$ and $\gamma(x, y \mid \Psi)$ for a fixed point $(x, y) \in \Psi$, and Kneip et al. (2015) provide CLT results enabling inference about the expected values of these measures over the random variables (X, Y). In addition, Theorem 3.1 of Simar and Wilson (2020) establishes consistency, rate of convergence, and the existence of a limiting distribution for the FDH and VRS estimators of cost efficiency. Moment properties are established by Theorems 3.2 and 3.3 of Simar and Wilson provides CLT results for cost efficiency. Similar results for FDH and VRS estimators of input allocative efficiency are provided by Theorems 3.6–3.8 of Simar and Wilson (2020).

4 Data and Variable Specification

Year-end data for 2006, 2008, ..., 2016 are taken from the FR Y-9C Consolidated Financial Statements for U.S. Bank Holding Companies. I specify $p = 4$ inputs (borrowed funds, consisting of purchased funds and core deposits (X_1); labor, measured in full-time equivalents (X_2); physical capital measured by the book value of premises and fixed assets including capitalized leases (X_3); and equity capital (X_4)) and $q = 2$ outputs (total loans and leases (Y_1); and total securities (Y_3)). In addition, prices W_1, W_2, and W_3 for the first three inputs are obtained by multiplying the reciprocals of X_1, X_2, and X_3 by the corresponding expenses incurred for each of these inputs. However, the price of equity capital is unobservable.[10] Consequently, I consider two input-output specifications, either with inputs X_1, X_2, and X_3 but without equity capital, or with all four inputs. In the former case, technical, cost, and input allocative efficiencies are estimated, but in the latter case only technical efficiency can be estimated. As will be seen below, the main results are broadly similar across the two specifications.[11] All dollar amounts are measured in constant 2016 U.S. dollars. Both input-output specifications used here reflect the view that banks borrow money from those with a surplus of cash, and lend to those who desire more cash than they have. The input-output specifications are typical and standard; e.g., see Wheelock and Wilson (2018).

I assume that all banks operate in the same production set Ψ defined by (2.1), and consequently face the same frontier in the five-dimensional input-output space. Note, however, that banks may have very different business plans, and hence may operate in different regions of the production set or under different parts of the frontier. To give an example, Bank of America became one of the largest banks operating in the USA in part by building an extensive retail network of branches, often by acquiring other banks. By contrast, JP Morgan Chase grew its business

[10] Conceivably one could estimate the shadow price of equity capital, but for inefficient firms this is problematic since the estimated shadow price would depend on the particular direction in which an inefficient firm is projected onto the estimated frontier.

[11] Note that equity capital can arguably be viewed as a free source of financial capital for banks. In each year 2006, 2008, ..., 2016, the median value of X_4/X_1 varies between 0.1005 and 0.1144, while the first quartiles range between 0.0802 and 0.0977 and the third quartiles range between 0.1229 and 0.1362. Hence equity capital typically amounts to around 10–11% of the financial capital of banks in the sample. One should perhaps not expect large differences between results from the two different specifications.

in large part through business lending. The two banks apparently operated under rather different business plans, and hence in different regions of the production set Ψ. More recently, Bank of America has shed many of its retail branches, perhaps adopting at least in part or moving closer to the business plan of JP Morgan Chase.

The view here contrasts with studies that assume different frontiers for different firms. Papers that do so invariably rely on fully parametric estimation methods, and allowing different frontiers buys some flexibility. The model described in Sect. 2 is fully nonparametric, and hence quite flexible. The assumptions listed in Sect. 2 impose only minimal restrictions involving free-disposability, continuity, and some smoothness of the frontier, etc. Note that there is no assumption of convexity of Ψ, which is tested below in Sect. 5.

The flexibility of the nonparametric model specified in Sect. 2 comes with a price, however, in terms of the well-known "curse of dimensionality." Wilson (2018) discusses dimension reduction in the context of nonparametric efficiency estimation, and presents several diagnostics to indicate when reducing dimensionality might be advantageous. As discussed in Sect. 3, FDH, VRS, and CRS estimators converge at rate n^{κ}, where $\kappa = 1/(p+q)$ for FDH estimators, $\kappa = 2/(p+q+1)$ for VRS estimators and $\kappa = 2/(p+q)$ for CRS estimators. With the $(p+q) = 5$ dimensional specification where equity capital is not included, the convergence rates are $n^{1/5}$, $n^{1/3}$, and $n^{2/5}$ for FDH, VRS, and CRS estimators, respectively. Moreover, the number of observations in each period that I consider range from 533 to 943. The *effective parametric sample size* defined by Wilson (2018) is then, in the worst case, $533^{2/5} \approx 12$ for FDH estimators, $533^{2/3} \approx 66$ for VRS estimators and $533^{4/5} \approx 152$ for CRS estimators. In other words, with a sample size of 533, FDH estimators should be expected to result in estimation error of the same order one would achieve with a typical parametric estimator and only 12 observations. With VRS (or CRS) estimators, one should expect estimation error of the same order that 66 (or 152) observations would provide in a parametric model. Of course, consistency of the VRS estimators requires convexity of Ψ, and consistency of the CRS estimators requires in addition CRS. It remains to be seen whether Ψ satisfies such restrictions.[12]

Wilson (2018) also suggests examining the ratios R_x, R_y of the largest eigenvalues of the moment matrices $\boldsymbol{XX'}$, $\boldsymbol{YY'}$ to the corresponding sums of eigenvalues for these moment matrices. Table 1 gives values of these ratios for each of the 6 periods represented in the data. The smallest value (97.13 for R_x in 2008) is well above the level needed for dimension reduction to be likely to reduce mean square error

---

[12]The situation becomes even worse if equity capital is included. Then the effective parametric samples sizes for the FDH, VRS, and CRS estimators are 3, 36, and 66 (respectively) for $n = 533$. Of course, the notion of *effective parametric sample size* defined by Wilson (2018) presupposes that one has a correctly specified parametric model. As Robinson (1988) notes, the root-n parametric convergence rate means that estimators converge quickly to the wrong thing in a mis-specified model, leading the author to refer to root-n *in*consistency.

Table 1 Eigensystem analysis by year

	Without equity	With equity	
Year	R_x	R_x	R_y
2006	97.65	97.37	97.14
2008	97.13	97.17	97.86
2010	97.62	98.04	97.75
2012	98.12	98.43	97.67
2014	97.32	97.70	98.41
2016	98.12	98.17	98.43

of either DEA or FDH estimates as indicated by the simulation results reported by Wilson (2018). Consequently, I compute $(1 \times n)$ vectors of principal components $X^* = E_x' \boldsymbol{X}$ and $Y^* = E_y' \boldsymbol{Y}$ where E_x and E_y are the $(p \times 1)$ and $(q \times 1)$ eigenvectors corresponding to the largest eigenvalues of the moment matrices $\boldsymbol{X}\boldsymbol{X}'$ and $\boldsymbol{Y}\boldsymbol{Y}'$, respectively. Given the values of R_x and R_y in Table 1, it is clear that these principal components contain most of the independent information in the $p = 3$ (or $p = 4$) inputs and $q = 2$ outputs specified above. Consistent with earlier observations, R_x is little changed when equity is included or omitted. Except as noted below, all estimation is done using the principal components X^* and Y^*. In this two-dimensional setting, the convergence rates of the FDH, VRS, and CRS estimators are $n^{1/2}$, $n^{2/3}$, and n^1, respectively. The simulation results of Wilson (2018) provide clear evidence that relying only on X^* and Y^* for estimation likely results in less estimation error than would be the case with five dimensions. This is true regardless of whether the technology is homothetic, contrary to what is suggested by Färe and Lovell (1988) and Olesen and Petersen (2016).

Table 2 gives summary statistics for the original input and output variables as well as the input prices W_1, W_2, and W_3, cost $C = W_1 X_1 + W_2 X_2 + W_3 X_3$, and the principal components X^* (both with and without equity capital) and Y^*. For each variable, the table shows the minimum value, first quartile (Q1), median, mean, third quartile (Q3), and the maximum value. Comparing differences between the median and Q1 and between Q3 and the median for the input and output variables reveals that the marginal distributions are heavily skewed to the right, reflecting the skewness of the distribution of bank sizes.

Table 3 shows total assets of the five largest institutions in each of the 6 periods represented in the data. The table reveals that the largest institutions grew larger throughout the financial crisis. Total assets of the five largest institutions amount to about 5.89 trillion dollars in 2006, and about 8.85 trillion dollars in 2016, for an increase of about 50%. Moreover, the results in Table 3 indicate that growth occurred throughout the financial crisis.

Table 2 Summary statistics

Variable	Min	Q1	Median	Mean	Q3	Max
X_1	$3.7140 \times 10^{+04}$	$6.0980 \times 10^{+05}$	$9.5950 \times 10^{+05}$	$1.3030 \times 10^{+07}$	$2.0110 \times 10^{+06}$	$2.3550 \times 10^{+09}$
X_2	$1.3000 \times 10^{+01}$	$1.6100 \times 10^{+02}$	$2.4800 \times 10^{+02}$	$2.2380 \times 10^{+03}$	$4.9900 \times 10^{+02}$	$3.6290 \times 10^{+05}$
X_3	$1.9600 \times 10^{+02}$	$1.0630 \times 10^{+04}$	$1.9280 \times 10^{+04}$	$1.1310 \times 10^{+05}$	$3.7240 \times 10^{+04}$	$1.4310 \times 10^{+07}$
X_4	$4.1180 \times 10^{+02}$	$6.3170 \times 10^{+04}$	$1.0290 \times 10^{+05}$	$1.5550 \times 10^{+06}$	$2.2370 \times 10^{+05}$	$2.6680 \times 10^{+08}$
Y_1	$1.1340 \times 10^{+02}$	$1.1380 \times 10^{+05}$	$2.2250 \times 10^{+05}$	$2.6350 \times 10^{+06}$	$4.7700 \times 10^{+05}$	$4.1340 \times 10^{+08}$
Y_2	$7.4680 \times 10^{+03}$	$4.8340 \times 10^{+05}$	$7.6630 \times 10^{+05}$	$7.6040 \times 10^{+06}$	$1.6100 \times 10^{+06}$	$1.0940 \times 10^{+09}$
W_1	6.6350×10^{-05}	4.9090×10^{-03}	1.0440×10^{-02}	1.4030×10^{-02}	2.3270×10^{-02}	7.9260×10^{-02}
W_2	$2.8410 \times 10^{+00}$	$6.1860 \times 10^{+01}$	$7.2060 \times 10^{+01}$	$7.7860 \times 10^{+01}$	$8.6760 \times 10^{+01}$	$3.7880 \times 10^{+02}$
W_3	1.2630×10^{-02}	1.5850×10^{-01}	2.1470×10^{-01}	3.0430×10^{-01}	3.1850×10^{-01}	$4.6340 \times 10^{+00}$
C	$1.9740 \times 10^{+03}$	$2.2290 \times 10^{+04}$	$3.4930 \times 10^{+04}$	$4.4580 \times 10^{+05}$	$7.1550 \times 10^{+04}$	$1.1190 \times 10^{+08}$
X^{*} [a]	$2.1730 \times 10^{+04}$	$3.5940 \times 10^{+05}$	$5.6480 \times 10^{+05}$	$7.5910 \times 10^{+06}$	$1.1860 \times 10^{+06}$	$1.3730 \times 10^{+09}$
X^{*} [b]	$2.2450 \times 10^{+04}$	$3.4530 \times 10^{+05}$	$5.4240 \times 10^{+05}$	$7.3650 \times 10^{+06}$	$1.1370 \times 10^{+06}$	$1.3090 \times 10^{+09}$
Y^{*}	$2.9140 \times 10^{+04}$	$4.5050 \times 10^{+05}$	$7.0420 \times 10^{+05}$	$7.2410 \times 10^{+06}$	$1.4520 \times 10^{+06}$	$1.0540 \times 10^{+09}$

[a]Does not include equity (X_4)
[b]Includes equity (X_4)

Table 3 Total assets of five largest BHCs by year in thousands of 2016 US dollars

Name	Total assets	Name	Total assets
2006		2012	
Citigroup	1,884,318,000	JP Morgan Chase	2,359,141,000
Bank of America	1,463,685,485	Bank of America	2,212,004,452
JP Morgan Chase	1,351,520,000	Citigroup	1,864,660,000
Wachovia	707,121,000	Well Fargo	1,422,968,000
Well Fargo	481,996,000	Bank of NY Mellon	359,301,000
2008		2014	
JP Morgan Chase	2,175,052,000	JP Morgan Chase	2,572,773,000
Citigroup	1,938,470,000	Bank of America	2,106,796,000
Bank of America	1,822,068,028	Citigroup	1,842,181,000
Well Fargo	1,309,639,000	Well Fargo	1,687,155,000
PNC FNCL SVC GROUP	291,092,876	US Bancorp	402,529,000
2010		2016	
Bank of America	2,268,347,377	JP Morgan Chase	2,490,972,000
JP Morgan Chase	2,117,605,000	Bank of America	2,189,266,000
Citigroup	1,913,902,000	Well Fargo	1,930,115,000
Well Fargo	1,258,128,000	Citigroup	1,792,077,000
US Bancorp	307,786,000	US Bancorp	445,964,000

5 Empirical Results

Before turning to the main results, as a further check on whether dimension reduction might be useful, I estimate hyperbolic efficiency in each year using first the full-dimensional data with five or six dimensions (omitting or including equity capital), and then using the reduced-dimension data with only two dimensions. For either case, I use FDH, VRS, and CRS estimators. Table 4 shows counts of the number of estimates equal to one in each of the resulting 6 scenarios. As discussed by Wilson (2018), large proportions of efficiency estimates equal to one are symptomatic of the need for dimension reduction.

The counts in Table 4 reveal show that the FDH estimator produces more estimates equal to one than either of the DEA estimators, and that the VRS estimator results in more estimates equal to one than the CRS estimator. This is to be expected. More importantly, however, the FDH estimator, when used on the full-dimensional data, results in 69.65 to 87.43% of observations in a given year having estimates equal to one when equity capital is omitted (or 87.75–95.31% when equity is included). The proportions for the DEA estimators are much smaller—4.24 to 7.13% with the VRS estimator, and 1.59 to 3.19% for the CRS estimator when equity capital is omitted (or 7.46–11.82% and 3.51–5.82%, respectively, when equity is included). The large proportion of ones obtained with the FDH estimator is clear evidence of too many dimensions for the given sample sizes (see Wilson 2018

Table 4 Numbers of observations with estimated hyperbolic technical efficiency equal to 1 in each year

		Without dim. reduction			With dim. reduction		
Year	n	FDH	VRS	CRS	FDH	VRS	CRS
Equity not included							
2006	912	727	49	19	154	9	1
2008	881	674	56	24	157	8	1
2010	898	637	52	20	145	8	1
2012	906	631	41	15	137	7	1
2014	943	683	40	15	149	8	1
2016	533	466	38	17	139	7	1
Equity included							
2006	912	834	68	32	201	12	1
2008	881	805	86	38	178	9	1
2010	898	791	101	45	166	10	1
2012	906	795	79	32	180	8	1
2014	943	847	91	45	190	10	1
2016	533	508	63	31	158	7	1

for discussion). Moreover, the large difference in the proportions obtained with the FDH estimator and those obtained with the VRS estimator suggest that Ψ may not be convex.

With dimension reduction, Table 4 indicates that the FDH estimator results in smaller proportions of estimates at one than when working in the full-dimensional space. However, the proportions obtained with the FDH estimator are roughly 15–20 times those obtained with the VRS estimator, again suggesting that perhaps Ψ is not convex. Overall, the results in Table 4 provide evidence (in addition to the values of R_x and R_y and the effective parametric sample sizes discussed in Sect. 4) that dimension reduction likely reduces estimation error relative to what would be obtained working in the full, five-dimensional space. Hence all results that follow are obtained using the principal components X^* (with or without equity) and Y^* described above in Sect. 4.

The next question to consider is which estimator should be used. In increasing order of restrictiveness lie the FDH, VRS, and CRS estimators. But this is also the increasing order of the estimators' rates of convergence. Using the principal components X^* and Y^*, I test the null hypothesis of convexity of Ψ versus the alternative hypothesis that Ψ is not convex using the test developed by Kneip et al. (2016). This test involves randomly splitting the sample for a given year into two subsamples of size $n_1 = \lfloor n/2 \rfloor$ and $n_2 = n - n_1$, where $\lfloor a \rfloor$ denotes the integer part of $a \in \mathbb{R}$. I do this by randomly ordering the observations using the randomization algorithm described by Daraio et al. (2018) and then taking the first n_1 observations as the first subsample, and the remaining n_2 observations as the second subsample. The randomization algorithm of Daraio et al. provides a machine-independent, pseudo-random sort of the observations and requires neither a random number generator nor an initial seed, thereby ensuring (1) that the results of the tests can be easily replicated and (2) that the results are not sensitive to the choice of an initial seed value. The first subsample is used to compute VRS estimates, and the second is used to compute FDH estimates. The test statistic given in equation (50) of Kneip et al. (2016) involves the difference of the means of these two sets of estimates, with generalized jackknife estimates of biases and corresponding sample variances, and is asymptotically normally distributed with mean zero and unit variance. The test is a one-sided test since under the null the two means should be roughly similar, but should diverge with increasing departures from the null resulting in the mean of the FDH estimates exceeding the mean of the VRS estimates. The statistic given in equation (50) of Kneip et al. (2016) is defined in terms of input-oriented estimators, but extends trivially to output-oriented and hyperbolic estimators. The tests are one-sided, and I define the statistics so that "large" positive values indicate rejection of the null hypothesis.

Table 5 gives the results of the convexity tests for each year and for both input-output specifications. The results reveal that neither of the three tests reject convexity in 2012 when equity is omitted, but all three tests reject convexity when equity is included. In 2006, omitting equity, convexity is soundly rejected in the input orientation, and at better than 5% in the hyperbolic direction, although convexity cannot be rejected in the output orientation. In all other cases, convexity is overwhelmingly rejected when equity is omitted. When equity is included, convexity is rejected in every case except for 2014 in the output orientation.

The results in Table 5 provide substantial evidence of non-convexity of Ψ except in 2012 when equity is omitted (but not when it is included). However, failure to reject the null does not mean the null is true. Moreover, the FDH estimator is the safer choice, as it is consistent regardless of whether Ψ is convex, while the DEA

Table 5 Results of convexity tests (with dimension reduction, $p = q = 1$)

	Input		Output		Hyperbolic	
Year	Statistic	p-value	Statistic	p-value	Statistic	p-value
Equity not included						
2006	5.8905	1.92×10^{-09}	−1.9925	9.77×10^{-01}	2.2268	1.30×10^{-02}
2008	35.7747	1.37×10^{-280}	31.6805	1.44×10^{-220}	34.7482	7.37×10^{-265}
2010	38.0250	1.11×10^{-316}	36.6606	1.55×10^{-294}	39.9191	9.27×10^{-349}
2012	0.5653	2.86×10^{-01}	0.3956	3.46×10^{-01}	0.4351	3.32×10^{-01}
2014	20.9089	2.22×10^{-97}	8.5365	6.92×10^{-18}	19.9513	7.30×10^{-89}
2016	44.0234	1.30×10^{-423}	18.1325	8.83×10^{-74}	39.3904	1.20×10^{-339}
Equity included						
2006	12.5929	1.16×10^{-36}	9.8292	4.21×10^{-23}	11.9265	4.31×10^{-33}
2008	10.1610	1.48×10^{-24}	6.8068	4.99×10^{-12}	10.1284	2.07×10^{-24}
2010	8.6850	1.89×10^{-18}	6.6418	1.55×10^{-11}	7.7757	3.75×10^{-15}
2012	7.5624	1.98×10^{-14}	5.8638	2.26×10^{-09}	6.5516	2.85×10^{-11}
2014	6.9305	2.10×10^{-12}	0.8491	1.98×10^{-01}	5.7448	4.60×10^{-09}
2016	7.4840	3.61×10^{-14}	2.9769	1.46×10^{-03}	6.6392	1.58×10^{-11}

estimators require convexity. In addition, the simulation results of Wilson (2018) indicate that the FDH estimator often yields smaller mean square error than the VRS estimator after dimension reduction, even if the underlying production set is convex. Consequently, for the remainder of the analysis, I use the FDH estimators.

Table 6 presents summary statistics on the FDH technical efficiency estimates in the input, output, and hyperbolic orientations for the case where equity is omitted. Table 7 presents similar summary statistics for the case where equity is included. In both tables, statistics for the reciprocals of the output-oriented estimates are shown so that all the estimates represented in Tables 6 and 7 are weakly less than 1 in order to facilitate comparisons. As might be expected, the hyperbolic estimates are more conservative on average, with mean efficiencies ranging from 0.9392 to 0.9636 in Table 6 and from 0.9620 to 0.9758 in Table 7. By contrast, the means of the input-oriented estimates range from 0.8845 to 0.9314 and from 0.9274 to 0.9538 in Tables 6 and 7 (respectively), while the means of the output-oriented estimates range from 0.8895 to 0.9280 and from 0.9268 to 0.9555 Tables 6 and 7 (respectively). These difference are due to the geometry of the efficiency measures as discussed by Wilson (2011). Nonetheless, overall patterns appear to be the same across the

Table 6 Summary statistics for FDH technical efficiency estimates (with dimension reduction, equity not included, $p = q = 1$)

Year	Min	Q1	Median	Mean	Q3	Max
Input orientation						
2006	0.4347	0.8892	0.9359	0.9198	0.9798	1.0000
2008	0.4507	0.8965	0.9426	0.9294	0.9830	1.0000
2010	0.4946	0.8625	0.9225	0.9074	0.9729	1.0000
2012	0.4049	0.8218	0.9069	0.8845	0.9715	1.0000
2014	0.1536	0.8645	0.9323	0.9116	0.9812	1.0000
2016	0.1580	0.9069	0.9608	0.9314	1.0000	1.0000
Output orientation						
2006	0.3799	0.8831	0.9339	0.9136	0.9800	1.0000
2008	0.4325	0.8925	0.9419	0.9290	0.9814	1.0000
2010	0.4536	0.8560	0.9229	0.9051	0.9750	1.0000
2012	0.4660	0.8364	0.9118	0.8895	0.9729	1.0000
2014	0.1197	0.8749	0.9328	0.9146	0.9774	1.0000
2016	0.1742	0.8990	0.9609	0.9265	1.0000	1.0000
Hyperbolic orientation						
2006	0.6678	0.9414	0.9679	0.9562	0.9906	1.0000
2008	0.6035	0.9463	0.9703	0.9636	0.9921	1.0000
2010	0.6549	0.9272	0.9611	0.9506	0.9876	1.0000
2012	0.6943	0.9061	0.9548	0.9392	0.9851	1.0000
2014	0.3574	0.9338	0.9640	0.9538	0.9891	1.0000
2016	0.4097	0.9536	0.9796	0.9620	1.0000	1.0000

Note: Statistics for the reciprocals of the output efficiency estimates are given to facilitate comparison with the input-oriented and hyperbolic estimates

Table 7 Summary statistics for FDH technical efficiency estimates (with dimension reduction, equity included, $p = q = 1$)

Year	Min	Q1	Median	Mean	Q3	Max
Input orientation						
2006	0.4398	0.9266	0.9631	0.9509	0.9954	1.0000
2008	0.3351	0.9232	0.9613	0.9469	0.9919	1.0000
2010	0.4793	0.8962	0.9439	0.9274	0.9879	1.0000
2012	0.3748	0.8979	0.9481	0.9285	0.9894	1.0000
2014	0.1141	0.9183	0.9576	0.9407	0.9914	1.0000
2016	0.1555	0.9375	0.9722	0.9538	1.0000	1.0000
Output orientation						
2006	0.4519	0.9289	0.9623	0.9502	0.9950	1.0000
2008	0.3154	0.9263	0.9612	0.9484	0.9916	1.0000
2010	0.5042	0.8938	0.9454	0.9273	0.9858	1.0000
2012	0.3789	0.8938	0.9493	0.9268	0.9893	1.0000
2014	0.0866	0.9139	0.9556	0.9390	0.9914	1.0000
2016	0.1300	0.9404	0.9743	0.9555	1.0000	1.0000
Hyperbolic orientation						
2006	0.6792	0.9644	0.9806	0.9744	0.9972	1.0000
2008	0.5780	0.9616	0.9801	0.9728	0.9966	1.0000
2010	0.7066	0.9463	0.9712	0.9620	0.9930	1.0000
2012	0.6229	0.9462	0.9743	0.9621	0.9948	1.0000
2014	0.2963	0.9574	0.9777	0.9686	0.9949	1.0000
2016	0.3682	0.9698	0.9865	0.9758	1.0000	1.0000

Note: Statistics for the reciprocals of the output efficiency estimates are given to facilitate comparison with the input-oriented and hyperbolic estimates

three sets of estimates and the two input-output specifications, with mean efficiency declining (though perhaps not monotonically) from 2006 to 2010 or 2012, after which the means rise again.

I use the test described by Kneip et al. (2016, Section 3.1.1) to test for significant differences between the means reported in Table 6 from one year to the next, as well as from the first year to the last year. As discussed in Kneip et al. (2015, 2016), even with the reduced dimensionality so that $p+q = 2$, the usual CLT results (e.g., the Lindeberg-Feller CLT) do not hold for means of FDH efficiency estimates. As with the convexity test discussed above, the test statistic given by equation (18) of Kneip et al. (2016) involves not only the difference in sample means of efficiency estimates in a pair of years, but also the corresponding difference in generalized jackknife estimates of bias. The test extends trivially to the output orientation, and due to Theorem 31 in Sect. 3 it also extends easily to the hyperbolic orientation. In each case, the statistic used here is defined so that a positive value indicates that efficiency increases from year 1 to year 2, while a negative value indicates that

Table 8 Tests of differences in means for FDH technical efficiency estimates (with dimension reduction, $p = q = 1$)

	Input		Output		Hyperbolic	
Period	Statistic	p-value	Statistic	p-value	Statistic	p-value
Equity not included						
2006–2008	7.7153	1.21×10^{-14}	9.1496	5.72×10^{-20}	7.7992	6.23×10^{-15}
2008–2010	− 8.7378	2.38×10^{-18}	−10.0008	1.51×10^{-23}	−10.4234	1.94×10^{-25}
2010–2012	− 9.9423	2.73×10^{-23}	− 8.6392	5.66×10^{-18}	−11.5666	6.09×10^{-31}
2012–2014	− 0.4688	6.39×10^{-01}	− 0.3685	7.12×10^{-01}	0.3247	7.45×10^{-01}
2014–2016	14.2125	7.67×10^{-46}	4.1348	3.55×10^{-05}	13.5037	1.49×10^{-41}
2006–2016	9.9013	4.11×10^{-23}	3.6628	2.49×10^{-04}	9.7570	1.72×10^{-22}
Equity included						
2006–2008	− 3.0179	2.55×10^{-03}	− 2.1029	3.55×10^{-02}	− 2.9811	2.87×10^{-03}
2008–2010	− 5.5593	2.71×10^{-08}	− 4.1699	3.05×10^{-05}	− 4.5160	6.30×10^{-06}
2010–2012	0.1097	9.13×10^{-01}	− 0.3467	7.29×10^{-01}	− 0.1998	8.42×10^{-01}
2012–2014	2.8955	3.79×10^{-03}	0.2732	7.85×10^{-01}	3.1004	1.93×10^{-03}
2014–2016	1.4422	1.49×10^{-01}	− 0.5556	5.79×10^{-01}	1.5738	1.16×10^{-01}
2006–2016	− 0.1643	8.70×10^{-01}	− 0.6141	5.39×10^{-01}	0.4869	6.26×10^{-01}

efficiency decreases from year 1 to year 2.[13] As shown by Kneip et al. (2016), the test statistics are asymptotically normal with zero mean and unit variance.

Note that the test of differences in means described by Kneip et al. (2016) requires that the two sample means to be compared be computed from independent samples. Here, where means from two periods are compared, many banks in the first period also appear in the second period. Consequently, the observations in period one are likely not independent of the observations in period two. Let n_1 denote the number of observations in period 1, and let n_2 denote the number of observations in period 2. Let n_0 denote the number of observations for banks appearing in both periods. Then clearly $n_0 \leq \min(n_1, n_2)$. to implement the test, I randomly sort the n_0 "common" observations, and then use the first $\lfloor n_0/2 \rfloor$ of these together with the $n_1 - n_0$ observations for banks represented in period one but not in period two to compute the sample mean for period 1. Similarly, I compute the sample mean for period 2 using the remaining $n_0 - \lfloor n_0/2 \rfloor$ common observations together with the $n_2 - n_0$ observations for banks that appear only in period two. This ensures that the sample means that are compared are independent, as required by Kneip et al. (2016).

Results of the tests of significant differences in mean efficiency are given in Table 8. With equity omitted, the tests provide clear evidence that mean efficiency increased from 2006 to 2008, then declined from 2008 to 2010 and from 2010 to 2012. No significant change is found for 2012–2104, and significant increases are

[13]Consequently, the statistic I use for the input orientation is the negative of the statistic appearing in equation (18) of Kneip et al. (2016).

found for 2014–2016 as well as for 2006–2016. then increased from 2012 to 2014. Except for 2012–2014, all of the p-values for two-sided tests are less than 0.001 in all three orientations. When equity is included, the tests show evidence of declines in mean efficiency in each of the three orientations for 2006–2008 and 2008–2010. For 2010–2012 the tests are insignificant, but two of the three orientations the tests find evidence of increasing mean efficiency for 2012–2014. The results for 2014–2016 as well as 2006–2016 are insignificant. For both input-output specifications, there is strong evidence of a decline in mean efficiency during 2008–2010, but otherwise the evidence is mixed. But of course the period 2008–2010 encompasses the recent financial crisis.

Estimates of cost efficiency and input allocative efficiency (with equity omitted, as discussed in Sect. 4) are shown in Table 9. In both cases, both mean and median efficiencies (as well as the first, second, and third quartiles) decline from 2006 to 2014, but rise from 2014 to 2016. Since estimation of cost efficiency involves estimating an input-oriented efficiency measure in cost-output space as discussed earlier in Sect. 3, the test statistic appearing in equation 18 of Kneip et al. (2016, Section 3.1) can be used without modification due to the results in Simar and Wilson (2020, Section 3.3) to test for significant changes in mean cost efficiency from one period to the next. In addition, Simar and Wilson (2020, Section 3.4) establish moment properties as well as CLT results for the FDH estimator of input allocative efficiency, and hence straightforward reasoning permits construction of a statistic analogous to the one in equation 18 of Kneip et al. (2016, Section 3.1) to test for significant differences in mean input allocative efficiency from one period to the next. As with the tests of differences in mean technical efficiency from one period

Table 9 Summary statistics for FDH cost and input allocative efficiency estimates (with dimension reduction, equity not included, $p = q = 1$)

Year	Min	Q1	Median	Mean	Q3	Max
Cost efficiency						
2006	0.1168	0.6211	0.7167	0.7234	0.8193	1.0000
2008	0.0294	0.6148	0.7071	0.7168	0.8162	1.0000
2010	0.0600	0.4942	0.6033	0.6178	0.7272	1.0000
2012	0.0429	0.4112	0.5210	0.5443	0.6521	1.0000
2014	0.0217	0.3856	0.4786	0.5189	0.6125	1.0000
2016	0.0549	0.4115	0.5220	0.5613	0.6832	1.0000
Input allocative efficiency						
2006	0.1286	0.6854	0.7785	0.7817	0.8847	1.0000
2008	0.0427	0.6667	0.7641	0.7662	0.8722	1.0000
2010	0.0804	0.5542	0.6633	0.6755	0.7947	1.0000
2012	0.0509	0.4815	0.5907	0.6092	0.7165	1.0000
2014	0.0549	0.4308	0.5262	0.5632	0.6650	1.0000
2016	0.0689	0.4359	0.5664	0.5981	0.7327	1.0000

Table 10 Tests of differences in means for cost and input allocative efficiency estimates (with dimension reduction, $p = q = 1$)

	Cost eff.		Input alloc. eff.	
Period	Statistic	p-value	Statistic	p-value
2006–2008	− 2.7604	5.77×10^{-03}	− 5.4293	5.66×10^{-08}
2008–2010	− 9.5337	1.52×10^{-21}	− 9.3787	6.68×10^{-21}
2010–2012	−12.2249	2.29×10^{-34}	−11.3125	1.14×10^{-29}
2012–2014	2.8068	5.00×10^{-03}	0.9022	3.67×10^{-01}
2014–2016	0.9465	3.44×10^{-01}	− 1.2896	1.97×10^{-01}
2006–2016	−14.8843	4.17×10^{-50}	−19.5096	9.10×10^{-85}

to the next, independence is crucial for the tests here, and similar care must be taken to split the observations for banks observed in both years as described above.

The outcomes of tests of significant changes in the means from one period to the next, as well as from 2006 to 2016, are shown in Table 10. The change in mean cost efficiency is not significant for 2014 to 2016, but is highly significant for all other pairs of years. Changes in mean input allocative efficiency are significant except for 2012–2014 and 2014–2016. The tests provide strong evidence of decreasing mean cost and input allocative efficiencies from 2006 through 2012. Over the entire period from 2006 to 2016, there is strong evidence of declines in both efficiencies, with p-values of order 10^{-50} and 10^{-85}.

In order to measure productivity, note that with the dimension reduction to $(p + q) = 2$ dimensions using the principal components X_i^*, Y_i^* as described in Sect. 4, (output) productivity can be measured by Y_i^*/X_i^* for firm i. Similarly, cost productivity is measured by Y_i^*/C_i, where C_i is the cost incurred by firm i as defined in Sect. 4. Summary statistics for both of these measures are displayed in Table 11 for each period. Note that the output-productivity measures and the cost-productivity measures involve different units of measurement and different scales. Consequently, one should resist temptation to compare values of one measure with those of the other measure. Nonetheless, one can examine changes from one period to the next, and it appears that both mean and median output productivity steadily decreases over the period covered by the data, except for a small increase in mean productivity from 2012 to 2014. By contrast, mean (and median) cost productivity steadily increases from one period to the next.

Since both output productivity and cost productivity are measured by simple ratios that do not involve estimators of efficiency, standard CLT results can be used to test for significant changes in means from one period to the next or from 2006 to 2016.[14] The results of these tests are shown in Table 12. The change in output productivity from 2012 to 2014 is insignificant when equity is included,

[14] Since standard CLT results apply here, one can use sample covariance to account for dependence across periods among observations for banks observed in both periods. There is, however, some subtlety. Details are given in Appendix.

Table 11 Summary statistics for productivity (with dimension reduction, $p = q = 1$)

Year	Min	Q1	Median	Mean	Q3	Max
Output productivity (equity not included)						
2006	0.6109	1.3283	1.3694	1.3603	1.4079	2.0872
2008	0.5781	1.2725	1.3200	1.3067	1.3599	1.6662
2010	0.6475	1.1753	1.2506	1.2295	1.3034	1.6864
2012	0.5888	1.1333	1.2150	1.1875	1.2654	1.8825
2014	0.1571	1.1583	1.2143	1.1948	1.2566	1.5355
2016	0.1915	1.1612	1.2036	1.1815	1.2314	1.7778
Output productivity (equity included)						
2006	0.6496	1.3756	1.4207	1.4053	1.4604	1.5821
2008	0.4581	1.3291	1.3777	1.3606	1.4159	1.5356
2010	0.6419	1.2367	1.3045	1.2812	1.3556	1.4862
2012	0.4862	1.1873	1.2591	1.2301	1.3069	1.4145
2014	0.1130	1.2043	1.2568	1.2344	1.2977	1.3828
2016	0.1685	1.2001	1.2428	1.2185	1.2722	1.3631
Cost productivity						
2006	2.4912	14.1331	15.5515	15.4151	16.8372	39.6868
2008	0.8107	14.7619	16.3845	16.4718	17.8742	62.7839
2010	1.2506	18.0673	20.7045	21.3348	23.5244	390.2392
2012	2.2836	20.7653	24.0726	24.2964	27.4853	65.2999
2014	0.7103	23.5049	27.2784	27.5346	31.2966	66.4672
2016	0.8283	25.2607	28.8047	29.0594	32.8342	71.1294

Table 12 Tests of differences in means of productivity estimates (with dimension reduction, $p = q = 1$)

	Output prod.		Cost prod.	
Period	Statistic	p-value	Statistic	p-value
Equity not included				
2006–2008	−18.3422	3.81×10^{-75}	9.8930	4.47×10^{-23}
2008–2010	−23.0461	1.61×10^{-117}	11.0725	1.71×10^{-28}
2010–2012	−13.2578	4.07×10^{-40}	6.5999	4.11×10^{-11}
2012–2014	2.4434	1.45×10^{-02}	20.7864	5.74×10^{-96}
2014–2016	− 3.6589	2.53×10^{-04}	6.0032	1.93×10^{-09}
2006–2016	−37.9799	3.85×10^{-631}	43.5253	1.49×10^{-827}
Equity included				
2006–2008	−15.7000	1.51×10^{-55}		
2008–2010	−24.3466	6.30×10^{-131}		
2010–2012	−17.4127	6.61×10^{-68}		
2012–2014	1.4492	1.47×10^{-01}		
2014–2016	− 4.5213	6.15×10^{-06}		
2006–2016	−38.2847	3.04×10^{-641}		

but significant and positive when equity is omitted. Otherwise output productivity declines significantly for all pairs of years in Table 12. All of the other changes in output productivity are negative and highly significant. All of the changes in cost productivity are positive and highly significant. For both output and cost productivity, the changes from 2006–2016 are numerically large and, to provide a comparison, have p-values 31–227 orders of magnitude smaller than the reciprocal of the Shannon number raised to a power of 5.[15] Note that although mean cost efficiency declined from 2006 to 2016 as seen in Table 10, mean cost productivity increased over 2006–2016.

The results presented so far provide clear evidence of changes in mean efficiency (i.e., technical efficiency, cost efficiency, and input allocative efficiency) as well as both output and cost productivity over the years represented in the sample. To gain further insight, I examine pairs of years 2006–2008, ..., 2014–2016 as well as 2006–2016 and apply the test of "separability" developed by Daraio et al. (2018) while treating time as a binary "environmental" variable (see Daraio et al. 2018 for details). The separability test in this case amounts to a test of whether time affects the frontier, i.e., whether the frontier changes over time.

Implementation of the separability test of Daraio et al. (2018) involves pooling the data for two periods and then randomly shuffling the observations using the randomization algorithm presented by Daraio et al. Then the pooled, randomly shuffled observations are split into two subsamples of equal size (or, if the combined number of observations is odd, one subsample will have one more observation than the other). Using the first subsample, efficiency is estimated as usual for each observation, ignoring which period a particular observation comes from, and the sample mean of the efficiency estimate is computed. The second subsample is split into the set of observations from period 1 and the set of observations from period 2. Efficiency is estimated for the period-1 observations using only the observations from period 1, while efficiency for the period-2 observations is estimated using only those observations from period 2. Then the sample mean of these two sets of efficiency estimates from the two sub-subsamples (of the second subsample) is computed. The resulting test statistic involves differences in the two sample means as well as differences in the corresponding generalized jackknife estimates of bias. See Daraio et al. for discussion and details.

Results of the separability tests using input- and output-oriented as well as hyperbolic FDH efficiency estimators are shown in Table 13. When equity is omitted, separability is rejected in every case with p-values less than 0.01, and in most cases well less than 0.01. When equity is included, separability is not rejected for 2014–2016, nor for 2012–2014 when working in the output orientation. But in all other cases when equity is included, separability is soundly rejected, with p-values less than 0.01. The separability tests provide clear evidence of changes in the

[15] What has come to be known as the Shannon number, i.e., 10^{120}, is a conservative lower bound on the game-tree complexity of chess calculated by Shannon (1950).

Table 13 Test for separability with respect to time (with dimension reduction; $p = q = 1$)

	Input		Output		Hyperbolic	
Period	Statistic	*p*-value	Statistic	*p*-value	Statistic	*p*-value
Equity not included						
2006–2008	14.0622	3.24×10^{-45}	16.7043	6.10×10^{-63}	16.8664	3.98×10^{-64}
2008–2010	3.2325	6.13×10^{-04}	2.8191	2.41×10^{-03}	2.8708	2.05×10^{-03}
2010–2012	19.6520	2.78×10^{-86}	15.1182	6.14×10^{-52}	17.5059	6.46×10^{-69}
2012–2014	9.4825	1.24×10^{-21}	6.0759	6.17×10^{-10}	10.0947	2.92×10^{-24}
2014–2016	9.3826	3.22×10^{-21}	3.4992	2.33×10^{-04}	7.2694	1.80×10^{-13}
2006–2016	11.8802	7.50×10^{-33}	6.9104	2.42×10^{-12}	10.4223	9.81×10^{-26}
Equity included						
2006–2008	6.1698	3.42×10^{-10}	3.3137	4.60×10^{-04}	5.2119	9.34×10^{-08}
2008–2010	4.4977	3.43×10^{-06}	4.2561	1.04×10^{-05}	5.6692	7.17×10^{-09}
2010–2012	6.1936	2.94×10^{-10}	4.3509	6.78×10^{-06}	5.9456	1.38×10^{-09}
2012–2014	4.2779	9.43×10^{-06}	0.2516	4.01×10^{-01}	2.7496	2.98×10^{-03}
2014–2016	0.4843	3.14×10^{-01}	– 1.2833	9.00×10^{-01}	– 0.4653	6.79×10^{-01}
2006–2016	11.8802	7.50×10^{-33}	6.9104	2.42×10^{-12}	10.4223	9.81×10^{-26}

technology between pairs of years (except perhaps 2014–2016) as well as over the entire period 2006–2016 covered by the data.[16]

In order to learn something about the *direction* in which technology may have shifted, I adapt new results from Simar and Wilson (2019) who provide CLT results for components of productivity changed measured by Malmquist indices. Simar and Wilson define the Malmquist index in terms of hyperbolic distances, and then consider various decompositions that can be used to identify components of productivity change. In particular, let Ψ^t represent the production set at time $t \in \{1,\ 2\}$ and let $Z_i^t = (X_i^t, Y_i^t)$ denote the i-th firm's observed input-output pair at time t. Then technical change relative to firm i's position at times 1 and 2 is measured by

$$\mathcal{T}_i = \left[\frac{\gamma(Z_i^2 \mid \Psi^1)}{\gamma(Z_i^2 \mid \Psi^2)} \times \frac{\gamma(Z_i^1 \mid \Psi^1)}{\gamma(Z_i^1 \mid \Psi^2)} \right]^{1/2}. \tag{5.1}$$

[16] A number of papers in the banking literature have regressed DEA efficiency estimates on some explanatory variables including categorical variables to capture differences in regulatory environments across countries. As far as I know, none of these tests the separability condition discussed by Simar and Wilson (2007, 2011b). Here, banks face the same regulatory environment at a given point in time, but the regulatory environment changes with passage of the Dodd-Frank Act in 2010. Rejection of separability with respect to time amounts to a rejection with respect to the different regulatory regimes before and after 2010. Hence my results cast some doubt on results from cross-country analyses that attempt to control for differing regulatory regimes across countries in second-stage regressions.

Table 14 FDH estimates of technical-change index (with dimension reduction; $p = q = 1$)

Period	$\widehat{T}^{1,2}$	p-value	# obs
Equity not included			
2006–2008	0.9713	8.04×10^{-207}	796
2008–2010	0.9825	2.41×10^{-72}	761
2010–2012	0.9953	3.13×10^{-12}	800
2012–2013	0.9891	3.02×10^{-84}	829
2014–2016	0.9940	1.87×10^{-02}	513
2006–2016	0.9173	4.33×10^{-284}	400
Equity included			
2006–2008	0.9849	2.48×10^{-142}	796
2008–2010	0.9812	2.80×10^{-624}	761
2010–2012	0.9802	6.26×10^{-915}	800
2012–2013	0.9948	3.57×10^{-71}	829
2014–2016	0.9874	4.88×10^{-59}	513
2006–2016	0.9293	2.16×10^{-1026}	400

This is the hyperbolic analog of the output-oriented technical-change index that appears in the decompositions of Ray and Desli (1997), Gilbert and Wilson (1998), and Wheelock and Wilson (1999). The first ratio inside the brackets in (5.1) measures technical change relative to firm i's position at time 2, while the second ratio measures technical change relative to the firm's position at time 1. The measure $\mathcal{T}_i$ is the geometric mean of these two ratios. Values greater than 1 indicate an upward shift in the technology, while values less than 1 indicate a downward shift (a value of 1 indicates no change from time 1 to time 2).

Estimates $\widehat{\mathcal{T}}_i$ are obtained by substituting the hyperbolic FDH estimator for each term in (5.1). Simar and Wilson (2019) develop CLT results for geometric means $\widehat{T}^{1,2}$ of $\mathcal{T}_i$ over firms $\imath = 1, \ldots, n$, for periods 1 and 2, and these results can be used to test significant differences of the geometric means from 1. The theoretical results obtained by Simar and Wilson (2019) are based on estimates of $\mathcal{T}_i$ using DEA estimators, but the results for the geometric mean of $\mathcal{T}_i$ extend trivially to FDH estimators, but with the slower convergence rate of the FDH estimator. Table 14 shows values of the geometric means $\widehat{T}^{1,2}$ for successive pairs of periods as well as for 2006–2016 and the corresponding p-values for tests of differences from 1. The last column of Table 14 gives the number of banks observed in both periods under consideration, and for which $\mathcal{T}_i$ can be estimated in each pair of years. All of the geometric means are less than one, suggesting downward shifts of the technology in each pair of years. The p-value for 2014–2016 is 0.0187 when equity is omitted, and all of the other p-values are well less than 0.01, with a number of p-values well less than the reciprocal of the Shannon number mentioned above. Consequently, the data provide clear and convincing evidence of downward shifts in the technology throughout the period from 2006 through 2016.

6 Summary and Conclusions

Among studies that use either FDH or DEA estimators to estimate efficiency and benchmark the performances of firms, the vast majority use VRS, DEA estimators which impose convexity on the production set. The test of convexity versus non-convexity of Ψ developed by Kneip et al. (2016) allows researchers to let the data tell them whether DEA estimators are appropriate in a given setting. Here, in the context of banks, convexity is strongly rejected. This is consistent with the results of Wheelock and Wilson (2012, 2018), who find evidence of increasing returns to scale among even the largest banks operating in the USA.

Because I reject convexity of the production set, I use FDH estimators which remain consistent when Ψ is not convex, whereas DEA estimators do not. I exploit collinearity in the data to reduce inputs and outputs to their first principal components, resulting in a two-dimensional problem. Results from Wilson (2018) indicate that this substantially reduces mean square error of efficiency estimates. Moreover, the simulation evidence provided by Wilson (2018) suggests that when production sets are convex, FDH estimates often have less mean square error than DEA estimators after dimension reduction.

By rigorously comparing estimates and testing differences across the years represented in my data, I find that technical efficiency declined during the financial crisis, but recovered afterward. By 2016, technical efficiency is significantly better than in 2006 when input-oriented and hyperbolic estimators are used. However, I also find that both cost and input allocative efficiency declined significantly from 2006 to 2016, and that the frontier shifted downward throughout the financial crisis and from 2006 to 2016. At the same time, output productivity declined from 2006 to 2016, while cost productivity increased from 2006 to 2016. These results are broadly consistent with the hypothesized effects of the Dodd-Frank Act discussed near the end of Sect. 1.

It is well known that despite unprecedented low interest rates, banks reduced their loan outputs through the financial crisis and beyond. My finding regarding output productivity is consistent with this. The result that cost productivity increased, together with the reduction in output, is consistent with the well-known observation that many banks ruthlessly cut costs during and after the crisis. However, the finding that cost inefficiency worsened suggests that banks could have cut costs even more.

Appendix: Technical Details

As discussed in Sect. 5, with dimension reduction productivity can be measured by simple ratios. In addition, since neither FDH nor DEA estimators are involved, the usual Lindeberg-Feller CLT can be used to make inference about differences in mean productivity between two periods. However, the samples in each period are unbalanced, and care must be taken to properly account for covariance.

Suppose banks are observed in two periods $t \in \{1, 2\}$. Let n_t be the number of banks observed only in period t, and let n_0 be the number of banks observed in *both* periods (here, n_1 and n_2 are defined differently than in the discussion about testing differences in mean technical efficiency in Sect. 5). Then the total numbers of observations in periods 1 and 2 are given by (n_1+n_0) and (n_0+n_1). Let P_{jti} denote productivity (measured by output/input or output/cost after reducing dimensionality to $p = q = 1$) for bank i in group $j \in \{0, 1, 2\}$ in period $t \in \{1\ 2\}$. Group 0 consists of banks observed in both periods, while groups 1 and 2 consist of banks observed only in periods 1 and 2 (respectively). We have sample means $\widehat{\mu}_1$, $\widehat{\mu}_2$ for periods 1 and 2, with

$$\widehat{\mu}_t = (n_0 + n_t)^{-1} \left[\sum_{i=1}^{n_1} P_{11i} + \sum_{i=1}^{n_0} P_{01i} \right] \tag{6.1}$$

for $t = 1$ or 2.

Due to Assumption 24, the Ps are independent within a given period, but may be dependent across periods. Hence any covariance between $\widehat{\mu}_1$ and $\widehat{\mu}_2$ can result only from the n_0 banks observed in *both* periods. Let

$$\sigma_t^2 := \text{VAR}(P_{11i}) = \text{VAR}(P_{01i}) \tag{6.2}$$

and

$$\sigma_{12} := \text{COV}(P_{01i}, P_{02i}) \tag{6.3}$$

for all i. Then

$$\text{VAR}(\widehat{\mu}_2 - \widehat{\mu}_1) = \frac{\sigma_1^2}{n_1 + n_0} + \frac{\sigma_2^2}{n_0 + n_2} - \frac{2n_0\sigma_{12}}{(n_1 + n_0)(n_0 + n_2)}. \tag{6.4}$$

The variances σ_t^2 and covariance σ_{12} can be estimated by the corresponding sample moments, i.e.,

$$\widehat{\sigma}_t^2 = (n_0 + n_2)^{-1} \left[\sum_{i=1}^{n_0} (P_{0ti} - \widehat{\mu}_t)^2 + \sum_{i=1}^{n_t} (P_{tti} - \widehat{\mu}_t)^2 \right] \tag{6.5}$$

for $t = 1$ or 2 and

$$\widehat{\sigma}_{12} = n_0^{-1} \left[\sum_{i=1}^{n_0} (P_{01i} - \widehat{\mu}_1)(P_{02i} - \widehat{\mu}_2) \right]. \tag{6.6}$$

Then the test statistic

$$\widehat{\tau} := \frac{\widehat{\mu}_2 - \widehat{\mu}_1}{\left[\frac{\widehat{\sigma}_1^2}{(n_1+n_0)} + \frac{\widehat{\sigma}_2^2}{(n_0+n_2)} - \frac{2n_0\widehat{\sigma}_{12}}{(n_1+n_0)(n_0+n_2)}\right]^{1/2}} \xrightarrow{d} N(0, 1) \tag{6.7}$$

as $(n_1 + n_0 \rightarrow \infty$ and $(n_0 + n_2) \rightarrow \infty$ by the Lindeberg-Levy CLT. For a two-sided test of size α, the null hypothesis $H_0: \mu_1 = \mu_2$ is rejected in favor of $H_1: \mu_1 \neq \mu_2$ whenever $|\widehat{\tau}| > \Phi^{-1}(1 - \frac{\alpha}{2})$ where $\Phi^{-1}(\cdot)$ is the standard normal quantile function.

Acknowledgments An early version of this work was presented at the North American Productivity Workshop, University of Miami Business School, Miami, Florida, 12–15 June 2018. I thank conference participants and Shirong Zhao for helpful comments.

References

Acharya, V. V., & Richardson, M. (2012). Implications of the Dodd-Frank act. *Annual Review of Financial Economics, 4*, 1–38.

Baba, N., Packer, F., & Nagano, T. (2008). The spillover of money market turbulence to FX swap and cross-currency swap markets. *BIS Quarterly Review*, 73–86.

Banker, R. D., Charnes, A., & Cooper, W. W. (1984). Some models for estimating technical and scale inefficiencies in data envelopment analysis. *Management Science, 30*, 1078–1092.

Bernanke, B. S. (2005). Remarks by Governor Ben s. Bernanke: The global saving glut and the U.S. current account deficit, Board of Governors of the Federal Reserve System. Speech delivered April 14, http://www.federalreserve.gov.boarddocs/speeches/2005/20050414/default.htm.

Bernanke, B. S. (2013). *The crisis as a classic financial panic, Board of Governors of the Federal Reserve System*. Speech delivered November 8 at the Fourteenth Jacques Polak Annual Research Conference, Washington, D.C., https://www.federalreserve.gov/newsevents/speech/bernanke20131108a.htm.

Bernanke, B. S. (2018). The real effects of the financial crisis. *Brookings Papers on Economic Activity Conference Drafts*, September 13–14.

Bolt, W., de Haan, L., Hoeberichts, M., van Oordt, M. R. C., & Swank, J. (2012). Bank profitability during recessions. *Journal of Banking and Finance, 36*, 2552–2564.

Boyd, S., & Vandenberghe, L. (2004). *Convex optimization*. New York: Cambridge University Press.

Daouia, A., Simar, L., & Wilson, P. W. (2017). Measuring firm performance using nonparametric quantile-type distances. *Econometric Reviews, 36*, 156–181.

Daraio, C., Simar, L., & Wilson, P. W. (2018). Central limit theorems for conditional efficiency measures and tests of the 'separability condition' in non-parametric, two-stage models of production. *The Econometrics Journal, 21*, 170–191.

Deprins, D., Simar, L., & Tulkens, H. (1984). Measuring labor inefficiency in post offices. In M. M. P. Pestieau & H. Tulkens (Eds.), *The performance of public enterprises: concepts and measurements* (pp. 243–267). Amsterdam: North-Holland.

Diamond, D. W., & Rajan, R. G. (2001). Liquidity risk, liquidity creation, and financial fragility: A theory of banking. *Journal of Political Economy, 109*, 287–327.

Färe, R. (1988). *Fundamentals of production theory*. Berlin: Springer.

Färe, R., Grosskopf, S., & Lovell, C. A. K. (1985). *The measurement of efficiency of production*. Boston: Kluwer-Nijhoff Publishing.

Färe, R., & Lovell, C. A. K. (1988). Aggregation and efficiency. In: W. Eichhorn (Ed.), *Measurement in economics* (pp. 639–647). Heidelberg: Physica-Verlag.

Farrell, M. J. (1957). The measurement of productive efficiency. *Journal of the Royal Statistical Society A, 120*, 253–281.

Gilbert, A., & Wilson, P. W. (1998). Effects of deregulation on the productivity of Korean banks. *Journal of Economics and Business, 50*, 133–155.

Gorton, G. (2018). Financial crises. *Annual Review of Financial Economics, 10*, 43–58.

Gorton, G., Lewellen, S., & Metrick, A. (2012). The safe-asset share. *American Economic Review, 102*, 101–106.

Hördahl, P., & King, M. (2008). Developments in repo markets during the financial turmoil. *BIS Quarterly Review*, 37–53.

Kashyap, A. K., Rajan, R. G., & Stein, J. C. (2008). Rethinking capital regulation, in *Maintaining Stability in a Changing Financial System*, Kansas City: Federal Reserve Bank of Kansas City, pp. 431–471. Economic Policy Symposium Proceedings.

Kneip, A., Park, B., & Simar, L. (1998). A note on the convergence of nonparametric DEA efficiency measures. *Econometric Theory, 14*, 783–793.

Kneip, A., Simar, L., & Wilson, P. W. (2008). Asymptotics and consistent bootstraps for DEA estimators in non-parametric frontier models. *Econometric Theory, 24*, 1663–1697.

Kneip, A., Simar, L., & Wilson, P. W. (2011). A computationally efficient, consistent bootstrap for inference with non-parametric DEA estimators. *Computational Economics, 38*, 483–515.

Kneip, A., Simar, L., & Wilson, P. W. (2015). When bias kills the variance: Central limit theorems for DEA and FDH efficiency scores. *Econometric Theory, 31*, 394–422.

Kneip, A., Simar, L., & Wilson, P. W. (2016). Testing hypotheses in nonparametric models of production. *Journal of Business and Economic Statistics, 34*, 435–456.

Kneip, A., Simar, L., & Wilson, P. W. (2020). *Inference in dynamic, nonparametric models of production: Central limit theorems for Malmquist indices*. Forthcoming.

Olesen, O. B., & Petersen, N. C. (2016). Stochastic data envelopment analysis—A review. *European Journal of Operational Research, 251*, 2–21.

Park, B. U., Jeong, S.-O., & Simar, L. (2010). Asymptotic distribution of conical-hull estimators of directional edges. *Annals of Statistics, 38*, 1320–1340.

Park, B. U., Simar, L., & Weiner, C. (2000). FDH efficiency scores from a stochastic point of view. *Econometric Theory, 16*, 855–877.

Patel, S. S. (2014). Citi will have almost 30,000 employees in compliance by year-end. July 14, 2014, https://blogs.marketwatch.com/thetell/2014/07/14/citi-will-have-almost-30000-employees-in-compliance-by-year-end/.

Ray, S. C., & Desli, E. (1997). Productivity growth, technical progress, and efficiency change in industrialized countries: Comment. *American Economic Review, 87*, 1033–1039.

Robinson, P. M. (1988). Root-n-consistent semiparametric regression. *Econometrica, 56*, 931–954.

Shannon, C. E. (1950) Programming a computer for playing chess. *The London, Edinburgh, and Dublin Philosophical Magazine and Journal of Science, 41*, 256–275.

Shephard, R. W. (1970) *Theory of cost and production functions*. Princeton: Princeton University Press.

Simar, L., & Wilson, P. W. (2007). Estimation and inference in two-stage, semi-parametric models of productive efficiency, *Journal of Econometrics, 136*, 31–64.

Simar, L., & Wilson, P. W. (2011a). Inference by the m out of n bootstrap in nonparametric frontier models, *Journal of Productivity Analysis, 36*, 33–53.

Simar, L., & Wilson, P. W. (2011b). Two-Stage DEA: Caveat emptor. *Journal of Productivity Analysis, 36*, 205–218.

Simar, L., & Wilson, P. W. (2019). Central limit theorems and inference for sources of productivity change measured by nonparametric Malmquist indices. *European Journal of Operational Research, 277*, 756–769.

Simar, L., & Wilson, P. W. (2020). Technical, allocative and overall efficiency: Estimation and inference. *European Journal of Operational Research, 282*, 1164–1176.

U.S. Congress. (2010). *Dodd-Frank Wall Street Reform and Consumer Protection Act*. Washington, DC: GPO. http://www.gpo.gov/fdsys/pkg/PLAW-111publ203/pdf/PLAW-111publ203.pdf.

Wheelock, D. C., & Wilson, P. W. (1999). Technical progress, inefficiency, and productivity change in U. S. banking, 1984–1993. *Journal of Money, Credit, and Banking, 31*, 212–234.

Wheelock, D. C., & Wilson, P. W. (2008). Non-parametric, unconditional quantile estimation for efficiency analysis with an application to Federal Reserve check processing operations. *Journal of Econometrics, 145*, 209–225.

Wheelock, D. C., & Wilson, P. W. (2012). Do large banks have lower costs? New estimates of returns to scale for U.S. banks. *Journal of Money, Credit, and Banking, 44*, 171–199.

Wheelock, D. C., & Wilson, P. W. (2018). The evolution of scale-economies in U.S. banking. *Journal of Applied Econometrics, 33*, 16–28.

Wilson, P. W. (2011). Asymptotic properties of some non-parametric hyperbolic efficiency estimators. In I. Van Keilegom & P. W. Wilson (Eds.) *Exploring research frontiers in contemporary statistics and econometrics*, pp. 115–150. Berlin: Springer.

Wilson, P. W. (2018). Dimension reduction in nonparametric models of production. *European Journal of Operational Research, 267*, 349–367.

Room to Move: Why Some Industries Drive the Trade-Specialization Nexus and Others Do Not

Jaap W. B. Bos and Lu Zhang

Abstract We investigate which industries drive the trade-specialization nexus in the European Union over the 1997–2006 period. We study the impact of the reallocation of resources within industries. We find that the true drivers of the trade-specialization nexus are productive firms, who benefit from the increase in trade openness by appropriating resources from less productive firms, coinciding with the expansion of the industry in which they operate, at the expense of other industries, in which there is no room to make such moves.

Keywords Trade barriers · Latent class model · Gravity model

1 Introduction

Over the past two decades, economic integration, mirrored by a rapid growth in international trade, has had a strong impact on specialization in the European Union (EU). During the 1997 to 2006 period, all EU14 countries except Portugal have experienced a significant increase in industrial specialization. Particularly large increases are observed in United Kingdom, Austria, and France, where Gini coefficients have risen by 14.5, 10.1, and 9.8%, respectively.[1]

[1]The Gini coefficient in Portugal has decreased by 5.6%.

J. W. B. Bos (✉)
Finance Department, Maastricht University, School of Business and Economics, Maastricht, The Netherlands
e-mail: j.bos@maastrichtuniversity.nl

L. Zhang
Financial Stability Division, Netherlands Central Bank, Amsterdam, The Netherlands
e-mail: l.zhang@dnb.nl

C. F. Parmeter, R. C. Sickles (eds.), *Advances in Efficiency and Productivity Analysis*, Springer Proceedings in Business and Economics,
https://doi.org/10.1007/978-3-030-47106-4_12

The economic literature has a long tradition of analyzing *what* drives the relationship between trade and specialization. Classical trade theories predict that trade integration will result in increasing specialization in sectors where a country has a comparative advantage due to cross-country differences in technology or factor endowment (Ricardo 1817; Ohlin 1933).[2] New trade theories stress the importance of increasing returns to scale and product differentiation in facilitating intra-industry trade and predict that international trade will induce a shift of increasing-return industries towards countries with good market access, i.e., the core (Krugman 1979, 1980). New economic geography theories emphasize agglomeration forces and suggest a non-monotonic relationship between trade liberalization and location of economic activities, depending on the level of trade costs (Krugman 1991; Venables 1996).[3]

Much less is known about *who* drives the relationship between trade and specialization. The reduction of trade barriers has caused major restructuring across industries and countries. The process of reallocation of production within and across sectors is likely to be a key determinant of aggregate productivity growth. The relative importance of these two types of reallocation depends on asset specificity. In particular, a growing literature has demonstrated the importance of within-industry reallocation in explaining industry growth. This phenomenon is often motived by the existence of significant and persistent gaps in productivity within industries (Bartelsman et al. 2013). Not all firms grow. Some firms may come out on top, whereas others lose market shares and eventually exit the market. Since the seminal work by Schumpeter (1942), these effects have been well-documented empirically. A key message from this literature is that firm-level dynamics are crucial to understand industry-level outcomes.

Recent work by Jones (2013) and Baqaee and Farhi (2017) has shown that a misallocation of resources can explain large differences in growth outcomes. Most of these misallocations occur within industries (Calligaris et al. 2017), and they are often related to the productivity of firms and establishments within these industries, thereby affecting aggregate output and productivity (Bhattacharya et al. 2013; Restuccia and Rogerson 2008, 2013; Hsieh and Klenow 2009). Indeed, the importance of misallocation has resulted in attempts to endogenize the development of firm-level productivity (Gabler and Poschke 2013). For the purpose of this paper, it is not the source of misallocation that we are interested in, but rather the subsequent reallocation that can help explain industry growth (Foster et al. 2008).

[2]Most neoclassical trade theories, with reference to the theory of comparative advantage, predict a positive relationship between trade liberalization and industrial specialization. For example, Dornbusch et al. (1977) demonstrate that falling trade costs result in a narrowing non-traded sector; it is therefore cheaper to import goods than to produce them domestically. Thus resources are freed up and used more intensely in fewer activities. The empirical studies are numerous. See for example, Sapir (1996), Brülhart (2001), Longhi et al. (2003) and Riet et al. (2004).

[3]Lower trade costs result in the agglomeration of economic activities into fewer locations. However, a further reduction in trade costs leads to a geographical dispersion of activities when labor mobility across sectors exhibits finite costs.

We demonstrate that the removal of trade barriers can in fact provide the impetus for reallocation within industries, but only if there was enough misallocation—and concomitant productivity differences—prior to the removal. The result then is an increase in the growth of industries where these circumstances indeed exist, but not in other industries, thus changing the trade-specialization relationship.[4]

We are further motivated by a growing body of empirical literature that documents the intra-industry reallocation process following trade openness. A substantial part of the effect of international trade is channeled into the reallocation of resources within the industry, which in turn shapes the industry aggregates (Tybout and Westbrook 1995; Pavcnik 2002; Trefler 2004; Bernard et al. 2006; Eslava et al. 2009). Pavcnik (2002) finds that trade liberalization in Chile during the 1979–1986 period has had substantial reallocation and productivity effects. Trefler (2004) examines the reallocation and productivity effect of the Canada–U.S. Free Trade Agreement (FTA) on Canadian industries, and finds that industries with the deepest Canadian tariff reduction experienced a reduction in employment by 12% plus a 15% increase in industry labor productivity due to the contraction of low-productivity plants. For the USA, Bernard et al. (2006) demonstrate that productivity gains are most pronounced in industries where trade barriers have declined the most.[5]

In our paper, the true drivers of the trade-specialization nexus are productive firms, who benefit from the increase in trade openness by appropriating resources from less productive firms, thus causing the industry in which they operate to expand, at the expense of other industries, in which there is no room to make such moves. Wacziarg and Wallack (2004) find that reallocation between industries is either not affected or negatively affected by trade liberalization. We argue and find, however, that the potential for reallocation *within* industries determines whether there is a trade-specialization nexus; in industries with little potential for reallocation, increased trade openness has no effect, or a negative effect, on that industry's share of total value added. As a result, the trade-specialization nexus is driven by a small number of industries, which nevertheless have a significant impact on concentration patterns.

In this paper, we investigate which industries are driving the trade-specialization nexus. We distinguish between industries that do and not drive the nexus using a conditional latent class model (Bos et al. 2010). We argue that industries need "room to move" in order for increasing trade openness to translate into increased specialization. We condition the potential for reallocation (a latent variable) on the within-industry spread in efficiency and scale elasticity, at the start of our sample period. Our latent class setup avoids the disaggregation bias that would otherwise exist when we test the trade-specialization nexus at the industry level. Furthermore, by allowing industries to switch classes over time, we enable our model to help

[4]In which direction this change occurs is not obvious, ex ante. Segerstrom and Sugita (2015) show that productivity may in fact increase more strongly in non-liberalized industries.

[5]For a comprehensive survey, see Tybout (2000).

explain the slow-down in the specialization trend. And we demonstrate that under certain conditions, we can infer quasi-treatment effects from our latent class estimations. To the best of our knowledge, our study is the first contribution to the literature on how firm-level dynamics affect the trade-specialization nexus, based on a unique sample of EU manufacturing firms.

To analyze who drives the trade-specialization nexus, we use a panel data set consisting of 390,350 manufacturing firms spanning 18 industries in 14 EU countries over the period 1997–2006. After we estimate firm-level economies of scale and technical efficiency levels for each industry, we use the *initial* dispersion in both productivity measures to endogenously sort each industry into one of two classes. We observe a positive, inverted-U shape trade-specialization relationship for the high-potential class; the same relationship is insignificant or slightly negative for the low-potential class. Our analysis is further supported by a detailed instrumentation strategy and an elaborate robustness analysis. In addition, we verify the relevance of our approach by demonstrating how closely our predicted specialization patterns match the actual specialization that took place in the EU over our sample period.

The remainder of the paper proceeds as follows. Section 2 presents the models used and the econometric strategy. Section 3 presents the data and the measures proposed. Section 4 discusses the results. Finally, Sect. 5 summarizes and concludes.

2 Methodology

In this section we first present a conditional latent class framework to examine the heterogeneous effect of trade integration on specialization, conditional on the within-industry potential for reallocation. Next, we discuss methodological concerns and our identification strategy.

2.1 *Empirical Framework*

In order to find out who drives the trade-specialization nexus, we need to estimate the nexus in a way that allows us to distinguish between those industries that can use trade liberalization to drive the increase in concentration of output and those that cannot.

We start with a straightforward parametrization that allows for a non-linear effect in the spirit of new economic geography theories (Krugman 1991; Venables 1996):

$$S_{iot} = \beta_0 + \beta_1 T_{iot} + \beta_2 T_{iot}^2 + \beta' Z_{iot} + \varepsilon_{iot}, \tag{2.1}$$

where S_{iot} is a measure describing the extent to which a country o at time t specializes in industry i, T_{iot} is that industry's trade openness at the same time, β' is a $1 \times n$ parameter vector, and Z_{iot} is a $n \times 1$ vector of control variables.

But can we use Eq. (2.1) to test the trade-specialization nexus? After all, whereas trade openness has increased for most industries in most countries, if a country specializes in some industries, the share of output produced by other industries is reduced. As a result, the trade-specialization nexus implies that $\frac{\partial \ln S_{iot}}{\partial \ln T_{iot}}$ is positive for some industries (differing from country to country, and possibly also over time) and zero or negative for other industries (idem).

Since (Melitz 2003), we know that industries that grow after an increase in trade openness largely do so through an intra-industry reallocation of resources. Melitz (2003) also teaches us that whereas *actual* reallocation is expected to be endogenous to trade openness, the *potential* for reallocation matters, as trade openness can act as the catalyst that facilitates the realization of this potential, as *reflected* in changes in specialization.

Consequently, we expect the trade-specialization nexus to be driven by those industries that have a large enough potential to reallocate resources, thus benefiting from the increased trade openness. Let us call these industries high-potential (HP) industries, as opposed to low-potential (LP) industries. Formally, for any industry i in country o at time t:

$$\epsilon_{iot} = \begin{cases} \epsilon_{iot}^{HP} \text{ if } HP_{iot} = 1; \\ \\ \epsilon_{iot}^{LP} \text{ if } HP_{iot} = 0, \end{cases} \tag{2.2}$$

where $\epsilon_{iot} = \frac{\partial \ln S_{iot}}{\partial \ln T_{iot}}$ and $\epsilon_{iot}^{LP} \leq 0 < \epsilon_{iot}^{HP}$. Therefore, in order to test the trade-specialization nexus and find out who drives it, we wish to estimate:

$$S_{iot} = \beta_{0|HP,LP} + \beta_{1|HP,LP} T_{iot} + \beta_{2|HP,LP} T_{iot}^2 + \beta_{HP,LP}' Z_{iot} + \varepsilon_{iot|HP,LP}, \tag{2.3}$$

where HP and LP industries have their own parameter vector β.

In practice, of course, HP is a latent variable. We can, however, estimate the likelihood that an industry i in a country o at time t is an HP industry, if we can measure the potential for reallocation in an industry. If we let θ_{iot} measure the odds of being an HP industry, conditional on the set of variables in the vector V_{iot}, then

$$\theta_{iot} = \frac{\exp\left(V_{iot}\theta^{HP}\right)}{\exp\left(V_{iot}\theta^{HP}\right) + \exp\left(V_{iot}\theta^{LP}\right)}. \tag{2.4}$$

Of importance in the light of our analysis is the vector V_{iot}: it should contain covariates that predict whether an industry will be able to reallocate from its least productive to its most productive firms, thus benefiting from the opportunities that have arisen as a result of increased trade openness and resulting in an increased share of this industry in total production or value added. In Sect. 3, we explain the variables contained in V_{iot} in detail. For now, we note that these variables capture productivity differences at the firm level *within* each industry i in country o at time

t. As a result, V_{iot} captures the potential for reallocation, and is then used to estimate θ_{iot}.

Since HP is a latent variable, we require the prior probability of being part of the HP class, for each industry i in country o at time t, so we can estimate θ_{iot} with a logit model. To this purpose, we estimate Eq. (2.3) jointly with Eq. (2.4) using an iterative procedure with an expectation-maximization (EM) algorithm, following Greene (2007). In this procedure, the unconditional likelihood for each industry i in country o at time t is obtained as a weighted average of its class-specific likelihood using the prior probabilities of being in classes HP and LP as the weights. Each industry i in country o at time t is thereby placed in the class where it contributes the most to the total likelihood of the estimated system, which is being maximized.[6]

It is natural in light of our investigation to estimate Eqs. (2.3) and (2.4) for two classes. Following Orea and Kumbhakar (2004), we use the Akaike Information Criterion (AIC) and Schwartz Bayesian Information Criterion (SBIC) to verify whether the specification with two classes is indeed the preferred specification.

In practice, the class allocation may exhibit a certain degree of persistence and is likely to be stable. However, following Bos et al. (2010), industries can switch classes over time, since an industry's allocation in a given period is *ex ante* independent of its allocation in other periods. We can thus study how changes in the potential for reallocation affect the dynamics of the trade-specialization relationship and can possibly explain the slow-down in the specialization process. In addition, adding this flexibility to the model may enable us to identify causality, as explained below.

To summarize, we employ a conditional latent class model to examine the heterogeneous relationship between trade integration and specialization in two endogenously determined groups of industries. The group membership probabilities are conditional on the potential for reallocation by exploring firm-level productivity characteristics within industries.

2.2 Identification

We aim to shed light on the real effect of trade openness on specialization. Obviously, the simple correlation between trade openness and specialization cannot be interpreted as evidence of causality because specialization itself also affects trade. For example, Imbs (2004) demonstrates a negative relationship

[6]The sum of all unconditional likelihoods over all industries i in countries o at time t is maximized with respect to the parameter vectors for each class in Eq. (2.3) and the parameters in the sorting equation (2.4). With these parameter estimates, a posterior estimate of the class membership probability for each industry i in country o at time t can be computed using Bayes' theorem. Each observation is assigned to a particular class with the largest posterior probability. The posterior estimate of the parameter vector β can also be obtained by multiplying the posterior membership probability.

running from specialization to trade, as a result of intra-industry trade. Furthermore, unobserved industry/country characteristics can influence both trade and specialization/production—such as industrial policies or demand shifts that are difficult to measure and control for.[7] Given these concerns, identification based on the direct impact of trade openness on specialization will yield inconsistent estimates.

2.2.1 Benefits of a Three-Dimensional Panel

As a first step to proper inference, we observe that the three-dimensional panel that we have (industry, country, time) makes it possible to include a wide array of fixed effects in order to control for the unobservables and resolve omitted variable bias concerns to a large extent. In particular, the possibility to introduce interacted fixed effects enables us to sweep out a much wider range of omitted variables.

For example, industry $\times$ time (it) effects would not only absorb industry fixed effects, but also the average effects of time-varying industry characteristics, such as industrial policy, economies of scale, research-orientation, technology level, and labor-intensiveness (Midelfart-Knarvik et al. 2000; Longhi et al. 2003). Similarly, country $\times$ time (ot) effects eliminate all time-varying country characteristics that affect specialization, such as market potential, R&D spending, or labor abundance (Midelfart-Knarvik et al. 2000; Longhi et al. 2003).

Furthermore, the industry $\times$ country effects capture various sources of comparative advantage that matters to understand the impact of trade openness on specialization. Chor (2010) presents a framework to quantify the importance of a wide range of sources of comparative advantage, e.g. Heckscher–Ohlin force, Ricardian effect, etc. He expresses comparative advantage as a function of industry-country characteristics, so that countries specialize in those industries whose production needs they can best meet with their endowment mix or institutional strengths.

Therefore, in our specification, we control for all these three types of interactive fixed effects, namely industry $\times$ time, country $\times$ time, and industry $\times$ country by demeaning both sides of Eq. (2.3) along these three dimensions. However, all these fixed effects may still not eliminate factors at the industry $\times$ country $\times$ time dimension. To deal with this concern, we incorporate output per worker as a control variable to correct for any technological shifts at the industry $\times$ country $\times$ time level that could affect specialization (López and Sánchez 2005).

[7]Another reason is that specialization is theoretically linked to the factor content of trade, as an industry that has a large share in GDP is likely to be an exporting sector. So the relationship between production patterns and endowments is not independent of the relationship between trade and endowments.

Essentially, our identification strategy thereby exploits the time variation within each industry in each country, in line with our aim of exploring the role of (time-varying) firm dynamics in the trade-specialization relationship.

2.2.2 Alternative Measures to Control for Endogeneity

It is notoriously difficult to use direct measures of trade barriers (e.g., tariffs) and exploit the time variation in the lifting of these barriers across industries and countries for identification. Because trade barriers and costs have declined significantly in the EU over the past few decades. Our second method for identifying causality involves the creation of two instrumental variables for trade openness, at the industry level.

First, we construct an instrument for trade openness using gravity estimates. The method we apply was developed by Frankel and Romer (1999) in the context of studying the relationship between trade openness and growth at the country level, and has been extended by Di Giovanni and Levchenko (2009) to the industry level. For each industry, Di Giovanni and Levchenko (2009) estimate a (cross-section) gravity equation to predict bilateral trade openness by means of distance, population, language, land border, land area, and land-locked status. The summation of the predicted trade openness across trading partners yields an industry-level natural openness measure, i.e., predicted trade volume as a percentage of output not only in each country, but also in each industry within each country. Gravity estimates provide a good instrumental variable as the geographical variables used are plausibly exogenous and highly correlated with the actual trade openness.

Our point of departure is to extend (Di Giovanni and Levchenko 2009) within a panel framework. Our approach corrects for important mis-specifications of gravity models commonly used in the literature, and yields a time-varying industry-level natural openness. The latter is particularly appealing in our context as we are interested in the evolution of the effects of trade openness on specialization over time, given the fact that trade barriers and costs have decreased significantly in the EU during the past few decades (Chen and Novy 2011).

Second, we construct an industry-specific time-varying trade integration measure as proposed by Chen and Novy (2011). They derive a micro-founded measure of bilateral sector-specific trade frictions, i.e., the inverse of bilateral trade integration. They model disaggregated trade flows at the industry level in a gravity framework, allowing trade costs to be heterogeneous across industries. This measure is proven to be theoretically consistent with a wide range of trade models and correlated with a large set of observable trade cost proxies.[8] The Appendix lays out the details of our approach.

Even though our identification strategy is comprehensive, we cannot rule out the possibility that other factors may still bias our results, such as the restrictiveness of the i.i.d. assumption.

3 Data

We use an extensive data set that contains firm-level, industry-level, and country-level data for 18 manufacturing industries in 14 EU countries over the period 1997–2006. For the firm-level data, we have compiled a comprehensive data set based on annual editions of the AMADEUS (Analyze Major Databases from European Sources) database.[9] We supplement this data set with industry- and country-level data from various sources. Industry-level data—disaggregated at NACE 2-digit—on value added, output, imports, exports, and employment are taken from the OECD (2008) Structural Analysis Database (STAN). Country-level data on manufacturing GDP and country-level GDP are retrieved from the World Bank (2008) *World Development Indicators* (WDI). Except for employment, all data are reported in current U.S. dollars. The industries and countries included in our sample are listed in Tables 5 and 6 in Appendix, respectively. Below, we explain how each of the variables we use is constructed.

Our aim is to construct an industry-specific specialization index, since we are primarily interested in examining the heterogeneity of the trade-specialization relationship across industries. Our starting point is Redding (2002), who uses neoclassical trade theory to derive a specialization measure (spe), defined as nominal industry value added as a percentage of a country's total GDP.[10] In

---

[8]It is worth noting that measurement error in independent variables can lead to misleading inferences in regression-type applications. Although employing the instrumental variable of trade openness we have constructed might introduce measurement errors in our estimations, using Chen and Novy (2011)'s measure does not have this problem. In addition, while the gravity approach in a panel setting can be subject to criticisms that most of the independent variables used in the estimation are time invariant, which poses challenges to the validity of this instrument, Chen and Novy (2011)'s micro-funded measure does not suffer from this issue. Essentially these two approaches complement each other. Therefore, we present results using both approaches to ensure the validity of our results.

[9]One of the characteristics of the AMADEUS database is that each edition only includes surviving firms. In addition, as time has gone by, the coverage of AMADEUS has increased. By using all annual editions of AMADEUS, and compiling the data set both backward looking (to reduce survivorship bias) and forward looking (to increase the coverage), we are able to construct the most comprehensive firm-level data set of European manufacturing firms.

[10]This measure has the advantage of being theory-consistent, in contrast with ad hoc definitions of specialization that have been used by other authors, such as the indexes of revealed comparative advantage, pioneered by Balassa (1965).

Eq. (3.1), we express Redding (2002)'s measure as the product of an industry's share of a country's manufacturing value added (S) and manufacturing's share of a country's GDP (MS). In our estimations, we log transform each of these components, which then allows us to include the log of MS as a control variable and the log of S as our dependent variable. In this manner, we isolate the impact of increased trade openness within manufacturing industries from the overall decline in manufacturing activity:

$$spe_{iot} = \frac{VA_{iot}}{GDP_{ot}} = \frac{VA_{iot}}{VA_{ot}^{\text{manufacturing}}} \times \frac{VA_{ot}^{\text{manufacturing}}}{GDP_{ot}} = S_{iot} \times MS_{ot}. \tag{3.1}$$

As a robustness test, we also construct an additional measure of specialization, S'. This measure is the log of the normalized value added, where for each country, normalization is based on the value added of the food industry (NACE 15–16), which is set at 100 at the beginning of our sample, in 1997. Essentially, this normalized variable captures the changes of industry composition within a country over time. We describe the results using this variable as a robustness check in Appendix. From Table 1, we observe that there is a wide variation in shares across manufacturing industries, as expected. The variation of the share of the manufacturing sector as a whole, however, varies much less. In addition, we control for industry-specific, time-varying productivity by including output per worker (Y/L), which varies significantly across our sample.

In a similar vein, we measure trade integration at the industry level. The existing literature distinguishes between *de jure* and *de facto* measures of trade integration (Sachs and Warner 1995; Wacziarg and Welch 2008). *De jure* measures capture the extent of government restrictions on trade flows, whereas *de facto* measures quantify the degree of openness through realized trade flows. Since *de jure* measures are typically not available at the industry level, we mainly rely on the measure of *de facto* openness (T), defined as the ratio of industry imports and exports to output (Di Giovanni and Levchenko 2009). Table 1 contains descriptives of both T and its instruments T' and T'', described in the previous section. The main observation from comparing the three trade openness measures is that the measure based on Chen and Novy (2011) has far less variance than the other two measures. The correlation between openness and natural openness is 0.9, whereas the correlation between openness and trade integration is 0.2. Both correlations are significant at the 1% level.

To capture the intra-industry potential for reallocation, we need a set of conditioning variables V_{iot}. Since this type of reallocation takes place *between* firms in the same industry, we require firm-level observations to construct industry-level measures. Our objective is to show the extent to which the most productive firms in an industry can grow by appropriating the assets of the least productive firms. Therefore, we need to measure the dispersion in productivity within each industry in each country. We measure the productivity of each firm in two ways. First, and most closely related to Melitz (2003), we estimate each firm's economies of scale.

Table 1 Descriptive statistics

	Variable	Source	Mean	Min	Max	Std
S	Specialization (S)	OECD STAN	5.877	0.016	23.585	4.267
	Normalized specialization (S')	OECD STAN	1.458	−4.110	3.161	0.905
T	Openness (T)	(imports+exports)/value added	153.290	16.677	5735.303	405.529
	Natural openness (instrument, T')	Di Giovanni and Levchenko (2009)	165.858	11.655	9344.317	562.117
	Trade integration (instrument, T'')	Chen and Novy (2011)	2.273	0.710	6.206	1.017
Z	Labor productivity, \$1000 (Y/L)	OECD STAN	281.449	17.895	8036.795	522.882
	Manufacturing share (MS)	OECD STAN	18.311	8.715	26.452	4.071
V	Efficiency dispersion, 25/75 ratio	AMADEUS, own calculations	1.151	1.001	13.085	0.279
	Efficiency dispersion, 10/90 ratio	AMADEUS, own calculations	1.435	1.001	13.516	0.576
	Efficiency dispersion, standard deviation	AMADEUS, own estimations	0.112	0.001	0.365	0.038
	Scale dispersion, 25/75 ratio	AMADEUS, own calculations	1.035	1.002	1.109	0.014
	Scale dispersion, 10/90 ratio	AMADEUS, own calculations	1.070	1.003	1.174	0.026
	Scale dispersion, standard deviation	AMADEUS, own calculations	0.028	0.002	0.073	0.009
	Initial efficiency level (weighted)	AMADEUS, own calculations	0.773	0.176	0.910	0.082
	Initial scale level (weighted)	AMADEUS, own calculations	1.091	0.886	1.623	0.149

Number of observations is 2138; based on specifications given in Table 3; Std = standard deviation

Second, and based on the same estimations, we estimate each firm's efficiency. Our primary measure of dispersion is the ratio of the productivity of firms in the top quantile (i.e., with the highest economies of scale, or the most efficient) to the productivity of firms in the bottom quartile (i.e., with the lowest economies of scale, or the least efficient), the 25/75 ratio. To check the robustness of our results, we also use two other measures of dispersion, the 10/90 ratio and the standard deviation of scale and efficiency, described in the robustness analysis in Appendix. For our identification approach, it is important that we control for the *initial* level of efficiency and scale elasticity in each industry. Therefore, we also include the average efficiency and scale elasticity in the first year of our sample, weighted by each firm's total assets.

We estimate each firm's scale elasticity and efficiency as follows. First, we estimate a stochastic production frontier for each industry, described in detail in Appendix. Our approach has three distinct features. First, by estimating a translog production function, we allow for increasing, decreasing, and constant economies of scale, within an industry, at any time. Second, by estimating this production function using stochastic frontier analysis (SFA), we can also measure efficiency, i.e., the extent to which firms with the *same* economies of scale and input levels produce different levels of output. In our approach, the error term of that stochastic production frontier is composed of two parts (Aigner et al. 1977; Battese and Corra 1977; Meeusen and Broeck 1977): a one-sided component with a truncated distribution that captures inefficiency, as well as a systematic component that allows for measurement errors or other random shocks around the production frontier. Third, we account for systematic differences in production technologies, which may otherwise be wrongly labeled as inefficiency (Orea and Kumbhakar 2004), by estimating true fixed effects frontiers (Greene 2005), with firm- and country-fixed effects for each industry-specific frontier. In so doing, we still assume that firms that produce similar products and thereby operate in the same industry can be benchmarked against each other, even if they operate in different countries. Put differently, even though we allow for structural differences in output (and productivity) between firms that operate in the same industry, but in different countries, we assume that these firms have access to the same production technology.[11]

For our firm-level productivity estimations, we use the all-companies module of AMADEUS, a database provided by Bureau Van Dijk Electronic Publishing. This pan-European database contains detailed financial and business data on more than ten million public and private firms in 44 European countries. The homogeneity of the data collecting process across countries and its fairly complete coverage, especially of privately held firms makes it well suited for our analysis. Our sample consists of 390,350 manufacturing firms across 14 EU countries over the 1997–2006 period. We choose manufacturing industries because in contrast to services, they are more involved in trade and more responsive to trade integration.[12] We group all firms into 18 industries to ensure a sufficient number of firms in each industry-country combination, and compatibility with other industry-level data. The choice of countries is based on the quality of firm-level coverage.[13] To estimate the stochastic production frontier, we use raw data on gross value added, tangible fixed assets, and number of employees to construct firm-level output (Y), capital (K), and labor (L), respectively. Appendix describes the AMADEUS database, the

[11]Bos et al. (2010) endogenize the allocation of European manufacturing industries in a low- and high-technology class. Although, in their paper, the same industry can belong to one class in one country and another class in another country, in their Table A4 they show that most industries cluster in the same class, confirming that technology difference, in EU manufacturing, are industry- rather than country-specific.

[12]On average, manufacturing trade accounts for 80% of total merchandize trade in the EU.

[13]We compare the total number of manufacturing firms and the number reported in OECD 2006 Structural and Demographic Business Statistics (SDBS) and select countries with more than 30% of firms covered.

sample selection procedure and the construction of our variables in detail. Table 1 summarizes the definitions, sources, and descriptive statistics of the main variables used in our analysis, respectively.

In Table 1, we observe that the most efficient quartile of firms is on average 15% more efficient than the least efficient quartile. However, if we move one standard deviation (0.279) above this average, the difference has increased to more than 40%. Results are similar for the other two efficiency dispersion measures. Average efficiency at the beginning of the sample period is 77.3%, indicating that the average firm should be able to increase its output by 22.7% without increasing its use of inputs. The average return to scale at the beginning of the sample period are 1.091, indicating that the average firm experiences increasing returns to scale, and can increase its output by 1.091% by increasing its inputs by 1%. The top quartile firms operate with return to scale that are on average 3.5% larger than the bottom quartile, although this difference can increase to more than 10% for some industries.

As explained in the previous section, for the purpose of our analysis, we aim to measure the potential for reallocation in each of the industries in each of the countries. But how valid are our measures introduced above? In order to validate them, we also calculate the actual degree of reallocation that takes place in each industry in each country over the sample period, using a decomposition method suggested by Olley and Pakes (1996). Consider the following decomposition of efficiency and scale for an industry i in country o at the period t:

$$Scale_{iot}=\sum_j w_{jiot}Scale_{jiot}=\overline{Scale_{iot}}+\sum_j(w_{jiot}-\overline{w_{iot}})(Scale_{jiot}-\overline{Scale_{iot}}) \tag{3.2a}$$

$$Eff_{iot}=\sum_j w_{jiot}Eff_{jiot}=\overline{Eff_{iot}}+\sum_j(w_{jiot}-\overline{w_{iot}})(Eff_{jiot}-\overline{Eff_{iot}}), \tag{3.2b}$$

where j indexes firms, and $Scale$ and Eff refer to efficiency and return to scale, respectively. In Eq. (3.2a), $Scale_{iot}$ represents the value-added weighted average scale in industry i in country o at time t and $\overline{Scale_{iot}}$ the unweighted average scale. Equation (3.2b) decomposes the value-added weighted average efficiency into a first component that is size invariant, and a second component that is not. It is this second component in which we are interested, as it measures the sample covariance between return to scale and value added. The larger this covariance, the higher the share of the value added that is produced by firms with higher return to scale, and consequently the higher the industry-level return to scale. The same applies to efficiency, in Eq. (3.2b). Validating our measures of the potential for reallocation therefore involves assessing whether they are positively correlated with the changes of these two covariance terms over time.

4 Results

In this section we present our results. First, we validate our measures of the potential for reallocation. Secondly, we examine whether the potential for reallocation has indeed driven the trade-specialization nexus. Thirdly, we explore the treatment effect from changes in trade openness, and fourthly we verify our results by comparing the actual shares of industries with the ones predicted by our model.

4.1 *The Potential for Reallocation and Subsequent Actual Reallocation*

Do we find that industries with the most "room to move" are also the ones where subsequently reallocation is most likely to take place? To validate our measures of the potential for reallocation, in Fig. 1a and b we compare them to the actual reallocation that took place during our sample period based on Eqs. (3.2a) and (3.2b).

Two concurrent developments can be noted from these figures. First, we observe that higher levels of dispersion, signifying the greater potential for reallocation, are positively correlated with actual reallocation, especially for return to scale. Second, as the changes of most covariance terms are positive, the reallocation is indeed in line with Melitz (2003), and can lead to the expansion of the industry in which firms are located.

4.2 *How Has the Potential for Reallocation Driven the Trade-Specialization Nexus?*

Our aim is to explain why some industries drive the trade-specialization nexus and others do not. Therefore, we start by determining the number of groups or classes

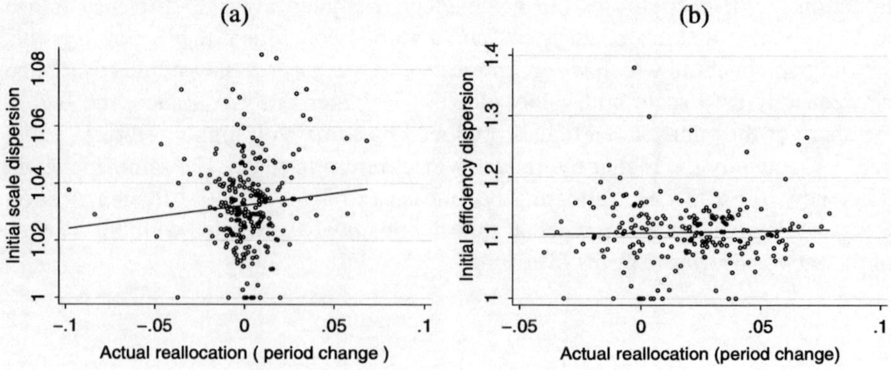

Fig. 1 Potential vs. actual reallocation. (**a**) Scale. (**b**) Efficiency

Table 2 Specification tests of the number of groups

	Natural openness				Trade integration			
Specification	Likelihood	Parameters	AIC	SBIC	Likelihood	Parameters	AIC	SBIC
Two-group	2313.357	15	14.507	100.734	2195.605	15	14.612	100.83
Three-group	2360.783	25	34.467	178.178	2256.219	25	34.557	178.269
Four-group	2415.082	35	54.421	255.617	No convergence			

Akaike Information Criterion (AIC) $= 2m - 2nLF(k)$, Schwartz Bayesian Information Criterion (SBIC) $= -2lnLF(k) + mln(n)$; m is the number of parameters, n is the number of observations, *LF(k)* is the log likelihood for groups. The preferred specification has the lowest AIC or the lowest SBIC. See Orea and Kumbhakar (2004). Obs = 2318; Natural openness based on Di Giovanni and Levchenko (2009); Trade integration based on Chen and Novy (2011)

of industries identified by our latent class model. Following Orea and Kumbhakar (2004), we estimate for two, three, and four classes, respectively, and formally test using the Akaike and Schwartz Bayesian information criteria (AIC and SBIC, respectively). We do so using the natural openness measure following (Di Giovanni and Levchenko 2009) and the trade integration measure from Chen and Novy (2011). As shown in Table 2, a specification with two classes is preferred for both measures, since this results in the lowest AIC and SBIC.[14]

Table 3 contains our estimation results. Panel B contains parameter equality tests and confirms what we have found so far: there are two distinct groups of industries, with significantly different parameters, both for trade openness and output per worker. Also, the parameters for variables used in the sorting equation are jointly significantly different from zero.

Turning to Panel C, we see that the industries in the first class are characterized by a higher efficiency dispersion, a lower initial efficiency level, and a higher initial return to scale level. Scale dispersion, however, is not higher in this first class. Most notable is the difference in $\Delta\bar{S}$, the average percentage change in the manufacturing share of industries. In the first class, the change is between 2.5 and 3.2%, whereas it is approximately -1.5% on average in the second class. Summing up, we henceforth refer to the first class as the high-potential or HP class, whereas the second class is referred to as the low-potential or LP class. The prior class probabilities (at data means) show that approximately between 7 and 9.2% of our sample belongs to the HP class, while the rest is assigned to the LP class.

Of course, what remains to be seen is whether the trade-specialization nexus is indeed driven by the HP class, as we conjecture. We therefore turn to Panel A, which contains the parameter estimates. We start with the parameters in the sorting equation. Scale and efficiency dispersion increase the likelihood of being in the HP class, as expected. High initial scale levels make it more likely that an industry will be driving the trade-specialization nexus, whereas high efficiency levels make it less likely that an industry is in the HP class. Overall, results are more significant for

[14]For a possible third group, we find that parameters are jointly not significant from zero, and the number of observations allocated in this additional group is rather small.

Table 3 The trade-specialization Nexus at the industry level

Parameter estimates	Natural openness				Trade integration			
	High-potential		Low-potential		High-potential		Low-potential	
Panel A								
Kernel								
T	0.708	(0.218)***	−0.171	(0.067)**	0.396	(0.320)	−0.261	(0.062)***
T^2	−0.087	(0.017)***	−0.016	(0.007)**	−0.421	(0.581)	0.077	(0.048)
Output per worker	0.251	(0.066)***	0.215	(0.021)***	0.408	(0.071)***	0.285	(0.021)***
Constant	0.001	(0.016)	0.000	(0.001)	0.007	(0.017)	0.000	(0.002)
Sorting								
Scale dispersion	17.719	(8.137)**	Reference		14.066	(9.459)	Reference	
Efficiency dispersion	5.940	(1.438)***	Reference		5.720	(1.411) ***	Reference	
Initial scale level	14.282	(1.426)***	Reference		14.998	(1.475)***	Reference	
Initial efficiency level	−4.144	(1.860)**	Reference		−2.499	(2.576)	Reference	
Constant	−39.846	(8.665)***	Reference		−38.130	(9.856)***	Reference	
Prior class probability	0.092		0.908		0.072		0.928	
Equality tests	Natural openness			Trade integration				
	Wald	P-value	Conclusion	Wald	P-value	Conclusion		
Panel B								
All parameters	14.519	0.000	Rejected	32.980	0.000	Rejected		
T and T^2	15.306	0.000	Rejected	19.362	0.000	Rejected		
Sorting variables	62.224	0.000	Rejected	50.380	0.000	Rejected		
Class characteristics	Natural openness			Trade integration				
	HP	LP	P-value	HP	LP	P-value		
Panel C								
Scale dispersion	1.033	1.036	0.000	1.032	1.036	0.000		
Efficiency dispersion	1.243	1.135	0.000	1.252	1.135	0.000		
Initial scale level	1.333	1.048	0.000	1.349	1.050	0.000		
Initial efficiency level	0.708	0.784	0.000	0.704	0.784	0.000		
$\Delta\bar{S}$ (%)	2.504	−1.511	0.001	3.203	−1.548	0.000		

Standard errors in parentheses; significance at the 10/5/1% level (**/***); Natural openness based on Di Giovanni and Levchenko (2009); Trade integration based on Chen and Novy (2011); in panel C, P values for significance of difference in means, HP is high-potential industry, LP is low-potential industry, $\Delta\bar{S}$ is the average percentage change in industry shares in a class the natural openness measure (Di Giovanni and Levchenko 2009) than for the trade integration measure (Chen and Novy 2011), which may be explained by the latter's low variance.

In the top part of panel A, we find the parameter estimates for trade openness and labor productivity. As expected, labor productivity always has a positive relationship to an industry's manufacturing share (López and Sánchez 2005). More interesting are the results for trade openness: in line with our expectations, an increase in natural openness (Di Giovanni and Levchenko 2009) increases an industry's share in manufacturing in the HP class, whereas it has a negative, but much smaller effect in the LP class. Both effects are similar, but less significant for an increase in trade integration (Chen and Novy 2011). For the HP class, results are in line with the trade-specialization nexus. For the LP class, increases in trade openness have a negative effect on an industry's share in manufacturing.

This is in line with López and Sánchez (2005), who find a negative relationship between openness and specialization for ten European countries. They assert that the convergence of industrial structures following the openness to foreign trade is consistent with the prediction of the Hechscher–Ohlin–Vanek theory: when factor prices are equalizing, the sources of comparative advantage arising from relative differences in factor prices disappear.[15]

An interesting question to ask at this point is whether there is a threshold point beyond which further opening-up to international trade may not lead to increased specialization. Thus, the relationship between trade openness and specialization may no longer be positive for industries with very high levels of openness—a phenomenon that is identified in new economic geography theories (Krugman 1991; Venables 1996). These theories postulate a non-linear relationship between trade costs and location of economic activity. The decrease in trade costs induces firms to agglomerate into fewer locations, and a further decline in trade costs can result in geographical dispersion of activities when mobility across sectors exhibits a finite cost. Beine and Coulombe (2007) document a similar positive short-run relationship and a negative long-run relationship between trade integration and specialization, i.e., short-run specialization and long-run diversification based on export data of Canadian regions.

Therefore, in order to further assess the economic nature of the relationship between trade openness and specialization, we calculate the marginal effect of trade on specialization, i.e., the partial derivative of S with respect to T in Eq. (2.3), conditional on the level of trade openness T for both the HP and the LP class. Fig. 2a and b illustrate these conditional marginal effects and the corresponding 95% confidence intervals (Brambor et al. 2006). We find for the HP class that although the effect of openness on specialization decreases as industries' natural

[15]Trade integration implies the creation of new exporting industries, which in turn leads to the expansion of aggregate production in those industries. This process could be driven by agglomeration forces and forward (large market)–backward (large input variety) linkages identified by new economic geography theories (Fujita et al. 2001).

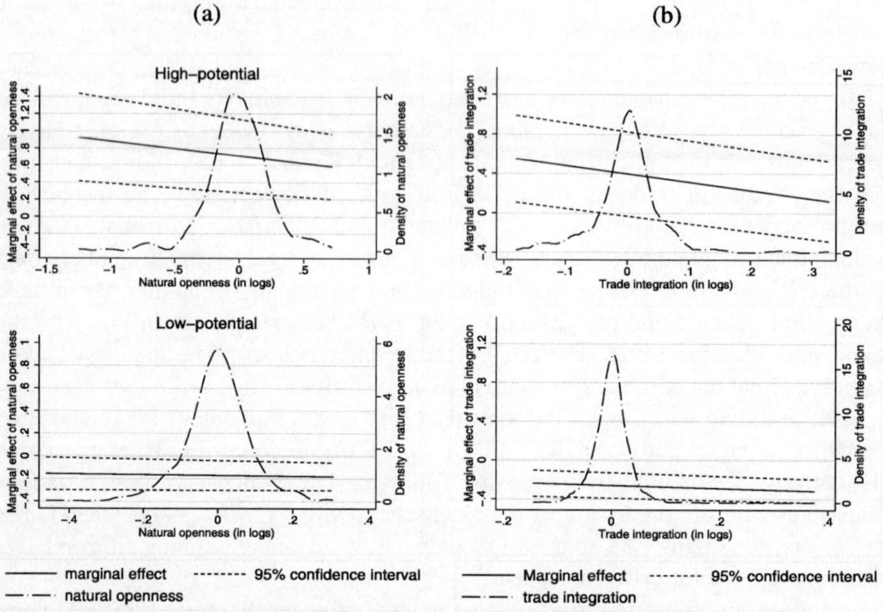

Fig. 2 Conditional marginal effect. (**a**) Natural openness. (**b**) Trade integration

openness (in the top part of Fig. 2a) and as trade integration increases (in the top part of Fig. 2b). However, the marginal effects remain positive. Thus, although there is some saturation with respect to trade openness, we do not find evidence of a threshold effect for the HP class.

Things are even clearer for the LP class, where the marginal effect of natural openness (in the bottom part of Fig. 2a) and trade integration (in the bottom part of Fig. 2b) is scarcely affected by changes in openness or integration and is consistently below zero.

To check the robustness of our results, we first consider an alternative measure of specialization, the log of normalized industry value added. The results are reported in Panel A of Table 7 in Appendix. We find that they are qualitatively and quantitatively very similar to those in Table 3, despite the lack of significance for two of the conditioning variables, namely scale dispersion and initial efficiency level. In addition, the division of the sample into a small HP and a large LP group resembles that of our main specification in Table 3.

We then consider two other measures of dispersion, namely the 10/90 ratio and the standard deviation. Panels B and C of Table 7 in Appendix display the results. We find no significant changes from our main results, except that the scale dispersion and/or initial efficiency level loses its significance when the dispersion is measured as 10/90 ratio in Panel B of Table 7. Similar results are found when using the standard deviation as the dispersion measure in Panel C of Table 7. We find no evidence of changes in the main parameter estimates. But the power of our conditioning variables becomes somewhat weaker—except for the initial return to scale level—as the individual significance of three variables drops and the efficiency dispersion appears to have the "wrong" sign. These results mainly highlight the problems of using the standard deviation as the dispersion measure, because firm efficiency and scale are not normally distributed within each industry. Overall, our results do not seem to be driven by the use of an alternative specialization measure, nor by the choice of a particular dispersion measure.

To summarize, we find that the effects of trade openness on specialization appear to be very different in the HP and LP class. The potential for reallocation, as measured by the four conditioning variables, determines the allocation of an industry into either the HP or LP class.

4.3 Can We Explain the Slow-Down in Specialization?

An interesting question that arises is how the changes in the potential for reallocation affect the dynamics of the trade-specialization nexus. The distinctive features of our latent class model allows us to explore this question. In our modeling framework, the probability of belonging to a certain group depends on the average of all four conditioning variables. As a result, the changes in these variables can alter this probability. Therefore, we prefer here to permit industries to switch groups over time, rather than imposing the assumption that they are restricted to one group.

Panel A in Table 4 shows the migration matrices, including the absolute number and percentage of group allocation changes over time. We can see that the diagonal elements carry the largest percentage as would be expected, which indicates that the potential for reallocation hardly changes drastically. Transitions from the LP to HP group are rare. At the same time, transitions from the HP to LP group are more frequent, suggesting that if industries react to the trade openness by realizing the potential for reallocation, the remaining potential is reduced. Thus, these industries are more likely to migrate to the LP group.[16]

Most of the industry transitions, i.e., 31.03% of all cases, take place in the petroleum industry (18 out of 58), followed by 13.8 and 12.07%, respectively, in basic metals and electronic equipment industries. In terms of country divisions, 22.41% of industries transit from the HP to LP group in Hungary (13 out of 58), which seems not surprising given that CEEC countries are expected to be mostly affected by trade integration. They are closely followed by Portugal and Sweden with 12.07 and 10.34% (7 out 58 and 6 out of 58), respectively. However, we find no trends with regard to when these transitions occur.

[16]We checked whether the occurrence of transition is due to the fact that the conditional probability of an industry being in one group our model assigned is close to 50%, which is the conventional cut-off point in the multinomial logit model of Eq. (2.4). However, the conditional probability of group membership is very high in almost all cases, i.e., above 90%. Therefore, the transition is not related to the flexibility of our model.

Table 4 Transitioning from high-potential to low-potential

Panel A: transition matrices

	Natural openness				Trade integration		
	To				To		
From	HP	LP	Total	From	HP	LP	Total
HP	215	58	273	HP	193	55	248
	(78.75)	(21.25)	(100)		(77.82)	(22.18)	(100)
LP	56	1574	1630	LP	54	1601	1655
	(3.44)	(96.56)	(100)		(3.26)	(96.74)	(100)
Total	271	1632	1903	Total	247	1656	1903
	14.24	85.76	(100)		(12.98)	(87.02)	(100)

Panel B: covariates

Variable	Mean	Sign	t-test	KW	Mean	Sign	t-test	KW
Efficiency dispersion	1.156	–	**	***	1.146	–	**	***
Scale dispersion	1.038	+	**	***	1.038	+	***	***
Initial efficiency level	0.766	+	***	***	0.776	+	***	***
Initial scale level	1.155	–	***	***	1.170	–	***	***

Percentages in parentheses; significance at the 10/5/1% level (**/***); Natural openness based on Di Giovanni and Levchenko (2009); Trade integration based on Chen and Novy (2011); in panel B, t-test for difference in means and Kruskal–Wallis (KW) rank test; HP is high-potential industry, LP is low-potential industry

Panel B in Table 4 provides some further insights into why and how some industries migrate from the HP to the LP group. We examine whether the potential for reallocation is significantly lower for these switchers. More specifically, we employ a t-test and a Kruskal–Wallis test to assess whether the four conditioning variables used to predict group membership differ significantly on average between industries that switch and those that stay in the HP group. A positive (negative) sign indicates the variable is higher (lower) than for the industries that stay in the HP group. For example, the first column in panel A indicates that efficiency dispersion is significantly lower (at 5 and 1%) than that of the average of the HP group. Overall, we find that the potential for reallocation of these switchers is significantly lower, evidenced by a lower efficiency dispersion, a higher efficiency level, and a lower scale level. The scale dispersion appears to have the "wrong" sign, however. These results provide additional support for the saturation effect of trade openness: the process of openness-driven-specialization is not monotonic, but rather, it is slowing down.

4.4 Actual and Predicted Industry Shares

Last but not least, we examine the predictive power of our model by looking at how well it predicts our specialization measure S_{iot}, i.e., the industry shares. To do so, the top parts of Fig. 3a and b plot the predicted S_{iot} against the actual S_{iot} on the

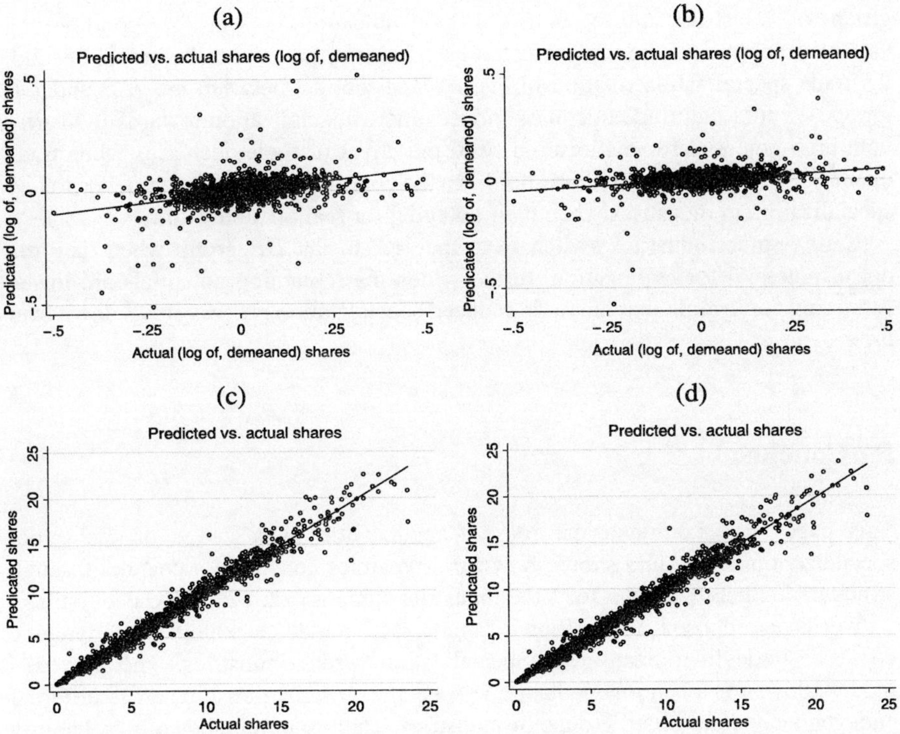

Fig. 3 Predictability of the latent class model. (**a**) Natural openness, demeaned. (**b**) Trade integration, demeaned. (**c**) Natural openness, not demeaned. (**d**) Trade integration, not demeaned

basis of Eq. (2.3) using natural openness and trade integration, respectively. It shows that the predicted S_{iot} captures a considerable amount of variation embedded in the actual S_{iot} (the correlation coefficient is 0.4 and 0.35, respectively).

One point which deserves noting here is that since the specialization measure used in the estimation is in logs and demeaned, our model essentially predicts the deviation from the means. To retrieve the predicted shares, we add back the actual means (i.e., country-time, industry-time, and industry-country averages discussed in the methodology section).

The bottom parts of Fig. 3a and b plot the predicted industry shares (in levels) against the actual shares. It is clear from the figures that they are highly correlated (the correlation coefficient is 0.99 and 0.98, respectively), confirming the predictive power of our model. The caveat to bear in mind is that the "means" we take out may contain important information in explaining specialization, that is beyond the scope of our model.

To summarize, three main findings emerge from our analysis so far. First, the trade-specialization nexus is not homogeneous across all industries, nor is the relationship entirely unique for each industry. Instead, we find two distinctive groups of industries, and the potential for reallocation, i.e., the four conditioning variables, determines the assignment of each industry into a specific group. Second, the trade-specialization relationship is in stark contrast between the HP and LP group. We find that trade openness induces more specialization towards industries with high potential for reallocation. And the effect of trade decreases when trade openness is beyond a certain threshold. On the contrary, trade openness leads to less specialization in industries when their potential for reallocation is low.

Lastly, some industries switch from the HP to the LP group when they run out of potential for reallocation, further when the remaining potentials are lower, furthering confirming that the trade-induced specialization process slows down over time.

5 Conclusion

This paper has examined the role of reallocation as a driver of the trade-specialization nexus, and shown how firm dynamics constitute a channel through which trade liberalization affects the industrial composition within EU economies.

We have proposed a conditional latent class model to examine the dynamic effect of trade liberalization on specialization across industries. The proposed model allows for a heterogeneous trade-specialization relationship across different endogenously determined groups of industries. The group membership probability is modelled as a function of four firm-based measures that encapsulate the intra-industry potential for reallocation, namely the dispersion of firm efficiency and scale and the initial level of industry average efficiency and scale. To obtain firm-specific efficiency and scale, we set up a model of production that permits the inefficient use of resources and estimate a stochastic production function. In order to overcome endogeneity problems, we employ two novel instrumentation strategies based on the exogenous geographic determinants of trade flows and a micro-founded measure of industry-specific trade frictions.

Using a unique panel of manufacturing firms in 14 EU countries during 1997–2006, we have found evidence that the trade-specialization relationship differs markedly between two distinctive groups of industries and that the relationship depends on the potential for reallocation. We have shown that the potential for reallocation appears to be positively associated with the future actual reallocation observed in reality. On the one hand, an inverted U-shaped trade-specialization pattern has been found in one group of industries which are characterized by greater potential for reallocation, indicating that trade openness induces specialization at a decreasing rate. On the other hand, trade openness results in less specialization in the other group when the potential for reallocation is small. Our results are consistent with the theoretical and empirical evidence that international trade acts as a catalyst in facilitating the intra-industry reallocation of economic activity.

Our findings have important policy implications. As reallocation is a key channel through which industries can benefit from trade liberalization, policies aimed at removing barriers in the factor and product markets are likely to enhance the reallocation of economic activity. The resulting gains in efficiency and return to scale appear to be an important source of long-run competitiveness and economic growth in the EU.

Appendix

Construction of Alternative Measures for Trade Openness

This appendix gives a detailed description of two time-varying industry-level alternative measures for trade openness used in the estimations of Eqs. (2.4) and (2.3).

Industry-Level Natural Openness

The first measure is a time-varying measure of industry-level natural openness. Our starting point is the use of the gravity model of trade that has enjoyed remarkable empirical success in predicting a large proportion of variations in observed trade volumes. Furthermore, the gravity model has a solid theoretical foundation and can be derived from almost any standard trade model, including the monopolistic competition model, the Heckscher–Ohlin model, and the latest trade models featuring firm heterogeneity. Frankel and Romer (1999) introduce a natural openness measure that can be used as an instrument. They propose a (cross-section) gravity equation to predict bilateral trade openness between each pair of countries based on a large set of geographical variables, such as distance, population, language, land border, land area, and land-locked status.[17] The summation of predicted trade openness across all trading partners yields a natural openness measure, i.e., the ratio of predicted trade volume to GDP for each country. This measure carries exogenous elements and permits the examination of the causal effect of trade on growth, and is later applied to a wide range of settings in which trade openness and other variables are potentially jointly determined.[18]

Recent literature has extended the gravity estimation using disaggregated data. Although the dependent variable in a gravity equation is generally observed at the country level and does not vary across industries, trade volumes react differently to geographical characteristics in different industries. In other words, the gravity coefficients are found to vary considerably across industries. Consider for example the coefficient for distance: assuming some industries are more sensitive to distance

[17] Instead of predicting trade volumes, Frankel and Romer (1999) predict trade openness, i.e., the trade volumes as a percentage of a country's GDP.

[18] See, for example, Rose et al. (2000), Glick and Rose (2002), Subramanian and Wei (2007).

than others, countries that are located further away from their trading partners will have less predicted trade in sectors that are distance-sensitive. Theoretically, Anderson and van Wincoop (2004) demonstrate that the estimated coefficient for distance in the gravity model is a function of trade costs and the elasticity of substitution between product varieties within the sector. Since both trade costs—direct and informational—and the elasticity of substitution differ significantly across industries, it is not surprising that the distance coefficient exhibits significant variations. Di Giovanni and Levchenko (2009) report an industry-specific distance coefficient ranging from −0.8 to −1.6, close to the range of −0.5 to −1.5 reported in Chaney (2008). Therefore, the variation in (all) gravity coefficients is the key for this procedure to work.

Di Giovanni and Levchenko (2009) apply the methodology of Frankel and Romer (1999) at the industry level and subsequently construct an industry-level natural openness measure. Following Di Giovanni and Levchenko (2009), we estimate the following gravity specification for each industry i:

$$\begin{aligned} ln(T_{iodt}) = {} & \alpha_i^0 + \eta_i^1 ldist_{od} + \eta_i^2 lpop_{ot} + \eta_i^3 larea_o + \eta_i^4 lpop_{dt} \\ & + \eta_i^5 larea_d + \eta_i^6 landlock_{od} + \eta_i^7 border_{od} + \eta_i^8 border_{od} \times ldist_{od} \\ & + \eta_i^9 border_{od} \times lpop_{ot} + \eta_i^{10} border_{od} \times larea_c \\ & + \eta_i^{11} border_{od} \times lpop_{dt} + \eta_i^{12} border_{od} \times larea_d \\ & + \eta_i^{13} border_{od} \times landlock_{od} + D_{ot} + D_{dt} + \epsilon_{iodt}, \end{aligned} \tag{5.1}$$

where c denotes sector, o denotes origin country, d denotes destination country, and t denotes time. $ln(T_{iodt})$ is the natural log of bilateral trade (imports plus exports) as a share of output in industry i, from country o to country d at time t. We follow Di Giovanni and Levchenko (2009), and include a series of gravity variables: $ldist_{od}$ is the natural log of the distance between two countries, defined as the distance between the capitals in the two countries; $lpop_{ot}$ is the natural log of the population of country o at t; $larea_c$ is the natural log of land area of country c; $lpop_{dt}$ is the natural log of the population of country d at t; $larea_d$ is the natural log of land area of country d; $landlock_{od}$ takes the value of 0, 1, or 2 depending on whether none, one, or both of the countries are land-locked; $border_{od}$ is a contiguity dummy that takes the value of 1 if countries o and d share a land border; D_{ot} and D_{dt} are a list of time-varying origin and destination country dummies, serving as proxy for multilateral resistance in Anderson and van Wincoop (2003); ϵ_{iodt} is a normally distributed random error term that has a zero mean and a constant variance.

Having estimated Eq. (5.1) for each industry i, we then obtain the predicted log of bilateral trade as a share of output from country o to each of its trading partners d at time t, i.e., $\widehat{ln(T_{iodt})}$. To construct the predicted overall trade in industry i from country o at t, we take the exponential of $\widehat{ln(T_{iodt})}$, and sum across all trading partner countries d as shown in Eq. (5.2):

$$T_{iot} = \sum_{d} \exp\,(\widehat{ln(T_{iodt})}). \tag{5.2}$$

Hence, we have created a time-varying measure of industry-level natural openness, i.e., the predicted trade volume as a share of output for each industry i in each country o at time t. Importantly, our instrument is entirely independent of trade liberalization, as all variables used to generate the instrument are deep parameters that are not themselves endogenous to the trade liberalization process.

It is worth noting that in contrast to past gravity literature based on cross sectional data, we use panel data. Therefore, our approach has three distinctive advantages, compared to Di Giovanni and Levchenko (2009). First, following Anderson and van Wincoop (2003), we recognize that the standard gravity specification may have been misspecified in ignoring a multilateral resistance term, since a country pair's relative distance to all other markets may have a punitively large effect on its bilateral trade. Failing to properly include this multilateral resistance term can result in a serious estimation bias, resulting the so-called 'gold medal error' of gravity model estimations (Baldwin and Taglioni 2006). An early study by Rose et al. (2000) includes a "remoteness" term. Anderson and van Wincoop (2004) suggest that the inclusion of time-invariant importer and exporter dummies captures multilateral resistance reasonably well in a cross-section setting; however, it does not address the time-varying nature of trade costs in panel data. Hence, we correct by including a series of time-varying importer and exporter dummies to avoid the gold medal error. Second, and equally important, by including these time-varying dummies we can avoid the "bronze medal error," i.e., the inappropriate deflation of nominal trade values by the US aggregate price index.

Thus, our ability to incorporate these time-varying dummies in a panel context allows us to properly address these two misspecification issues. Third, the panel setup permits the construction of an industry-level natural openness that is time-varying. This is much more appealing in our context as we are interested in the evolution of trade openness and specialization over time, given the fact that trade barriers and costs have decreased significantly in the EU over the past few decades.[19]

To estimate Eq. (5.1), we use the OECD STAN Bilateral Trade Database to obtain information on bilateral trade flows (imports and exports) for 18 manufacturing industries in 14 EU countries across 53 trading partner countries over the 1997–2006 period. The industry output data is obtained from the same source. Table 5 lists the

[19]As robustness checks, we estimate two extended specifications. The first one adds additional covariates, such as language, trade agreement, colonial history, monetary union as commonly used in the gravity literature (Rose et al. 2000). The second one introduces a set of country-pair dummies to capture any unobserved factors that are influencing bilateral trade. As a result, some country-pair specific covariates may be absorbed into the pair fixed effects. We find that the industry-level natural openness derived from these two specifications is highly correlated with our preferred specification.

Table 5 Industries and NACE codes

Industry	NACE code
Food products, beverages, and tobacco products	15–16
Textiles, wearing apparel, footwear	17–19
Wood and products of wood and cork	20
Pulp, paper products, and printing	21–22
Coke, refined petroleum, and nuclear fuel	23
Pharmaceuticals	24
Rubber and plastics products	25
Other non-metallic mineral products	26
Basic metals	27
Fabricated metal products	28
Machinery, NEC	29
Office, accounting, and computing machinery	30
Insulated wire, other electrical machinery	31
Electronic valves and tubes, telecommunication equipment	32
Scientific instruments	33
Motor vehicles, trailers, and semi-trailers	34
Building and repairing of ships and boats, aircraft, and spacecraft	35
Manufacturing nec, recycling	36–37

Table 6 Country of origin and destination

Country of Origin (14)
Austria, Belgium, Denmark, Estonia, Finland, France, Hungary, Italy, Netherlands, Norway, Portugal, Spain, Sweden, United Kingdoms
Country of Destination (53)
Argentina, Australia, Austria, Belgium, Bangladesh, Brazil, Canada, Switzerland, Chile, China, Cyprus, Czech Republic, Germany, Denmark, Spain, Estonia, Finland, United Kingdoms, Greece Hong Kong, Hungary, Indonesia, India, Ireland, Iceland, Israel, Italy, Japan, Korea, Lithuania, Latvia Mexico, Malta, Malaysia, Netherlands, Norway, New Zealand, Philippines, Poland, Portugal, Russia, Saudi Arabia, Singapore, Slovakia, Slovenia, Sweden, Thailand, Turkey, Taiwan, USA, Vietnam, South Africa

18 industries and their corresponding NACE codes. The countries included in our sample are listed in Table 6. All gravity variables are taken from the database, which was compiled by Centre d'Études Prospectives et d'Informations Internationales (CEPII).

Industry-Level Trade Integration

Our second approach to address the endogeneity of trade openness is to compute a time-varying measure of industry-specific trade integration proposed by Chen and Novy (2011). They derive a micro-founded measure of bilateral sector-specific trade frictions measured as the inverse of bilateral trade integration. This measure is derived from a model of disaggregated trade flows at the sector level in a gravity framework, allowing trade costs to be heterogeneous across sectors. This measure is shown to be consistent with a wide range of theoretical trade models. Empirically, Chen and Novy (2011) regress it on a large set of observable trade cost proxies and find that technical barriers to trade as well as high transportation costs associated with heavy-weight goods are the most important factors in explaining the variation in their bilateral trade integration measure.

Following Chen and Novy (2011), we compute the following for each industry:

$$\theta_{iodt} = (\frac{x_{ioot} \cdot x_{iddt}}{x_{iodt} \cdot x_{idot}})^{\frac{1}{2(\sigma_i - 1)}}, \tag{5.3}$$

where i denotes industry, o denotes origin country, d denotes destination country, t denotes time, and x represents export flows. The more two countries trade with each other, i.e., the higher $x_{iodt} \cdot x_{idot}$ is, the lower the trade frictions, ceteris paribus. Conversely, the more two countries trade domestically, i.e. the higher $x_{ioot} \cdot x_{iddt}$, the higher the trade frictions, ceteris paribus. Domestic trade in industry i is defined as gross industry output minus total industry exports to the rest of the world. A higher elasticity of substitution σ_i means that consumers are price sensitive; a small price difference induced by bilateral trade costs can lead to a high ratio of domestic to bilateral trade, resulting in a lower θ_{iodt}. The elasticity of substitution is taken from Imbs and Mejean (2009). Therefore, θ_{iodt} not only captures bilateral trade barriers but also a low degree of product differentiation. We take the weighted average of θ_{iodt} across all trading partners d using the bilateral trade volumes as the weights and then invert it, yielding a time-varying industry-level trade integration measure.

A Stochastic Frontier Production Model

We model the firm performance by means of a stochastic frontier production function (Aigner et al. 1977). A frontier production function defines the maximum output achievable, given the current production technology and available inputs. If all firms in produce on the boundary of a common production set that consists of an input vector with two arguments, physical capital (K) and labor (L), output of each firm can be described as:

$$Y^*_{jiot} = f(K_{jiot}, L_{jiot}, t; \beta) \exp\{v_{jiot}\}, \tag{5.4}$$

where Y^*_{jiot} is the firm's frontier (optimum) level of output; f and parameter vector β characterizes the production technology; t is a time trend variable that captures neutral technical change (Solow 1957); and v_{jiot} is an i.i.d. error term distributed as $N(0, \sigma_v^2)$, which reflects the stochastic nature of the frontier.

Some firms, however, may lack the ability to employ existing technologies efficiently and therefore produce less than the frontier output. If the difference between the optimum and actual (observable) output is represented by an exponential factor, $\exp\{-u_{jiot}\}$, then the actual output, Y_{jiot} can be written as $Y_{jiot} = Y^*_{jiot}\exp\{-u_{jiot}\}$, or equivalently:

$$Y_{jiot} = f(K_{jiot}, L_{jiot}, t; \beta)\exp\{-u_{jiot}\}\exp\{v_{jiot}\}, \tag{5.5}$$

where $u_{jiot} \geq 0$ is assumed to be i.i.d., with a normal distribution truncated at zero $|N(0, \sigma_u^2)|$ and independent from the noise term, v_{jiot}.[20]

To operationalize Eq. (5.5), we test different functional forms, and find that a translog production function is preferred. Thus, the stochastic frontier production specification function becomes:

$$\begin{aligned}\ln Y_{jiot} = {} & \beta_i + \beta_1 \ln K_{jiot} + \beta_2 \ln L_{jiot} + \tfrac{1}{2}\beta_{11} \ln K^2_{jiot} \\ & + \tfrac{1}{2}\beta_{22} \ln L^2_{jiot} + \beta_{12} \ln K_{jiot} \ln L_{jiot} + \gamma_t D_t \\ & + \delta_1 \ln K_{jiot} D_t + \delta_2 \ln L_{jiot} D_t + \alpha X + v_{jiot} - u_{jiot},\end{aligned} \tag{5.6}$$

where β_i are firm-specific fixed effects, and X is a vector of country dummies. We include a set of time dummies D—which also interact with the vectors K and L—to encapsulate a general index of technical changes (Baltagi and Griffin 1988). We estimate Eq. (5.6) using a true fixed effects model, following Greene (2007). In this model, the fixed effects β_i are allowed to be correlated with other parameters, but are truly independent of the inefficiency and the error term.

Recent studies have shown that industries employ different technologies, and are therefore likely to be characterized by different production frontiers (Bos et al. 2010). Imposing a common frontier across industries can create biased estimates of the true underlying technology. Moreover, omitted technological differences may be wrongly labeled as inefficiency (Orea and Kumbhakar 2004). We account for the heterogeneity in production technology by estimating a separate frontier for each of the 18 industries, and including country dummies. In other words, we assume technology is industry-specific, with (limited) country-level variation. As a result, we obtain efficiency and economies of scale for each firm that reflects the distance to an industry-specific technology.

[20]When estimating Eq. (5.5), we obtain the composite residual $\exp\{v_{jiot}\}=\exp\{-u_{jiot}\}\exp\{v_{jiot}\}$. Its components, $\exp\{-u_{jiot}\}$ and $\exp\{v_{jiot}\}$, are identified by the λ ($=\sigma_u/\sigma_v$) for which the likelihood is maximized (for an overview, see Coelli and Battese 2005).

Two final aspects are worth noting regarding our approach. First, the production frontier represents a set of maximum outputs for a range of input vectors. It is defined by the observations from a number of firms in a specific industry at each time period, in contrast to the conventional approach of assuming that the leading firm constitutes the frontier (Cameron et al. 2005). Second, our approach treats the frontier as stochastic through the inclusion of the error term u_{jiot}, which accommodates noise in the data and therefore allows for statistical inference. In this respect, it differs fundamentally from other non-parametric frontier analysis.[21]

After obtaining the estimated parameters of frontier, the efficiency score for each $jiot$ is computed as the ratio of actual over maximum output, $\exp\{-u_{jiot}\} = \frac{Y_{jiot}}{Y^*_{jiot}}$, where $(0 \leqslant \exp\{-u_{jiot}\} \leqslant 1$ and $\exp\{-u_{jiot}\} = 1$ implies full efficiency.

The return to scale of each firm j in industry i in country o at time t is computed by taking the derivative of the production function with respect to K and L in Eq. (5.6) as follows:

$$scale_{jiot} = \underbrace{\beta_1 + \beta_{11} \ln K_{jiot} + \beta_{12} \ln L_{jiot} + \delta_1 D_t}_{\frac{\partial lnY_{jiot}}{\partial lnK_{jiot}}} + \underbrace{\beta_2 + \beta_{22} \ln L_{jiot} + \beta_{12} \ln K_{jiot} + \delta_2 D_t}_{\frac{\partial lnY_{jiot}}{\partial lnL_{jiot}}} . \quad (5.7)$$

If $scale_{jiot}$ is equal to one, the production of the firm is subject to constant returns to scale, referring to a situation where the output change is proportional to the change in all inputs. If the value is larger (smaller) than one, this indicates increasing (decreasing) return to scale, where output increases by more (less) than that proportional change in inputs.

Data and Variables

The AMADEUS Database

We take the core data used in our analysis from the AMADEUS database. This is a firm-level panel created by the Bureau Van Dijk Electronic Publishing (BvD), which collects standardized commercial data from 50 regional information providers (IPs)

[21] Comprehensive reviews of frontier approaches can be found in Kumbhakar and Lovell (2003), and Coelli and Battese (2005).

across Europe. The AMADEUS 2007 edition, for example, covers more than ten million private and public firms in 44 European countries.[22] It not only contains detailed information about the profile of companies, such as legal status, year of incorporation, activity code, etc., but also includes financial information on standard balance sheet and income statement items. The AMADEUS database comprises all sectors with the exception of the financial sector and consists of observations for up to 10 years per firm, although the coverage varies by industry and country.[23] The coverage improves significantly over time.

The AMADEUS database has several important advantages, which make it especially well suited to our analysis (Gomez-Salvador et al. 2004). First, the data collection process is fairly homogeneous, ensuring the comparability of results across industries and countries. This overcomes the drawbacks of other cross-country firm panels which are typically constructed using different sources of data (administrative vs. survey), various units of measurement (firm vs. establishment), inconsistent inclusion criteria (large firms vs. small firms), and uneven sector coverage (manufacturing vs. service) and periods of observation (cross-section vs. panel). Secondly, AMADEUS covers a large proportion of privately held firms, which account for more than 99.5% of the total number of firms in the 2007 edition. Previous firm samples which only cover public/large firms are far from representative and may have yielded misleading conclusions regarding the overall behavior of firms. Therefore, the availability of data on private firms in AMADEUS provides a better representation of the entire population of firms, which is the key to measuring the intra-industry dispersion in a more accurate manner. Lastly, one unique advantage of our sample is that the "attrition bias" has been corrected by using different editions of the AMADEUS database. We are able to retrieve data on firms that no longer exist in the current version, but did exist in the previous editions.

Sample Selection

In constructing the sample for our analysis, we face a number of considerations. First, having a sufficiently complete set of firms within each industry-country combination is crucial in order to derive an accurate measure of dispersion. Additionally, the choice of industry aggregation needs to be compatible with other industry data, in particular industry-level trade and production data. A third consideration lies

[22]The AMADEUS database is supplied at three levels of coverage, depending on the number of firms included, namely the Top 250,000 module, the Top 1.5 million module, and the All-companies module. We use the All-companies module, which is the most complete version.

[23]Information on banks and insurance companies are not included in the AMADEUS database. They are presented in two separated databases, i.e., BankScope and ISIS, provided also by BvD.

in the fact that we require a relatively broad set of countries to ensure sufficient variations in industry structural patterns. Last but not least, a longer time span is preferred to show the effects of trade integration as this is a complex process that requires time to develop.

Our main source is the 2007 edition of AMADEUS, which is the latest edition at our disposal. We limit our sample to manufacturing firms, based on the premise that manufacturing industries are more involved in trade and more responsive to trade liberalization. We aggregate these firms into 18 industries. We follow additional steps to complete our sample. We correct for attrition bias by obtaining data from previous editions of AMADEUS on exiting firms that no longer exist in the current edition. For example, we compare the 2007 edition with the 2006 edition of AMADEUS and detect the firms which are included in the 2006 edition, but no longer in the 2007 edition. We then retrieve data on those firms from the 2006 edition. Similarly, data on those firms that exited in 2006, but remained active in 2005 are extracted from the 2005 edition. The same procedure is repeated between three other pairs, i.e., the 2005 and 2004 editions, the 2004 and 2003 editions, and the 2003 and 2002 editions.[24] Following this step, we have assembled the data on a series of exiting firms that are not overlapping with those in 2007 edition. The combination of the main source, together with these non-overlapping firms ensures the unique coverage of our sample.[25] We find that on average, the exit rate is between 5 to 10% on an annual basis.[26]

We apply several exclusion restrictions to our sample. First, our frontier estimation requires firms to have some basic information in their annual accounts. Specifically, we drop all firm-year observations where input (capital, labor) and/or output (value added) information is missing. The reasons for dropping these non-reporting firms are twofold (Klapper et al. 2006). One, there could be country differences in the criteria for including firms with no account information. The other reason is that this restriction eliminates any "phantom" firms established for tax

[24]The 2002 edition is the earliest edition in which AMADEUS substantially improves its coverage by including private firms; editions prior to 2002 only covered listed firms. As the coverage of firms increases from 200,000 in the 2001 edition to 3,500,000 in the 2002 edition, this makes prior data less comparable in this respect.

[25]In order to maximize the time-series dimension, we also retrieve some observations in 1994, 1995 and 1996 from the 2004, 2005, and 2006 editions, respectively. Since company accounts are typically published annually at the end of March, the AMADUES 2007 edition records data for the 10 years from 1997 to 2006. Thus, we extract additional data going back to 1996 from the 2006 edition, and similarly, to 1995 from the 2005 edition and 1994 from the 2004 edition. However, the quality of the early data is rather poor and we decide to begin our sample in 1997.

[26]Arguably, the AMADEUS database may be subject to selection bias as well. Since it is not census data, there is no legal commitment for firms to provide information. Firms can self-select into the sample or stay out, as, for example, in the case of small and medium sized German firms which are not legally required to disclose (Gomez-Salvador et al. 2004). However this bias appears to be less severe, as coverage of most firms in Europe is provided—i.e., 95% guaranteed by the IPs.

or other purposes. Secondly, to minimize measurement error in the data, we also drop firms where the absolute value of either the output or the input growth rate is above 500% over the entire sample period. Next, we exclude consolidated accounts if firms also have unconsolidated accounts, to avoid double counting.[27] After data cleaning, our final sample consists of 390,350 firms in 14 countries over the 1997–2006 period.

Variable Definitions

To estimate the stochastic frontier, we require data on firm output (Y), capital (K), and labor (L) from the AMADEUS database. We take gross value added as the preferred measure of firm output.[28] Since value added is measured in local currency units at current prices, we apply an industry-level value added deflator extracted from the EU KLEMS database and convert each series to constant prices based on the year 1995. For cross-country comparisons, we then use purchasing-power parity (PPP) exchange rates, taken from the Penn World Table, Version 6.3 (PWT 6.3) to convert the local currency measures into 1996 international PPP dollars.

We construct capital stocks using data on tangible fixed assets in local currency at current prices. Next, we use a gross fixed capital formation (GFCF) deflator, extracted from the EU KLEMS and AMECO database, and a PPP exchange rate, taken from PWT 6.3, to convert each series.[29] We take the number of employees as the labor input.

[27] The accounting practice in AMADEUS is classified into six types. (1) Consolidated accounts C1—accounts of the company headquarters of a group, aggregating all companies belonging to the group (affiliates, subsidiaries, etc.), where the company headquarters has no unconsolidated account. (2) Consolidated accounts C2—accounts of the company headquarters of a group, aggregating all companies belonging to the group (affiliates, subsidiaries, etc.), where the company headquarters does have an unconsolidated account. (3) Unconsolidated accounts U1—accounts of a company with no consolidated accounts. (4) Unconsolidated accounts U2—accounts of a company which does have a consolidated account. (5) Limited number of financial items LF—accounts of a company with only a limited number of information/variables included. (6) No financial items at all NF—accounts of a company with no financial items/variables included. Therefore, we drop firms with the type C2.

[28] Value added is defined as total staff costs plus depreciation plus profit before tax. We impute some missing value-added data using this formula. We have also calculated an alternative measure of value added without depreciation. However, the two measures are highly correlated (correlation coefficient 0.88) and results using both measures are quantitatively similar.

[29] We use the industry-level GFCF deflator from the EU KLEMS database whenever it is available. Otherwise, we employ the country-level GFCF deflator from the AMECO database instead.

Robustness Checks

Our robustness tests are included in Table 7 below.

Table 7 Robustness tests

Panel A: normalized industry value added as the dependent variable

	Natural openness				Trade integration			
	High-potential		Low-potential		High-potential		Low-potential	
Kernel								
T	0.871	(0.240)***	−0.089	(0.074)	0.513	(0.285)*	−0.252	(0.065)***
T^2	−0.098	(0.019)***	−0.023	(0.008)**	−0.159	(0.443)	0.116	(0.052)**
Output per worker	0.237	(0.069)***	0.226	(0.022)***	0.395	(0.069)***	0.283	(0.023)***
Constant	−0.005	(0.015)	0.000	(0.016)	0.004	(0.015)	0.000	(0.002)
Sorting								
Scale dispersion	8.995	(7.629)	Reference		2.718	(8.316)	Reference	
Efficiency dispersion	5.260	(1.228)***	Reference		5.334	(1.210) ***	Reference	
Initial scale level	10.256	(0.999)***	Reference		10.111	(0.987)***	Reference	
Initial efficiency level	−1.062	(1.869)	Reference		−0.544	(1.852)	Reference	
Constant	−27.643	(7.816)***	Reference		−21.529	(8.379)**	Reference	
Prior class probability	0.129		0.871		0.123		0.877	

Panel B: 10/90 ratio as the dispersion measure

	Natural openness				Trade integration			
	High-potential		Low-potential		High-potential		Low-potential	
Kernel								
T	0.716	(0.222)***	−0.158	(0.066)**	0.389	(0.320)	−0.260	(0.061)***
T^2	−0.087	(0.018)***	−0.017	(0.007)**	−0.438	(0.576)	0.077	(0.048)
Output per worker	0.247	(0.067)***	0.216	(0.021)***	0.405	(0.071)***	0.288	(0.014)***
Constant	0.001	(0.016)	0.000	(0.016)	0.008	(0.017)	−0.000	(0.002)
Sorting								
Scale dispersion	1.924	(4.721)	Reference		0.321	(5.347)	Reference	
Efficiency dispersion	0.881	(0.381)**	Reference		0.844	(0.444) **	Reference	
Initial scale level	13.675	(1.351)***	Reference		14.678	(1.454)***	Reference	

(continued)

Table 7 (continued)

Panel C: standard deviation as the dispersion measure								
	Natural openness				Trade integration			
	High-potential		Low-potential		High-potential		Low-potential	
Initial efficiency level	−3.189	(1.871)**	Reference		−2.558	(2.536)	Reference	
Constant	−18.078	(5.341)***	Reference		−18.140	(5.974)***	Reference	
Prior class probability	0.091		0.909		0.072		0.928	
Kernel								
T	0.749	(0.235)***	−0.148	(0.066)**	0.411	(0.335)	−0.281	(0.062)***
T^2	−0.089	(0.019)***	−0.018	(0.007)**	−0.489	(0.613)	0.065	(0.048)
Output per worker	0.250	(0.069)***	0.213	(0.020)***	0.409	(0.073)***	0.284	(0.021)***
Constant	0.000	(0.001)	0.000	(0.001)	0.006	(0.017)	0.000	(0.000)
Sorting								
Scale dispersion	19.047	(12.971)	Reference		18.461	(15.325)	Reference	
Efficiency dispersion	−3.408	(2.799)	Reference		−4.126	(3.073) ***	Reference	
Initial scale level	13.164	(1.328)***	Reference		14.820	(1.515)***	Reference	
Initial efficiency level	−3.148	(1.910)*	Reference		−2.084	(2.604)	Reference	
Constant	−14.528	(1.987)***	Reference		17.346	(2.675)***	Reference	
Prior class probability	0.080		0.920		0.061		0.939	

Standard errors in parentheses; significance at the 10/5/1% level (*/**/***); Natural openness based on Di Giovanni and Levchenko (2009); Trade integration based on Chen and Novy (2011); HP is high-potential industry, LP is low-potential industry

Acknowledgments We thank participants at the 2013 European Workshop on Efficiency and Productivity Analysis in Helsinki (Finland), the Netherlands Economists Day 2012 (The Netherlands), the 2012 European Trade Study Group Conference in Leuven (Belgium), the 2011 European Workshop on Efficiency and Productivity Analysis in Verona (Italy), the 2010 Asia-Pacific Productivity Conference in Taipei (Taiwan), and the 2010 North American Productivity Workshop in Houston (USA) for their valuable comments. We also thank seminar participants at Copenhagen University, the European Bank for Reconstruction and Development, the University of Cyprus, Groningen University, UNU Merit at Maastricht University, and Utrecht University as well as Victoria Purice for most helpful comments. An earlier working paper version of this paper appeared as a Central Bank of Cyprus workshop paper on February 13, 2013, after our presentation at the joint seminar series of the University of Cyprus and the Central Bank of Cyprus. We thank Caroline

Studdert for excellent editorial services. Lu Zhang gratefully acknowledges the financial support from the Netherlands Organization for Scientific Research (NWO). The usual disclaimer applies.

References

Aigner, D., Lovell, C. A. K., & Schmidt, P. (1977). Formulation and estimation of stochastic frontier production function models. *Journal of Econometrics, 6*(1), 21–37.

Anderson, J. E., & van Wincoop, E. (2003). Gravity with gravitas: A solution to the border puzzle. *American Economic Review, 93*(1), 170–192.

Anderson, J. E., & van Wincoop, E. (2004). Trade costs. *Journal of Economic Literature, 42*(3), 691–751.

Balassa, B. (1965). Trade liberalisation and "revealed" comparative advantage. *The Manchester School, 33*(2), 99–123.

Baldwin, R., & Taglioni, D. (2006). *Gravity for dummies and dummies for gravity equations*. CEPR Discussion Papers 5850, CEPR.

Baltagi, B. H., & Griffin, J. M. (1988). A general index of technical change. *Journal of Political Economy, 96*(1), 20–41.

Baqaee, D. R., & Farhi, E. (2017). *Productivity and misallocation in general equilibrium*. Working Paper 24007, National Bureau of Economic Research.

Bartelsman, E., Haltiwanger, J., & Scarpetta, S. (2013). Cross-country differences in productivity: The role of allocation and selection. *American Economic Review, 103*(1), 305–34.

Battese, G. E., & Corra, G. S. (1977). Estimation of a production frontier model: With application to the pastoral zone of eastern Australia. *Australian Journal of Agricultural Economics, 21*(3), 169–179.

Beine, M., & Coulombe, S. (2007). Economic integration and the diversification of regional exports: Evidence from the Canadian-U.S. free trade agreement. *Journal of Economic Geography, 7*(1), 93–111.

Bernard, A. B., Jensen, J. B., & Schott, P. K. (2006). Survival of the best fit: Exposure to low-wage countries and the (uneven) growth of U.S. manufacturing plants. *Journal of International Economics, 68*(1), 219–237.

Bhattacharya, D., Guner, N., & Ventura, G. (2013). Distortions, endogenous managerial skills and productivity differences. *Review of Economic Dynamics, 16*(1), 11–25.

Bos, J., Economidou, C., & Koetter, M. (2010). Technology clubs, R&D and growth patterns: Evidence from EU manufacturing. *European Economic Review, 54*(1), 60–79.

Brambor, T., Clark, W., & Gold, M. (2006). Understanding interaction models: Improving empirical analyses. *Political Analysis, 14*(1), 64–81.

Brülhart, M. (2001). Growing alike or growing apart? Industrial specialization of EU countries. In C. Wyplosz (Ed.), *The impact of EMU on Europe and the developing countries* (pp. 1–35). Oxford: Oxford University Press.

Calligaris, S., Gatto, M. D., Hassan, F., Ottaviano, G. I., & Schivardi, F. (2017). *The Productivity puzzle and misallocation: An Italian perspective*. Working Paper CRENoS 201710, Centre for North South Economic Research, University of Cagliari and Sassari, Sardinia.

Cameron, G., Proudman, J., & Redding, S. (2005). Technological convergence, R&D, trade and productivity growth. *European Economic Review, 49*(3), 775–807.

Chaney, T. (2008). Distorted gravity: The intensive and extensive margins of international trade. *American Economic Review, 98*(4), 1707–1721.

Chen, N., & Novy, D. (2011). Gravity, trade integration, and heterogeneity across industries. *Journal of International Economics, 85*(2), 206–221.

Chor, D. (2010). Unpacking sources of comparative advantage: A quantitative approach. *Journal of International Economics, 82*(2), 152–167.

Coelli, T., & Battese, G. (2005). *An introduction to efficiency analysis* (2nd ed.). New York: Springer.

Di Giovanni, J., & Levchenko, A. A. (2009). Trade openness and volatility. *The Review of Economics and Statistics, 91*(3), 558–585.

Dornbusch, R., Fischer, S., & Samuelson, P. A. (1977). Comparative advantage, trade, and payments in a Ricardian model with a continuum of goods. *The American Economic Review, 67*(5), 823–839.

Eslava, M., Haltiwanger, J. C., Kugler, A. D., & Kugler, M. (2009). *Trade reforms and market selection: Evidence from manufacturing plants in Colombia.* NBER Working Papers, No. 14935.

Foster, L., Haltiwanger, J., & Syverson, C. (2008). Reallocation, firm turnover, and efficiency: Selection on productivity or profitability? *The American Economic Review, 98*(1), 394–425.

Frankel, J. A., & Romer, D. (1999). Does trade cause growth? *American Economic Review, 89*(3), 379–399.

Fujita, M., Krugman, P., & Venables, A. J. (2001). *The spatial economy: Cities, regions, and international trade.* Cambridge: The MIT Press.

Gabler, A., & Poschke, M. (2013). Experimentation by firms, distortions, and aggregate productivity. *Review of Economic Dynamics, 16*(1), 26–38.

Glick, R., & Rose, A. K. (2002). Does a currency union affect trade? The time-series evidence. *European Economic Review, 46*(6), 1125–1151.

Gomez-Salvador, R., Messina, J., & Vallanti, G. (2004). Gross job flows and institutions in Europe. *Labour Economics, 11*(4), 469–485.

Greene, W. (2007). LIMDEP, Version 9.0: Reference Guide. Econometric Software.

Greene, W. H. (2005). Reconsidering heterogeneity in panel data estimators of the stochastic frontier model. *Journal of Econometrics, 126*(2), 269–303.

Hsieh, C.-T., & Klenow, P. J. (2009). Misallocation and manufacturing TFP in China and India. *The Quarterly Journal of Economics, 124*(4), 1403–1448.

Imbs, J. (2004). Trade, finance, specialization, and synchronization. *The Review of Economics and Statistics, 86*(3), 723–734.

Imbs, J., & Mejean, I. (2009). *Elasticity optimism.* CEPR Discussion Papers 7177, CEPR.

Jones, C. I. (2013). *Misallocation, economic growth, and input–Output economics.* Econometric Society Monographs (Vol. 2, pp. 419–456). Cambridge: Cambridge University Press.

Klapper, L., Laeven, L., & Rajan, R. (2006). Entry regulation as a barrier to entrepreneurship. *Journal of Financial Economics, 82*(3), 591–629.

Krugman, P. (1979). Increasing returns, monopolistic competition, and international trade. *Journal of International Economics, 9*(4), 469–479.

Krugman, P. (1980). Scale economies, product differentiation, and the pattern of trade. *The American Economic Review, 70*(5), 950–959.

Krugman, P. (1991). Increasing returns and economic geography. *Journal of Political Economy, 99*(3), 483–499.

Kumbhakar, S., & Lovell, C. K. (2003). *Stochastic frontier analysis.* Cambridge: Cambridge University Press.

Longhi, S., Nijkamp, P., & Traistaru, I. (2003). *Determinants of manufacturing location in EU accession countries.* European Regional Science Association Conference Papers, 310.

López, E., & Sánchez, R. (2005). Specialization and openness to foreign trade in the European Union. *Applied Economics Letters, 12*(13), 805–810.

Meeusen, W., & Broeck, J. V. D. (1977). Efficiency estimation from Cobb-Douglas production functions with composed error. *International Economic Review, 18*(2), 435–444.

Melitz, M. J. (2003). The impact of trade on intra-industry reallocations and aggregate industry productivity. *Econometrica, 71*(6), 1695–1725.

Midelfart-Knarvik, K. H., Overman, H. G., & Redding, S. J. (2000). The location of European industry. *European Commission Working Paper, 142*, 1–68.

Ohlin, B. (1933). *Interregional and international trade.* Cambridge: Harvard University Press.

Olley, G. S., & Pakes, A. (1996). The dynamics of productivity in the telecommunications equipment industry. *Econometrica, 64*(6), 1263–97.

Orea, L., & Kumbhakar, S. C. (2004). Efficiency measurement using a latent class stochastic frontier model. *Empirical Economics, 29*(1), 169–183.

Pavcnik, N. (2002). Trade liberalization, exit, and productivity improvement: Evidence from Chilean plants. *Review of Economic Studies, 69*(1), 245–76.

Redding, S. (2002). Specialization dynamics. *Journal of International Economics, 58*(2), 299–334.

Restuccia, D., & Rogerson, R. (2008). Policy distortions and aggregate productivity with heterogeneous establishments. *Review of Economic Dynamics, 11*(4), 707–720.

Restuccia, D., & Rogerson, R. (2013). Misallocation and productivity. *Review of Economic Dynamics, 16*(1), 1–10.

Ricardo, D. (1817). *On the principles of political economy and taxation*. London: John Murray.

Riet, A. V., Ernst, E., Madaschi, C., Orlandi, F., Rivera, A. S., Robert, B., et al. (2004). Sectoral specialisation in the EU a macroeconomic perspective. *ECB Occasional Paper Series, 19*, 1–59.

Rose, A. K., Lockwood, B., & Quah, D. (2000). One money, one market: The effect of common currencies on trade. *Economic Policy, 15*(30), 7–45.

Sachs, J. D., & Warner, A. (1995). Economic reform and the process of global integration. *Brookings Papers on Economic Activity, 26*(1), 1–118.

Sapir, A. (1996). The effects of Europe's internal market program on production and trade: A first assessment. *Review of World Economics (Weltwirtschaftliches Archiv), 132*(3), 457–475.

Schumpeter, J. (1942). *Capitalism, socialism and democracy*. New York: Harper and Row.

Segerstrom, P. S., & Sugita, Y. (2015). The impact of trade liberalization on industrial productivity. *Journal of the European Economic Association, 13*(6), 1167–1179.

Solow, R. (1957). Technical change and the aggregate production function. *Review of Economic and Statistics, 39*(3), 312–320.

Subramanian, A., & Wei, S.-J. (2007). The WTO promotes trade, strongly but unevenly. *Journal of International Economics, 72*(1), 151–175.

Trefler, D. (2004). The long and short of the Canadian-U.S. free trade agreement. *American Economic Review, 94*(4), 870–895.

Tybout, J. R. (2000). Manufacturing firms in developing countries: How well do they do, and why? *Journal of Economic Literature, 38*(1), 11–44.

Tybout, J. R., & Westbrook, M. D. (1995). Trade liberalization and the dimensions of efficiency change in Mexican manufacturing industries. *Journal of International Economics, 39*(1–2), 53–78.

Venables, A. J. (1996). Equilibrium locations of vertically linked industries. *International Economic Review, 37*(2), 341–359.

Wacziarg, R., & Wallack, J. S. (2004). Trade liberalization and intersectoral labor movements. *Journal of International Economics, 64*(2), 411–439.

Wacziarg, R., & Welch, K. H. (2008). Trade liberalization and growth: New evidence. *World Bank Economic Review, 22*(2), 187–231.

Expansionary Investment Activities: Assessing Equipment and Buildings in Productivity

Jasper Brinkerink, Andrea Chegut, and Wilko Letterie

Abstract We study firm-level expansionary investment activities in *both* equipment *and* buildings—the so-called investment spikes. Our identification strategy decomposes firm investment spikes into three streams: a spike in equipment only, buildings only, or a simultaneous spike. Empirically, we find that the timing and size of investment in equipment and buildings are not independent. Firms conducting a simultaneous spike enhance firm scale more than in the case of a spike in equipment or buildings alone. Employment growth occurs when a firm builds structures. Investment in equipment affects the optimal input mix and high productivity in equipment and buildings provides investment timing signals. In low-tech sectors firm production growth depends on investment in buildings. In contrast, a necessary condition for firms in high-tech sectors to grow their production is investment in equipment.

Keywords Investment spikes · Equipment · Buildings · Interrelation · Scale · Productivity · Input mix · Efficiency · Low- and high-tech · Labour intensity

1 Introduction

Buildings are an important production factor; they house employees and shield equipment. In this chapter we investigate whether investment in structures drives

J. Brinkerink
Free University of Bozen-Bolzano, Faculty of Economics and Management, Centre for Family Business Management, Bolzano, Italy

A. Chegut
Massachusetts Institute of Technology, Center for Real Estate, Cambridge, MA, USA

W. Letterie (✉)
Maastricht University, School of Business and Economics, Department of Organization and Strategy, Maastricht, The Netherlands
e-mail: w.letterie@maastrichtuniversity.nl

C. F. Parmeter, R. C. Sickles (eds.), *Advances in Efficiency and Productivity Analysis*, Springer Proceedings in Business and Economics,
https://doi.org/10.1007/978-3-030-47106-4_13

employment, production technology, and firm capacity in manufacturing industries, and also distinguish industries by research and labour intensity. Our empirical results inform investment in buildings and equipment is interrelated—the timing and size of investment in equipment and buildings are not independent phenomena. We also find that adding investments in buildings to a firm's decision set improves understanding of key firm-level performance and production metrics. Our conclusion is that to properly understand firm-level production processes one should incorporate investment in buildings.

Capital adjustment patterns are lumpy. Generally, annual firm investment activity is low until there is an investment trigger. Then, evidence suggests, firms experience investment spikes (Doms and Dunne 1998; Cooper et al. 1999; Caballero et al. 1995). This investment pattern holds internationally (Nilsen and Schiantarelli 2003; Letterie and Pfann 2007) and for expansionary investment and capital replacement (Letterie et al. 2010). Economically, these irregular investment patterns have implications for understanding the dynamic behaviour of micro-level investment decisions by firms and may have implications for macroeconomic activity (Caballero et al. 1995; Caballero 1999; Caballero and Engel 1999; Bachmann et al. 2013) or not (Thomas 2002).

A nascent literature investigates investment in equipment to understand its triggers and economic productivity after investment spikes occur. Empirical analysis is consistent with the notion of firm expansion. At the time of an investment burst, both output and the number of employees increase (Sakellaris 2004; Nilsen et al. 2009). Firms also invest in the latest technologies incorporated in equipment to stave off economic obsolescence (Goolsbee 1998), to adopt changes in production technology (Klassen and Whybark 1999), or derive a new optimal mix between labour and capital (Acemoglu 2015; Dunne et al. 1989; Hémous and Olsen 2013). Moreover, subsequent to the investment spike, firms may anticipate improved productivity, but quite some economists have found that there is no improvement in labour productivity (Power 1998; Sakellaris 2004; Nilsen et al. 2009). This phenomenon may point at a "missing link" between technology, investment, and productivity (Power 1998).

We have learned that microeconomic models of firm behaviour need to incorporate fixed adjustment costs, investment irreversibility, and/or indivisibilities to be able to replicate the behaviour observed in firm investment data (Cooper and Haltiwanger 2006; Bloom 2009; Asphjell et al. 2014). In this way, these studies inform the extensive margin in microeconomic investment. A caveat of this area of research is the sole focus on identifying investment in capital equipment, but not other components of capital that are factors of production.

This chapter explores the consequences of firm-level investment spikes in productive capital, like equipment, *and* non-productive capital, like buildings. Hence, in our study we also investigate the impact of investment spikes concerning structures. By doing that, we (1) separate expansionary investment from that of replacement—which further calibrates the extensive margin; (2) identify distinct investment profiles of the firm—in buildings, equipment, or a simultaneous spike of both. By broadening the examination of how the composition of firms' investment spikes (equipment, buildings, and both) affects the scale of production and employment, productivity, the input mix, and operational efficiency we aim to contribute to the goals of the productivity literature (Sickles and Zelenyuk 2019) and the role of buildings in microeconomics.

To disentangle the drivers and implications of firms' investment composition, we use yearly data from Statistics Netherlands (CBS) concerning 652 firms for the 2000–2008 period. We investigate firm-level investment decisions and production statistics for manufacturing industries in the Netherlands. Firm-level data allows us to identify when an investment spike in either equipment or buildings occurs and when a simultaneous spike occurs in both buildings and equipment. Our empirical strategy reveals individual firm's microeconomic activity before and after an episode of intense capital adjustment. To obtain more detailed insight we follow Robertson et al. (2009) and Czarnitzki and Thorwarth (2012) in accounting for differences across high- and low-tech sectors. Similar to Ramirez et al. (2005), we assess firms by industry labour intensity to understand variation in the cross-section by low, medium and high labour intensity.

Identifying investment spikes in buildings and equipment has implications for the productivity literature. First, the extensive margin of firm investment activity can be decomposed further. We observe that 14% of the datapoints concern spikes related to capital equipment expansion. However, single equipment investment spikes, not coinciding with spikes in buildings, are observed in 11% of the observations. Thus, neglecting simultaneity of spikes in buildings and equipment represents inadequately the breadth of the extensive margin. In fact, we show that about 20% of the equipment spikes, i.e. those that concur with building spikes, have a very different character according to our empirical results.

Second, the decomposition further calibrates the intensive margin. A measure of the investment size is more informative when including both expenditures on buildings and equipment. Our empirical results document that firms who signal expansion through simultaneous investment spikes in both buildings and equipment experience a higher post investment expansion in production and number of workers than firms that experience a spike in either equipment or buildings only. However, the results also reveal that large investments do not improve firm-level productivity. Instead high productivity acts as a signal of when to invest. What we observe is that before an investment takes place firm productivity is high and afterwards it decreases. Our results also suggest investment in equipment tends to increase the employee wage rate at a firm on average; based on this result we infer that firms buying new machinery display an increase in the skilled worker ratio. Likewise we deduce firms investing in structures hire more unskilled workers. Furthermore, when firms invest in equipment, the labour intensity decreases as well. These latter findings suggest that capital investments also affect the production technology employed by the firm.

Finally, our empirical study highlights that production processes are fundamentally different across industry sectors. Firms in high-tech sectors rely more on investment in equipment to be able to grow, whereas companies in low-tech sectors need investment in buildings to be able to expand.

The paper proceeds with providing a theoretical grounding in Sect. 2. Next, Sect. 3 describes the data isolating details on firm-level panel data, our investment spike identification strategy. We outline our methodology including our model of investment spikes and estimation strategy in Sect. 4. In Sect. 5, we report empirical results and in Sect. 6 an industrial cluster analysis. Finally, we discuss our findings in relation to the investment literature in Sect. 7.

2 Theoretical Grounding

Our analysis is based on the notion of investment spikes. Spikes represent large capital expenditures. We aim to identify these as they reflect major retooling or expansionary efforts of a firm. In Appendix 2, we show under which conditions lumpy investments take place. If the evolution of input factors is characterized by the occurrence of spikes, we expect that the production level of the firm will increase substantially upon large investment, especially if more types of capital goods are adjusted at the same time. A CES production technology, i.e.

$$Y_t = \phi_t L_t^{\alpha} \left(a \left(K_t^B \right)^{\rho} + (1-a) \left(K_t^E \right)^{\rho} \right)^{\beta/\rho}, \quad (1)$$

yields this prediction. We also expect that if investment in equipment and stuctures is interrelated and if at least one of them is subject to fixed adjustment costs, other input factors will display a lumpy adjustment pattern as well (Abel and Eberly 1998). It is likely that if the firm buys capital, the number of workers will increase. This can be seen as follows. Let $p_t = \varphi_t (Y_t)^{-1/\varepsilon}$ denote an isoelastic demand function where$\varepsilon > 1$ and the wage is given by w_t. Assuming labour is a flexible input factor, the optimal number of employees L_t is determined by maximizing $p_t Y_t - w_t L_t$. The first-order condition is given by:

$$\varphi_t \alpha \left(\frac{\varepsilon - 1}{\varepsilon} \right) L_t^{\frac{\varepsilon(\alpha-1)-\alpha}{\varepsilon}} \left(\phi_t \left(a \left(K_t^B \right)^{\rho} + (1-a) \left(K_t^E \right)^{\rho} \right)^{\beta/\rho} \right)^{1-\frac{1}{\varepsilon}} = w_t \quad (2)$$

As $\varepsilon(\alpha - 1) - \alpha < 0$ with higher stocks of capital, the number of workers needs to increase as well to restore equality of the first-order condition.

Power (1998) investigated whether investment affects productivity of a firm. When investment embodies more recent technology available in the market one would expect that over time productivity will increase (Jovanovic and Nyarko 1996). There may be a delay in improved productivity, in that firms need to learn about the new technology. Technology specific human capital may be lost when new machines are present. However, results by Abel and Eberly (1998) imply that factor productivity is a signal for a firm of when to invest. If productivity is high, meaning that the level of input (capital) is low relative to the level of output, this signals the firm is running at high capacity and that it may be sensible to start investing. In Appendix 2, we also show that investment in buildings, for instance, is driven by expectations about its future productivity. Hence, investment tends to become more likely if the firm expects higher future productivity. If current productivity is high and also transmits into high future productivity, for instance, due to persistent technology shocks ϕ_t being governed by an autoregressive process, current productivity acts as a signal for a firm of when and how much to invest. Obviously, immediately after investment productivity will be lower. For this reason it may be difficult to investigate investment causing productivity.

We investigate the dynamics of productivity surrounding major investment events at the firm level to determine whether productivity acts as a signal for the firm of when to invest or whether it is possible to see improvements in productivity after investments. Note that our framework discriminating between buildings and equipment is more suitable to do that. We will be able to separate expansionary from replacement investment, assuming that investing in equipment alone represents replacing older with newer technology. In addition, we distentangle operating expenditures in buildings from that of large scale capital expenditures or new development.

Investment may not only affect the scale of a firm's operations or firm productivity. It may also imply production technology changes when new capital enters the firm (Acemoglu, and Restrepo 2020, Acemoglu 2015; Dunne et al. 1989; Hémous and Olsen 2013). For instance, upon investment the parameters of the production function depicted in Eq. (1) may change, which potentially affects the optimal mix of input factors or productivity of input factors. In our study we explore this issue in two different ways. First, we aim to analyse average wage costs. Changes in the average wage signal either changes in the composition of the workforce or changes in labour productivity. Second, we assess how investment types affect capital intensity of firms. The final issue we address in our study is whether major investment episodes affect the cost efficiency experienced by firms.

3 Data Description

Statistics Netherlands (CBS) annually collects data on production statistics and investment figures at the firm level. Specifically, a random selection of all Dutch companies employing less than 50 people is sent questionnaires and all Dutch firms with 50 or more employees receive a survey.[1] We merge the annual data sets on production statistics and investments of the manufacturing sector using a firm specific identifier, resulting in a panel for 2000–2008. Importantly, we aim to capture regular firm investment intensity dynamics and not extreme events like divestments

[1]Detailed information (in Dutch only) on sampling strategies and collection methods of Statistics Netherlands can be retrieved from http://www.cbs.nl/nl-NL/menu/themas/industrie-energie/methoden/dataverzameling/korte-onderzoeksbeschrijvingen/productie-statistiek.htm.

or mergers. To do so, we analyse a balanced set of panel data (cf. Letterie et al. 2004). In this way, the balanced panel conservatively controls for firm entry and exit, major (dis)investment decisions like mergers, acquisitions, bankruptcies, and/or geographic relocations. Moreover, as we want to assess empirical data, imputed observations are deleted. The panel data set isolates investment behaviour for a 9 year period, concerning 652 firms and for a total of 5868 yearly investment observations.[2]

3.1 Identifying Investment Spikes

In line with the literature, we identify an investment spike as the investment ratio of a firm i in year t, $\frac{I_{it}^z}{K_{it}^z}$, that exceeds the median investment ratio of that firm by an investment threshold (Power 1998). An investment spike is identified as follows:

$$S_{it}^z = \begin{cases} 1 \text{ if } \left[\frac{I_{it}^z}{K_{it}^z} > \theta \cdot \underset{\tau}{\text{median}} \left(\frac{I_{it}^z}{K_{i\tau}^z} \right) \text{and} \frac{I_{it}^z}{K_{it}^z} > \delta^z \right] \\ 0 \text{ otherwise} \end{cases}, \tag{3}$$

where I is the financial capital investment, K is the existing physical capital stock of firm i for investment in capital type z. The variable z represents investment in equipment, E, or buildings, B.[3] Importantly, we exogenously define θ as the investment threshold factor. We set the value of $\theta = 1.75$.[4] Based on the latter, if a firm does not invest at all (i.e., $\frac{I_{it}^z}{K_{it}^z} = 0$) in at least 5 out of 9 observed years t, even a miniscule investment in any of the remaining years will classify as an investment spike, since the median investment rate will be 0. To remain conservative, we therefore incorporate a second condition in our investment spike definition. Specifically, the investment rate should also exceed the depreciation ratio for the asset in casu. The depreciation ratio is denoted by δ^z. A strictly positive number for depreciation tends to limit the number of spikes in buildings because of the restriction $\frac{I_{it}^z}{K_{it}^z} > \delta^z$ in the spike definition. For buildings we set depreciation at 0.02, which is fairly conservative for the commercial building sector in Europe (Bokhari and Geltner 2018; Bokhari and Geltner 2014; Chegut et

[2]To prevent potential contamination of our findings by extreme outliers, we decided to remove the 1% largest investment ratios to obtain the final data.

[3]The appendix documents our calculations for assessing the initial physical capital stock K.

[4]We have tested three values for θ, a low (1.75), medium (2.5), and high (3.25) threshold (cf. Power 1998). Our empirical results are robust to the θ value.

al. 2015). Following Letterie and Pfann (2007), who also employ Dutch data for equipment, the depreciation rate is set at 0.05.[5,6]

Investment spikes may signal significant expansion when investment in both buildings and equipment occurs, and may have important consequences in identifying changes in productivity, firm scale, input mix, and operational efficiency. To measure significant expansion, we include a simultaneous investment spike variable:

$$S_{it}^{C} = \begin{cases} 1 \text{ if } \left[S_{it}^{B} = 1 \text{ and } S_{it}^{E} = 1\right] \\ 0 \text{ otherwise} \end{cases} \quad (4)$$

So, the variable S_{it}^{C} identifies the event of a simultaneous spike.

Table 1 documents the descriptive statistics for the investment spikes in buildings, equipment, or simultaneously in both. We have 5868 observations from general firm investments, representing general capital expenditures on equipment and buildings. According to Table 1 our assumptions imply that the frequency of equipment spikes is somewhat larger than that of the spike frequency of buildings. This is consistent with the notion that equipment is a more flexible input factor than structures. In fact, in our dataset firms abstain from investing in buildings far more often than they refrain from investing in equipment. More specifically, we observe 2896 year observations without building investment (i.e., in roughly 49% of the observations) and only 552 year observations without investment in equipment (i.e., about 9%). In case we also add the simultaneous spikes to the spikes in equipment we observe a ratio of about 14% in equipment spikes. Hence, the equipment spike frequency is in line with Power (1998) who observes investment spikes in equipment in 13.6% of her observations for a θ of 1.75.[7]

The average investment rate of firms in buildings is 1.0% and for equipment about 5.9%. The average investment rate in the single spike regimes is 6.8% for buildings and 21.6% for equipment. Noticeably, the average rate of investment increases with the occurrence of a spike. The occurrence of a simultaneous investment spike in buildings and equipment we observe in 3% of the sample. The average conditional investment rates are at their largest across the sample, 7% and

[5]Our depreciation rates for buildings and equipment are consistent with the geometric depreciation approach employed by the US Bureau of Economic Analysis calculating the depreciation rate dividing the declining balance rate by the service life using the information provided by Görzig (2007) and van den Bergen et al. (2009).

[6]Following a helpful suggestion by one of our reviewers we tested the robustness of our results to a higher equipment depreciation rate (12.6%), based on rates used by the US Department of Labor, Bureau of Economic Analysis (see Feenstra et al. 2015, Online Appendix Table 2). Although the coefficients tend to be slightly (though not significantly) larger, in terms of sign and significance the results are stable.

[7]Various studies have also employed an absolute spike definition. For instance, one may define a spike to realize if the investment rate exceeds 0.2. We have a relative spike definition, because the absolute spike definition is not well suited for capturing spasmodic investment bursts that cannot be seen as large in an absolute sense (Power 1998).

Table 1 Descriptive statistics investment rates

Investment rate	Observations	Percentage of total ($N = 5868$)	Mean	Std. dev.
All observations				
Rate buildings	5868	100%	0.010	0.028
Rate equipment	5868	100%	0.059	0.105
Building spikes				
Rate buildings	486	8%	0.068	0.054
Rate equipment	486	8%	0.046	0.066
Equipment spikes				
Rate buildings	651	11%	0.004	0.007
Rate equipment	651	11%	0.216	0.171
Simultaneous spikes				
Rate buildings	155	3%	0.070	0.047
Rate equipment	155	3%	0.240	0.199

This table documents the distribution of investment rates for all observations and spikes in buildings, equipment, and simultaneous. Percentage of total is a frequency measure representing the number of data points observed

24% for buildings and equipment, respectively, when simultaneous investments in both buildings and equipment are identified.

3.2 Identifying Firm Scale, Productivity, and Efficiency

Table 2 documents the mean and standard deviation of firm scale operations, productivity, and operational efficiency under the scenarios of (1) all observations, (2) *no* investment spikes, and in case of (3) single spikes in buildings, (4) single spikes in equipment and (5) simultaneous spikes. The variables used in the empirical analysis as dependent variable have received a natural log transformation.[8]

We measure the scale of firm operations by production output (firm revenues) and the number of workers (full time equivalent, i.e., FTE). For estimation, production has been deflated by the producer price index (PPI) for the industrial sector to reflect *real* production.[9] Conditional on firms making an investment spike, the mean statistics for levels and natural logarithms suggest it is larger firms that experience an investment spike involving equipment (a single equipment spike or a simultaneous spike).

Micro-level productivity is measured by dividing output by the number of workers, the stock of buildings or the stock of equipment. In the cross-section, we

[8]Kernel density plots of all natural log-transformed dependent variables available upon request from the authors show near-perfect normal distributions.

[9]All these indices were retrieved from the Statistics Netherlands (CBS) Statline online datacenter.

Table 2 Firm activity descriptive statistics

	All observations		No spikes		Building spikes		Equipment spikes		Simultaneous spikes	
	$N = 5868$		$N = 4576$		$N = 486$		$N = 651$		$N = 155$	
Dependent variable	Mean	Std. dev.	Mean	Std. dev.	Mean	Std. dev.	Mean	Std. dev.	Mean	Std. dev.
Level										
Production (in 1000's of euro)	58,566	208,175	56,142	215,859	42,925	63,886	83,819	239,011	73,100	94,659
Number of workers (in full time equivalents)	196	236	187	230	199	230	238	253	297	307
Natural logarithms										
Production	10.03	1.29	9.95	1.29	9.97	1.19	10.44	1.21	10.58	1.17
Number of workers	4.79	1.01	4.73	1.01	4.80	1.02	5.09	0.88	5.25	0.97
Productivity labour	5.23	0.63	5.22	0.63	5.18	0.54	5.35	0.68	5.33	0.57
Productivity buildings	1.08	0.43	1.06	0.43	1.14	0.42	1.11	0.44	1.18	0.44
Productivity equipment	0.48	1.50	0.34	1.52	0.31	1.38	1.37	1.09	1.22	1.05
Average wage	3.61	0.25	3.60	0.25	3.58	0.24	3.65	0.25	3.66	0.21
Capital stock buildings/number of workers	4.16	0.65	4.16	0.65	4.04	0.58	4.24	0.67	4.14	0.63
Capital stock equipment/number of workers	4.76	1.42	4.88	1.44	4.87	1.37	3.98	1.05	4.10	1.07
Operational efficiency (total costs/sales)	−0.07	0.10	−0.07	0.10	−0.08	0.09	−0.06	0.10	−0.07	0.08

This table documents the descriptive statistics, the mean and standard deviation, of the dependent variables by level and natural logarithm. The variables are decomposed into all observations, general investments—no spikes, investment spikes in buildings, equipment, and simultaneous spikes see productivity of equipment and labour conditional on observing an equipment spike is high. We also measure features of the overall production technology, or to put it differently, the mix of physical capital and labour. A number of variables provide information in this respect. Our data do not provide a distinction between various types of workers, but to measure the composition of the work force we employ the average real wage per worker of the firm.[10] We expect lower values of this variable to indicate that a firm hires relatively more unskilled employees. We identify the mix between capital and labour by dividing the stock of buildings and the stock of equipment by the number of workers. Table 2 reveals spikes involving equipment are associated with firms paying higher wages on average. The latter observation may hint at relatively more skilled workers employed by firms that increase the stock of equipment (together with structures).

The final variable we analyse accounts for the overall efficiency of the firm: the ratio of total costs to sales. Within the cross-section, the efficiency variable is considerably constant at about −0.07 over the observed period regardless of investment activity. In the next section we depict our methodology by which we can analyse the dynamic consequences of investment activity.[11]

4 Methodology

In our analysis of investment spike consequences for some firm-level metrics—production and employment scale as well as productivity, the input mix, and firm efficiency—as denoted by DV_{it}, we adhere to the following model:

$$DV_{it} = \mu_i + \alpha_i + \sum_{z \in \{B,E,C\}} \beta_z' X_{it}^z + \varepsilon_{it}, \tag{5}$$

where μ_i is a firm specific time-invariant effect.[12] Furthermore, α_t is a year dummy vector (2001–2008, base year is 2000) that captures potential macro-economic shifts. The idiosyncratic error is given by ε_{it}. Based on earlier work by Sakellaris (2004), Letterie et al. (2004), and Nilsen et al. (2009), X_{it}^z is an independent variable vector. It identifies the relative position of the firm in a series of annual observations around investment spikes for both capital types (i.e., buildings where $z = B$ and equipment where $z = E$), as well as for an event named a simultaneous spike, $z = C$, where a simultaneous investment spike in buildings and equipment takes place (i.e.,

[10] Labour costs have been deflated by the wage development index for the industrial sector obtained from Statistics Netherlands (CBS) Statline online datacenter.

[11] A table with correlations of variables used in the empirical analysis is available upon request.

[12] The fixed effect controls for heterogeneity due to, for instance, cross sectional variation in managerial ability, local input market conditions, and strategic interaction at output markets unobserved to the econometrician.

where $S_{it}^{B} = S_{it}^{E} = 1$). It behaves as described below:

$$\left[X_{it}^{B}\right] = \begin{bmatrix} X_{1it}^{B} \\ X_{2it}^{B} \\ X_{3it}^{B} \\ X_{4it}^{B} \\ X_{5it}^{B} \\ X_{6it}^{B} \end{bmatrix} = \begin{bmatrix} \left(1 - S_{it}^{B}\right)\left(1 - S_{it+1}^{B}\right) S_{it+2}^{B}\left(1 - S_{it+2}^{E}\right) \\ \left(1 - S_{it}^{B}\right) S_{it+1}^{B}\left(1 - S_{it+1}^{E}\right) \\ S_{it}^{B}\left(1 - S_{it}^{E}\right) \\ \left(1 - S_{it}^{B}\right) S_{it-1}^{B}\left(1 - S_{it-1}^{E}\right) \\ \left(1 - S_{it}^{B}\right)\left(1 - S_{it-1}^{B}\right) S_{it-2}^{B}\left(1 - S_{it-2}^{E}\right) \\ \left(1 - S_{it}^{B}\right)\left(1 - S_{it-1}^{B}\right)\left(1 - S_{it-2}^{B}\right) \cdot \max\limits_{\tau \le t-3}\left\{S_{i\tau}^{B}\right\} \end{bmatrix} \quad (6)$$

$$\left[X_{it}^{E}\right] = \begin{bmatrix} X_{1it}^{E} \\ X_{2it}^{E} \\ X_{3it}^{E} \\ X_{4it}^{E} \\ X_{5it}^{E} \\ X_{6it}^{E} \end{bmatrix} = \begin{bmatrix} \left(1 - S_{it}^{E}\right)\left(1 - S_{it+1}^{E}\right) S_{it+2}^{E}\left(1 - S_{it+2}^{B}\right) \\ \left(1 - S_{it}^{E}\right) S_{it+1}^{E}\left(1 - S_{it+1}^{B}\right) \\ S_{it}^{E}\left(1 - S_{it}^{B}\right) \\ \left(1 - S_{it}^{E}\right) S_{it-1}^{E}\left(1 - S_{it-1}^{B}\right) \\ \left(1 - S_{it}^{E}\right)\left(1 - S_{it-1}^{E}\right) S_{it-2}^{E}\left(1 - S_{it-2}^{B}\right) \\ \left(1 - S_{it}^{E}\right)\left(1 - S_{it-1}^{E}\right)\left(1 - S_{it-2}^{E}\right) \cdot \max\limits_{\tau \le t-3}\left\{S_{i\tau}^{E}\right\} \end{bmatrix} \quad (7)$$

$$\left[X_{it}^{C}\right] = \begin{bmatrix} X_{1it}^{C} \\ X_{2it}^{C} \\ X_{3it}^{C} \\ X_{4it}^{C} \\ X_{5it}^{C} \\ X_{6it}^{C} \end{bmatrix} = \begin{bmatrix} \left(1 - S_{it}^{C}\right)\left(1 - S_{it+1}^{C}\right) S_{it+2}^{C} \\ \left(1 - S_{it}^{C}\right) S_{it+1}^{C} \\ S_{it}^{C} \\ \left(1 - S_{it}^{C}\right) S_{it-1}^{C} \\ \left(1 - S_{it}^{C}\right)\left(1 - S_{it-1}^{C}\right) S_{it-2}^{C} \\ \left(1 - S_{it}^{C}\right)\left(1 - S_{it-1}^{C}\right)\left(1 - S_{it-2}^{C}\right) \cdot \max\limits_{\tau \le t-3}\left\{S_{i\tau}^{C}\right\} \end{bmatrix} \quad (8)$$

For $z\{B, E\}$ X_{1it}^{z} takes the value 1 if a spike occurs in year $t + 2$ for investment in asset z, but not a spike of the other kind, and no spikes of asset z occur in years t and $t + 1$. In this case, the variable will be 0 otherwise. For $z = C$,X_{1it}^{C} takes the value 1 if a simultaneous spike occurs in year $t + 2$, but not in t and $t + 1$. The variables with the sub-index 2 measure how a dependent variable behaves 1 year before a specific investment spike. X_{2it}^{z}, $z \in \{B, E\}$ takes the value 1 if a spike of the asset z (but not of the other kind of asset) occurs in year $t + 1$, but not in year t; it takes value 0 otherwise. X_{2it}^{C} is 1 if a simultaneous spike occurs in year $t + 1$, but not in year t. To measure changes in the dependent variable at the time of a spike we define variables with the sub-index 3. X_{3it}^{z}, $z \in \{B, E\}$ takes the value 1 if a spike of type z occurs in year t, and there is no spike of the other kind in t and it will be 0 otherwise. If $z = C$, X_{3it}^{C} is 1 if a simultaneous spike occurred in year t. The variables X_{4it}^{z} and X_{5it}^{z} function like X_{2it}^{z} and X_{1it}^{z}, with the difference that it concerns a spike in year $t - 1$ $(t - 2)$ rather than $t + 1$ $(t + 2)$. Hence these variables identify what happens 1 and 2 years after a spike event, respectively. Finally, X_{6it}^{z} takes the value 1 if a spike took place before year $t - 2$, but not in $t - 2$, $t - 1$, and t. This last variable therefore captures the effect of investment spikes that occurred at least 3 years and at most 8 years (i.e., in case a firm experiences an investment spike in 2000 and no subsequent spikes are observed for that firm) in the past.

After performing Hausman tests on all models, all dependent variables DV_{it} except for total costs/sales required a fixed effects specification. For comparability reasons, we therefore decided to apply a fixed effects specification for all dependent variables. The models are estimated using fixed effects, within estimators. Time-invariant variables are omitted from the model due to differencing fixed effects. Hence, we abstract from such variables.[13]

In our estimations of Eq. (3), the regression coefficients β_z obtained for independent variables X_{it}^z, $z \in \{B, E, C\}$ identify what happens to any dependent variable DV_{it} for firms i that find themselves in the situation described by the specific variable, relative to firms that do not. Note that due to the fixed effects specification the estimates compare the within variation of the dependent variable across various types of investment experiences of firms. The dependent variables are in natural logarithms. The β_z coefficients thus indicate percentage differences in the dependent variable between firms that are, and firms that are not in situation X_{it}^z. For instance, if the dependent variable is the natural logarithm of production in year t and the parameter estimate for X_{3it}^C receives a value of 0.01, then relative to a firm that does not conduct a (simultaneous) spike, a firm that simultaneously does invest in equipment and structures experiences an output level 1% higher than its mean.

5 Empirical Results

In Fig. 1 and Table 3 we depict the results of an analysis to determine to what extent investment rates are interrelated.[14] We observe from the figure that at the time of an investment spike in either buildings or equipment the investment rate of the other investment component is significantly higher. Especially at the time of a spike in buildings the rate of investment in equipment is higher by almost 4% points. Strikingly, the figure depicts, that firms on average start to invest in equipment already 2 years before the firm builds new structures. Perhaps before expanding the firm first replaces older machinery or uses its existing buildings more efficiently. Once the firm is more certain about future growth prospects, it also decides in favour

[13]Within our analysis, within estimators in principle should be more efficient than first differencing, assuming that the idiosyncratic error terms ε_{it} are i.i.d. Since we do not (for example) include any lagged variables in the regression, we think this should be a safe assumption after averaging out the fixed effects. Note, we do not intend to estimate a model obtaining causal insights. We rather aim at obtaining insight of a descriptive nature regarding dynamic patterns of some key firm level variables.

[14]To avoid endogeneity issues in the analysis where investment rates are dependent variables, the vectors X_{it}^B and X_{it}^E have been constructed such that $\left(1 - S_{iq}^E\right) = 1$ and $\left(1 - S_{iq}^B\right) = 1$ for $q \in \{-2, \ldots, 2\}$ respectively.

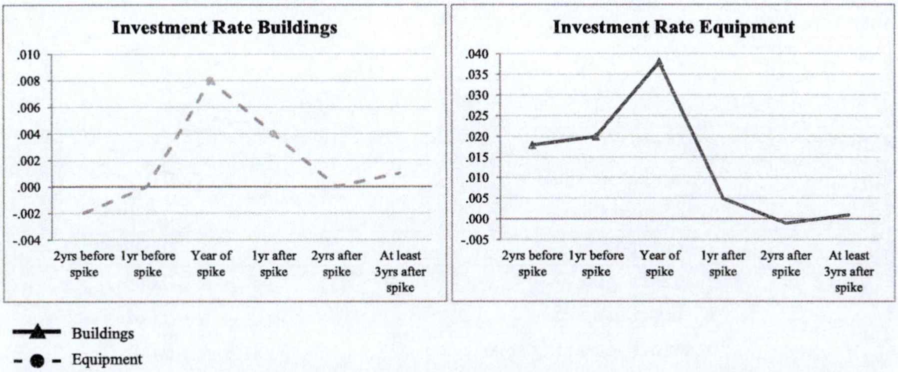

Fig. 1 Interrelation between investment types. This figure depicts investment rate of either equipment or buildings before, during, and after the investment spike in the other investment type. The vertical axis represents the difference relative to firms that experienced no spike event. Markers represent estimates significant at $p < 0.10$ level (two-tailed)

of more risky and larger investments by investing simultaneously in buildings and equipment. These results suggest that investments in equipment and buildings are interrelated in the sense that the timing of these decisions is not independent. Using country level data Garcia-Belenguer and Santos (2013) find evidence of interrelation as well. The firm-level data employed in our paper allow identification of a richer dynamic interaction between investment in buildings and equipment.

Our previous discussion of the shadow value of investment in Eq. (10) is in line with these findings. There we argued that investments are interrelated through the production technology. In fact, investment in one type of capital tends to raise the marginal profit of the other type, making it more likely to conduct simultaneous investment. Or, if the firm invests in only one type, it becomes more likely that in the near future the firm also invests in the other type of capital. Figure 1 confirms these thoughts.

Empirical results for the estimation of Eq. (14) are presented in Table 4. The table reports the coefficients and statistical significance at the 1%, 5%, and 10% levels. The dependent variables outlined in Sect. 3 are on the horizontal axis and the independent timing variables are on the vertical axis for buildings, equipment, and for simultaneous spikes.

5.1 *Changes in Scale: Production and Employment*

Table 4 documents the differences in production and number of workers—FTE employees—across the investment spike horizon in Columns (1) and (2). Figure 2 depicts these changes—2 to 1 years before an investment spike, the year of the investment spike, 1–2 years after the investment spike as well as three or more years after the investment spike. First, in Column (1) production increases significantly

Table 3 Interrelated investment

		(1) $\frac{I^B}{K^B}$	(2) $\frac{I^E}{K^E}$
Vector X_{it}^B	*Buildings*		
X_{1it}^B	2 years before spike		0.018***
X_{2it}^B	Year before spike		0.020***
X_{3it}^B	Year of spike		0.038***
X_{4it}^B	Year after spike		0.005
X_{5it}^B	2 years after spike		−0.001
X_{6it}^B	At least 3 years after spike		0.001
Vector X_{it}^E	*Equipment*		
X_{1it}^E	2 years before spike	−0.002	
X_{2it}^E	Year before spike	0.000	
X_{3it}^E	Year of spike	0.008***	
X_{4it}^E	Year after spike	0.004***	
X_{5it}^E	2 years after spike	0.000	
X_{6it}^E	At least 3 years after spike	0.001	

This table presents the results of the estimation parameters for the impact of investment spikes in equipment and buildings. Dependent variables across regressions are on the horizontal row. Dependent variables: (1) Investment rate of buildings and (2) investment rate of equipment. The vertical axis presents independent variables. The vectors X_{it}^B and X_{it}^E have been constructed such that $\left(1 - S_{iq}^E\right) = 1$ and $\left(1 - S_{iq}^B\right) = 1$ for $q \in \{-2, \ldots, 2\}$. Parameter estimates, conditioned upon observing an investment spike, are documented by investment spike time and investment type. Statistical significance is reflected by: $*p \leq 0.10$, $**p \leq 0.05$, $***p \leq 0.01$. The models include year dummies, that are however not displayed to save space

when a firm invests in both buildings and equipment, in the immediate 0–2 year horizons by 8–15% and an impact on production of about 8% after 3 years. This finding is distinct from firms who invested in equipment or buildings alone where firms saw short-term marginal gains in production of about 0% and 8%, respectively. Investment in buildings does not yield production changes beyond 3 years after the spike, but equipment does increase production scale by about 4% then. A notable finding is that the production level is highest at the time of the investment spike. The data indicate that once investment payments have been booked, production capacity has increased substantially. In case increased capacity is not fully installed yet a larger demand has been met by increasing factor utilization rates. Altogether, the empirical observation that production increases with higher input levels is in line with a standard production technology.

Second, as expected and highlighted in Column (2), the number of workers increases after an investment in buildings, equipment, or a simultaneous investment. In fact, we find that employment may increase by 3–15% in the short-run. However, only in instances where investment in buildings is involved, a longer-lasting effect

Table 4 Economic impact from investment spikes in equipment, buildings, and simultaneously both

		(1) PR	(2) NW	(3) AW	(4) CB/NW	(5) CE/NW	(6) PRL	(7) PRB	(8) PRE	(9) TC/S
Vector X_{it}^{B}	*Buildings*									
X_{1it}^{B}	2 years before spike	0.044***	0.031**	−0.001	−0.044***	−0.004	0.013	0.057***	0.017	−0.005
X_{2it}^{B}	Year before spike	0.062***	0.055***	−0.016*	−0.069***	−0.020	0.007	0.076***	0.027	−0.007
X_{3it}^{B}	Year of spike	0.079***	0.085***	−0.023**	−0.089***	−0.047*	−0.006	0.084***	0.042	−0.004
X_{4it}^{B}	Year after spike	0.057***	0.073***	−0.017**	−0.015	−0.038	−0.016	−0.001	0.022	0.005
X_{5it}^{B}	2 years after spike	0.058***	0.068***	−0.017*	−0.017	−0.037	−0.009	0.008	0.027	0.003
X_{6it}^{B}	At least 3 years after spike	0.022	0.051***	−0.006	0.012	−0.029	−0.029**	−0.041**	−0.001	0.010**
Vector X_{it}^{E}	*Equipment*									
X_{1it}^{E}	2 years before spike	0.009	0.007	−0.010	−0.011	−0.087***	0.003	0.014	0.090***	−0.004
X_{2it}^{E}	Year before spike	0.038**	0.020*	−0.009	−0.019	−0.112***	0.018	0.036**	0.129***	−0.011**
X_{3it}^{E}	Year of spike	0.069***	0.049***	−0.005	−0.051***	−0.178***	0.019	0.070***	0.197***	0.002
X_{4it}^{E}	Year after spike	0.029	0.046***	−0.009	−0.044***	−0.002	−0.017	0.028	−0.014	0.009*
X_{5it}^{E}	2 years after spike	0.020	0.031**	0.003	−0.029**	0.026	−0.011	0.018	−0.037*	0.014**
X_{6it}^{E}	At least 3 years after spike	0.038**	0.010	0.014*	−0.004	0.130***	0.028**	0.032**	−0.102***	−0.008*
Vector X_{it}^{C}	*Simultaneous*									
X_{1it}^{C}	2 years before spike	0.071**	0.034	0.007	−0.047	−0.081***	0.037*	0.084***	0.118***	−0.027
X_{2it}^{C}	Year before spike	0.104***	0.079***	−0.003	−0.091***	−0.156***	0.025	0.116***	0.180***	−0.008
X_{3it}^{C}	Year of spike	0.150***	0.119***	−0.003	−0.190***	−0.192***	0.031	0.161***	0.222***	0.002
X_{4it}^{C}	Year after spike	0.134***	0.101***	−0.003	−0.049*	0.006	0.032	0.081***	0.026	0.007
X_{5it}^{C}	2 years after spike	0.083***	0.082***	−0.006	−0.023	0.031	0.001	0.024	−0.030	0.013
X_{6it}^{C}	At least 3 years after spike	0.080***	0.067***	−0.010	−0.003	0.132***	0.012	0.016	−0.120***	−0.000

This table presents the results of the estimation parameters for the economic impact of investment spikes in equipment, buildings, and simultaneously both. Dependent variables across regressions are on the horizontal row and all dependent variables have received a (natural) logarithmic transformation. Dependent variables: (1) Production (2) number of workers (3) average wage (4) capital stock-buildings/number of workers (5) capital stock-equipment/number of workers (6) productivity labour (7) productivity buildings (8) productivity equipment (9) total costs/sales. Parameter estimates, conditioned upon observing an investment spike, are documented by investment spike time and investment type. Statistical significance is reflected by: * $p \leq 0.10$, ** $p \leq 0.05$, *** $p \leq 0.01$. The models include year dummies that are however not displayed to save space

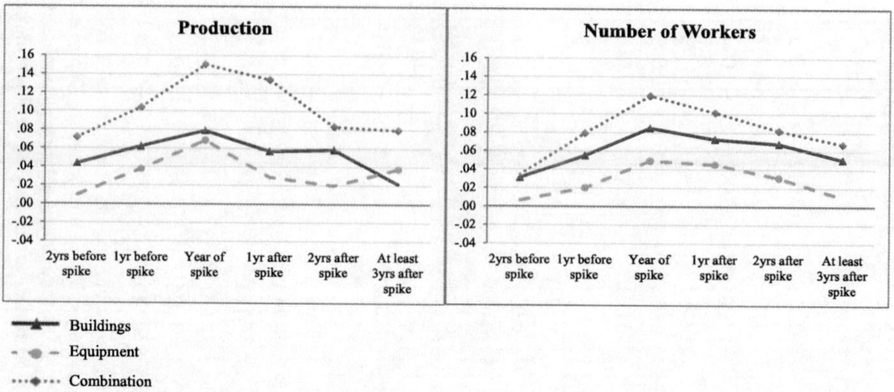

Fig. 2 Production scale and number of workers. This figure depicts the production scale and number of workers before, during, and after the investment spike. The vertical axis represents the percentage difference relative to firms that experienced no spike event. Markers represent estimates significant at $p < 0.10$ level (two-tailed)

on employment is observed represented by a 5–7% increase.[15] Apparently, it is investment in buildings that increases the marginal profit of labour inducing the firm to attract more workers even after 3 years.

5.2 *Change of Average Wage and Capital Intensity*

Table 4 Column (3) and Fig. 2 depict that when the firm experiences a spike in equipment the average wage bill becomes higher 3 years afterwards. This may indicate more skilled workers were hired by the firm. Alternatively, productivity has become higher in general due to investment justifying a higher wage on average. However, when the firm only invests in buildings, the wage decreases before, during,

[15]Using a Wald statistic we have tested whether parameters of the model in Eq. (11) are statistically different between investment types. For instance, we have tested the hypotheses whether for $k \in \{1, \ldots, 6\}$ the coefficient of X^B_{kit} equals that of X^E_{kit}, whether the coefficient of X^B_{kit} equals that of X^C_{kit}, and whether the coefficient of X^E_{kit} equals that of X^C_{kit}. For the dependent variable production we find that in general, i.e. for $k \leq 5$, the coefficients relating to the equipment and combination spikes are statistically different. We find the same for the coefficients relating to the building and the combination spikes after the spike occurred, i.e. for $k \geq 3$. For the dependent variable number of workers, coefficients relating to equipment spikes in general, i.e. for $k \geq 2$, are different from those of the combination spikes. Those relating to buildings are generally significantly different from those concerning the equipment spikes, for $k \geq 2$. These tests are significant at least at the 10% significance level, but often at 5%. They are not reported in the paper, but are available upon request.

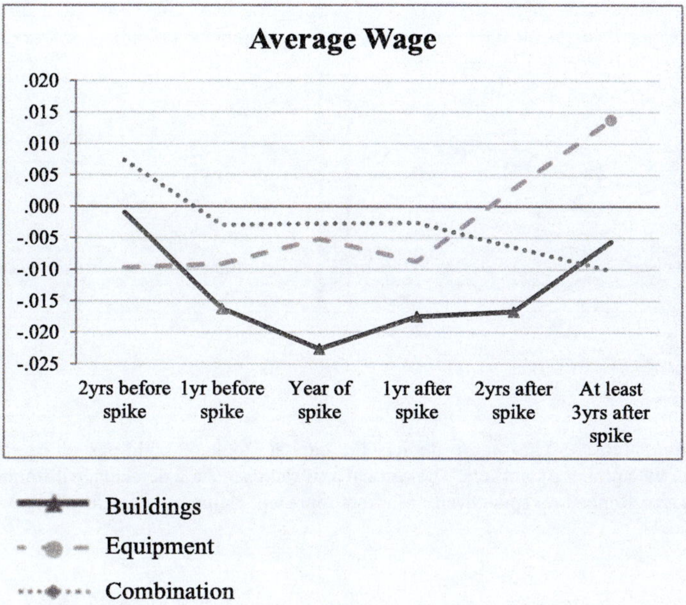

Fig. 3 Development Wage. This figure depicts the average wage per worker before, during, and after the investment spike, relative to firms that experienced no spike event. Markers represent estimates significant at $p < 0.10$ level (two-tailed)

and after the investment spike. This hints at firms hiring relatively more unskilled workers in those instances or productivity going down.[16]

Table 4, Columns (4) and (5), and Fig. 3 reveal that before a spike the firm becomes more labour intensive. The capital intensity for both buildings and equipment drops considerably in anticipation of the investment. The capital intensity for buildings gets back to the pre-spike period, but the equipment intensity increases by 12% in the post-spike period when a spike in equipment is involved. These numbers indicate that a change occurs in the input factors' optimal mix.[17] This may be due to capital investment causing a change in the parameters of the production technology.

The event order described above is consistent with the real option investment theory (Dixit and Pindyck 1994). Firms tend to first adjust factors of production that are relatively flexible. Labour is flexible compared to fixed capital assets (Asphjell et al. 2014). Firms adjust inflexible inputs like structures once uncertainty has been resolved to a large extent (Dixit 1998; Eberly and van Mieghem 1997).

[16]The Wald test tells that the coefficient of X^B_{6it} is not equal to that of X^E_{6it}.

[17]The Wald test informs that coefficients of X^B_{kit}, where $k \notin \{4, 5\}$ do not equal that of either X^E_{kit} or X^C_{kit}.

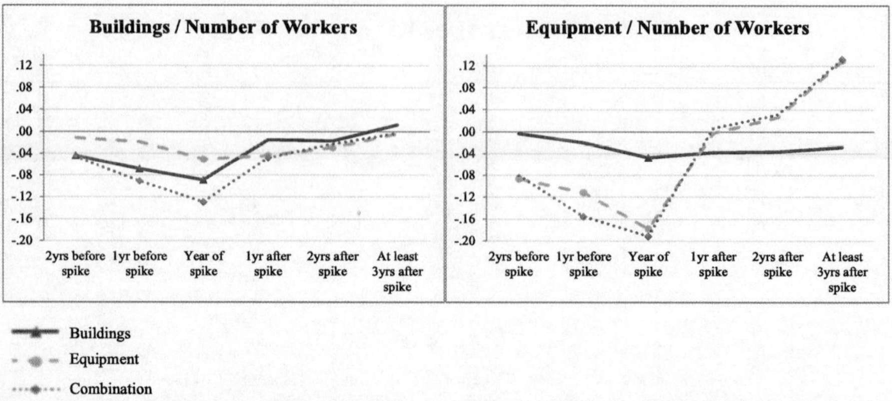

Fig. 4 Capital intensity. This figure depicts the capital stock of buildings or equipment as a percentage of the number of workers. The vertical axis represents the percentage difference relative to firms that experienced no spike event. Markers represent estimates significant at $p < 0.10$ level (two-tailed)

The study period 2000–2008 includes two recessionary periods and a boom. The period is marked by real wages increasing 6.6% in 9 years. In addition, long- and short-term interest rates have not increased, but have followed a U-shaped pattern consistent with the state of the economy during contraction and expansion.[18] This implies that during the period we have considered labour has become more expensive relative to the cost of financing capital. In this way, our findings are largely in line with the dynamics of the Dutch economy. Investment in buildings reflects an expansion of production in the economy. We also found that during events where firms invest in buildings they increase the number of workers (Fig. 2). When firms invest in equipment, we find that the share of workers decreases relative to the stock of capital employed by the firm (Fig. 4). This potentially reflects the need for firms to design a production process that is less labour intensive due to wages increasing over time.[19]

5.3 Changes in Firm Productivity and Efficiency

Columns (6), (7), and (8) of Table 4 further document, that most often productivity is higher before investment spikes. However, in the years subsequent to the investment

[18]The relevant statistics can be found at https://data.oecd.org/netherlands.htm.

[19]Note that the models we estimated control for year fixed effects. These will account for the general state of the Dutch economy (real wages and interest rates). Disaggregate data on relative input factor prices are not available. Persistent heterogeneity of these relative prices will be controlled for by the fixed effect panel data estimation technique we employed.

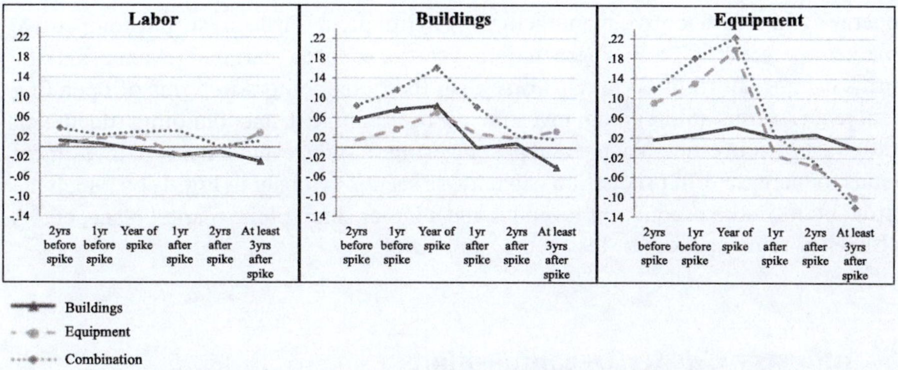

Fig. 5 Labour, buildings, and equipment productivity. This figure depicts productivity for labour, buildings, and equipment. The vertical axis represents the percentage difference relative to firms that experienced no spike event. Markers represent estimates significant at $p < 0.10$ level (two-tailed)

spike, productivity gains are lower and even negative in some cases. Figure 4 depicts the sharp contrast in labour, building, and equipment productivity pre and post investment, where productivity reaches a summit just as investment occurs.

Our results confirm Power's (1998) finding of a "Missing Link" between technology, investment, and productivity. Her conclusion was based on investigating the relationship between the history of large investment outlays and labour productivity. Recalling Fig. 2 our two firm scale measures, production and number of workers, display very similar behaviour. Hence, it is not surprising that labour productivity is hardly affected by investment dynamics according to Table 4 and Fig. 5.

In line with Abel and Eberly (1998), in Sect. 2 of this chapter we have argued that productivity may act as a signal of when to invest. Hence, high productivity should precede investment. We find small labour productivity gains of about 2–4% in case of investment in equipment after 3 years. However, productivity from equipment drops by as much as 10–12% when equipment is involved. At the same time productivity of structures improves beyond 3 years. In order to be able to understand productivity consequences of capital adjustment, our findings suggest one probably needs to conduct a structural estimation approach identifying the process that generates firm productivity.

Lastly, we see in Table 4 Column (9) and Fig. 5 that there is an impact on firm operational efficiency after investment spikes. Capital expenditures for equipment improve cost efficiency by 1% after 3 years. In contrast, investment in buildings decreases cost efficiency by 1% or so. This means there is a small but notable difference in cost efficiency between a single spike in equipment and buildings of about 2% after 3 years.[20] One way of interpreting this finding is that firms are

[20]Interestingly, the Wald test signals that the coefficient of X^B_{6it} does not equal that of X^E_{6it}.

operating in a competitive manufacturing environment. Firms in such a competitive market operate efficiently where marginal cost is equal to marginal revenue, and the firms cannot afford to do much worse than their competitors in terms of operating efficiency. Firms undergoing investments in equipment and buildings document little variation in efficiency pre and post investment spike events. Instead, investment tends to increase firm production capacity, as seen previously in Fig. 1, by which the firm obtains more production revenues and a larger share of the market place, but its efficiency remains more or less at the same level.

6 Industry Cluster Decomposition

Recent empirical work argues that firms in high-tech and low-tech are different along various dimensions (Robertson et al. 2009; Czarnitzki and Thorwarth 2012). To obtain more detailed insight, we run our firm-level analysis in Eq. (3) by innovation industry clusters as well. In addition, we distinguish industries in terms of labour intensity. We adopt a classification developed by Raymond et al. (2006), which identifies high- and low-tech industry categories for Dutch manufacturing firms. A low-tech firm is categorized by its low propensity to engage in innovation seeking activities, e.g., R&D activities and innovation subsidy achievement.[21] In addition, we employ a Dutch industry grouping established by Ramirez et al. (2005) who document labour intensity. Table 5 provides results for our sample's firm industry classification by innovation and labour intensity.[22] High-tech and low-tech sectors account for 39% and 45% of the investment sample's sectors, respectively. Innovation intensity in high-tech sectors is observed largely in the oil and coal, chemicals, and machines and apparatuses sector, which also corresponds with low-labour-intensity manufacturing. High-, medium- and low-labour-intensive industries reflect 22%, 30%, and 49% of the investment sample's sectors, respectively. Interestingly, low-labour-intensive industries are split almost evenly between high-tech and low-tech industries.

Figure 6 depicts production and number of employees for high- and low-tech industries. Compared to establishments operating in high-tech industries, low-tech firms tend to expand firm size by adding structures rather than equipment. Instead, high-tech industries need equipment to expand production. Apparently, in the low-tech industries the production process is rather labour intensive. In this way, should a low-tech firm want to grow, it needs to create a workplace for its workers.

[21] The model developed by Raymond et al. (2006) identifies three categories of innovation intensity: high-technology, low-technology, and wood. Wood is a distinctively non-innovative industry.

[22] We have also estimated Eq. (3) for industries separated by employing the twodigit SIC classification code. However, we generally find no statistically significant patterns. One reason might be that breaking up by SIC codes yields relatively few observations per industry classification.

Table 5 Sample breakdown by sector, innovation intensity, and labour intensity

1993 SBI code	Sector	N	%	Innovation intensity	Labour intensity
15–16	Food and drinks; tobacco	918	16	Low-tech	Low
17–19	Textile; clothes; leather goods	180	3	Low-tech	High
20	Wood	162	3	Wood	High
21	Paper and pulp	461	8	Wood	Medium
22	Publishers, printing companies, etc.	351	6	Wood	Low
23–24	Oil and coal; chemicals	638	11	High-tech	Low
25	Rubber and plastics	241	4	High-tech	Medium
26	Non-metallic minerals	441	8	Low-tech	Medium
27	Metals	237	4	Low-tech	Low
28	Metal products	662	11	Low-tech	High
29	Machines and apparatuses	700	12	High-tech	Low
30–32	Office machinery and computers; electronic machines and equipment; audio, video, and telecom devices	294	5	High-tech	Medium
33	Medical and optical apparatuses and instruments	139	2	High-tech	Medium
34	Cars and trailers	178	3	High-tech	High
35	Other transportation means and products	95	2	High-tech	High
36	Furniture and other products	171	3	Low-tech	Medium
	Total	5868	100		

This table documents the frequency of our sample by industry classification, technology intensity, and labour intensity. Sectors have been aggregated into bigger groups, as Statistics Netherlands (CBS) requires reported statistics to be based on some minimum number of firms to ascertain anonimity of findings. The SBI classification system is the Dutch equivalent of the United States SIC system. Innovation intensity classification based on Raymond et al. (2006) and labour intensity classification based on Ramirez et al. (2005)

Figure 7 graphs the dynamics of production and number of employees in industries distinguished by different levels of labour intensity. Notably, firms in labour-intensive industries do not expand production and number of employees by investing in structures or equipment. Production processes in these industries are less dependent on capital inputs overall. Apparently, then the share of capital in the production technology is too small to make capital accounting for variation in firm size measures. We find a more pronounced influence of capital investment on firm

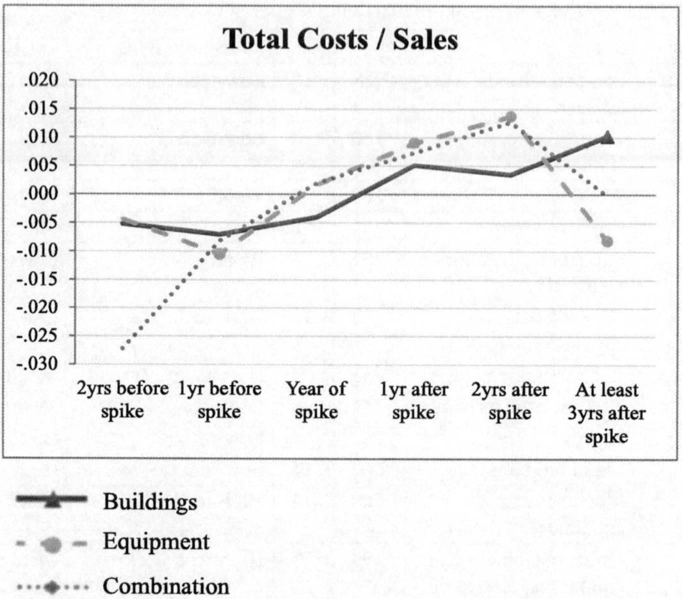

Fig. 6 Operational efficiency. This figure depicts total costs relative to total sales of the firm, reflecting a basic measure of firm operating efficiency. The vertical axis represents the percentage difference relative to firms that experienced no spike event. Markers represent estimates significant at $p < 0.10$ level (two-tailed)

size measures in industries characterized by low- and medium-labour-intensity. In particular, simultaneous investment spikes increase production scale and number of workers.

Our results based on a firm investment panel dataset, presented in the previous section, stress the role of simultaneous spikes in understanding firm growth. In particular, capital intensive industries (i.e., low- and medium-labour-intensive sectors) exhibit features that are common to what we observed for the entire sample. For these industries simultaneous spikes are important to understand both employment and production growth. Firms operating in high-tech industries are more dependent on investment in equipment to increase production volume after 3 years, but employment growth is established by all investment spike types. To grow in low-tech industries firms build structures. Simultaneous spikes in low-tech industries increase production, whereas in high-tech industries they increase employment (Fig. 8). Figure 8 documents a similar breakdown by production and number of workers by low, medium and high labor intensity. The results document significant variation by labor intensity, where medium labor intensity faces significant investment impact from a combination of buildings and equipment.

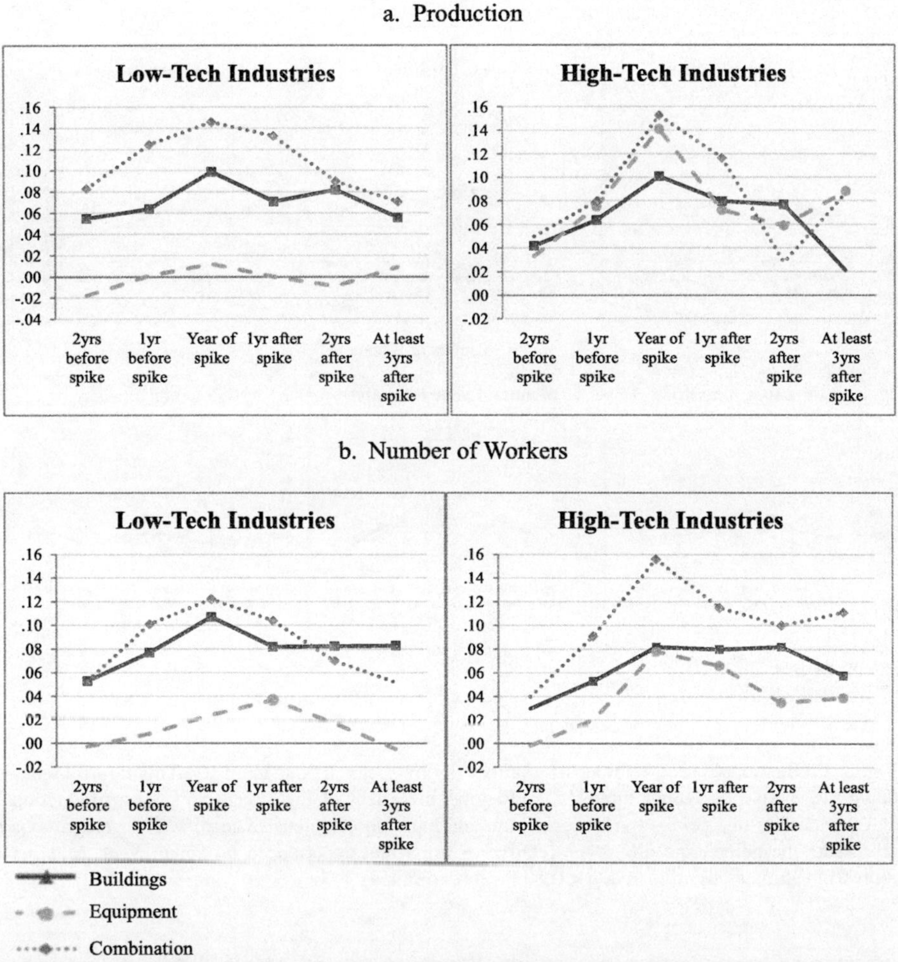

Fig. 7 Production (**a**) and number of workers (**b**) by sector innovation intensity. This figure depicts production and the number of workers, broken down by different levels of innovation intensity. The vertical axis represents the percentage difference relative to firms that experienced no spike event. Markers represent estimates significant at $p < 0.10$ level (two-tailed)

7 Conclusion

Central to firm production is investment in capital. We find the distinction between productive capital, like equipment, and non-productive capital, like buildings, is critical for understanding the scale and production technology of a firm. This chapter documents the impact of decomposing investment spikes in buildings and equipment on scale, productivity, mix of input factors, and firm efficiency. Firms that

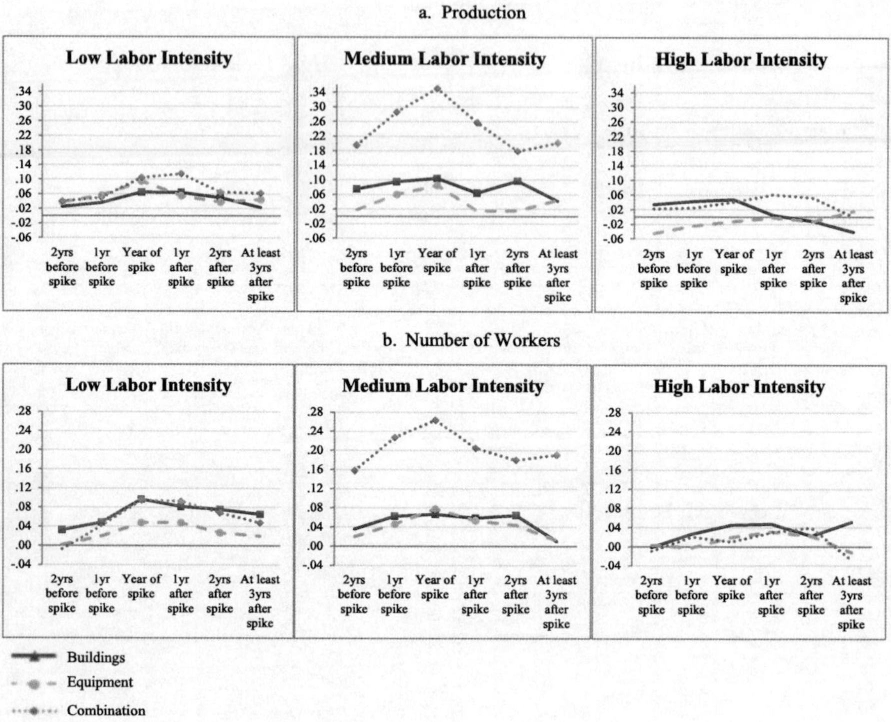

Fig. 8 Production (**a**) and number of workers (**b**) by sector labour intensity. This figure breaks down the sample by labour intensity, and shows the effect of investment spikes on production and the number of workers for low, medium, and high labour-intensive sectors. The vertical axis represents the percentage difference relative to firms that experienced no spike event. Markers represent estimates significant at $p < 0.10$ level (two-tailed)

invest in buildings, equipment, or simultaneously in both obtain different outcomes concerning production technology and performance metrics.

Our results reveal high productivity acts as a signal for firms to invest. Furthermore, firms conducting simultaneous investment spikes experience the largest post investment expansion in production and number of workers. We find employment growth does not come from spikes in equipment only. Especially, when buildings are constructed the number of workers increases. Investments involving equipment affect the optimal input mix. In those instances, labour tends to be substituted by equipment. Additionally, operational efficiency is economically affected by spike investments in equipment.

We also conducted a more fine-grained analysis by type of industry. We distinguished high- and low-tech sectors and employed a classification based on labour intensity. The industry analysis reveals that simultaneous spikes drive firm production growth in capital intensive industries (i.e., low- and medium-labour-intensive sectors) and in low-tech industries. Simultaneous spikes enhance employment in capital intensive industries and in a high-tech environment. In order to grow production a necessary condition for low-tech firms is building structures to house workers. High-tech firms depend more on equipment to be able to grow production. These results tell production processes are different across industries. Furthermore they reveal how revenue and employment growth are advanced in different industrial settings.

For future research we recommend three opportunities. First, production processes are different across sectors and there could be gains in our analysis by looking at stochastic frontier analysis (SFA) that can accommodate potential time-varying or invarying inefficiencies with panel data (Schmidt and Sickles 1984; Kumbhakar et al. 2017). Moreover, within sectors processes may alter over time according to our results, possibly depending on technological developments and changes in factor input costs and could be looked at in an SFA framework (Cornwell et al. 1990; Sickles and Zelenyuk 2019). An interesting topic for future research concerns whether, how, and with what speed firms are capable of adjusting in response to such developments.

Second, our results based on distinguishing between firm expenses on structures and equipment suggest adding firm-level investment dimensions to the micro investment literature is worth the effort. We propose a research agenda resulting in a better understanding of investment in both equipment and buildings. Studies on interrelated factor demand have revealed that models of more flexible input factors need to be complemented with less flexible ones. In particular, Bloom (2009) and Asphjell et al. (2014) observed that performance of labour demand models improves by also incorporating the dynamics of investment in equipment. However, models concerning the stock of equipment do not have to include labour demand to be able to match important moments of the data. Likewise, we expect that to properly model the dynamics of equipment accounting for investment in buildings is mandatory.

Third, the distinction between firms' investment choices underscores different expected outcomes for economic growth and macroeconomic activity. Caballero and Engel (1999) document lumpiness in firm investment is critical for understanding macroeconomic activity. Bachmann et al. (2013) further advance the role of investment lumpiness in impacting business cycle activity. However, other studies inspired by Thomas (2002) are more critical regarding the role of investment lumpiness in driving the business cycle. A more recent strand in the literature suggests it is particularly uncertainty that drives macro-economic outcomes through investment (Bloom 2009; Bloom et al. 2012), but this can be further amplified by the firm's timing in the business cycle as well as the type of industry that is implementing change (Samaniego and Sun 2015). Due to irreversibility firms tend to become cautious when experiencing higher uncertainty (Guiso and Parigi 1999; Ghosal and Loungani 2000) and this could especially be the case when investing in buildings (Driver et al. 2005). In fact, investment in structures is subject to a larger degree of lumpiness than equipment hinting at fixed adjustment costs or indivisibility. Hence, uncertainty potentially affects investment in structures to an even larger extent than investment in equipment.

Furthermore, distinct capital investments result in specific financing frictions, due to varying degrees of irreversibility. Additionally, capital market stakeholders for buildings and equipment differ (Bayer 2006). Hence, the timing and size of investment depend on capital type, business cycle properties like uncertainty, and access to the capital market (Fiori 2012). Decomposing investment into structures and equipment will be an important contribution in understanding micro and macro level growth. It will also provide better insight into which policies need to be in place to advance growth and employment at both the national and sectoral level.

Appendix 1: Construction of Capital Stock Variables

We construct the starting value of a firm's capital stock for buildings and for equipment as follows. The initial capital stock for a firm is the contemporaneous ratio of firm to industy output multiplied by the industry's capital stock of an asset. More specifically, for a given firm i in period t, the firm's capital stock, i.e. K_{it}^{c} is calculated using $K_{it}^{c} = K_{jt}^{c} \cdot \frac{Y_{it}}{Y_{jt}}$, where j denotes the industry a firm is operating in, Y_{it} (Y_{jt}) depicts output of firm i (industry j) in year t, $K_{it}^{c}(K_{jt}^{c})$ denotes the capital stock of asset z of company i (industry j) at the beginning of year t. The industry level data are obtained from the Statline online datacenter of Statistics Netherlands (CBS). To construct the starting values of the capital stock series, data from the year prior to the start of the sample are collected. Hence, these series start in the year 2000.

The capital stock for the remaining years is determined by the perpetual inventory method. Importantly, in the analysis we employ real investment and capital figures. The nominal numbers have been deflated using producer price indices on buildings or equipment assets. The nominal numbers refer to investments done in the book year.

Appendix 2: Available upon Request: Derivation of Investment Model

Few recent studies have analysed firm decisions along more than one dimension when it comes to input demand. Those that have done so usually have focused on two types: investment in equipment and labour (Bloom 2009; Asphjell et al. 2014) and investment in equipment and structures (Bontempi et al. 2004; Del Boca et al. 2008). An exception is Ghosal and Nair-Reichert (2009) who distinguish between four categories: investment in mechanical devices, chemical devices, monitoring devices, and information technology. Bloom and Asphjell et al. conclude that adding a margin to the decision problem of the firm improves the empirical performance of models. Often part of the model relating to a relatively flexible input factor (labour when compared to equipment, or equipment when compared to buildings) gains accuracy in being able to explain the data when analysed jointly with the less flexible factor. This finding reflects the insight by Eberly and van Mieghem (1997) that the adjustment timing of flexible input factors is driven by the fundamentals of the less flexible inputs as well.

We present a simple model to guide our empirical analysis of firm-level investment decisions. Consider a firm that at time t uses two capital inputs—the stock of buildings is given by K_t^B and the stock of equipment is given by K_t^E—to produce a non-storable output. The firm's objective function is given by

$$V_t = E_t\left(\sum_{s=0}^{\infty}\beta^s\left[F\left(A_{t+s}, K_{t+s}^B, K_{t+s}^E\right) - AC\left(I_{t+s}^B, K_{t+s}^B, I_{t+s}^E, K_{t+s}^E\right)\right]\right) \tag{9}$$

The term E_t indicates that expectations are taken with respect to information available at time t. The discount rate is given by β with $0 < \beta < 1$. The expression $F\left(A_t, K_t^B, K_t^E\right) = p_t Y_t - w_t L_t$ denotes sales minus wage costs. Note that a CES production technology takes on the shape of a Cobb–Douglas production technology if $\rho \rightarrow 0$. In the derivation below we employ the Cobb–Douglas example for ease of exposition. Consider a standard Cobb–Douglas production technology $Y_t = \phi_t(K_t^B)^\nu(K_t^E)^\mu(L_t)^\kappa$, where Y, L, and ϕ denote production, labour, and a technology parameter, respectively, and where $0 < \nu, \mu, \kappa < 1$. Labour is a fully flexible factor of production. Let $p_t = \varphi_t(Y_t)^{-\frac{1}{\varepsilon}}$ denote an isoelastic demand function where $\varepsilon > 1$, then $p_t Y_t - w_t L_t = \varphi_t\left(\phi_t(K_t^B)^\nu(K_t^E)^\mu(L_t)^\kappa\right)^{1-\frac{1}{\varepsilon}} - w_t L_t$. The term $A_t = \varphi_t\phi_t^{1-\frac{1}{\varepsilon}}$ captures randomness in both total factor productivity and demand that the firm is facing.

The firm incurs adjustment costs when investment takes place given by

$$AC\left(I_t^B, K_t^B, I_t^E, K_t^E\right) = \begin{bmatrix} p_t^B I_t^B + \alpha^B \cdot \mathrm{I}\left(I_t^B \neq 0\right) + \frac{b^B}{2}\left(\frac{I_t^B}{K_t^B}\right)^2 \cdot K_t^B \\ + p_t^E I_t^E + \alpha^E \cdot \mathrm{I}\left(I_t^E \neq 0\right) + \frac{b^E}{2}\left(\frac{I_t^E}{K_t^E}\right)^2 \cdot K_t^E \end{bmatrix} \tag{10}$$

The indicator function I(.) takes the value 1 if the condition in brackets is satisfied and equals zero otherwise. As usual the adjustment cost function allows for convex costs. The size of these costs is reflected by the parameters b^B and b^E. Such costs imply a penalty on large capital expenditures and hence induce firms to smooth investment over time. The cost function also allows for non-convexity.[23] For instance, the prices of the input factors are expressed as p_t^B and p_t^E, where for $z \in \{B, E\}$, $p_t^z = p^{z+} \cdot \mathrm{I}\left(I_t^z > 0\right) + p^{z-} \cdot \mathrm{I}\left(I_t^z < 0\right)$. The purchase price for a unit of capital c is p^{z+}, while the value of one unit of sold capital would be $p^{z\text{-}}$. Due to

[23] Such costs may be skipped when the level of aggregation is high (see, for example, Groth 2008). However, we use plant level data featuring lumpy capital adjustment patterns.

irreversibility of investment decisions, the purchase price of capital is higher than the resale price: $p^{z+} > p^{z-}$. Another non-convexity is due to fixed costs given by α^B and α^E. We assume these to be symmetric by being independent of whether the inputs are positive or negative.

Investment in buildings and equipment is denoted by I_t^B and I_t^E, respectively. By investment the firm decides upon the optimal size of the capital stocks, K_{t+1}^B and K_{t+1}^E. If the parameters δ^B and δ^E measure the rate of capital depreciation of buildings and equipment, respectively, the evolution of capital is governed by

$$K_{i,t+1}^z = \left(1 - \delta^z\right) K_{i,t}^z + I_{i,t}^z \tag{11}$$

where $z \in \{B, E\}$. To obtain the optimal values for I_t^B and I_t^E Eq. (9) is optimized with respect to these decision variables subject to Eq. (11). The variables λ_t^B and λ_t^E are the shadow values of an additional unit of capital. Their formal expression for $z \in \{B, E\}$ is

$$\lambda_t^z = E_t\left(\sum_{s=0}^{\infty}\left(1 - \delta^z\right)^s \beta^{s+1}\right.$$
$$\left.\left[\frac{\partial F\left(A_{t+s+1}, K_{t+s+1}^B, K_{t+s+1}^E\right)}{\partial K_{t+s+1}^z} - \frac{\partial AC\left(I_{t+s+1}^B, K_{t+s+1}^B, I_{t+s+1}^E, K_{t+s+1}^E\right)}{\partial K_{t+s+1}^z}\right]\right) \tag{12}$$

They measure how the value of the firm changes if the constraints in Eq. (11) are relaxed or equivalently, if capital is increased by one unit. The shadow values represent the expected present discounted value of the marginal profit of capital minus the marginal adjustment costs in future periods. For $z \in \{B, E\}$ the first-order condition for capital adjustment is given by

$$\lambda_t^z - p_t^z - b^z\left(\frac{I_t^z}{K_t^z}\right) = 0 \tag{13}$$

In line with Abel and Eberly (1994) and Eberly (1997) optimal factor demand adjustment equals:

$$\frac{I_t^z}{K_t^z} = \left(\frac{\lambda_t^z - p_t^z}{b^z}\right) \tag{14}$$

The equation determining whether to change the stock of capital for $z \in \{B, E\}$ is given by

$$\lambda_t^z I_t^z \geq AC\left(I_t^z, K_t^z\right) \tag{15}$$

The left-hand side of Eq. (15) measures the expected benefits of investing. The right-hand side denotes the cost associated with the firm's decisions.[24] Using Eq. (14) it can be shown that Eq. (15) holds if $\frac{1}{2b^z}\left(\lambda_t^z - p_t^z\right)^2 K_t^z \geq \alpha^z > 0$. Hence, the sufficient condition for changing the amount of capital $z \in \{B, E\}$ is

$$\left|\lambda_t^z - p_t^z\right| > \sqrt{\frac{2b^z\alpha^z}{K_t^z}} \equiv A^z \tag{16}$$

Equation (16) shows that if the net benefits of adjusting capital do not exceed a certain minimum threshold, the firm decides to abstain from adjusting. The thresholds are also caused by the presence of the fixed adjustment costs α^B and α^E. With larger fixed costs, the threshold will increase. Hence, investment becomes less likely, all else equal. In addition, we observe that with larger fixed costs, once the firm decides to invest, the size of the investment will be larger, because with a larger threshold the left-hand side of Eq. (16) must be higher and this expression drives the size of investment as can be seen from Eq. (14). Hence, fixed costs largely explain the phenomenon of investment spikes as mentioned before.

Acknowledgements We thank David Geltner, Rogier Holtermans, Øivind Nilsen, Jaap Bos, Lyndsey Rolheiser and seminar participants at Maastricht University and MIT for useful comments on preliminary drafts of this chapter.

References

Abel, A. B., & Eberly, J. C. (1994). A unified model of investment under uncertainty. *American Economic Review, 84*, 1369–1384.

Abel, A. B., & Eberly, J. C. (1998). The mix and scale of factors with irreversibility and fixed costs of investment. In *Carnegie Rochester Conference Series on Public Policy* (Vol. 48, pp. 101–135).

Acemoglu, D. (2015). *How the machines replace labor?* Paper presented at the annual meeting of the Allied Social Science Associations, American Economic Association, Boston.

Acemoglu, D., & Restrepo, P. (2020). Robots and jobs: Evidence from US labor markets. *Journal of Political Economy, 128*(6), 2188–2244.

Asphjell, M., Letterie, W. A., Nilsen, Ø. A., & Pfann, G. A. (2014). Sequentiality versus simultaneity: Interrelated factor demand. *Review of Economics and Statistics, 96*, 986–998.

Bachmann, R., Caballero, R. J., & Engel, E. M. (2013). Aggregate implications of lumpy investment: New evidence and a DSGE model. *American Economic Journal: Macroeconomics, 5*, 29–67.

Bayer, C. (2006). Investment dynamics with fixed capital adjustment cost and capital market imperfections. *Journal of Monetary Economics, 53*(8), 1909–1947.

Bloom, N. (2009). The impact of uncertainty shocks. *Econometrica, 77*, 623–685.

[24]The expression $\lambda_t^z I_t^z$ approximates the benefits allowing for a closed form solution. In a continuous time framework with one production factor a similar expression holds exactly.

Bloom, N., Floetotto, M., Jaimovich, N., Saporta-Eksten, I., & Terry, S. J. (2012). *Really uncertain business cycles (no. w18245)*. Cambridge: National Bureau of Economic Research.

Bokhari, S., & Geltner, D. (2014). Characteristics in commercial and multi-family property: An investment perspective. *Center for real estate working paper series*.

Bokhari, S., & Geltner, D. (2018). Characteristics of depreciation in commercial and multifamily property: An investment perspective. *Real Estate Economics, 46*(4), 745–782.

Bontempi, E., Del Boca, A., Franzosi, A., Galeotti, M., & Rota, P. (2004). Capital heterogeneity: Does it matter? Fundamental Q and investment on a panel of Italian firms. *RAND Journal of Economics, 35*, 674–690.

Caballero, R. J. (1999). Aggregate investment. *Handbook of Macroeconomics, 1*, 813–862.

Caballero, R. J., & Engel, E. M. (1999). Explaining investment dynamics in US manufacturing: A generalized (S, s) approach. *Econometrica, 67*, 783–826.

Caballero, R. J., Engel, E. M., & Haltiwanger, J. C. (1995). Firm-level adjustment and aggregate investment dynamics. *Brookings Papers on Economic Activity, 26*, 1–54.

Chegut, A., Eichholtz, P. M., & Rodrigues, J. M. (2015). Spatial dependence in international office markets. *Journal of Real Estate Finance and Economics, 51*(2), 317–350.

Cooper, R., & Haltiwanger, J. (2006). On the nature of capital adjustment costs. *Review of Economic Studies, 73*, 611–634.

Cooper, R., Haltiwanger, J., & Power, L. (1999). Machine replacement and the business cycle: Lumps and bumps. *American Economic Review, 87*, 921–946.

Cornwell, C., Schmidt, P., & Sickles, R. C. (1990). Production frontiers with cross-sectional and time-series variation in efficiency levels. *Journal of Econometrics, 46*(2), 185–200.

Czarnitzki, D., & Thorwarth, S. (2012). Productivity effects of basic research in low-tech and high-tech industries. *Research Policy, 41*, 1555–1564.

Del Boca, A., Galeotti, M., Himmelberg, C. P., & Rota, P. (2008). Investment and time to plan and build: A comparison of structures vs. equipment in a panel of Italian firms. *Journal of the European Economic Association, 6*, 864–889.

Dixit, A. (1998). Investment dynamics in the short run and long run. *Oxford Economic Papers, 49*, 1–20.

Dixit, A., & Pindyck, R. (1994). *Investment under uncertainty*. Princeton: Princeton University Press.

Doms, M., & Dunne, T. (1998). Capital adjustment patterns in manufacturing firms. *Review of Economic Dynamics, 1*, 409–429.

Driver, C., Temple, P., & Urga, G. (2005). Profitability, capacity, and uncertainty: A model of UK manufacturing investment. *Oxford Economic Papers, 57*(1), 120–141.

Dunne, T., Roberts, M. J., & Samuelson, L. (1989). Firm turnover and gross employment flows in the US manufacturing sector. *Journal of Labor Economics, 7*, 48–71.

Eberly, J. C. (1997). International evidence on investment and fundamentals. *European Economic Review, 41*, 1055–1078.

Eberly, J. C., & van Mieghem, J. A. (1997). Multi-factor dynamic investment under uncertainty. *Journal of Economic Theory, 75*, 345–387.

Feenstra, R. C., Inklaar, R., & Timmer, M. P. (2015). The next generation of the Penn world table. *American Economic Review, 105*(10), 3150–3182.

Fiori, G. (2012). Lumpiness, capital adjustment costs and investment dynamics. *Journal of Monetary Economics, 59*(4), 381–392.

Garcia-Belenguer, F., & Santos, M. S. (2013). Investment rates and the aggregate production function. *European Economic Review, 63*, 150–169.

Ghosal, V., & Loungani, P. (2000). The differential impact of uncertainty on investment in small and large firms. *Review of Economics and Statistics, 82*, 338–343.

Ghosal, V., & Nair-Reichert, U. (2009). Investments in modernization, innovation and gains in productivity: Evidence from firms in the global paper industry. *Research Policy, 38*, 536–547.

Goolsbee, A. (1998). The business cycle, financial performance, and the retirement of capital goods. *Review of Economic Dynamics, 1*, 474–496.

Görzig, B. (2007). Characteristics of depreciation in commercial and multifamily property: An investment perspective. *Real Estate Economics, 46*(4), 745–782.

Groth, C. (2008). Quantifying UK capital adjustment costs. *Economica, 75*, 310–325.

Guiso, L., & Parigi, G. (1999). Investment and demand uncertainty. *The Quarterly Journal of Economics, 114*, 185–227.

Hémous, D., & Olsen, M. (2013). *The rise of the machines: Automation, horizontal innovation and income inequality*. Paper presented at the annual meeting of the Allied Social Science Associations, American Economic Association, Boston.

Hemous, David and Olsen, Morten, The Rise of the Machines: Automation, Horizontal Innovation and Income Inequality (November 2014). CEPR Discussion Paper No. DP10244. Available at SSRN: https://ssrn.com/abstract=2526357.

Jovanovic, B., & Nyarko, Y. (1996). Learning by doing and the choice for technology. *Econometrica, 64*, 1299–1310.

Klassen, R. D., & Whybark, D. C. (1999). The impact of environmental technologies on manufacturing performance. *Academy of Management Journal, 42*, 599–615.

Kumbhakar, S., Parmeter, C., & Zelenyuk, V. (2017). *Stochastic frontier analysis: Foundations and advances (no. 2017–10)*. Miami: University of Miami, Department of Economics.

Letterie, W. A., & Pfann, G. A. (2007). Structural identification of high and low investment regimes. *Journal of Monetary Economics, 54*, 797–819.

Letterie, W., Pfann, G. A., & Polder, J. M. (2004). Factor adjustment spikes and interrelation: An empirical investigation. *Economics Letters, 85*, 145–150.

Letterie, W. A., Pfann, G. A., & Verick, S. (2010). On lumpiness in the replacement and expansion of capital. *Oxford Bulletin of Economics and Statistics, 72*, 263–281.

Nilsen, Ø. A., & Schiantarelli, F. (2003). Zeroes and lumps in investment: Empirical evidence on irreversibilities and nonconvexities. *Review of Economics and Statistics, 85*, 1021–1037.

Nilsen, Ø. A., Raknerud, A., Rybalka, M., & Skjerpen, T. (2009). Lumpy investments, factor adjustments, and labor productivity. *Oxford Economic Papers, 61*, 104–127.

Power, L. (1998). The missing link: Technology, investment, and productivity. *Review of Economics and Statistics, 80*, 300–313.

Ramirez, C. A., Patel, M., & Blok, K. (2005). The non-energy intensive manufacturing sector. An energy analysis relating to the Netherlands. *Energy, 30*, 749–767.

Raymond, W., Mohnen, P., Palm, F., & Schim van der Loeff, S. (2006). A classification of Dutch manufacturing based on a model of innovation. *De Economist, 154*, 85–105.

Robertson, P., Smith, K., & Von Tunzelmann, N. (2009). Innovation in low-and medium technology industries. *Research Policy, 38*, 441–446.

Sakellaris, P. (2004). Patterns of firm adjustment. *Journal of Monetary Economics, 51*, 425–450.

Samaniego, R. M., & Sun, J. Y. (2015). Technology and contractions: Evidence from manufacturing. *European Economic Review, 79*, 172–195.

Schmidt, P., & Sickles, R. C. (1984). Production frontiers and panel data. *Journal of Business & Economic Statistics, 2*(2), 367–374.

Sickles, R. C., & Zelenyuk, V. (2019). *Measurement of productivity and efficiency*. Cambridge: Cambridge University Press.

Thomas, J. (2002). Is lumpy investment relevant for the business cycle? *Journal of Political Economy, 110*, 508–534.

van den Bergen, D., de Haan, M., de Hey, R., & Horsten, M. (2009). *Measuring capital in the Netherlands* (Statistics Netherlands Discussion Paper 09036).

Applying Statistical Methods to Compare Frontiers: Are Organic Dairy Farms Better Than the Conventional?

Mette Asmild, Dorte Kronborg, and Anders Rønn-Nielsen

Abstract The Malmquist index is widely used in empirical studies of productivity change over time. The index is based on estimates of the frontier obtained from the convex envelopment of the data as in DEA. The statistical properties of the Malmquist index and its components, i.e. the frontier shift and the efficiency change, have until recently only been subject to a limited number of studies. The asymptotic properties of the geometric mean of the individual Malmquist indexes have been studied in the literature. Permutation tests for performing statistical inference in finite samples have recently been proposed and are easily performed. In the present paper we illustrate the permutation methods by an analysis of data comprising organic and conventional dairy farms in Denmark from 2011–2015. Further, differences between the frontiers of the production possibility sets for two separate samples are studied, specifically those of the organic and the conventional producers. We suggest to use jackknife methods when estimating the differences to ensure that these are not affected by the well-known bias originating from estimation of the frontier. In summary, the paper offers an illustration of how to analyse productivity data, in particular a comparison of two independent groups, and furthermore an analysis of how the separate groups evolve over time is provided.

Keywords Malmquist index · Frontier differences · Data envelopment analysis (DEA) · Independent samples · Permutation tests · Organic farming

M. Asmild (✉)
Department of Food and Resource Economics, University of Copenhagen, Frederiksberg C., Denmark
e-mail: meas@ifro.ku.dk

D. Kronborg · A. Rønn-Nielsen
Center for Statistics, Department of Finance, Copenhagen Business School, Frederiksberg, Denmark

C. F. Parmeter, R. C. Sickles (eds.), *Advances in Efficiency and Productivity Analysis*, Springer Proceedings in Business and Economics,
https://doi.org/10.1007/978-3-030-47106-4_14

1 Introduction

Using the Malmquist index to measure productivity change over time was proposed by Caves et al. (1982). Following Färe et al. (1992), the productivity change is frequently calculated using non-parametric data envelopment analysis (DEA) to estimate the relevant frontiers. The Malmquist index and its components, measuring changes in efficiency and in technology between two time periods, respectively, are subsequently determined, and typically the geometric means of the individual indexes are reported. However, these indexes are often interpreted without any associated measures of uncertainty. Simar and Wilson (1999) propose methods for calculating confidence intervals for the Malmquist index and its components using bootstrapping. Kneip et al. (2018) note that this bootstrap method is not based on theoretical results, and provide a method for calculating asymptotic confidence intervals for the Malmquist index. However, this method is only applicable for the Malmquist index itself and not for the frontier shift or the efficiency change components. To the best of our knowledge, Asmild et al. (2018) are the first to suggest exact statistical tests to assess the significance of the Malmquist index as well as of its components. The present paper reviews the permutation tests recently developed by Asmild et al. (2018) and provides an application hereof. Furthermore, where the Malmquist index is used to analyse changes over time for balanced panel data, comparisons of frontiers for separate groups in terms of the relative location of the group specific frontiers, provide information about which group technology offers superior production possibilities. Comparison of frontiers can be performed by calculating an index almost similar to the frontier change index for two time periods which is also presented in the present paper.

The various approaches are used to analyse the case of dairy farms in Denmark, over a number of years, with focus on comparison of the performance over time of organic and conventional dairy farming. The development of the dairy industry over time is, of course, relevant to practitioners and policy makers alike. Furthermore, it is of particular importance to distinguish between organic and conventional farms, not only with respect to the relative locations of their frontiers, but also concerning the development over time of the productivity within each of the groups. This has implications for, for example, policy interventions.

2 Methodology

Using standard notation, let input and output quantities be denoted by $(x, y) \in \mathbb{R}_+^{p+q}$. Under the usual assumptions of closedness, convexity, and strong disposability in both inputs and outputs, the production possibility set is given as

$$\Psi = \{(x, y) \in \mathbb{R}_+^{p+q} \mid x \text{ can produce } y\},$$

and the efficient frontier of Ψ is defined as

$$\Psi^{\delta} = \{(x, y) \in \Psi \mid (\gamma^{-1}x, \gamma y) \notin \Psi, \ \forall \gamma > 1\}.$$

The technical input efficiency index of Farrell (1957) is defined as

$$\theta(x, y) = \inf\{\theta > 0 | \ (\theta x, y) \in \Psi\}.$$

The production possibility set Ψ is unobserved and can in empirical applications be estimated from a set of n observations of random variables, $(X_i, Y_i), i = 1, \ldots, n$, which are assumed to be independent and identically distributed, such that (X_i, Y_i) has distribution F for all $i = 1, \ldots, n$. Denoting $\mathbf{X} = (X_1, \ldots, X_n)$ and $\mathbf{Y} = (Y_1, \ldots, Y_n)$, the estimate, $\hat{\Psi}$, of the production possibility set assuming constant return to scale (CRS) is

$$\hat{\Psi} = \{(x, y) \in \mathbb{R}_{+}^{p+q} \ | \exists \omega \in \mathbb{R}_{+}^{n} : x \geq \mathbf{X}\omega, y \leq \mathbf{Y}\omega\},$$

and the input efficiency for (x, y) can be estimated as $\hat{\theta}(x, y) = \inf\{\theta \in \mathbb{R}_{+} | \ (\theta x, y) \in \hat{\Psi}\}$ or equivalently using the standard DEA linear programming formulation:

$$\hat{\theta}(x, y) = \min_{\theta, \omega}\{\theta \mid \theta x \geq \mathbf{X}\omega, \ y \leq \mathbf{Y}\omega, \ \omega \in \mathbb{R}_{+}^{n}\}.$$

Consider a situation, where each unit is observed in two time periods, t_1 and t_2, such that we are given observations from the random variables $(X_i^{t_1}, Y_i^{t_1})$ and $(X_i^{t_2}, Y_i^{t_2})$ for the two time periods, respectively. We will allow the possibility set and the distribution of the variables to differ between the two time periods, and therefore we introduce the notation Ψ_t, Ψ_t^{δ}, and F_t for the possibility set, the frontier, and the distribution of the random variables (X_i^t, Y_i^t) in time period $t \in \{t_1, t_2\}$. We shall allow dependence between variables from the same unit in different time periods, i.e. $(X_i^{t_1}, Y_i^{t_1})$ and $(X_i^{t_2}, Y_i^{t_2})$, while there is (still) independence between variables concerning different units.

The traditional Malmquist index of productivity change (see e.g. Färe et al. 1992), from one period t_1 to another t_2 for unit i observed in both time periods is defined as

$$M(X_i^{t_1}, Y_i^{t_1}, X_i^{t_2}, Y_i^{t_2}) = \prod_{t \in \{t_1, t_2\}} \left(\frac{\hat{\theta}^t(X_i^{t_2}, Y_i^{t_2})}{\hat{\theta}^t(X_i^{t_1}, Y_i^{t_1})}\right)^{\frac{1}{2}},$$

where $\hat{\theta}^t$ denotes the input efficiency estimated relative to the frontier for time t, i.e.

$$\hat{\theta}^t(x, y) = \min_{\theta, \omega}\{\theta \mid \theta x \geq \mathbf{X}^t\omega, \ y \leq \mathbf{Y}^t\omega, \ \omega \in \mathbb{R}_{+}^{n}\}, \ \ t \in \{t_1, t_2\}.$$

We consider the geometric mean of the calculated Malmquist indices, i.e.

$$T_M = \prod_{i=1}^{n} M(X_i^{t_1}, Y_i^{t_1}, X_i^{t_2}, Y_i^{t_2})^{\frac{1}{n}}, \tag{1}$$

which can be interpreted as the productivity change for the whole technology, similar to the logic of the global indexes of Asmild and Tam (2007). The Malmquist index is often decomposed into two effects; the frontier shift and the efficiency change. The frontier shift for an individual unit (X_i^t, Y_i^t) is defined as

$$FS_i^t = \frac{\hat{\theta}^{t_1}(X_i^t, Y_i^t)}{\hat{\theta}^{t_2}(X_i^t, Y_i^t)}, \quad t \in \{t_1, t_2\},$$

and the frontier shift component of the Malmquist index is the geometric mean of FS_i^t over $t \in \{t_1, t_2\}$,

$$FS(X_i^{t_1}, Y_i^{t_1}, X_i^{t_2}, Y_i^{t_2}) = \left(FS_i^{t_1} \times FS_i^{t_2}\right)^{\frac{1}{2}}.$$

The efficiency change between t_1 and t_2 for unit i is given as

$$EC(X_i^{t_1}, Y_i^{t_1}, X_i^{t_2}, Y_i^{t_2}) = \frac{\hat{\theta}^{t_2}(X_i^{t_2}, Y_i^{t_2})}{\hat{\theta}^{t_1}(X_i^{t_1}, Y_i^{t_1})}.$$

With the above notation, the geometric mean of the frontier shift component can be written

$$T_{FS} = \prod_{i=1}^{n} FS(X_i^{t_1}, Y_i^{t_1}, X_i^{t_2}, Y_i^{t_2})^{\frac{1}{n}}, \tag{2}$$

and similarly the geometric mean of the efficiency change is

$$T_{EC} = \prod_{i=1}^{n} EC(X_{t_1}^i, Y_{t_1}^i, X_{t_2}^i, Y_{t_2}^i)^{\frac{1}{n}}. \tag{3}$$

Note that $M(X_i^{t_1}, Y_i^{t_1}, X_i^{t_2}, Y_i^{t_2}) = FS(X_i^{t_1}, Y_i^{t_1}, X_i^{t_2}, Y_i^{t_2}) \times EC(X_i^{t_1}, Y_i^{t_1}, X_i^{t_2}, Y_i^{t_2})$ and $T_M = T_{FS} \times T_{EC}$. All these statistics are positive.

The statistic T_{FS} can be used as a measure of how the two possibility sets Ψ_{t_2} and Ψ_{t_1} are placed relative to each other. A T_{FS} greater than 1 indicates that the possibility set generally is smaller in time t_1 than in time t_2. Since intersections of the frontiers are possible, when $T_{FS} > 1$ we cannot generally conclude that Ψ_{t_1} is a subset of Ψ_{t_2}. For a more thorough discussion of the properties and the interpretation of the statistic see Asmild et al. (2018).

While the Malmquist Index and the efficiency change component are only defined for balanced panel datasets, the (geometric mean of the) frontier shift can also be estimated for unbalanced panels, with n_{t_1} and n_{t_2} observations in the two time periods, respectively:

$$T_{FS}^{u} = \prod_{t \in \{t_1, t_2\}} \prod_{i=1}^{n_t} (FS_i^t)^{\frac{1}{n_{t_1}+n_{t_2}}}. \tag{4}$$

If, like in the present analysis, there are separate (independent) groups within the dataset, the above analysis can be done within each of the groups, letting $(X_i^{g,t}, Y_i^{g,t})$, $i = 1., \ldots, n_g$ denote observations from group g, $g = 1, \ldots, G$ in time period t. In the empirical example we consider $G = 2$ separate groups of organic and conventional farms, respectively, as well as analysis done on the full dataset.

Besides comparing frontiers over time (possibly within a given group), we are here also interested in comparing the frontiers for the two independent groups, g_1, g_2 (organic and conventional producers) at a fixed time. Similar to the definitions above, the geometric mean of the difference between the two groups' frontiers is defined as the ratio of the efficiencies relative to each of the two frontiers

$$T_{FD}^{g_1,g_2} = \prod_{g \in \{g_1, g_2\}} \prod_{i=1}^{n_g} \left(\frac{\hat{\theta}^{g_1}(X_i^g, Y_i^g)}{\hat{\theta}^{g_2}(X_i^g, Y_i^g)} \right)^{\frac{1}{n_{g_1}+n_{g_2}}}, \tag{5}$$

which for subsequent use can be decomposed as

$$T_{FD}^{g_1,g_2} = \left(\prod_{i=1}^{n_{g_1}} \left(\frac{\hat{\theta}^{g_1}(X_i^{g_1}, Y_i^{g_1})}{\hat{\theta}^{g_2}(X_i^{g_1}, Y_i^{g_1})} \right)^{\frac{1}{n_{g_1}}} \right)^{\frac{n_{g_1}}{n_{g_1}+n_{g_2}}} \times \left(\prod_{i=1}^{n_{g_2}} \left(\frac{\hat{\theta}^{g_1}(X_i^{g_2}, Y_i^{g_2})}{\hat{\theta}^{g_2}(X_i^{g_2}, Y_i^{g_2})} \right)^{\frac{1}{n_{g_2}}} \right)^{\frac{n_{g_2}}{n_{g_1}+n_{g_2}}}, \tag{6}$$

i.e. a weighted product of geometric means of the difference between the two groups' frontiers for observations from each of the two groups, which indicates the relative location of the two possibility sets.

It is well known that the estimate of the production possibility set is downward biased and therefore the efficiency scores are biased too. The bias decreases with increasing number of observations, so with large differences between the sizes of the two groups, the numerator and the denominator in (4) and (5) are determined with quite different biases. For a review of the asymptotic properties of the efficiency estimates see Simar and Wilson (2015).

Jackknifing methods can be used to address the issue of (differences in) biases by ensuring that whenever two frontiers are compared, the frontier estimates are based on groups of equal sizes: From the larger group, draw without replacement the same number of observations as in the smaller group, and calculate the relevant statistic (T_{FS}^{u} or $T_{FD}^{g_1,g_2}$). Repeat this a large number of times, say 1000, and calculate the geometric mean of the frontier difference measures (4) resp. (5) over the jackknife replications.

If the jackknifed $T_{FD}^{g_1,g_2}$ is greater than 1, this indicates that the possibility set for g_1 is smaller than that for g_2, implying that the g_2 technology (on average) offers better production possibilities (and similarly for T_{FS}^{u}). However, considering the two components of $T_{FD}^{g_1,g_2}$ in (6) provides additional information. Particularly, if one of the components is larger than 1 and the other smaller than 1, this implies that neither production possibility set is a subset of the other, meaning that their frontiers intersect. Furthermore, it also implies that the observations in the two groups are located differently in the production space. This can be further investigated by considering the input- and output mixes in the groups, for example, represented by the dimension-specific contributions to the overall length of the input- (or output) vector, $\frac{X_i}{||X_i||}$ (respectively $\frac{Y_i}{||Y_i||}$). Analysis hereof can, for example, be performed using the methodology of Asmild et al. (2016), by transforming the contributions into angles, ϕ, using the inverse cosine.[1]

2.1 Statistical Inference of the Malmquist Index and Its Components

To test the significance of the changes over time, i.e. of the Malmquist Index and its components, within each of the separate groups, we utilize permutation tests. Overall, the hypothesis we wish to test is that $(X^{t_1}, Y^{t_1}, X^{t_2}, Y^{t_2})$ and $(X^{t_2}, Y^{t_2}, X^{t_1}, Y^{t_1})$ have the same distribution, i.e. that the distribution in time period t_1 can be interchanged with the distribution in time period t_2. For this we use three tests designed to detect different forms of deviations from this hypothesis.

We first present the test procedures for *balanced* panels as described in detail in Asmild et al. (2018). The procedure compares the observed values of the test statistics T_M, T_{FS}, and T_{EC} given in (1), (2), and (3), respectively, with N similar values of the test statistics calculated based on appropriate permutations of the original dataset: Each of the permuted datasets are obtained by interchanging every pair of observations $(X_i^{t_1}, Y_i^{t_1})$ and $(X_i^{t_2}, Y_i^{t_2})$ randomly with probability 0.5 and independently for different $i = 1, \ldots, n$.

Under the hypothesis being tested, the test statistics T_M, T_{FS}, and T_{EC} based on the original dataset all have the same distributions as their N permuted counterparts calculated from permuted versions of the dataset. Thus, significance probabilities are obtained by finding the proportion of simulated test statistics that are further away from one than the observed test statistic.

[1]It is here worth noting that these angles are not scale invariant. Therefore, one should ensure that all input (output) variables are measured in similar metrics, like, e.g. in the present case where all inputs are costs and the outputs are revenues.

As discussed in Asmild et al. (2018) a set of three tests can be used to identify the nature of any differences between the two time periods: If the value of T_M is significantly different from one, an overall deviation from the null hypothesis can be concluded, i.e. that there is some difference between the distributions F_{t_1} and F_{t_2} in the two periods. If, furthermore, the test associated with T_{FS} is significantly different from one, the deviation from the null hypothesis is of such nature that the two frontiers are different or at least that the distributions F_{t_1} and F_{t_2} are different near the frontier. If, on the other hand, T_{EC} has a value significantly different from one, the null hypothesis is rejected because the efficiency distributions are different in the two periods.

As mentioned in the previous section, the test statistic for frontier shift, T_{FS}, can be generalized to an *unbalanced* version, T^u_{FS}, as formulated in Eq. (4) in order to take all available information into consideration. To perform a significance test, the permutation procedure for producing N permuted datasets also has to be modified: All complete observation pairs $(X_i^{t_1}, Y_i^{t_1})$ and $(X_i^{t_2}, Y_i^{t_2})$ are randomly interchanged as before. All remaining observations, that by assumption are independent and furthermore are identically distributed under the null hypothesis, are permuted and divided randomly into the two groups such that the two group sizes remain unchanged in the permuted dataset. Finally, a significance probability is obtained by comparing the observed (original) value of T_{FS} with the empirical distribution of the test statistic when based on each of the N permuted datasets.

It should be noted that while there is unequal bias when estimating the frontiers for the two groups of different sizes, this will not give problems in the described test procedure as long as the sizes of the groups are fixed in all permutations of the dataset. Thereby the observed test statistic is still comparable with the permuted counterparts.

3 Danish Dairy Farms

The dataset is provided by SEGES (who amongst other things provide specialist advisory services to the Danish agricultural sector) and contains annual farm-level accounting data from the years 2011–2015. For the current analysis, only full-time farmers specialized in dairy production and with at least 100 dairy cows and at least 25 hectares of cultivated land are included. Observations with problematic data based on various screening criteria are excluded (as detailed in Lillethorup 2017), resulting in an only partly balanced dataset comprising between 1355 and 1567 observations in each year.

The variables included in the efficiency models are as follows:

Inputs:

- Feed costs (costs of purchasing grains and fodder)
- Labour costs (estimated value of family labour plus paid labour)

- Other variable costs, OVC (including energy, fuel, fertilizer, veterinary costs, etc.)
- Fixed costs, FC (including costs of maintenance, taxes, insurances, etc.)
- Capital costs (defined as 4% of the value of the tangible assets, including land)

Outputs:

- Milk revenue
- Other (output) revenue, OO (revenue from all other outputs)

Descriptive statistics of the variables in each year, for both the conventional and the organic producers, are provided in Table 1.

In Sect. 4 below we illustrate how the approaches outlined in Sect. 2, when used together can provide various insights on the development over time of the Danish dairy producers, as well as on the differences between conventional and organic farms.

4 Results

4.1 Frontier Differences

Comparison of the organic and conventional farms is performed within each of the 5 years. The frontier differences are here defined as the efficiency scores relative to the frontier for the organic farms divided by the efficiency scores relative to the frontier for the conventional farms. Frontier difference measures (T_{FD}) larger than 1 mean that the observations on average are closer to the organic frontier than to the conventional frontier, implying that the conventional technology (on average) offers better production possibilities.

First, consider the geometric mean frontier difference within each of the two subgroups, accounting for different sample sizes using the described jackknife technique. The results are shown in the upper part of Table 2 where it is seen, that during the study period the organic farms on average are located nearer the production frontier for the conventional farms than that for the organic farms, implying that the organic technology (on average) offers better production possibilities in the directions determined by the locations of the organic farms. Conversely, for the conventional farms the frontier difference measures are larger than one in 2012–2014, implying that the conventional technology (on average) offers better production possibilities in the directions determined by the locations of the conventional farms in 2012–2014. However, in 2015 the frontier difference measure for the conventional farms is smaller than one, implying that the organic technology now offers better possibilities for the conventional farms (as well as for the organic farms). The (geometric) average of the frontier differences for the organic and the conventional farms is in all years smaller than or equal to one, indicating that the

Table 1 Averages and standard deviations (in parenthesis) within year and group (in 1000 DKK)

Type	Year	Feed	Labour	OVC	FC	Capital	Milk	OO
Conv	2011	1353 (833)	976 (448)	1585 (749)	1393 (826)	1640 (794)	4590 (2268)	1083 (953)
	2012	1494 (992)	1006 (481)	1658 (822)	1414 (776)	1641 (791)	4652 (2468)	1182 (1010)
	2013	1798 (1133)	1057 (531)	1722 (841)	1456 (732)	1681 (819)	5558 (2922)	1001 (1013)
	2014	1703 (1081)	1116 (576)	1788 (870)	1568 (860)	1726 (850)	5811 (3056)	952 (1017)
	2015	1702 (1154)	1137 (615)	1757 (874)	1571 (956)	1768 (902)	4968 (2824)	1183 (916)
Org	2011	1096 (803)	1002 (472)	1352 (600)	1493 (833)	1925 (846)	4490 (2246)	1076 (728)
	2012	1271 (1010)	1036 (463)	1413 (644)	1498 (639)	1983 (861)	4542 (2314)	1138 (794)
	2013	1561 (1357)	1087 (543)	1488 (759)	1561 (729)	2019 (902)	5324 (2964)	957 (701)
	2014	1569 (1422)	1163 (629)	1558 (807)	1679 (842)	2079 (990)	5815 (3463)	954 (728)
	2015	1486 (1272)	1168 (608)	1482 (677)	1656 (796)	2106 (974)	5504 (3067)	1257 (826)

Table 2 Group frontier differences, $T_{FD}^{g_1,g_2}$ and its components (as in (6))

	2011	2012	2013	2014	2015
With jackknife					
Organic	0.840	0.900	0.864	0.934	0.786
Conventional	0.988	1.023	1.041	1.071	0.920
Average	0.911	0.959	0.948	1.000	0.850
Without jackknife					
Organic	0.949	1.008	0.994	1.084	0.872
Conventional	1.070	1.115	1.167	1.206	0.991
All	1.054	1.102	1.144	1.191	0.976

organic technology overall tends to be superior (after controlling for sample size biases).

Calculating the frontier differences without jackknifing yields the results in the lower part of Table 2, which give substantially different (and misleading) conclusions. In particular, that the mean frontier difference across all the observations is larger than one all years besides 2015, would lead to the (wrong) conclusion that the conventional technology is superior in those years. This highlights the importance of controlling for sample size biases using, e.g. jackknifing.

As the organic technology (on average) offers better production possibilities for the organic farms, but the conventional technology (on average) offers better production possibilities for the conventional farms in 2012–2014, is evidence of the two frontiers intersecting in (at least) those years. That the organic farms tend to be located with an input-output mix where the organic technology offers better possibilities, and similarly for the conventional farms, makes perfect sense from an economic point of view.

4.2 *Mix Differences*

To investigate the differences in input-output mix between the organic and the conventional farms we express the dimension-specific contributions to the overall length of the input and the output vectors by the angles ϕ. The average angles for the organic and the conventional farms in 2015 for each dimension are shown in the top part of Table 3. In the bottom part of the table test statistics and corresponding p-values for equality of the mean direction in the truncated ($[0, \pi/2]$) approximative normal distribution of the angles (c.f. Asmild et al. 2016)[2] are shown.

From the mean angles we observe that the average ϕ_{Milk} is much smaller than the average ϕ_{OO} (for both conventional and organic farms), which implies that the share of revenue from milk is much larger than that from other outputs.

[2]Note that since there are only two outputs, the angles are complementary and therefore the test statistics and p values for the two output angles are identical.

Table 3 Average input- and output angles ϕ in 2015, and test statistics for comparisons (conventional and organic) and corresponding p-values

Type	ϕ_{Feed}	ϕ_{Lab}	ϕ_{OVC}	ϕ_{FC}	ϕ_{Cap}	ϕ_{Milk}	ϕ_{OO}
Conv	1.098	1.249	1.060	1.125	1.057	0.239	1.332
Org	1.177	1.244	1.146	1.097	0.950	0.229	1.342
LR	40.26	0.758	123.74	12.71	120.68	1.835	1.835
p	0.0000	0.384	0.0000	0.0004	0.0000	0.176	0.176

In terms of the comparison of the organic and the conventional farms we note that there are significant differences on four out of the five inputs. The differences on labour and on the outputs are not significant. The organic farms have a larger angle on feed than the conventional farms, meaning a smaller contribution from feed to the overall length of the input vector. Correspondingly, the organic farms have a larger contribution from capital than the conventional farms. This is likely due to the fact that being classified as an organic dairy farm in Denmark entails requirements for animal welfare, which means that the organic dairy cows in Denmark must be on pasture for around 6 month during the summer. This requires additional farmland, but results in saving on hard feed, thus more capital but less feed costs are necessary for the organic farmers compared to the conventional. Furthermore, the organic farms have a larger angle thus smaller contribution from other variable costs than the conventional farms, which is likely because of less veterinary costs and/or costs associated with pesticides, etc.

Performing similar analysis in the other years shows that the main changes over time are on the contribution from milk to the overall length of the output vector. Specifically it was large in 2013 and 2014 (for both organic and conventional farms) but dropped substantially in 2015. The latter is likely due to a drop in the raw milk prices in the European Union in 2015, as also discussed below.

4.3 *Permutation Tests for Productivity Change and Its Components*

To further investigate the changes over time the T_M (1), T_{FS} (2), and T_{EC} (3) are calculated for the balanced subsets of the organic, respectively, the conventional farms as well as T^u_{FS} (4) for the unbalanced groups. Further, permutation tests as described in Sect. 2.1 are performed and shown in Tables 4 and 5.

Considering the Malmquist indexes for all the year-on-year shifts, we note that the test statistics for comparisons are extreme, so the null hypothesis is rejected, meaning that the distributions F_{t_1} and F_{t_2} are not interchangeable for either the organic or the conventional farms. This can be interpreted as significant productivity changes within both groups between all consecutive time periods. To understand the nature of the productivity changes we next consider its components, i.e. T_{FS} and

Table 4 Test statistics and significance probabilities for the subset of conventional farms (based on 1000 permutations)

	2011–12	2012–13	2013–14	2014–15
No. obs. balanced	1373	1348	1332	1220
No. obs. first year	1567	1530	1499	1454
No. obs. second year	1530	1499	1454	1355
Balanced dataset				
T_M	0.970 (0.000)	1.050 (0.000)	1.026 (0.000)	0.871 (0.000)
T_{EC}	1.002 (0.836)	0.991 (0.510)	1.000 (0.982)	1.059 (0.002)
T_{FS}	0.968 (0.000)	1.059 (0.000)	1.026 (0.145)	0.823 (0.000)
Unbalanced dataset				
T_{FS}^u	0.971 (0.000)	1.081 (0.000)	1.031 (0.063)	0.811 (0.000)

Table 5 Test statistics and significance probabilities for the subset of organic farms (based on 1000 permutations)

	2011−12	2012−13	2013−14	2014−15
No. obs. balanced	200	186	178	166
No. obs. first year	223	214	206	196
No. obs. second year	214	206	196	179
Balanced dataset				
T_M	0.9511 (0.000)	1.0383 (0.000)	1.0152 (0.009)	1.0172 (0.002)
T_{EC}	1.0119 (0.477)	1.0159 (0.228)	1.0477 (0.006)	0.9928 (0.412)
T_{FS}	0.9399 (0.000)	1.0220 (0.123)	0.9689 (0.191)	1.0246 (0.009)
Unbalanced dataset				
T_{FS}^u	0.926 (0.000)	1.089 (0.000)	0.961 (0.027)	1.021 (0.023)

T_{EC}. For T_{FS} we do not need a balanced dataset and more information is included when considering the unbalanced version T_{FS}^u shown in the last rows of the tables. As these all are significant, the frontiers are significantly different for all time shifts (or the distribution of points near the frontiers are different). Furthermore, when the efficiency changes T_{EC} are insignificant, we conclude that the productivity changes are likely to be due to frontiers movements.

The change from 2014 to 2015 is particularly interesting: The conventional farms exhibit worse production possibilities in 2015 compared to 2014, whereas the organic farms experienced significantly better productions possibilities in 2015 than in 2014. This explains the findings from Table 2, where the conventional farms in 2015 found the organic technology to be superior, unlike earlier years. It is here worth noting that this does not imply that the organic frontier strictly dominates the conventional frontier in 2015, since the frontiers might still intersect.

The likely reason for the change in 2015 that made organic farming superior to conventional farming for most input-output mixes is the abolishment of the milk quotas in Europe on March 31, 2015. While it (especially in the long run) enables an increased production, it in the short run led to a 25% drop in EU raw milk prices from 40 €per 100 kg in January 2014 to 30 €per 100 kg in January 2016, c.f.

e.g. the EU Milk Market Observatory (2018). This price drop had a relatively larger impact on the conventional farms since the premium paid for the organic milk in Denmark is fixed/independent of the price level.

This result is also supported by the more standard profitability analysis in Jørgensen (2017) which show that the profitability of the organic farms became much higher than that of the conventional farms in Denmark in 2015.

5 Final Remarks

This paper has focused on measures of productivity changes over time as well as frontier differences between independent groups. Statistical inference for productivity change measured by the Malmquist index, and the corresponding measures of frontier shift and efficiency change can be performed as permutation tests. These are exact tests and are in a recent paper by Asmild et al. (2018) found to be very powerful. We also suggest a method to measure frontier differences for separate independent groups, which accounts for the inherent bias in DEA estimated frontiers by using a jackknife method to minimize the effect of differences in sample sizes.

Formal tests for the significance of the differences between independent groups can be implemented in line with the methods in Asmild et al. (2018) using permutations. These methods, as well as the power of the tests, will be presented in a forthcoming paper.

The types of analyses presented here can have important policy implications, since the Danish government is focused on enhancing the competitiveness of the agricultural sector in Denmark at the same time as aiming at doubling the organic production between 2007 and 2020. Thus, formal analysis comparing the economic production possibilities associated with organic and with conventional farming is important as is the analysis of their respective productivity changes over time.

The results of the analysis presented in this paper showed that there might not have been a compelling argument for organic dairy production up until 2014, since the conclusion in terms of which production technology is superior differed depending on the input-output mix. However, in 2015 both the organic and the conventional farmers on average agreed to the organic technology being superior. An explanation for this pattern could be that the conventional farms have been "protected" by high milk prices, partly caused by the quota system. After the abolishment of the milk quotas and the corresponding drop in milk prices, which had a relatively larger impact on the conventional farms than on the organic, the frontier for the organic farming became superior to that of the conventional. This is also evident from the Malmquist index results which showed a large and significant productivity decrease for the conventional farms from 2014 to 2015 likely caused by a significant deterioration of the frontier, but a significant productivity (and frontier) improvement for the organic farms in the same period.

If subsequent analysis find that the difference between the organic and the conventional frontier is indeed significant (once the permutation based tests for comparisons of the frontiers for independent groups are fully investigated and can be applied), and persistent over the subsequent years, the business case for conversion to organic farming may be straightforward (at least if ignoring transition costs). This could also potentially be a solution to the lack of competitiveness for Danish dairy farming identified by Asmild et al. (2019).

References

Asmild, M., Balezentis, T., & Hougaard, J. L. (2019). Industry competitiveness indicators. IFRO Working Paper 2019/01.

Asmild, M., Kronborg, D., & Matthews, K. (2016). Introducing and modeling inefficiency contributions. *European Journal of Operational Research, 248*, 725–730.

Asmild, M., Kronborg, D., & Rønn-Nielsen, A. (2018). Testing productivity change, frontier shift, and efficiency change. IFRO Working Paper 2018/07.

Asmild, M., & Tam, F. (2007). Estimating global frontier shifts and global Malmquist indices. *Journal of Productivity Analysis, 27*, 137–148.

Caves, D., Christensen, L., & Diewert, E. (1982). The economic theory of index numbers and the measurement of input, output, and productivity. *Econometrica, 50*, 1393–1414.

EU Milk Market Observatory. (2018). https://ec.europa.eu/agriculture/market-observatory/milk/latest-statistics/prices-margins_en

Farrell, M. J. (1957). The measurement of productive efficiency. *Journal of the Royal Statistical Society, 120*, 253–281.

Färe, R., Grosskopf, S., Lindgren, B., & Roos, P. (1992). Productivity changes in Swedish pharmacies 1980–1989: A non-parametric Malmquist approach. *Journal of Productivity Analysis, 3*, 85–101.

Jørgensen, T. V. (2017). Økologi, økonomi og din strategi (in Danish). https://www.agrinord.dk/UserFiles/file/Nyheder%202017/oekonomi_i_oekologi.pdf

Kneip, A., Simar, L., & Wilson, P. W. (2018). Inference in dynamic, nonparametric models of production: central limit theorems for Malmquist indices. Discussion Paper #2018/10. Institut de Statistique, Biostatistique et Sciences Actuarielles, Université Catholique de Louvain, Louvain-la-neuve, Belgium.

Lillethorup, T. R. (2017). Linking animal welfare and yields to economic performance in Danish dairy production: A non-parametric approach using data envelopment analysis. Unpublished MSc dissertation, IFRO, University of Copenhagen.

Simar, L., & Wilson, P. W. (1999). Estimating and bootstrapping Malmquist indices. *European Journal of Operational Research, 115*, 459–471.

Simar, L., & Wilson, P. W. (2015). Statistical approaches for non-parametric frontier models: A guided tour. *International Statistical Review, 83*, 77–110.

Nutrient Use and Precision Agriculture in Corn Production in the USA

Roberto Mosheim and David Schimmelpfennig

Abstract This is a timely study of precision agriculture as both data management (mapping) and field production technologies for agricultural production are changing rapidly. We compare the performance of producers who adopt precision agriculture tools versus those that do not. We estimate both their own frontier performance and a metafrontier that enables the research to compare the efficiency of producers across technologies. To make these comparisons we pre-processed the data with a matching procedure in order to have a sample of producers of equal size for each category who faced similar conditions. In the metafrontier results we find that GPS yield maps, guidance auto-steering precision agriculture technologies, and managerial ability save input costs and increase farm production efficiency which has environmental benefits. Maps created from soils or aerial data and input applications using VRT did not produce useable results.

Keywords Crop production · Information technologies · On-farm ecosystem · Stewardship

Thanks to Chris O'Donnell, Spiro Stefanou, and our branch chief, Jim MacDonald, and attendants to the North American Productivity Workshop X at the University of Miami for their valuable feedback. The article uses confidential U.S. Department of Agriculture (USDA), National Agricultural Statistics Service data from the Agricultural Resource Management Survey. The findings and conclusions in this preliminary paper have not been formally disseminated by the U.S. Department of Agriculture and should not be construed to represent any agency determination or policy. This research was supported by the intramural research program of the U.S. Department of Agriculture, Economic Research Service.

R. Mosheim (✉) · D. Schimmelpfennig
Resources and Rural Economics Division (RRED), Economic Research Service, U.S. Department of Agriculture, Washington, DC, USA
e-mail: rmosheim@ers.usda.gov

C. F. Parmeter, R. C. Sickles (eds.), *Advances in Efficiency and Productivity Analysis*, Springer Proceedings in Business and Economics,
https://doi.org/10.1007/978-3-030-47106-4_15

1 Introduction

This study uses US corn production as a case study of precision agriculture (PrecAg). Such a study is timely as both data management (mapping) and field production technologies for agricultural production are changing rapidly. These information-based crop technologies allow farmers easier access to data and are increasing the effectiveness of production practices that use that data; their use is likely to accelerate in the near future. Sensor technologies for crop plants and soil, for example, are poised to increase the volume of data on crop conditions available to farmers. Internet-of-things devices are under development that can collect and store sensor data and produce crop practice recommendations in real-time in a farmer's fields. Field View, for instance, developed by Bayer AG, could be placed in the back of a combine to detect soil health resulting in reduction of nitrogen application by 10 pounds per acre, increasing yield by 2–3 bushels per acre, and increasing profitability by $12 per acre (Condon 2018).

Corn production in the USA and its associated use of agricultural chemicals (fertilizer and pesticides) has a significant effect on soil erosion and water quality and thus provides a valuable window onto the attempts to tackle the grand challenge problem of global sustainable agriculture and use of the world's land and water resources in the twenty-first century. As Purdue University's Global to Local Analysis of Systems Sustainability (GLASS), for one, emphasizes, sustainability is a local concept with global significance. Global forces drive local (un)sustainability, and local responses to individual stresses can have global consequences. PrecAg can enhance the benefits and diminish the costs of fertilizer use in corn production by better targeting the various nutrients to crop needs, thus reducing waste and environmental damage.

Profitability evaluations by Swinton and Lowenberg-DeBoer (1998), Griffin et al. (2004), and Schimmelpfennig (2016) are unanimous that precision technologies can be profitable on a large scale, notably in US corn production. These studies also agree with Griliches (1957) that profitability drives adoption, and as Lusk (2016) and Schimmelpfennig (2018) point out, their use has resource stewardship and environmental benefits brought about by fact-based crop management. This study tackles the question of whether these groundbreaking technologies also make field-crop farms more efficient. Paraphrasing economist Robert Solow's famous saying we see precision agriculture everywhere and our study shows where it is making an impact on the data.

Three technologies have been the most popular across a range of field crops, growing regions, and farm sizes. First, data management technologies that map harvester yield data and soil-test data using global positioning systems (GPS) coordinates can inform a wide range of production management decisions. Second, tractor guidance systems use GPS computer programs to self-steer farm machinery, and third, variable rate technology (VRT) seeding, fertilizer, and pesticide applications use GPS coordinates and are programmed from yield and soil maps.

2 Description of Precision Agricultural Technologies

Yield-by-location data from harvesters with yield-monitoring sensors and GPS receivers record latitude/longitude coordinates that use geographic information systems (GIS) to produce a yield map. Usually several years of yield data are necessary to discern consistent yield patterns. Soil tests show soil properties on a map using GPS data collected from a smaller number of locations often using core samples. Aerial maps show growing conditions using data collected from remotely sensing satellites with various light-spectrum sensitivities, small aircraft mounted with sensors, and unmanned aerial vehicles (UAVs) commonly referred to as drones. These UAVs may be quadcopters with four sets of propellers and are smaller versions of the jet engine drones used in military applications. Together these maps help to inform production management decisions.

Producers often use tractor or combine auto-guidance systems that self-steer farm equipment using maps that include the GPS boundaries of their fields. Auto-guidance has the benefit of relative simplicity, with one piece of steering equipment mounted on a steering column attached to a GPS receiver. In case studies, guidance systems have helped farmers efficiently reduce input costs by increasing the accuracy of row cut-offs and reducing overlapping or missed applications, that can also increase yields, while reducing operator fatigue.

VRT uses mapped data to program machinery controllers and servo motors to apply different levels of inputs, even seeds, at different rates across one field. VRT planters that can site-specifically select from different multiple-hybrid seeds are becoming available. Machinery with VRT is more expensive to purchase and time-consuming to maintain than other PrecAg options. In addition to production management support, maps also help identify conditions when VRT may not save costs or increase profit. Crop farmers hire custom service providers (CSPs) to perform routine production tasks that they are unable to perform, and the use of PrecAg technologies by CSPs is increasing. Erickson and Widmar (2015) and Erickson and Lowenberg-DeBoer (2017) report three-quarters of dealers offer GPS field mapping services and VRT fertilization in the Midwest, West, and Southern United States. CSPs are also heavy users of guidance systems, providing evidence for the practical and cost-effective usefulness of the technologies.

To estimate the productivity effect of PrecAg, this paper extends distance function models by Bravo-Ureta et al. (2012) and Henningsen et al. (2015) by accounting for technological heterogeneity of the corn sector in the USA using a stochastic metafrontier following Huang et al. (2014) and Amsler et al. (2017). Three frontiers are estimated: (1) One for those firms that use PrecAg; (2) another for those firms that are not users of PrecAg; and (3) metafrontier that includes both.

2.1 Data Sources and Variable Construction

This project uses nationally representative data from the 2016 Agricultural Resource Management Survey (ARMS) (ERS-ARMS 2017). The ARMS, administered jointly by USDA's Economic Research Service and National Agricultural Statistics Service, collects field-level data on practices and resource use for a rotating set of field crops in Phase II. Respondents to the Phase II survey are also surveyed as part of Phase III, which collects farm-level financial data. Detailed data provide crucial information on inputs used for agricultural production like nutrients and pesticides, machinery, labor, and the use of precision technologies, including GPS mapping, guidance systems, and variable rate application (VRT). ARMS Phase II asks over thirty questions about PrecAg use, and the identification of precision technologies is now an integral part of the ARMS survey. This dataset, in other words, is particularly well-suited to our analysis.

Technology adoption is estimated using sample responses to individual technology use questions, expanded to the number of farms using sample weights, to estimate the share of corn farms adopting a technology.[1] Table 1 presents the

Table 1 Variables description

Variable	Units	Definition
Output quantity		
y_1	Units	Corn for grain
Input quantities		
x_1	Acres	Field planted with corn
x_{2_a}	Paid hours	Direct labor used for corn production
x_{2_b}	Imputed hours	Operator + partner + unpaid labor hours
x_3	Horsepower	Sum power all machinery
x_{4a}	$	Other inputs
x_{4b}	$	Contract + custom + consulting work
Further explanatory variables in production function		
Farm size		
Precision Ag. adoption		
Variables hypothesized to affect inefficiency		
Operator identifies main occupation as farming		
Random component		
Yield goal		
Other variables in the metafrontier equation		
Yield monitor (data creates a map) P2463		
GPS-enabled guidance auto-steering P2148		
Managerial ability (Yield goal - Actual output)^2		

[1]This survey method means that each sample farm represents multiple farms from the same state and size class, and that the stratum weights have to be adjusted for nonresponse. Samples are expanded to population estimates with sample weights.

variable definitions and description of the output and input quantity information employed in the input distance frontier. Output quantity measures corn for grain in bushels. We distinguish four input quantities: first, land used is measured in acres of corn planted on the farm. The opportunity cost of land is measured as its rental rate. Second, labor is hours of labor and management employed in the field. Hired labor is collected on an hourly basis for time spent operating machinery, scouting for weeds, insects, and diseases, and other work-by-hand. Different wage rates are used for labor hours by part-time/seasonal and full-time workers as well as contract laborers. Unpaid labor is commonly family labor in some kind of actual or implied partnership with the farm owner. The cost of unpaid labor is an opportunity cost estimated from whole farm financial data. The attributes of unpaid operators—such as age, education, marital status, and location—allow estimation of foregone off-farm hourly earnings. In Griffin et al.'s (2004) profitability survey, only one-fifth of reviewed PrecAg studies include operator time, but those studies found it was significant.

Third, capital, is approximated by the sum of the horsepower of all equipment employed on the farm. Fourth, we include the sum in dollars of miscellaneous expenses and contract and custom expenditures. These expenses include fuel and oil, taxes, and insurance, while custom service costs are for custom seeding, fertilizer, or pesticide applications. Costs include specific operations paid by task rather than by hour and are separated from the cost of inputs used by custom applicators. We integrate two additional variables in the distance function: farm size and corn field size. Farm size is in acres which is larger than corn field size in ARMS Phase II. A correlation test together with a multicollinearity test between corn acreage and farm size is also included in Table 2. The size of the condition number excludes concerns of multicollinearity between these two variables.

We model heteroskedasticity in both the random and the inefficiency terms of the frontier model. We also model heteroskedasticity in the random portion of the error term employing the variable yield goal which captures the information the farmer has about the agroeconomic conditions of his or her fields and hence is used to control for location. We hypothesized that an operator that identifies his or her occupation as primarily in farming affects the performance of the agricultural enterprise. Following Huang et al. (2014) we hypothesize that different variables affect the enterprise performance and the metafrontier: yield monitors, GPS-enabled auto-steering, and a variable we call managerial ability and define as yield goal minus actual output squared. See Table 1 for a tabulation of these definitions.

We followed Bravo-Ureta et al. (2012) in using propensity score matching utilizing 1-to-1 nearest neighbor in order to impose common conditions that farmers face. In our case we employ the R software MatchIt on the adoption or non-adoption of PrecAg to ensure that both groups face similar observed characteristics. In the following table we present summary statistics for matched and unmatched data for adopters and non-adopters of PrecAg and present means difference tests.

Table 2 Summary statistics for the pooled and the matched sample[a]

	Pooled		Precision Ag.		Conventional		t Mean
Variables	Mean	Std. Dev.	Mean	Std. Dev.	Mean	Std. Dev.	Test
Unmatched sample							
y	175	47	177	47	168	45	2.87***
x_1	74	82	81	80	56	84	4.01***
x_2	13,547	52,548	15,047	60,337	9774	23,129	1.90*
x_3	882	397	900	384	837	428	2.08**
x_4	472,948	818,554	549,124	885,952	281,328	575,728	5.36***
Precision Ag.	0.72	0.45	1	0	0	0	
Ocuppd	0.91	0.29	0.92	0.27	0.88	0.33	1.83*
Fsz	817	1358	971	1475	429	898	6.74***
Yg	176	40	179	39	168	41	3.84***
	Correlation (significance in parentheses) and condition number for x_1 and Fsz						
Correlation	0.230 (0.000) 0.213 (0.000) 0.230 (0.000)						
Cond. number	2.539 2.764 2.088						
Observations	907		649		258		
Matched sample							
y	179	45	190	43	168	44.96716	5.75***
x_1	85	94	114	94	56	84.26028	7.36***
x_2	16,950	67,757	24,125	92,529	9774	23128.57	2.40**
x_3	902	393	967	343	837	427.5712	3.81***
x_4	631,971	1,034,740	982,614	1,251,886	281,328	575728.3	8.17***
Precision Ag.	0.5	0.5					
Ocuppd	0.92	0.27	0.97	0.18	0.88	0.33	3.79***
Fsz	1146	1146	1863	2014	429	898	10.45***
Yg	180	40	192	35	168	41	7.40***
	Correlation (significance in parentheses) and condition number for x_1 and Fsz						
Correlation	0.219 (0.000) 0.061 (0.331) 0.230 (0.000)						
Cond. number 2.585 3.400 2.089							
Observations	516		258		258		

[a] A t-test for testing whether the mean values of the variables are the same for precision Ag. adopter farmers and non-adopter farmers

Source: USDA, Agricultural Resource Management Survey (ARMS) 2016

Notes: *P = <0.10; **P = <0.05; ***P = <0.01

3 Input Distance Function Model

3.1 *Metaproduction Technology*

The metafrontier was introduced by Hayami (1969) and Hayami and Ruttan (1970). It captures the idea that relative differences in production environments (for example, economic resources, relative prices, regulation) inhibit firms in some groups from choosing the best technology from the potential technology set creating a so-called production technology gap. To estimate the most appropriate technology and corresponding efficiency for a sector like corn production by simply pooling all data on inputs and outputs is not justified because the frontier may not cover some producer groups. Also, there is the problem of benchmarking a group by a production technology estimated for another group. In the interest of measuring performance across groups of producers that employ different technologies, Battese and Rao (2002) and Battese et al. (2003) pioneered the idea of the metafrontier in the productivity literature. They applied a two-step procedure: first, they estimated stochastic frontiers for different groups of producers, and second, they employed a nonparametric method to envelop all the technologies of the different groups. The metafrontier, T^*, is conceptualized as the "totality" of group technologies. For example, if output y can be produced employing input vector x with a non-precision type of technology, then the input–output bundle (x, y) belongs to T^*. Huang et al. (2014) and Amsler et al. (2017) proposed fully stochastic methods to estimate metafrontiers that we employ in this study.

Formally, the metatechnology is defined as:

$$T^* = \{(x, y) : x \geq 0 \; and \; y \geq 0, such \; that \; x \; can \; produce \; y \; employing \; precision \; \text{Ag} \; or \; not, T^1, T^2\Big\}, hence, T^* \supseteq \{T^1 \cup T^2\}. \tag{1}$$

If T^1, T^2satisfy the production axioms, then T^* also satisfies all production axioms, except the convexity property. Then T^* is defined as a convex hull of the union of the specific technologies:

$$T^* \equiv Convex \; Hull \left\{T^1 \cup T^2\right\}. \tag{2}$$

Farmers produce output, y, using input vector, x, and technology k, T^k, $k = 1, 2$ correspond, respectively, to adoption or non-adoption of PrecAg technologies.

Given the output, y, define the input set as

$$L^k(y) = \left\{x : (x, y) \in T^k\right\}. \tag{3}$$

Define $D_i^k\,(x, y)$ as the input distance function for technology k given by

$$D_i^k y, x\Big) = \max_\lambda \left[\lambda : {}^x\!/_\lambda \in L^k(y)\right]. \tag{4}$$

If vector x lies in the boundary of $L^k(y)$, then $D_i^k\,(x, y) = 1$ is defined as the maximum contraction in input usage while still remaining within the production possibilities of the firm. If x lies in its interior $D_i^k\,(x, y) > 1$. The expression $D_i^*\,(x, y)$

denotes the input distance function defined using the metatechnology, T^*. Battese et al. (2003) established that for any given k, $D_i^k(x, y) \leq D_i^*(x, y)$, $(k = 1, 2)$, which follows from the fact that the input sets for any particular technology are a subset of the corresponding sets constituting the metatechnology.

The input-oriented technical efficiency of an observed pair (x, y) with respect to technology k is defined as:

$$TE_i^k(x, y) = \frac{1}{D_i^k(x, y)}. \tag{5}$$

The input-oriented technology gap ratio can be defined using the input distance functions for technologies T^k and T^* as:

$$TGR_i^k(x, y) = \frac{D_i^k(x, y)}{D_i^*(x, y)} = \frac{TE_i^*(x, y)}{TE_i^k(x, y)}. \tag{6}$$

It follows that

$$TE_i^*(x, y) = TGR_i^k(x, y) \times TE_i^k(x, y). \tag{7}$$

We can use Eq. (7) to test for the coverage of the metafrontier, i.e. to test whether the metafrontier covers every group of producers entirely and Eqs. (5), (6), and (7) comprehensively measure efficiency and decompose the metafrontier.

4 Econometric Estimation and Results

The samples we used for the estimations consist of 907 farms before matching and 516 after matching. We started the examination of the empirical model by specifying a Cobb–Douglas input distance function, $\ln D_i = \beta_o + \phi \ln y_1 + \sum_{n=1}^{4} \beta_n \ln x_n + v$. We follow Coelli et al. (2003, 2005) who point out that this function must be non-decreasing, linearly homogeneous, and concave in inputs, $\beta_n \geq 0$ for all n and $\sum_{n=1}^{4} \beta_n = 1$ and non-increasing in output if $\phi \leq 0$. We estimate a homogeneity-constrained Cobb–Douglas frontier:

$$-\ln x_1 = \beta_o + \phi \ln y + \sum_{n=2}^{4} \beta_n \ln(x_n/x_1) + v_i - u_i. \tag{8}$$

In the above equation $-\ln D_i = v_i - u_i$. Distance is conceptualized as the radial distance between the data points and the frontier, having both an inefficiency and a stochastic element. We assume a normal distribution for the random error term

$v \sim N\left(0, \sigma_v^2\right)$ and a half-normal distribution for inefficiency, $u \sim N^+\left(0, \sigma_u^2\right)$. The input-oriented efficiency and the random error terms are heteroskedastic. As in Greene (2008, p. 219) the variance is doubly heteroskedastic (Hadri et al. 1999, 2003a, b) which means that both variances are a linear function of a set of covariates, Z. We assume that both the inefficiency and the error terms are heteroskedastic, depending on different sets of covariates:

$$\begin{aligned} Var\left(u|z_i\right) &= \sigma_u^2 \exp\left(w_i\delta\right) \\ Var\left(v|z_j\right) &= \sigma_v^2 \exp\left(w_j\delta\right). \end{aligned} \quad (9)$$

Input-oriented technical inefficiency is $TI = \frac{1}{D_I} = \exp\left(-u_i\right)$.

We estimate Eq. (9) above employing the input, output, and covariate variables described in Table 1. Table 2 shows a comparison of matched and unmatched variables employed in the econometric estimation. There are several aspects worth noticing about this table. First, difference in means statistical tests points to significant differences in the means of the variables between adopters of PrecAg and non-adopters. Second, the most important difference is that farm size of adopters is more than twice that of non-adopters. Third, yield goal and self-identification as in the farming profession are surprisingly similar but still statistically different between adopters and non-adopters. Fourth, the table presents a strong justification against using a model where both adopters and non-adopters of PrecAg are pooled. Last, the matching procedure resulted in more significant difference of means tests between adopters of precision and non-adopters for all variables.

Table 3 shows the estimates of the unmatched and matched samples. The result from the matching procedure brought that sample down from 907 to 516 observations, 258 adopters and 258 non-adopters. In the estimated input distance function labor, power (capital) and other inputs were divided by land, x_1, to impose linear homogeneity. Output was not so divided. Hence $-$ ln $(1/x_1)$serves as the measure of distance for the enterprise. The signs of the input and output elasticities of the unmatched and matched samples correspond to expectations from economic theory. Overall the estimates using the unmatched sample are more significant than those using the matched sample. However, they have the drawbacks controlled during the matching process.

The variable "adopt" in both the pooled and matched samples is highly significant and shifts the distance function inward, that is, farms that employ PrecAg use less of every input to produce the same quantity of corn than those that do not use it. The effect of PrecAg is higher for the matched sample. The effect of the variable "farm size" is also to economize resources. On average, larger farms are more efficient than smaller farms. Yield goal is highly significant when modeling heteroskedasticity of the error term. Yield goals are generally associated with farm size and what the farmer estimates the farm can produce according to its agroecological conditions determined by the location of the farm.

Table 4 compares the individual matched samples of farmers that use PrecAg tools in their farms with those that do not. This table highlights some important

Table 3 Estimates of inefficiency effects model

	Unmatched sample		Matched sample	
Variables	Coefficient	Rbst. Std. Err.	Coefficient	Rbst. Std. Err.
di				
lny	−0.177***	0.043	−0.104	0.066
ln(x2/x1)	0.060***	0.010	0.057***	0.014
ln(x3/x1)	0.785***	0.019	0.766***	0.024
ln(x4/x1)	0.101***	0.016	0.112***	0.022
adopt	−0.206***	0.035	−0.426***	0.048
const	−0.327**	0.053	−6.408***	0.384
lnsig2v				
yield goal	−0.006***	0.001	−0.006***	0.002
const	−0.608***	0.236	−0.672**	0.326
lnsig2u				
farm size	−0.0005***	0.0001	−0.0003***	0.0001
const	−3.377***	0.492	−3.975***	1.023
Log-likelihood	−566.20		−302.85	
Observations	907		516	

Note: *P = <0.10; **P = <0.05; ***P = <0.01

Table 4 Estimates of inefficiency effects model

	Precision Ag. farmer	Non-precision Ag. farmer	
Variables	Coefficient	Rbst Std. Err.	Coefficient
di			
lny	−0.073	0.036	−0.026
ln(x2/x1)	0.030**	0.010	0.046**
ln(x3/x1)	0.494***	0.042	0.786***
ln(x4/x1)	0.345***	0.038	0.141***
farm size	−0.00008***	0.00002	−0.0002***
const	−8.234***	0.425	−6.903***
lnsig2v			
yield goal	−0.001	0.003	−0.0003
const	−3.521***	0.417	−1.460***
lnsig2u			
farming occupation	27.296***	4.034	24.185***
const	−31.149***	3.778	−26.884***
Log-likelihood	−39.29		−182.37
Observations	258		258

Note: *P = <0.10; **P = <0.05; ***P = <0.01

results for adopters of PrecAg. First, technology coefficients have the same theoretically consistent effects as to input and output elasticities though they are slightly weaker. Second, yield goal, the variable that we use to model heteroskedasticity is not significant. Third, the effect of farm size is strong and shifts the frontier towards the origin, that is, efficiency improves with farm size. Fourth, farmers can have various occupations apart from farming. The variable "farming" points to whether the farmer's main occupation was indeed farming, and an operator that identifies as a farmer is more efficient than those that do not. This effect is also quite strong. For non-adopters of PrecAg, however, if a farmer identifies as a farmer the variable has a much stronger effect. Specialization makes up for the expanded skill set brought to the farm by adopters. In contrast, the effect of farm size is stronger for adopters than non-adopters which makes sense as well since many technologies become economical for larger farms. Relative to their respective frontiers, group 1 (adopters) has an average technical efficiency score of 0.832 with a std. dev. of 0.101, and group 2 (non-adopters) has one of 0.675 with a std. dev. of 0.194. We can infer that the level of competition is higher for adopters than non-adopters. The results presented in Table 4 also represent the first step of the two-step procedure used to estimate a metafrontier where we specify $D_i^k(x, y)$ for adapters and non-adapters of PrecAg, as was mentioned above.

The striking difference in the structure of the output elasticities shown in Tables 3 and 4 needs to be explained. Table 3 shows similar estimates for output elasticities for both matched and unmatched models. Table 4 shows pretty wide differences in output elasticities between PrecAg and Non-PrecAg farmers. It is important to remember that the matching process makes the conditions that both PrecAg and Non-PrecAg farmers face as similar as possible, including their sample size. The matching process reduced the overall sample from 907 to 516. The matching process attempts to make the conditions that both types of firms face as similar as possible. We hypothesize it is desirable that the unmatched and matched sample estimations generate similar output elasticity results. For the process to not introduce a statistical bias, the end result should produce an overall matched sample with very similar mean and variance for all variables. These results are presented in Table 3.

Table 4 presents estimates for the two distinct types of firms after elimination of firms in each group with the most dissimilar external conditions. The matching process does not attempt to make the elasticities of the two different groups as similar as possible but to ensure they face the same external conditions.

Table 5 shows the coefficient estimates of the metafrontier using an almost identical procedure as in Huang et al. (2014) in which the predictions of the individual frontiers are employed to construct the stochastic metafrontier. Here we use Battese and Coelli (1995) in both steps. We followed Huang et al. (2014) in choosing different sets of exogenous variables for the first and the second steps. The estimated coefficients on output are non-increasing and the ones on inputs are non-decreasing meeting the theoretical properties of the input distance function. All these coefficients are strongly significant. We also include two PrecAg variables for the technology in the distance function, finding that GPS-enabled auto-steering decreases the usage of all inputs. This result is significant at the 1% level. Yield monitors also decrease input usage shifting the isoquant downward. However, this result is significant only at the 10% level. We used "farm size" to model heteroskedasticity in the error with the variable significant at the 1% level. Farmers' ability to predict future production (yield goal—realized yield squared) is a strong indicator of managerial ability. Greater variance in this metric results in a lower efficiency score. The effect of this latter variable is significant at the 5% level. Larger farms are more efficient as they are able to exploit the cost-cutting effect of size through scale economies.

We checked the predicted metafrontier distance against both adopter and non-adopter predicted distances to verify that the metafrontier covered both groups.[2] The results of this initial probe were that the metafrontier encompassed totally the group that adopted PrecAg but almost also encompassed the group that did not. We will follow this finding by examining the random error relation between groups as in Amsler et al. (2017). Nevertheless, the results we got from following Huang et al. (2014) are valuable as an initial step as seen below.

Table 5 shows the estimates of the metafrontier. Of note is that the metafrontier meets all of the theoretical properties of an input distance function. Here we tested two PrecAg variables directly into the technology. We also employed "farm size" to model heteroskedasticity in the random error term. At the same time, we tested the performance metric yield goal minus realized production directly into the distance frontier. We also included farm size concurrently with that of managerial ability to isolate the effects. The estimates are significant at the 1% level. These preliminary results point to a strong impact of PrecAg on technology, shifting the distance function downward, i.e. saving in the input bundle to produce the output, corn. The bottom of Table 5 shows the implied group efficiencies for adopters versus non-adopters of PrecAg which were presented in Table 4. The most interesting aspect is that the implied average efficiency of both groups in the metafrontier is close to one, a result of the use of the best available production technology overall. The technology gap hence matters quite a bit here in that it tells producers how far they still need to go to achieve overall best practice. Not surprisingly non-adopters are further away than adopters.

5 Summary of Results and Conclusion

In the above study, we estimated Cobb–Douglas distance models for all corn producers in the USA. These functions met the basic theoretical properties of distance functions. In the metafrontier results we find that GPS yield maps, guidance auto-steering PrecAg technologies, and managerial ability save input costs and

[2]O'Donnell's (2018, personal communication), suggestion.

Table 5 Coefficients of econometric metafrontier (robust standard errors)

Variables	Prec. Ag.	Non-prec. Ag.		Metafrontier
di			pred2	
lny	−0.073	−0.026	lny	−0.070***
ln(x2/x1)	0.030**	0.046**	ln(x2/x1)	0.051***
ln(x3/x1)	0.494***	0.786***	ln(x3/x1)	0.785***
ln(x4/x1)	0.345***	0.141***	ln(x4/x1)	0.135***
farm size	−0.00008***	−0.0002***	P2463	−0.095*
const	−8.234***	−6.903***	P2148	−0.342***
			const	−6.628***
lnsig2v				
yield goal	−0.001	−0.0003	lnsig2v	
const	−3.521***	−1.460***	fsz	0.001***
lnsig2u			Const	−6.521***
farming occup.	27.296***	24.185***		
const	−31.149***	−26.884***	lnsig2u	
			diff	−0.00005**
			fsz	0.0008***
			const	−3.669***
Log-likelihood	−38.40	−182.37		227.73
Observations	258	258		516

Predicted group efficiencies		
	Prec. Ag.	Non-prec. Ag.
Mean	0.832	0.675
Std. Dev.	0.101	0.194
Min	0.439	0.207
Max	1	1
Metafrontier		
	Prec. Ag.	Non-prec. Ag.
Mean	0.999	0.962
Std. dev.	0.001	0.029
Min	0.987	0.898
Max	1	1
Technology gap		
Mean	0.831	0.652
Std. dev.	0.101	0.195
Min	0.437	0.199
Max	1	1
OBS	258	258

Note: *P = <0.10; **P = <0.05; ***P = <0.01

increase farm production efficiency which has environmental benefits. Maps created from soils or aerial data and input applications using VRT did not produce useable results, however. In the end, this study confirms that PrecAg can have important benefits to farmers on a local level which also translates into important results for global sustainable agriculture.

References

Amsler, C., Donnell, C. O.'., & Schmidt, P. (2017). Stochastic metafrontiers. *Econometric Reviews, 36*(6–9), 1007–1020.

Battese, G. E., & Prasada Rao, D. S. (2002). Technology gap, efficiency, and a stochastic metafrontier function. *International Journal of Business and Economics, 1*(2), 87–93.

Battese, G. E., Rao, D. S., & Donnell, C. O'. (2003). *Metafrontier functions for the study of inter-regional productivity differences* (Working Paper Series No. 01/2003). Centre for Efficiency and Productivity Analysis.

Battese, G. E., & Coelli, T. J. (1995). A model for technical inefficiency effects in a stochastic frontier production function for panel data. *Empirical Economics, 20*, 325–332.

Bravo-Ureta, B. E., Greene, W., & Solis, D. (2012). Technical efficiency analysis correcting for biases from observed and unobserved variables: An application to a natural resource management project. *Empirical Economics, 43*(1), 55–72.

Coelli, T., Estache, A., & Trujillo, L. (2003). *A primer on efficiency measurement for utilities and transport regulators*. Washington, DC: World Bank Institute.

Coelli, T., Rao, D. S., O'Donnell, C. J., & Battese, G. E. (2005). *An introduction to efficiency and productivity analysis* (2nd ed.). New York, NY: Springer.

Condon, L. (2018, September 27). Crop Science Division, Bayer AG, 2018 *Wall Street Journal*, Global Food Forum, NY.

Erickson, B., & Lowenberg-DeBoer, J. (2017). *2017 Purdue Dealer Survey*, CropLife.

Erickson, B., & Widmar, D.A. (2015). *2015 precision agricultural services dealership survey results*. Dept. of Agricultural Economics and Dept. of Agronomy, Purdue University, W. Lafayette, IN. http://agribusiness.purdue.edu/precision-ag-survey

ERS-ARMS. (2017). *ARMS farm financial and crop production practices*. Retrieved October 15, 2017, from https://www.ers.usda.gov/data-products/arms-farm-financial-and-crop-production-practices/

Greene, W. (2008). The econometric approach to efficiency analysis. In H. Fried, C. A. K. Lovell, & S. S. Schmidt (Eds.), *The measurement of productive efficiency and productivity growth* (pp. 92–250). New York, NY: Oxford University Press.

Griffin, T. W., Lowenberg-DeBoer, J., Lambert, D. M., Peone, J., Payne, T., & Daberkow, S. G. (2004). *Adoption, profitability, and making better use of precision farming data* (Staff Paper #04–06). Dept. of Agricultural Economics, Purdue University.

Griliches, Z. (1957). Hybrid corn: An exploration in the economics of technical change. *Econometrica, 25*(4), 501–522.

Hadri, K., Guermat, C., & Whittaker, J. (1999). *Doubly heteroscedastic stochastic production frontiers with an English cereal farms* (Discussion Paper 99–08). University of Exeter, School of Business and Economics.

Hadri, K., Guermat, C., & Whittaker, J. (2003a). Estimation of technical inefficiency effects using panel data and doubly heteroscedastic stochastic production frontiers. *Empirical Economics, 28*(1), 203–222.

Hadri, K., Guermat, C., & Whittaker, J. (2003b). Estimating farm efficiency in the presence of double heteroscedasticity using panel data. *Journal of Applied Economics, 6*(2), 255–268.

Hayami, Y. (1969). Sources of agricultural productivity gap among selected countries. *American Journal of Agricultural Economics, 51*(3), 564–575.

Hayami, Y., & Ruttan, V. W. (1970). Agricultural productivity differences among countries. *American Economic Review., 40*, 895–911.

Henningsen, A. Mpeta, D., Daniel, F., Adem, A, Anwar, J. K., & Czekaj, T, et al. (2015). *A meta-frontier approach for causal inference in productivity analysis: The effect of contract farming on sunflower productivity in Tanzania.* 2015 AAEA & WAEA joint annual meeting, July 26-28, San Francisco, CA.

Huang, C., Huang, T. H., & Liu, N. (2014). A new approach to estimating the metafrontier production function based on a stochastic frontier framework. *Journal of Productivity Analysis, 42*(3), 241–254.

Lusk, J. (2016, September 23). Why industrial farms are good for the environment. *New York Times*. https://www.nytimes.com/2016/09/25/opinion/sunday/why-industrial-farms-are-good-for-the-environment.html?mcubz=0

Schimmelpfennig, D. (2016). *Farm profits and adoption of precision agriculture* (Economic Research Report ERR-217). U.S. Department of Agriculture, p. 46.

Schimmelpfennig, D. (2018). Crop production costs, profits, and ecosystem stewardship with precision agriculture. *Journal of Agricultural and Applied Economics, 50*(1), 81–103.

Survey, A. R. M. (2016). United States Department of Agricluture, Washington D.C. 20250, November. 2016. In *ARMS 3 agricultural resource management Survey phase 3 Interviewer's manual.*

Swinton, S. M., & Lowenberg-DeBoer, J. (1998). Evaluating the profitability of site-specific farming. *Journal of Production Agriculture, 11*(4), 439–446.

Index

C. F. Parmeter, R. C. Sickles (eds.), *Advances in Efficiency and Productivity Analysis*, Springer Proceedings in Business and Economics,
https://doi.org/10.1007/978-3-030-47106-4

E

F

G

H